Life, Death and Representation

Millennium-Studien

zu Kultur und Geschichte des ersten Jahrtausends n. Chr.

Millennium Studies

in the culture and history of the first millennium C.E.

Band 29

De Gruyter

Life, Death and Representation

Some New Work on Roman Sarcophagi

Edited by
Jaś Elsner and Janet Huskinson

De Gruyter

ISBN 978-3-11-048231-7
e-ISBN 978-3-11-021678-3
ISSN 1862-1139

Library of Congress Cataloging-in-Publication Data

Life, death and representation : some new work on Roman sarcophagi / edited by Jaś Elsner and Janet Huskinson.
p. cm. – (Millennium-Studien ; Bd. 29)
Includes bibliographical references and index.
ISBN 978-3-11-020213-7 (hardcover : alk. paper)
1. Sarcophagi, Roman. I. Elsner, Jaś. II. Huskinson, Janet.
NB1810.L47 2010
733'.5–dc22
2010028071

Bibliographic information published by the Deutsche Nationalbibliothek

The Deutsche Nationalbibliothek lists this publication in the Deutsche Nationalbibliografie; deatailed bibliographic data are available in the Internet at http://dnb.d-nb.de abrufbar.

Printing: Hubert & Co. GmbH & Co. KG, Göttingen
∞ Printed on acid-free paper
Printed in Germany
www.degruyter.com

Contents

Abbreviations

AE	*L'Année Épigraphique*
Aquarius	*La catalogazione automatica dei sarcofagi reimpiegati. La stampa dei documenti. (user name: F. Martorana)* (Pisa, 4.8.1982).
ASR	*Die antiken Sarkophagreliefs* (Berlin 1890 –).
ASR I, 2	Andreae, B. *Die Sarkophage mit Darstellungen aus dem Menschenleben. Die römischen Jagdsarkophage* (Berlin, 1980).
ASR I, 3	Reinsberg, C. *Die Sarkophage mit Darstellungen aus dem Menschenleben. Vita Romana-Sarkophage* (Berlin, 2006).
ASR I, 4	Amedick, R. *Die Sarkophage mit Darstellungen aus dem Menschenleben. Vita privata* (Berlin, 1991).
ASR III, 1	Robert, C. *Einzelmythen – Actaeon bis Hercules* (Berlin, 1897).
ASR III, 2	Robert, C. *Einzelmythen – Hippolytos bis Meleagros* (Berlin, 1904).
ASR III, 3	Robert, C. *Einzelmythen – Niobiden bis Triptolemos* (Berlin, 1919)
ASR IV, 1	Matz, F. *Die dionysischen Sarkophage. Die Typen der Figuren. Die Denkmäler 1-71 B* (Berlin, 1968).
ASR IV, 2	Matz, F. *Die dionysischen Sarkophage. Die Denkmäler 72-161* (Berlin, 1968).
ASR IV, 3	Matz, F. *Die dionysischen Sarkophage. Die Denkmäler 162-245* (Berlin, 1969).
ASR IV, 4	Matz, F. *Die dionysischen Sarkophage. Die Denkmäler 246-385* (Berlin, 1975).
ASR V, 1	Rumpf, A. *Die Meerwesen auf den antiken Sarkophagreliefs* (Berlin, 1939).
ASR V, 2, 1	Kranz, P. *Die stadtrömischen Eroten-Sarkophage 1: Dionysische Themen: Ausnahme der Weinlese- und Ernteszenen* (Berlin, 1999).
ASR V, 2, 2	Bielefeld, D. *Die stadtrömischen Eroten-Sarkophage – Weinlese- und Ernteszenen* (Berlin, 1997).
ASR V, 2, 3	Schauenburg, K. *Die stadtrömischen Eroten-Sarkophage 3: Zirkusrennen* (Berlin, 1995).
ASR V, 3	Wegner, M. *Die Musensarkophage* (Berlin, 1966).
ASR V, 4	Kranz, P. *Jahreszeiten-Sarkophage. Entwicklung und Ikonographie des Motivs der vier Jahreszeiten auf klassischen Sarkophagen und Sarkophagdeckeln* (Berlin, 1984).
ASR VI, 1	Stroszeck, J. *Die dekorativen römischen Sarkophage. Die Löwen-Sarkophage. Die Sarkophage mit Löwenköpfen, schreitenden Löwen und Löwenkampfgruppen* (Berlin, 1998).

ASR VI,2,1 Herdejürgen, H. *Die dekorativen römischen Sarkophage. Stadtrömische und italische Girlandensarkophage. Die Sarkophage des ersten und zweiten Jahrhunderts* (Berlin, 1996).
ASR VII Herbig, R. *Die Jüngeretruskischen Steinsarkophage* (Berlin, 1952)
ASR VIII,2 Kollwitz, J. and Herdejürgen, H. *Die Sarkophage der westlichen Gebiete des Imperium Romanum. Die ravennatischen Sarkophage* (Berlin, 1975).
ASR IX,1 Rogge, S. *Die Sarkophage Griechenlands und der Donauprovinzen. Die attischen Sarkophage. Achill und Hippolytos* (Berlin, 1995).
ASR XII, 1 Grassinger, D. *Die mythologischen Sarkophage. Achill, Adonis, Aeneas, Aktaion, Alkestis, Amazonen* (Berlin, 1999).
ASR XII,2 Sichtermann, H. *Die mythologischen Sarkophage. Apollon, Ares, Bellerophon, Daidalos, Endymion, Ganymed, Giganten, Grazien* (Berlin, 1992).
ASR XII,6 Koch, G. *Die mythologischen Sarkophage. Meleager* (Berlin, 1975).
CIG *Corpus Inscriptionum Graecarum*
CIL *Corpus Inscriptionum Latinarum*
Digest *The Digest of Justinian*. Edited by A. Watson (Philadelphia, 1998).
EphEp *Ephemeris Epigraphica. Corpus Inscriptionum Latinarum Supplementum*
ICUR *Inscriptiones christianae urbis Romae*
ILCV *Inscriptiones latinae christianae veteres*
LIMC *Lexicon Iconographicum Mythologiae Classicae* (Zurich and Munich,1981-1999)
MNR Museo Nazionale Romano
PLRE Jones, A.H.M., Martindale, J.R. and Morris, J. *Prosopography of the later Roman empire* (Cambridge, 1971–)
PPM Baldassare, I., Lanzillotta, T. and Salomi, S. *Pompei. Pitture e Mosaici, vols. 1-9* (Rome, 1990–2000).
Rep. *Repertorium der christlich-antiken Sarkophage*
Rep. I Deichmann, F., Bovini, G. and Brandenburg, H. *Repertorium der christlich-antiken Sarkophage I. Rom und Ostia* (Wiesbaden, 1967).
Rep. II Dresken-Weiland, J. *Repertorium der christlich-antiken Sarkophage II. Italien mit einem Nachtrag Rom und Ostia, Dalmatien, Museen der Welt* (Mainz, 1998).
Rep. III Christern-Briesenick, B. *Repertorium der christlich-antiken Sarkophage III. Frankreich, Algerien, Tunisien* (Mainz, 2003).
SEG *Supplementum Epigraphicum Graecum*

All dates are AD unless indicated otherwise.

Introduction

Jaś Elsner

This book was born out of two impulses. First, there is no single volume of essays on Roman sarcophagi in English, despite the great antiquity of their systematic study (for well over a century). Nor is there a good introduction for purely Anglophone students to the rich and thoughtful traditions of continental research on sarcophagi, particularly in German scholarship. Second, current research has focused insistently on a relatively small corpus – the sarcophagi carved with ancient mythological subjects, usually studied within the timeframe and cultural context of their place and moment of production. This body of material is small by comparison with the vast surviving quantity of Roman sarcophagi which certainly number over 10,000 examples and may stretch to as many as 20,000 including fragments (many unpublished). Large areas of great interest in the big picture of what the production and survival of ancient sarcophagi mean, have been relatively little discussed – especially questions of reception and the longevity of sarcophagi through reuse and spoliation into the middle ages, and questions related to their material nature (the kinds of marble used for them and what this means for the industries of their production and distribution in antiquity). Our aim here is not a radical rethink of all the assumptions guiding the long study of sarcophagi, but rather a blend of new approaches with new thinking on traditional questions, coupled with an insistence on the bigger picture of production and reception as well as a refusal to follow the scholarship's strange division between sarcophagi with Christian subjects and those without, which were produced in the same places by the same workshops for very similar patrons and clients.

The study of sarcophagi (Sarkophagstudien, to give the subject its most professional terminology,[1] and one that reveals the subject's fundamental German origins) is an odd discipline. It is on the one hand the result of a focus on a very particular kind of object and on the other of the remarkable quantity of such objects that have survived in the archaeological record. By far the greatest number of our surviving sarcophagi is from the Roman Empire rather than from anywhere in the Mediterranean before imperial times. Of these, again the largest number by far are what German scholarship calls 'stadtrömische' – that is made often from imported marble in the City of Rome itself, either for use

1 See e.g. Koch 1998, 2002 and 2007 for the series *Sarkophag-Studien.* For a recent general review of the field see Baratte 2006.

there or for export across the empire, but significant numbers were produced elsewhere in Italy, in Greece, Asia Minor, the eastern provinces and southern France in late antiquity. While the essays in this book are in principle concerned with sarcophagi from all over the empire, it is inevitable – given the bulk of our examples and the resulting stress of the large majority of the literature – that most focus on examples from the city of Rome.

Sarcophagi are typically body-sized boxes (made for one or more bodies, and many of the surviving examples include the bones of more than one individual) with a lid. The decorated instances number thousands, which means they are susceptible to statistical and quantitative analysis in ways most other classes of surviving ancient art are not.[2] They may be carved only on the front, more typically on the front and on the two ends (with the ends often sculpted in lower relief than the front), relatively rarely on all four sides (but commonly so in sarcophagi from Attica or the east). Hardly any are decorated on the interior, and these are from the provinces.[3] The extent of decoration can be very simple or highly complex, from 'abstract' (as in the large number of strigillated examples that survive – perhaps more than a thousand, including fragments) via relatively non-complex designs such as garlands to vivid realisations of visual narratives. The lid may emulate the roof of a building, turning the whole sarcophagus into a form of body-sized micro-architecture; or it may show an individual or couple reclining as if in life, in three-dimensional form by contrast with the relief-decoration of the main base; or it may add a further band of imagery to run alongside, perhaps also to comment on, the images of the main base; and it often includes a panel for an inscription (which may have been painted, in which case it is now lost). It is not surprising that the major scholarly emphasis has been on the visually richer examples with figures or subjects taken from Greco-Roman mythology or Christian scripture, since they are among our most impressive surviving monuments of Roman art; but it is worth mentioning that to emphasise such examples (as does this volume, and almost all other discussions) is to stress a small sample within the much larger surviving body of sarcophagi which are decorated with non-narrative subjects, such as garlands, paired images of lions and strigillation.

The richness and diversity of types of decoration within a highly restricted material format goes with two intriguing chronological issues, neither of which has been fully or finally explained. First, sarcophagi came into significant de-

2 For some statistical discussions of iconographical matters in published sarcophagi see Ewald 2004, 234–7, 250–3; Zanker 2005; and for a chronological overview of changes in the spectrum of themes between the second and fourth centuries, see Ewald 2003, 563–5.

3 For instance, the Simpelveld sarcophagus with Holwerda, 1933 and Bastet, 1979, no. 32, or the Kertch sarcophagus with Rostovtzeff, 2004, vol. 1, 474–92.

mand rather suddenly towards the beginning of the second century in Italy,[4] and somewhat later in Greece.[5] This has been tied to a fundamental social move from cremation to inhumation in the disposal of the dead, with ash chests and urns seen as the precursors of sarcophagi.[6] But we need to use some circumspection here – it is clearly the case that sarcophagi come to outnumber ash chests in the course of the second and third century, but they never wholly replace them. Moreover, it is by no means certain that all sarcophagi were always used for inhumation – we have some examples where (despite their body-shaped form and size) sarcophagi appear to have been used for ashes.[7] Second, and no less problematic, is the sudden end of large-scale and high-quality decorated sarcophagus production at the inception of the fifth century – at least in Rome, although production continued at a much reduced scale in local centres such as the South of France, where the material used shifted from imported marble to local stone, and at an elite level in imperial centres such as Ravenna and Constantinople.[8] The general phenomenon has been tied to wider changes in aesthetics, material production and burial practices in late antiquity,[9] but it has never been adequately explained. Yet – even if clear explanations and causes for the beginning and end of the vast numbers of Roman sarcophagi produced between the early second and the early fifth centuries cannot be certainly grasped – the remarkable growth and development of a spectacular artistic phenomenon in a very specific medium and type of object is itself worthy of study as a process; it remains astonishing that there has never been an attempt at a full, single synoptic account.

The 'scientific' field of sarcophagus studies reaches back to the seminal enterprise of Friedrich Matz the elder and Carl Robert from the 1870s in establishing what became the *Antiken Sarkophagreliefs* series (*ASR*) and before that (as Bjoern Ewald reminds us in this volume) to Winckelmann and the inception of Classical archaeology as an academic discipline in the eighteenth century. But we may fairly say that the regular (re-)discovery and reuse of

4 See especially Brandenburg 1978; Koch and Sichtermann 1982, 35–61; Müller 1994, 139–70. In Italy at any rate there was a significant traditions of Etruscan forerunners in stone from c. 350 BC: See *ASR* VII and van der Meer, 2004. Nor was the occasional use of sarcophagi unknown in the first centuries BC and AD.

5 See Ewald 2004, 231. Herdejürgen 1981 is correct to note some first century examples (as there were some in Italy) but the key issue is the production of large quantities.

6 Toynbee 1971, 39–40; Brandenburg 1978, 324–6; Davies in this volume.

7 On sarcophagi as ash urns: Cumont 1931, 352; Nock 1932, 333 and n.61; Toynbee 1971, 40 and n.107.

8 On the end of sarcophagus production, see Brandenburg 2002, and Brandenburg 2004. On Ravenna see *ASR* VIII.2, *Rep* II. 118–26 and Koch 2000, 379–98; on Constantinople, see *Rep.* II, 126–30; Koch 2000, 399–443; Deckers 2004; on Gaul, Benoit 1954, 5–7.

9 See Elsner 2004, 277–86.

sarcophagi has been a fundamental constant in the European artistic tradition since late antiquity itself.[10] From within antiquity sarcophagi were reused for reburials. By the early middle ages, more sacred and decorative re-employments were added to this fundamental and continuing function – notably with sarcophagi serving as caskets for saints' relics (that is, as the ancient tombs of the very special dead)[11] and their carved fronts as the display spolia in the façades of churches (the cathedrals of Genoa in Italy and Tarragona in Spain spring to mind).[12] The above-ground display throughout the middle ages of carved sarcophagi now in the Camposanto at Pisa,[13] as a veritable art gallery of ancient relief sculpture, clearly led to significant imitation and inspiration for the likes of Nicola Pisano and others in the development of early Renaissance sculptural styles in their work on the pulpits of the cathedral and baptistery in the same complex.[14]

This very long history of excavation, display and re-use is itself a signal of the great problem in finding examples that have any significant archaeological context. Indeed, it is only in very recent years than an attempt has been made, in the path-breaking book of Jutta Dresken-Weiland on the Western empire, to create any kind of systematic catalogue of sarcophagi that can be contextualised.[15] The difficulties, however, are great. We must rely on old records of finds to attempt even a general sense of archaeological context (rarely anything as specific as a find-spot). We must believe the epigraphic data (more than I do) to trust that a sarcophagus apparently made for a woman, for instance, (like that of

10 In the history of the reuse of antiquities sarcophagi hold a privileged place. For a general conspectus, see Settis 1986, with further and more nuanced thoughts in Settis 2004 and 2008.

11 For instance, the small sarcophagus said to have housed the relics of St Caesarius of Arles from as early as 883: See Benoit 1935 and 1946, *Rep.* III, no. 79; or the sarcophagus said to be of St Martha which appears to have had a reliquary function since1187, see *Rep.* III no. 511; or the sarcophagi found in 1279 at La Ste. Baume and interpreted as the reliquary containers of a series of saints including Mary Magdalene: see Saxer 1955, *Rep.* III nos 497–500, Fixot 2001. For the charged issue of what happens when the bones a coffin holds are discovered to be holy, see the modern debate on the first century ossuary of James, the brother of Jesus in e. g. Byrne and McNary-Zak 2009.

12 The literature is large. See e. g. Andreae and Settis 1984 (where Genoa is discussed by Lucia Faedo; on Tarragona, see Rodà 1998, 154); Greenhalgh 1989, 194–201; Greenhalgh 2009, 207–212.

13 See Arias, Cristiani and Gabba 1977. They lined the outside walls of the Cathedral until they were removed to the Camposanto when Pisa came under Florentine occupation in 1406: just one example of the intricate political complications underlying display choices in the history of the reception of sarcophagi. See Tolaini 2008.

14 E.g. Seidel 1975. For a general overview, Zanker and Ewald 2004, 9–24.

15 Dresken-Weiland 2003. For the special and limited case of Aphrodisias, see Smith 2008. On tombs in context (not specifically sarcophagi) see Feraudi-Gruénais 2001. Of great importance in this area will be Borg forthcoming, and Meinecke forthcoming.

Bassa, discussed in this volume by Dennis Trout) was certainly not intended to include also the bodies of her husband and children, despite the absence of their mention on a given inscription.[16] With osteological evidence of bones inside sarcophagi, we are on equally difficult ground, since it is not certain that any given group of bones actually belonged to the person initially intended for or buried inside a given coffin. All this prompts some doubts as to some of the more optimistic conclusions about gender, influences of customers on image-choices and questions of arrangement and display in Dresken-Weiland's book, despite its outstandingly important catalogue and discussion.[17]

However, as the essays by Ben Russell and Frances Van Keuren et al. in this volume demonstrate, the application of modern technologies and methods from the sciences and social sciences can – even in this uncertain archaeological terrain – throw substantial light on some aspects of the making and trading of sarcophagi. Notably, scientific analysis can tell us much about where different kinds of marble came from, and this in turn illuminates the remarkable breadth and extent of the marble trade in the Roman Empire. John Herrmann's note, arising from the scientific evidence that some fourth century sarcophagi were made from Carrara marble – that is, from a quarry largely out of service after the second century – suggests that the practice of using old blocks (whether previously carved or uncarved) for sarcophagus-production in the late antique period was in fact extremely widespread, with sarcophagi playing a full part in the well-attested culture of spoliation and reuse that appears to have become frequent in the course of the third century.[18] The movement of sarcophagi – some decoratively roughed-out and some uncut – to workshops in Rome or Athens from quarries in Asia Minor, Greece and Italy, and the movement of finished artefacts to Southern France, Sicily and Dalmatia as well as all over Italy has the potential to be a very rich source for the dynamics of demand, the economics of the market and the analysis of questions of 'industry' and 'mass production' in the Roman world.[19]

From the points of view of both art history and social history, the loss of archaeological context for almost all our surviving sarcophagi (except any dis-

16 On inscriptions see Wischmeyer 1982, 117–57; Dreken-Weiland 2003, 18–80, Dresken-Weiland 2004.

17 It may be added that sarcophagi are by no means unique in having been studied so late in a contextualised model. See now Audley-Miller 2010, for a catalogue of Roman funerary portraits with archaeological context. Some recent discussion of funerary ritual in archaeological context may be found in Heinzelmann, Ortilli, Fasold and Witteyer 2001 and in relation to the materials from Ostia in Heinzelmann 2000, 97–101.

18 On third century spolia see e.g. Pensabene 1993, 762–8; Pensabene and Panella 1993–4, 112–25; on spolia in general see e.g. Lachenal 1995 and Hansen 2003.

19 On sarcophagi from Gaul, see Turcan 1999, 269–332 and *Rep.* III; on Sicily, see Tusa 1957; on Dalmatia, see Cambi 1998.

covered very recently) has been little short of catastrophic. A good example of the problem is the outstanding second and third century group of sarcophagi discovered together in 1885 in two underground chambers on the Via Salaria in Rome, of which 7 are now in Baltimore, 2 in Rome and 1 (an undecorated sarcophagus) was destroyed shortly after excavation.[20] A third chamber – the first chronologically and probably part of the same tomb (though this has been contested) contained a series of high quality statues, busts and funerary altars.[21] The sarcophagi offer a collection of examples, some of exceptional quality, that belonged together in antiquity and were placed in a single tomb – which has been identified as belonging to an extremely distinguished Senatorial family, the Licinii and Calpurnii – which appears to have had continuous usage of the site for some 200 years from the first to the early third century.[22] The original excavation reports fail to record any kind of context, including the arrangement or placement of the items, their contiguity or otherwise, or any issue that might respond to a bigger visual question than the specific iconography of given examples in isolation.[23] Yet we know enough in general to say that the majority of second and early third century sarcophagi were placed in mausolea,[24] that many of these were not only carefully laid out – so that some kind of attention was at least potentially paid to the visual arrangement of sarcophagi in relation to each other – but also that the walls and ceilings of these spaces were painted with frescoes, the mythological subjects of which may have emulated the subjects carved on the sarcophagi.[25] Precisely the same considerations apply to sarcophagi placed in decorated underground hypogea and cubicula in catacombs.[26] Of course this picture of carefully created integral contexts of display is too simple. Many such tombs, as family complexes, were added to over time as in the Via Salaria burials mentioned above, and every available space may have eventually been stuffed with items which will have confused any original visual co-ordination or conceptual planning. Something like this may have been the case in the so-called Tomb of the Pancratii on the Via Latina in Rome, from which some stucco decoration survives and at least 7 sarcophagi were recovered

20 Lehmann-Hartleben and Olsen 1942, 10 and esp. Kragelund, Moltesen and Østergaard 2003, 55–79.

21 See e.g. Kragelund, Moltesen and Østergaard 2003, 46–54 and 109–111 (altars), 81–100 and 113–115 (portraits).

22 See e.g. Bentz 1997/8; van Keuren 2002; Kragelund, Moltesen and Østergaard 2003.

23 Especially Fiorelli 1885. Full original documentation is in Kragelund, Moltesen and Østergaard 2003, 55–65 and 116–25. Discussion of the dig is *ibid* 13–18.

24 Dresken-Weiland 2003, 98–107.

25 For an outstanding discussion of one such example in Rome, see Bielfeldt 2003.

26 For an example, see the Crypt of the Twelve Apostles in the Catacomb of Marcellus and Marcellinus, with Saint-Roch 1981, 219–23 and Saint-Roch 1999, 34–6, 97–99, 119–122.

after the original find of 1858, of which 5 still exist.[27] The question of when such tombs were available to visitors or to display is also an open one – and it may be no more often than on the anniversary of decease or when a new burial was added; likewise, the issue of to whom such display was made possible (just family? chosen visitors? slaves and freedmen? long-standing clients?) is unresolved and likely never to be soluble.

Yet not only are there hardly any studies of such integrated contexts – either in their original form or as developments over time – but the job is in fact difficult for the archaeological reasons laid out in my lament about the group of sarcophagi now mainly in Baltimore.[28] However, in principle the issues are extremely interesting. There is a potential for linking the different narrative directions of different sarcophagi (some 'reading' left to right, some right to left and some with highly centralised designs) to placement in different positions in the same site – for instance in left and right hand niches or *arcosolia* that comprised tomb spaces. There is the further issue that sarcophagi place decoration on the exterior of the coffin space, protecting or encasing the dead as it were with imagery designed to be viewed by the living, while the spaces containing sarcophagi – mausolea or cubicula – are decorated on their interiors, with a range of painted imagery that itself encases a viewer, that plays with or against the sarcophagi within them, and that relates as a flat pictorial field to the carved relief surface of the sarcophagi. Questions of the apotropaic function of imagery, of whether sarcophagus decoration was for the edification of the dead in their tomb-houses or for the living who occasionally visited them to mourn and remember, of whether imagery – like the representation of garlands and other offerings – might function as a replacement for (or a perpetual performance of) funerary ritual,[29] would all be profoundly advanced if we had more by way of context.

It is worth noting, however, that the contextual turn is historiographic in that it inevitably goes with a reaction to the long history of reception and of the kind of archaeology that demolished contexts as it unearthed trophy objects, and demolished objects (like the uncarved sarcophagus in the tomb of Licinii) which did not make display pieces. It is also profoundly limited – at any rate for sarcophagi – because with the best will in the world it can never be applicable to more than a few hundred sarcophagi at most (and many of these in only the vaguest terms) out of the thousands that survive.

27 Herdejürgen 2000, 220–34; Feraudi-Gruénais 2001, catalogue K48, 108–114 and Dresken-Weiland 2003, catalogue A.55, 313–4.

28 That said, in cases where something might be attempted it usually has not been – witness Saint-Roch 1999, who discusses the room, the paintings and the sarcophagi separately as if they had no potential integral relations.

29 On sarcophagi decorated with implements of cult see Herdejürgen 1984.

As so often with fields that boast a venerable and ancient historiography of continuous study over more than a century, there have been some very eccentric turns taken in the discussion of these objects, which remain influential in circumscribing the field.[30] Some issues – such as the question of sarcophagi as micro-architecture, to which Edmund Thomas returns in this volume – had brief outings in the course of the last 150 years and were promptly forgotten.[31] The great question of stylistic change in Roman art and how it could be traced most intimately and precisely through the vast empirical archive of sarcophagi was arguably the dominant aspect of the field for most of the twentieth century, but appears entirely to have dropped out of fashion in the last 30 years.[32] The attempt to write a social history of the Roman upper class through the ways imagery on sarcophagi has emulated so-called state reliefs is an old one which remains in play – it is closely inter-related with the *ASR* category of catalogues of sarcophagi showing images of public and private life (*Die Sarkophage mit Darstellungen aus dem Menschenleben*).[33]

Most notable is the rigorous separation of 'pagan' from Christian sarcophagi, not only in the vast majority of discussions but even in the main handbooks and the key fundamental corpora which catalogue and reproduce the surviving examples.[34] Indeed, institutionally different disciplines – *Klassische*

30 One historiographic survey is Koch and Sichtermann 1982, 3–19 and 621–3.

31 See Altmann 1902 for the last extensive account of architectural structure.

32 This was how Alois Riegl used sarcophagi in his seminal *Spätrömische Kunstindustrie:* Riegl 1901, 71–81. The obsession with stylistic change (*Stilwandel*) became the driving force in the work of the giants of twentieth century Roman art history including Gerhard Rodenwaldt and Ranuccio Bianchi Bandinelli: see especially Rodenwaldt 1935 as well as Rodenwaldt 1925, 1935–6, 1936, 1939 and 1944 with Effenberger 1986, Thümmel 1986 and Zimmermann 1986; also Bianchi Bandinelli 1970, 313–28 (although this is focused on historical reliefs). For this topic as late as the 1980s, see Jung 1984. For a recent discussion of formal and iconographic changes, and also the move to pre-Constantinian Christian sarcophagi, see Zanker and Ewald 2004, 247–66.

33 See e.g. Koch and Sichtermann 1982, 88–126; Wrede 2001.

34 Handbooks: Pagan – Koch and Sichtermann 1982 (also Koch 1993a); Christian: Koch 2000 (also Koch 1996, 107–24). Corpora: the great 'pagan' series is *ASR*, on which see Koch 1998 ix-x for a brief history and 318–20 for a conspectus of the envisaged volumes; the Christian series is *Rep.* Note the way that the edited volumes of the *Sarkophag-Studien* series (e.g. Koch 1998 and 2007; also Koch 1993b), systematically exclude Christian material (although Koch 2007 has a short piece on Jewish ossuaries and Koch 1993b has a piece on a relief from a sarcophagus from Constantinople which is necessarily Christian), yet Koch himself is perhaps the foremost expert on Christian sarcophagi; the same observation may be made of the early Christian side of the field: Koch 2002, and Bisconti and Brandenburg 2004, contain hardly any non-Christian material. One exception to this obsessive divisionalisation is when the scholarly focus is on the extant remains in a given province or region: Noguera Celdrán and Conde Guerri 2001, is an admirable mix of Christian and pre-Christian material in Spain. However, for Southern France, Drocourt-Dubreuil 1989 eccentrically excludes the non-Christian

Archäologie and *Christliche Archäologie* – have been traditionally responsible for the two areas of study. All this despite the fact that from the later third century the same workshops in Rome appear to have been making sarcophagi with 'pagan' and Christian and Jewish iconography for patrons of broadly the same social standing.[35] This division is an example of the larger institutional split between the study of late antique art, seen as a branch of Classical archaeology, and the study of early Christian art, seen as the inception of Byzantine and medieval art history.[36] In respect of logic, materials, historical context and artists – that is, the sociology of production – the division makes absolutely no sense at all, since it is dependent on the separation of Christian *iconography* from other iconographies (in ways we do not adopt or accept when thinking about Dionysiac or Meleager iconographies, let alone erotes or garlands). At the same time, insofar as some Christian patrons may have partaken of a different eschatology, and hence a different view of life and death, from other Romans, one can see that different ways of viewing and patron-relations to the finished object are potentially at play in Christian iconographies. This however is a subtle nuance within what ought to be one field; but the divide of sarcophagus studies into two different fields is fundamental to the history and evolution of disciplines, including the differentiation of secular subjects from theology in the early modern period. It is not so easily overcome.

In interpretative terms – and ones not wholly unconnected with the Christian/Pagan divide – the great shift that took place in the field in the 1940s remains of huge importance to the ways scholarship is still practiced. In 1942, Franz Cumont (1868–1947), the great Belgian scholar of ancient religions and their archaeology, published his *Recherches sur le symbolisme funéraire des Romains.*[37] Although by no means only about sarcophagi, this book was – and remains – the most systematic and relentless attempt to find religious, allegorical and symbolic meanings in the non-Christian sarcophagi. It is hard to resist the conclusion that Cumont's interpretative model is ultimately Christianising in that it is driven by Christian-modulated assumptions about religion, such as the centrality of belief, which are at least contestable and need to be enticed out

material from the site of St Victor at Marseilles, while Gaggadis-Robin 2005 publishes only the pagan sarcophagi in the Arles Museum.

35 The Jewish question is complex: see Elsner 2003. Clearly there are many sarcophagi with Old Testament themes used in a Christian context. There are a few which may be seen as made for Jews (or re-used by them) with specifically Jewish imagery like the menorah: see Konikoff 1986 and Rutgers 1995, 77–81. What is not clear is whether any of the sarcophagi we think of as Christian might have also been used by Jewish patrons or perceived as inoffensive by Jewish viewers.

36 See Elsner 2004, 271–86.

37 Cumont 1942.

of the material evidence.[38] Cumont's position, although influential on a small number of scholars and most especially the great French expert on sarcophagi, Robert Turcan,[39] remains largely a road no longer travelled. In 1946, Cumont's book received a brilliant, sceptical, thirty-page review from A. D. Nock.[40] This consisted of a series of demolitional vignettes of some of Cumont's stronger proposals resulting in the following general proposition about the nature of Roman sarcophagi:

> We are left with classicism and culture as a prime factor when we look at these representations [on sarcophagi] or at a grave altar with the tale of Pasiphae. They mean no more than do the garland sarcophagi and it matters not whether the garlands hang by themselves or are carried by Erotes. Literary classicism is the predominant factor, but there was also a similar feeling towards many art works of the great past.

And again:

> In spite of local variations there is massive unity in this sepulchral art; but is it not a unity of cultural inheritance and to some extent of feeling rather than a unity of belief?[41]

I think it little exaggeration to say that where Nock led, just about the entire field has followed for well over half a century. Whether in the direction of mythological narratives and classicising interpretations,[42] or into the world of social meanings and mourning,[43] let alone more directly archaeological issues of formal influence, typology and iconography,[44] Nock's twin formula of 'classicism and culture' reigns supreme. Nock's intervention allowed Classicists to heave a collective sigh of relief and leave issues of belief and symbolic meaning to their early Christian brethren. But it is worth asking if the secularist agenda which has been ascendant since Nock is not itself limiting and potentially

38 However, Cumont's model of ancient religion should not be lead to the assumption that he was himself a Christian apologist. He was prevented from occupying the Chair of Roman History at Ghent in 1910 specifically because he was seen as not Catholic enough. His thinking may be better placed in the context of Belgian symbolism and pre-World War I mysticism, which included a strong tradition of Freemasonry in Belgium.

39 See for instance Turcan 1966, 1999 and 2003 and especially his riposte to the rejection of Cumont in Turcan 1978; also Engemann 1973.

40 Nock 1946. For an interesting account of Cumont and Nock in relation to epiphanic sarcophagi, see Platt, forthcoming, chapter 8.

41 Nock 1946, 166 and 169.

42 For example, books: Müller 1994; Koortbojian 1995 (explicitly at p. 3, n. 3); Bielfeldt 2005; significant shorter pieces (out of vast numbers) Blome 1978: Brilliant 1984, 124–65; Giuliani 1989; Blome 1992; Zanker 1999: Zanker 2000, and Zanker 2005.

43 Magisterially Zanker and Ewald 2004; on the image of the intellectual see Zanker 1995, 267–97; esp. Ewald 1999; Borg 2004b, 167–71.

44 For instance, Himmelmann 1979.

restrictive,[45] as if some questions of belief and the search for meaning after death were not in play for at least some viewers and users of sarcophagi in antiquity.[46] The opening of Nock's final sentence in his famous review is worth citing here: 'Our decisions are personal; at all times students of ancient religion are almost necessarily maximizers or minimizers....'[47] Insofar as sarcophagi touch on questions of the aftermath of death, Nock is quite right to see the burden of explanation as an interpretative and personal one for the modern interpreter just as much as for the ancient viewer. It may be that the 'minimizers' may have dominated the field for too long.

The result of Classical archaeology's abandonment of the Cumontian arena of belief has meant that little work has been done on the potential parallelisms of Christian visual promises of salvation and afterlife by comparison with those in pagan sarcophagi (even when – as in the case of Dionysus' epiphany to Ariadne or Selene's appearance to Endymion – there may be some implication of a better future in a better place). Similarly the appropriation of 'paradisal' themes from pagan to Christian iconographies – one thinks of bucolic or seasonal imagery, or the sleeping Ariadne and Endymion reconfigured as the type of the resting Jonah – while frequently noted, have never been the subject of sustained and systematic analysis that explores the transformation of culture through iconography in the carefully limited context of a single type of monument with a funerary function. At the same time, Christian sarcophagi have rarely been subjected to the kinds of social, functional and economic analysis that Nock's 'culture and classicism' opened for the non-Christian corpus. They have for too long remained in a scripturally-determined ghetto of iconographic and typological description. Yet, in testing for instance the kinds of rhetorical emphasis of praise or polemic offered by Christian sarcophagi (as Jaś Elsner begins to do here), and alternatively by pagan sarcophagi, as well as comparing the two approaches – something may be learned on both sides of a largely false divide.

45 See Horden and Purcell 2000, 447 for problems with the 'extreme secularising tendency' governing studies of ancient religion in general in the second half of the twentieth century.

46 It is interesting that Nock's model for reading sarcophagi anticipates by a generation that primarily adopted for understanding the so-called 'Second Sophistic', especially in seminal work of Ewen Bowie 1970, and those who have followed him in a cultural interpretation, such as Anderson 1993; Swain 1996; Whitmarsh 2001; Borg 2004. It is only relatively recently that religion has been integrated into this cultural mix in e.g. Egelhaaf-Gaiser 2000; Galli 2004 and 2005; the essays in the third part of Cardovana and Galli 2007. It is time, in the study of sarcophagi (arguably the supreme artistic phenomenon of the period of the Second Sophistic), that the 'classicism and culture' brigade remembered that religion (including belief) is part of their enterprise.

47 Nock 1946, 170.

It is worth noting how 'spotty' our ability for detailed focus remains, despite the long history and sporadic intensity of scholarly study. Many iconographic categories of Roman mythological sarcophagi – by far the most popular for scholarly discussion – remain without a fundamental catalogue: only three volumes of the projected six in the new edition of the mythological sarcophagi (*ASR* XII. 1, 2 and 6) have been published.[48] In the case of sarcophagi from the Greek-speaking East, only one volume of the projected eleven on Greece itself has seen the light (*ASR* IX 1.1) – which means that detailed studies of the material have been reduced to the mythological corpora made available there (the themes of Achilles and Hippolytus), as Bjoern Ewald remarks in the acknowledgment note to his paper here.[49] Likewise no *ASR* volume of the projected eight for the Asia Minor sarcophagi has yet been published;[50] nor any of the three for Syria, Palestine, Arabia and Egypt.[51] As a result the literatures on these topics remain weak in general and by contrast with sarcophagi from Rome – despite the outstanding nature of the material – with the exception of Bjoern Ewald's important article of 2004 and in this volume (which make a huge advance in the field of Attic sarcophagi)[52] and the work of Fahri Işik and Bert Smith on Aphrodisias,[53] which puts the material from that particular city on an entirely different basis of contextual and archaeological knowledge from anything else in the East.

The current volume, born from a conference at Corpus Christi College, Oxford, represents a series of new essays in English. It makes no claims and has no pretensions to do more than sketch some dimensions in which the gaps might be filled and the field might develop. We see the totality of Roman sarcophagus production and receptions from Asia to Spain as part of a wide and complex phenomenon – differently motivated and enacted in different contexts, to be sure. The book opens with a chapter by Glenys Davies that assesses the inception of sarcophagi and their relation to funerary urns and ash chests. This is followed by four chapters that stress different aspects of the big picture within which Roman sarcophagi must be placed. Janet Huskinson looks at the long

48 The full projected agenda was advertised in Koch 1998, 318–20. It has been radically reduced in the last 10 years – see now http://www.dainst.org/index_89d21121bb1f14a137510017f0000011_de.html for the current project.

49 In the new model the eleven Greek volumes have been reduced to three projected volumes (all on mythological subjects) for Attica and one in the *Sarkophag-Studien* series on Thessalonike.

50 Although I take it that what Koch 1998, 319 advertised as *ASR* X.2.1 on garland sarcophagi at Aphrodisias has now emerged elsewhere as Işik 2007. Korkut 2006, discusses garland ossuaries in limestone from Pamphylia and Cilicia. On some aspects of Phrygian sarcophagi, see Strocka 1984.

51 On Palmyrene sarcophagi, for instance, see Parlasca 1984 and 1998.

52 Ewald 2004 and in this volume.

53 Işik 2007 and Smith 2008.

story of sarcophagi from their documentable reuse in antiquity to some aspects of their 'lives' in the Middle Ages and the Counter Reformation. Francisco Prado-Vilar, beginning with a specific instance of medieval appropriations of a striking iconography on a particular sarcophagus, traces aspects of that long story in the history of art itself – thinking especially about the tradition of Aby Warburg. Frances van Keuren and her collaborators offer new scientific analyses and resulting reflections on where the marble comes from – issues that stress wide movement of marbles from different provenances and raise questions about the extent of the use of spolia (reused blocks of stone recycled from some earlier function) in the making of sarcophagi in late antiquity. Ben Russell takes a fresh synoptic look at the economics of production, trade and the sarcophagus market.

The volume then turns to three groups of studies that home in more directly on the iconographic and detailed art-historical study of objects. The first group deals with questions of portraiture, gender and identity. In the spirit of giving a fresh outing to some old and perennial themes, Zahra Newby undertakes a new exploration of the significance of portrait heads within sarcophagi with mythological subjects.[54] Stine Birk examines one of the great emergent themes in archaeology and Classical studies since the 1980s, namely, the place of gender in the visual and material culture. Björn Ewald turns to questions of identity and sexuality in both modern and ancient reception in the spectacular corpus of Attic sarcophagi. The second group pairs two essays that give deep readings of individual objects. Katharina Lorenz confronts the problem of how to read the mythological material and how its visual representations may respond to the actualities of mourning in which the sarcophagus itself was a centre piece by focusing on the great Borghese sarcophagus with the theme of Meleager that is now in Paris. Dennis Trout examines the remarkable Christian sarcophagus of Bassa from the Praetextatus catacomb in Rome with its long poetic inscription, to explore the ways mourning and identity were constructed in the Christian fourth century. Our final group pairs two chapters that explore frameworks and categories across multiple examples of sarcophagi. Jaś Elsner looks at the subject of the Arrest and Trial of Jesus in a series of fourth-century sarcophagi to examine questions of polemic and apologetics. Edmund Thomas reflects on the complex relationship between Asian and Italian columnar sarcophagi as brilliant examples of ancient 'micro-architecture'.

As a whole, the book actively seeks to deny the disciplinary divide between 'pagan' and Christian sarcophagi (or more correctly between those with iconographies identified as Christian and all the rest), and so includes three papers

54 See for instance Wrede 1981, 139–57; Koch and Sichtermann 1982, 607–14; Fittschen 1984; Andreae 1984b; Huskinson 1998; Koch 2000, 107–118; Dresken-Weiland 2003, 85–95; Zanker and Ewald 2004, 45–50.

– by Dennis Trout, Janet Huskinson and Jaś Elsner – that deal with material from Christian contexts. Likewise, we contest the usually too firm line that has been drawn between studies of antiquity and studies of its reception – since in the case of our objects, their 'lives' as artefacts in the experiential record of European culture encompass both.[55] Hence the papers of Francisco Prado-Vilar and Janet Huskinson actively take on questions of reception, interpretation and influence in periods after the ancient world itself came to an end.

Sarcophagi are our richest single source of Roman iconography – translating the realms of Greek and Roman myth, the subjects of Roman public art, some themes of spiritual or directly religious content into images that were designed to resonate in the most personal and intense of private contexts, when a family mourned for its deceased. We cannot know how often the tombs, in which sarcophagi were kept, were opened and for whom – but their showing was clearly ritualised, exceptional, candle- or lamp-lit and special in every way (like the later *ostentiones* of relics or icons in Christian culture). The patterning and arrangement of visual narratives, the replication but also differentiation of similar imagery, the wide distribution of marble types and of finished examples from workshops based in urban centres – all this goes to the heart of a series of key issues in Roman artistic production. Moreover, although some sarcophagi were clearly purchased by the very highest echelons of the Roman aristocracy (witness the items in the Licinian tomb or the sarcophagus of Junius Bassus, who was city prefect when he died in 359), many surviving examples take us somewhat deeper down the social pyramid into the world of wealthy freedmen and the more aspiring middle classes. Their visual negotiation of the ideals, realities and fantasies of Roman people, both the deceased and their mourners, at the interface of the public and the personal where death is marked and the rites of burial performed, makes them of quite exceptional importance for understanding Roman culture.[56]

Acknowledgements

The Editors are extremely grateful to the Centre for Greek and Roman Antiquity at Corpus Christi College, Oxford, for hosting the colloquium from which this collection of papers arose, and to the Arts Faculty of the Open

55 Note the rigorous separation of the 'reception' papers from those on sarcophagi in antiquity when the Pisa conference on 1982 came to be published: Reception was Andreae and Settis 1984 (*Marburger Winckelmann Programm* 1983) and sarcophagi in Roman antiquity was Andreae 1984 (*Marburger Winckelmann Programm* 1984).

56 My particular thanks for their careful reading and responses to this Introduction are due to Janet Huskinson and Björn Ewald.

University for its financial support. We thank the Charles Oldham fund in Corpus for help towards indexing and copy-editing. We are most grateful to Barbara Borg for facilitating our collaboration with the Millennium Supplements series and to Sabine Vogt and Sabina Dabrowski at De Gruyter for their efficient command of all aspects of publication. Above all, we thank Emma-Jayne Graham for the enthusiastic help she has given us in copy-editing, commenting on and indexing the volume.

Bibliography

Altmann, W. *Architektur und Ornamentik der antiken Sarkophage* (Berlin, 1902).

Anderson, G. *The Second Sophistic: A Cultural Phenomenon in the Roman Empire* (London, 1993).

Andreae, B.(ed.). *Symposium über die antiken Sarkophage* (Marburg, 1984a) = *Marburger Winkelmann Programm,* 1984.

Andreae, B. Bossierte Porträts auf römischen Sarkophage – ein ungelöstes Problem, in: *Symposium über die antiken Sarkophage,* edited by B. Andreae (Marburg, 1984b), 109–28.

Andreae, B. and Settis, S. (eds.). *Colloquio sul reimpiego dei sarcofagi romani nel medioevo* (Marburg, 1984) = *Marburger Winkelmann Programm,* 1983.

Arias, P. Cristiani, E. and Gabba, E. (eds.). *Camposanto monumentale di Pisa* (Pisa, 1977).

Audley-Miller, L. *Tomb Portraits under the Roman Empire: Local Contexts and Cultural Styles.* (D.Phil. dissertation, Oxford, 2010).

Baratte, F. Les sarcophages romains: Problèmes et certitude. *Perspective* 1 (2006), 38–54.

Bastet, F. *Beeld en Relief* ('s-Gravenshage, 1979).

Benoit, F. La tombe de saint Césaire d'Arles et sa restauration en 883. *Bulletin monumental* 94 (1935), 137–43.

Benoit, F. Les reliques de saint Césaire, archevêque d'Arles. *Cahiers archéologiques* 1 (1946), 51–62.

Benoit, F. *Sarcophages paléochretiens d'Arles et de Marseille* (Paris, 1954).

Bentz, K. Rediscovering the Licinian Tomb. *Journal of the Walters Art Gallery* 55/6 (1997/8), 63–88.

Bianchi Bandinelli, R. *Rome: the Centre of Power* (London, 1970).

Bielfeldt, R. Orestes im Medusengrab: Ein Versuch zu Betrachter. *Römische Mitteilungen* 110 (2003), 117–50.

Bielfeldt, R. *Orestes auf römischen Sarkophagen* (Munich, 2005).

Bisconti, F. and Brandenburg, H. (eds.). *Sarcofagi tardoantichi, paleocristiani e altomedievali: atti della giornata tematica dei seminari di archeologia Cristiana* (Vatican, 2004).

Blome, P. Zur Umgestaltung griechischer Mythen in der römischen Sepulkralkunst. Alkestis-, Protesilaos- und Proserpinasarkophage. *Römische Mitteilungen* 85 (1978), 435–457.

Blome, P. Funerärsymbolische Collagen auf mythologischen Sarkophagreliefs. *Studi Italiani di Filologia Classica* 10 (1992), 1061–1073.

Borg, B. (ed.). *Paideia: The World of the Second Sophistic* (Berlin, 2004a).

Borg, B. Glamorous Intellectuals: Portraits of Pepaideumenoi in the Second and Third Centuries AD, in: *Paideia: The World of the Second Sophistic,* edited by B. Borg (Berlin, 2004b), 157–178.

Borg, B. A *Matter of Life and Death: a social history of tombs and burial customs in second and third century AD* Rome (Oxford, forthcoming).

Bowie, E. Greeks and their Past in the Second Sophistic. *Past and Present* 46 (1970), 3–41.

Brandenburg, H. Der Beginn der stadtrömische Sarkophag Produktion der Kaserzeit. *Jahrbuch des Deutsches Archäologisches Instituts* 93 (1978), 277–327.

Brandenburg, H. Das Ende der antiken Sarkophagkunst in Rom. Pagane und christliche Sarkophage im 4. Jahrhundert, in: G. Koch (ed.), *Akten des Symposions 'Frühchristliche Sarkophage',* Marburg, 1999. (Mainz, 2002), 19–39.

Brandenburg, H. Osservazioni sulla fine della produzione e dell' uso dei sarcofagi a rilievo nello tarda antichità nonché sulla loro decorazione, in: F. Bisconti and H. Brandenburg (eds.), *Sarcofagi tardoantichi, paleocristiani e altomedievali: atti della giornata tematica dei seminari di archeologia Cristiana* (Vatican, 2004), 3–34.

Brilliant, R. *Visual Narratives: Storytelling in Etruscan and Roman Art* (Ithaca, 1984).

Byrne, R. and McNary-Zak, B. *Resurrecting the Brother of Jesus: The James Ossuary Controversy and the Quest for Religious Relics* (Chapel Hill, 2009).

Cambi, N. Sarkophage aus salonitanischen Werkstatten, in: G. Koch (ed.), *Akten des Symposiums 125 Jahre Sarkophag-Corpus. Sarkophag-Studien Band 1* (Mainz, 1998), 169–81.

Cardovana, O. and Galli, M. (eds.). *Arte e memoria culturale nell' età della Seconda Sofistica* (Catania, 2007).

Cumont, F. In: *Comptes rendus de l'académie des inscriptions* 1931, 4 (1931), 351–353.

Cumont, F. *Recherches sur le symbolisme funéraire des Romains* (Paris, 1942).

Deckers, J. G. Theodosianische Sepulkralplastik in Konstantinopel 380–450 n. Chr., in: F. Bisconti and H. Brandenburg (eds.), *Sarcofagi tardoantichi, paleocristiani e altomedievali: atti della giornata tematica dei seminari di archeologia Cristiana* (Vatican, 2004), 35–52.

Dresken-Weiland, J. Sarkophagbestattungen des 4.–6. Jahrhunderts im westen des römischen Reiches. *Römische Quartalschrift für christliche Altertumskunde und Kirchengeschichte, Supplementband* 55 (Rome, Freiburg and Vienna, 2003).

Dresken-Weiland, J. Ricerche sui committenti e destinatari dei sarcofagi paleocristiani a Roma, in: F. Bisconti and H. Brandenburg (eds.), *Sarcofagi tardoantichi, paleocristiani e altomedievali: atti della giornata tematica dei seminari di archeologia Cristiana* (Vatican, 2004), 149–153.

Drocourt-Dubreuil, G. *St Victor de Marseille: Art funéraire et prière des mors aux temps paléochrétiens (VIe – Ve siècles)* (Marseilles, 1989).

Effenberger, A. Rodenwaldts Bedeutung für die Sarkophagforschung. *Wissenschaftliche Zeitschrift der Humboldt-Universität zu Berlin. Gesellschaftswissenschaftliche Reihe* 35 (1986), 698–704.

Egelhaaf-Gaiser, U. *Kulträume im römischen Alltag: das Isisbuch des Apuleius und der Ort von Religion im kaiserzeitlichen Rom* (Stuttgart, 2000).

Engemann, J. *Untersuchungen zur Sepulkralsymbolik der späteren römischen Kaiserzeit* (Münster, 1973).

Elsner, J. Archaeologies and Agendas: Reflections on Late Ancient Jewish Art and Early Christian Art. *Journal of Roman Studies* 93 (2003), 114–128.

Elsner, J. Late Antique Art: The Problem of the Concept and the Cumulative Aesthetic, in: *Approaching Late Antiquity: The Transformation from Early to Late Empire,* edited by S. Swain and M. Edwards (Oxford, 2004), 271–309.

Ewald, B. *Der Philosoph als Leitbild: Ikonographische Untersuchungen an römischen Sarkophagreliefs* (Mainz, 1999).

Ewald, B. Sarcophagi and Senators: The Social History of Roman Funerary Art and its Limits. *Journal of Roman Archaeology* 16 (2003), 561–571.

Ewald, B. Men, Muscle and Myth. Attic Sarcophagi in the Cultural Context of the Second Sophistic, in: *Paideia: The World of the Second Sophistic,* edited by B. Borg (Berlin, 2004), 229–276.

Feraudi-Gruénais, F. *Ubi diutius nobis habitandum est: Die Innendekoration der kaiserzeitlichen Gräber Roms* (Wiesbaden, 2001).

Fiorelli, V. *Notizie degli scavi di antichità* (1885), 188–191 and 251–254.

Fittschen, K. Über Sarkophage mit Porträts verschiedener Personen, in: *Symposium über die antiken Sarkophage,* edited by B. Andreae (Marburg, 1984), 129–161.

Fixot, M. *La crypte de Saint-Maximin-la-Sainte-Baume* (Aix-en-Provence, 2001).

Gaggadis-Robin, V. *Sarcophages païens du musée de l'Arles antique* (Arles, 2005).

Galli, M. 'Creating Religious Identities': Paideia e religione nella Seconda Sofistica, in: *Paideia: The World of the Second Sophistic,* edited by B. Borg (Berlin, 2004), 315–356.

Galli, M. Pilgrimage as Elite Habitus: Educated Pilgrims in Sacred Landscape during the Second Sophistic, in: *Pilgrimage in Graeco-Roman and Early Christian Antiquity: Seeing the Gods,* edited by J. Elsner and I. Rutherford (Oxford, 2005), 253–290.

Giuliani, L. Achill-Sarkophage in Ost und West: Genese einer Ikonographie. *Jahrbuch der Berliner Museen* 31 (1989), 25–39.

Greenhalgh, M. *The Survival of Roman Antiquities* (London, 1989).

Greenhalgh, M. *Marble Past, Monumental Past: Building with Antiquities in the Mediaeval Mediterrannean* (Leiden, 2009).

Hansen, M. *The Eloquence of Appropriation: Prolegomena to an Understanding of Spolia in Early Christian Rome* (Rome, 2003).

Hederjürgen, H. Frühkaiserzeitliche Sarkophage in Griechenland. *Jahrbuch des Deutsches Archäologisches Instituts* 96 (1981), 413–435.

Hederjürgen, H. Sarkphage mit Darstellungen von Kultgeräten, in: *Symposium über die antiken Sarkophage,* edited by B. Andreae (Marburg, 1984), 7–26.

Hederjürgen, H. Sarkophage von der Via Latina: Folgerungen und dem Fundkontext. *Römische Mitteilungen* 107 (2000), 2009–2034.

Heinzelmann, M. *Der Nekropolis von Ostia* (Munich, 2000).

Heinzelmann, M., Ortilli, J., Fasold, P. and Witteyer, M. (eds.). *Römischer Bestattungsbrauch und Beigatensitten* (Wiesbaden, 2001).

Himmelmann, N. *Typologische Untersuchungen an römischen Sarkophagreliefs des 3. und 4. Jahrhunderts n. Chr.* (Mainz, 1973).

Holwerda, J. Der römische Sarkophag von Simpelveld. *Archäologischer Anzeiger* (1933), 56–75.

Horden, P. and Purcell, N. *The Corrupting Sea* (Oxford, 2000).

Huskinson, J. 'Unfinished Portrait Heads' on Later Roman Sarcophagi: Some New Perspectives. *Papers of the British School at Rome* 46 (1998), 129–158.

Işik, F. *Girlanden-Sarkphage aus Aphrodisias* (Mainz, 2007).

Jung, H. Zur Vorgeschichte des spätantoninischen Stilwandels, in: *Symposium über die antiken Sarkophage,* edited by B. Andreae (Marburg, 1984), 59–103.

Koch, G. *Sarkophage der römischen Kaiserzeit* (Darmstadt, 1993a).

Koch, G. (ed.). *Grabeskunst der römischen Kaiserzeit.* (Mainz, 1993b).
Koch, G. Early *Christian Art and Architecture* (London, 1996).
Koch, G. (ed.). *Akten des Symposiums 125 Jahre Sarkophag-Corpus. Sarkophag-Studien* Band 1 (Mainz, 1998).
Koch, G. *Frühchristliche Sarkophage* (Munich, 2000).
Koch, G. (ed.). *Akten des Symposiums 'Frühchristliche Sarkophage',* Marburg, 1999, (Mainz, 2002).
Koch, G. (ed.). *Akten des Sarkophag-Corpus 2001. Sarkophag-Studien* Band 3 (Mainz, 2007).
Koch, G. and Sichtermann, H. *Römische Sarkophage* (Munich, 1982).
Konikoff, A. *Sarcophagi from the Jewish Catacombs of Ancient Rome: A Catalogue Raisonnée* (Stuttgart, 1986).
Koortbojian, M. *Myth, Meaning, and Memory on Roman Sarcophagi* (Berkeley, 1995).
Korkut, T. *Girlanden-Ostotheken aus Kalkstein in Pampylien und Kilikien. Untersuchungen zu Typologie, Ikonographie und Chronologie. Sarkophag-Studien* Band 4 (Mainz, 2006).
Kragelund, P., Moltesen, M. and Østergaard, J. S. *The Licinian Tomb: Fact or Fiction* (Copenhagen, 2003).
de Lachenal, L. *Spolia: Uso e reimpiego dell' antico dal III at XIV secolo* (Milan, 1995).
Lehmann-Hartleben, K. and Olsen, E. *Dionysiac Sarcophagi in Baltimore* (Baltimore, 1942).
van der Meer, L. *Myths and More on Etruscan Stone Sarcophagi* (Louvain, 2004).
Meinecke, K. *Sarcophagum posuit. Römische Steinsarkophage im Kontext* (Mainz, forthcoming).
Müller, F. *The So-Called Peleus and Thetis Sarcophagus in the Villa Albani* (Amsterdam, 1994).
Nock, A. D. Cremation and Burial in the Roman Empire. *Harvard Theological Review* 25 (1932), 321–359.
Nock, A. D. Sarcophagi and Symbolism. *American Journal of Archaeology* 50 (1946), 140–170.
Noguera Celdrán, J.-M. and Conde Guerri, E. (eds.). *El sarcófago romano: contribuciones al estudio de su tipología, iconografía y centros de producción* (Murcia, 2001).
Parlasca, K. Probleme der palmyrenischen Sarkophage, in: *Symposium über die antiken Sarkophage,* edited by B. Andreae (Marburg, 1984), 283–296.
Parlasca, K. Palmyrenische Sarkophage mit Totenmahlreliefs – Forschungsstand und Ikonographische Probleme, in: G. Koch (ed.), *Akten des Symposiums 125 Jahre Sarkophag-Corpus. Sarkophag-Studien* Band 1 (Mainz, 1998), 311–317.
Pensabene, P. Il reimpiego nell' età Costantina a Roma, in: G. Bonamente and F. Fusco (eds.), *Costantino il Grande dall'antichità all'umanesimo. Colloquio sul cristianesimo nel mondo antico,* Macerata 1992. Vol. 2. (Macerata, 1993) 749–768.
Pensabene, P. and Panella, C. Reimpiego e progettazione architettonica nei monumenti tardo-antichi di Roma. *Rendiconti* 66 (1993–1994), 111–283.
Platt, V. *Facing the Gods: Epiphany and Representation in Graeco-Roman Art, Literature and Religion* (Cambridge, forthcoming).
Riegl, A. *Spätrömische Kunstindustrie* (Vienna, 1901).
Rodà, I. Sarcófagos cristianos de Tarragona, in: G. Koch (ed.), *Akten des Symposiums 125 Jahre Sarkophag-Corpus. Sarkophag-Studien* Band 1 (Mainz, 1998), 150–161.
Rodenwaldt, G. *Der Sarkophag Caffarelli: Winckelmannsprogramm der archäologischen Gesellschaft zu Berlin* 83 (Berlin, 1925).

Rodenwaldt, G. *Über den Stilwandel in der antoninische Kunst. Abhandlungen der preussischen Akademie der Wissenschaften* (Berlin, 1935).
Rodenwaldt, G. Römische Löwen. *Critica d' arte* 1 (1935–1936), 225–228.
Rodenwaldt, G. Zur Kunstgeschichte der Jahre 220 bis 270. *Jahrbuch des Deutschen Archäologischen Instituts* 51 (1936), 82–113.
Rodenwaldt, G. The Transition to Late-Classical Art. *Cambridge Ancient History* vol. 12 (Cambridge, 1939), 544–570.
Rodenwaldt, G. Jagdsarkophage in Reims. *Römische Mitteilungen* 59 (1944), 191–203.
Rostovtzeff, M. I. *La peinture décorative antique en Russie méridionale* (Paris, 2004).
Rutgers, L. The *Jews in Late Ancient Rome: Evidence of Cultural Interaction in the Roman Diaspora* (Leiden, 1995).
Saint-Roch, P. La region centrale du cimetiere connu sous nom de 'Cimetière des Saints Marc et Marcellien et Damase'. *Rivista di archeologia cristiana* 57 (1981), 209–251.
Saint-Roch, P. *Le cimetière de Basileus ou coemeterium Sanctorum Marci et Marcelliani Damasique* (Vatican, 1999).
Saxer, V. La crypte et les sarcophages de saint-Maximin dans la literature Latine de Moyen-Age. *Provence Historique* 5 (1955), 196–231.
Seidel, M. Studien zur Antikenrezeption Nicola Pisanos. *Mitteilungen des Kunsthistorischen Institutes in Florenz* 19 (1975), 307–392.
Settis, S. Continuità, distanza, conoscenza. Tre usi dell' antico, in: *Memoria dell'antico nell'arte italiana: 3. Dalla tradizione all'archeologia,* edited by S. Settis (Turin, 1986), 375–486.
Settis, S. Riusare l'antico, mutare il presente, in: *Roma: il riuso dell'antico: fotografie tra XIX e XX sec.*, edited by G. Borghini (Bologna, 2004), 11–18.
Settis, S. Collecting ancient sculpture: the beginnings, in: *Collecting Sculpture in Early Modern Europe* (*Studies in the History of Art* 70), edited by N. Penny and E. D. Schmidt (Washington, 2008), 13–31.
Smith, R. R. R. Sarcophagi and Roman Citizenship, in: *Aphrodisias Papers* 4. *New Research on the City and its Monuments. JRA Supplement* 70, edited by C. Ratté and R.R.R. Smith (Providence, RI, 2008), 347–394.
Strocka, V. M. Sepulkral-Allegorien auf dokimeischen Sarkophage, in: *Symposium über die antiken Sarkophage,* edited by B. Andreae (Marburg, 1984), 197–241.
Swain, S. *Hellenism and Empire: Language, Classicism and Power in the Greek World* A.D. 50–250 (Oxford, 1996).
Thümmel, H. G. Heidnisches und Christliches auf spätantiken Sarkophagen. *Wissenschaftliche Zeitschrift der Humboldt-Universität zu Berlin. Gesellschaftswissenschaftliche Reihe* 35 (1986), 688–693.
Tolaini, E. Pisa. Quando i sarcofagi entrarono in Campo Santo. *Critica d'Arte* 33–34 (2008), 51–56.
Toynbee, J. M. C. *Death and Burial in the Roman World* (London, 1971).
Turcan, R. *Les Sarcophages romains à représentations dionysiaques: essai de chronologie et d'histoire religieuse* (Paris, 1966).
Turcan, R. Les sarcophages romaines et le problème du symbolisme funéraire. *Aufstieg und Niedergang der römischen Welt* II.16.2 (1978), 1700–1735.
Turcan, R. *Message d'outre-tombe: L'iconographie des sarcophages romains* (Paris, 1999).
Turcan, R. *Études d'archéologie sépulcrale: sarcophages romains et gallo-romains* (Paris, 2003).
Tusa, V. *I sarcofagi romani in Sicilia* (Palermo, 1957).
Wischmeyer, W. *Die Tafeldeckel der christlichen Sarkophage konstantinischer Zeit in Rom: Studien zur Struktur, Ikonographie und Epigraphik* (Freiburg, 1982).

Whitmarsh, T. *Greek Literature and the Roman Empire: the Politics of Imitation* (Oxford, 2001).

Wrede, H. *Consecratio in formam deorum: vergöttlichte Privatpersonen in der römischen Kaiserzeit* (Mainz, 1981).

Wrede, H. *Senatorische Sarkophage Roms: der Beitrag des Senatorenstandes zur römischen Kunst der hohen und späten Kaiserzeit* (Mainz, 2001).

Zanker, P. *The Mask of Socrates: The Image of the Intellectual in Antiquity* (Berkeley, 1995).

Zanker, P. Phaidras Trauer und Hippolytos Tod, in: *Im Spiegel des Mythos – Lo Specchio del Mito,* edited by S. Muth and F. De Angelis (Wiesbaden, 1999), 131–142.

Zanker, P. Die mythologischen Sarkophagreliefs und ihre Betrachter. *Sitzungsberichte Bayerische Akademie der Wissenschaften, Philosophisch-Historische Klasse* 2 (2000), 3–47.

Zanker, P. Zur Veränderung mythologischer Bildthemen auf den kaiserzeitlichen Sarkophagen aus der Stadt Rom, in: *Lebenswelten. Bilder und Räume in der römischen Stadt der Kaiserzeit,* edited by P. Zanker and R. Neudecker (Wiesbaden, 2005), 243–252.

Zanker, P. and Ewald, B. *Mit Mythen leben: die Bilderwelt der römischen Sarkophage* (Munich, 2004).

Zimmermann, K. Rodenwaldts Beitrag zur Sarkophagforschung. *Wissenschaftliche Zeitschrift der Humboldt-Universität zu Berlin. Gesellschaftswissenschaftliche Reihe* 35 (1986), 681–685.

1.
Before Sarcophagi

Glenys Davies

Elaborately decorated sarcophagi came into use in the city of Rome and its environs from c. 120 onwards.[1] Only a handful of sarcophagi can be dated to the first century or first two decades of the second century, the best known of which is perhaps the very early and anomalous Caffarelli sarcophagus in Berlin (c. 40).[2] Of the three early sarcophagi illustrated here two belong to the Trajanic period (i. e. between c. 100 and 120) (Figures 1.8 and 1.9), and the third (Figure 1.10) is Hadrianic.[3] Inhuming the unburnt body in a sarcophagus was at this time an exceptional form of burial, presumably undertaken for personal or family reasons, and it would not be seen as the usual Roman funerary custom at the time.[4] Instead the dead were usually cremated, and the funerary monuments of choice for those who could afford them were the marble ash chest (designed to hold the cremated remains taken from the pyre), the grave altar (which did not have a cavity inside to hold the ashes and therefore had a more purely commemorative function) or the ash altar (which was larger in size than an ash

---

1 The date at which production of the main series of imperial sarcophagi began will be discussed in more detail below.

2 Caffarelli sarcophagus, now in the Pergamon Museum, Berlin (inv. SK 843a): *ASR* VI, 2, 1, 77, no. 1. Although this sarcophagus is decorated with garlands its style is quite different from that of the Trajanic and Hadrianic series of garland sarcophagi which belong to the beginning of the vogue for using sarcophagi in the second century.

3 Sarcophagus of C. Bellicus Natalis Tebanianus (Figure 1.8), Camposanto, Pisa: *ASR* VI, 2, 1, 79–81, no. 6 (dated c. 100); child's sarcophagus with biographical scenes (Figure 1.9), Museo Nazionale Romano inv. 65199: *ASR* I, 4, no. 190, pl. 45, 1–5 (c. 100); Huskinson 1996, 10 and 22, no. 1.29 (c. 120); child's sarcophagus with griffins in Ostia with inscription to Ostorius Ostorianus (Figure 1.10) (Ostia Museum inv. 1156): Huskinson 1996, 63, no. 9.14; Eberle1990, 53, fig. 2; Herdejürgen 1990, 97–8, fig. 2 (130–40).

4 Herdejürgen suggests that only 15 garland sarcophagi can be assigned to the period from Augustus to c. 120, and that literary sources provide three possible reasons for the choice of such an anomalous form of burial: being a member of a Pythagorean sect, family tradition, and sensitivity to the burning process (*ASR* VI, 2, 1, 17). Petronius (*Satyricon* 111.2) describes inhumation as a Greek custom, and Tacitus (*Annals* 16.6), commenting on the exceptional practice of embalming used for Poppaea, says that cremation was the Roman custom.

chest, and combined the functions of both ash chest and grave altar).[5] The change from ash chests and grave altars to sarcophagi, and from cremation to inhumation, took the best part of a century to achieve, but by the early 3rd century the practice in Rome had completely reversed: the usual form of funerary monument for those who could afford it was the sarcophagus, and ash chests and grave altars had practically disappeared.[6] Whereas in the early empire tombs were built to accommodate cremated remains only, in the 3rd century they were designed to contain inhumed bodies, whether these were placed in sarcophagi or more basic forms of coffin or trench grave.[7] This chapter examines issues concerning this change in practice by focussing on the decoration of the monuments themselves. It concentrates on the types of funerary containers and monuments that were used before sarcophagi arrived and those sarcophagi which can be dated to the earliest decades of the second century: it considers the salient differences between them, and asks whether we can ever confidently answer the question of why the changes took place.

The nature of the question

When this phenomenon was considered in the early and mid twentieth century it was assumed that the reason for such a change in burial practice should be sought in the area of religious belief, and that the explanation must involve changes in beliefs about and attitudes to the fate of the body and soul after death. Even A.D. Nock's article on inhumation and cremation published in 1932, which argued that the change was one primarily of 'fashion', examined the question from the point of view of the attitude of different religious groups

5 For these monuments see Altmann 1905, Sinn 1987, and Boschung 1987.

6 As Jaś Elsner has pointed out to me, it is an assumption (if a plausible one) that sarcophagi represent inhumation as a burial rite: the size and shape of sarcophagi leads to the supposition that they were designed to, and always did, contain unburnt and fully articulated bodies, but the form of the human remains inside is not known for most sarcophagi. It is conceivable that on occasion they might have contained ashes or a secondary deposit of bones. Some cases of ashes placed in sarcophagi have been recorded, but these are generally at sites outside the city of Rome or at periods later than that considered here (Toynbee 1971 and 1982, 40 and n.107; Nock 1932, 333 and n.61). From the available evidence it does seem that there was a general correlation between sarcophagi and inhumation, but this is a particularly pertinent issue when considering 'children's sarcophagi' which are often defined as such by size (see below, n. 76).

7 This change can be seen particularly clearly in the excavated cemeteries under the Basilica of St. Peter in the Vatican and in the Isola Sacra near Ostia, where tombs of the later 2nd century provided for both cremation and inhumation, and contained both ash containers and sarcophagi.. For a brief discussion of the evidence see Morris 1992, 56–62; for details of the tombs, Toynbee 1971 and 1982, 132–143.

to death and the afterlife. Franz Cumont's monumental study of Roman funerary symbolism (1942) interpreted the decoration of Roman funerary monuments as expressions of complex and deeply held afterlife beliefs and hopes. Nock, in his review of Cumont, and in line with his previous article, queried the idea that the majority of those buying sarcophagi held or were trying to express such complex religious/philosophical beliefs.[8] Some scholars, however, were persuaded by Cumont's approach and adopted it enthusiastically in their analysis of specific monuments,[9] while others instead developed a more general approach to funerary symbolism which toned down some of Cumont's more extravagant arguments but nevertheless assumed that the motifs used should be explained primarily in relation to afterlife belief.[10] Nock's scepticism nevertheless struck a cord with many, and scholars studying these monuments in the later part of the 20th century have on the whole tended to react against Cumont's interpretations, seeing them as too often resting on obscure texts and arcane philosophies unlikely to be known by the public at large.

Even so, many would agree with Toynbee when she states that: 'The view that mere fashion or a purely ostentatious taste for elaborate and expensively decorated coffins could have brought about a change in burial rite so widespread and lasting is not convincing'.[11] Instead she suggests that 'it is in the development of this "other-worldly" thought that we have to seek the reason for the striking and enduring change in the method of disposing of the dead'.[12] Toynbee's idea that the use of inhumation is 'somehow a gentler and more respectful way of laying to rest the mortal frame'[13] is echoed by McCann who considers, but rejects, the idea that the production of sarcophagi was inspired by the emperor Hadrian's taste for Classical forms, which resulted in an influx of

8 Cumont 1942; Nock 1946. On the whole Cumont deals with later Roman monuments, but he does discuss the ash chest of T. Flavius Abascantus in some detail in an Appendix, and the ash chest of Ti. Claudius Vitalis in the text (Cumont 1942, 162–8).

9 See, for example, the interpretation of the decoration of the ash chest of Ianuaria (now in the Museo Gregoriano Profano, inv. 9858/9) in Farnoux 1960, and of the ash chest of Volusia Arbuscula (in the Musée Condé, Chantilly) in Berard 1974, 15. Cumont's views continue to be more highly regarded by French-speaking and Italian scholars, while English and German speakers tend to be more sceptical or dismissive of his approach.

10 See especially the work of Toynbee. For example, Toynbee writes that: 'A charioteer winning a race on a tombstone, or a hunting- or battle-scene on a sarcophagus, speak of the soul's triumph over death and evil; a man or woman reclining at a banquet expresses the soul's endowment with heavenly bliss' (Toynbee 1956, 210). I discuss the issue of different approaches to the symbolism of the decoration of ash chests and grave altars more fully in Davies 2003.

11 Toynbee 1971 and 1982, 40. But Toynbee adds 'despite the fact that ashes have occasionally been discovered in sarcophagi'.

12 Toynbee 1971 and 1982, 33.

13 Toynbee 1971 and 1982, 41.

artists from Asia Minor to Rome: 'Artistic considerations may in part explain this change, but concern with inhumation of the body and the wish to honour it with a more sumptuous and lasting home must reflect more than a change in fashion and taste'.[14] 'Fashion', however, is increasingly seen by many modern social historians as something that should not be considered too trivial for academic study – as the phrase 'mere fashion' implies – but rather as a phenomenon worthy of study in its own right, revealing many insights into the thought and concerns of the culture that created it. Thus recent studies have tended to focus on the ways the monuments express identity and status rather than afterlife belief: the focus has switched to social rather than religious reasons for commissioning and buying expensive and elaborately decorated funerary containers and monuments. The switch in interest can be seen clearly, for example, in the contrast between Cumont's interpretation of the scene on the grave altar of Flavius Abascantus showing him (presumably) reclining holding a cup as a 'festin célèste', a banquet taking place in a celestial afterlife, with Roller's recent assessment of the scene of C. Calpurnius Beryllus (see Figure 1.6) reclining on a couch with a table in front and a serving boy at either end as an expression of his social aspirations.[15]

At the same time important work was being done on the typology and chronology of the monuments, and on catalogues which considerably enhanced the known corpus of material for study, refined their chronology, and began to identify workshop groupings.[16] Such studies have tended to be rather cautious in their consideration of the significance and in particular the symbolic content of the decoration of the monuments; moreover, the various types of monuments have generally been considered in isolation, rather than in relation to one another. It is this relationship that this chapter aims to explore.

No surviving ancient text discusses, let alone explains, the change in burial rite and type of funerary monument that occurred in Rome in the 2nd century (which might in itself suggest that contemporary Romans did not see the change in burial rite as of particular significance or interest). In the absence of any such

14 McCann 1978, 20. The idea that Hadrian's Hellenism was an important factor in the introduction of inhumation to Rome is reconsidered positively in Morris 1992, 53–61.

15 Cumont 1942, 457–462. He interprets the wreath often held by the reclining figure as a 'couronne d'immortalité', and the little winged boy flying above Abascantus' legs holding a torch as Phosphorus, who 'shows the heroised dead the pathway in the sky' (Cumont 1942, 458). For the discussion of the altar of Calpurnius Beryllus see Roller 2006, 31–37; for him the 'banquet' scene evokes 'high-style elite conviviality', while 'certain details assert a freedman's achieved status and belonging' – 'The message for the viewer, correspondingly, is one of both social differentiation and social integration' (Roller 2006, 36).

16 Sinn 1987 for ash chests; Boschung 1987 (which provided an update on Altmann 1905); *ASR* VI, 2, 1 for garland sarcophagi.

literary evidence the main source of information is the monuments themselves. The first question I shall be considering therefore is the extent to which the decoration of ash chests and grave altars differs from that of the earliest sarcophagi: was there a complete break in pictorial tradition, or was there continuity? Can we discern changes in the motifs and designs used which might suggest significant changes in concerns and attitudes? Another set of questions, which are more difficult to answer given the available information, concerns the people who were buying or commissioning the monuments. What kinds of people elected to use the new monuments, and, once sarcophagi had become well-established, who were the most likely to hold onto the old monuments and methods of burial? Equally important to consider are the suppliers of the monuments – the sculptors who made them: to what extent were they responsible for creating or fostering the demand for a different type of monument? Were sarcophagi made in the same workshops as grave altars and ash chests? Or were sarcophagi promoted by new workshops (possibly indeed by sculptors newly arrived in Rome from the eastern provinces), or by workshops which had hitherto specialised in non-funerary art (such as the sculpted decoration of temples and other public buildings)? And finally, what was the motivation that inspired an individual's decision to be inhumed (or to inhume a relative) in a sarcophagus rather than be cremated and commemorated by a grave altar and/or an ash chest? Which was the more important factor in making the decision: the burial rite or the type of monument?

Dating and chronology

Only a very small proportion of the monuments can be dated at all precisely. As the majority of ash chests and grave altars have inscriptions which provide some information about the person or people commemorated it might be expected that these would give some fixed dates on which a chronology could be based. But the date of death is only very rarely mentioned: Boschung lists only six altars which give the names of the consuls at the time of death.[17] Very few of the people concerned were famous enough for us to know the date of their death from other sources, and any other information provided can usually only suggest an approximate date of death: the best we can hope for from the inscriptions is a 20-year period in which the person commemorated is likely to have died. Occasionally we know the date of events in the deceased's life (e.g.

17 Boschung 1987, 57–8, Appendix I, nos. I.1-I.6. The grave altar of Volusia Prima and Volusia Olympias in the Villa Albani (Boschung 1987, 57, no. I.1), for example, has inscriptions on the sides naming the consuls of 89 and 97 (CIL VI 9326). This altar is richly decorated and belongs to the period of particular interest to this chapter.

the date of a consulship), but not how long after that date the person concerned died: this is true of two of the monuments illustrated here, the sarcophagus of C. Bellicus Natalis Tebanianus, who was consul in 87 (Figure 1.8), and the grave altar of Licinia Magna, who was the daughter of a consul of 27 and wife of a consul of 57 (Figure 1.2).[18] Many ash chests, too, are dedicated to imperial freedmen whose names indicate the regime or even the emperor who granted their freedom – but again this provides only a *terminus post quem*, with a long potential survival period after that (although this may be limited to some extent by the stated age at death, and likely lifespan).[19] The presence of portraits with fashionable hairstyles is also evidence that can be fairly closely dated, but again only quite a small proportion of the corpus has this feature.[20] The early sarcophagi are even less helpful in that very few of them have inscriptions or portraits. Occasionally the context in which the monument was found provides some clue about the date of the monument, such as the brick stamps in the structure of the tomb with three sarcophagi in it found at the Porta Viminalis: these date the construction of the tomb to c. 134, but this provides only indirect evidence for the dates of the sarcophagi (which might have been made some

---

18 Tebanianus, consul in 87, may have died soon afterwards, but may well have survived into the reign of Trajan, or even have died early in the reign of Hadrian: Herdejürgen's date for his sarcophagus of c. 100 seems rather too early to many, including the present author (*ASR* VI, 2, 1, 22–23). Eberle 1990, 50 for example suggests that Tebanianus died c. 120–125. See also the section on dating with the help of prosopography in Boschung's appendix I (1987, 58–63): coincidentally, two other inscriptions name consuls of 87 – one is the grave altar which commemorated C. Calpurnius Crassus Frugi Licinianus who probably died in the reign of Hadrian (Boschung 1987, no. 856 and appendix I.10; CIL VI 31724); the other names a L. Volusius who was the husband of Licinia Cornelia Volusia Torquata and who seems also to have been consul in 87 (Boschung 1987, no. 13 and appendix I. 15; CIL VI 31726). The circumstances which date the altar of Licinia Magna are also discussed in Boschung 1987, 58–9, no. I.17: he suggests the altar dates to c. 80 (Boschung 1987, 97, no. 657).

19 So, for example, someone who has the *nomen* Flavius and who is described as an *Augusti libertus* cannot have died before 69, but equally he could have outlived the Flavian dynasty by several decades and could easily have survived into (even beyond) the reign of Hadrian. Some limitation to the likely date of death may be provided if the inscription gives the age at death. Similar calculations can sometimes be made for slaves and freedmen of other families whose members held consulships: the best studied of these is the large group of funerary monuments for the household of the Volusii Saturnini, a family which provided several consuls over the course of the first century (Boschung 1987, 62–3, App. I.49-I.61; Buonocore 1984).

20 The grave altars with portraits have been collected and studied in Kleiner 1987. Many such altars however make such a feature of the portrait itself that there is little other decoration, which means that they do not provide as much information about the stylistic development of other features as one might wish. The female hairstyles on the sarcophagus illustrated here in Figure 1.9 are important evidence for its date in the Trajanic period.

time after, or indeed before, the tomb was built), but does at least give a broad indication of the period concerned.[21]

Frustratingly imprecise though all this information is, it does provide a rough chronological framework on which various scholars have built complex and detailed chronologies for the groups of monuments concerned. To fill in the gaps in the chronology and to assign specific pieces to their place within the framework scholars have relied primarily on the assessment of their style and of the direction and speed of stylistic development within the corpus.[22] In the absence of more objective criteria this system has worked reasonably well and has resulted in what appear to be convincing and remarkably coherent dates for the series of ash chests, grave altars, and garland sarcophagi,[23] but it should be recognised that there is a fair amount of subjectivity involved in coming to these conclusions, with consequent room for disagreement. Herdejürgen's method, for example, relies heavily on the assumption that there were recognisable and rapidly evolving period styles, and that sculptors working at the same time, even in different workshops, would share the same definable stylistic characteristics – but at the same time she acknowledges that individual workshops had their own quirks.[24] It is not always as easy as some would maintain to decide which characteristics belong to a workshop and which to a period, and different scholars interpret the stylistic evidence in different ways. Thus the absolute dates that are assigned to an individual piece by two different scholars may be quite different, and it has to be recognised that the dates cited in most cases are relative rather than absolute, and they should be regarded as useful guidelines rather than definitive in any sense. Nevertheless, in seeking to understand why some Romans chose to be buried in sarcophagi rather than be cremated and

21 Three sarcophagi were found in this tomb: the garland sarcophagus placed opposite the door of the tomb was probably the earliest burial, but can the sarcophagus also be securely dated to the years around 134? (*ASR* VI, 2, 1, no. 78 dates it 130–140; *ASR* V, 2, 3, 91, no. 124 dates it (or, rather, its lid) to c. 120). And how much later should we date the other two sarcophagi (both mythological frieze sarcophagi, one decorated with the death of the Niobids and the other with the Orestes story)? Indeed, even within the same book (Zanker and Ewald 2004) the Niobid sarcophagus is dated 'after the middle of the second century' (captions to figures 28 and 29) and 'c. 130–140' (359), and the Orestes sarcophagus to c. 150 (caption to fig. 62) and 130–140 (364).

22 Early and pioneering work was done, for example, on the stylistic development of garlands: Toynbee 1934 established that the main series of garland sarcophagi belonged to the Hadrianic period and were not Augustan as had previously been thought, and Honroth 1971 continued the study by comparing the garlands on undated funerary monuments with more closely dated reliefs in both state and funerary art.

23 Sinn 1987; Boschung 1987; *ASR* VI, 2, 1.

24 See for example Herdejürgen 1990, where she identifies a number of workshops making garland sarcophagi at Ostia, but maintains that, although their decorative repertoires and styles were distinct from those of metropolitan Roman workshops, they did not have enough in common with each other to constitute a distinctive Ostian style.

commemorated by an ash chest or grave altar, and why this change in burial practice might have caught on more generally, we have to have some idea of what was being produced when.

In this chapter I shall be looking specifically at those ash chests and grave altars which have been dated to the end of the first and beginning of the second century, and the earliest of the main series of the sarcophagi made and used at Rome (and its environs, especially Ostia). If one looks at the catalogues of sarcophagi in the *Antiken Sarkophagreliefs* (*ASR*) series it becomes clear that very few sarcophagi are assigned dates before 150, but that a much larger number fall into the bracket of c. 150–160, or are described as early-mid Antonine (some authors prefer to use absolute dates, albeit covering quite wide periods of time, while others are more comfortable with periods expressed in terms of the ruling emperor or dynasty). Clearly the general consensus is that until c. 150 the use of sarcophagi could be considered experimental and unusual, but that around or shortly after 150 a much larger number of people were opting to use them, and workshops were established which were sufficiently familiar with sarcophagi that they had begun to make standard designs. (I leave open for now the question of whether these were the same workshops that had up until then made ash chests and grave altars or were new workshops that were created to provide for a new form of demand).

Schemes and themes of decoration: ash chests and grave altars

The decorative repertoire for ash chests and grave altars (and the hybrid ash altars) evolved over the course of the first century: a general trend was simply for the addition of more motifs, but some items went in and out of fashion.[25] Although there were always some very plain monuments, and also some idiosyncratic pieces that were presumably specially commissioned and had special meaning for the commissioner, for the majority there was a large repertoire of commonly-used motifs which could be combined in a large number of different ways, to the extent that it is difficult to find any two monuments decorated in exactly the same way. The possible decorative schemes can be divided into two broad categories: those based on the hanging garland and those which rely on more architectonic motifs, particularly columns or pilasters at the corners. Examples of the garland variety illustrated here are the

25 This can be seen, for example, in the changing preferences for garland supports: *bucrania* were used early on but became less popular in the later first century, only to experience a revival in the Hadrianic period. Their place had been taken successively by rams' heads, the head of Jupiter-Ammon and cupids (*erotes*) – each of these had its period of greatest popularity.

grave altars of Licinia Magna (Figure 1.2),[26] of L. Aufidius Aprilis (a *corinthiarius* or bronze-smith who worked in the area of the Theatre of Balbus) (Figure 1.3),[27] and of T. Apusulenus Caerellianus (Figure 1.5),[28] all three of which have been dated to the late Flavian period; the architectonic variety is represented by the ash chest of L. Lepidius Epaphra (Figure 1.1),[29] the ash altar of Ti. Claudius Callistus (Figure 1.4),[30] and the grave altar of C. Calpurnius Beryllus (Figure 1.6).[31] Both types of decorative scheme involve combining a variety of individual motifs in a design which is symmetrical and emphasises the front of the monument – indeed in most cases the attention of the viewer is drawn to the inscription in a panel placed in the centre of the upper part of the front.

Standard motifs on the garland variety include the garland itself (made up of fruit and flowers, laurel or oak leaves, or occasionally other plants) slung from bulls' skulls (*bucrania*), rams' heads or the head of Zeus/Jupiter Ammon, or from other supports such as cupids (*erotes*), torches or candelabra at the upper corners of the front: there might be other items under the front corner supports, such as eagles, swans, sphinxes or griffins (the dancing figures on the grave altar of L. Aufidius Aprilis, seen in Figure 1.3, are unusual), and small garden birds, insects and lizards are often shown around the garland. The small semi-circular space above the garland, which was just under the inscription panel and near the centre of the front, was often the location for a less standard, perhaps more personally chosen and meaningful, motif such as a small mythological or animal scene or a portrait, but a popular motif was the head of Medusa, sometimes flanked by swans (as on the grave altar of Licinia Magna, see Figure 1.2). The sides of such monuments would often be decorated in a similar way, but usually without the more complex scenes and commonly (especially on the grave altars)

26 Grave altar of Licinia Magna, Vatican Museums, Gabinetto delle Maschere 811: Altmann 1905, 36, no. 3; Boschung 1987, 97 no. 657, pl. 18; *CIL* VI 1445/31655.

27 Grave altar of L. Aufidius Aprilis, discovered in 1965 on the Via Flaminia, now on display in the Crypta Balbi museum: Caronna 1975, 205–214; Panciera 1975, 222–229 (inscription); Boschung 1987, 99, no. 693, pl. 34.

28 Grave altar of Apusulenus Caerellianus, Museo Nazionale Romano inv. 23892: Boschung 1987, 102, no. 754, pl. 30; *CIL* VI 38027.

29 Ash chest of Lepidius Epaphra, British Museum 2368: Sinn 1987, 132, no. 161; *CIL* VI 21188. Sinn dates this late Claudian-Neronian.

30 Large ash chest or ash altar of Ti. Claudius Callistus, an imperial freedman: this monument was found on the Via Flaminia placed back to back to and on the same base as the altar of Aufidius Aprilis. The inscription on the base shows that it was only Aprilis's altar that was originally intended for this site. It too is now on display in the Crypta Balbi museum. Caronna 1975, 214–222; Panciera 1975, 231–2 (inscription); Boschung 1987, 104, no. 782, pl. 35.

31 Grave altar of C. Calpurnius Beryllus, Capitoline Museum inv. 1967: Altmann 1905, no. 182; Boschung 1987, 107, no. 830, pl. 42; *CIL* VI 14150.

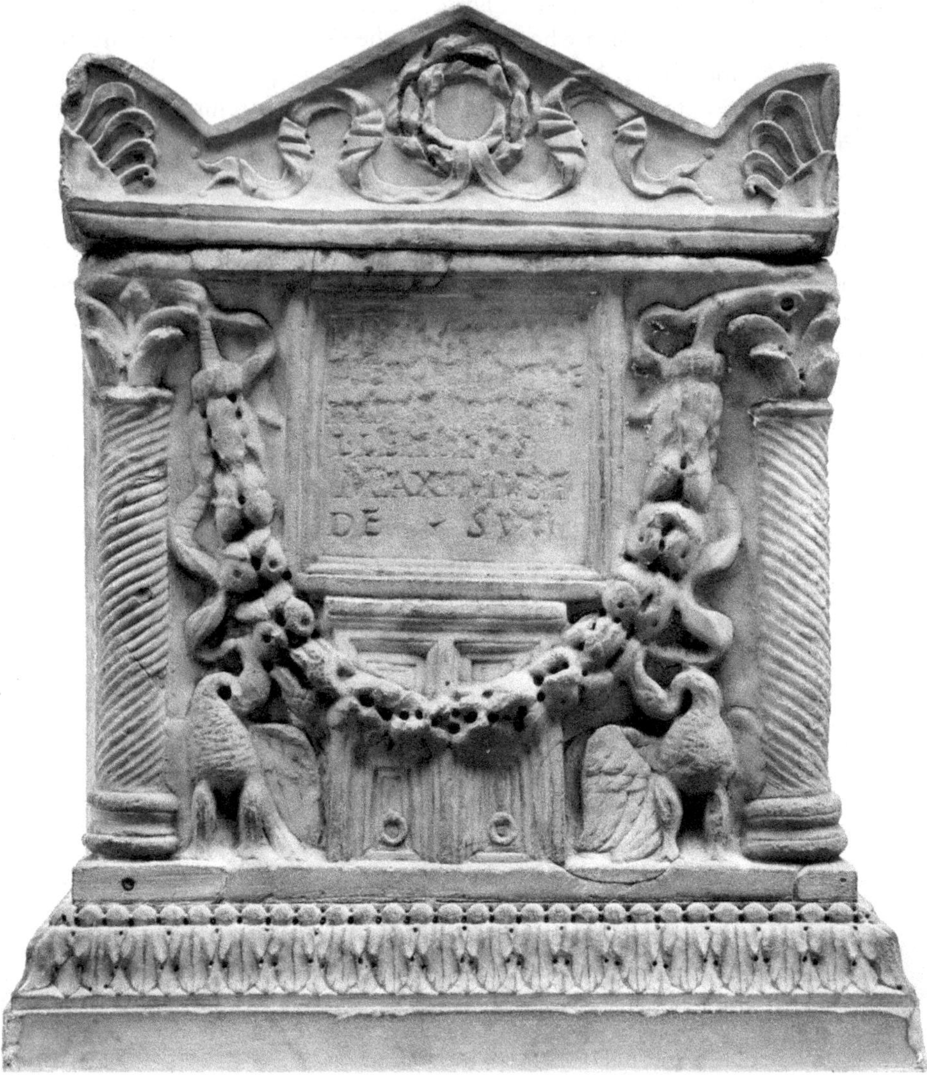

Figure 1.1: Ash chest of L. Lepidius Epaphra in the British Museum (2368) (late Claudian-Neronian). Photograph: © The Trustees of the British Museum.

with a jug and an offering bowl (*patera*) above the garlands: these are objects associated with making offerings to the gods and to the dead.[32]

32 Several authors have pointed to the importance within the repertoire used on grave altars, ash chests and some early sarcophagi of motifs associated with sacrifice and religious ritual in general: in addition to the jug and *patera* the garlands themselves could come into this category, especially when combined with *bucrania*. Such motifs could refer to

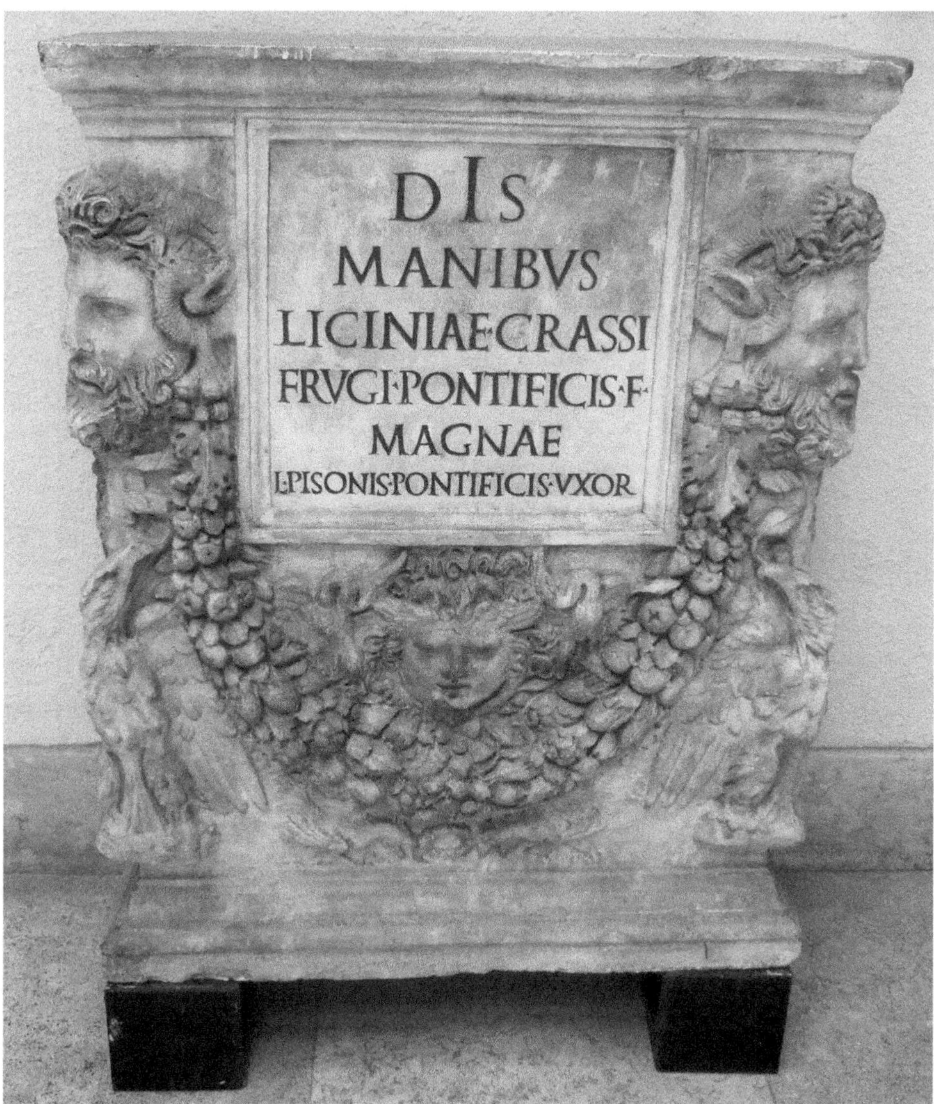

Figure 1.2: Grave altar of Licinia Magna. Vatican Museums, Gabinetto delle Maschere 811 (AD 70–80). Photograph of the cast in Civiltà Romana Museum, EUR, by the author.

Standard motifs to be found in the 'architectonic' format include those designed to make the monuments look like a building, such as columns and pilasters (usually placed at the corners and so flanking the inscription panel on the front), imitation ashlar masonry, doors and niches (*aediculae*) (see the closed

---

the cult of the *Dii Manes* or to the piety of the deceased (or , of course, both). Boschung 1993, 38; *ASR* VI, 2, 1, 24; Morris 1992, 44.

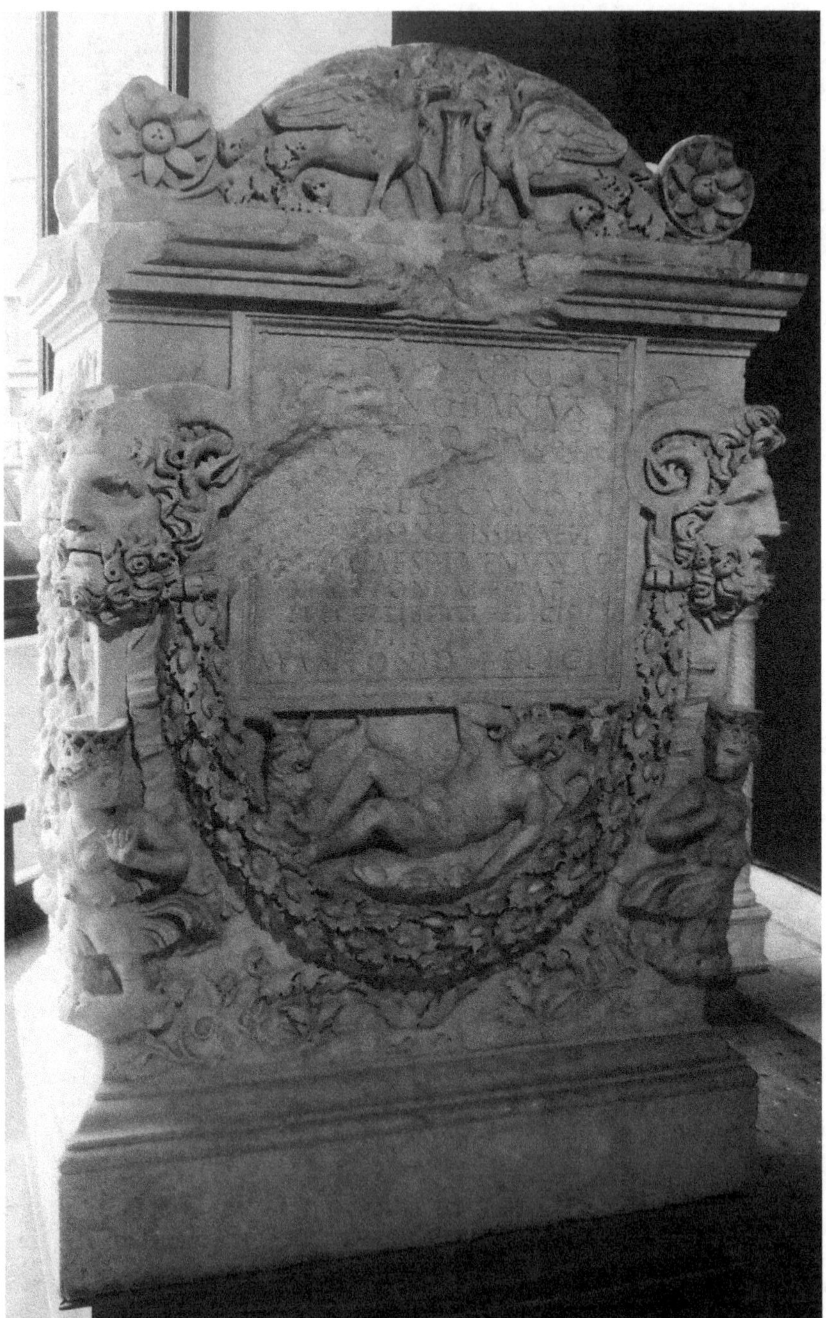

Figure 1.3: Grave altar of L. Aufidius Aprilis in Crypta Balbi (found on Via Flaminia) (late 1st century AD). Photograph: author.

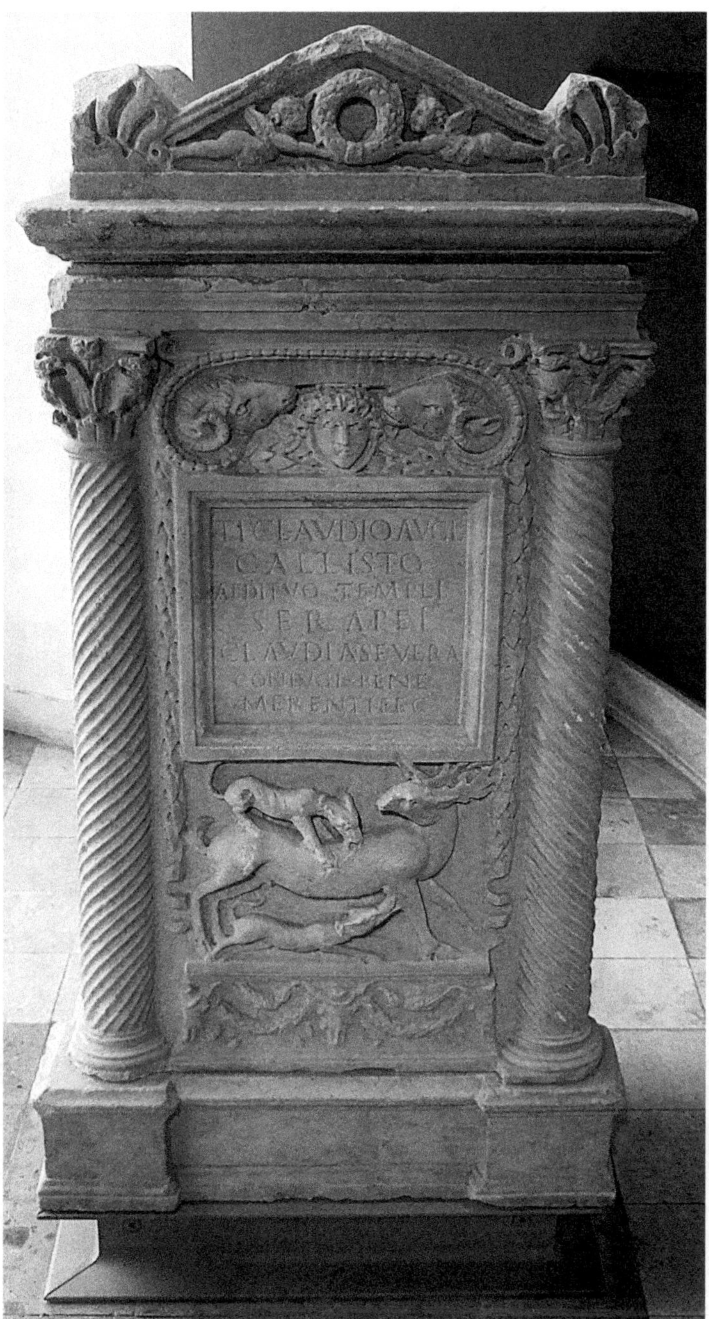

Figure 1.4: Large ash chest of Ti. Claudius Callistus in Crypta Balbi (found on Via Flaminia) (late first century AD). Photograph: author.

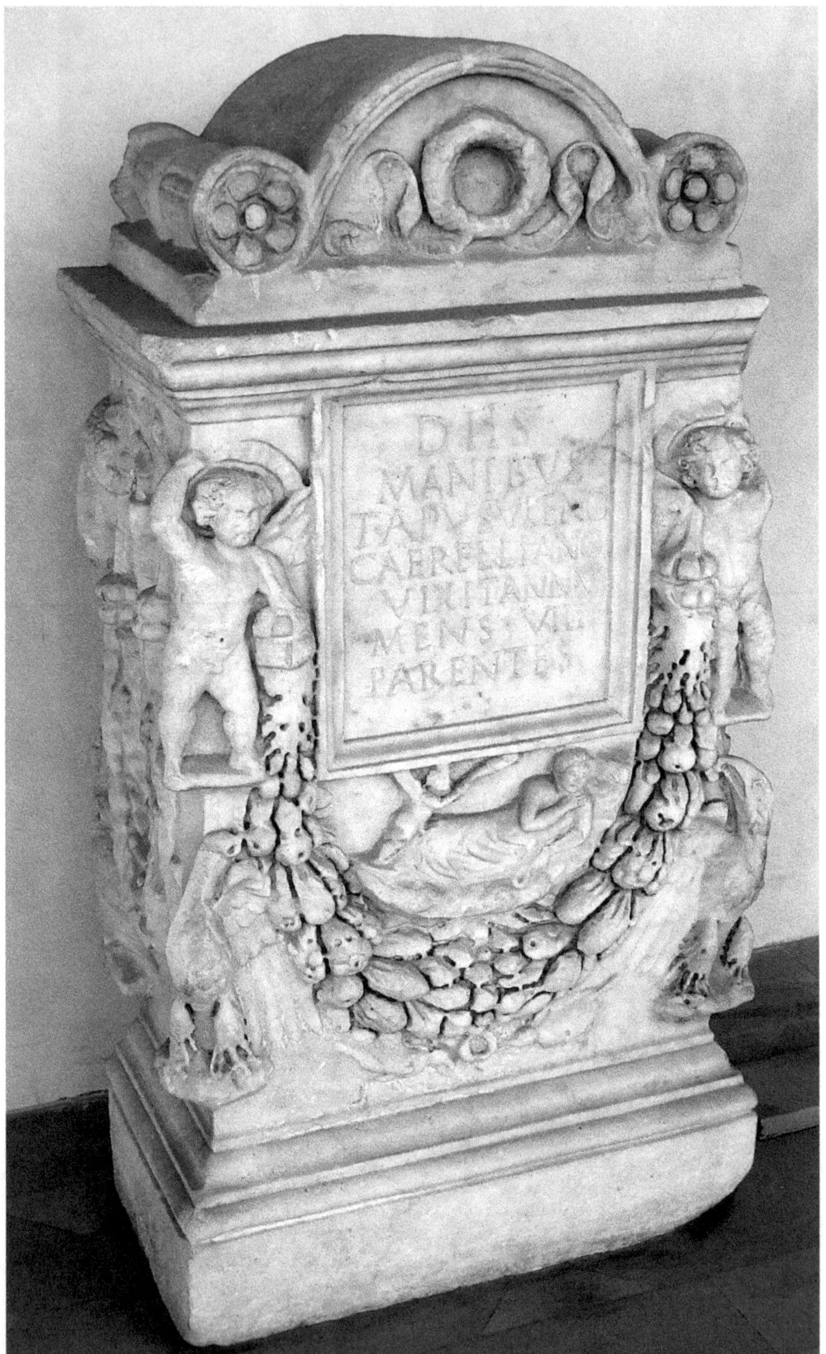

Figure 1.5: Grave altar of T. Apusulenus Caerellianus in Museo Nazionale Romano (23892) (late first century AD). Photograph: author.

door flanked by swans on the ash chest of Lepidius Epaphra, Figure 1.1). Here too there might be garlands hanging down beside the columns, looped in a frieze across the top of the front or hanging across the field as in the garland type. The space below the inscription panel may also provide a rectangular field for the representation of a small scene – as before this may be mythological, but is just as likely to involve animals or the deceased him/herself in some way (heraldically arranged pairs of griffins and sphinxes, for example, are quite popular; see also the scene of two dogs attacking a stag in Figure 1.4 or the 'funerary banquet' of Calpurnius Beryllus in Figure 1.6). The space above the inscription panel might also provide a narrower field for decoration, often with plant or animal motifs, or again the head of Medusa – in the case of Calpurnius Beryllus's altar this is flanked by rams' heads. The sides of these monuments might be decorated with motifs such as a tree with birds, a seated griffin (see Figure 1.6) or sphinx, or the ubiquitous jug and offering bowl.

An important principle in the case of both the garland and architectonic schemes is that the design relies on a mix-and-match approach: the motifs chosen from a large and flexible repertoire are not combined into a single visibly coherent picture, and do not necessarily have any thematic connection with each other. It is debatable whether they were individually or collectively conceived of as having a 'meaning', although they did perhaps evoke associations which were seen as appropriate to the context in which they were used.[33] Figured scenes play a limited part: only a small number of monuments are decorated with such scenes as the only form of decoration, and they are clearly one-off commissions where the decoration had particular meaning for the person who commissioned them (and they also tend to be late in date).[34] More commonly the figured scene is only part of and is subordinated to the decorative scheme.

33 In my view they did not form a coherent symbolic 'picture language' as advocated by Jocelyn Toynbee (Toynbee 1956): see Davies 2003.

34 For example, the scene of a woman with cupid and a little girl with birds and a dog on the ash chest of T. Apusulenus Alexander (Sinn 1987, no. 172); scenes involving cupids and boys on the ash chest of Publius Severeanus and Blolo (Sinn 1987, no. 173), both dated Claudian-Neronian; cupids wrestling in the *palaestra* on the ash chest of C. Minicius Gelasinus in Liverpool (Sinn 1987, no. 607 and Davies 2007, 85–90, no. 41), mid second century; battle scenes on a round urn without inscription (Sinn 1987, nos. 631); Meleager, Medea and Hippolytos/Phaedra scenes (Sinn 1987, nos. 633 and 634, 635 and 636): Sinn dates all of these urns/chests to the mid Antonine period, by which time frieze sarcophagi with similar scenes had become established. On grave altars such scenes tend to represent the deceased's work or family: L. Calpurnius Daphnus is shown at work in the Macellum Magnum on the front of his altar in the Palazzo Massimo alle Colonne (Boschung 1987, no. 953, dated between 41–110), L. Cornelius Atimetus's tool-making business and shop are shown on the sides of his altar in the Galleria Lapidaria, Vatican Museums (Boschung 1987, no. 968, dated 'soon after AD

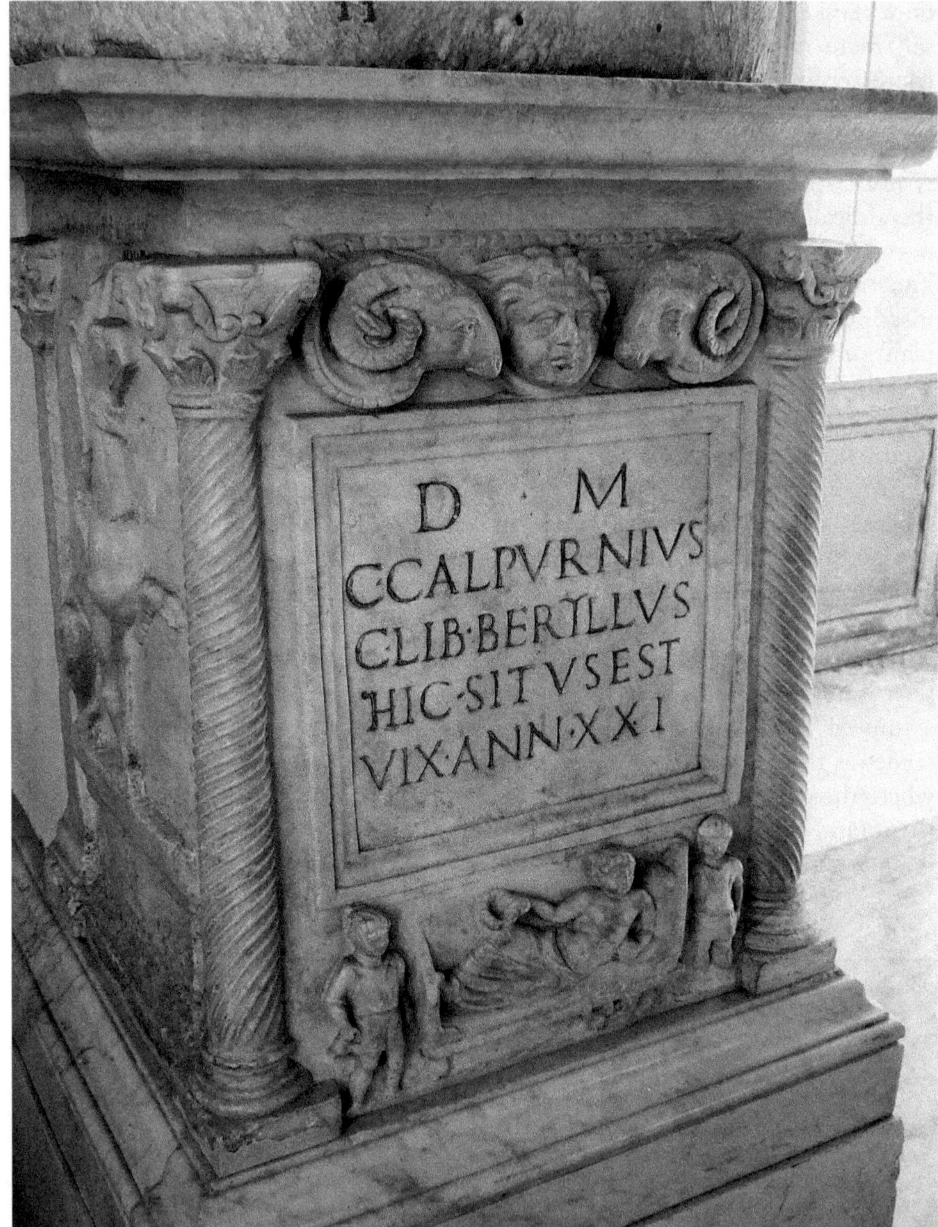

Figure 1.6: Grave altar of C. Calpurnius Beryllus in Capitoline Museums (1967) (early 2nd century AD). Photograph: author.

80'). Passienia Gemella is also shown with each of her two sons on the sides of her altar in Liverpool (Boschung 1987, no 329; Davies 2007,140–145, no. 104, Hadrianic).

Broadly speaking such scenes depict either the deceased him/herself, a mythological incident, or a scene from nature. The most common of the scenes involving the deceased are the so-called funerary banquet scene, as on the grave altar of C. Calpurnius Beryllus (Figure 1.6) (the deceased is seen lying on a couch with a drinking vessel, with or without paraphernalia such as a small table standing in front of the couch with further cups on it, servants, and a spouse seated at the end of the bed), a couple linking right hands (the '*dextrarum iunctio*' gesture), or, more rarely, other scenes from their working or domestic lives.

Specific mythological scenes are not very common and represent a wide range of rather disparate stories: the only mythological episodes represented on several monuments are the Rape of Persephone (Persephone/Proserpina being carried off in a chariot by Hades/Pluto) (see Figure 1.7)[35] and Romulus and Remus being suckled by the she-wolf:[36] otherwise scenes appear only once or twice in the surviving corpus (though Venus bathing does appear three times,[37] and the doe suckling the infant Telephos was also quite popular as a pendant, or perhaps alternative, to the wolf and twins).[38] The scenes which can be identified as specific mythological episodes are otherwise very disparate, and appear to be one-off special commissions: these include: Daedalus making the cow for Pasiphae, Oedipus and the sphinx, Leto fleeing with her children, the death of Archemoros, and Mercury with the infant Dionysus.[39] These scenes are typically

35 Ash chest without inscription in the Museo Nazionale Romano (inv. 65197): Sinn 1987, 237, no. 603, pl. 87c (mid second century); Boschung 1987,107, no. 830, pl. 42 (beginning of second century). I know of eight other ash chests/grave altars decorated with this motif: all would appear to date to the late first/early second century.

36 It is perhaps debatable whether this should really be classed as a 'scene', as it only ever consists of the wolf and two babies, without any other figures. It is found, for example, above the garland on the front of the grave altar of Volusia Prima and Volusia Olympias, dated by consular dates to c. 90 (see note 17 above) (Buonocore 1984, 135–7, no. 106, fig. 5), and below the garland on the front of the altar of L. Volusius Urbanus (Buonocore 1984, 65–7, no. 7, fig. 1; Sinn 1990, 79–80, no. 46, pl, 133–4).

37 On the grave altar of A. Albius Graptus (Capitoline Museums 2101: Montemartini): Boschung 1987, 103, no, 763, pl. 31 (Domitianic); ash altar of M. Coelius Superstes in the British Museum 2360 (Altmann 1905, 161. no. 203, fig. 131), and on a grave altar in Nazzano.

38 The doe suckling Telephos appears on several monuments: it appears, for example, below the garland on the ash altar of L. Volusius Phaedrus (Buonocore 1984, 97–98, no. 51, fig. 4; Sinn 1990, 80–81, no. 47, pl. 135–6). Also used on a smaller number of monuments was the similar scene of a goat suckling a child (presumably Amaltheia and Zeus): all three 'suckling' scenes (she-wolf, doe and goat) appear together on one altar, that of P. Annius Eros and Ofillia Romana in New York, Zanker, 1988.

39 Daedalus: ash chest of C. Volcacius Artemidorus, Museo Nazionale Romano inv. 125407 (Sinn 1987, 200, no. 456, pl. 70 f, late first century); Oedipus: grave altar of Ti. Claudius Geminus, lost (Altmann 1905, 105, no. 90); Leto: grave altar of

small and involve only a few figures, and there is no obvious pattern or explanation for why they were chosen. In addition there are scenes which allude more vaguely to mythology or deities (such as Mercury watching a goat eating the leaves of a tree).[40] Also quite numerous are scenes which involve the followers of Dionysus (such as the scene above the garland on the grave altar of L. Aufidius Aprilis which shows a sleeping satyr reminiscent of the Barberini Faun watched by two goats, see Figure 1.3): although these scenes sometimes include Dionysus himself, they more often show Silenus riding a donkey in the company of satyrs, maenads and/or Pan, dancing maenads, or other vignettes involving the Dionysiac *thiasos.*[41] Other scenes involve playful cupids[42] and Nereids, Tritons and other sea creatures swimming through the ocean.[43]

Animal scenes frequently involve combat: a lion or dogs attacking some other animal such as a deer (see Figure 1.4) and cock fights:[44] usually these scenes are just presented as scenes, but in some examples, as that of the scene of two dogs attacking a deer on the ash chest of Ti. Claudius Callistus (Figure 1.4)

Luccia Telesina, Museo Chiaramonti, Vatican (Altmann 1905, 83, no. 46, pl. 47; Boschung 1987, 101, no. 732, pl. 28); Archemoros: grave altar of P. Egnatius Nicephorus, Detroit Institute of Arts 38.167 (Altmann 1905, 102, no. 84; Boschung 1987, 103, no. 765, pl. 32, Domitianic). An almost identical altar dedicated to Herbasia Clymene has been lost for so long that one wonders whether it ever actually existed: it is known only from drawings (Altmann 1905, 103, no. 85; Boschung 1987, 103, no. 766); Mercury and the infant Dionysus appear on a grave altar in Amelia and on the altar of Passiena Prima on display in the Vatican car park excavation site (where seated Mercury dangles a large bunch of grapes in front of the child, in the presence of female figures, presumably the Nymphs about to take over the task of caring for the baby).

40 Ash chest of Ianuaria from the Volusii tomb, in the Museo Gregoriano Profano: Buonocore 1984, 110–111, no. 70, fig. 42; Sinn 1987, 202–3, no. 463, pl. 72e, c. 90–120; Sinn 1990, 98–9, no. 78, pl. 196–7. See also Farnoux 1960 for an elaborate and ingenious Cumont-style interpretation of the scene as an allegory of Orphic/neo-Pythagorean beliefs.

41 For example, the ash chest of Callityche in Bologna (Sinn 1987,161, no. 280, pl. 50b, Flavian?) with Silenus riding a donkey with satyrs, maenads and other figures.

42 Naked little boys, sometimes with, sometimes without, wings appear in a variety of different scenes. Particularly charming are those on an ash altar in the Museo Gregoriano Profano (inv. 9819): those placed under the garland on the front have just finished a cock fight – the winner approaches the prize table and the loser leaves the scene in dejection; on the right side two little boys are represented in drunken revelry, and on the left they appear with a panther (Buonocore 1984, 184–5, no. 186, figs. 37–9; Sinn 1987, 121–2, no. 119, l. 30 a and b; Sinn 1990, 106–7, no. 93, pl. 227–32).

43 For example the grave altar of Agria Agathe in the British Museum (2350) has underneath the inscription panel a scene of a sea-centaur with a Nereid seated on its back and two cupids on its tail; on the ash chest of Flavia Sabina in the Louvre (MA 2148) a child-like sea centaur with a lyre-playing cupid on his back gallops through the waves side by side with a sea-horse (Sinn 1987, 233–4, no. 584, pl. 86b).

44 See also the scene of a lion attacking a donkey above the garland on the altar of T. Statilius Hermes in Cambridge. For the cock fight motif see Bruneau 1965.

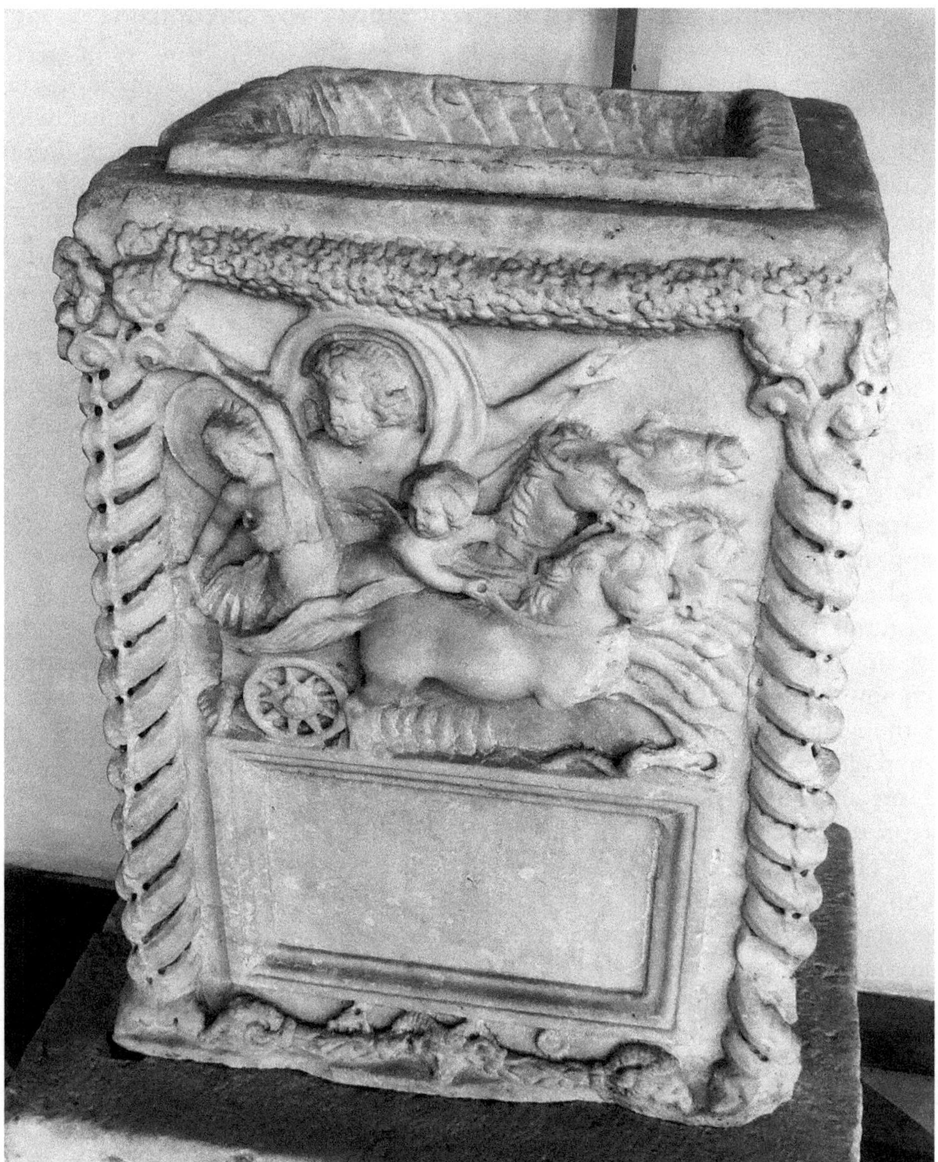

Figure 1.7: Ash chest without inscription with Rape of Persephone scene in Museo Nazionale Romano (65197) (early or mid 2nd century AD). Photograph: author.

the group is placed on a low base, making it look like a statue group rather than a scene from nature, but this is unusual.

Schemes and themes of decoration: early sarcophagi

The biggest coherent group of sarcophagi which appear to be made in the period before the middle of the second century are those decorated with garlands: this in itself might suggest that their decoration followed a tradition established by ash chests and grave altars and that the new form of monument did not immediately entail the introduction of radically new designs or motifs. There were however quite a number of differences in the repertoire used for garland sarcophagi compared to that used on ash chests and grave altars. The garland supports are usually human figures (especially cupids) and not *bucrania* or animal heads (and never the head of Zeus/Jupiter Ammon). The field is not cluttered with small birds or other subsidiary scenes or motifs: instead the fields in the lunettes above the garlands are given prominence, and are usually filled with a detailed and often quite specific mythological scene. These scenes, moreover, do not have to compete with an inscription panel for the viewer's attention: in the very few instances where these sarcophagi have an inscription it appears to have been an afterthought and is not placed in a panel but rather has had to be fitted in along the top edge of the chest, as on the sarcophagus of Ostorius Ostorianus (Figure 1.10), or between the various elements of the decoration (as on the sarcophagus of Tebanianus (Figure 1.8).[45] Many motifs common on grave altars and ash chests are absent from these sarcophagi – although the sculptors appear to be more inventive when it comes to composing mythological scenes their repertoire of small motifs, especially those involving birds and animals, appears to have shrunk, and they show little interest in representing the deceased him/herself in any form.

The subjects chosen for the mythological scenes on garland sarcophagi appear just as disparate (but on the whole not the same) as those used on the grave altars and ash chests but at the same time they are not the myths or mythological episodes that were to become most popular later on frieze sarcophagi. One difference however is that the larger format of the sarcophagus allows for more than one episode in a story to be shown, and several sarcophagi take advantage of this. The sarcophagus in the Metropolitan Museum, New York, dated Trajanic by Herdejürgen, has three episodes from the story of Theseus and Ariadne in the three lunettes above the garlands on the front;[46] the

45 Another early sarcophagus with the inscription fitted in along the top edge is that of Malia Titia (*ASR* VI, 2, 1, 109, no. 50): like that of Ostorius Ostorianus it seems it was made in Ostia. Two sarcophagi which do have central inscription panels are discussed in Herdejürgen 1990: dedicated to Volusia Prosodos and M. Aemilius Posidonianus, both are from Ostia and differ in style from Roman Metropolitan sarcophagi. It would seem that patrons in Ostia were keener on including an inscription than those in Rome itself.

46 Inv. no. 90.12: *ASR* VI, 2, 1, 90–92, no. 23, dated 'shortly after AD 120'; Brilliant 1984, 133–4, pl. 4.4. The three scenes (from left to right) show Theseus and Ariadne

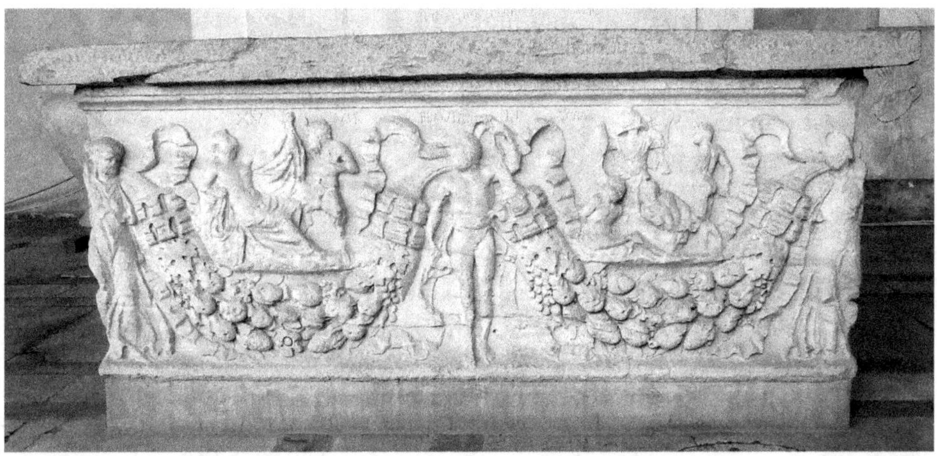

Figure 1.8: Sarcophagus of C. Bellicus Natalis Tebanianus in Pisa, Camposanto (Trajanic?). Photograph: author.

early Hadrianic sarcophagus from the same workshop in the Palazzo Barberini has three episodes from the story of the punishment of Marsyas by Apollo;[47] the garland sarcophagus now in Basle has four episodes of the story of Philoctetes in the two lunettes on the front and two on the sides,[48] and the well-known sarcophagus in the Louvre similarly has four episodes from the Actaeon story.[49] In all of these cases the designer of the sarcophagus has taken the opportunity given by the multiple fields available to tell a story through two or more episodes using the same figures in much the same way as later sarcophagus designers were to do with frieze sarcophagi. Even the two scenes on the front of the sarcophagus of Tebanianus (Dionysus revealing himself to Pan and a trophy with two prisoners and a satyr) could be said to be linked thematically, although they are not two episodes in the same story – and the same is true of the scenes of a drunk Silenus supported by Pan and a satyr, and the sleeping Ariadne, on a sarcophagus in Liverpool.[50] On the other hand the sarcophagus front in the Palazzo Mattei combines Oedipus and the sphinx with Polyphemus and Galatea, and it is difficult to see what link (if any) the viewer was expected to make between the two scenes.[51] Many of the pieces surviving from this early

before the door to the labyrinth; Theseus fighting the Minotaur; Theseus abandoning Ariadne on Naxos. Above the garlands on the sides are a theatrical mask (right) and the bust of a boy (possibly Dionysus as a child) (left). The sarcophagus contained the skeleton of a man of mature years (McCann 1978, 25–9, no. 1).

47 *ASR* VI, 2, 1, 96–7, no. 30 (dated 120–130).

48 *ASR* VI, 2, 1, 85–7, no. 16 (dated 120–130).

49 *ASR* VI, 2, 1, 93–5, no. 26 (dated c. 130). The narrative scenes are also discussed by Brilliant (1984, 125–33, pl. 4.1–4.3).

50 Ince Blundell Hall collection: *ASR* VI, 2, 1, no. 42.

51 *ASR* VI, 2, 1, 97–8, no. 31 (dated 120–130).

period however are too fragmentary for us to know what other scenes they were combined with (e.g. fragments with the Rape of Persephone in Venice, Ariadne in Pisa, the childhood of Dionysus, Medea);[52] and in addition to the sarcophagi with specific mythological scenes in the lunettes there were many with more generic scenes of the followers of Dionysus,[53] Nereids and other sea creatures,[54] cupids (on animals, on dolphins, with fighting cocks),[55] animal scenes, bucolic scenes,[56] and the ubiquitous Medusa heads.[57] Masks of various kinds were also to become very popular on garland sarcophagi.[58] Motifs previously popular on grave altars and ash chests, where they occur, tend to be displaced from the front onto the sides and lid,[59] and even when a motif like the Rape of Persephone, relatively popular on the earlier monuments, appears on a sarcophagus it is noticeable that the sculptors were not following the same design original.[60]

Although garland sarcophagi would appear to represent the largest category of sarcophagus types used in the period between c. 100 and 140, other types of design were also used in the period. The largest single group is that of griffin sarcophagi, decorated usually with heraldically placed pairs of seated or standing winged griffins (which may be of the eagle-headed or lion-headed variety). A very early example is the so-called 'priest's sarcophagus' in the Vatican Museums, dated by Herdejürgen to the end of the first century:[61] others include a child's sarcophagus in the Fitzwilliam Museum, Cambridge, a griffin sarcophagus from the tomb of the Licinii Crassi now in Baltimore,[62] and a child's sarcophagus from Ostia (Figure 1.10).[63] Another child's sarcophagus in Malibu combines

---

52 *ASR* VI, 2, 1, 99–100, no. 35 (Persephone in Venice); 96, no. 29 (Ariadne in Pisa); 127–8, no. 80 (Childhood of Dionysus, lost); 103–4, no. 40 (Medea, once in Florence).

53 Dionysiac scenes: *ASR* VI, 2, 1, no. 46 (cupids carry a drunk Silenus).

54 Nereids and sea-creatures: *ASR* VI, 2, 1, nos. 17, 19,22, 24, 34, 56, 70, 75.

55 Cupids riding sea-animals: *ASR* VI, 2, 1, nos. 36, 41, 44, 53, 60, 66, 76; with fighting cocks no. 50. Cupids riding animals or sea creatures also appear in friezes on lids.

56 Animal and bucolic scenes: *ASR* VI, 2, 1, nos. 33, 38, 39, 50 (cock fight), 58, 59, 71.

57 Medusa Heads: *ASR* VI, 2, 1, nos. 15, 20, 52, 78 (from the Porta Viminalis tomb).

58 Masks: *ASR* VI, 2, 1, nos. 45, 46, 51, 54, 60, 61, 64.

59 This is particularly noticeable in the case of a sarcophagus once on the London art market (*ASR* VI, 2, 1, no. 44) with four small scenes along the front of the lid of the wolf and twins, doe and Telephos, Pan fighting cupid, and Pan confronting a goat.

60 *ASR* VI, 2, 1, pl. 33.1: here Persephone's body is extended almost horizontally across the picture in front of that of Hades; the usual depiction on ash chests and grave altars has Persephone's body arched back over Hades' outstretched arm (see Figure 1.7).

61 *ASR* VI, 2, 1, 23; the priest's sarcophagus is illustrated in Strong 1961, 47, pl. 85.

62 Cambridge sarcophagus: Huskinson 1996, 63, no. 9.12; Baltimore sarcophagus: Lehmann-Hartleben and Olsen 1942, 17–18 and 63–4; Huskinson 1996, 63, no. 9.11.

63 Sarcophagus from the Isola Sacra with inscription to Ostorius Ostorianus (Ostia Museum inv. 1156): see note 3 for references. Herdejürgen (1990, 97–8 and *ASR* VI, 2,

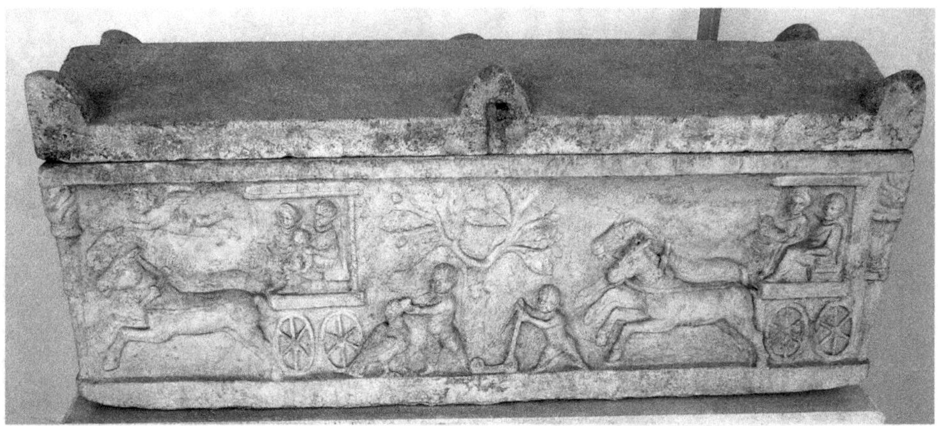

Figure 1.9: Sarcophagus in Museo Nazionale Romano (65199) with scenes of travelling carriages and children (Trajanic). Photograph: author.

four scenes of cupids pouring liquid from a jug in front of a standing griffin with two more cupids holding up the portrait bust of a girl.[64] Griffins also appear on the sides of garland sarcophagi and some early strigillated sarcophagi.[65] The idea of heraldically placed griffins, seated or standing either side of an object such as a tripod or incense burner, was not new: they appear on a number of ash chests and grave altars ranging in date from the reign of Tiberius to that of Hadrian, but were particularly popular at the turn of the first-second centuries.[66]

Also dating to the period before or around 140 is a small number of other sarcophagi, such as the one illustrated here in Figure 1.9. This shows the life course of a small child in poignant scenes of his arrival into the world in a carriage (where he is shown as a baby in his mother's arms), his progress as a toddler learning to walk and playing with a pet goose, and his early exit from the world, again in a carriage, sitting on his father's knee: that this is not an ordinary everyday journey is indicated by the cupid flying above.[67] The woman's hairstyle in the two scenes dates the sarcophagus to the reign of Trajan. Another child's sarcophagus, in Agrigento, with scenes of childhood and parents mourning their

1, 45) argues that this sarcophagus belongs to the same date (c. 130–140) and workshop as the garland sarcophagus of Malia Titia, also from Ostia.

64 Eberle 1990, figs. 1a-d.Eberle dates the sarcophagus to early in the reign of Hadrian (i. e. c. 120) and discusses its unusual iconography with reference to other griffin sarcophagi and architectural friezes from buildings in Rome, including Trajan's Forum.

65 For example, a strigillated sarcophagus at Ostia with horned lion griffins on the sides, on the left with a ram's head and on the right starting back from a snake emerging from a hole under a tree: *Notizie degli Scavi* 1972, 432–441 and 484–487.

66 Sinn 1987, nos. 36, 154, 164, 259, 260, 271, 298, 412, 413, 446, 550.

67 Sarcophagus in the Museo Nazionale Romano, inv. 65199: *ASR* I, 4, no. 190, pl. 45, where it is dated to c. 100; Huskinson 1996, 22, no. 1.29 (dated c. 120).

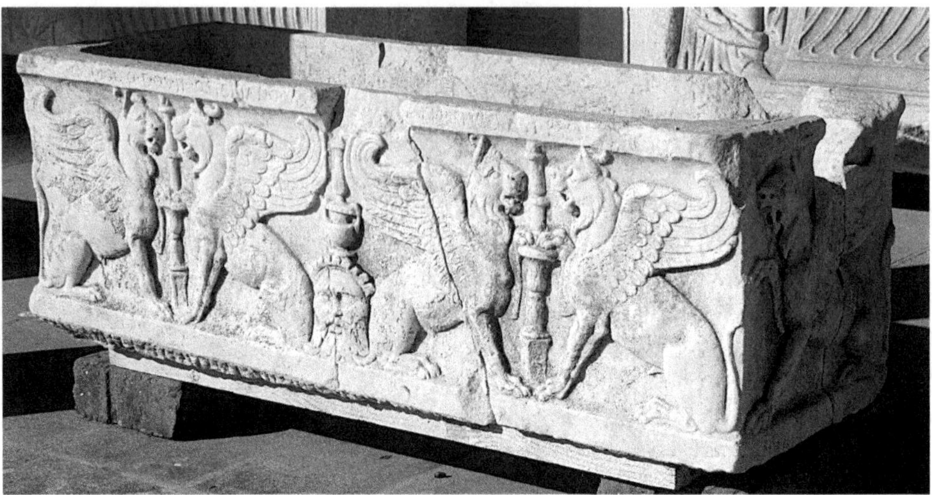

Figure 1.10: Sarcophagus of Ostorius Ostorianus decorated with griffins in Ostia (1156) (Hadrianic). Photograph: author.

child's early death, is also generally considered to be early in date (Hadrianic).[68] A very small number of sarcophagi decorated with mythological scenes in a frieze that takes up the whole of the front (i. e. without garlands) may also date to the Hadrianic or very early Antonine period (140 or earlier) – for example, an Endymion sarcophagus in the Capitoline Museums.[69] A small number of sarcophagi depicting Dionysus and his followers may also have been made as early as 140,[70] and also a few with cupids or children at play,[71] but the main series of most themes seems to have started up around the middle of the second century.

This survey of the designs and motifs used on ash chests, grave altars and early sarcophagi does not point to a major shift in iconography or its meaning in the early second century, but on the other hand the repertoire used to decorate sarcophagi is not exactly the same as that found on the cremation monuments. Garland sarcophagi continue in the tradition of large grave altars

68 *ASR* I, 4, no. 2, pl. 53 (c. 120–130); Huskinson 1996, 20, no. 1.1 (120–130); Zanker and Ewald 2004, 66, figs. 47 and 48 (dated 130 in the caption to fig. 47 but 'Antonine' in the text).

69 Zanker and Ewald 2004, 249, fig. 221 and pp. 317–9; *ASR* XII, 2, no. 27.

70 A sarcophagus in the Museo Nazionale Romano with the childhood of Dionysus (inv. 124736), and a sarcophagus with the followers of Dionysus involved in various erotic activities in Naples, are both dated Hadrianic by Turcan (1966, 136).

71 Cupids racing in chariots: *ASR* V, 2, 3, nos. 35 (Louvre Ma 1350), 87 (Vatican, Sala della Biga), 113 (Berlin); boys playing with nuts: *ASR* I, 4, no. 63 (British Museum); cupids playing: *ASR* V, 2, 1, nos. 5 (in Berlin), 82 (Palazzo Mattei), 106 (Villa Albani).

decorated with garlands, although with the perhaps significant omission of the prominent inscription panel. But this particular design of altar (seen in Figure 1.2, 1.3 and 1.5) is in the minority compared with the many other decorative schemes used on grave altars and ash chests, some of which privilege the inscription panel over all other elements of the decoration. The people who chose to buy sarcophagi and inhume their loved ones, and the sculptors who made the sarcophagi for them, seem on the whole to have had a similar mindset to those who previously bought and made grave altars, and were content to draw on a familiar repertoire of motifs, but they chose from it selectively. There appear to have been subtle shifts in emphasis as far as the iconography is concerned rather than major changes in direction. So, in the final section of this chapter I shall consider the question of whether we can deduce anything of significance about the patrons and the workshops who opted to switch from one form of funerary monument to the other, and what their motivation might have been for doing so.

Patrons and sculptors

The inscriptions usually placed on ash chests and grave altars provide a lot of information about the social groups who bought and erected these monuments: obviously only the comparatively well-off could afford to buy even a small and very ordinary sculpted marble monument, but this economic class included a wide range of social groups, including both slaves and noble families. Freedmen/women seem to be the most prominent group, as many monuments name the deceased and/or their relatives as freed slaves, often of the imperial household. The proportion of freedmen to freeborn named in the inscriptions is unlikely to reflect the makeup of Roman society in the first and early second centuries, but it may say something about which groups were most anxious to commemorate themselves and to provide adequate and appropriate funerary provision. The find contexts of most ash chests and grave altars have not been recorded, but when we do know it would seem that many ash chests come from the large *columbaria* of the slaves and freedmen of the imperial family or from tombs which housed the monuments of the *familia* (slaves and freedmen) of other prominent Roman families.[72] It is much less common to find such monuments dedicated to people who can be identified as belonging to the senatorial aristocracy, but clearly they too might be commemorated by a grave altar or have their ashes placed in a marble ash chest. The Licinii Crassi at least used

72 Such as the three *columbaria* of the Vigna Codini (Toynbee 1971 and 1982, 113–5), the huge *columbaria* on the Via Appia of the slaves and freedmen of Augustus and Livia, or the tombs of the Volusii, or the Passienii.

grave altars as memorials to even the most prominent of their family members, as a group of nine altars found together in 1884 testifies.[73] These altars are decorated in much the same way as altars to those of lower status in Roman society, although they could perhaps be said to be characterised by a degree of tasteful minimalism: they include altars decorated with garlands as well as those which put more emphasis on the inscription and confine the decoration to the pedimental area. The altar to Licinia Magna illustrated in Figure 1.2 is one of the more highly decorated altars in this group, but compared to the altar of the bronze-worker Aufidius Aprilis (Figure 1.3) it seems quite restrained, and it would seem that the noble families of Rome were not the ones to commission the most flamboyant monuments.[74]

The altars of the Licinii Crassi are also of interest because it would seem that this may be one instance where we can see the transition from cremation to inhumation monuments in action within a single aristocratic family. A group of sarcophagi were found in two chambers close by the place where the grave altars were found, and it has been presumed that these sarcophagi were used for the burial of the same family: the fact that the latest of the grave altars dates to about the same time as the earliest of the sarcophagi (the Hadrianic period) suggests that the family might have decided to change its usual burial habits at this time.[75] However, it should be emphasised that the circumstances of the discovery and excavation make certainty that the two sets of monuments have anything to do with each other impossible, and, as is usually the case, none of the sarcophagi have inscriptions. Thus we cannot be sure that the same aristocratic family used the sarcophagi as was commemorated by the altars. But if they were, it is interesting that the first member of the family for whom the

73 The altars were found in the grounds of the Villa Bonaparte near the Porta Salaria on land which may well have been part of the family's suburban estates, but not, apparently, in their original tomb: see Kragelund 2003 esp. chapter 7, 101–8. For details of the altars and the identification of the people commemorated see also Altmann 1905, 36–43; Boschung 1987, 58–9 and nos. 1, 13, 287, 593, 643, 657, 745, 856, 857; and Kragelund 2003 chapters 2, 18–45 and 8, 109–11.

74 The slaves and freedmen of the Volusii were also commemorated by conspicuously large and highly decorated ash and grave altars (catalogued and illustrated in Buonocore 1984 and Sinn 1990).

75 According to Boschung 1987, 59, no. 1.10 the last of the datable altars is that of C. Calpurnius Crassus Frugi Licinianus, who died under Hadrian; the earliest of the sarcophagi is a child's garland sarcophagus in the Museo Nazionale Romano (inv. 441; *ASR* VI, 2, 1, 116–8, no. 60, c. 130) closely followed by a griffin sarcophagus in Baltimore (inv. 2335) (Lehmann-Hartleben and Olsen 1942 passim and Kragelund 2003).

new burial rite was adopted was a child, and that the family no longer felt that the most important part of a funerary monument was the inscription.[76]

It is tempting to assume that the fashion for sarcophagi began with the Roman aristocracy and then trickled down to lower levels of society:[77] after all, one of the earliest of the garland sarcophagi of the 'new' type belonged to C. Bellicus Natalis Tebanianus, a man who had been a consul, was a *XV vir sacris faciundis* and a member of the *sodalitas* attached to the imperial cult of Vespasian.[78] On the other hand, the flashiest grave altars commemorated wealthy freedmen and other members of the new bourgeoisie, and it is just as plausible that they might have introduced the new fashion into Roman funerary practice, a fashion that involved making larger and more expensive monuments, i.e. sarcophagi. There simply is not enough evidence to be able to say with confidence that one or another social group started the new fashion for burial in sarcophagi.

The surviving evidence does, however, suggest that the new burial practice was not (as might have been expected) the preserve of adult males: although many of the Trajanic-Hadrianic sarcophagi were made for adults a considerable number were of a size that suggests they were made for children. Iconography suitable for children was also developed early on for these sarcophagi, suggesting that there might be a positive correlation between the death of a loved child and the choice of inhumation as a burial rite, that some parents did consider inhumation a gentler and less traumatic option than cremation in such circumstances.

The amount that can be deduced about the people buried in these earliest sarcophagi is limited because of the general lack of inscriptions (and provision

---

76 This garland sarcophagus is designated that of a child primarily because of its size (length 1.27 m.): Janet Huskinson in her study of Roman children's sarcophagi took size as an important criterion in defining a child's sarcophagus, with a length of 1.70 m. as the notional maximum (Huskinson 1996, 2). She does however recognise that children might be buried in larger sarcophagi, and that smaller ones could have been designed to hold ashes or bones of adults. Only an inscription or appropriate iconography can make ascription to a child more certain. In the case of the sarcophagus under discussion (*ASR* VI, 2, 1, 11–8, no. 60) there is no inscription and the decoration on the front (garlands and theatrical masks) does not apply particularly to a child, but the playful cupids riding on animals on the sides could be seen as more of a pointer towards use for a child's burial.

77 Morris (1992, 54 and 59) mentions but rejects the opposite view that inhumation began among the lower orders and worked its way up through society. He concludes that 'All that we can really say is that the richer classes at Rome, from the emperors down to wealthy non-magistrates, probably all took up the new rite within the space of a generation or so, between about 140 and 180; the lower orders took to it rather more slowly' (Morris 1992, 54).

78 *C.I.L.* XI 1430; Arias 1977, 117–8, B4 Est.

for inscriptions in the form of a panel) on these sarcophagi: we do not know who the Louvre Actaeon sarcophagus was commissioned for, or who built and furnished the tomb at the Porta Viminalis with its three sarcophagi, or why it was not felt necessary to inscribe the names of those buried inside on most early sarcophagi. One possible explanation is that sarcophagi were not intended to be placed in tombs with large numbers of other burials but rather in small family tombs, and each sarcophagus was expected to hold a single body: this is different from the ash chests and grave altars which were generally placed in tombs where large numbers of people were buried, often belonging to a number of different nuclear families, so that there was a need for the inscription to identify a particular monument or niche as the burial place of a an individual or a number of related individuals. This need might not be as great if the whole tomb belonged to a small family unit. But it may also be that the patrons of the earliest sarcophagi were more concerned with other issues than the commemoration of the deceased and his/her family.

One reason why these sarcophagi were not provided with space for an inscription may be due to the craftsmen who made them rather than the patrons who bought them.[79] If they were not the sculptors who had previously made ash chests and grave altars but came from a different artistic tradition (e.g. immigrants from Asia Minor) they might not see the inscription panel as a central and all but indispensable element in a Roman funerary monument.[80] This raises the question of who was more instrumental in defining the decorative repertoire (and monument type) in vogue at any one time: the buyers or the makers. The individual nature of some commissions suggests that the purchaser of an altar or sarcophagus did have some freedom to ask for a specific design, even something not in the sculptor's repertoire, but the formulaic nature of the majority suggests that the designs were largely dictated by the sculptors, and it seems likely that in many cases the purchaser chose from what the sculptor had in stock, or ordered from a limited selection of design options.[81]

79 Clearly some patrons did wish to include an inscription, but in these circumstances it had to be fitted in awkwardly around the decoration at the top of the chest (sarcophagi of Tebanianus and Malia Titia) or along the moulding at the top of the chest (sarcophagus of Ostorius Ostorianus). Herdejürgen sees the central inscription panel as a motif characteristic of provincial Italian sarcophagus production, and as an element which was only later re-introduced to Metropolitan Roman workshops – in this respect the Ostian workshops were in the forefront of Roman fashion. It is however possible that the inscription panel was reinvented in Ostia because of the wishes of the clientele there.

80 The idea that sarcophagi were introduced to Rome from Asia Minor has frequently been suggested, but without any solid evidence to back it up: the close affinities of the earliest sarcophagi with Roman grave altars would seem to me on balance to argue against such a view.

81 It is significant that Boschung's identification of workshop groups shows that particular motifs were favoured by each group, to the extent that he names the groups according to

Nevertheless, it is perhaps more plausible that the earliest second-century sarcophagi were requested by the clients, and the artists had to adapt their repertoire to fit, rather than that the artists tried to interest their customers in a new form of monument (and its associated burial rite).

The fact that the iconographic repertoire of the Trajanic and Hadrianic garland sarcophagi largely coincides with that of at least some of the grave altars might indicate that the craftsmen who made the two types of monument came from the same artistic tradition and indeed were the same people.[82] But Herdejürgen, who has carried out the most detailed assessment of the stylistic characteristics of the garland sarcophagi, is of the opinion that, as far as the sarcophagi made in Rome itself were concerned, the three workshops she has identified as making sarcophagi in the Hadrianic period were not the same as those that had previously made grave altars and ash chests.[83] These sarcophagi, she suggests, rather have stylistic affinities with relief friezes from buildings, which may suggest that it was sculptors who had worked on architectural projects who began to diversify their production with the introduction of sarcophagi rather than the established workshops making ash chests and grave altars. The situation, she believes, was otherwise in Ostia, where the locally made sarcophagi have iconographic and stylistic characteristics which differentiate them from sarcophagi made in Rome, and which have greater affinities with grave altars and urns.[84] One of the earliest of the sarcophagi made in an Ostian workshop is that of Malia Titia, with its scenes of cock fights in the spaces above the garlands on the front – a motif relatively common on ash chests and grave altars, but rare on sarcophagi.[85]

---

their characteristic motifs (the Medusa Group, the Tripod Group etc.): Boschung 1987, 47 and passim.

82 Specifically the larger grave altars decorated with garlands which date to the late first century: Boschung 1993, 41 remarks that it is clear that the altars of the late first century had a massive influence on the sarcophagi.

83 *ASR* VI, 2, 1, 33. The earliest of these three workshops (the 'Via Cassia', which made the garland sarcophagi now in New York and the Palazzo Barberini) she believes started sarcophagus production in the late Trajanic period. Although she thinks that grave altars and garland sarcophagi were not made in the same workshops she assigns the two mythological sarcophagi from the Porta Viminalis tomb to the Via Labicana workshop, which made the garland sarcophagus from the same tomb: i. e. the same workshop made different types of sarcophagi, but not grave altars and sarcophagi.

84 Herdejürgen 1990, 95–8 and 109–11; *ASR* VI, 2, 1, 45 and 68. She estimates that production of garland sarcophagi at Ostia began in the 130s (earlier examples found at Ostia were made in Roman workshops).

85 The closest parallel for these scenes is the scene below the garland on a large ash chest from the Tomb of the Volusii, now in the Museo Gregoriano Profano: Sinn 1991, 106–7, no. 93.

Conclusion

If one compares a cremation monument of the mid first century (such as that of Lepidius Epaphra illustrated in Figure 1.1) with any typical frieze sarcophagus of the mid second century (such as the 'Pianabella' Iliad sarcophagus, Figure 2.1) there appear to be quite considerable differences between them in form, iconography and purpose. It is not unreasonable to deduce that there must have been a considerable shift in mentality over the course of this hundred-year period, nor is it implausible that the change from cremation to inhumation was in some way related to this shift. But a more nuanced analysis of the monuments reveals that this was a gradual process and suggests that the attitudes that produced some of the more elaborate grave altars of the last two decades of the first century were not so very different from those that resulted in the earliest sarcophagi. The motifs used on the early second-century sarcophagi such as garlands, cupids, medusa heads, mythological scenes, griffins, and even scenes of childhood[86] were used on grave altars before they were used on sarcophagi, but the iconographic repertoire used on these sarcophagi is more limited and their decorative schemes have subtly different emphases. We do not know for certain that the same kinds of people bought these monuments: the evidence does not point to any particular social group being at the forefront of the move towards inhumation and the use of richly decorated sarcophagi, except in so far as the people concerned must have been wealthy.

We can at least be sure that large and showy grave altars and the earliest sarcophagi were not reserved for the most important people in Roman society (mature male citizens), although they were used for them: they were also used for both women and children.[87] It may be that Romans at the turn of the first/second centuries were beginning to find the cremation of loved ones too traumatic an experience to bear, as is suggested by Statius in his description of Abascantus's abhorrence of cremation for his wife Priscilla's corpse – she was therefore inhumed.[88] Pliny the Younger also describes the extravagant (and in Pliny's view unseemly) mourning of Regulus for his dead son: the boy was apparently cremated, but the incident reveals the depths of feeling that could be generated at the death of a child in Roman society at precisely the period when sarcophagi were beginning to be used.[89] Many of the early sarcophagi are in sizes

86 Childhood scenes are not common on grave altars and ash chests, but are found for example on the altar of C. Iulius Philetus in the Vatican Museums (Museo Gregoriano Profano 9934): Sinn 1990, 65–7, no. 33, pl. 96–9 (Tiberian-Caligulan).

87 E.g. the grave altars of Licinia Magna (Figure 1.2) and T. Apusulenus Caerellianus (Figure 1.5): the latter commemorates a boy who died aged five years and eight months, and was dedicated by his parents (*CIL* VI 38027).

88 *Silvae* 5.1.226–7.

89 Pliny, *Letters* 4.2 and 4.7.

appropriate to the burial of a child who has not yet reached adult stature. Sentimental impulses on the part of the bereaved husband or parent may explain the decision to inhume the loved one's body in a sarcophagus in some cases, and can therefore be seen as one factor in the changes in funerary practice, but it does not explain everything. When looking back from the perspective of the mid-Antonine sarcophagi a crucial development appears to be the expansion of the mythological subject matter, seen in the range of the myths represented, the amount of space dedicated to them, and sophistication of the narrative techniques used. But were sarcophagi introduced to Rome in order to provide the scope for such developments? This does not seem likely. It does not seem to me that Tebanianus's sarcophagus (Figure 1.8) is designed to communicate ideas essentially different from those presented by the grave altar of Aufidius Aprilis (Figure 1.3): it is not clear in either case why the Dionysiac scenes were thought to be appropriate, any more than it is evident why Aprilis was cremated and Tebanianus was inhumed.[90] It was only after sarcophagi had begun to be used in Rome as more than an occasional anomaly that the possibilities this form of monument presented for the representation of myth was fully realised – and from the sculptors' point of view the combination of sarcophagus and myth provided excellent opportunities for the expansion of their production in a no doubt very lucrative direction.

Bibliography

Altmann, W. *Die römischen Grabaltäre der Kaiserzeit* (Berlin, 1905).

Amedick, R. *Vita Privata auf Sarkophagen. Die Sarkophage mit Darstellungen aus dem Menschenleben* (ASR 1.4) (Berlin, 1991).

Arias, P.E., Gabba, E., and Cristiani, E. *Camposanto Monumentale di Pisa 1: Le Antichità* (Pisa, 1977).

Bérard, C. Silène porte-van. *Bull. Ass. Pro Aventico* 22 (1974), 5–16.

Boschung, D. *Antiken Grabaltäre aus den Nekropolen Roms* (Acta Bernensia 10) (Bern, 1987).

Boschung, D. Grabaltäre mit Girlanden und früher Girlandensarkophage, Zur Genese der kaiserzeitlichen Sepulkralkunst, in: *Grabeskunst der römischen Kaiserzeit,* edited by G. Koch (Mainz, 1993), 37–42.

Brilliant, R. *Visual Narratives. Storytelling in Etruscan and Roman Art* (Ithaca and London, 1984).

Bruneaux, P. Le motif des coqs affrontés dans l'imagerie antique. *Bulletin de Correspondance Hellenique* 89 (1965), 90–121.

90 Turcan (1999, 102) attempts to relate the trophy scene on Tebanianus' sarcophagus with possible events in the deceased's life by suggesting that he took part in Trajan's Parthian War: thus the Indian Triumph of Dionysus, the civilising god, could be equated to the Roman imperialist mission, and Tebanianus is himself equated with the deity and merits apotheosis.

Buonocore, M. *Schiavi e Liberti dei Volusi Saturnini. Le iscrizioni del colombario sulla via Appia antica* (Rome, 1984).

Calza, R. Un Nuovo Sarcophago Ostiense. *Bollettino d'Arte* 39 (1954), 107–113.

Caronna, E.L. *Notizie degli Scavi* 29 (1975), 205–222.

Cumont, F. *Recherches sur le symbolisme funéraire des romains* (Paris, 1942).

Davies, G. Roman funerary symbolism in the early Empire, in: *Inhabiting Symbols. Symbol and image in the ancient Mediterranean* (Accordia Specialist Studies on the Mediterranean vol. 5), edited by J.B. Wilkins and E. Herring (London, 2003), 211–222.

Davies, G. *The Ince Blundell Collection of Classical Sculpture Volume 2: The ash chests and other funerary reliefs* (Mainz am Rhein, 2007).

Eberle, A. F. Un sarcophage d'enfant au J. Paul Getty Museum, in: *Roman Funerary Monuments in the J. Paul Getty Museum vol. 1*, edited by M. True and G. Koch (California, 1990), 47–58.

Farnoux, B. Combet. L'inspiration pythagoricienne et dionysiaque dans un autel funéraire du Musée du Latran. *Mélanges de l'École française de Rome, Antiquité* 72 (1960), 147–165.

Herdejürgen, H. Girlandensarkophage aus Ostia, in: *Roman Funerary Monuments in the J. Paul Getty Museum vol. 1*, edited by M. True and G. Koch (California, 1990), 95–114.

Honroth, M. *Die Stadtrömische Girlanden* (Sonderschriften of the Österreichischen Archäologischen Institut in Wien no. 17) (Vienna, 1971).

Huskinson, J. *Roman Children's Sarcophagi. Their decoration and social significance* (Oxford, 1996).

Kragelund, P., Moltesen, M. and Østergaard, J. *The Licinian Tomb. Fact or Fiction?* (Copenhagen, 2003).

Kleiner, D.E.E. *Roman Imperial Funerary Altars with Portraits* (Rome, 1987).

McCann, A.M. *Roman Sarcophagi in the Metropolitan Museum of Art* (New York, 1978).

Morris, I. *Death-Ritual and Social Structure in Classical Antiquity* (Cambridge, 1992).

Nock, A. D. Cremation and Burial in the Roman Empire. *Harvard Theological Review* 25.4 (1932), 321–359.

Nock, A. D. Sarcophagi and Symbolism. *American Journal of Archaeology* 50.1 (1946), 140–170.

Panciera, S. *Notizie degli Scavi* 29 (1975), 222–232.

Roller, M. B. *Dining Posture in Ancient Rome. Bodies, values and status* (Princeton and Oxford, 2006).

Sinn, F. *Stadtrömische Marmorurnen* (Mainz am Rhein, 1987).

Sinn, F. *Vatikanischen Museen Museo Gregoriano Profano ex Lateranense: Die Grabdenkmäler 1 Reliefs Altäre Urnen* (Mainz am Rhein, 1990).

Strong, D.E. *Roman Imperial Sculpture* (London, 1961).

Toynbee, J. M. C. *The Hadrianic School. A chapter in the history of Greek art* (Cambridge, 1934).

Toynbee, J. M. C. Picture-language in Roman Art and Coinage, in: *Essays in Roman Coinage presented to Harold Mattingly* edited by R. A. G. Carson and C. H. V. Sutherland (Oxford, 1956), 205–226.

Toynbee, J. M. C. *Death and Burial in the Roman World* (London and Southampton, 1971 and 1982).

Turcan, R. *Les sarcophages romains à representations Dionysiaques* (Paris, 1966).

Turcan, R. *Messages d'outre-tombe. L'iconographie des sarcophages romains* (Paris, 1999).

Zanker, P. Bilderzwang: Augustan Political Symbolism in the Private Sphere, in: *Image and Mystery in the Roman World, Papers given in memory of Jocelyn Toynbee,* edited by J. Huskinson, M. Beard and J. Reynolds (Gloucester, 1988), 1–20.
Zanker, P. and Ewald, B. C. *Mit Mythen leben. Die Bilderwelt der römischen Sarkophage* (Munich, 2004).

2.
Habent sua fata: Writing life histories of Roman Sarcophagi

Janet Huskinson

'Quel che il poeta dice dei libelli, vale anche e sopra tutto per i sarcofagi: questi pure habent sua fata': thus the great scholar of early Christian sarcophagi Josef Wilpert started his 1923–24 article about some particular examples which he had recently recorded for his corpus of *I sarcofagi cristiani.*[1] Many of these had been cut up or wrongly re-assembled for display in new contexts that were quite different to their original funerary purpose, leading him to lament the post-classical fortunes of Roman sarcophagi as so often 'rather sad'.[2]

This rather negative assessment of their reception is perhaps not surprising since Wilpert himself was primarily interested in the iconography of their figured decoration and its relationship to contemporary religious ideas, and subsequent changes of use and setting often caused damage – physical and conceptual – that made it near impossible to retrieve these original values. But, as the papers in this volume show so well, the study of Roman sarcophagi in their ancient contexts now draws on many different approaches – commercial, cultural, aesthetic, as well as iconographical – and these may also be applied to evaluating their re-use in post-classical societies. This too involved a broad range of values, for evidence shows that at one time or another ancient sarcophagi were regarded as classical art-works or antiquities, chosen as suitable tombs, fountains or decorative containers, or taken as symbols of the Roman tradition or even as poetic metaphors for life and death.[3] Yet on the other hand they were sometimes re-deployed with little apparent interest in their ancient past. This wide range of possibilities opens the way to more positive evaluations of how later societies re-used Roman sarcophagi than Wilpert could give. But at the

1 Wilpert 1929–1936; Wilpert 1923–1924: 'What the poet said about books, is true too – and most of all – of sarcophagi: they have their own fates.' The poet was Terentianus Maurus. Wilpert's statement echoes that made by C.Robert 1900, 98 on a sarcophagus at Cliveden.

2 Wilpert 1923–24, 168–69.

3 The theme of sarcophagi having a new existence as life-giving fountains or fonts was treated by several baroque poets interested in exploring 'metamorfosi e la dilettica fra Vita e Morte': Federici 2002, 277–279. This is a reminder of how re-used material objects, such as sarcophagi, also have values as literary symbols.

same time it is also a potential obstacle to finding a single interpretative approach that could be used to accommodate all the different circumstances of re-use.

For to avoid ending up with a virtual list of individual types of re-use, what is needed is an evaluative framework that can transcend all this variability. But this is particularly hard to identify because of the essentially functional nature of sarcophagi, which as durable, useful, and often beautiful containers, could be re-deployed in many different ways and settings. The values involved in this re-use could shift from one context to another, and vary between locations and over time, creating a complex and many-layered set of meanings even for a single sarcophagus. This means that interpretative approaches that have been evolved for assessing the re-use of one particular type of ancient material may only work for some sarcophagi, some of the time, and are not generally applicable. For instance, not all sarcophagi can be usefully discussed in terms of architectural *spolia* (a category of ancient material which has rather dominated recent studies of re-use); and, although some sarcophagi were copied by later artists as influential stylistic models, as a whole they did not attract the rich array of visual and literary responses needed to support the kind of reception-based approach useful for ancient art works which became established cultural icons.[4]

Multi-disciplinary approaches, on the other hand, have proved much more effective in coping with the variations, especially where they have been employed to survey the full range of values attached to the re-use of Roman sarcophagi within a specific context. These contexts have usually involved a particular time or place, as, for instance, in the studies of Ragusa 1951 and Elsner 2009, and in the papers included in Andreae and Settis 1984. But in the quest for a single transcendent approach, some of the most helpful work has dealt with conceptual contexts, as two recent articles by Settis exemplify.

The first (Settis 2004) was written as the introduction to a catalogue of photographs which document the re-use of ancient material – including sarcophagi – in the city of Rome; and in it Settis systematically sets out a series of questions and criteria for addressing different aspects of this kind of re-use. These involve five 'key words' – *Assenza* (representing an emptiness waiting to be filled), *Presenza* (of models surviving from antiquity, to be re-used in new contexts and functions), *Selezione* (process of choosing models for new uses), *Citazione* (using *spolia* to create quotations from the past), and *Topos* (repeatable formulae which help to construct the visual argument).[5] Together these form a sequential process for analysis and evaluation, which can accommodate even the

4 For a survey of some recent work on *Spolia* see Stenbro, 2005. For Vasari on Nicola Pisano, see Settis 2004, 14; and also Bober-Rubinstein 1986. For reception of an ancient work of art: Prettejohn 2006 (on the Venus de Milo).

5 Settis 2004, 15–19.

multifarious situations presented by sarcophagi. (These key words recall terms proposed in other studies, which are also useful for evaluating re-used sarcophagi: *Continuità, distanza, conoscenza,* which were formulated by Settis himself in 1986, and '*spolia in se*' and '*spolia in re*', by Brilliant 1982, to which Cutler 1999 added '*in spe*').[6] The second discussion (Settis 2008) has a more specific historical focus, as Settis explores the great popularity of Roman sarcophagi amongst various elite groups in the Middle Ages, who used them as a way of confirming contemporary power through the authority of the past. This chapter (which appears in a volume on collecting sculpture in early modern Europe) is a brief but pointed discussion, which presents the sarcophagi rather as commodities in which different values are invested according to the specific context of their re-use.[7]

Here, then, is one single approach – namely, the treatment of sarcophagi as commodities, or potentially valuable objects – that can accommodate variations in value that arise from different circumstances. It offers a pathway through all the shifts and fluctuations that characterise their use and re-use right from the time of manufacture, which the rest of this paper will aim to follow.

An obvious way to test out where it can lead is to take individual sarcophagi and trace the various contexts in which they have been used and re-used over time – in other words, to write something akin to their 'life histories'. This kind of biographical approach has been developed recently as an interpretative tool in social history (with the 'life-course' of individuals) and in archaeology and material studies for evaluating the changing significance of objects.[8] It '… seeks to understand the way objects become invested with meaning through the social interactions they are caught up in. These meanings change and are re-negotiated through the life of the object'.[9] In other words, this is a method which is actually geared to deal with the kind of changes and fluctuations which the sarcophagi present across their entire existence. Although Kopytoff, in a seminal essay on

6 Settis 2004, 15–18; Settis 1986; Brilliant 1982, 2–17: '*in se*' represents the physical re-use of an object itself; '*in re*' the use of an ancient object as a model; and Cutler 1999, 1064, '*spolia in spe*' 'are things used in the anticipation that they will be seen to complete an object, or at least add to a new creation valences that are not communicated in their absence'.

7 E.g. Settis 2008, 14; 19. Verkerk 2007 also considers sarcophagi as objects of re-use (rather than for art-historical classification), but from the point of view of the secondary patron rather than 'object biography' *per se.*

8 For discussions of this approach e.g. Gosden and Marshall 1999, Hoskins 2006. Appadurai 1986 was a major influence from material studies. Biography and the life-cycle are now frequently used as approaches to ancient social history and archaeology: e.g. Robb 2002; Harlow and Laurence 2002. Greenhalgh 1989 describes his study of the survival of Roman antiquities into the Middle Ages as partly 'an interpretative "biography" of various classes of antiquities'.

9 Gosden and Marshall 1999, 170.

writing artefact biographies, focused on objects as commodities in a strict economic sense, sarcophagi may benefit from taking a wider, more inclusive approach to writing their life stories. After all, their contexts of use may involve not only the kinds of circulation and transaction that define commodities, but also the need to keep and preserve in respect of some intrinsic value (attached to them as antiquities or reliquaries, for instance); and this variation means that they may get invested with a wide array of cultural, religious, political and social meanings.[10]

In addition to the meanings they derive from such social interactions, there is a particular metaphorical connection between sarcophagi and biography which makes this kind of approach especially relevant. For more than almost any other object, they are intimately related to the life of the human body and its changes over time: as containers for the dead they 'consumed' the physical body inside, while providing it with an enduring 'monumental body' which represented ideal social qualities or life-events.[11] As biography is an obvious way of presenting the changing values of a human life, so it should be for the different phases of a sarcophagus' existence.[12]

So this paper will test out the merits of a biographical approach by focusing on three Roman sarcophagi, which have been chosen because their long life histories contain an interesting range of 'events' and are well-documented in published sources.[13] It will first attempt to draft their outline biographies, from their creation to the present-day, and then move on to discuss some of the changing values and meanings that these represent.

'The Pianabella Sarcophagus', Ostia Museum inv. No. 43504, on permanent loan from Antikenmuseum, Berlin (Figure 2.1 a, b and c)

Imported Proconnesian marble was used for this sarcophagus, and its decoration seems to have been carved around 160 by sculptors in or near Rome.[14] On the front are three scenes inspired by the Iliad – on the left, the arming of Achilles in the presence of his mother Thetis, followed by Achilles'

10 Kopytoff 1988; Rowlands 2005.

11 For funerary monuments and the physical body: e.g. Llewellyn 1991, 46–49.

12 But while the lives of those once buried within them are finished, sarcophagi continue to exist (although others were destroyed, by being converted into lime – ultimately another form of re-use).

13 Because the prime point of this paper is to illustrate the opportunities of this approach, these narratives are simply written from published sources without recourse to archives or private correspondence etc., that could perhaps fill out (or even alter) some of the details given here.

14 Morandi 1993, 152. Paroli 1999, 219 gives the dimensions as H. 54.5, L.195, D. 62. Lid: H: 23.5, L. 200cms, greatest depth 15. For main bibliographic references to the piece see Paroli 1999, 221–222, no. B8; *ASR* XII,1 44–48, 204–05, no. 27 pl 28–31; Dresken-Weiland 2003, 331, A91; Zanker and Ewald 2004, 283–285.

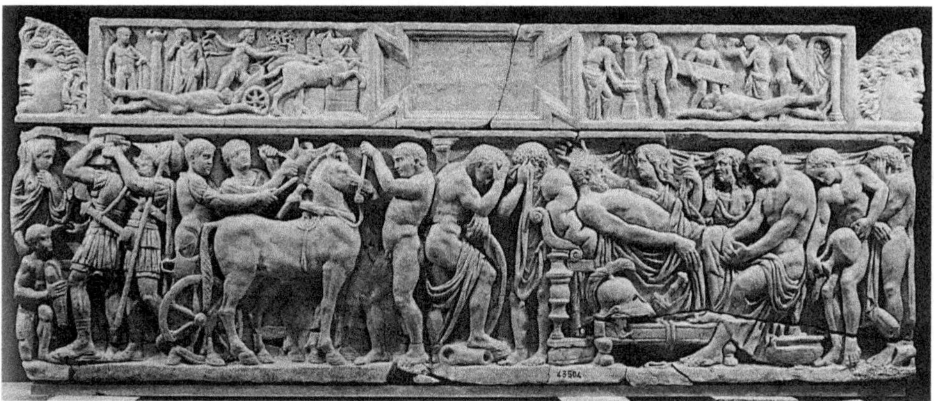

Figure 2.1: ' The Pianabella Sarcophagus' Ostia Museum inv. No. 43504, on permanent loan from Antikenmuseum, Berlin. Photograph: courtesy of the Archivio Fotografico della Soprintendenza per i Beni Archeologici di Roma, Sede Ostia Antica.

chariot guided by Automedon, and on the right an extended scene of Achilles mourning the dead Patroclus. Griffins decorate the side panels. The lid has further scenes from the Iliad flanking the inscription panel: on the left Achilles is shown in his chariot dragging Hector's corpse around Patroclus' tomb, and on the right the washing of Hector's body prior to its restoration to Priam.

Individually these scenes resemble episodes in the life of Achilles as represented on Attic sarcophagi, but they include iconographical features in the iconography (such as the death-bed scene) of Roman derivation. From this it has been deduced that the sarcophagus was decorated in or around Rome, possibly taking an Attic sarcophagus imported through Ostia as its model.[15]

These Roman elements in the imagery of Achilles are unique and suggest that the sarcophagus may have been specially commissioned. The choice of Greek literature as the basis of its decoration and the conspicuously high quality of the figured scenes, exquisitely carved on expensive marble, suggest that whoever commissioned it was wealthy and cultivated. A possible candidate has been proposed – a leading Ostian family, the Egrili, who appear – from other archaeological traces – to have had a funerary complex in the necropolis of Pianabella, outside Ostia.[16] Whatever the case, no evidence survives to show where the sarcophagus was deposited, or how it might have been displayed within the tomb.

The next attested stage in the life of the sarcophagus is its re-use, sometime in the third century, in another mausoleum in the Pianabella cemetery. Its

15 E.g. Koch and Sichtermann 1982, 130; Giuliani 1989; *ASR* IX,1, 72; *ASR* XII,1, 44–48.

16 Morandi 1993,154.

original inscription was erased, making it ready to accommodate another generation of dead whose family must have been pleased to have acquired (but how?) such a high quality marble sarcophagus to use for burial.

This mausoleum was at the northern end of the row of tomb-buildings in the cemetery.[17] It was originally erected sometime in the first half of the second century but underwent various re-arrangements during the second and third centuries.[18] In one of these the sarcophagus was installed below floor-level, in a *forma* which was specially made to accommodate it; a wall was built along its front and mortar poured in to fill the spaces left around it.[19] The sarcophagus was now out of sight, buried below ground, presumably to protect it (as both a valuable piece of marble and a container of the dead) against any further re-use.

Over seventeen centuries passed before the next known episode in the life of this sarcophagus, which turned it into an object of value in the illicit trade in antiquities, and then in international negotiations about the return of cultural property. Sometime, probably, in 1976 it was discovered *in situ* by clandestine excavators, who looted the front, parts of the side panels and the lid, leaving the rest behind.[20] Obviously they managed to take most of the figured reliefs, which were high-value commodities in the art market, but were presumably frustrated in attempts to get the whole sarcophagus out of the ground. By 1982 these fragments had entered the Berlin Antikenmuseum at Charlottenburg. They had been acquired on the assurance of a 'previous owner' that they had come from a Swiss private collection where they had been for at least a generation, and where they had once been set into a wall to serve as a flower container.[21] But by then the rest of the sarcophagus, left in situ by the clandestini, was found at Pianabella, and the freshness of the breaks gave strong suggestion that the story of a previous Swiss owner was untrue. From 1988 to 1991 Italian archaeologists carried out a systematic excavation of the mausoleum and discovered how the sarcophagus had been installed below ground, as described above. What is more they found impressions left in the mortar by the figures carved on the front and sides of the sarcophagus. These were the final proof that the reliefs in Berlin had come from this tomb.

But even so – to follow Heilmeyer – criminal investigations proved fruitless. There also seemed to be no legal grounds for requiring that the fragments should be restored to Ostia. On the other hand, scholarship was seen to provide

17 Paroli 1999, 20. The mausoleum is designated as L1 in area 7000 of the necropolis excavations.

18 Morandi 1993, 149; 151 fig.8.

19 Morandi 1993, 149; 152 fig. 9; Paroli 1999, 220, Fig 9.

20 Morandi 1993, 150 figs 2 and 3 for sections of the sarcophagus in Berlin and Ostia, and fig 4 for the sarcophagus re-composed.

21 Giuliani 1989, 27, n.8 and Heilmeyer 1992, 265–267.

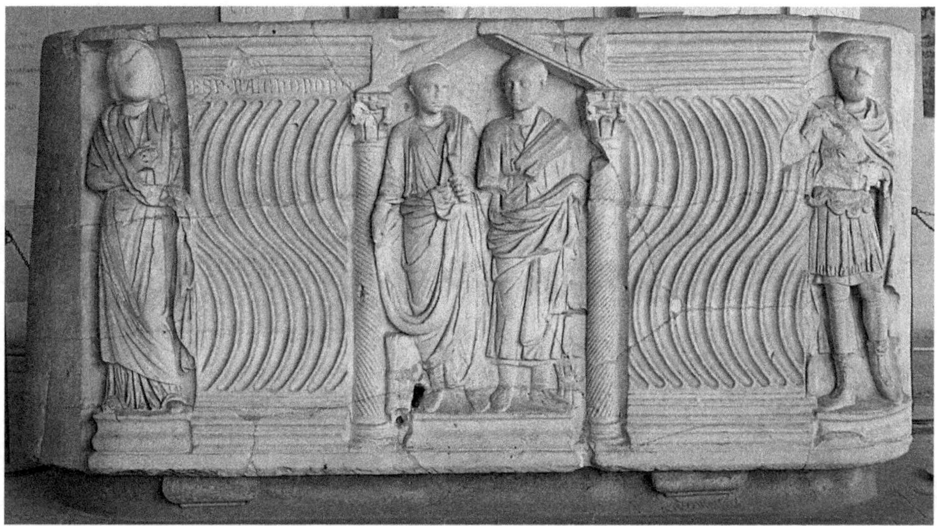

Figure 2.2: Pisa, Camposanto B 1 est,‘ The Brothers’ sarcophagus’. Pisa, Camposanto. Photograph: J. Elsner.

cogent arguments for reuniting the different parts of the sarcophagus, and as an agreed solution the sections in Berlin were sent on permanent loan to Ostia, where they are now displayed together with the rest, creating a whole, but badly damaged, sarcophagus with lid.

‘The Brothers’ sarcophagus’, Pisa, Camposanto, B 1 est. inv. no. (1963) 188 (Figure 2.2)

This sarcophagus has the tub-like form of a *lenos*, with curved sides.[22] The front is decorated by three figured panels separated by two sections of curved fluting which are set between heavy borders. In the centre two young men are shown standing within an *aedicula*, which is supported by two spirally fluted columns. They wear togas (of different styles) and shoes of a type that suggests senatorial status; the youth on the left holds a scroll, and there are bundles of scrolls at their feet. They stand on a low plinth, as do the single figures in the corner panels – a draped woman on the left and a military man on the right. Both of these figures half turn towards the centre, and were intended to have portrait features, which were never carved. The sides and back of sarcophagus are smooth, but the back is decorated with two lion heads, with rings in their

22 The main references, with detailed descriptions and bibliographies are: Arias, Cristiani and Gabba 1977, 113–14, B1 est; *Aquarius* (entry compiled by F. Donati) Doc. no SNSSARC00150; *ASR* VI,1,110 Kat 50; Wrede 2001, 124–25 no. 15; and *ASR* I,3, 36, 208, Kat no. 54. Reinsberg there gives the measurements as: H. 1.30, L. 2.80, D. 1.54 ms. The front figures, in particular, are quite damaged in places.

mouths, carved in high relief (and placed, unusually, at the very top of the sarcophagus).

These lion heads, and their unusual position on what is now the back of the sarcophagus suggest several things about the earliest stages in its life. As a large number of other examples testify, they were originally intended to decorate the front, within a decoration of strigillations.[23] Evidence shows that sarcophagi of this type were exported from quarries in Asia Minor partly prefabricated, for their decoration to be finished in Rome.[24] Some found in the San Pietro shipwreck off Taranto were said to have been made of a marble similar to this example in Pisa, which probably came from quarries in Thasos.[25] In this case, it looks as if decisions were taken to alter the planned decoration after the half-finished sarcophagus had arrived in Rome: the lion heads were completed (though not the strigils that usually surrounded them), and a set of figured scenes was carved on the other long side, thus turning it into the front.[26] But quite how many stages of work this involved and quite when these may have been completed is uncertain: opinions have diverged about the relative dating of the portraits (generally assigned to 220s) and lion heads, and about whether all the decoration was carved at the same time.[27]

The figured scenes – which show a couple in the centre and a man and woman individually in the corners – have clear resonances with those on what Reinsberg has termed the 'Feldherrn/Hochzeit-Sarkophage' in which men and women are shown both as individuals and also together, usually in a central scene of *dextrarum iunctio* representing their marriage.[28] Even so there are significant differences: here neither the man nor the woman is shown engaged in any activity, such as sacrifice, while the central scene contains the portrait figures of two young men. This is a unique deviation from the conventional iconography, and may have been specially commissioned to commemorate the premature death of the couple's sons: that is the suggestion.[29] But plausible though it is, the reality is that this explanation cannot be confirmed. All in all, just who was responsible for this re-design, when and why it happened, and

23 Cf. examples depicted in *ASR* VI,1, pls. 8–19.

24 Ward-Perkins and Throckmorton 1965.

25 Ward-Perkins and Throckmorton 1965, 205; and Russell, this volume note 84 for further references (Cf. also Walker 1985, 62–64: this was the only sarcophagus in her sample of this type not to have been made of Proconnesian marble).

26 Andreae 1984, 110–112 and for illustrations of the back; *ASR* VI,1 1998, 23.

27 For views on several phases: Arias, Cristiani, and Gabba 1977,114; Walker 1985, 60; Andreae 1984, 110–11; *ASR* I,3, 36 n.177. But Stroszeck in *ASR* VI,1, 110 dates it much later, to between 280 and 300, from the type of the lion heads (but without discussion).

28 *ASR* I,3, 19–39. This composition is usually found on rectangular sarcophagi.

29 E.g. Reinsberg in *ASR* I,3, 36.

where the sarcophagus was finally placed in Rome have to remain unknown. Although it is a monumental piece, the carving of the figured scenes is not of the highest quality: the woman is sculpted on the front of the sarcophagus and the man on its curved corner, so that their plinths and also the adjacent panels of fluting are of different dimensions.

The next documented stage in the life of the sarcophagus occurs in fourteenth century Pisa. There it was re-used as a tomb by the Falconi family, as is revealed by the inscription added above the left-hand panel of strigillations. They were rich and influential merchants, who were regularly named amongst the Anziani, the principal Pisan magistracy.[30] For many such families in Pisa at that time, to be buried in an ancient Roman sarcophagus was a symbol of their status. The attraction lay in its commercial value as an expensive import (possibly purchased direct from Rome), in its aesthetic qualities, and above all in its symbolism, as a Roman antiquity. Since the eleventh century Pisa had consciously identified itself with Rome, using Roman inscriptions and reliefs as *spolia* in the Duomo and other major buildings to reinforce the historical reference; by choosing Roman sarcophagi for their tombs the elite were also allying themselves to the past from which their city claimed authority. Until the Camposanto was built in the early 1300s, these sarcophagi were placed around the outer walls of the Duomo, on public view in the heart of the city.[31] This was a fitting burial-place for the Pisan elite, who were identified by inscriptions on the wall above. The Falconi may have been represented there, but this seems unlikely since the re-use of this particular sarcophagus apparently dates from after the move to the Camposanto.[32]

Although it still remains there, this Roman sarcophagus has further stages in its life to be described since changes in the use and nature of the Camposanto itself altered the way in which its contents would be viewed and valued.[33] The Camposanto had from the start a complex range of roles, sacred and civic: its cemetery had a religious function, but it was also the place where distinguished Pisans were commemorated, many buried in ancient Roman sarcophagi. Gradually, it seems, the balance came to shift, and the Camposanto changed from being a sacred space to become a secular museum of art and Pisan

30 Donati and Parra 1984, 112; 118, n. 40. The historical context of the re-use of sarcophagi from Rome and Ostia at Pisa is very well-discussed and well-documented: see e.g. Donati and Parra 1984, Donati 1984, 1993, 1996. For their influence on Pisan artists, notably Nicola Pisano, see e.g. Milone 1993, 20; Settis 2004, 14.

31 See Tolaini 2008, 54 for current debate about the date of their removal into the Camposanto. He claims that this did not happen until the early fifteenth century.

32 Cf. sources given in Donati 1984, 28–32 (Appendice) and Donati 1996, 93–96.

33 Here too developments in Pisa are well documented: e.g. Baracchini 1993; Baracchini and Castelnuovo, 1996.

history.[34] In 1706–7 the sarcophagi were brought inside from its garden, where they had originally been placed, to shelter under the cloisters, and a printed catalogue made in 1708.[35] Further changes came with the appointment in 1807 of Carlo Lasinio as Conservatore del Camposanto, who set out to consolidate the collection as a celebration of Pisa's past, and as a museum of art, along the lines of great European museums that had recently been created.[36] Under Lasinio, the sarcophagi became part of the collection to be curated. He added to the collection – and its value as a secular museum – by bringing into the Camposanto sarcophagi from elsewhere in town, including some from churches.[37] He improved the visibility of the display, set some sarcophagi on marble bases, reallocated lids or disposed of the sarcophagus' contents.[38] The Falconi sarcophagus was originally sited in the eastern part of the Camposanto, but in 1810 was moved into the western cloister, to be positioned at the end of the central row of monuments.[39]

Like other sarcophagi that remain in the Camposanto, it is a survivor of the antiquarium which Lasinio fostered, even though many of the other artefacts he collected as a museum of the arts have been dispersed to other locations in Pisa when new collections were set up.[40] It is also a survivor of the massive war damage that afflicted the Camposanto on 27 July 1944. Today it stands with a commanding view down the south-western side of the cloister.

'The Borghese sarcophagus', Louvre MA 2980 and Rome Musei Capitolini, Centrale Montemartini inv. no. 2071. (Figures 2.3 a,b, and c).

This large sarcophagus was decorated with figured scenes on all four sides, and would originally have had a decorated lid.[41] It belongs to the so-called 'City gate' series of prestigious sarcophagi that date to the late fourth century, and was probably made in Rome, and its similarity to another in Milan, raises questions

34 Milone 1993. Also Tolaini 2008 for the display element, from the early fifteenth century.

35 Donato 1984, 13–14; Milone 1993, 25–27.

36 Baracchini 1993.

37 Donati and Parra 1984, 103; Donati 1993, 97–100.

38 Donati 1993, 94; Casini 1993, 65, fig.15.

39 Settis 1984, Piantina/Itinerario nos. 1 and 2 show the location of the sarcophagus in 1708 and 1760 outside the cover of the cloister on the south-east side. Baracchini 1993, 129 ('ricostruzione grafica'); Baracchini 1996, 203, 212 for alterations to the display in this cloister soon after Lasinio's death; cf. pl.28 for recent picture of that side.

40 Baracchini, 1993 13–16 also Donati 1993, 102; 1996, 71.

41 The main references, with detailed descriptions and bibliographies are: for the back: *Rep.* I, no. 829; for the rest: Baratte and Metzger, 1985, no 212 ; Koch 2000, 325, no 139 ; *Rep.* III, no. 428; Dresken-Weiland, 2003, 378, Kat E 26. These also give the measurements as: Front and sides: H. 1.10; L. 2.52 right side: 1.4; left side 1.46. Back: H. 0.98; L. 2.45 ms.

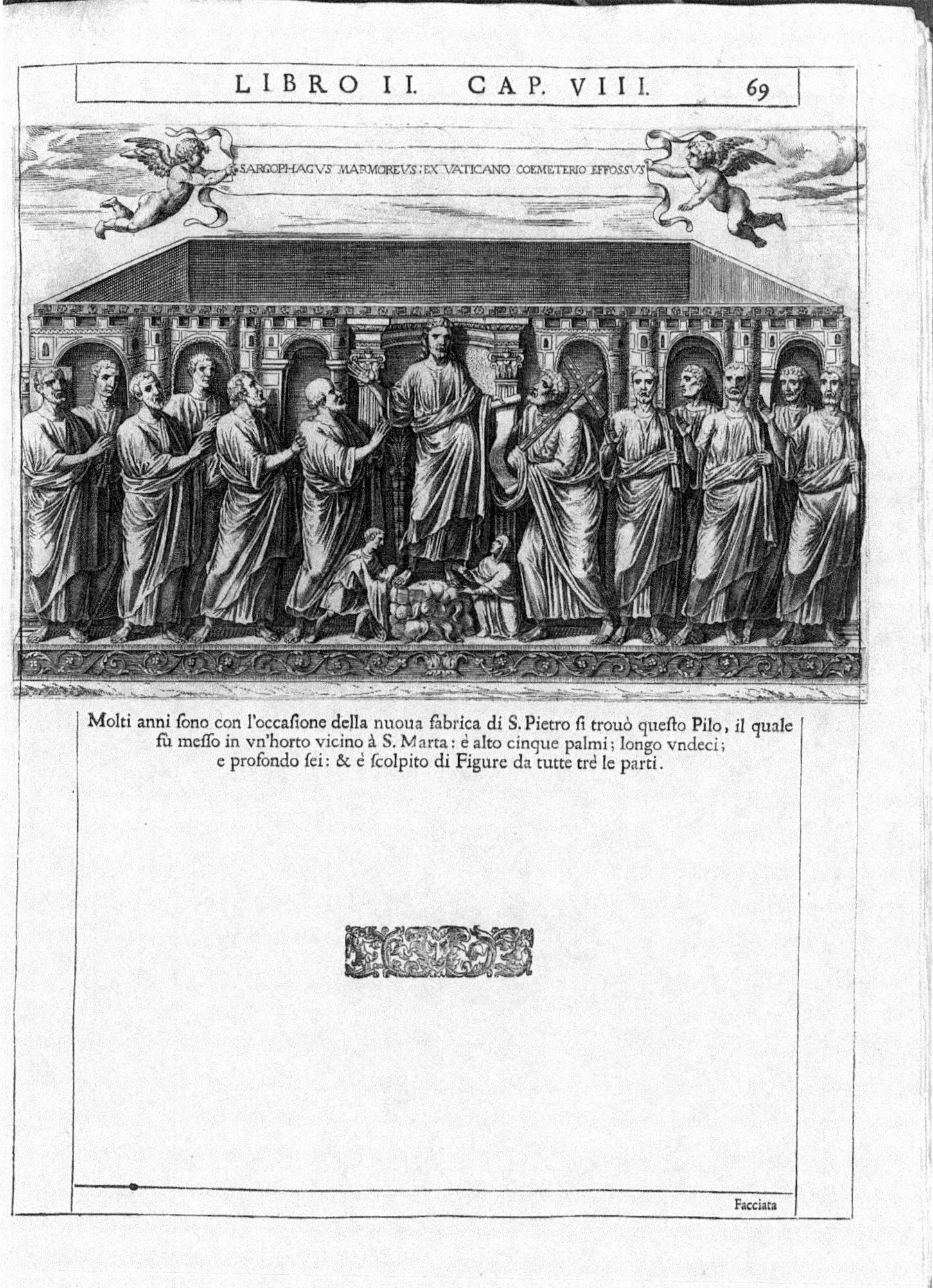

LIBRO II. CAP. VIII. 69

SARGOPHAGVS MARMOREVS: EX VATICANO COEMETERIO EFFOSSVS

Molti anni ſono con l'occaſione della nuoua fabrica di S. Pietro ſi trouò queſto Pilo, il quale fù meſſo in vn'horto vicino à S. Marta: è alto cinque palmi; longo vndeci; e profondo ſei: & è ſcolpito di Figure da tutte trè le parti.

Facciata

Figure 2.3 a: 'The Borghese sarcophagus': front. Photograph: from Antonio Bosio, *Roma Sotterranea*, Rome 1632, 69 (by kind permission of the Syndics of Cambridge University Library).

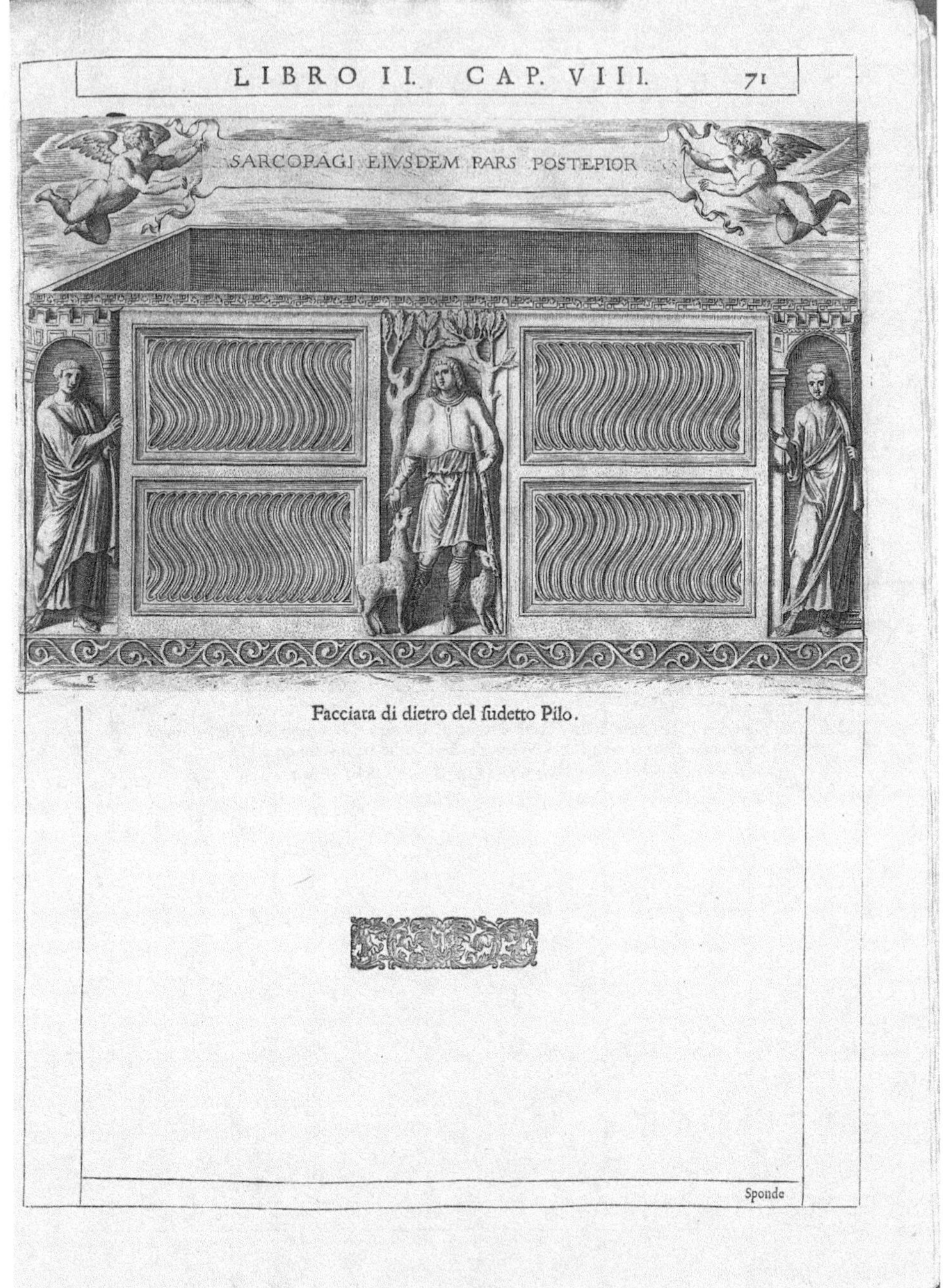

Figure 2.3b: 'The Borghese sarcophagus': back. Photograph: from Antonio Bosio, *Roma Sotterranea*, Rome 1632, 71 (by kind permission of the Syndics of Cambridge University Library).

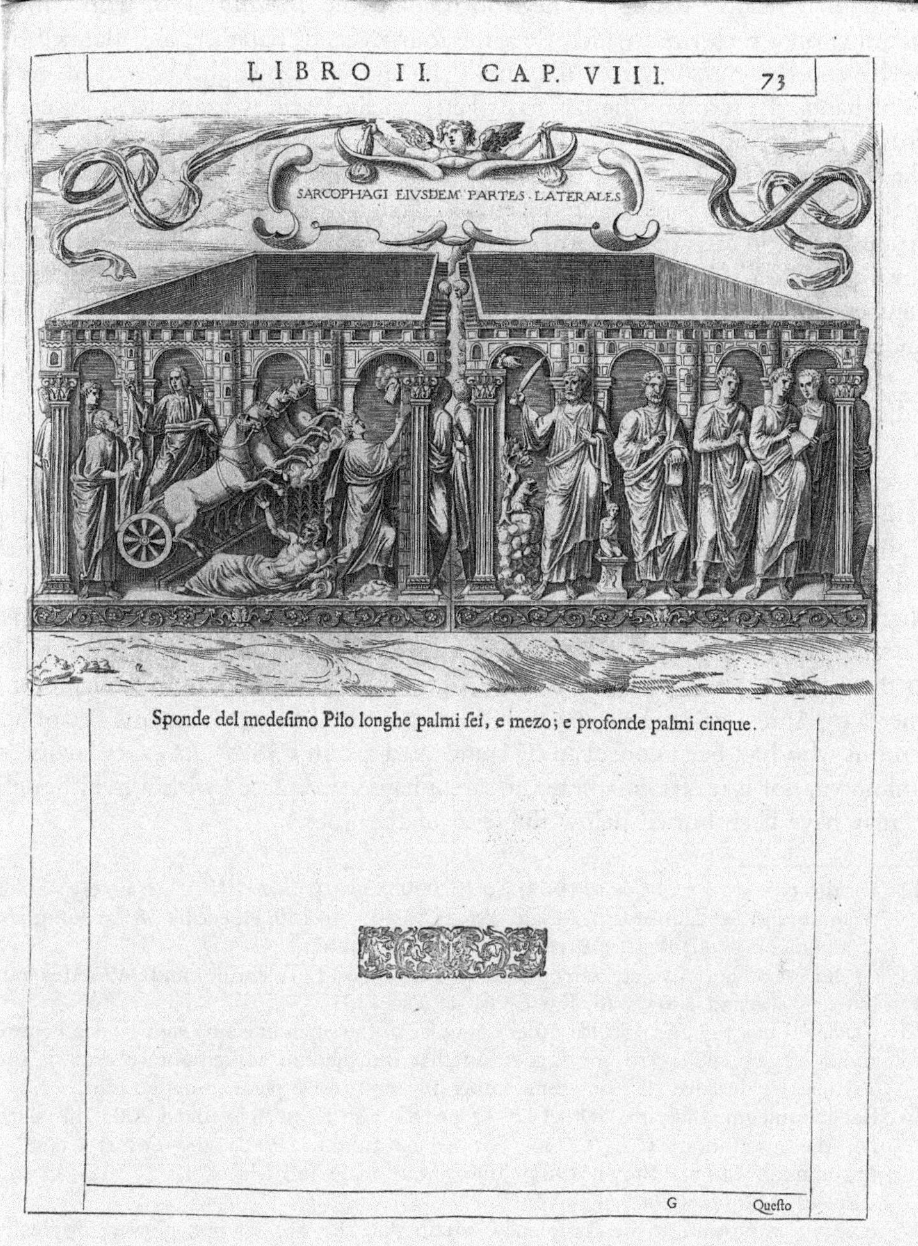

LIBRO II. CAP. VIII. 73

SARCOPHAGI EIVSDEM PARTES LATERALES

Sponde del medeſimo Pilo longhe palmi ſei, e mezo; e profonde palmi cinque.

G Queſto

Figure 2.3 c: 'The Borghese sarcophagus': sides. Photograph: from Antonio Bosio, *Roma Sotterranea*, Rome 1632, 73 (by kind permission of the Syndics of Cambridge University Library).

about their relative dating.[42] The front depicts the *Traditio Legis*, with Christ standing on a rock from which flow the four rivers of paradise, and flanked by twelve apostles. Small figures of a man (left) and woman (right) bow at his feet, as he hands the scroll of the law to St Peter on the right, who carried a jewelled cross. The left side panel depicted the ascension of Elijah and Moses receiving the Tablets of the Law, and the right the sacrifice of Isaac and four standing men. The back had three figured scenes separated by double registered panels of strigillations: in each of the corners the figure of an apostle stands half-turned to the figure of a young shepherd at the centre. He is framed by trees, but the figures in all the other scenes are shown in front of a city wall, with crenellations and arches.

It is not known who actually commissioned the sarcophagus (although the lid, now lost, probably carried a dedicatory inscription).[43] But circumstances of its discovery, as will become apparent, suggest that it was for the burial of a member or members of the Anicii family.[44] Their high social standing is reflected in the quality of the sarcophagus, and possibly also in the central male figure on the right side panel who is dressed like some contemporary court official (and not in a tunic and mantle like the others).[45] The sarcophagus was then placed, with at least one other (see below), in their family mausoleum. Located in a prestigious site behind the apse of St. Peter's basilica, this was built at the end of the fourth century and dedicated (according to inscriptions found there) by Anicia Faltonia Proba to her late husband, Sextus Claudius Petronius Probus who had been consul in 371 and died around 388.[46] Its exact layout is unknown, nor is it certain where the sarcophagus was placed within it, although it may have been buried below the level of the floor.[47]

42 For this type see e.g., Sansoni 1969; Koch 2000, 304–07; *Rep.* III, 201. It is very similar to another in Sant'Ambrogio, Milan: *Rep.* II 56–58, no.150, especially 58 for summary of arguments about their relative dating and relationship.

43 Cf. lids of other 'City gate' sarcophagi: *Rep.* II nos. 148 (Tolentino) and 149 (Ancona).

44 Dresken-Weiland 2003, 378, Kat E 26; see also 119.

45 Cf. *Rep* II nos.149 and 150 for other examples of the small kneeling figures. See Baratte and Metzger, 1985, 316 for suggestion that the man in contemporary dress is the 'destinataire du cuve'; if so it seems rather an unobtrusive place to depict him.

46 Re. mausoleum: Liverani 1999 ,147–48 no. 68; also Dresken-Weiland 2003, 118–19. For the inscription: *CIL* 6.1756. For Anicia Faltonia Proba and Sextus Claudius Petronius Probus see Brown 1961; Jones, Martindale and Morris 1971, 732–33 and 736–40; Matthews 2009, 134–38.

47 It seems impossible to be completely certain that the two sarcophagi were originally buried, even if that is how they were found in the fifteenth century: e.g. Schoenebeck 1935, 108–09, amongst lime and debris. Dresken-Weiland 2003, 119 adds arguments to support the case for the original burial: i.e. that the objects found in the so-called Probus sarcophagus would not otherwise have escaped robbery, and that as fifteenth century popular belief thought the mausoleum was the tomb of St. Peter, no sarcophagus was to be seen in it.

This is the inference to be made from the report of its discovery given by Maffeio Vegio (1405–1457), who visited the Mausoleum shortly before it was demolished in 1453 in preparation for the rebuilding of St. Peter's.[48] But his description primarily focused on the other, columnar sarcophagus found there, in which garments with gold thread were discovered alongside the skeletal remains.[49] This obvious sign of wealth, along with the depiction of a married couple on the back, meant that this sarcophagus was quickly associated with Probus and his wife, while the 'Borghese Sarcophagus' was assigned less distinguished inhabitants. Cesare Baronio (1538–1607), who illustrated it with two women at the feet of Christ, suggested that it was the sarcophagus of Anicia Proba Faltonia and her daughter-in-law Anicia Juliana; his inaccuracy was roundly criticised by Antonio Bosio (1575–1629), who then proposed that the man depicted was her son, Anicius Hermogianus Olybrius with his wife Juliana.[50]

The sarcophagus was discovered without its lid and, to judge from copies of some late sixteenth century drawings, even by then many of its figures were badly damaged.[51] When Bosio saw it, it was presumably still intact and located in the garden near the church of Santa Marta to which it had been taken sometime after its discovery.[52] But soon after this it was moved to another setting in Rome, the Villa Borghese.

The Villa was developed for Cardinal Scipione Borghese (1576–1633) as a place of leisure, where he could display his collection of antiquities.[53] He bought sarcophagi from various sources and was also given antiquities by his uncle Pope Paul V.[54] Like many others this sarcophagus was dismembered, and its front and two side panels used to decorate facades of the Casino, while the back was cut into seven pieces which were inserted into decorative facades near the so-called 'Teatro' in the Villa grounds. This new function as an object of conspicuous display sealed the fortunes of this sarcophagus to this present day.

The decoration of the Casino's facades with ancient marble sculptures was done between 1616 and 1624 to the designs of Giovanni Vasanzio, creating '… in effect a great outdoor gallery of sculpture'.[55] The original layout can be

48 Valentini and Zuchetti 1953, 385.

49 For this sarcophagus: *Rep.* I, no. 678; Dresken-Weiland 2003, 377, Kat E 25; and 118–19 for the discovery.

50 Baronio 1601, 724; Bosio 1632, 55.

51 Baratte and Metzger, 1985, 314.

52 Bosio 1632, 69.

53 Paul 2000, 23–27 for a summary of development and brief description of the Villa; also Baratte and Metzger, 1985, 9–11.

54 Baratte and Metzger, 1985, 9–10; Kalveram 1995, 17–25 (especially 23 for gift from Paul V of sarcophagi discovered in excavating foundations of S. Peter's), 156–58.

55 Hermann Fiore 2008, 219, and 221–26 for other examples in Rome.

largely reconstructed from early guide-books to the Villa; but just how far there was an underlying theme to the choice and arrangement of the ancient images has been disputed by recent scholars.[56] It is hard to believe that there was none, yet nothing obvious seems to have emerged. A recent study has suggested a general theme to do with 'magnificence and the 'presence' of a Rome triumphing in the sign of Christian love', in which fragments of Christian sarcophagi were used to play an important symbolic role – in fact it was the first case of Christian antiquities being incorporated into the decoration of such a building, and a reflection of the interest stimulated by the new Christian archaeology, and in how it related to the pagan past.[57]

The front panel of this sarcophagus, showing Christ and the apostles, was immured on the front face of the southern belvedere overlooking the giardino segreto of the Villa, and the two side panels placed together in a corresponding position on the north.[58] In each case they occupied quite a prominent position, for though the walls they decorated stood back some way from the Villa's front facade, they technically formed part of this, its most important aspect, and were the sole decorative feature at that register of decoration. Looking up and down on the south side a viewer would see the relief of Christ and apostles set below a roundel with a bust of Claudius, and a relief of putti with swags, and above a roundel depicting a philosopher and two panels of a mounted soldier and a battle. The north showed a similar melange of subjects: above the panel composed of the two small sides of the sarcophagus was a roundel containing a now unidentified subject and a boar-hunt, while below it was a roundel with a putto with a griffin, and reliefs of Hercules and of a youth. Thus the walls presented a balance of forms and ideologies, juxtaposing subjects that had been prominent in Roman imperial and early Christian art.

The back of the sarcophagus was divided into seven pieces which were similarly immured with other ancient fragments and contemporary ornament in decorative facades in the second recinto of the Villa's gardens.[59] The figure of the shepherd was described *in situ* by both Manilli (who identified it as Christ)

56 Guide-books: Manilli 1650, and Montelatici 1700. For reconstructions and discussions: Kalveram 1995 and Hermann Fiore 2008, especially 220 for a summary.

57 Hermann Fiore 2008, 226, 239. Cf. also Federici 2002, 277.

58 Manilli 1650; Montelatici 1700; Kalveram 1995, Anghang III; Hermann Fiore 2008, 233, 236–37, figs, 24, 25 and 235, fig.23. For the two side panels placed together Martinez 2004, 469, no. 0949 (I am very grateful to Jean Luc Martinez for this reference).

59 Wilpert 1923–24, 172–74, fig.4 (in the so-called Prospettiva di Levante, not the Teatro, as Wilpert calls it); cf. Campitelli 2003, 154–56 for present day review, with replacement figures. For display of ancient sculptures in the Villa's grounds: Kalveram 1995, 80–88.

and Montelatici.[60] Figured panels were placed under ornamental niches and strigillated panels decorated areas of the wall below the main relief. During the cutting up of this back panel the upper borders of the strigillated panels seem to have been discarded.

While these sections of the back remained *in situ* until 1920s, when they were identified for what they were, published by Wilpert (in the article from which this paper's opening quotation was taken), and removed to the Capitoline collections in Rome (and now to the Centro Montemartini), the front and side panels of the sarcophagus entered yet another stage in their history. Nearly two hundred years after they were put on the façade, the reliefs were removed and transported to Paris, sold with other antiquities by Camillo Borghese to his brother-in-law, Napoleon Buonaparte in the agreement of 27 September 1807.[61] It is not entirely clear if Camillo Borghese initiated the sale as a solution to financial difficulties, or whether he was forced by Napoleon who wanted to add this great collection to the Italian art-works he had already removed to France as spoils of war.[62] In 1816, after Napoleon's defeat and the restitution to Italy of the plundered art-works, Camillo Borghese made an unsuccessful bid to retrieve them.[63]

Once in France the sculptures were displayed in the courtyard of the Musée Napoléon which had been established in 1793 at the Palais du Louvre, as a public museum, where they joined other artistic masterpieces taken by Napoleon from European cities.[64] Despite the different function of the building in which they now found themselves, they were still treated primarily as decorative items, and had simply exchanged their position on the Villa's walls for display on the Museum's.[65] This view may explain why it was not until some restoration work was done on the three panels in 1983 that the two side panels

60 Manilli 1650,143; Montelatici 1700, 70–71.

61 Hermann Fiore 2008, 219–220 for uncertainty about when the sculptures were actually removed from facades; she argues that it was on the sale to Napoleon. The Louvre Inventory of 1810 quotes a price of 4000 francs for the two small sides together, and 3000 for the front: Martinez 2004, 469, nos. 0949 and 0950. (I have been unable to access the recent book on the sale by J.-L.Martinez, *1807 L'achat de la collection Borghèse*).

62 Baratte and Metzger 1985, 11.Boyer 1969, 197, n. 2 cites the relevant archival sources, and (198) claims that Camillo Borghese was in financial difficulties. For other views see Paul 2000, 80 n. 177. For art-works taken by Napoleon from Italy during 1796, and their later restitution: Miles 2008, 319–348.

63 But afterwards he and his successor, managed to restore the Villa and its collections to much of its earlier splendour through new acquisitions and displays: Boyer 1969, 202; Paul 2000, 80–81; Hermann Fiore 2005, 123.

64 For setting: Martinez 2004, 469.

65 Baratte and Metzger, 1985, 11.

were separated, and re-assembled with the front, so that as now they could be shown for what they were – namely, three panels of a city gate sarcophagus.

In 2000–2001 they were temporarily reunited with the back (now in the Capitoline Collections in Rome) for the exhibition 'Aurea Roma. Dalla città pagana alla città Cristiana'. They were displayed separately (and have two separate catalogue entries, written by a French and by an Italian scholar).[66]

Conclusions

Constructing biographies like these is intricate work, with details to be pieced together and gaps and discrepancies to be negotiated (and unfortunately contains plenty of scope for creating and perpetuating errors). At this stage it might seem the ultimate exercise in positivism, but the point is to record the various events in the lives of the sarcophagi so that they provide '…a rich array of vantage points and approaches for understanding different trajectories in the human valuation of things'.[67] This section of the paper now moves on to do this. It first revisits each biography to identify particular 'vantage points' in the different values they involve, and then looks at all three together.

'The Pianabella sarcophagus', Ostia

The biography of 'The Pianabella sarcophagus' immediately suggests two important themes, to do with financial and cultural value. Its value as an expensive and beautiful commodity may explain why it was selected for re-use in the third century, and almost certainly was a reason – if not the only one – why it was then buried in the tomb, with liquid mortar used to secure a tight fit. Its commercial value to robbers was enduring, as is shown by the action of the twentieth century looters and of the dealers who bought from them. More precisely, it was the value that resided in the high quality of the figured decoration that counted to them, as they left behind the rest of the sarcophagus which was presumably not worth their while extracting from the site. At any rate the figured scenes had enough financial value to make even the fragmentary piece attractive to the art-market; their fate raises ethical issues which involve a whole series of players, from looters to dealers, collectors, and museum authorities.[68]

66 Ensoli and La Rocca 2000, 607–608, nos. 308 (C. Metzger for the Louvre panels) and 309 (S. Ensoli for the Capitoline).

67 Binsbergen 2005, 22.

68 As discussed for instance in Lundén 2004, 222.

The figured scenes also proved valuable to twentieth century scholars because of their iconographical worth. Although the clandestini were most likely unaware of this additional value, the images turn out to be unique in combining elements from Greek and Roman iconographies of Achilles. Thus the sarcophagus drew on two cultures. Reflecting contemporary Roman interest in Hellenic culture in the wake of the 'Second Sophistic', it celebrated Hellenism in choosing to depict events from the Iliad; but in using them to stand for universal experiences of death and loss, it was part of a Roman tradition of representing the human condition by reference to mythology and the heroic past. This linking of two cultures through the decoration is paralleled in the life of the sarcophagus itself, through the solution negotiated between cultural authorities in Germany and Italy in the late twentieth century. After its Ostian provenance was clarified, it was agreed that the sarcophagus should go to the Museum of Ostia as a permanent loan from Berlin, and hopes were expressed that this might lead to mutual benefits in terms of collaborative publications and a focus on authenticated excavated material.[69]

'The Brothers sarcophagus', Pisa

The biography of the sarcophagus in Pisa offers two major themes, which give rather different trajectories to the evaluation. The first is more historicist, and relates to the meaning which the sarcophagus and its decoration seems to have had in terms of family and society. Just as the Roman parents might have taken this half-finished sarcophagus for the chance it offered to personalise the decoration for their dead sons, so too the Falconi may have chosen it because the figures added by the Roman family – the soldier, the young men engaged in public affairs, and the decorously presented woman – also represented their own ideals. As if to confirm this, they inscribed their own family name upon it and added a heraldic device between the central figures.

The second theme is to do with space, and the contrasting states of fixed and mobile, religious and secular, and the different values these entail. Mobility, represented by the long journeys from quarry to Rome and centuries later from Rome to Pisa, involved commercial transactions and the value of the sarcophagus as a prestige import. But then 'fixed' in the Camposanto its values changed and accumulated as the significance of the Camposanto changed around it, from religious shrine and burial place to a secular museum of both Roman and Pisan antiquities. Decorated with figures that embodied Roman civic virtues, the sarcophagus acquired further value as a symbol of Pisa's own glorious past as a new Rome.

69 Heilmeyer 1992, 267.

'The Borghese sarcophagus', Paris and Rome

'Fixed' and 'mobile' are qualities also important in the biography of the 'Borghese sarcophagus' – especially in the move from religious, interior space to secular, external display – but it also offers two other themes to consider.

The first is the agency of powerful men, whose famous names dominate its life history. Its precise connection with the earliest of these, Sextus Claudius Petronius Probus, is hard to clarify although the sarcophagus was found in his mausoleum (and may even have been intended for him). For the Borgheses, Scipione and Camillo, and for Napoleon, the sarcophagus meant something collectable, a possession which represented civilisation, learning, the authority of the past, and money. But valued in this way it was also exposed to unsympathetic treatment, in transactions of power and money, and worse still, to be dismembered for display. Napoleon's acquisition of the Borghese antiquities resulted from his power (in whatever respect) over Camillo Borghese at the time, and although it came at the very high price of 13 million francs (which was far more than the 'expert' valuations had predicted) it was seen in Rome at least as little short of plunder.[70] Protests raised against the sale emphasised the loss to the Roman people in aesthetic, historic and legal terms; it was a loss more acute since the city had already lost many of its classical masterpieces as spoils of war.[71] But for Napoleon the purchase was intended to reinforce the cultural power of France, to turn Paris into '… the new Rome, the artistic capital of the Western world, superseding even its model and symbolising, inseparably, the succession of France to the centre of Western power, its line of descent ultimately reverting to antiquity'.[72] Once again the *romanitas* of the sarcophagus was of prime importance.

The second aspect is didactic – which underlies the display of this sarcophagus ever since its discovery. Even though damaged, it aroused great interest in Counter-Reformation Rome since its images could be directly linked with one of the most prominent families of early Christian Rome. So the 'Father of Ecclesiastical History', Cardinal Cesare Baronio published it in his great *Annales ecclesiatici* (1598–1607) as evidence for the piety of early Christians which he could set before his readers for their spiritual edification.[73] The Anicii made good exemplars for his cause since Probus was a famous senatorial convert to Christianity, and Proba celebrated for her good works and the head of several generations of leading Christian women. To support his text he provided a (rather inaccurate) illustration of the front panel. In contrast, Antonio Bosio's

70 Boyer 1969, 197–202.

71 Hermann Fiore, 2005; Miles 2008, 319–348.

72 Paul 2000, 80.

73 Baronio 1601, 724. He directly addresses the reader in the second person.

approach to the sarcophagus made a particular point of archaeological accuracy, and he systematically illustrated all four sides of the sarcophagus which he claimed to have inspected personally. This new interest in early Christian archaeology in early seventeenth century Rome presumably explains why these Christian reliefs were included in the decoration of the Casino of the Villa Borghese (particularly if this was to be read as a programmatic exploration of links between pagan and Christian antiquity). The culmination of this didactic aspect was in the systematic displays of the Louvre (which had become a public state museum in 1793), designed as they were to educate the visiting public.[74]

Looking now at all three biographies together, certain common features emerge which suggest the effectiveness of this as a methodology. To begin with a caveat: in terms of their record, all three show a similar imbalance in the evidence on which they are based, with large gaps for the start of the 'lives' and much better documentation towards the end. This is scarcely surprising given how hard it is to piece together anything much about the earliest stages in the production and usage of any Roman sarcophagus (let alone the identities of their original owners), while more recent situations are often well documented in museum inventories or catalogues. Yet even so, each involves a 'life event' or visual feature which helps fill some of these gaps in their record. For instance, particular iconographical details suggest that they all may have started life as special commissions, while information from other imported lion heads' sarcophagi allows more to be understood about the background to the decoration on the sarcophagus in Pisa. As for establishing evidence for more recent events in their existence, two involved contrasting means: at Pianabella it took a systematic investigation to ascertain the provenance of the front panel, while a fortuitous recognition appears to have identified the back panel of the 'Borghese sarcophagus' in the Villa grounds. All three sarcophagi now display the physical effects of their major life events: the 'Pianabella sarcophagus' is badly damaged, the 'Borghese sarcophagus' separated into sections (distributed across two countries), while the Pisan sarcophagus has been inscribed with an owners' name.

On the other hand, these biographies offer two distinctive opportunities as an interpretative tool – to look across the entire 'life-span' of an individual sarcophagus, and to allow the identification of common values or recurring patterns in significance.

The chance to review the whole existence of a sarcophagus, from quarry (if possible) to its present-day location, is especially important as it does away with the artificial boundaries of period (especially between antiquity, the Middle ages and the Renaissance), and is also a reminder of how often other accounts of re-

74 Paul 2000, 88. For the opening of the Louvre, McClellan, 1994, 94–98.

use tend to privilege the sarcophagus at one particular point in time. In fact it is clear from the Pianabella and Pisa sarcophagi (and from many other cases recorded by Dresken-Weiland 2003, for instance) that the adaptation, re-use, and re-location of sarcophagi frequently happened in antiquity (often not long after a sarcophagus first came into use), and that it would be more accurate to see this as a practice that happened as a continuum across centuries, rather than with supposedly decisive breaks between antiquity and the Middle ages. But it does also demand a tighter analysis than is often made of changes in social and cultural values that took place in Rome during antiquity, to achieve a better understanding of what was signified by the burial of the re-used Pianabella sarcophagus, for instance, or whether the (apparent) burial of Christian sarcophagi in the Mausoleum of the Anicii had the same meaning a century or so later. Were they both interred for reasons of security, for instance, or were there ideological grounds for burying the Christian sarcophagi below the mausoleum floor?[75] The need to consider closely what was involved at every stage seems a very positive aspect of the biographical method.

Comparing biographies, such as these, offers the important chance to identify common or recurrent elements. The discussion which follows will focus on three which, in different ways, are particularly useful for identifying how meanings get attached to sarcophagi through different human social actions.

Each biography has demonstrated re-use for aesthetic or ideological motives (sometimes both together, as in the decoration of the Villa Borghese). These are aspects of re-use which are well-known from studies that are period- or location-based; but biography makes it possible to see how they varied across time and function. Take, for example, the re-use of sarcophagi as an appeal to the authority of the past which occurs as a virtual constant, but in several different forms. In medieval Pisa it had particular value to the elite who used *romanitas* as an ideal which confirmed their own power and that of their city. In early seventeenth century Rome, the past which was cited through aesthetic and ideological references was both pagan and early Christian, and provided a theme through which leading figures in Papal Rome could negotiate their own contemporary priorities, whether cultural or driven by the needs of the Counter Reformation. Yet another aspect of the authority of the past emerges in the museological drives of the late eighteenth and early nineteenth centuries when systematic displays become important means of showing the value of local heritage or universally important art-works. In Rome, Paris and Pisa questions were asked about cultural ownership which show that the past at issue was not exclusively that of ancient Rome; for by that time the Borghese collection of antiquities is perceived of as being part of the patrimony of contemporary

75 Cf. also Barbavara di Gravellona 2002, 208 for invisibility of tombs, buried '*humile e depressum*' below church floors.

Rome, and the sarcophagi in Lasinio's Camposanto important as evidence of Pisa's glorious medieval past. Nearly two centuries later 'the Pianabella sarcophagus' is returned to be displayed as part of Ostia's history (although on permanent loan from Berlin). Biography, in short, is a good way of revealing how values attached to a particular sarcophagus can accumulate across centuries, but may also shift in emphasis in response to changing historical contexts.

Another theme that emerges from these three biographies concerns display, and more precisely the states of being hidden and viewable; and this is especially interesting given recent debate about the role of the viewer in relation to Roman sarcophagi, in terms of giving meaning to the visual image.[76] 'The Pianabella' and 'the Borghese' Sarcophagi are powerful illustrations of how one sarcophagus may move from one of these states to another, changing not only significant context but also the degree of visibility to a viewer. It is not known how 'the Pianabella' sarcophagus was originally displayed, but there is no particular reason to suspect that it was hidden entirely from view, but the way it was buried in the third century made it conclusively invisible, until centuries later its more spectacular sections were sheared off and ended up on public display (now happily visible with the rest in Ostia Museum). If burial was a strategy to ensure the security of this sarcophagus, then it was successful for a long while. The fate of 'the Borghese sarcophagus' was even more striking in this respect: long hidden from view (and perhaps even buried) it escaped destruction along with its mausoleum, only to be 'preserved' by being dismembered and publically displayed on a high profile building. This new context enforced new readings on to its separated panels through association with the other reliefs with which they were juxtaposed. Even in its current places of display, this sarcophagus is no longer visible as an entity, leaving visitors to supply the missing sections from a combination of knowledge and imagination. Again, comparisons of biographies can show how such vicissitudes are a regular feature of the lives of sarcophagi, but they also suggest that things can change again: perhaps the separated panels of the 'Borghese sarcophagus' might yet again be permanently reunited like that of Pianabella. The fates of sarcophagi need not end up as 'rather sad'.[77]

A third feature to emerge from comparing these biographies is just how often sarcophagi are regarded as 'empty vessels' waiting to be filled with a personal identity. There is a real sense that as one set of bones gets removed from the sarcophagus (and to where?), some new, living body is ready to appropriate it for a fresh purpose and a fresh identity.[78] The Falconi literally

76 E.g. Dresken-Weiland 2003, 185–98; also Barbavara di Gravellona 2002 for this as an issue in the re-use of sarcophagi.

77 Wilpert 1923–24, 168–69.

78 I am grateful to Jessica Hughes for reminding me to put the bodies back into these sarcophagi, but tracing – even generally – the comings and goings of bones and bodies is

inscribed their new identity on to the Roman sarcophagus which they re-used – in contrast to the new Roman owner of the sarcophagus at Pianabella, who seems to have erased its original inscription before he buried it.[79] Wilpert even saw one of the heads restored on the Borghese sarcophagus in the Louvre as having the features of Napoleon III.[80] But even now it is apparently hard to resist suggesting personal identities and motivations for the unknown people who commissioned or used the sarcophagi (such as the Roman and Pisan families, or the Egrili at Ostia). The whole debate about which of the two sarcophagi found in the Mauseoleum of the Anicii actually contained the body of Probus shows how important a 'big name' might be for the future evaluation of a sarcophagus – and also much may hang on a twist of fate. For, as Schoenbeck observed, a quirk of preservation – of the gold-threaded fabric allegedly found inside the columnar sarcophagus – instantly gave that one a glorious and certain identity, and consigned the other to a life in its shadow.[81] The power of the label in shaping the meanings invested in a sarcophagus has been demonstrated by Elsner in his discussion of how sacred and secular values were constructed for Roman sarcophagi re-used in Provence across several centuries.[82]

Another facet of the attachment of value through names is the naming of the sarcophagi themselves. It is noticeable how each of these three sarcophagi has acquired a title – 'the Pianabella sarcophagus', 'the Brothers' or 'the Tabernacle sarcophagus' at Pisa, and 'the Borghese sarcophagus'. (The first comes from provenance, the second from iconographical features, and the third from the collection: so like the naming of Pompeian houses or Greek vase painters, the process is rather random and privileges one particular aspect of the objects' life). Names like these make for obvious ease of reference in discussions (as here), but each of these is used in a principal publication of the sarcophagus concerned as if it is some official term, or has some intrinsic proprietorial value.

In conclusion, writing biography is necessarily a partial affair, and this is true for objects as it is for people: I have written and interpreted these three sarcophagi conscientiously, but from my own viewpoint and inevitably imperfect knowledge. These biographies are also limited, as they can only ever be partial accounts of the whole phenomenon of re-used Roman

not so easy, apart from occasional insights. For instance, Baronio 1601, 723 recorded the re-burial of bones from the so-called Probus sarcophagus in the Vatican, and see Donati 1993, 94 for Lasinio's treatment of the human remains he found in sarcophagi entering the Camposanto in Pisa.

79 Paroli 1999, 221.

80 Wilpert 1923–24, 173–74.

81 Schoenebeck 1935, 112–13 despite what he saw as its stronger claims to be that of Probus and his wife.

82 Elsner 2009.

sarcophagi, illuminating only those aspects which are represented in the individual life histories. Inevitably they yield much more when they can be compared with each other. Yet necessary as they are, these provisos are small in comparison with the benefits to be gained from treating sarcophagi as 'things', or 'objects' and approaching them biographically. This method '...can make salient what might otherwise remain obscure,' and this has the great advantage of being able to accommodate the wide variety of uses and contexts that they involve.[83] It thus provides an inclusive base from which to consider the values and meanings that different societies have invested in their use of them.

Bibliography

Andreae, B. Bossierte Porträts auf römischen Sarkophagen – ein ungelöstes Problem, in: B. Andreae (ed.), *Symposium über die antiken Sarkophage, Pisa 5.–12. September 1982* (Marburger Winckelmann-Programm, 1984), 109–128.

Andreae B. and Settis, S. (eds.). *Colloquio sul reimpiego dei sarcophagi romani nel Medioevo, Pisa , 5–12 settembre 1982, Marburger Winckelmann-Programm* 1983 (Marburg, 1984).

Appadurai, A. (ed.). *The Social Life of Things* (Cambridge, 1988).

Arias, P. E. Cristiani, E. and Gabba, E. *Camposanto monumentale di Pisa. Le antichità. II sarcofagi romani, iscrizioni romane e medioevali* (Pisa, 1977).

Baracchini, C. (ed.). *I marmi di Lasinio. La collezione di sculture medievali e moderne nel Camposanto di Pisa* (Florence, 1993).

Baracchini, C. and Castelnuovo, E. (eds.). *Il Camposanto di Pisa* (Biblioteca di storia dell'arte 27) (Turin, 1996).

Baracchini, C. Il restauro infinito, in: *Il Camposanto di Pisa* (Biblioteca di storia dell'arte 27), edited by C.Baracchini and E. Castelnuovo (Turin, 1996), 201–212.

Baratte, F. and C. Metzger. *Catalogue des sarcophages en pierre d'époques romaine et paléochrétienne* (Paris: Éditions de la Réunion des musées nationaux, 1985).

Barbavara di Gravellona, T. Visibilità effimera, visibilità negata: sarcofagi romani reimpiegati e obliterati nel medioevo, in: *Senso della rovine e riuso dell'antico* (*Annali della scuola normale Superiore di Pisa Quaderni* 14), edited by W. Cupperi (2002), 199–217.

Baronio, C. *Annales Ecclesiastici* IV (Antwerp, 1601).

Binsbergen, W. van and Geschiere, P. (eds.). *Commodification. Things, agency and identities; the social life of things revisited* (Münster, 2005).

Bober, P. and Rubinstein, R. *Renaissance artists and antique sculpture* (Oxford, 1986).

Bosio, A. *Roma sotterranea* (Rome, 1632).

Boyer, F. L'achât des antiques Borghèse, in: *Le monde des arts en Italie et la France de la Révolution et de l'Empire,* (*Biblioteca di studi francesi,* 4), edited by F. Boyer (Turin, 1969), 197–202.

Brilliant, R. I piedistalli del giardino di Boboli: *spolia in se, spolia in re. Prospettiva* 31.4 (1982), 2–16.

83 Kopytoff 1988, 67.

Brown, P. Aspects of the Christianization of the Roman Aristocracy. *Journal of Roman Studies* 61 (1961), 1–11.

Campitelli, A. *Villa Borghese da giardino del principe a parco dei romani* (Rome, 2003).

Casini, C. *Ultimus morientis et primus resurgentis artis gradus* La disposizione delle sculture in Camposanto, in: *I marmi di Lasinio. La collezione di sculture medievali e moderne nel Camposanto di Pisa*, edited by C. Baraccini (Florence, 1993), 61–72.

Cupperi, W. (ed.). *Senso della rovine e riuso dell'antico* (*Annali della scuola normale Superiore di Pisa Quaderni* 14) (2002), 273–285.

Cutler, A. Re-use or use? Theoretical and practical attitudes towards objects in the early middle ages' in: *Ideologie e practiche del reimpiego nell'alto medioevo. Settimane d studio del centro italiano di studi sull'alto medioevo 26. 16–21 aprile 1998* (Spoleto, 1999), 1055–1079.

Donati, F. and Parra, M. C. Pisa e il reimpiego 'laico': la nobiltà di sangue e d'ingegno, e la potenza' in: *Colloquio sul reimpiego dei sarcophagi romani nel Medioevo, Pisa , 5–12 settembre 1982, Marburger Winckelmann-Programm* 1983 (Marburg, 1984), edited by B. Andreae and S. Settis, 103–119.

Donati, F. Storia della collezione. Raccolta delle opera antiche in: *Camposanto monumentale di Pisa. Le antichità II*, edited by S. Settis (Modena,1984), 9–34.

Donati, F. Genesi e formazione della collezione di antichita del Camposanto, in: *I marmi di Lasinio. La collezione di sculture medievali e moderne nel Camposanto di Pisa*, edited by C. Baraccini (Florence, 1993), 87–107.

Donati, F. Il reimpiego dei sarcofagi. Profilo di una collezione, in: *Il Camposanto di Pisa* (Biblioteca di storia dell'arte 27), edited by C. Baracchini and E. Castelnuovo (Turin, 1996), 69–96.

Dresken-Weiland, J. *Sarkophagbestattungen des 4–6 Jahrhunderts im Westen des römischen Reiches (Römische Quartalschrift 55 Supplementband)* (Rome, 2003).

Elsner, J. The Christian Museum in the South of France: Antiquity, Display and Liturgy from the Counter-reformation to Aftermath. *Oxford Art Journal* 32, 2 (2009), 181–204.

Ensoli, S. and La Rocca, E. (eds.). *Aurea Roma. Dalla città pagana alla città Cristiana* (Rome, 2000).

Federici, F. *Veterum signa tanquam spolia.* Aspetti del reimpiego di sculture antiche a Roma nel seicento, in: *Senso della rovine e riuso dell'antico* (*Annali della scuola normale Superiore di Pisa Quaderni* 14), edited by W. Cupperi (2002), 273–285.

Giuliani, L. Achill-Sarkophage in Ost und West: Genese einer Ikonographie. *Jahrbuch der Berliner Museen* 31 (1989), 24–39.

Gosden, C. and Marshall, Y. The cultural biography of things. *World Archaeology* 31.2 (1999), 169–178.

Greenhalgh, M. *The Survival of Roman Antiquities in the Middle Ages* (London, 1989).

Harlow, M. and Laurence, R. *Growing up and Growing old in ancient Rome. A life course approach* (London, 2002).

Heilmeyer, W.D. Antikenwanderungen. Ostia und Berlin tauschen Skulpturen und Wandmalereien aus, *Antike Welt* 23.4 (1992), 263–267.

Hermann Fiore, K. Antonio Canova 1807: un memoriale a Pio VII in difesa del diritto del populo romano contro la vendita dei marmi della collezione Borghese a Napoleone, in: *Villa Borghese. Storia e gestione. Atti del convegno internazionale di Studi Roma, British School at Rome 19–21 giugno 2003*, edited by A. Campitelli (Milan, 2005), 113–129.

Hermann Fiore, K. The exhibition of sculpture on the Villa Borghese Facades in the time of Scipio Borghese, in: *Collecting Sculpture in early modern Europe (Studies in the History of Art 70. Symposium Papers 47)*, edited by N. Penny and E. D. Schmidt (Washington 2008), 219–245.

Hoskins, J. Agency, biography and objects, in: *Handbook of Material Culture*, edited by C. Tilley (London, 2006), 74–84.

Jones, A.H.M., Martindale, J. and Morris, J. *The Prosopography of the Later Roman Empire* Vol. I, AD 260–395 (London, 1971).

Kalveram, K. *Die Antikensammlung des Kardinals Scipione Borghese (Römische Studien della Biblioteca Hertziana Band 11)* (Worms, 1995).

Koch, G. *Frühchristliche Sarkophage. Handbuch der Archäologie* (Munich, 2000).

Koch, G. and Sichtermann, H. *Römische Sarkophage. Handbuch der Archäologie* (Munich, 1982).

Kopytoff, I. The cultural biography of things: commoditization as process, in: *The Social Life of Things*, edited by A. Appadurai (Cambridge, 1988), 64–91.

Liverani, P. *La topografia antica del Vaticano* (Vatican City, 1999).

Llewellyn, N. *The Art of Death. Visual Culture in the English Death Ritual c. 1500 – c.1800* (London, 1991).

Lundén, S. The Scholar and the Market. Swedish scholarly contributions to the destruction of the world archaeological heritage, in: *Swedish archaeologists on ethics*, edited by H. Karlsson (Lindome, 2004), 197–247.

Manilli, J. *Villa Borghese fuori di Porta Pinciana* (Rome, 1650).

Martinez, J.L. *Les antiques du Musée Napoléon. Édition illustré et commentée des volumes V et VI de l'Inventaire du Louvre de 1810. Notes et documents des musées de France 39* (Paris, 2004).

Matthews, J. Four Funerals and a Wedding: This World and the Next in Fourth-Century Rome, in: *Transformations of Late Antiquity: essays for Peter Brown*, edited by P. Rousseau and E. Papoutsakis (Farnham, 2009), 129–146.

McClellan, A. *Inventing the Louvre. Art, politics, and the origins of the modern museum in eighteenth century Paris* (Berkeley and London, 1994).

Miles, M. *Art as Plunder. The ancient origins of debate about cultural property* (New York and Cambridge, 2008).

Milone, A. Il camposanto, museo immaginato, tra seicento e settecento, in: *I marmi di Lasinio. La collezione di sculture medievali e moderne nel Camposanto di Pisa*, edited by C. Baraccini (Florence, 1993), 19–36.

Montelatici, D. *Villa Borghese fuori di Porta Pinciana con l'ornamenti, che si osservano nel di li palazzo, e con le figure delle statue più singolari* (Rome, 1700).

Morandi, A. Il sarcofago di Pianabella. *Archeologia Laziale* 11 (1993), 149–154.

Paroli, L. *La basilica cristiana di Pianabella, Scavi di Ostia XII* (Rome, 1999).

Paul, C. *Making a Prince's Museum: Drawings for the late eighteenth century redecoration of the Villa Borghese* (Los Angeles, 2000).

Penny N. and Schmidt, E. D. *Collecting Sculpture in early modern Europe (Studies in the History of Art 70. Symposium Papers 47)* (Washington, 2008).

Prettejohn, E. Reception and ancient art: the case of the Venus de Milo, in: *Classics and the Uses of Reception*, edited by C. Martindale and R. Thomas (Malden, Mass. and Oxford, 2006), 227–249.

Ragusa, I. *The Re-use and Public Exhibition of Roman sarcophagi in the Middle Ages and early Renaissance.* (Unpublished MA Dissertation, New York University, 1951).

Robb, J. Time and biography. Osteobiography of the Italian Neolithic Lifespan, in: *Thinking through the Body*, edited by Y. Hamilakis, M. Pluciennik and S. Tarlow (New York and London, 2002), 153–171.

Robert, C. Roman sarcophagi at Clieveden *Journal of Hellenic Studies* 20 (1900), 81–98

Rowlands, M. Value and the cultural transmission of things, in: *Commodification. Things, agency and identities; the social life of things revisited*, edited by W. van Binsbergen and P. P. Geschiere (Münster, 2005), 267–281.

Sansoni, R. *I sarcofagi paleocristiani a porte di città (Studi di antichità cristiane 4)* (Bologna, 1969).

Schoenebeck, H. von. *Der Mailänder Sarkophag und seine Nachfolge* (Vatican City, 1935).

Settis, S. *Camposanto monumentale di Pisa. Le antichità II* (Modena, 1984).

Settis, S. Continuità, distanza, conoscenza, tre usi dell' antico, in: *Memoria dell'antico nell'arte italiana,* edited by S. Settis (Turin, 1986), 375–486.

Settis, S. Riusare l'antico, mutare il presente, in: *Roma: il riuso dell'antico: fotografie tra XIX e XX sec.*, edited by G. Borghini, P. Callegari and L. Nista (Bologna, 2004), 11–18.

Settis, S. Collecting ancient sculpture: the beginnings, in: *Collecting Sculpture in early modern Europe (Studies in the History of Art 70. Symposium Papers 47)*, edited by N. Penny and E. D. Schmidt (Washington 2008), 219–245.

Stenbro, R. Kunstwollen und Spolia. On the methodological and theoretical foundation of spolia research and the positions adopted towards it. *Analecta Romana Instituti Danici* 31 (2005), 59–76.

Tolaini, E. Pisa. Quando i sarcofagi entrarono in Campo Santo. *Critica d'arte* 33–34 (2008), 51–56.

Valentini, R. and Zuchetti, G. *Codice topografico della città di Roma* IV (Rome, 1953).

Verkerk, D. Life after Death: the afterlife of Sarcophagi in medieval Rome and Ravenna, in: *Roma Felix: Formation and Reflections of Medieval Rome*, edited by E. Ó Carragáin and C. Neuman de Vegvar (Aldershot and Burlington VT, 2007), 81–96.

Walker, S. The marble quarries of Proconnesos: isotopic evidence for the age of the quarries and for lenos-sarcophagi carved at Rome, in: *Marmi antichi. Problemi d'impiego, di restauro, e d'identificazione. Studi Miscellanei 26*, edited by P. Pensabene (Rome, 1981–1982 [1985]), 57–65.

Ward-Perkins, J. B. and Throckmorton, P. New Light on the Roman Marble trade. The San Pietro Wreck. *Archaeology* 18 (1965), 201–209.

Wilpert, J. *I sarcofagi cristiani antichi* I – III (Vatican City, 1929–36).

Wilpert, J. Appunti su alcuni sarcofagi cristiani. *Rendiconti della pontificia accademia romana di archeologia* (1923–24), 169–184.

Wrede, H. *Senatorische Sarkophage Roms: der Beitrag des Senatorenstandes zur römischen Kunst der hohen und späten Kaiserzeit (Monumenta artis Romanae 29)* (Mainz, 2001).

Zanker, P. and Ewald, B. C. *Mit Mythen leben. Die Bilderwelt der römischen Sarkophage* (Munich, 2004).

3.
Tragedy's Forgotten Beauty: the Medieval Return of Orestes

Francisco Prado-Vilar

> The father prayed, called to his men to lift her
> with strength of hand swept in her robes aloft
> and prone above the altar, as you might lift
> a goat for sacrifice, with guards
> against the lips' sweet edge, to check
> the curse cried on the house of Atreus
> by force of bit and speech drowned in strength.
> Pouring then to the ground her saffron mantle
> she struck the sacrificers with
> the eyes' arrows of pity,
> lovely as in a painted scene, and striving
> to speak.
>
> Aeschylus, *Agamemnon* 231–43,
> transl. Lattimore

It is a poignant piece of history that Spanish Romanesque sculpture finds one of its stylistic and emotional foundations in a Greek tragedy. The ancient myth's unexpected point of entry into the historical reality of medieval Iberia materialised in the Castilian church of Santa María de Husillos (Palencia), where a magnificent Roman sarcophagus decorated with episodes of the saga of Orestes was reused in a Christian burial (Figures 3.1,3.2, and 3.3).[1] For over a century, the sarcophagus had lain silent in the small church, holding the remains of one of those noblemen who, at the dusk of the first millennium, prepared the way for the emergence of the Kingdom of Castile.[2] Yet, in the spring of 1088,

1 Now in the Museo Arqueológico Nacional, Madrid (inv. no. 2839); see García y Bellido 1949, 212–17; and also Fernández-Guerra y Orbe 1872 (written when the sarcophagus was transferred to Madrid) especially for its beautiful lithograph. Dated to the first decades of the 2nd century, the sarcophagus must have found its way into Hispania in antiquity.

2 Since its foundation in the 10th century, Santa María de Husillos was connected to the powerful Ansúrez family – which has led scholars to speculate that the Orestes sarcophagus could have been used for the burial of one its most prominent members, Fernando Ansúrez, count of Monzón. Other leaders of the Kingdom of León received burials in antique sarcophagi during the 10th century, showing how these were valued as status-symbols by the Castilian elite. The famous first independent count of Castile, Fernán González, a rival and

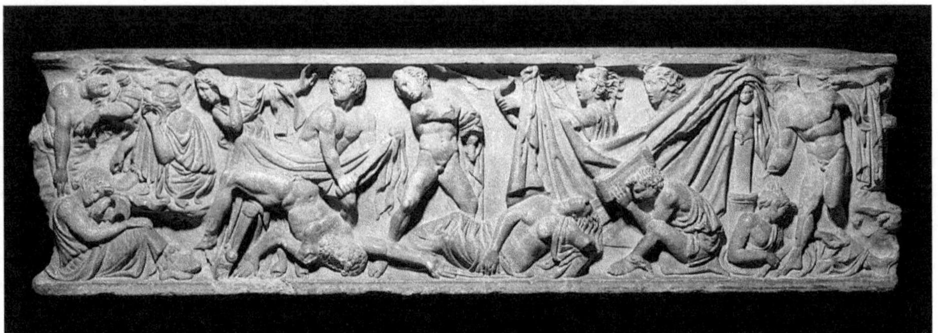

Figure 3.1: Orestes sarcophagus (early second century A.D.). Front: the revenge of Orestes. Madrid, Museo Arqueológico Nacional, inv. 2839. Photograph: courtesy of Museo Arqueológico Nacional.

when King Alfonso VI of León-Castile summoned the bishops and nobles of his realm to meet at Husillos for a momentous council, its imagery of crime, revenge and sacrifice seemed to be speaking, once more, to the present.

Their urgent task was to restore peace and social order after a year of political, military and ecclesiastical unrest that had almost split the kingdom.[3] During the council, there were disputes punctuated by episodes of high drama almost recalling the tableaux carved on the sarcophagus that stood nearby. One may imagine the Castilian nobles entering the church of Husillos, some for the

contemporary of Fernando Ansúrez, and his wife Sancha were also interred in two antique sarcophagi, originally located in the family monastery of San Pedro de Arlanza and now in the Colegiata de Covarruvias in Burgos (see Moralejo 1984a). The literature on the reutilization of antique sculpture in the Middle Ages is vast but the standard study remains Adhémar 1939. See also Greenhalgh 1989. In his excellent new book on Roman mythological sarcophagi (Zanker and Ewald 2004), P. Zanker includes a chapter on the re-use of examples such as the Hippolytus sarcophagus in Pisa.

3 The magnates of Galicia, led by count Rodrigo Ovéquiz, had revolted against the king, presumably due to his decision to hand over the administration of the region to count Raymond of Burgundy, a nephew of abbot Hugh of Cluny, who had settled at the Leonese court a few years earlier. The early-12th-century chronicle known as the *Historia Compostellana* suggests that the ultimate goal of the rebels, aided by the bishop of Santiago de Compostela, Diego Peláez, was the severance of Galicia from León-Castile and its surrender to William the Conqueror. Anglo-Norman epic sources seem to recall this possible connection between William and the Galician aristocracy signalling that the horse that led him to victory at the Battle of Hastings had been raised in Santiago de Compostela (see Moralejo 1994, 175). However, with the defeat of the rebels, the incredible historical possibility of a Norman takeover of Northwestern Spain was thwarted, bishop Diego Peláez was put in prison by Alfonso VI and later brought in chains before the papal legate at the council of Husillos, where 'the bishop, proclaiming before the council that he was unworthy of the episcopate, surrendered his pastoral ring and staff' (Falque Rey 1988, 15). For the background of these events, see Fletcher 1984, 29–50, Fletcher 1978, 7–10, Reilly 1988, 185–209, and Reilly 1982, 3–43, esp. 14–17.

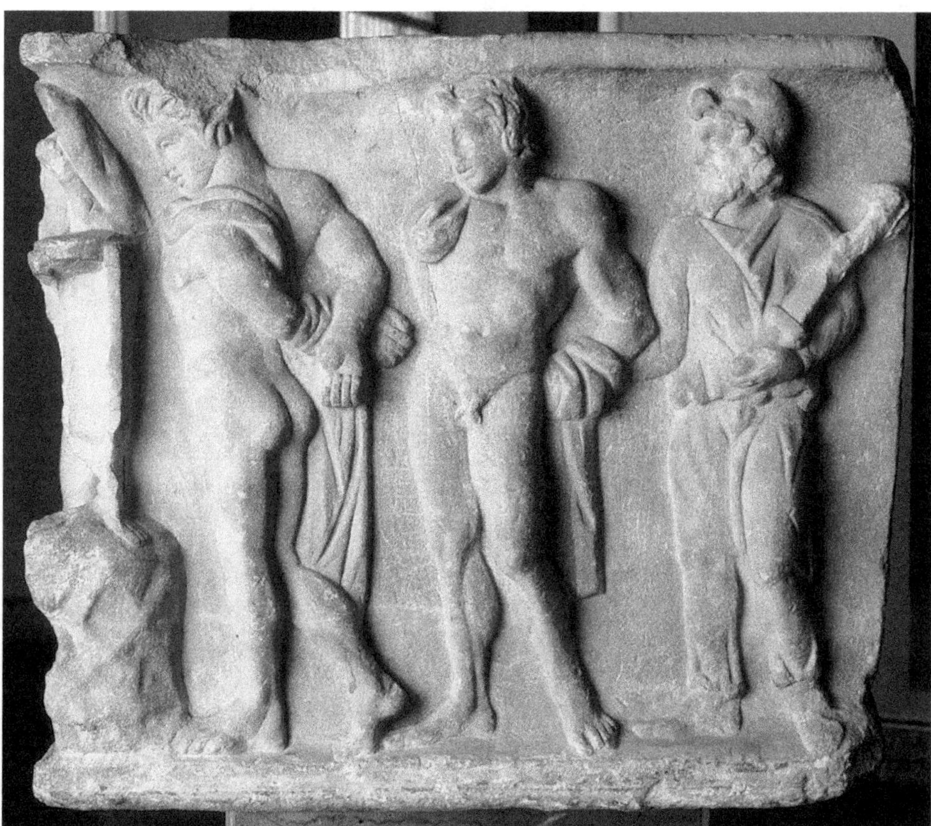

Figure 3.2: Orestes sarcophagus (early second century A.D.). Right side: Orestes and Pylades captured by the tauri. Madrid, Museo Arqueológico Nacional, inv. 2839. Photograph: courtesy of Museo Arqueológico Nacional.

first time, being mesmerised by the beauty and strangeness of the images on the sarcophagus, such as Orestes, naked and with hands tied, led to sacrifice by his captors (Figure 3.2), only later to experience, in the flesh, similarly gripping scenes, such as the detention and disrobing of the bishop of Santiago de Compostela, Diego Peláez, before the papal legate. Art and life might suddenly seem to merge in a series of echoing gestures, as if the ancient myth provided the background and choreography for the unfolding of history.

No document records the impact of the Roman reliefs on those who attended the council (nor on the chronicler of the *Historia Compostellana* who would recreate in writing, a few decades later, episodes such as Diego Peláez's deposition).[4] But, it

4 We will probably never know whether the 12th-century author of the *Historia Compostellana*, having visited Husillos sometime in his life, was inspired by the sarcophagus in his literary recreation of the council. Little remains of the building where it happened, or of the building

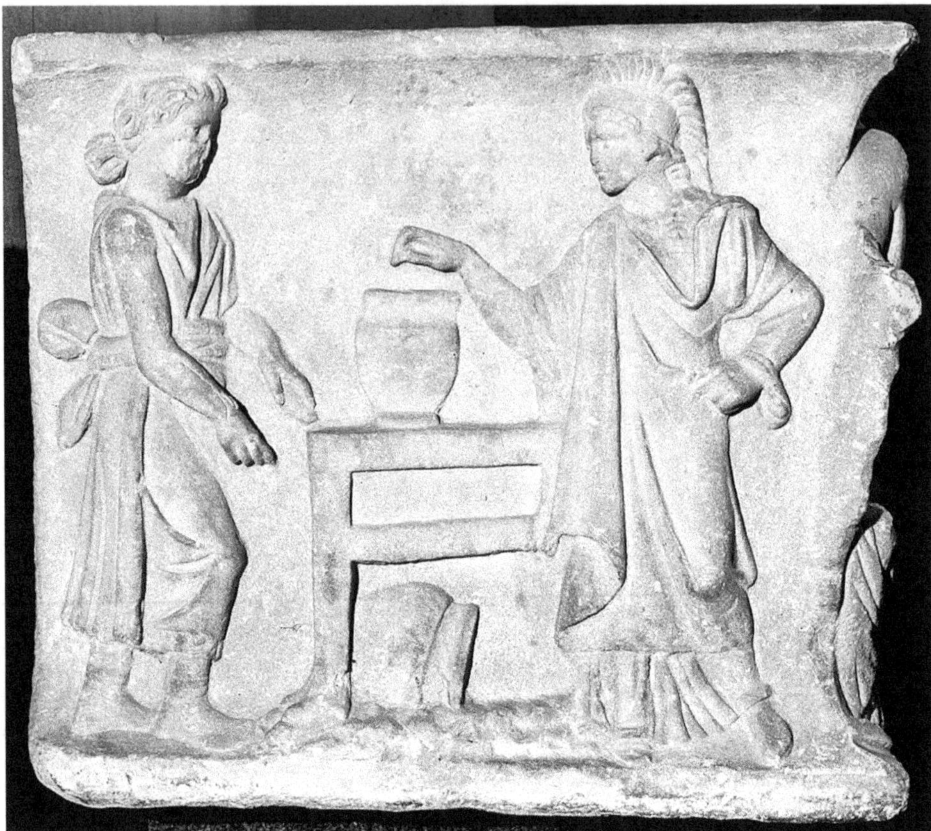

Figure 3.3: Orestes sarcophagus (early second century A.D.). Left side: Athena at the trial of the Areopagus. Madrid, Museo Arqueológico Nacional, inv. 2839. Photograph: courtesy of Museo Arqueológico Nacional.

is hardly a coincidence that soon after that memorable event, which exposed the sarcophagus to a large gathering of potential art patrons, a paraphrase of its frieze was carved on a capital decorating the main apse of the nearby church of San Martín de Frómista (Figure 3.4).[5] 'Traces of the ancient model,' observed Serafín Moralejo, the scholar who first noticed the striking correspondence between the 'Roman' and the 'Romanesque' works, 'are as intense as the interpretation creative, which suggests that the piece represents the genesis of a style. In the subtle compositional cadences of the sarcophagus frieze, the master

that the author of the *Historia Compostellana* could have seen in the early 12th century. The church of Husillos was completely rebuilt in the 13th century and drastically renovated several times since, so the sarcophagus is one of the few points of continuity, and the only extant material witness to the council. For the history of Santa María de Husillos, see Hernando Garrido 2002.

5 The capital is now in the Museo Provincial de Palencia (Palencia), inv. no. 227.

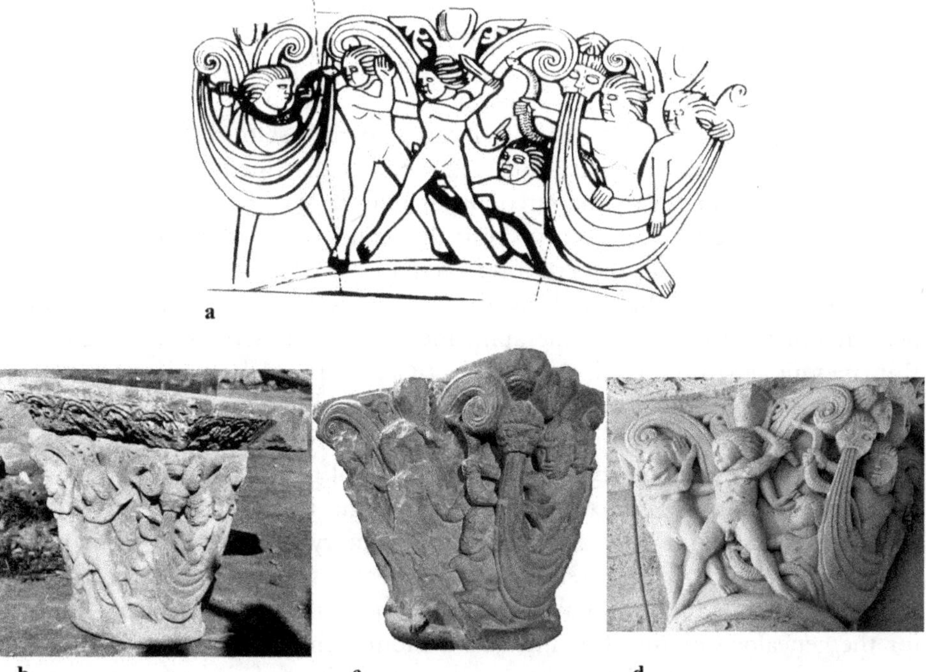

Figure 3.4: Capital representing Cain killing Abel from the church of San Martín de Frómista. **a.** Scheme of the capital by Serafín Moralejo (published by courtesy of Serafín Moralejo). **b.** Photograph of the capital during restoration ca. 1900. Photograph: courtesy of Fundación Eugenio Fontaneda. **c.** Capital in its current display at the Museo Arqueológico Provincial de Palencia, inv. 227. Photograph: author. **d.** Modified modern copy in the central apse of San Martín de Frómista. Photograph: author.

of Frómista discovered rhythmic accents that he used to articulate the plastic architecture of the capital, such as the x-shaped postures of the figures stretched across the fork formed by the volutes, and the ample curves describing the draperies with which he closes and gives balance to the composition of the side faces.'[6] This creative encounter, first described by Moralejo in a paper delivered at the International Congress of the History of Art in Granada in 1973, was just the beginning of an extraordinary artistic watershed that would forge the seminal place of the Orestes sarcophagus from Husillos in the history of medieval art.[7]

Moralejo followed this initial observation with a series of remarkable studies, which pursued this medieval artist's obsession with the classical model, its dissemination in later commissions of the workshop (especially the Cathedral

6 Moralejo 1994b, 211.
7 Moralejo 1976.

of Jaca), and contribution towards shaping the visual morphology of the so-called 'Hispano-Languedocian' Romanesque style (Figure 3.5).[8] Moralejo was primarily interested in elucidating the formal genealogy of the style, tracing the lineage of figures from Romanesque monuments back to their classical ancestors in the sarcophagus. He limited his findings to the establishment of a formal aetiology partly because he assumed (reasonably) that medieval viewers would find the subject-matter of the sarcophagus remote and inaccessible, and partly because he had some uncertainty about the iconography of the first link in its Romanesque succession, the Frómista capital.

In this article I shall address those two issues as I explore the subtle permutations of form and iconographic meaning that link the sarcophagus to its Romanesque offspring. I will show how a thematic parallel runs alongside to the formal lineage outlined by Moralejo. By understanding the ways in which these two genealogies – formal and iconographic – evolved in response to the historical, political and psychological conditions of patronage and reception, we may begin to grasp the function of the sarcophagus in larger cultural terms, as a true *lieu de mémoire* where the artistic memory of Spanish Romanesque sculpture 'crystallizes and secretes itself.'[9] As we will see, like the *lieux de mémoire* conceptualized in Pierre Nora's historical project, the Husillos sarcophagus is, for the genealogy of the Romanesque, a monument that 'exists because of its capacity for metamorphosis, an endless recycling of its meaning and a unpredictable proliferation of its ramifications.'[10] In the course of this analysis, we will discover two more genealogical ramifications, one historic and the other historiographic, which will allow us to view the sarcophagus as an active witness to history and a nexus that links history (and the present) to the time of myth.

La Beauté Oubliée

Moralejo's discovery occurred in the realm of memory. He was guided by the recollections of Émile Bertaux who, visiting Frómista in 1905, saw sculptures that reminded him of the *beauté oubliée* of Roman sarcophagi:

> L'artiste … a étudié des sarcophages antiques, pour y copier des figures entières, qu'il a laissées nues, et qui, dans les formes de leurs corps et dans le sourire de leur

8 See, especially, Moralejo 1979, 1985, and 1987. For the influence of formal elements derived from the sumptuary arts in the definition of the style, see Moralejo 1982. For an overview of Hispano-Languedocian sculpture, see Gaillard 1938, and Durliat 1990.

9 Nora 1989, 7.

10 Ibid.,9.

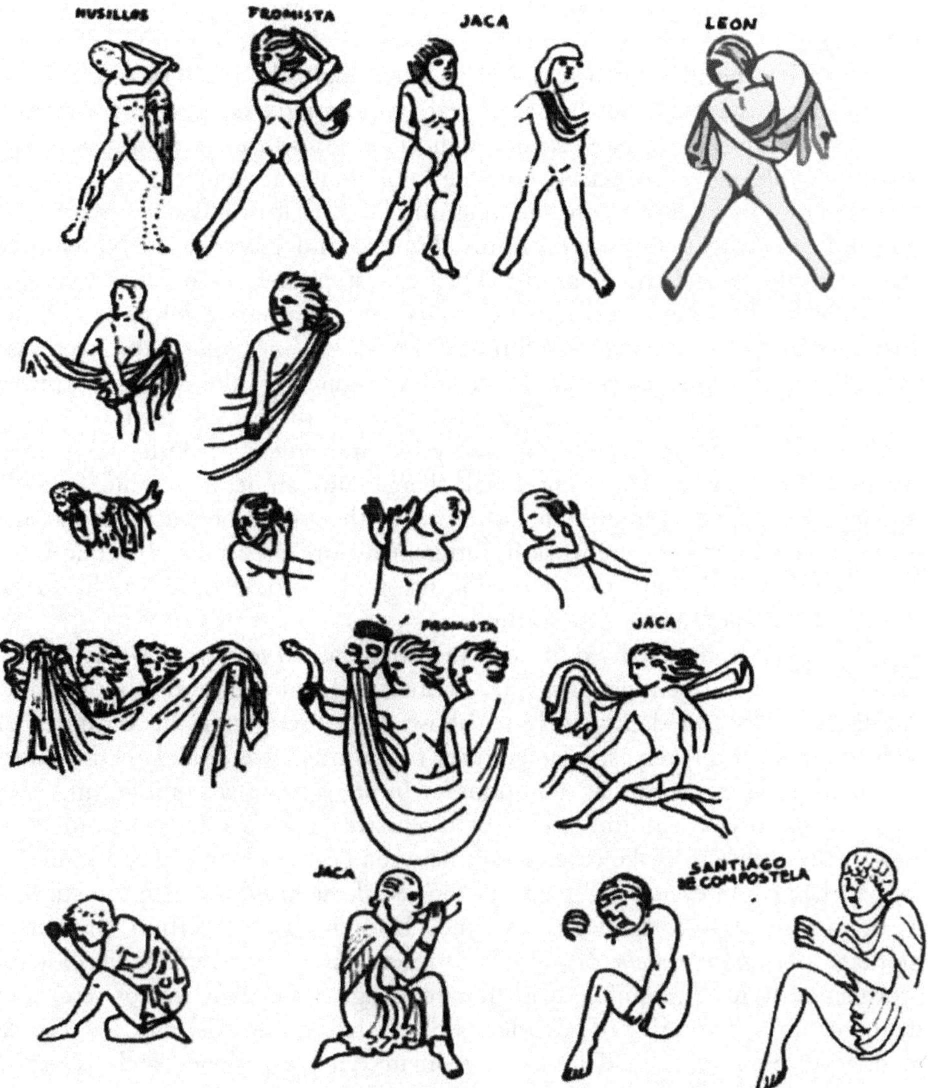

Figure 3.5: Scheme showing the Romanesque descendancy of the figures from the Orestes sarcophagus (by Serafín Moralejo and published with his kind permission).

visage, font apparaitre, au milieu des monstres barbares qu'elles combattent au chevauchent, une vision fugitive de la beauté oubliée.[11]

11 Bertaux 1906, 244. For a brief account of Bertaux's trip to Spain and Portugal, where he spent 'longues semaines, pour relever, étudier, photographier tant monuments remarquables et presque ignores,' see Bertaux 1924, 2–3.

This observation inspired Moralejo to follow his own memory trail, finally reuniting two works that had once been closely connected in the Middle Ages, but which had been by then removed to museums – the Husillos sarcophagus and the Frómista capital. The same year that Bertaux delighted in catching glimpses of an Apollonian beauty amidst the *monstres* at Frómista, Aby Warburg, a scholar more sensitive to the Dionysian undercurrent of antiquity, gave a lecture in Hamburg on 'the long migration that brought superlatives of gesture from Athens, by way of Rome, Mantua and Florence, to Nuremberg and into the mind of Albrecht Dürer.'[12] Expounding on his previous investigations on 'the circulation and exchange of expressive forms in art,' he traced the origins of the composition of Dürer's *Death of Orpheus* to Greek vase painting via Italian Renaissance art. The figure of the dying Orpheus constituted what he would call a *Pathosformel,* or pathos formula – the condensed gestural expression of a psychic movement.[13] Both the primal corporeal expression of an emotional charge and an iconographic formula containing the fundamental kernel of meaning that could be reactivated at any point of encounter with the work in different historical periods, the concept of the *Pathosformel* became the centre of his project to retrieve an 'historical psychology of the human expression.'[14]

This project materialised in the picture atlas *Mnemosyne,* where, using *Pathosformel* as an operative principle, Warburg created a series of photographic montages placed on dark panels to 'show that throughout the centuries of history the same or very similar gestures or formulas were used in the visual presentation of basic human emotions.' *Mnemosyne* was a complex machine intended to surpass the limitations of discursive analysis and to stimulate in viewers the ability to make connections between gesture, memory and mimesis, so that they could eventually 'map out the visual memory of European culture, its origins and transformations.' In panel 5, for instance, Warburg presents a montage of *Pathosformeln* of women from works of different archaeological provenance (Greek ceramics, Roman sarcophagi, Pompeian frescos, etc) and thematic context (stories of Cybele, Niobe, Medea, Alcestis, etc) as a visual meditation on the essential forms of woman's vital experience such as panic, fury, crime, sacrifice (Figure 3.6).

---

12 Warburg 1999, 558.

13 Only recently have scholars begun to delve into the epistemological complexities of Warburg's project, read for years through the more positivistic, taxonomic, and textually oriented lens of his famous successors such as Panosfky or Gombrich. This Warburgian revival has produced extensive scholarship; most relevant here are: Didi-Huberman 2002; Michaud 2007; and Rose 2001.

14 Gombrich 1970, 223.

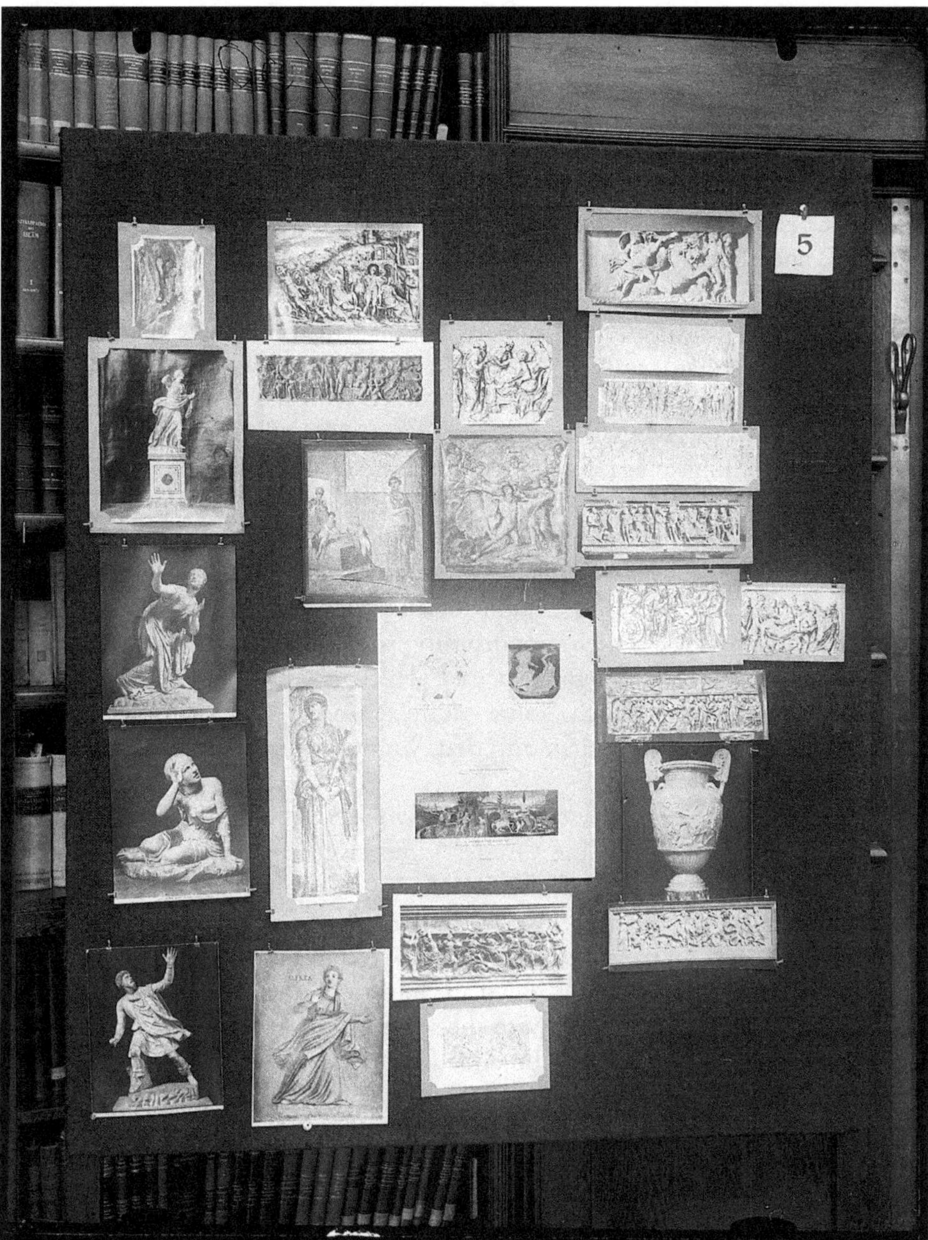

Figure 3.6: Panel 5 of the *Mnemosyne Atlas*. Formulas of female *pathos*. London, Warburg Institute. Photograph: courtesy of the Warburg Institute.

If Bertaux's *beauté oubliée* represents the acknowledged Apollonian inspiration for Moralejo's inquiry, Warburg's project emerges as its Dionysian repressed subtext. As in his case, Moralejo's interest in the question of the afterlife of antiquity centred on the observation of a trans-historical gestural vocabulary of the human expression that originated in the Greco-Roman world and re-emerged periodically in later works. But if Moralejo focused primarily on *gesture as form* and its implications for the history of style, Warburg was more concerned with *gesture as psychic movement*, and with the complexities of its recurrent historical materialisations at the intersection of iconography, cultural memory and human psychology. However, even if they were originally conceived as diagrams of classical formal sources, Moralejo's charts, seen from a Warburgian perspective, unintentionally double as psychic tableaux outlining a repertoire of *Pathosformeln* that defines the emotional space of the style (Figure 3.5).[15] It is a space teeming with bodies imbued with the pathos of ancient art, and with faces whose Dionysian intensity leaves an indelible mark on those who walk along the Pilgrimage Road to Compostela, from the corbels of Saint-Sernin de Toulouse (Figure 3.7), to the capitals of San Martín de Frómista (Figures 3.4 and 3.8b), and the architectural sculpture in the cathedral of Santiago de Compostela.[16] Embedded, therefore, in Moralejo's outline of the artistic genealogy of Hispano-Languedocian Romanesque sculpture, is a case study which provides a rich opportunity to explore the full potential of Warburg's theoretical paradigm – a case which is much more elegant in its formal premises and much more comprehensive in its historical and psychological ramifications than any that Warburg himself might have had at his disposal.

To explore the complex conditions involved in the reactivation of the *Pathosformeln* derived from the Orestes sarcophagus at the specific historical moment of the emergence of the Romanesque at the end of the eleventh century (such as formal processes, religious imagination, historico-political circumstances, and human psychology), I propose to build incrementally a new *Mnemosyne* panel that could be added to Warburg's unfinished 'ghost story for truly adult people' (Figure 3.8). With the sarcophagus as the classical, generative kernel, Romanesque works will be added in a series of analytical movements (*motecta*). When the panel is complete, at the end of this article, all those movements will relate to each other in complex contrapunctual harmonies which should be fully apprehended, to use a musical metaphor, like the

15 Thus they recall the famous tabular gestural taxonomies developed in the context of the clinical studies on hysteria conducted by Charcot at the Salpetrière. For the influence of Charcot's clinical studies on hysteria and his *Iconographie photographique de la Salpetrière* on Warburg's concept of the *Pathosformel*, see Schade 1995 and Didi-Huberman 2001.

16 For stylistic connections between the corbel from Saint-Sernin de Toulouse and the figural tradition inspired by the Husillos sarcophagus: Moralejo 1984b, 32–33.

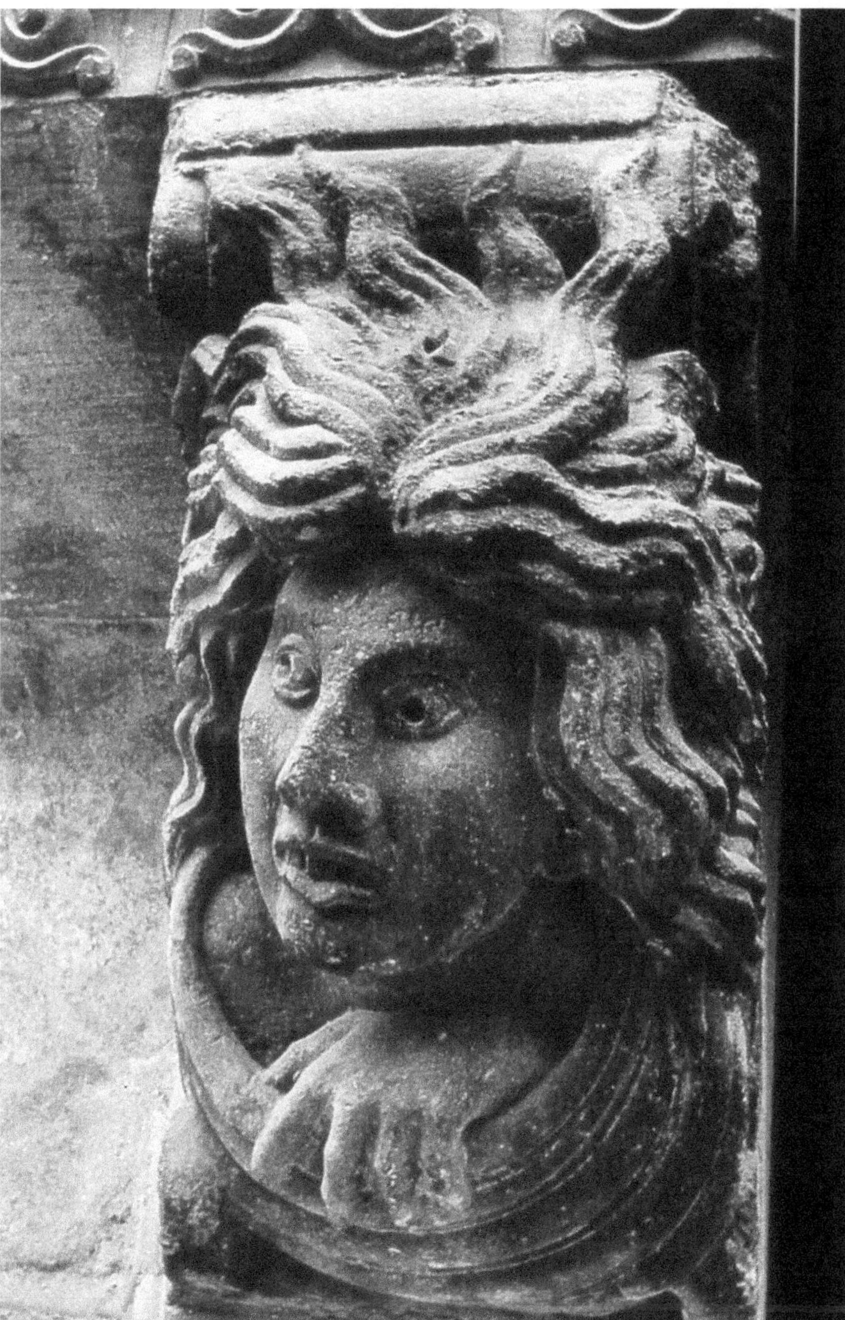

Figure 3.7: Corbel from the *Porte Miègeville* of Saint-Sernin de Toulouse. Photograph: author.

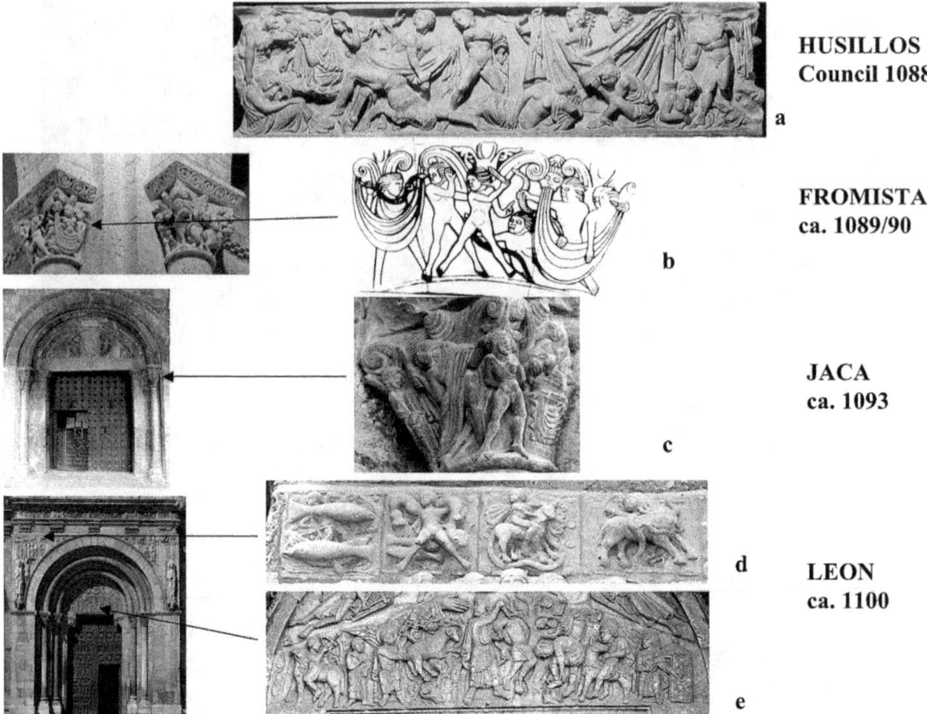

Figure 3.8: The Orestes sarcophagus in Spanish Romanesque sculpture **a.** Orestes sarcophagus (early second century A.D.). Madrid, Museo Arqueológico Nacional, inv. 2839. Photograph: courtesy of Museo Arqueológico Nacional. **b.** Capital with Cain killing Abel, central apse of San Martín de Frómista. Photograph: author. **c.** Capital with the Sacrifice de Isaac, South Portal of the Catedral de Jaca. Photograph: author. **d.** Frieze with the Signs of the Zodiac, Portal of the Lamb of San Isidoro de León. Photograph: author. **e.** Tympanum with the Sacrifice of Isaac, Portal of the Lamb of San Isidoro de León. Photograph: author.

polyphonic structure of a medieval motet.[17] Over the *cantus firmus* of Moralejo's formal lineage, we will hear an elegiac chant around the themes of family crime and sacrifice – one that reverberates almost simultaneously and at different intensities, at four levels: mythical, biblical, historical, and historiographical.

17 *Mnemosyne* has been described as a symphony, see Gombrich 1970, 282.

Husillos: the Return of Orestes

The starting place is the sarcophagus itself. Drawing principally on Aeschylus's famous trilogy, *The Oresteia*, its scenes represent the revenge of Orestes and his subsequent quest for expiation (Figure 3.1).[18] From left to right, the narrative unfolds chronologically in a continuous series of interconnected tableaux, beginning with a peaceful scene where the Erinyes, goddesses of revenge, rest quietly before the crime around the funerary cairn of Agamemnon, who had been assassinated by his wife Clytemnestra and her lover Aegisthus. Then, suddenly, in the centre, the drama explodes into a chiastic movement, springing from the double portrait of Orestes in his murderous rampage to avenge his father's death, and the slain bodies of Clytemnestra and Aegisthus, toppled from his throne.[19] Forming emotional brackets to this central scene are two supporting characters, which will have illustrious Romanesque descendants, an old nurse who shields her face from the violence, and a manservant hiding behind a stool beside Clytemnestra's corpse.

The Roman artist cleverly incorporated subtle elements of the Aeschylian *mise-en-scène:* for instance the cloth with which Orestes cleans his sword after killing Aegisthus recalls the carpet and robe which Clytemnestra used in Agamemnon's murder, and so expands the dramatic span of the story by introducing a reminder of the earlier crime that had sparked the whole cycle of revenge. Another dramatic peak of the play is evoked by the figure of Orestes brandishing his sword over Clytemnestra's partially naked body. Despite the fact that matricide seems to have been committed already, Orestes appears still caught up in the agonising moment of hesitation that preceded the crime, when the queen pleaded for mercy by showing him her breasts, to remind him of her motherhood. It is then that Orestes utters the most famous line of the play 'What am I to do Pylades? Be ashamed to kill my mother?' If we identify the figure to the left of Orestes as his companion Pylades, that is exactly the tragic question reverberating through the reliefs. When viewers of the sarcophagus follow the interpretative sequence movement activated by the multivalent visual narrative of the frieze (Orestes progressively killing his mother and her lover, Orestes posing the 'tragic question' to Pylades, the piece of cloth that recalls the

18 First performed in 458 B.C., *The Oresteia* inspired a lasting iconographic tradition. From the Greek stage, the saga of Orestes entered Latin literature, and during the Hadrianic Hellenic revival it became the subject of a magnificent series of Roman sarcophagi, of which the Husillos sarcophagus is a prime example: See Toynbee 1934, 166–77, McCann 1978, and Neils 1984.

19 An alternative interpretation sees the two figures as Orestes, centre, and his friend Pylades, to the left.

original crime), they can experience the sculptures in their dynamic dimension, as a true 'life' performance of the play.

The next episode on the sarcophagus (to the right of centre) begins with the entrance of two Furies who, woken by the blood spilled in matricide, pursue Orestes, brandishing a snake and a torch. Finally, the right end of the frieze introduces the first stage in the process of purification – Orestes' visit to the temple of Apollo in Delphi: en route to Athens, he steps gingerly over a sleeping Fury who has fallen victim to Apollo's spell.

The short sides of the sarcophagus represent the expiatory rites that would eventually cleanse Orestes of his crime. The right side features a scene showing Orestes and Pylades being captured by the Tauri, who have the custom of sacrificing all strangers to Artemis, but Iphigenia, the high priestess of the goddess, eventually recognizes her brother and the three manage to escape to Athens carrying the sacred statue (Figure 3.2). On the left, Athena casts the deciding vote in favour of Orestes at the trial of the Areopagus, which would put an end to his persecution by the Erinyes (Figure 3.3).

Not until the nineteenth century was the iconography of this typology of so-called 'Orestes sarcophagi' determined with any certainty. Even the knowledgeable seventeenth-century Roman antiquarian Giovanni Bellori failed to give a satisfactory interpretation of an almost identical piece housed at the Palazzo Giustiniani.[20] In his *Admiranda Romanorum antiquitatum ac veteris sculpturae vestigia* (1693), Bellori wrote a poetic commentary to accompany a delicate engraving of the sarcophagus by Pietro Santi Bartoli, where he emphasised the themes of crime and sacrifice as central to its meaning.[21]

But more than a century before Bellori, and writing about the Husillos sarcophagus, the Spanish humanist Ambrosio de Morales had come closer to the original meaning of the typology by framing the themes of crime and sacrifice within the context of an interfamilial conflict. Morales drew upon his knowledge of Roman history, mediated through Livy, to speculate that it might represent the story of the Horatii and Curiatii (described in *Ab Urbe Condita* I, 24–26).[22] He identifies the central figure (of Orestes who had killed his mother Clytemnestra) as Horatius who had just murdered his sister Camilla claiming 'So perishes any Roman woman who mourns the enemy,' for she had shown

20 Although its iconography was not properly understood during the Renaissance, this sarcophagus was revered by many artists who used it as a source of figural models: see Bober and Rubinstein 1986, 137–138.

21 For the online edition of the *Admiranda Romanorum antiquitatum*, with an image of Pietro Santi Bartoli's engraving, see the *Corpus Informatico Belloriano* http://biblio.signum.sns.it/cgi-bin/bellori//blrCGI?cmd=1&w=12&u=Palazzo+Giustiniani.+Strange&pg=052

22 Ambrosio de Morales visited Husillos in the course of his trip, at the command of Philip II in 1572, to document the treasures of his kingdom: Morales 1765 [1977], 26–27.

grief at the death of one of the Curiatii to whom she was betrothed. This story has some parallels with Orestes's tragedy, because, like Orestes, Horatius should have been condemned to death for killing his sister but was absolved because of the motivating circumstances and the advocacy of his father. To expiate his crime, Horatius' father obliged him to carry out a series of sacrifices, amongst which was to walk under a beam 'as if set under the yoke.' Morales identifies the figure on the sarcophagus of the crouching servant with a stool as Horatius passing under this beam, which came to be known as the *tigillum sororium* (sister's beam). In sum, Morales' knowledge of an ancient text (Livy) allowed him to identify a classical story of family crime and expiation similar to the one that was actually represented in the sarcophagus.

But more relevant to this inquiry is the process of interpretation that enabled Morales to access the core of Orestes' story, exclusively through the evocative power of a *Pathosformel.* He identifies the Erinyes who sleep around Agamemnon's cairn in the sarcophagus as mourners grieving the death of Camilla; he then identifies as her corpse the body of the sleeping Erinys lying by Aegisthus'; and he interprets his body as that of the slain Curiatius. At this point Morales makes a startling comment about the crouching Erinys whose face is hidden by a veil, saying that 'she conveys more sadness than any of the other figures whose faces are visible to us. It is as if the artist wanted this figure to be the Agamemnon of Timanthes, whose grief was covered with a gesture in order to be more intensely revealed by art.'[23] The humanist recalls here the famous story of the Greek painter Timanthes of Sicyon whose artistic capacity to represent grief-stricken faces reached its limits when he attempted to render that of Agamemnon at the sacrifice of his daughter Iphigenia, deciding finally to cover his face with a veil.[24] This painting is now lost but a possible echo survives in works such as a fresco of the Sacrifice of Iphigenia from the House of the Tragic Poet in Pompeii and a mosaic of the same theme from Ampurias, both showing Agamemnon covering his face with a veil, in a gesture that closely resembles that made by the Erinys in the sarcophagus.[25] It is a testimony to the evocative power of the images of the sarcophagus that the gestural expression of the Erinys could bring to mind for Morales the sacrificial drama (the murder of Agamemnon) at the origin of the actual story represented in the frieze. Here Morales' interpretation shows a process of transmission whose complexity

23 Morales 1765 [1977], 26.

24 See Pliny (*Naturalis Historia*, 35.73), Quintillian (*Institutio Oratoria*, 2. 13. 13) and Cicero (*Orator*, 74).

25 For an illustration of the Sacrifice of Iphigenia from Pompeii, now in the National Archaeological Museum of Naples, see Prado-Vilar 2008, 179, fig. 6. For the mosaic from Ampurias, see Blázquez 1993, 388–389. For later use of the motif of the veiled face to represent inexpressible grief, e.g. Nicolas Poussin in his famous *Death of Germanicus*, see Montagu 1994, and Crow 1999, 79–103.

surpasses any example studied by Warburg: we see how the *Pathosformel* invented by Timanthes as the paradigmatic representation of the inexpressibility of paternal grief was textually transmitted by several Roman authors (Pliny, Quintillian, Cicero) and visually recreated by Pompeian painters, who inserted the image of the veiled Agamemnon in their representations of the myth. Later, in the context of the Greek revival of the time of Hadrian, the *Pathosformel* of the veiled face was deployed by the sculptors responsible for the Orestes sarcophagus, which much later on would end up in medieval Husillos. Arriving there centuries later, Morales observed the *Pathosformel* of the veiled face, recalling immediately, through textual memory and mimesis, the story of Timanthes' veiled Agamemnon. Therefore, remarkably, the *Pathosformel* caused Morales to invoke the 'ghost' of Agamemnon in the very same location on the sarcophagus where, unbeknown to him, the cairn of the murdered king is represented.[26]

Morales' account is also illuminating about the different reception accorded to the sarcophagus by ecclesiastical dignitaries and artists. An Italian church official, Cardinal Poggio, praised the work saying: 'this tomb deserved to be in Rome among the most precious antiquities preserved there, because it is as good as all of them.' And a prominent Spanish Renaissance artist, Alonso de Berruguete, was similarly admiring: 'I haven't seen anything better in Italy, and a few things which are as good.' In addition to the opinion of such well-informed patrons and artists, Morales relates a personal anecdote that attests to the mythopoetic power of the work: noting that the head of Orestes in the Delphi scene seems to have been deliberately struck off, rather than broken accidently, he concludes that this must have been the act of an artist eager to take it as a 'token of such a marvellous work.'[27]

In trying to match the gestural language of the sarcophagus frieze with a written source they deemed appropriate to its original context, these commentators allow us to reflect on the various responses of medieval audiences, which ranged from learned appraisals based on classical sources to

26 This analysis helps elucidate an aspect of my interpretation of the Husillos Orestes frieze about which scholars disagree. Toynbee (1934, 167), amongst others, suggested that the mound around which the Erinyes rest represents Agamemnon's cairn, arguing from comparison with other types of Orestes sarcophagi which at that point show, instead, Agamemnon's ghost. I would suggest that the Roman sculptors who designed the typology of Orestes sarcophagus to which the Husillos example belongs, intentionally included the *Pathosformel* of the veiled face at the site of Agamemnon's cairn, as a visual trigger to set off in viewers familiar with the story of Timanthes' Agamemnon, the same interpretive process that Morales later underwent: i. e. to recall Agamemnon's ghost, and by extension Iphigenia's sacrifice – the crime that initiated the tragic cycle represented on the reliefs.

27 These quotes in Morales 1765 [1977], 27.

popular anecdotes inspired by the mythopoetic power of its imagery.[28] In the absence of documentary records informing us of the medieval reception of the Orestes sarcophagus, the principal evidence for the continuous interest in the interpretation of its imagery is the trail of Romanesque works inspired by its reliefs. Indeed, it is no coincidence that themes of genealogy, crime and sacrifice are at the core of the iconography of the three Romanesque works more intensely indebted to the imagery of the sarcophagus: the capital from the apse of San Martín de Frómista (Figures 3.5 and 3.8b, depicting Cain killing Abel), a capital from the Cathedral of Jaca (Figure 3.8c), and the tympanum of the so-called Portal of the Lamb of the basilica of San Isidoro in León (Figure 3.8e), both representing the Sacrifice of Isaac. It is as if style and iconography, mimicking the Erinyes, were relentlessly following the trail of family blood.

Frómista: the Mark of Cain

Appropriate to its position at the head of the formal genealogy which sprang from the imagery of the sarcophagus, the capital from the church of San Martín de Frómista also emerges as the closest conceptual translation of its iconographic message into a new Christian context.[29] Indeed, both the sarcophagus and the capital deal with themes of the shedding of family blood and its divine punishment. The iconography of the capital has long eluded scholars, largely because the two nude figures on it were defaced (in what seems to have been a deliberate act of censorship during a restoration of the church in the early twentieth century), and their original gender has been disputed.

The capital visible in the apse of the church today is a copy, made before the two nudes on the original were destroyed: it shows them as a man and a woman

28 For an example of the *mythopoetic* power of figures on Roman sarcophagi to spark biographical legends around the medieval personages who re-used them for their burials, see Moralejo 1984, 189–90.

29 San Martín de Frómista was a small Benedictine community founded by Alfonso VI's grandmother, Muniadomna, Countess of Castile and widow of Sancho III the Great of Navarre. Through her, Fernando I, Alfonso's father, inherited the Kingdom of Castile. In her foundational charter, Muniadomna expressedly bequeathed San Martín de Frómista to her 'stirpe' entrusting her descendants with its care and aggrandisement as a special dynastic possession. Her will of 1066 mentions work under construction, but the present church was built c. 1090 and belongs, typologically and stylistically, to a group of churches in the area of Tierra de Campos (Palencia) connected with the Leonese dynasty. All of these churches underwent building campaigns in a new mature Romanesque style right after the council of Husillos (see Prado-Vilar 2008, 183–184).

(Figure 3.4d).[30] Moralejo, and every other scholar after him, never questioned the reliability of this copy. 'The calm nudes, man and woman,' he wrote, 'who find themselves threatened by sinister individuals flourishing serpents, seem to suggest an allegory of the fallen human condition, impossible to translate verbally.'[31] There is in fact a photograph of the capital taken before its defacement, which shows one of the nudes (clearly male), but, unfortunately, only part of the other (Figure 3.4b).[32] Yet it clearly shows how far the copy diverged from the original, and particularly how the restorer engaged in a 'genital reconstruction' of what he thought was a female figure.[33] But this figure was probably male like the other (although the restorer may have been confused because its penis was missing and because the medieval sculptor had exaggerated the muscled chest of the Roman figures he was copying, so they looked rather like female breasts).

Analysis of the process by which individual figures from the Orestes sarcophagus were assigned new roles within the thematic environment of the capital leaves no doubt that this scene represents Cain killing Abel. On the capital Cain adopts the heroic pose of the murderous Orestes, while the terrified nurse of the sarcophagus becomes Abel recoiling from the blow.[34] More startling is the transformation of the figure of Aegisthus, which has been turned upside down on the capital to join the demonic forces that emerge from the underworld to punish Cain. This metamorphosis was with all probability suggested by the biblical passage (Genesis 4: 3–10) that describes how Abel's blood cried out to denounce the crime and curse the murderer.

Comparison with two other artworks, which feature separate episodes of this biblical narrative, shows quite how brilliantly the whole story was visualised at Frómista. The first is a capital from the cathedral of Saint-Lazare in Autun showing God asking Cain for his brother, whose corpse lays hidden in the bushes, his legs partially visible in the frontal face of the capital while the rest of the body occupies the lateral face.[35] The other is a drawing from an early eleventh-century Anglo-Saxon manuscript now in the Bodleian Library (MS

30 For the socio-historical context of the restoration of San Martín de Frómista, see the two collections of essays published on the occasion of its 100 anniversary: *Frómista* 2004; and *San Martín de Frómista* 2005.

31 Moralejo 1994b, 211.

32 The photograph was first published in Serrano Fatigati 1901.

33 He inflated the genital area and inserted a slit where there was originally none, resulting in a strange *unicum* in 'medieval' vaginal iconography. For medieval vaginal iconography, see Caviness 2007.

34 The medieval artist adopted the sword from the Orestes sarcophagus to fill the gap in the biblical narrative which says nothing of the instrument Cain used. For the iconography of Cain's weapon, see Schapiro 1979, 249–65; and for the blade as weapon in twelfth-century Iberian examples, see Patton 2005.

35 See Grivot and Zarnecki 1961, 68; and Prado-Vilar 2008, 181, fig.9.

Junius 11, fol. 49) which focuses on the moment when the blood of Abel (represented in anthropomorphic form as is typical in medieval iconography) denounces the crime to God.[36] In contrast, the Frómista artist, inspired by the narrative theatricality of the Hadrianic reliefs, manages to create a more dynamic composition that combines three episodes in one explosive moment: Abel's murder, the denunciation of the crime to God, and the following curse, resulting in one of the most spectacular evocations of Abel's death in medieval art.

The Furies of the sarcophagus, who in classical mythology were specifically devoted to avenging the shedding of kindred blood, re-emerge on the capital, with function and meaning unchanged, as if their persecuting rage had carried them directly from mythical to biblical times.[37] This iconographic continuity from sarcophagus to capital parallels their survival in written texts, notably in their description in Isidore's *Etymologies* which was widely read through the Middle Ages, and specially in eleventh-century Castile:

> They also say that the three Furies are women with serpents for hair, on account of the three passions that give rise to many disturbances in people's spirits, and they sometimes so drive a person to do wrong that they allow him to give no consideration to his reputation or his own danger. The passions are Anger, which desires revenge, Desire, which wishes for wealth, and Lust, which seeks pleasure. They are called Furies (*Furiae*) because they strike (*ferire*) the mind with their goads and do not allow it to be tranquil (VIII. Xi. 95).[38]

As in the Greek drama, where the Erinyes pursue Orestes relentlessly, on the Frómista capital they seem to enforce God's curse to Cain, 'you will be a fugitive and a wanderer on earth' (Genesis 4:12). The disgrace that befalls sinners, condemned to wander in the wilderness for letting animal impulses control their actions is, appropriately, the theme of the adjacent capital, by the same sculptor – the original is also in the Museo de Palencia, replaced by a copy in the church (Figure 3.8b). This group of partially naked men riding fierce lions brings to mind 'the passions [of] Anger, which desires revenge, Desire, which wishes for wealth, and Lust, which seeks pleasure,' described by Isidore in the aforementioned passage.

The identification of the iconography of the famous capital as Cain's murder of Abel is confirmed by its narrative and allegorical relationship with neighbouring capitals. The narrative context is defined by the axis that connects this capital with the capitals of the nave, where we find, supporting the arcade that gives access to the crossing, a pair depicting two other episodes from Genesis: the Temptation of Adam and Eve (north) and the Reprimand and

36 See Kauffmann 2003, 37–55, and Prado-Vilar 2008, 181, fig.10.
37 For the function of the Erinyes in the Aeschylan stage, see Frontisi-Ducroix 2007.
38 Isidore 2006, 189.

Expulsion from Paradise (south). In turn, the allegorical context is provided by its pendant capitals on the north side of the apse: one shows a series of heraldic birds, probably doves – an iconography of clear Eucharistic/sacrificial connotations appropriate to this area of the church – and the capital next to that, which has lush vegetal decoration evoking paradise.[39] So if the figurative programme of the south side of the apse (Cain killing Abel and men riding lions) focuses on the martyrial and penitential dimension of sacrifice (Abel as a type of the first martyr and prefiguration of the Passion of Christ), then the north side focuses on its salvific and paradisiacal aspects, through eucharistic birds and vegetation.

Located in the most prestigious area of the church, the Cain capital is not only the masterpiece of the sculptural decoration of San Martín but also the cornerstone of its iconographic programme. To be sure, this direct quotation of the frieze of the Orestes sarcophagus in the most visible place of the church at Frómista, in the aftermath of the Council of Husillos, might respond to a more specific set of circumstances than mere aesthetic appeal for the classical model. The capital might have been created as a *lieu de mémoire* meant to recall its ancient model, not only artistically but also iconographically, contextually and historically. As mentioned earlier, the circumstances that compelled Alfonso VI to summon the council at Husillos were extremely grave as the unity and stability of the kingdom had been seriously threatened by political insurgency (a rebellion of Galician nobles), and ecclesiastical turmoil (the bishops' resistance to the adoption of the Roman rite and to the advance of Cluniac influence). Various pieces of surviving evidence show how the council then dealt with political pacification, reorganisation of the church, and the resolution of conflicts over ecclesiastical jurisdiction.[40] So, for those who attended, the imagery of the sarcophagus must have been artistically impressive and also very evocative in its significance. In the eleventh century, in a church setting, images apparently representing a family crime associated with scenes of offering and sacrifice would probably recall episodes from the cycle of Cain and Abel – the nudity of the figures, rather than signalling a referent to classical antiquity, might, in that context, have suggested a Biblical narrative of origins.[41] And so the Frómista artist, following the directions of his patron, might have

39 Illustation in Prado-Vilar 2008, 183, fig. 12.

40 For the historical significance of the council of Husillos, see above, n. 3.

41 For a comparison between the scene of Athena at the trial of the Areopagus from the Husillos sarcophagus (Figure 3.2) and a compositionally similar Romanesque representation of the Offering of Cain and Abel in a twelfth-century capital from Moutiers Saint-Jean, now at the Fogg Museum, Harvard University, see Prado-Vilar 2008, 184, fig. 13.

deliberately copied the 'Orestes' scenes for the iconographic value that had been assigned to it in Husillos during the council.

It is, therefore, not a coincidence that, like the council of Husillos, with its aims of peace and stability, the iconographic programme at Frómista presented biblical and moral condemnations of fratricidal violence, and the church as the agent restoring peace.[42] The Genesis capitals of the crossing illustrate the fall of man, its causes and consequences: pride, discord, violence, damnation. The pairs of capitals decorating each of the interior arcades of the two entrances articulate moralising messages by establishing deliberate compositional and thematic connections with the crossing capitals, whose Biblical stories provide the Scriptural background.

In sum, the direct paraphrase of the Husillos Orestes sarcophagus in the capital at Frómista, and the connections between the iconographic programme of San Martín de Frómista and the issues discussed at the council of Husillos, opens the possibility to speculate that the Frómista programme might actually have been inspired by the council's pacifying mission. In other words, the council's proceedings may still survive at San Martín de Frómista, written in stone in a new Romanesque language, and with the Cain capital as its seal of provenance.

The council of Husillos also provides clues about the kind of personal and institutional connections that might have brought to Spain an artist such as the sculptor of the Cain-Orestes capital, whose artistic genealogy has been traced back to the figural arts of Gascony and, particularly, to the naturalistic pictorial tradition represented by the magnificent *Beatus* of Saint-Sever (Paris, Bibliothèque nationale, Ms. Lat. 8878, fol. 85, ca. 1070).[43] This was made by an artist, Stephanus Garsia, who had a sensibility for the tautness of the flesh, the diaphanous fluidity of folds and the emotional extremes of the human experience. It is from that teeming ferment of *Pathosformeln*, beautifully illustrated by the miniature of the Flood from the *Beatus*, where we find the

42 The historiated capitals at Frómista articulate the interior space of the church in what Moralejo rightly understood as a series of 'programmatic sequences' (Moralejo 1990, 23). Figured capitals concentrate in meaningful groups in three principal areas: the crossing, where, as we have seen, there are capitals depicting episodes from Genesis; the interior arcade of the northern entrance (the access to the laity) with capitals featuring popular fables and moralising themes; and the interior arcade of the southern entrance (the access for the monks) decorated with capitals featuring ecclesiastical themes. For a detailed discussion of this iconographic programme and its historical significance in the context of eleventh-century Romanesque, see Prado-Vilar 2008, 182–184.

43 For the connections between Frómista and the Southwest of France, see Moralejo 1987, 94–95; and Moralejo 1985, 77–80.

DNA of the eye and the hand of the *Orestes-Cain master.*[44] He may have arrived in Husillos with his patron for the council, and there found the myth that changed both his life and the art of the time.[45]

Jaca: the Inventory of Forms

During the time that the group of artists trained at Frómista moved along the pilgrimage road to Jaca, the forms of the Husillos sarcophagus had come to dominate the visual morphology of their style – nudes in chiastic poses with thick, deeply-carved hair, undulating draperies, and figures brandishing serpents are ubiquitous (cfr. Figure 3.5).[46] For this reason Moralejo called the artist responsible for the Cain-Orestes capital at Frómista 'The Jaca Master'.

But there was a substantial difference, for unlike the sculptor of the Frómista capital, who looked at the Orestes frieze as a compositional and iconographic unit, the masters of the Jaca workshop used the images as a repertory of forms, dissecting its individual *Pathosformeln* to recast them in different Biblical roles (such as Balaam, Daniel, and Habbakuk). Using the ancient forms in this way, the masters of Jaca emerge as the direct forerunners of Renaissance artists, such as Raphael and Titian, who would later subject other ancient Orestes sarcophagi to a similar taxonomic gaze.[47] To the transitional period between the Middle Ages and the Renaissance, belongs a series of drawings compiled in the so-called Vallardi codex, which artists of the circle of Pisanello produced to use for figurative models.[48] One folio gives an idea of the repertory of models that might have been used by the Jaca sculptors. It shows three figures copied from an Orestes sarcophagus: one brandishing a club, which is taken from the central Orestes; a woman derived from the figure of Aegisthus, here returned to life as in the Frómista capital; and a crouching man that recalls the figure of the servant.[49]

44 An illustration of this miniature in Prado-Vilar 2008, 185, fig. 16. For the interest of Stephanus Garsia in recycling motifs from antique sources, especially from the iconography of battles, see Werckmeister 1973, 612–616.

45 For a possible patron, Bernard of Sédirac, a prominent Cluniac monk with Gascon connections who became archbishop of Toledo and attended the council of Husillos, see Prado-Vilar 2008, n. 59, and Prado-Vilar 2009, n. 36.

46 For a comprehensive discussion of the chronology and stylistic filiation of the sculpture of Jaca, see Moralejo 1979, and 1984.

47 For Titian, see Brendel 1955. The figure of Orestes/Pylades provides the blueprint for the Bacchus in his *Bacchus and Ariadne* at the National Gallery of London.

48 For this codex, now in the Louvre (Cod. Vallardi, inv. 2397v), see Scheller 1995, 341–356.

49 Illustration in Prado-Vilar 2008, fig. 17.

The transformation of the legacy of the Husillos sarcophagus into a workshop undertaking must have occurred in an intermediate stage situated chronologically between Frómista (c. 1089/90) and Jaca (c. 1093/94), which is now difficult to locate but, for reasons I have outlined elsewhere, we can point to San María la Real de Nájera as a good candidate – an important monastery on the route from Palencia to Aragón, which had become, since its incorporation to the Kingdom of Castile in 1076 and its donation to Cluny in 1079, one of the most important monastic centres of the kingdom.[50] We might speculate that it was in Nájera where the *Orestes-Cain master* passed on his knowledge to younger members of his workshop who would then exploit it with a new vitality. The principal master of Jaca would belong to this new generation, for his work exudes, as Marcel Durliat perceptively observed 'un esprit de jeunesse, une vivacité et une spontanéité remplis de séduction.'[51]

If the Nájera capital is the missing link between the sculpture of San Martín de Frómista and that of the Cathedral of Jaca, a capital from the South Portal of the latter provides a link towards the future (Figure 3.8c). It is an artistic experiment that foreshadows the high levels of formal and conceptual sophistication, which this new generation of artists would reach in their dialogue with the Husillos sarcophagus when they finally returned to the Kingdom of León. On this capital, the heroic pathos of the Orestes frieze is fully revived when its morphology and syntax are put to serve the most gripping family drama of the Old Testament, the sacrifice of Isaac (Genesis 22). The sculptor of this capital radically transformed the central group of the sarcophagus, so that the nurse turned into the figure of Abraham, who holds by the hair the naked body of Isaac, which in turn was modelled on the central Orestes. The figure of Pylades reappears as a woman holding a ram by the altar (identical disposition of head and upper body and drapery covering the lower portion). The result is a dramatic immediacy not found in other Romanesque representations of this theme.

This led Moralejo to relate the capital to a personal statement written by King Sancho Ramírez, the patron who oversaw the early construction of the cathedral. In a charter of 1093, Sancho Ramirez offered his own son Ramiro as oblate to the monastery of Saint-Pons de Tomières, allegedly as a sacrifice to gather divine help to fight the enemies of the Christians.[52] As was standard in this type of donation, he compared himself to Abraham who was willing to immolate Isaac. Yet the terms of this invocation more clearly recall the

50 A single capital with vegetal decoration, now preserved in the Cathedral of Jaca, stands as a token of its Romanesque fabric and shows direct connections with both Frómista and, specially, Jaca (an illustration in Prado-Vilar 2008, 186, fig. 18).

51 Durliat 1990, 220.

52 Moralejo 1985, 30–32. For an edition of this document, see Lacarra 1946.

motivation behind the mythological sacrifice – of Iphigenia by Agamemnon – that was the source of imagery which permeates the composition of this capital.

In addition to these formal echoes of the sarcophagus frieze give the story of Orestes a subliminal 'presence' on the capital, the woman derived from the figure of Pylades offers a more direct point of connection. In form and iconography, she links the biblical sacrifice, which is explicitly represented, and the mythological sacrifice which is latent. To be sure, she does not occur in the biblical narrative (which simply says that the ram appeared caught up in a thicket) and more closely brings to mind the figure of Artemis who saved Iphigenia by sending a deer to be killed in her place. The iconography of this episode was widely disseminated in antiquity through works in various media, such as aforementioned painting from the House of the Tragic Poet in Pompeii or the mosaic from Ampurias. Although the classical iconography of the Sacrifice of Iphigenia has no direct relation to the Abraham capital at Jaca, distant echoes of it resonate in the figure of this woman.[53] This brief analysis of the complex network of formal, iconographic and historical threads that meet in the Jaca capital underscores its status as a *lieu de mémoire* that holds the 'essence' of the concept of ritual sacrifice in Mediterranean culture.

Compositionally, iconographically, and stylistically, the design of the South Portal of Jaca is an essential introduction to the next work in the Romanesque succession from the Orestes sarcophagus, the South Portal of the Basilica of San Isidoro in León, which is also known as the Portal of the Lamb (c. 1100).

León: the Iconology of the Interval

The product of a workshop trained in Jaca, the Portal of the Lamb at León reproduces in its general layout the original arrangement of the South Portal of Jaca cathedral, but on a monumental scale and with a more extensive sculptural programme. It has a richly carved tympanum featuring the Agnus Dei and the Abraham story, and a large frieze above the doorway which depicts the signs of the Zodiac (Figures 3.8 d, e).

Moralejo noted that the figure of Aquarius in this frieze derived from the central Orestes of the sarcophagus (Figures 3.5 and 3.8d).[54] However, the influence of the classical reliefs is more extensive, and can be felt in the syntax that connects Aquarius with its adjacent signs: Sagittarius and Capricorn, with wild hair and threatening attitudes (using arrows instead of serpents) mirror the two Furies who charge towards Orestes in the sarcophagus, while behind the

53 For further details on the complex network of exegetical and iconographic traditions that inform the presence of this woman in the Jaca capital, see Prado-Vilar 2008, 185–186.

54 Moralejo 1977.

fish in the sign of Pisces, is a figure (a fisherman?) which faithfully reproduces the backward movement of the old nurse. Furthermore, the curve of the cloth that links Pylades and the nurse on the sarcophagus is reproduced in the Pisces panel to create the shape of a boat (just behind the lower fish). So here the artists show an understanding of the compositional syntax of the Orestes frieze and of the dynamics generated by the correlation among the figures that transcends the simple cataloguing of *Pathosformeln.* This offers a preview of what they accomplished in the tympanum.

Although, surprisingly, this tympanum has never been mentioned in connection with the Husillos sarcophagus, it is unquestionably the Romanesque work that most profoundly engages the classical model (Figure 3.7d). The Sacrifice of Isaac is situated at its centre, at the intersection of two axes, a vertical one encapsulating the Eucharistic idea of sacrifice by drawing a typological connection with the Agnus Dei, and a horizontal one that dramatises the theme of genealogy and its implications for salvation history by playing out the contrast between Abraham's two sons, Isaac and Ishmael. The biblical narrative that unfolds in the horizontal axis is rare in Romanesque tympana. From right to left appears Sarah, seated in front of a tent house overseeing the departure of her son Isaac. Next he is shown removing his shoes to enter the sacred ground where the sacrifice will be performed (the repetition of Isaac on his way to the sacrifice and his representation with a halo stress the Christological implications which are explicitly symbolised in the vertical axis). In the centre is Abraham at the fateful moment in which he is stopped by God's injunction. To his left, an angel offers the lamb that will take the place of Isaac. Next to the angel is Abraham's slave concubine Hagar and her son Ishmael, both represented following the biblical narrative, as they wander in the wilderness of Beersheba.

The elongated field of the tympanum allowed the artist to adopt faithfully the sarcophagus frieze as a compositional blueprint, reproducing closely the poses and positions of individual figures. From right to left, the figure of Sarah, extending her left arm backwards as she turns her head towards the direction of the action, is a variation of Orestes at Delphi; Isaac taking off his sandals recalls the crouching pose of the servant; the figure of Abraham is a clothed version of the central Orestes, as if he had grabbed from the ground the corpse of Clytemnestra, here transformed into Isaac; the Angel, with his right arm crossing over his chest to bring forth the lamb, replicates the position of the Orestes/Pylades; and finally, Hagar strikes a pose similar to the sleeping Fury on the left end of the sarcophagus.

The León artist also shows a masterful understanding of the rhythmic cadences of the Roman sarcophagus reliefs. In both works, the forceful chiastic centre sets off a kinetic reaction that ripples laterally in undulating sequences. The ample curves of fluted drapery created, on the right side of the sarcophagus, by the cloth hanging before the Furies and the fabric held by the Orestes at Delphi are echoed in the tympanum by the rhythmic waves described by the tree branches, Isaac's discarded garments suspended between the branches and the altar, and his billowing cape as he rides off to Mount Moriah. Similarly, on the left side of the tympanum, the elongated body of the sheep held by the angel occupies the same position as the stretched cloth that connects Aegisthus's corpse to the hand of his murderer in the sarcophagus. At an even more subtle level, the tympanum emulates the narrative technique of the sarcophagus down to its clever use of syncopated temporality. The replication of the figure of Isaac progressing rapidly in three different temporal sequences recalls the heightening rhythm effected by the triplication of the figure of Orestes, from his single appearance at Delphi to his doubling during the killing spree.

Yet the most brilliant artistic and conceptual communion between the tympanum and the sarcophagus occurs in an empty space – the charged area where the gaze of the sacrificer meets the hand that tries to stop him. The hand of the nurse facing Orestes/Pylades morphs into the Hand of God halting Abraham, in a formal translation that amounts to a profound visual meditation, contained in one gesture, on the relationship between ritual murder in Greek myth and Biblical sacrifice.

The Orestes frieze provides not only the *formal master-image* but also the *exegetical metanarrative* behind the León tympanum. Like the hand of the nurse, God's commanding hand acts as the indictment of crime, but here it is no longer the impotent gesture of a servant unable to prevent the crime but the almighty Hand of God directly intervening in the course of events. On the tympanum, sacrifice is not condemned by reproach but stopped by interdiction. It is not framed morally by the emotional response of a fellow human, but legally by the unquestioned judgment of the Father. Yet the way in which, in the formal genealogy of the tympanum, the hand of the nurse exists within God's, introduces an unintentional level of exegesis to the Biblical episode – the realisation that deep inside God's ostensibly detached command lies a very human consideration for the consequences of the crime.

But if this act of artistic translation inspires a meditation on the human kernel of Biblical sacrifice such as I have just outlined, it also facilitates a meditation on the sacred dimension of murder in Greek tragedy. As Jean-Pierre Vernant observes, religious sacrifice in Greek tragedy seems to be an empty ritual performance, and it is in human murder, rather, where the sacred dimension of sacrifice is fully released:

> The normal form of communication between gods and men is sacrifice, the invention of Prometheus. But, there are, precisely, no regular sacrifices in Aeschylus' tragic world: on the contrary, every sacrifice is 'corrupt'... Every attempt to sacrifice is brought to a halt ... Conversely, every murder, whether of a brother, a daughter, a spouse, or a father, is depicted as a sacrifice .... In Greek tragedy, the norm is

> presented only to be transgressed or because it has already been transgressed. It is in this respect that Greek tragedy derives from Dionysus, the god of confusion and transgression.[55]

The León artist, in transforming the scene of matricide from the sarcophagus into a sacred sacrifice in the tympanum, has revealed the sacred sacrificial nature contained, as Vernant says, in every murder in Greek tragedy, and clearly implied in Aeschylus's description of Clytemestra's execution.

It is difficult to find a more beautiful and complex artistic realisation of an 'iconology of the interval.' This cryptic phrase, introduced by Warburg in his 1929 journal, has been interpreted in reference to the montage structure of the *Mnemosyne* panels, which, as Philip-Alain Michaud points out, were meant to generate meaning through correlations between images:

> This iconology is based not on the meaning of the figures – the foundation of interpretation for Warburg's disciples, beginning with Panofsky – but on the interrelationships between the figures in their complex, autonomous arrangement, which cannot be reduced to discourse.[56]

It is precisely in its understanding of the meanings generated by the intervals and correlations between the different figures, or *Pathosformeln,* of the Husillos sarcophagus, that the work of the León artist surpasses both that of his Jaca forerunners, and his late-Gothic (Pisanello) and Italian Renaissance counterparts. It is also by adopting an *iconology of the interval* as an analytical strategy that we can discover the profound reflection on sacrifice that emerges, only at the level of the visual, 'which cannot be reduced to discourse,' from a comparative analysis of the Orestes sarcophagus and the León tympanum. And, as generative kernel at the centre of it all we find the transcendental gesture of a hand that travels artistically the ontological distance between man and God, and stands as a brilliant materialisation of how Warburg, in Agamben's words, viewed gesture in the context of his project, 'as a crystal of historical memory.... which stiffened and turned into a destiny.'[57]

Bend Sinister: Tragedy, History, and Historiography

These three illustrious examples suggest that, parallel to Moralejo's stylistic genealogy, we can trace a second, iconographic, lineage emerging from the Husillos sarcophagus – one that centres on the themes of family crime and sacrifice. By following the Erinyes in their avenging wrath, we can witness myth

55 Vernant 1990, 263–264.
56 Michaud 2007, 251–52.
57 Agamben 2000, 53.

bleeding over Christian iconography ... and over history. Indeed, the specific historical events, revolving around the question of dynastic genealogy, which inspired the commission of those monuments, especially San Martín de Frómista and San Isidoro de León, provide yet a third link connecting the Romanesque descendants of the Husillos sarcophagus.

The 'Orestes' and 'Electra' of this story are Alfonso VI, King of León-Castile (r. 1065–1109), and his older sister, the infanta Urraca. Their father, Fernando I (r. 1037–1065), divided his empire among his three sons, leaving Castile to the eldest, Sancho, León to Alfonso, and Galicia to García, the youngest. In the dynastic dispute that ensued among the brothers after Fernando's death in 1065, Urraca helped Alfonso overcome defeat, imprisonment and exile to be finally crowned king of the united realms of León, Castile and Galicia in 1072. To achieve this goal, she conspired in the murder of Sancho, and the life imprisonment of Garcia, who would spend the next 18 years, until his death in 1090, confined in a castle in the remote mountains of León. A true medieval Electra, Urraca was an unmarried princess dedicated to the dynastic heritage of her family, whose symbolic centre was the complex of San Isidoro de León, which she inherited through the institution of the *infantazgo*.[58]

When Garcia died, still in captivity, in 1090, Alfonso VI seemed to be at the height of his power and prestige, having achieved renown in the rest of Europe by conquering Toledo in 1085, and having crushed several rebellions and other internal dissensions, which were finally settled at the Council of Husillos in 1088. Poignantly, art again provided a silent commentary to history, for, around the time Alfonso and Urraca attended, with considerable amounts of hypocrisy, Garcia's royal exequies at San Isidoro de León, presided over, like the council of Husillos, by the papal legate Rainier (future pope Paschal II), the Orestes-Cain capital surely must have dazzled visitors to the recently built apse of San Martín de Frómista. The presence of this representation of Cain's crime, endowed with

58 The *infantazgo* was the portion of the royal patrimony comprising monastic foundations and was given to a princess on the condition that she remained unmarried, as a *deo vota*. Through this endowment, the infanta acted like a lay abbess exercising total dominion and economic control over the monastic estates of the realm, including the administration of justice (see Walker 1999). San Isidoro was the most important monastery of the kingdom, and the centre of a larger palatine complex integrated by the royal palace, the church, and a double monastery, dedicated to Saint Palagius (nuns) and San Isidoro (monks). In addition to keeping the relics of the most revered saint and cultural authority of the Visigothic age, which had been translated from Seville with great pomp by Fernando I in 1063 when the former church of St. John the Baptist was rebuilt and rededicated to San Isidore, the complex also housed the royal cemetery of the Kings of León. Due to this, the monastery was the symbolic heart of the memory of the Leonese dynasty, which regarded itself as the direct continuator of the lineage descending from the Visigothic monarchs that governed the peninsula in the 'Golden Age' before the Muslim invasion. For the historical context of San Isidoro, see Williams 1995.

the patina of ancient tragedy, at the heart of Tierra de Campos – the area Alfonso had directly inherited from his father – could not offer a more suitable image for the original sin marking his ascent to power. It was only fitting that the monastery founded by the matriarch of the dynasty, Muniadomna, and entrusted to her *stirpe*, was sealed by the mark of Cain – a mark that run deep in their genealogical makeup.

As their Greek counterparts, therefore, Urraca and Alfonso were bound by fratricide, revenge and dynastic restoration. However, by the time of García's death, a sibling dissension had been slowly brewing between these 'Electra' and 'Orestes' who had triumphantly seized power in 1072. Tinged with the complex psychological underpinnings of a Greek tragedy, the progressive distancing between Urraca (motherly sister/mentor/lover) and Alfonso VI would have immense artistic ramifications because it was fought, not in the battlefield with the sword, but, rather, in the infanta's seat of power, San Isidoro, with stone, tempera, and parchment.[59]

The direction of Alfonso's policies since the 1080's, which implied a progressive marginalisation of León and of San Isidoro, run counter to Urraca's profound alliance to the Leonese dynastic heritage and her role as the main benefactress of the institution. In the infanta's eyes, her brother seemed to be betraying the dynastic memory – with the creation of a new royal pantheon in the monastery of San Benito de Sahagun, which had become the centre of Cluniac reform in the kingdom –, and the prospective descendancy, with his insistence that his only son, Sancho Alfónsez, born of a Muslim concubine named Zaida, the widowed daughter-in-law of King al-Mutamid of Seville, be appointed as heir to the kingdom. It is within the context of this divergence of interests between Urraca and Alfonso in relation to the question of León that I propose to interpret the infanta's frantic patronage activity at San Isidoro at the end of the eleventh century, reflected mainly in the building of Royal Pantheon, with its famous frescos, and the construction of the new Romanesque basilica with the Portal of the Lamb.

It is in the iconographic programme of the Portal of the Lamb, with its central representation genealogical drama of Abraham, where the split between the two siblings, triggered by the urgency of the question of dynastic succession, can be more clearly detected. Here again the Orestes sarcophagus presents the mythological background that ripples through history because, if the figure of the older sister Electra appears as the instigator behind the dynastic tragedy carved on its main frieze, so is Urraca behind the genealogical drama carved on the tympanum of the Portal of the Lamb, where Abraham's choice between his

59 Rumours of the incestuous relationship between Urraca and Alfonso circulated early and were echoed by Islamic sources, see Menéndez Pidal and Lévi-Provençal 1948, and Cantarella 2007.

legitimate heir Isaac and his discarded progeny Ishmael (regarded as progenitor of the Arabs in medieval chronicles) seems to address directly the dilemma that Alfonso had to face regarding the succession to his kingdom. Through the genealogical drama of the story of Abraham, the tympanum dramatises the position of a father who needed to make a series of difficult choices regarding his inheritance. At the time the tympanum was conceived Alfonso VI had to face a combination of Abraham's two most difficult choices. Sancho Alfónsez was the product of his union with a Muslim concubine (reminiscent of Ishmael) but he was also his firstborn son and chosen one (Isaac) – the one whom he would have to be willing to sacrifice in order to keep the covenant between God and his people. I believe it is from this context that the tympanum emerges, as an attempt to address the difficult situation of an impatient father wanting to recognise his only son as his legitimate heir and a Leonese party championed by his sister Urraca, who demanded from him the ultimate sacrifice that Abraham had to face and relinquish the position of his most beloved son, while they waited for his new marriage to yield an heir by a Christian mother.

Therefore Abraham's choice was really Alfonso's. It was the choice he had to make in the final years of his reign, it is the choice that was at stake when the Portal of the Lamb was built, and it is the final lesson given to Alfonso by his sister, the matriarchal gate-keeper of the Leonese dynastic line. By understanding the tympanum as a matriarchal work disguised within a patriarchal narrative, we can begin to visualise the spectral confrontation between Urraca, as the embodiment of the matriarchal tradition of the Leonese dynasty, and Alfonso VI that takes place there, in the guise of Sarah and Abraham. Comparative iconography reveals that the figure of Sarah is designed in clothing and disposition as a royal Leonese *deo vota* – an association which could not escape contemporary viewers. More strikingly, the head of Abraham, which represents a radical departure from the head types of all the other figures produced by this workshop, seems to consciously reflect the facial type afforded to the Kings of León in contemporary portraiture, and, in particular, to several portraits of Alfonso VI.[60]

60 In addressing these specific historical circumstances, the iconography of the Portal constitutes a larger statement asserting the birth of the rightful Christian prince as a divinely sanctioned occurrence, and the identity and mission of Christian kingship. The Zodiac functions in connection with the genealogical iconography of the tympanum and with the images of King David and St. Isidore, which are represented nearby, to form a statement defining the perfect Leonese monarch: genealogical purity (tympanum), moral character and destiny (Zodiac), and militant mission (emphasised by the anti-Muslim dimension of the iconography and by the Christian soldier which appears next to the figure of St. Isidore). See Prado-Vilar 2009, where taking the *Aeneid* as a methodological environment and *ekphrasis* as an analytical principle, I explore the imbrications between

When the infanta Urraca died in 1101, with the Portal recently built, Alfonso moved steadily towards having Sancho Alfónsez accepted as his heir, finally confirming him officially in a Council held in León in 1107.[61] It is another poignant piece of history that, soon after having been officially proclaimed heir to the Kingdom of León-Castile, Sancho Alfónsez, the son of the Muslim princess, was killed fighting the Murabit at the battle of Uclés (1108).[62] 'Ishmael' had truly become 'Isaac' but, this time, there was no divine hand to stop the sacrifice, and Abraham/Alfonso had to give up his son in the service of God. Returning to León after the tragedy of Uclés, the king of León-Castile could have observed how the imagery of the tympanum doubled as a specular representation of his own pain.

We have thus completed the outline of a hypothetical *Mnemosyne* panel that makes visible the trans-historical legacy of the Orestes sarcophagus in three genealogical movements: formal, iconographic, and historic. Yet a fourth tragic 'historiographic' genealogy inevitably emerges as a subtext for my present discussion, pointing towards a larger project which takes up where the work of M. Schapiro, S. Moralejo, and M. Camille left off. By outlining the genesis and formal vocabulary of an artistic tradition engaged in an incessant exploration of the semantic possibilities of the human body in direct dialogue with Roman art, Moralejo presented us with a unique case study to undertake a comprehensive analysis of the multivalent functions of the body in Romanesque sculpture, which not only accounts for the abstract and the social, as Schapiro had done, but also for the organic, the somatic and the tragic. In his perceptive review of Schapiro's essays on Romanesque art, entitled 'How New York stole the Idea of Romanesque Art,' Camille pointed out, more than a decade ago, the necessity to break with the textually oriented epistemology still dominating the field, and pursue the path of a sophisticated formalism. 'In my view,' wrote Camille, 'a far more innovative and powerful model for the art historian today are the essays Schapiro wrote in the thirties, where the body in all its materiality, conflicted desire and psychological subjectivity, rather than the text in its rationalisation through language, is the focus of exploring visual history.'[63] Even if here Camille credits Schapiro with doing something that, I believe, he never did, misreading his formalism as an interest in the body, the statement contains an insightful diagnosis of the state of the field and its possible future developments. To be sure, Schapiro's formalism, nurtured in the sensibility of the New York artistic avant-garde, was mostly concerned with the abstract and geometric aspects of

art, politics, and tragedy in the Kingdom of León-Castile during the reigns of Fernando I and Alfonso VI treating at length the themes outlined in this section.

61 See Reilly 1988, 326–344. According to Reilly, Alfonso VI finally married Zaida, who had been baptised as Isabel, in 1106 in order to legitimise their son.

62 See Reilly 1988, 345–363.

63 Camille 1994, 72.

Romanesque sculpture, but did not pursue at all the body as an independent site of meaning. The explanatory drawings accompanying his famous essay on Souillac, unlike those illustrating Moralejo's (Figure 3.5), clearly show that, unlike the Spanish scholar, Schapiro was mainly interested in the shapes that the body describes in space and the relations they establish with the surrounding field, but not in the body as a somatic entity.[64] It is not surprising, therefore, that when Schapiro turned his eyes to Spanish Romanesque sculpture, he found in the cloister of Silos a style more in tune with his own interests. Closely related to Moissac and Souillac – monuments that had already attracted Schapiro's attention – Silos represented within the stylistic trends of Spanish Romanesque sculpture a self-consciously conservative ensemble. In their adherence to strict geometrical patterns and linear figural design, the Silos artists largely side-stepped the experiments on plasticity and organic articulation that, as we have seen, were engaging the workshops of Languedoc and northern Spain, from Toulouse to Compostela at the turn of the twelfth century. Therefore, taking a cue from the title of Camille's essay on Shapiro, we could say that New York might indeed have been the place to steal a specific idea of Romanesque art and re-package it for the progressive intellectual circles of the mid-twentieth century, but not the place to undertake a full exploration of an important variant of the style tinged with classical models and deeply engaged with the somatic dimension of form. In Camille's wishful projection, however, there is an insightful prescription to rescue the study of Romanesque sculpture from the stagnation to which both the tyranny of the text and the abuse of the discourses of fantasy and marginality has brought it, signalling the way to a rediscovery of its tragic *beauté oubliée.*

Bibliography

Adhémar, J. *Influences antiques dans l'art du Moyen âge français: recherches sur les sources et les thèmes d'inspiration* (London, 1939).

Agamben, G. *Means Without End. Notes on Politics* (Minneapolis, 2000).

Baschet, J. *Le sein du père. Abraham et la paternité dans l'occident médiéval* (Paris, 2000).

64 Following his characterisation of Schapiro's Souillac essay as a prime example of his interest on the body, Camille states that 'Schapiro's iconographic argument … is almost somatic in its constant play upon the body as the site of meaning, and his descriptive teeth never lose hold of the flesh of the forms, no matter how many layers of meaning are being sucked from them' (Camille 1994, 67). However, I would argue that, on the contrary, Schapiro's descriptive teeth never get hold of the flesh of the forms. His prose, purged of colouring and lyrical inflection, bared down to its basic logical relations, and tied up to a syntax that plays elegantly with symmetry and dissonance, echoes the geometrical network he strives to map for the reader (illustrated by the accompanying schemes).

Bertaux, É. Sculpture chrétienne en Espagne dès origines au XIVe siècle, in: *Histoire de l'art, vol. 2, pt. 1*, edited by A. Michel (Paris, 1906), 244.

Bertaux, E. *Recueil de Travaux dédié a la mémoire d'Émile Bertaux* (Paris, 1924), 2–3.

Blázquez, J. M. *Mosaicos romanos de España* (Madrid, 1993).

Boder, P. Pray and Rubinstein, R. *Renaissance Artists and Antique Sculpture: A Handbook of Sources* (London, 1986).

Boswell, J. *The Kindness of Strangers: The Abandonment of Children in Western Europe from Antiquity to the Renaissance* (Hew Haven, 1988).

Braude, P. F. 'Cokkel in oure Clene Corn': Some Implications of Cain's Sacrifice. *Gesta* 7 (1968), 15–28.

Brendel, O. J. Borrowings from Ancient Art in Titian. *Art Bulletin* 37.2 (1955), 113–125.

Cahn, W. and Seidel, L. *Romanesque sculpture in American collections*, vol. 1 (New York, 1979), 120–28.

Camille, M. How New York Stole the Idea of Romanesque Art. *Oxford Art Journal* 17 (1994), 65–75.

Camille, M. Obscenity Under Erasure: Censorship in Medieval Illuminated Manuscripts, in: *Obscenity: Social Control, and Artistic Creation in the European Middle Ages*, edited by J. M. Ziolkowski (Leiden, 1998), 139–54.

Cantarella, T. Doña Urraca and Her Brother Alfonso VI: Incest as Politics. *La Coronica.* 35.2 (2007), 39–68.

Caviness, M. H. Retomando la Iconografía Vaginal. *Quintana* 6 (2007), 13–37.

Cazes, D. Sarcófago peleocristiano llamado 'de Saint-Clair', in: *Exhibition. El Románico y el Mediterráneo: Cataluña, Toulouse y Pisa (1120–1180)*, edited by M. Castiñeiras, J. Camps, and I. Lorés (Barcelona, 2008), 330–331.

Crow, T. *The Intelligence of Art* (Chapel Hill, NC.: University of North Carolina Press, 1999), 79–103.

Didi-Huberman, G. Dialektik des Monstrums: Aby Warburg and the symptom paradigm. *Art History* 24.5 (2001), 621–645.

Didi-Huberman, G. *L'image survivante: histoire de l'art et temps des fantômes selon Aby Warburg* (Paris, 2002).

Durliat, M. *La sculpture romane de la route de Saint-Jacques: de Conques à Compostelle* (Mont-de-Marsan, 1990).

Falque Rey, E (ed.). *Historia Compostellana*, Corpus Christianorum. Continuatio Mediaevalis 70 (Turnhout, 1988).

Fernández-Guerra y Orbe, A. Sarcófago pagano en la Colegiata de Husillos, recién traído al Museo Arqueológico Nacional. *Museo Español de Antigüedades* I (Madrid, 1872), 11–48.

Fita, F. Texto correcto del concilio de Husillos. *Boletín de la Real Academia de la Historia* 51 (1907), 410–413.

Fletcher, R. A. *The Episcopate in the Kingdom of León in the Twelfth Century* (Oxford, 1978).

Fletcher, R. A. *Saint James's Catapult: The Life and Times of Diego Gelmírez of Santiago de Compostela* (Oxford, 1984).

Frómista 1066–1904. San Martín, centenario de una resturación (Valladolid: Fundación del Patrimonio Histórico de Castilla y León, 2004).

Frontisi-Ducroix, F. The Invention of the Erinyes, in: *Visualizing the Tragic: Drama, Myth and Ritual in Greek Art and Literature. Essays in Honour of Froma Zeitlin*, edited by C. Kraus, S. Goldhill, H. P. Foley and J. Elsner (Oxford, 2007), 165–176.

Gaillard, G. *Les débuts de la sculpture romane espagnole: Leon, Jaca, Compostelle* (Paris, 1938).

García y Bellido, A. *Esculturas romanas de España y Portugal* vol. 1 (Madrid, 1949).

Gombrich, E. H. *Aby Warburg: An Intellectual Biography, with a Memoir of the History of the Library by F. Saxl* (London, 1970), 223.

Greenhalgh, M. *The Survival of Roman Antiquities in the Middle Ages* (London 1989).

Grivot, D. and Zarnecki, G. *Gislebertus. Sculptor of Autun* (New York, 1961), 68.

Gómez-Moreno, M. *El arte románico español: Esquema de un libro* (Madrid, 1934), 84–89.

Hernando Garrido, J. L. Husillos, in: *Enciclopedia del Románico en Castilla y León*, Palencia, vol. 2 (Aguilar de Campoo, 2002), 1059–1069.

Hernando Garrido, J. L. El contexto de la restauración de San Martín de Frómista (1895–1904): El Edificio de la gran patria castellana y la propaganda católica, in: *Frómista 1066–1904. San Martín, centenario de una resturación* (Valladolid, 2004), 87–118.

Hernando Garrido, J. L. Apostillas a la restauración de San Martín de Frómista (1895–1904): el contexto sociopolítico, in *San Martín de Frómista, paradigma o historicismo?* (Valladolid, 2005), 85–118.

Isidore of Seville. *The Etymologies of Isidore of Seville*, trans. S. A. Barney, W.J. Lewis, J.A. Beach, O. Berghof (Cambridge, 2006).

Kauffmann, C.M. *Biblical Imagery in Medieval England 700–1550* (London, 2003).

Lacarra, M. Documentos para la Reconquista del Valle del Ebro, in: *Estudios de la Edad Media de la Corona de Aragón, sección de Zaragoza*, vol. 2 (Zaragoza, 1946), 473–477.

Lyman, T. W. The Pilgrimage Roads Revisited. *Gesta* 8.2 (1969), 30–44.

McCann, A. M. Fragments on an Orestes Sarcophagus, in *Roman Sarcophagi in the Metropolitan Museum of Art* (New York, 1978), 53–60.

Menéndez Pidal, R, and E. Lévi-Provençal. Alfonso VI y su hermana la infanta Urraca. *Al-Andalus* 13 (1948), 157–66.

Michaud, Ph-A. *Aby Warburg and the Image in Motion*, translated by S. Hawkes (New York, 2007).

Montagu, J. Interpretations of Timanthes's *Sacrifice of Iphigenia*, in: *Sight and Insight. Essays on Art and Culture in Honour of E. H. Gombrich at 85*, edited by J. Onians (London, 1994), 305–325.

Moralejo, S. Sobre la formación del estilo escultórico de Frómista y Jaca, in: *Actas del XXIII Congreso Internacional de Historia del Arte, Granada 1973*, vol. 1 (Granada, 1976), 427–434.

Moralejo, S. Pour l'interprétation iconographique du Portail de l'Agneau à Saint-Isidore de León: Les signes du zodiaque. *Les cahiers de Saint-Michel de Cuixa* 8 (1977), 137–173.

Moralejo, S. La sculpture romane de la Cathédrale de Jaca: Etat des questions. *Les cahiers de Saint-Michel de Cuxa* 10 (1979), 79–106.

Moralejo, S. Les arts somptuaires hispaniques aux environs de 1100. *Les cahiers de Saint-Michel de Cuixa* 13 (1982), 285–310.

Moralejo, S. La reutilización e influencia de los sarcófagos antiguos en la España medieval, in: B. Andreae and S. Settis (eds.), *Colloquio sul reimpiego dei sarcofagi romani nel medievo. Pisa, 5–12 settembre 1982* (Marburg-an-der-Lahn, 1984), 187–203 = Moralejo 1984a.

Moralejo, S. Un reflejo de la escultura de Jaca en una moneda de Sancho Ramírez (+ 1094), in: *Scritti di Storia dell'arte in onore di Roberto Salvini* (Florence, 1984), 29–35 = Moralejo 1984b.

Moralejo, S. Artistas, patronos, y público en el arte del Camino de Santiago. *Compostellanum* 30 (1985), 395–430.

Moralejo, S. The Tomb of Alfonso Ansúrez (+1093): Its Place and the Role of Sahagún in the Beginnings of Spanish Romanesque Sculpture, in: *Santiago, Saint-Denis, and Saint Peter. The Reception of the Roman Liturgy in León-Castile in 1080*, edited by B. F. Reilly (New York, 1985), 63–100.

Moralejo, S. Modelo, copia y originalidad, en el marco de las relaciones artísticas hispano-francesas (siglos XI-XIII), in: *Ve Congrès Espanyol d'Història de l'art. Barcelona, 29 d'octubre al 3 de novembre de 1984*, vol. 1 (Barcelona, 1987), 89–115.

Moralejo, S. Cluny y los orígenes del románico palentino: El contexto de San Martín de Frómista, in *Jornadas sobre el arte de las órdenes religiosas* (Palencia, 1990), 23.

Moralejo, S. On the Road: The *Camino de Santiago*, in: *Exhibition. The Art of Medieval Spain, A.D. 500–1200.* (New York, 1994), 175–183.

Moralejo, S. Two Capitals, in: *Exhibition. The Art of Medieval Spain, A.D. 500–1200* (New York, 1994), 211.

Morales, Ambrosio de. *Viage de Ambrosio de Morales por orden del rey D. Phelipe II. A los Reynos de Leon, y Galicia, y Principado de Asturias* (Madrid, 1977).

Neils, J. The Orestes Sarcophagus and Other Classical Marbles. *The Bulletin of the Cleveland Museum of Art* 71 (1984), 103–115.

Nora, P. Between Memory and History: Les Lieux de Mémoire. *Representations* 26 (1989), 7–24.

Patton, P. Cain's Blade and the Question of Midrashic Influence in Medieval Art, in: *Church, State, Vellum and Stone. Essays on Medieval Spain in Honor of John Williams*, edited by T. Martin and J. A. Harris (Leiden, 2005), 413–441.

Prado-Vilar, F. *Saevum facinus:* estilo, genealogía y sacrificio en el arte románico español. *Goya* 324 (2008), 173–199.

Prado-Vilar, F. *Lacrimae rerum:* San Isidoro de León y la memoria del padre. *Goya* 328 (2009), 195–221.

Reilly, B. F. *The Kingdom of León-Castilla under Queen Urraca* (Princeton, 1982).

Reilly, B. F. *The Kingdom of León-Castilla under King Alfonso VI, 1065–1109* (Princeton, 1988).

Rose, L. *The Survival of Images: Art Historians, Psychoanalysts, and the Ancients* (Detroit, 2001).

Scheller, R. W. *Exemplum. Model-Book Drawings and the Practice of Artistic Transmission in the Middle Ages (ca. 900 – ca. 1470)* (Amsterdam, 1995).

Serrano Fatigati, E. Esculturas de los siglos IX al XIII astures, leonesas, castellanas y gallegas. *Boletín de la Sociedad Española de Excursiones* 9 (1901), 35–45.

Siedel, L. *Legends in Limestone. Lazarus, Gislebertus, and the Cathedral of Autun* (Chicago, 1999).

Schade, S. Charcot and the Spectacle of the Hysterical Body: The 'pathos formula' as an aesthetic staging of psychiatric discourse – a blind spot in the reception of Warburg. *Art History* 18.4 (1995), 499–517.

Schapiro, M. Cain's Jawbone That Did The First Murder, in: *Late Antique, Early Christian and Medieval Art. Selected Papers* (New York, 1979), 249–265.

Schapiro, M. The Angel with the Ram in Abraham's Sacrifice: A Parallel in Western and Islamic Art, in: *Late Antique, Early Christian and Medieval Art* (New York, 1979), 289–318.

Toynbee, J. M. C. *The Hadrianic School: A Chapter in the History of Greek Art* (Cambridge, 1934), 166–177.

Vernant, J.-P. Aeschylus, the Past and the Present, in: *Myth and Tragedy in Ancient Greece* (New York, 1990), 249–272.

Walker, R. Sancha Urraca and Elvira: the virtues and vices of Spanish royal women 'dedicated to God'. *Reading Medieval Studies*, XXIV (1998), 113–138.

Warburg, A. Dürer and Italian Antiquity, in: *The Renewal of Pagan Antiquity: Contributions to the Cultural History of the European Renaissance*, edited by K. W. Forster (Los Angeles, 1999), 553–558.

Werckmeister, O. K. Pain and Death in the Beatus of Saint Sever. *Studi Medievali* 14 (1973), 565–626.

Williams, J. J. A Source for the Capital of the Offering of Abraham in the Pantheón of the Kings in León, in: *Scritti di Storia dell'arte in onore di Roberto Salvini* (Florence, 1984), 25–28.

Williams, J. J. Leon: The Iconography of the Capital, in: *Cultures of Power: Lordship, Status, and Process in Twelfth-Century Europe*, edited by T. N. Bisson (Philadelphia, 1995), 231–258.

Zanker, P. and B. Ewald. *Mit Mythen Leben: Die Bilderwelt der römischen Sarkophage* (Munich, 2004).

4.
The Roman Sarcophagus 'Industry': a Reconsideration

Ben Russell

> The visual arts are rooted in handicrafts ..., a heightened manual skill grown from the exercise of manual labour as a whole. Every artist has more than a practical interest in labour.
>
> (Stokes 1934, 109)

That a work of art can be better understood through an analysis of its mode of production is not a novel idea. The finished form of any work of art is the product of a number of manual tasks or processes, all of which have an economic, as well as artistic dimension.[1] Even in antiquity the economic foundations of artistic production were well-understood; as the sophist Apollonius of Tyana is said to have observed: 'all the arts that exist among mankind have different spheres of action, but all aim at money, whether little or much or simply enough to subsist on.'[2]

Of all the arts, stone-carving is the most physically laborious. Stone is an obstinate material, and an expensive one, difficult to shape and to transport. The appeal of stone as a medium is its durability: a stone monument is an expression of permanence. It is no surprise, therefore, that the Roman obsession with personal immortality acquired its physical form in stone. And of all Roman funerary monuments, sarcophagi are perhaps the most emblematic – they survive in large numbers and present some of the finest examples of ancient stone-carving. The apparent ease with which they can be categorised according to material, place of production and type makes them particularly useful for economic studies. Additionally, and like all stone objects, sarcophagi describe their own manufacture; the working traces on them allow for an analysis of the stages of their production, the carving techniques used, even the organisation of the workshop. Indeed, in few other areas of ancient art history are discussions of the economics of artistic production so commonplace. However, most of these discussions follow the single, highly influential model formulated by Ward-Perkins.[3] At its heart lies the idea that, in the period of peak demand for their products, a limited handful of massive quarry-based sarcophagus producers

1 On this point with regard to sculpture, see Rockwell 1993, 9–13.
2 Philostratos, *Life of Apollonios of Tyana* VIII.7.3 (transl. C. P. Jones).
3 See especially Ward-Perkins 1980a and 1980b.

dominated the market, mass-producing sarcophagi in standard forms for the inter-regional export market. This newly rationalised mode of production engendered a shift away from a responsive production-to-order system towards a more efficient production-to-stock arrangement – 'stock' being products manufactured and stored in anticipation of an order. It became increasingly common, so the argument goes, for the individual customer to purchase their sarcophagus, nearly or entirely finished, from stock or 'off the shelf'. This has become the background against which sarcophagi, as funerary monuments as well as works of art, are typically interpreted and evaluated in both specialist studies and volumes intended for a more general readership.[4]

Although, in effect, this model has become the *status quo*, it turns out to be more problematic than often acknowledged. The focus on the producer, especially the quarry-based producer, sits somewhat awkwardly with much recent work on stylistic aspects which has emphasised the role of the customer (or patron or buyer) in the process of artistic production, the decisions made by them in their choice of images, and the social context in which they were operating.[5] The language of modern industrial manufacturing, centred on the idea of 'mass production' (sometimes 'serial production'), is especially divisive when applied to this debate; for many it conjures up images of mechanised production lines, churning out neatly identical objects; the individuality of the product is lost, as is any hint of customer choice or personalisation. Similar concerns are echoed in the words of the twentieth-century painter Albert Gleizes: 'the new masters of production … had no particular reason to love or respect the product, so they preferred *quantity* to *quality*.'[6] Modern commercial terminology need not necessarily be abandoned, but it does require definition. Too often discussion of sarcophagus production is framed in such terms without any discussion of their meaning or implications – for example, the term 'mass production' is regularly employed and treated as if synonymous with the notion of 'production-to-stock'.[7] Since the question of their production is now so central to analyses of sarcophagi many of our assumptions warrant reconsideration. In particular, if the customer, typically the prime instigator of production, is reinstated in such discussions, a more nuanced view of the relationship between producer and consumer may well emerge.

4 Examples of the latter include Penny 1993, 44, and Stewart 2008, 37.

5 See Smith 2002, 71.

6 From a lecture delivered in Warsaw in 1932; see Gleizes 1999, 108.

7 See Ward-Perkins 1980a, 25, on the convenience of such terminology; for use of the term 'mass production' see, for example, Waelkens 1982, 126–7; Koch 1993, 147; Heilmeyer 2000, 129 ('Serienproduktion'), and Stewart 2008, 37; in the context of the 'marble trade', see Pensabene 2002, 58 ('produzioni di massa').

Industry and mass production

'Industry' in the modern sense, that is the large-scale mechanical production of a limited range of standardised objects, is unattested in antiquity.[8] Machines existed, of course: water-powered stone-cutting saws are a pertinent example, the introduction of which can probably now be dated to the third century thanks to the newly discovered relief from Hierapolis.[9] But it is difficult to identify any form of manufacturing in antiquity which was greatly revolutionised by mechanisation; and indeed stone-working remains only limitedly mechanised today.[10] This has dissuaded many – notably Pucci, in his study of the Arretine ceramic workshops – from talking of 'industry' at all.[11] However, 'industry' is not necessarily reliant on mechanisation. In fact, as Harris has argued, 'any production of artefacts in large numbers can without great discomfort be called industry.'[12] More important from our perspective is the organisation of this production.

In his discussion of ancient manufacturing Wilson takes this discussion further, defining 'mass production', the key feature of 'industrial production', as 'the production of very large quantities of the same artefact, or of essentially similar artefacts, by the same production means.'[13] He argues that mechanisation is simply a development of the process of labour division whereby each section of the production process is broken down as much as possible. The essential features of 'mass production', therefore, are the division of labour and the large-scale production of standardised objects. For Adam Smith, this division of labour, both in a society generally and within individual enterprises more specifically, was key to the problem of economic growth, leading to a level of specialisation which could greatly increase per capita productivity; in its most efficient form this division of labour is facilitated by a simplification of the stages of the productive process.[14] This is not how the term 'mass production' is typically used in sarcophagus studies.

---

8 See Manning 1987, 586 and Wilson 2008, 393.

9 On machines in the Roman world more generally, see Wilson 2002. The use of water-powered stone-cutting saws on a tributary of the Moselle is famously described by Ausonius (*The Moselle*, ll. 363–4), and late antique examples have been excavated at Ephesos (Mangartz 2006) and Jerash (Seigne 2002); the relief of just such a saw from Hierapolis was found on the short end of a sarcophagus lid (see Ritti, Grewe and Kessener 2007).

10 See Rockwell 1993, 205.

11 Pucci 1973, 261–5; for detailed criticism of the term see Love 1991, 110–53.

12 Harris 1980, 127.

13 Wilson 2008, 394.

14 Adam Smith, *On the Wealth of Nations*, I.1 (2003 edn., ed. Cannan, 10–11).

The key features of 'mass production', as defined by Wilson, are identifiable in a number of ancient industries – notably ceramic production and the baking sector.[15] But, of course, not everything that we can say about the production of a ceramic vessel or loaf of bread applies equally well to a sarcophagus. For a start, the only built structure which tells us anything about the division of labour in stone-working is the six-aisled hall near to the quarries at Chemtou, the lay-out of which, it has been argued, was arranged to facilitate the production of small statuettes and vessels.[16] These objects were small and could easily have been passed between workers. Sarcophagi and other large objects, on the other hand, were probably carved outside or under impermanent structures.[17] In addition, anyone who has carved stone appreciates how difficult and unyielding a medium it is to work in.[18] Stone-working is seriously labour intensive and at almost every stage of the process requires high skill levels. Just the quarrying and shaping of a medium-sized rectangular sarcophagus chest might occupy a skilled quarryman, with two assistants, for as long as a month.[19] This investment in labour was justified by the permanence of the end product, but it would have cost. The only sarcophagus cost known – inscribed on a late third-century, undecorated, limestone piece from Salona – is 15 *solidi.*[20] Based on the price of gold in the Price Edict (72 *solidi* = 1 pound of gold = 72,000 *denarii*), this sum is equivalent to 15,000 Diocletianic *denarii*, or approximately 150 late first-century *denarii.*[21] Even this most basic, undecorated chest in local limestone, therefore, cost roughly five times the minimum annual subsistence figure proposed by Jongman (115 *sesterces* or approximately 29 late first- or early second-century *denarii*).[22] In the end, the real cost of a sarcophagus was determined by its material and the level of its decoration. While Attic or Dokimeian pieces would have been out of the reach of all but the richest individuals, more affordable – though still expensive – alternatives were available. At Rome the most commonly attested purchasers of sarcophagi were

15 See Wilson 2008.

16 On this structure, see Rakob 1994, and Mackensen 2005.

17 See Heilmeyer 2004, 405: 'a specific form of building for stone workshops is not to be expected, even in cases of mass production.'

18 I am very grateful to Martin Jennings for discussing some of these matters with me and for allowing me to work in his studio.

19 Like DeLaine 1997 and Barresi 2003, I use the figures given by Pegoretti 1863–4, 159–65 for the quarrying (40 man-hours per cubic metre for one skilled and two unskilled labourers) and shaping (12.5 man-hours per square metre for one skilled labourer) of white marble, assuming that the chest measures 2 × 1 × 1 m, and that the minimum effort involved in hollowing-out would be roughly equivalent to that for shaping.

20 See *EphEp* IV.653, which gives its measurements as 212 × 85 × 80 cm.

21 On the value of a *solidus* in the Price Edict, see Corcoran 2000, 226; the relationship between Diocletianic and late first-century *denarii* is discussed by Barresi 2003, 168.

22 Jongman 2007, 599–600.

individuals of middling to high rank in the military or civil administration; elsewhere, priests, town counsellors, and tradesmen are recorded – only rarely are persons of lowlier status identifiable.[23] For most of these individuals a sarcophagus would have been a massive, once in a lifetime, investment in the monument by which posterity would judge them.

The labour required in the production of a sarcophagus – or statue, or column or capital, for that matter – was of a different order of magnitude than that for almost any other commodity. However, we should be wary of assuming for this reason alone, that the production of objects like sarcophagi took place outside of the normal sphere of commercial activity. It was still in the interest of the producer to reduce unnecessary costs and waste, and to organise the work in such a way as to make it profitable. The core features of 'mass production' – the division of labour and specialisation – are just as relevant, therefore, to sarcophagus production as to any other industry.

Modelling sarcophagus production

Ward-Perkins never defined exactly what he meant by the term 'mass production', but the contexts in which he uses it suggest that he is talking about the large-scale production of standardized objects, often in a prefabricated form, to stock.[24] Less emphasis is placed on the organisation of the stages of production than in Wilson's definition, and much more on the importance of prefabrication and production to stock – 'the fundamental innovation'.[25] Ward-Perkins was concerned above all with sarcophagus production at the various large white marble quarries which dominated the supply of high-quality stone in the first three centuries A.D. However, sarcophagus production defies simplistic modelling and before looking at the evidence from the quarries it is worth considering this quarry-based activity in some context.

Three main parties were involved in the production of a sarcophagus (Figure 4.1): the customer who paid for it, the sculpting workshop that carved it, and the quarry-based workshop that supplied the materials. In a basic scenario, the customer orders a sarcophagus from the sculpting workshop (Stage 1), this sculpting workshop orders material from the quarry-based workshop (Stage 2), this quarry-based workshop supplies the material (Stage 3), the sculpting

23 On Rome, see Dresken-Weiland 2003, 23–6; on Hierapolis, Ritti 1987, 113; on Aphrodisias, Reynolds and Roueché 2007, 150; and at Tyre, see, for example, Chéhab 1984 and 1985, no. 217–8, 248–9, 418–9, 659–60, 931–2 and 4078–9.

24 Ward-Perkins 1980b, 326–7.

25 Ward-Perkins 1980a, 25; in fact, in his own discussion of stone objects Wilson 2008, 402–05 largely follows the model established by Ward-Perkins.

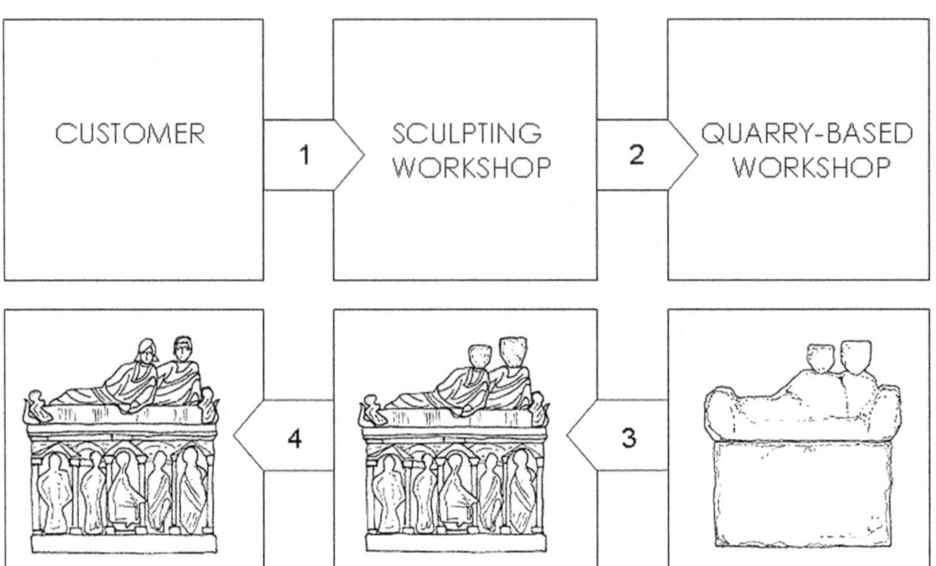

Figure 4.1: Simplified diagram showing the basic relationship between the three main parties involved in sarcophagus production. Diagram: author.

workshop carves the sarcophagus and supplies it to the customer (Stage 4). When all three parties were closely located and there was no particular time pressure such a scenario was entirely feasible and was probably even fairly routine: at least a third of all sarcophagi produced in the Roman period were carved in local stone for the local market. However, a number of variables, especially pertinent to the long-distance sarcophagus trade, complicate this arrangement:

1. The distances between these three respective parties. These could vary considerably. The Attic workshops were close to the source of their materials (Mount Pentelikon) but often far from their customers; the same is probably true of the workshops which produced 'Asiatic' sarcophagi, most in Dokimeian marble, though they rarely supplied clients outside of Asia Minor;[26] while the Metropolitan workshops were located far from the sources of their materials but were usually close to their core market.[27] Distance need not necessarily alter the arrangement of the scenario given

26 Although Waelkens has argued that the so-called 'Asiatic' sarcophagi were carved in the immediate vicinity of the Dokimeian quarries, no fully-finished examples are known from the quarries and we cannot rule out the possibility that these objects were actually carved in the nearby towns (Prymnessos, or Synnada, for example) or even elsewhere.

27 On the distribution of Attic and Metropolitan sarcophagi, see Koch and Sichtermann 1982, 267–72 and 461–70.

above but it did introduce gaps that had to be filled, either by travelling sculptors or by independent traders or other middlemen.[28] The location of these different parties respective to each other also determined at what stages in the production process these objects had to be transported, as Figure 4.2 shows. If Attic and Dokimeian sarcophagi had to travel, to Rome in this case, they were transported furthest once the bulk of their decoration was already completed, unless they were accompanied by a team of sculptors. For an example of an Attic sarcophagus in transit we might look to the example from the sea-bed off Punta de la Mora, near Tarragona.[29] Metropolitan sarcophagi, on the other hand, were usually transported furthest at the preceding stage in process, between quarry-based workshop and sculpting workshop, as the blank chests from the Torre Sgarrata and San Pietro shipwrecks show.[30]

2. The relationship between sculpting workshop and quarry-based workshop. In certain situations these two parties might well have been operated as a single enterprise. This seems to be most probable when they were located close to each other – as at Dokimeion – and less likely when they were further apart. Either way, work was clearly divided between these two stages, as we will see.
3. The form in which the quarry-based workshops supplied material (at Stage 3). In most cases this was probably decided by the sculpting workshop – the client at this stage in the process – but certain quarry-based workshops produced material that was useable without additional work (blank chests (*Rohlingen*) or roughed-out (*Halbfabrikat*) garland sarcophagi on Prokonnesos, for example). In this case it was possible that customer and quarry dealt with each other, perhaps again through middlemen. A variant of this scenario might see customers buying blanks or roughed-out chests from the quarries themselves and then taking them to a local sculpting workshop for finishing.[31]
4. How customers chose to have sarcophagi finished (at Stage 4). If the design of the product allowed for personalisation, for the addition of portrait details or an inscription on chest or lid, the customer could choose to have all or some of these elements finished at the time of purchase or to leave them to

28 Examples of such individuals might include the *negotiator artis lapidariae* recorded at Cologne (*AE* 1904, 23), the *negotiator marmorarius* from Rome (*CIL* VI 33886), or the Bithynian based at the *Horrea Petroniana* in Rome who describes himself as *prōtos lithemporos*, or a 'prime stone-seller' (*SEG* IV 106).

29 For the most recent discussion of this piece, see Arata 2005, 197.

30 On these shipwrecks, Throckmorton 1969; Ward-Perkins and Throckmorton 1965.

31 The numerous examples of Prokonnesian chests from the area around the Propontis which have only small carved panels inserted into their façades were possibly produced in this way; see Koch and Sichtermann 1982, 343–6.

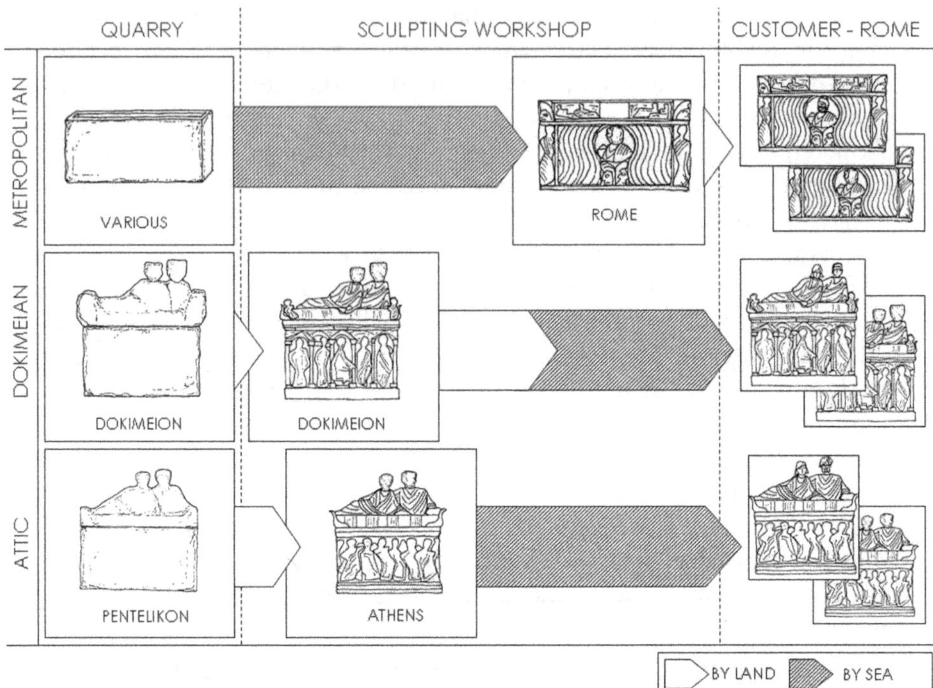

Figure 4.2: Diagram showing the three main stages in the production of three different sarcophagus types – Metropolitan, Dokimeian and Attic – and their spatial arrangement, assuming a customer based in Rome. Diagram: author.

be finished after their death. This introduces the possibility of a later stage of carving after the main commission had been completed.

The basic scenario offered above assumes that each stage of this process was commissioned; in other words both sculpting workshop and quarry-based workshop were responding to definite demand. However, three alternative forms of non-commissioned production could also have existed.

1. Instead of waiting for an order the quarry-based workshops could produce material (blank chests most obviously) to stock, in response to indefinite rather than definite demand – this is what Ward-Perkins argued for.
2. Likewise, the sculpting workshop, instead of waiting for a specific commissioner could acquire a stock of blank chests ready for further carving as required – this stock could be ordered from the quarry or possibly purchased from their stock.
3. Finally, the sculpting workshop could produce finished or near-finished objects for producers to purchase 'off the shelf'.

Since a large number of customers for sarcophagi needed them urgently, so the traditional argument goes, this last mode of production was probably relatively common, even normal.[32] Most discussions of sarcophagus production have focused on this point. But despite the obvious benefit of efficiency, production-to-stock only made sense in certain situations. First, when the capital necessary to invest in stock was available. Stock is costly; it ties up capital, and producers without this capital were reliant on orders – on definite demand. The smaller the workshop, the lower the capital investment, the less feasible production-to-stock became. Secondly, production-to-stock was only profitable when the market was predictable – when a clear, albeit indefinite, market was identifiable. And the indefinite market for a chest that lacked decorative definition and could thus be put to use in numerous ways would always be greater than that for a fully-finished chest. The feasibility of production-to-stock, therefore, depended both on the scale of production – and the amount of capital investment – and the relationship between producer and consumer.

Scale

How large-scale was sarcophagus production? Between 12,000 and 15,000 sarcophagi of all types datable to the second and third centuries are known. If, as Koch has argued, the surviving number account for between only 2 % and 5 % of the original number, then we are looking at very rough production totals of between 300,000 and 750,000 for the years of peak production (defined by Koch as 120 to 310).[33] The lower total gives an annual average of 1,579 sarcophagi, the higher an average of 3,947. In the years of peak production one should imagine figures of up to ten times these. These are high figures, of course, and probably too high. Away from those sites largely obliterated by later settlement, a far higher proportion of sarcophagi have probably survived. Unlike statues, sarcophagi remained functional, and continued to be used and re-used.[34] A more conservative average survival rate, therefore, might be in the order of 20 %.

These totals mean little, however, unless they can be broken down by individual sculpting or quarry-based workshop; only in this way can the scale of

32 See Koch and Sichtermann 1982, 613–4, and Stewart 2008, 37; for a full discussion of this last point with regard to children's sarcophagi, see Huskinson 1996, 79–80.

33 Koch 1993, 1.

34 Greenhalgh 1989, 189–90: sarcophagi 'were prized by later centuries as a very symbol of *romanitas*'.

production at individual establishments, and their productivity, be assessed.[35] It is customary in ancient art history to group together objects with shared characteristics as products of the same workshop or group of workshops, often with topographical identifiers – Attic, Asiatic, Metropolitan.[36] Material analysis and finds from the quarries have helped to pin down some of these vague identifications. We can now be sure that the majority of the ornate columnar sarcophagi traditionally described as 'Asiatic', for example, were carved from Dokimeian marble.[37]

Only occasionally, however, is it possible to break down these broad categories further. This has been attempted for Attic sarcophagi.[38] These objects are the products of a limited body of highly skilled sculptors trained in a common artistic tradition and there is widespread agreement that a number of distinct workshops were involved in their production. From the number of extant pieces we can acquire some indication of the scale of this production and the number of sculptors involved. If we use Koch's estimate of 1,500 preserved Attic sarcophagi (itself probably on the high side) and a 20 % survival rate then these workshops might have been producing as many as 75 sarcophagi annually (over 100 years).[39] Unfortunately labour figures for sculpting, of the kind documented by Pegoretti for architectural carving, are hard to come by.[40] Wiegartz, however, has estimated that it would require 1,000–1,200 man-days to produce a fully-finished Attic sarcophagus with a *kliné* lid.[41] This figure – equivalent to 5–6 large (1 m high) Corinthian capitals using Pegoretti's calculations – is justified by the detail of the carving on both chest and lid, the depth of the relief, and the extra effort involved in hollowing-out.[42] Assuming, therefore, that four sculptors working together could have produced an Attic sarcophagus in a year, a minimum workforce of 300 skilled sculptors might reasonably be conjectured. This is a large number but divided between multiple workshops – Giuliano and Palma tentatively identify at least 21 individual sculptors or working groups, for example – it becomes much more reasonable

35 On this point, see Garnsey and Saller 1987, 52, who argue that industry in the Roman world 'could achieve expanded output (not to be confused with higher productivity) merely through the multiplication of small producers working in isolation or in integrated enterprises.'

36 On this problem generally, see Heilmeyer 2004.

37 Waelkens 1982 and 1988.

38 See Giuliano and Palma 1978, 11–25.

39 Koch 1993, 110.

40 Pegoretti 1863–4; the most detailed carving work mentioned by him is for Corinthian capitals.

41 See Wiegartz 1974, 364–6; Koch 1993, 110, uses these figures.

42 See Pegoretti 1983–4, 397–9.

and more in line with what can be observed in other areas of the Roman economy.[43]

In his discussion of the Roman ceramic industry, Peacock argues that most Roman pottery was produced at single workshops, by single artisans and their assistants, but it was often beneficial for artisans to group together in larger nucleated industries in order to take advantage of access to raw materials, labour, transport or a particular market.[44] Based on modern parallels, Peacock suggests that most workshops would have contained fewer than twelve workers; for the Greek world, Hasebroek proposed a figure of ten to fifteen workers.[45] The stage up from the workshop, the manufactory, is marked 'by the size of its premises, the degree of specialisation in the product, the scale of output, and by the evidence of worker specialisation.'[46] But even at the important centres of ceramic manufacture, such as Arezzo or La Graufesenque, large-scale production was apparently spread across groupings of individually small workshops, and only occasionally anything resembling manufactories.[47] In the broader context of Roman manufacturing it seems most likely, therefore, that Attic sarcophagi were produced by a number of 'nucleated workshops', grouped together to take advantage of the high-quality marble of Mount Pentelikon; we might even posit relationships between workshops, perhaps through apprenticeships or family links.[48] Substantial capital investment in the stone-carving industry did exist – at Aphrodisias, for example – but was probably irregularly spread.[49]

These parallels from other sectors of the economy should also encourage us to challenge, if not necessarily reject, other assumptions about the size of sarcophagus workshops. In Phrygia, for example, Waelkens has argued that the stylistic homogeneity of the sarcophagi produced in Dokimeian marble identifies them as the products of a single large 'workshop', located at the

43 Giuliano and Palma 1978, 11–25.

44 Peacock 1982, 8–11; see also Kehoe 2007, 561: 'industries tended to be organised on a modest scale'.

45 See Hasebroek 1965, 75.

46 Peacock 1982, 9.

47 See Fülle 1997, 133–9, and Wilson 2008, 397–8.

48 Like so many other specialist crafts stone-working was probably often a family affair; on this point, see Lucian, *The Dream or Lucian's Career* 7–8.

49 A certain M. Ulpius Carminius Claudianos, a member of the local elite at Aphrodisias, provided many donations of both buildings and statues to the city in the second century; the statues, in particular, are noted as having come from 'his house' – *oikothen kateskeuakota* – which might well indicate a workshop or marble-production facility, a hypothesis supported by the fact that the Carminii were from Attouda, over the hill beyond the quarries (see *CIG* 2782). In fact, Reynolds 1996, 122 has hypothesised that many benefactors at Aphrodisias were also quarry-owners.

quarries.[50] The extant Dokimeian sarcophagi, however, might represent as many as 1,500 originals (using a 20 % survival rate; 6,500 using Koch's figure of 5 %).[51] This equates to an average annual production of 12 pieces over the 130 years of production (50 with the 5 % figure), with up to double this number in periods of peak demand like the 160s.[52] Estimating that the more ornate columnar Dokimeian sarcophagus took up to 1,500 man-days to carve, five sculptors working together could probably have finished one sarcophagus a year, necessitating a minimum workforce of 60 skilled sculptors (250 with the 5 % figure). This is a large number and, though Waelkens' well-constructed argument cannot be disproved, the idea that production of these sarcophagi was split between multiple units operating in a shared artistic tradition but without any overriding direction might fit more plausibly with patterns observable elsewhere. The absence of finished sarcophagi close to the quarries, as already noted, might suggest that these workshops were located elsewhere, possibly in the nearby cities, or alternatively that they were mobile: it is entirely likely that sculptors from Dokimeion travelled with their materials, finishing commissions in situ.[53]

The idea of nucleated workshops certainly seems most appropriate in the case of Rome. Approximately 6,000 metropolitan sarcophagi have been identified, the vast majority in and around the capital though others were exported to the western Mediterranean.[54] The range of marbles used by these workshops (Prokonnesian, Luna, Thasian, Ephesian, Parian, Pentelic), alongside the stylistic variety observable across all types of metropolitan sarcophagi, make it likely that production was again spread across numerous small-scale workshops and was never dominated by a single mega-producer; on this there has been general agreement.[55] But how large the quarry-based workshops

50 Considering the evidence for imperial involvement at Dokimeion, Waelkens 1982, 124–127 suggested that this workshop was probably also imperially-run; this proposal received initial support from Fant 1985, 661, though now he doubts whether imperial involvement in sarcophagus production is likely. In practice, the white marble at Dokimeion never seems to have attracted imperial attention like the *pavonazzetto* – quarry-inscriptions are rarely found on blocks of white marble, the quarrying of which was probably contracted out to private enterprises.

51 This calculation is based on the 311 examples catalogued by Wiegartz 1965; Ferrari 1966; Waelkens 1982; Koch 1989; and Özgan 2003.

52 Note, however, that only around half of the examples listed in the above catalogues are given dates and some of these are dubious.

53 Dokimeion was certainly an important artistic centre and Dokimeian sculptors, like Athenians and Aphrodisians, are found elsewhere: see Hall and Waelkens 1982; McLean 2002, no. 45; and Pensabene 2007, 297–9.

54 Koch 1993, 94, and Walker 1990, 10.

55 On the materials used, see Walker 1990, 15–36, and Van Keuren et al. (this volume); see also Koch 1993, 13–14, and for the later period, Koch 2000, 79–80.

supplying the metropolitan sculptors were is less agreed upon. The arguments discussed above with regard to the Attic and Dokimeian workshops apply equally to quarry-based workshops in other large white marble quarries. Epigraphic evidence for ownership is limited and the layout of many of these sites suggests a decentralised process.[56] These factors suggest that it would be wrong to assume, *a priori,* that individual quarries were worked by single large workshops.

Quarry-based production

Ward-Perkins' model of the imperial marble trade was centred on the idea of 'a completely new quarry-consumer relationship, based upon bulk-production at the quarries and upon stock-piling'.[57] The prefabrication of objects in standardised forms was 'a natural development' of this shift in focus, he argued, which in turn encouraged specialisation.[58]

Sarcophagus evidence lies at the heart of this model. Finds of roughed-out chests at the quarries show that a certain amount of work was undertaken on these objects before they were exported and that particular forms of sarcophagi can be linked to specific quarries. On this basis typologies can be constructed, the most comprehensive being those of the Asiatic garland sarcophagi.[59] The distinct roughed-out form of these pieces, which became valued in its own right, varied subtly between production centres, allowing for five main workshops to be identified – at Prokonnesos, Ephesos, Aphrodisias, somewhere else in Karia, and somewhere in the Hermos valley (Figure 4.3).[60] Roughed-out chests and lids on Prokonnesos, preserved in the necropolis as well as in the quarries, show that producers on the island also specialised in the shaping of four other chest-types: two sizes of plain-sided ones, one version with a lower moulding, and another with upper and lower mouldings (Figure 4.4).[61] Like the roughed-out garland sarcophagi, all of these types were useable as they were, without further

56 Quarry inscriptions are much scarcer on white marble than coloured marbles: inscriptions attesting to imperial involvement are found on blocks of Parian (Pensabene 1994, 121–2), blocks of Prokonnesian, but only in the Byzantine period (Asgari and Drew-Bear 2002), and also on blocks of Luna, but only ever alongside other inscriptions attesting to private or municipal quarrying (see Dolci 2004, 59–61, and Pensabene 2002, 15). On this point with regard to the Thasian quarries, see Marc 1995.

57 Ward-Perkins 1980a, 25.

58 Ward-Perkins 1980b, 327.

59 See Asgari 1977, and Işik 1992, 1998 and 2007.

60 The discovery of an abandoned roughed-out garland sarcophagus in the quarry at Selvioğlu, near Uşak, might indicate the origin of the type used in the Hermos valley: Pralong 1980, 254–5, Figs. 4a and 4b).

61 Asgari 1990, 110–15; see also Koch and Sichtermann 1982, 486 (Fig.10: 2a and 2b).

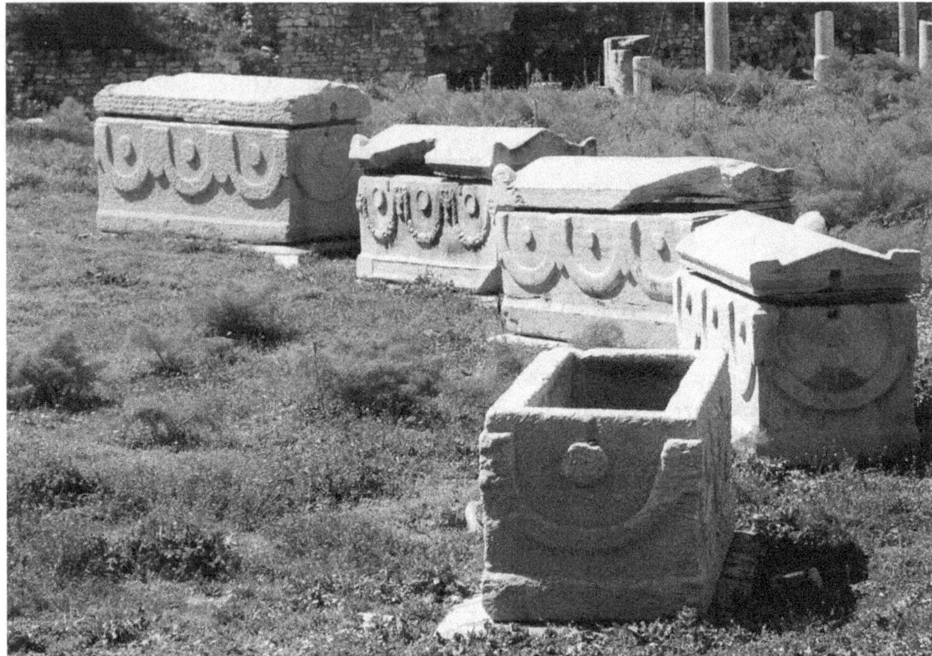

Figure 4.3: Various types of Ephesian garland sarcophagi. Ephesos. Photograph: author.

ornamentation, and were certainly valued in this form. But these chests typically received some level of further carving at sculpting workshops elsewhere around the Mediterranean, where they could be decorated according to local tastes.[62] More recently an additional category of roughed-out chests has been identified in the quarries at Vathy and Saliari on Thasos. This round-ended, so-called *lēnos* (ληνός) or tub-shaped type with projecting bosses was shipped primarily to Rome, where the bosses could be carved into either lion-head protomes or relief lions with raised heads, two of the canonical forms of the so-called 'lion sarcophagus' (*Löwensarkophag*).[63]

These finds are important for our understanding of the dynamics of production. Certain quarry-based workshops specialised in the production of roughed-out stone objects, sarcophagus chests and lids amongst them, and this

62 Major concentrations of sarcophagi in Prokonnesian marble which were carved by local workshops can be identified in the Balkans (Cermanović 1965; Cambi 1998, 169), northern Italy (Gabelmann 1973), and at Tyre (Ward-Perkins 1969; Koch 1989). A part-finished example from Constanţa (ancient Tomis) shows how these local decorative schemes, in this case a *tabula* framed by *genii*, were cut into the side of these plain Prokonnesian chest-types (see Alexandrescu-Vianu 1970, no. 15).

63 On Thasos: Koželj et al. 1985, and Wurch-Koželj and Koželj 1995. On the sarcophagi from which these types were carved, see ASR VI, 1.

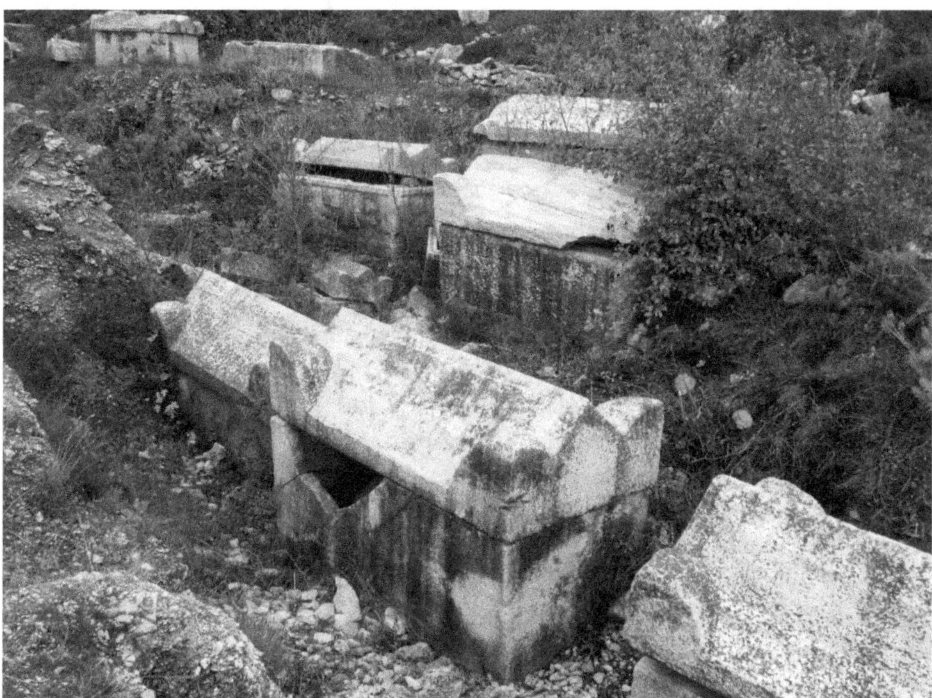

Figure 4.4: Plain-sided and roughed-out garland sarcophagi from the necropolis at Saraylar, on Prokonnesos (modern Marmara Adası). Photograph: author, published with the kind permission of Professor Nuşin Asgari.

suggests further specialisation at the workshops that received these roughed-out objects. That different phases of this process were completed in different locations indicates a geographically differentiated division of labour.[64] Labour could be divided further at each point in the process. Between quarryman and carver at the quarry and between any number of sculptors at the sculpting workshop – Eichner distinguishes nine stages in the carving process between receipt of a roughed-out chest and final polish.[65] Stone-working is highly methodical and it makes sense to divide the 'process', as Rockwell calls it, into different stages so as to avoid risk of over-cutting.[66] Part-finished sarcophagi help to reveal these stages. However, the objects alone cannot tell us whether these working stages were divided between different individuals or different

64 See Wilson 2008, 405–06.

65 Eichner 1981, 103–104; see Koch 1993, 32–33, for a similar reconstruction. For discussion of this point with regard to statue production, see Boschung and Pfanner 1988, 14 (Fig. 7), and on Corinthian capitals, Asgari 1988, 122 (Fig. 1); for labour division at the quarry, Rockwell 1993, 96.

66 Rockwell 1993, 12–13.

locations. The smaller the workshop the less likely this was, not simply because fewer workers were employed but because the level of production could not sustain it; what did eight specialist workers do while the ninth finished his stage unless there was a queue of pieces waiting to be finished?[67] Overall, therefore, the broad division of labour between quarry workshop and sculpting workshop is significant, and must have encouraged specialisation; it was probably also accompanied by division of labour at each of these stages, but the articulation of this system depended on the size of the workshop and the number of personnel. Again the question of scale is paramount.

All this being said, we should be wary of getting carried away by the idea of quarry-based specialisation – the idea, in Ward-Perkins' words, of 'certain quarries producing certain particular shapes, and in some cases even certain particular designs.'[68] The typological approach, in particular the focus on standardisation, can provide a false sense of uniformity. As already noted, a single 'quarry' was probably associated with numerous independent workshops. And at the same time we cannot rule out the possibility that individual sculptors or groups of sculptors travelled to the quarries to carry out commissions or select materials, as was customary in later periods; for large commissions the same individuals might have been present at every stage of the production process.[69] In fact, a variety is visible in quarry-based production that may well reflect the presence of a number of workshops or individual sculptors working or responding to orders in different ways. This is clear on Prokonnesos, where Asgari's on-going research has highlighted the range of objects which received shaping on the island prior to export. Alongside the chest types traditionally identified as 'Prokonnesian' it is clear that several varieties of roughed-out *lēnos* chests, finished to different degrees, were also shaped on the island; a strigillated example in the open-air museum at Saraylar, which is due to be published in full by Asgari, shows that these objects were sometimes carved further before export.[70] That sculptors capable of detailed work were present on the island is additionally shown by a single gable-lid with a roughed-out portrait bust on one

67 Adam Smith (*On the Wealth of Nations*, III (2003 edn., ed. Cannan, 27) made this point explicitly: 'as it is the power of exchanging that gives occasion to the division of labour, so the extent of this division must always be limited by the extent of that power, or, in other words, by the extent of the market.'

68 Ward-Perkins 1980a, 25.

69 See Klapisch-Zuber 1969, 62; it is quite normal today for sculptors from outside of Italy to travel to Carrara and work there on large commissions for at least part of the year. Dio Chrysostom certainly travelled to the local quarries to oversee the selection of stone when paying for a new stoa at Prusa (*Orations* XL, 7).

70 All of these objects will be discussed in more detail in Nuşin Asgari's forthcoming monograph.

acroterion, a decorative scheme common in northern Italy and the Balkans.[71] Analysis of finished sarcophagi at Rome and elsewhere helps to fill in the picture provided by the material from the quarries. Around half of the *lēnos* sarcophagi tested by Walker were carved in Prokonnesian, as were over half of the metropolitan sarcophagi analysed in the British Museum.[72] As reported in this volume, the analysis of twenty sarcophagus chests and five lids from the Museo Nazionale Romano revealed the use of Prokonnesian for thirteen chests and one lid, compared to Luna for three chests and four lids, and Pentelic for four chests.[73] Roughed-out types suitable for the production of these metropolitan sarcophagi are not represented on Prokonnesos but this does not mean that they were not shaped on the island before export. Equally, the Pentelic chests identified at Rome show that different sculpting workshops, specialising in very different types of product, dealt with the same quarries – not all Pentelic marble ended up as Attic sarcophagi. Recognising this kind of variety is key because it casts doubt on the link drawn by Ward-Perkins and others between the finds from the quarries and the controversial notion of production-to-stock. The more types of different products produced the less likely it was that they were produced-to-stock. In other words, this variety suggests a more nuanced picture, of multiple workshops, at or near the quarries, responding separately to the demands of a range of clients, themselves mainly sculpting workshops located elsewhere.

The crucial question here is where the stimulus for production came from. Ward-Perkins regarded it as 'a natural development, convenient both to the suppliers and to the far-off customers', that the quarries should introduce a degree of 'standardisation' and 'prefabrication'.[74] The quarries, consequently, are seen as the main instigators. However, 'standardisation' and 'prefabrication' are problematic terms, as too is the link drawn between them and the notion of production-to-stock. The 'pre-' of 'prefabrication', for example, suggests that these objects were shaped before they had a buyer.[75] But, whether a commission or a stock piece, it made good sense to reduce the weight of any object before export.[76] The hollowing-out of sarcophagi was especially worthwhile in this regard, reducing its weight by half – 2,500 kg for a chest measuring 2 × 1 × 1 m.[77] The practice of shaping objects prior to export additionally reduced the

71 Asgari 1990, 113 (Fig. 6).

72 See Walker 1985, 61, and 1990, 15–36.

73 Van Keuren et al. (this volume).

74 Ward-Perkins 1980b, 327.

75 Ward-Perkins 1980b, 327.

76 Klapisch-Zuber 1969, 69, and Manning 1987, 594–5; marble weighs between 2,563 and 2,700 kg/m^3, granite around 2,700 kg/m^3, and limestone around 2,620 kg/m^3.

77 See Wurch-Koželj and Koželj 1995, 45, for similar calculations for the round-ended chests on Thasos.

likelihood that flaws concealed within the block would be passed on to the client; and, as Conlin has remarked, since stone is at its softest, and easiest to carve, when initially quarried, it also made sense to carry out as much bulk shaping at this stage as possible.[78] This shaping took place even when quarry and customer were closely located and when the piece was a commission. Even though 90 % of the catalogued sarcophagi at Hierapolis in Phrygia were carved from the local travertine, they were still supplied in roughed-out form from the quarries.[79] And these were not stock pieces: decorated examples from the city's necropolis show that sides on which relief decoration was planned were shaped at this early stage to be thicker than sides on which no decoration was planned; in other words, the desires of the client were known from the earliest stage in the production process. Roughed-out sarcophagus chests have been identified in a number of other quarries which served only a local market.[80] At Dokimeion, where the sarcophagus workshops operated in the immediate vicinity of the quarries, chests and lids still received some shaping at the quarry-face before being moved: this was simply a stage in the working process that made the object more moveable.[81]

Equally problematic from this perspective is the concept of 'standardisation'. For though the term itself refers to a conscious and directed process, the similitude of a given class of object, in form or dimensions, need not necessarily result from choices made by their producer (the 'quarry' in Ward-Perkins' model) and need not automatically indicate a production-to-stock system. There was, in fact, massive consumer demand for such objects in what might be regarded as 'standard' forms: this is arguably one of the most striking characteristics of Roman art and architecture.[82] This was not because this was 'a society that placed no value on innovation, originality or progress', as Cornell put it, but arguably because these objects were required to function in very specific ways in a social context which had an accepted visual language.[83] In other words, objects produced in standard forms could just as easily be commissions as stock pieces.

A large quarry-based workshop, with access to the necessary capital, could quite reasonably have produced blank chests to stock without worry of the market for them evaporating. As we have seen stock production was feasible in

78 Conlin 1997, 36.

79 Vanhaverbeke and Waelkens 2002; see Ronchetta 1987, 105, for a roughed-out example still attached to the quarry-face.

80 On Brač, see Cambi 1998; on Aphrodisias, Işik 2007; and on the French quarries, Bedon 1984, 116 and Fig. 19 which lists seventeen sites (though he is unspecific about dates).

81 For roughed-out lids and chests, see Fant 1985, and Waelkens 1988.

82 On this point with regard to statue types, see Daehner 1997, and Trimble 2000.

83 Cornell 1987, 32–3.

such a situation. It is entirely possible that certain workshops on Prokonnesos or even Thasos did operate in this way. However, there is no direct connection between quarry-based shaping, standardisation and production-to-stock. Equally, even objects of apparently neutral or multi-purpose form – like blank sarcophagi chests – were not necessarily produced to stock. The cargo of the San Pietro shipwreck shows this well. This ship, wrecked in the early third century, was carrying twenty-three Thasian sarcophagi of three main types: ten *lēnos* sarcophagi (seven with projecting protomes, three without), nine rectangular chests, and four rectangular chests with round-ended interior cavities.[84] Six of these were stacked in pairs, a smaller one within a larger one to economize on space during transit; a further six were produced in joined pairs, for separation after arrival; while at least two had lids attached to one of their long sides. As Ward-Perkins and Throckmorton originally noted, the fact that one of these lids was not meant for the sarcophagus to which it was attached but for a smaller chest in the cargo showed that these two pieces at any rate were destined for the same workshop.[85] This also proves that this one chest at least was not a stock piece. The same can be proposed for the examples joined in pairs, which would require significant additional work to separate, but were structurally stronger in this form. Overall it seems unlikely that the range of chest-types from the San Pietro wreck could have been supplied from stock, especially considering the different sizes represented – essentially three of each type. This cargo probably represents at least one large order of material placed by a workshop, or multiple workshops, at Rome with the quarries on Thasos.

Instead, therefore, of thinking of quarry-based workshops as proactive enterprises – setting fashions rather than responding to them – it is perhaps more realistic to see them by and large as reactive ones. Production at the quarries responded to the demands of the client – either the customer directly or a sculpting workshop. The concentrations of particular sarcophagus types in particular regions – Prokonnesian garland sarcophagi at Alexandria, Attic sarcophagi at Cyrene – is more plausibly explained as resulting from decisions made by the customer or local workshops at these locations than the quarries.[86] Certain quarry-based workshops clearly specialised in producing certain objects, typically partially shaped before export, but this does not mean that the stimulus for production lay with them.

84 See Alessio and Zaccaria 1997, 215 (Fig. 2).

85 Ward-Perkins and Throckmorton 1965, 205–207.

86 On the apparent selective focus of different quarry-based workshops, see Ward-Perkins 1980a, 40–9.

Production and the customer

The feasibility of production-to-stock already discussed with regard to the quarry-based workshops applies equally to the sculpting workshops that dealt directly, in most cases, with the customer. A large workshop at Rome, with the necessary capital, could import a cargo of blank chests like that found off San Pietro with little risk. They could be kept in stock in this form ready for an order to be placed and the indefinite market was such that any workshop could be confident of selling them. Even the roughed-out pieces that had a more defined form – like the *lēnos* sarcophagi or the roughed-out garland sarcophagi – could easily be altered into a different form if necessary.[87] Any further work carried out on these roughed-out chests by the workshop that was not in response to definite demand might have made them better able to respond quickly but it also added risk, since it effectively reduced the market for the product. If the workshop was specialised, and if it was known for a particular product, then its market was already more defined and this was not as problematic. An obvious example might be a workshop specialising in strigillated sarcophagi. Several part-finished strigillated sarcophagi from Rome show that the main strigillated panels could be finished before any figured decoration was added (see Figure 4.5). The workshop could still complete much of the work necessary without depriving the customer of choice over the key features of their monument.[88]

This is the context in which the well-known corpus of 'unfinished' or blank portraits are usually discussed.[89] One common explanation of this phenomenon links it to the idea of production-to-stock: sarcophagi with standard motifs were produced near-finished to stock with such portraits left for personalisation, but because these objects were often needed quickly, following a sudden death, these portraits were never worked. Of course, the more formulaic the decoration and the more predictable the market the more feasible it was for a workshop with sufficient capital to produce a sarcophagus with blank portrait to stock. In third-century Rome, when the market for sarcophagi reached its zenith, such a situation is plausible. However, this does not mean that blank portraits indicate stock pieces. Indeed a number of arguments can be made against this connection. First, blank portraits are found on sarcophagi that were clearly

87 See Ward-Perkins and Throckmorton 1965, 205, on the sarcophagus from Acilia carved from a roughed-out *lēnos* sarcophagus; for altered garland sarcophagi, see Adriani 1961, no. 24 (Fig. 65–72), Asgari 1977, 332 (Istanbul A), and Mendel 1912–1914, no. 26.

88 A sarcophagus in the collection of the *Museo Nazionale Romano* with a delineated *clipeus* medallion could also be interpreted in this context (see Giuliano 1984, no. IX.4).

89 Unfinished here warrants inverted commas because of the recent suggestion that some of these portraits were perhaps never meant to be finished; see Huskinson 1998, 155.

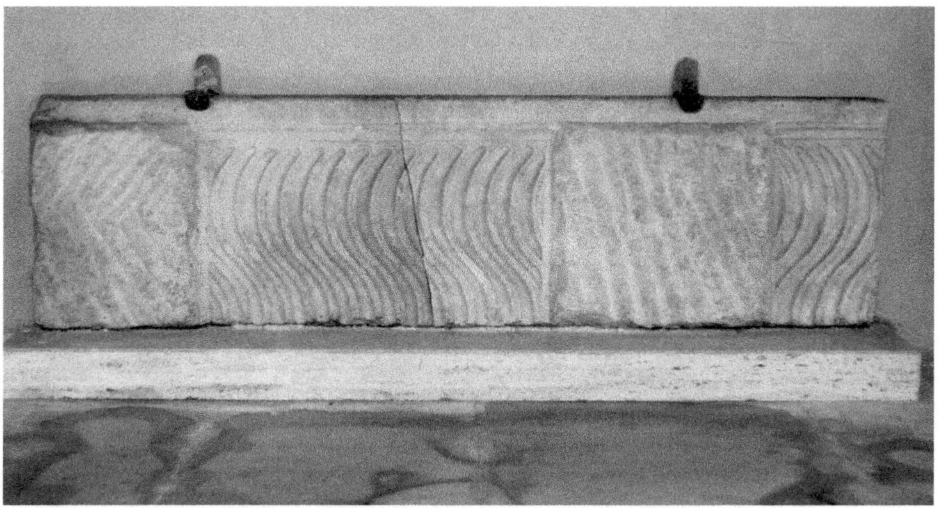

Figure 4.5: Fragment of a strigillated sarcophagus with roughed-out bosses, now in San Paolo fuori le Mura, Rome. Photograph: author.

commissions. The central figure on the front of the chest of the Portonaccio sarcophagus, for instance, has a blank portrait, and four others are incorporated into the biographic scene on its lid.[90] At the other end of the empire, at Aphrodisias, the sarcophagus of Aurelia Tate has two blank portraits on its façade alongside a central *tabula*, fully-inscribed, and a small depiction of a blacksmith's workshop (Figure 4.6).[91] Secondly, blank portraits are found on sarcophagi at a number of sites where the market appears too small to have sustained production to stock. At somewhere like Aphrodisias, with an estimated population living within the fourth-century wall circuit of around 15,000 inhabitants, the market for sarcophagi was considerably smaller than at Rome. Nevertheless, the majority of sarcophagi from Aphrodisias display some level of un-finish and frequently incorporate blank portraits.[92]

What the Aphrodisian material clearly shows is that sarcophagi were not simply functional containers for corpses. They were monuments, more akin to tombs than coffins.[93] Most were purchased during the lifetime of those commemorated.[94] As the sarcophagus of Aurelia Tate shows they were often commissioned with spaces for portraits that could be finished at the time of

90 Koch and Sichtermann 1982, 92.
91 Smith 2008, 374–6.
92 See Smith 2008, 347.
93 On the words used to describe tombs in the Greek East, see Kubrińska 1968, 32–57.
94 For Kalchedon, see Asgari and Fıratlı 1978, 34, and for Aphrodisias, Reynolds and Roueché 2007, 149.

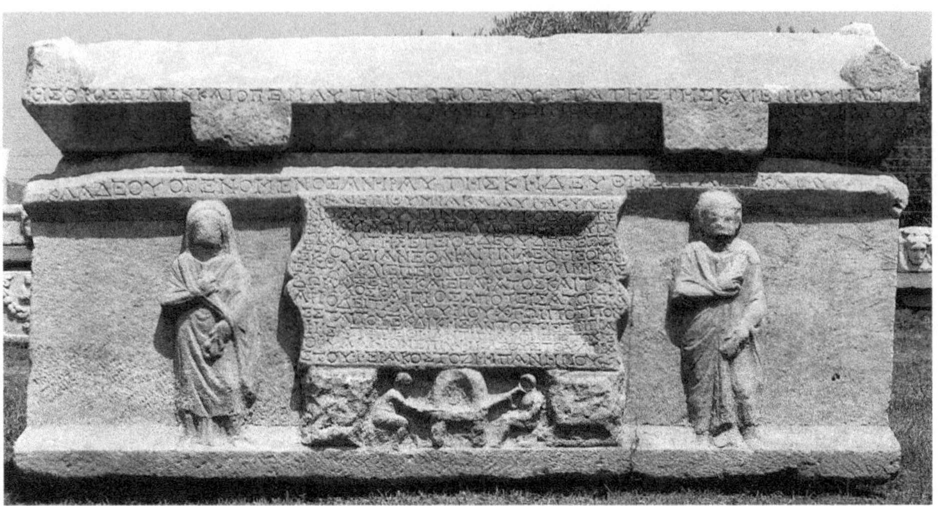

Figure 4.6: Sarcophagus of Aurelia Tate. Aphrodisias. Photograph: courtesy of the New York University excavations at Aphrodisias.

purchase or left until after their death. The epigraphic evidence shows that these objects were sometimes even exchanged between families. One example from the city, originally produced with four roughed-out busts on its façade, was ceded from one family to a married couple who then completed the middle two busts with their portraits; the number of busts suggests this was a commission that for some reason never got used and so was sold on.[95] If the purchaser did choose to leave these portraits for later finishing then any number of reasons might explain their incompletion: negligence on the part of the heir, or even the death of the heir; perhaps the context in which the sarcophagus was erected prevented its finishing. Alternatively, there is the intriguing possibility that some of these blank portraits were never intended to be finished, their blankness an expression of 'collective and spiritual values'.[96] Purchasing a sarcophagus, like buying a plot of land, building a tomb, or making a will, was part of the process of planning for death. Some tomb-buildings were even built around sarcophagi – the large sarcophagus in the so-called Tomb of the Pancratii on the Via Latina, for example, is too sizeable to have been placed there after the tomb's construction.[97] Individuals often purchased multiple sarcophagi. At Tyre local notables jostled for space in the crowded necropolis, reserving plots and sarcophagi for themselves and their families; a murex fisherman (and hence

95 Işik 2007, no. 6; see Reynolds and Roueché 2007, 152–3.

96 For a summary of these reconstructions, see Koch and Sichtermann 1982, 611–4, and Huskinson 1998, 143–5.

97 Coarelli 1981, 140–2.

probably also a purple-dyer) named Heraclitos reserved three sarcophagi in his name.[98] It was common for them to contain more than one body. All of the examples from Söğütlüçeşme near Kadıköy (ancient Kalchedon) which give appropriate details in their inscriptions commemorate multiple individuals, usually of the same family.[99]

Although it may have been the norm, patently not all sarcophagi were purchased during the lifetime of the deceased. As Huskinson has noted, in the case of children's sarcophagi in particular there would not have been time to commission one from scratch.[100] Presumably certain workshops specialised in producing children's sarcophagi to stock, typically with generic scenes; this was the kind of defined market, as discussed above, that made production to stock feasible. However, we should also be open to the idea that simply because an individual died suddenly did not mean their monument had to be purchased fully-finished. The late fourth-century sarcophagus of Catervius from the cathedral in Tolentino mentions that forty days passed between the death of the individual commemorated and his burial inside the sarcophagus.[101] Where Catervius' body was in the meantime is unclear but this raises the possibility that corpses intended for burial in a sarcophagus could be interred elsewhere first, perhaps in a wooden or lead coffin. The possibility that corpses were not interred in their final resting place immediately is even hinted at in a passage of the Digest which talks of bodies being held in one place for transferral elsewhere later.[102] Even if this was an extreme case there was still time between the death of an individual and their burial, and even after their burial further carving could have been carried out in the necropolis. A chest with pre-worked strigillated panels bought from stock could probably be personalised with figurative scenes relatively quickly by a team of sculptors. The ideas of production to stock and consumer choice, therefore, are not always mutually exclusive.

Conclusions

'Systems changed and methods doubtless changed; and right down the line, down to the individual workmen, it would be wrong to expect absolute uniformity and absolute standardisation.'[103] Ward-Perkins was well aware that

98 See Chéhab 1984 and 1985, no. 1341–2, 4950 and 4864.

99 See Asgari and Fıratlı 1978, 32–4; in all but one case, however, more skeletons were found inside the sarcophagus than there were individuals listed in its inscription.

100 Huskinson 1996, 79.

101 See Märki-Boehringer et al. 1966, 39, and Koch 2000, 79.

102 *Digest* XI.7.42.

103 Ward-Perkins in his Fourth Shuffrey Lecture, see Dodge and Ward-Perkins 1992, 39.

his model did not explain everything. Between customer and producer any number of relationships could exist. At every stage of the production process changes could be made, specifications altered, or complications arise. Equally, from quarry to finished article any single sarcophagus could follow a number of different trajectories. There is no single, one-size-fits-all, model that can adequately account for this heterogeneity. The decisions of innumerable individual customers determined the pattern of sarcophagus production. It is not a question, therefore, of either 'production-to-stock' or 'production-to-order', 'mass production' or 'small-scale production', 'industry' or 'craft'; the evidence is more nuanced than these dichotomies suggest. Instead it is helpful to think about what we mean by these terms and what the logic behind different modes of production was. Above all, we need to question many of our assumptions about sarcophagus production, what was normal and what was not. For instance, it is unclear what proportion of sarcophagi were produced in response to definite as opposed to indefinite demand but there are good reasons to doubt that production-to-stock was the norm; only in certain circumstance did it make sense. Equally, viewed against the broader background of the ancient economy, the notion that sarcophagus production was dominated by a handful of mega-producers becomes questionable.

The controversial notion of production-to-stock has somewhat dominated most discussions of sarcophagus production. Mass production – the large-scale production of standardised objects – and production-to-stock are not the same thing; one is not necessarily a symptom of the other. The division of labour between the quarry-based workshops, producing roughed-out chests, and the sculpting workshops, more closely connected to the customer and responsible for finishing these pieces, is suggestive of a level of specialisation that must have helped to increase productivity. This does not, however, equate to production-to-stock. The stimulus appears to have come from the customer and the sculpting workshop; the quarry-based workshops responded to their requests. Specialisation rendered both sets of workshops more efficient and better able to respond to demand. Therefore, though Roman sarcophagus production bore little similarity to modern industrial production, it was highly articulated, specialised, and responsive. Most importantly, it relied on the cooperation and interaction of individuals across large distances. From this perspective it adds significantly to our understanding of the connectivity, physical, cultural and artistic, of the Roman Mediterranean.

Acknowledgements

I am very grateful to Amanda Claridge, Andrew Wilson, Frances Van Keuren, Janet Huskinson and Jaś Elsner for their helpful comments on a first draft on this paper, and to Bert Smith for his assistance with Figure 4.6. I would also like to thank Martin Jennings and Stephen Cox for discussing the practicalities of stone-carving with me. The research on which this paper is based was undertaken at the University of Oxford, as part of the Oxford Roman Economy Project, and at the British School at Rome, and was funded by the Arts and Humanities Research Council and the Leverhulme Trust respectively.

Bibliography

Adriani, A. *Repertorio d'arte dell'Egitto Greco-Romano* (Palermo, 1961).

Alessio, A. and Zaccaria, A. Nuove ricerche sul relitto di San Pietro in Bevanga (Manduria –Taranto), in: G. Volpe (ed.), *Atti del convegno nazionale di archeologia subacquea: Anzio, 30–31 maggio e 1 giugno 1996* (Bari, 1997), 211–224.

Alexandrescu-Vianu, M. Les sarcophages romains de Dobroudja. *Revue des Études Sud-Est Européennes* 8.2 (1970), 269–328.

Arata, F. *Opere d'arte dal mare. Testimonianze archeologiche subacquee del trasporto e del commercio marittimo di prodotti artistici* (Rome, 2005).

Asgari, N. Die Halbfabrikate kleinasiatischer Girlandensarkophage und ihre Herkunft. *Archäologischer Anzeiger* (1977), 329–380.

Asgari, N. The stages of workmanship of the Corinthian capital in Proconnesus and its export form, in: *Classical Marble: Geochemistry, Technology and Trade, NATO ASI Series E: Applied Sciences, vol. 153*, edited by N. Herz and M. Waelkens (Dordrecht, 1988), 115–126.

Asgari, N. Objets de marbre finis, semi-finis et inachevés du Proconnèse, in: *Pierre Éternelle du Nil au Rhin. Carrières et prefabrication*, edited by M. Waelkens (Brussels, 1990), 106–126.

Asgari, N. and Drew-Bear, T. The quarry inscriptions of Prokonnesos, in: J. Herrmann, N. Herz and R. Newman (eds.), *ASMOSIA 5. Interdisciplinary Studies on Ancient Stone. Proceedings of the Fifth International Conference of the Association for the Study of Marble and Other Stones in Antiquity, Museum of Fine Arts, Boston, 1998* (London, 2002), 1–19.

Asgari, N. and Fıratlı, N. Die Nekropole von Kalchedon, in: *Studien zur Religion und Kultur Kleinasiens. Festschrift F. K. Dörner*, 2 vols. *Études Preliminaries aux Religions Orientales dans l'Empire Romain, vol. 66*, edited by S. Şahin, E. Schwertheim and J. Wagner (Leiden, 1978), 1–92.

Barresi, P. *Province dell'Asia Minore: costo dei marmi, architettura pubblica e committenza* (Rome, 2003).

Bedon, R. *Les carrières et les carriers de la Gaule romaine* (Paris, 1984).

Boschung, D. and Pfanner, M. Antike Bildhauertechnik. Vier Untersuchungen an Beispielen in der Münchner Glyptothek. *Münchner Jahrbuch der bildenden Kunst*, series 3, 39 (1988), 7–28.

Cambi, N. Sarkophage aus salonitanischen Werkstätten, in: G. Koch (ed.), *Akten des Symposiums '125 Jahre Sarkophag-Corpus', Marburg, 4.–7. Oktober 1995. Sarkophag-Studien, vol. 1* (Mainz am Rhein, 1998), 169–181.

Cermanović, A. Die dekorierten Sarkophage in den römischen Provinzen von Jugoslavien. *Archaeologia Iugoslavica* 6 (1965), 89–103.

Chéhab, M. *Fouilles de Tyr. La nécropole II: description des fouilles. Bulletin du Musée de Beyrouth 34* (Paris, 1984).

Chéhab, M. *Fouilles de Tyr. La nécropole III: description des fouilles. Bulletin du Musée de Beyrouth 35* (Paris, 1985).

Coarelli, F. *Dintorni di Roma* (Rome, 1981).

Conlin, D. *The Artists of the Ara Pacis. The Process of Hellenization in Roman Relief Sculpture* (Chapel Hill, 1997).

Corcoran, S. *The Empire of the Tetrarchs: Imperial Pronouncements and Government AD 284–324* (Oxford, 2000).

Cornell, T. Artists and patrons, in: *Art and Production in the World of the Caesars*, edited by T. Cornell, M. Crawford and J. North (Milan, 1987), 17–36.

Daehner, J. The statue types in the Roman world, in: *The Herculaneum Women. History, Context, Identities*, edited by J. Daehner (Malibu, 2007), 85–112.

DeLaine, J. *The Baths of Caracalla: a Study in the Design, Construction, and Economics of Large-Scale Building Projects in Imperial Rome. JRA Supplementary Series, vol. 25.* (Portsmouth, R.I, 1997).

Dodge, H. and Ward-Perkins, B. (eds.). *Marble in Antiquity: Collected Papers of J. B. Ward-Perkins* (London, 1992).

Dolci, E. Sui marmi lunensi recentemente scoperti. *Quaderni del Centro di Studi Lunensi* 8 (2004), 47–78.

Dresken-Weiland, J. *Sarkophagbestattungen des 4.–6. Jahrhunderts im westen des römischen Reiches. Römische Quartalschrift für christliche Altertumskunde und Kirchengeschichte, Supplementband 55* (Rome, Freiburg and Vienna, 2003).

Eichner, K. Die Produktionsmethoden der stadtrömischen Sarkophagfabrik in der Blütezeit unter Konstantin. *Jahrbuch für Antike und Christentum* 24 (1981), 85–113.

Fant, J. C. Four unfinished sarcophagus lids at Docimium and the Roman imperial quarry system in Phrygia. *American Journal of Archaeology* 89 (1985), 655–662.

Ferrari, G. *Il Commercio dei Sarcofagi Asiatici* (Rome, 1966).

Fülle, G. The internal organization of the Arretine terra-sigillata industry: Problems of evidence and interpretation. *Journal of Roman Studies* 87 (1997), 111–155.

Gabelmann, H. *Die Werkstattgruppen der oberitalischen Sarkophage* (Bonn, 1973).

Garnsey, P. and Saller, R. *The Roman Empire: Economy, Society and Culture* (London, 1987).

Giuliano, A. and Palma, B. *La maniera ateniese di età romana. I maestri dei sarcofagi attici. Studi Miscellanei 24* (Rome, 1978).

Giuliano, Antonio (ed.). *Museo Nazionale Romano: le sculture* (Roma, 1984), vol. 1.7.2.

Gleizes, A. *Art and Religion. Art and Science. Art and Production*, transl. Peter Brooke (London, 1999).

Greenhalgh, M. *The survival of Roman antiquities in the Middle Ages* (London, 1989).

Hall, A. and Waelkens, M. Two Dokimeian sculptors in Iconium. *Anatolian Studies* 32 (1982), 151–155.

Harris, W. Roman terracotta lamps: the organization of an industry. *Journal of Roman Studies* 70 (1980), 126–145.

Hasebroek, J. *Trade and Politics in Ancient Greece* (New York, 1965).

Heilmeyer, W.-D. Kunst und Material, in: *Klassische Archäologie: eine Einführung*, edited by A. H. Borbein, T. Hölscher and P. Zanker (Berlin, 2000), 129–146.

Heilmeyer, W.-D. Ancient workshops and ancient 'art'. *Oxford Journal of Archaeology* 23.4 (2004), 403–415.

Huskinson, J. *Roman Children's Sarcophagi: their Decoration and Social Significance* (Oxford, 1996).

Huskinson, J. 'Unfinished portrait heads' on later Roman sarcophagi: some new perspectives. *Papers of the British School at Rome* 66 (1998), 129–158.

Işik, F. Zum Produktionsbeginn von Halbfabrikaten kleinasiatischer Girlandensarkophage. *Archäologischer Anzeiger* (1992), 121–145.

Işik, F. Zu Produktionsbeginn und Ende der kleinasiatischen Girlandensarkophage der Hauptgruppe, in: G. Koch (ed.), *Akten des Symposiums '125 Jahre Sarkophag-Corpus', Marburg, 4.–7. Oktober 1995. Sarkophag-Studien, vol. 1* (Mainz am Rhein, 1998), 278–294.

Işik, F. (ed.). *Girlanden-Sarkophage aus Aphrodisias. Sarkophag-Studien, vol. 5* (Mainz am Rhein, 2007).

Jongman, W. The early Roman Empire: consumption, in: *The Cambridge Economic History of the Greco-Roman World*, edited by W. Scheidel, I. Morris and R. Saller (Cambridge, 2007), 592–618.

Kehoe, D. The early Roman Empire: production, in: *The Cambridge Economic History of the Greco-Roman World*, edited by W. Scheidel, I. Morris and R. Saller (Cambridge, 2007), 543–569.

Klapish-Zuber, C. *Les maîtres du marbre: Carrare, 1300–1600* (Paris, 1969).

Koch, G. Das Import kaiserlicher Sarkophage in den römischen Provinzen Syria Palaestina und Arabia. *Bonner Jahrbücher* 189 (1989), 161–211.

Koch, G. *Sarkophage der römischen Kaiserzeit* (Darmstadt, 1993).

Koch, G. *Frühchristliche Sarkophage* (Munich, 2000).

Koch, G. and Sichtermann, H. *Römische Sarkophage* (Munich, 1982).

Koželj, T., Lambraki, A., Muller, A. and Sodini, J.-P. Sarcophages découvertes dans les carriers de Saliari (Thasos), in: *Marmi Antichi: problemi d'impiego, di restauro e d'identificazione. Studi Miscellanei 26*, edited by P. Pensabene (Rome, 1985), 75–82.

Kubrińska, J. *Les monuments funéraires dans les inscriptions grecques de l'Asie Mineure.* Travaux du Centre d'Archéologie Méditerranéenne de l'Academie Polonaise des Sciences, vol. 5 (Warsaw, 1968).

Love, J. *Antiquity and Capitalism: Max Weber and the Sociological Foundations of Roman Civilisation* (London, 1991).

Mackensen, M. *Militärlager oder Marmorwerkstätten. Neue untersuchungen im Ostbereich des Arbeits- und Steinbruchlagers von Simitthus/Chemtou* (Mainz am Rhein, 2005).

Mangartz, F. Zur Rekonstruktion der wassergetriebenen byzantischen Steinsägemaschine von Ephesos, Türkei – Vorbericht. *Archäologisches Korrespondenzblatt* 36.4 (2006), 573–590.

Manning, W. Industrial growth, in: *The Roman World*, edited by J. Wacher (London and New York, 1987), 586–610.

Marc, J.-Y. Who owned the marble quarries of Thasos during the imperial period?, in: Y. Maniatis, N. Herz and Y. Basiakos (eds.), *The Study of Marble and Other Stones Used in Antiquity. Papers from the Third Meeting of ASMOSIA at 'Demokritos', the National Centre for Scientific Research, Paraskevi, near Athens, Greece, May 17–19, 1993* (London, 1995), 33–38.

Märki-Boehringer, J., Deichmann, F. and Klauser, T. *Frühchristliche Sarkophage in Bild und Wort. Antike Kunst, Beiheft 3* (Olten, 1966).

McLean, B. *Greek and Latin inscriptions in the Konya Archaeological Museum. Regional Epigraphic Catalogues of Asia Minor, vol. 4* (London, 2002).

Mendel, G. *Catalogue des sculptures grecques, romaines et byzantines*, 3 vols. (Istanbul, 1912–1914).

Özgan, R. (ed.). *Die kaiserzeitlichen Sarkophage in Konya und Umgebung. Asia Minor Studien, vol. 46* (Bonn, 2003).

Peacock, D. *Pottery in the Roman World: an Ethnoarchaeological Approach* (London, 1982).

Pegoretti, G. *Manuale pratico per l'estimazione dei lavori architettonici, stradali, idraulici e di fortificazione per uso degli ingegneri ed architetti*, 2nd edn., 2 vols. (Milan, 1863–1864).

Penny, N. *The Materials of Sculpture* (New Haven and London, 1993).

Pensabene, P. *Le Vie del Marmo: i blocchi di cava di Roma e di Ostia, il fenomeno del marmo nella Roma antica* (Rome, 1994).

Pensabene, P. Il fenomeno del marmo nel mondo romano, in: *I Marmi Colorati della Roma Imperiale*, edited by M. De Nuccio and L. Ungara (Padua, 2002), 3–68.

Pensabene, P. Gli elementi marmorei della scena. Classificazione tipologica e inquadramento nella storia della decorazione architettonica in Asia Minore, in: *Il teatro di Hierapolis di Frigia. Restauro, architettura ed epigrafia*, edited by D. De Bernardi, G. Ciotta and P. Pensabene (Genoa, 2007), 229–338.

Pralong, A. Trouvailles dans une carrière phrygienne inconnue: une inscription rupestre et un sarcophage 'in situ'. *Revue Archéologique* (1980), 251–262.

Pucci, G. La produzione della ceramica aretina. Note sull' 'industria' nella prima età imperiale romana. *Dialoghi di Archeologia* 7 (1973), 255–293.

Rakob, F. Das römische Steinbruchlager (Praesidium) in Simitthus, in: *Simitthus II: der Tempelberg und das römische Lager*, edited by F. Rakob (Mainz am Rhein, 1994), 51–140.

Reynolds, J. Honouring benefactors at Aphrodisias: a new inscription, in: *Aphrodisias Papers 3. The setting and quarries, mythological and other sculptural decoration, architectural development, Portico of Tiberius, and Tetrapylon. JRA Supplementary Series, vol. 20*, edited by C. Roueché and R. Smith (Ann Arbor, 1996), 121–126.

Reynolds, J. and Roueché, C. The inscriptions, in: *Girlanden-Sarkophage aus Aphrodisias. Sarkophag-Studien, vol. 5*, edited by F. Işik (Mainz, 2007), 147–192.

Ritti, T. Epigrafi sepolcrali, in: *Hierapolis di Frigia, 1957–1987* (Turin, 1987), 113–115.

Ritti, T., Grewe, K. and Kessener, P. A relief of a water-powered stone saw mill on a sarcophagus at Hierapolis and its implications. *Journal of Roman Archaeology* 20.1 (2007), 139–163.

Rockwell, P. *The Art of Stoneworking. A Reference Guide* (Cambridge, 1993).

Ronchetta, D. Necropoli, in: *Hierapolis di Frigia, 1957–1987* (Turin, 1987), 104–112.

Seigne, J. A sixth-century water-powered sawmill at Jerash. *Annual of the Department of Antiquities of Jordan* 26 (2002), 205–213.

Smith, R. The use of images: visual history and ancient history, in: *Classics in Progress. Essays on Ancient Greece and Rome*, edited by T. Wiseman (Oxford, 2002), 59–102.

Smith, R. Sarcophagi and Roman citizenship, in: *Aphrodisias Papers 4: New Research on the City and its Monuments. JRA Supplementary Series, vol. 70*, edited by C. Ratté and R. Smith (Portsmouth, R.I, 2008), 347–394.

Stewart, P. *The Social History of Roman Art* (Cambridge, 2008).

Stokes, A. *The Stones of Rimini* (London, 1934).

Throckmorton, P. Ancient shipwreck yields new facts – and a strange cargo. *National Geographic* 135 (1969), 282–300.

Trimble, J. Replicating the body politic: the Herculaneum Women statue types in Early Imperial Italy. *Journal of Roman Archaeology* 13 (2000), 41–68.

Vanhaverbeke, H. and Waelkens, M. The northwestern necropolis of Hierapolis (Phrygia). The chronological and topographical distribution of the travertine sarcophagi and their way of production, in: *Hierapolis. Scavi e ricerche, IV: Saggi in onore Di Paolo Verzone*, edited by D. De Bernardi (Rome, 2002), 119–146.

Waelkens, M. *Dokimeion. Die Werkstatt der repräsentativen kleinasiatischen Sarkophage. Chronologie und Typologie ihrer Produktion. Archäologische Forschungen, vol. 11* (Berlin, 1982).

Waelkens, M. Production patterns of sarcophagi in Phrygia, in: *Classical Marble: Geochemistry, Technology and Trade NATO ASI Series E: Applied Sciences, vol. 153*, edited by N. Herz and M. Waelkens (Dordrecht, 1988), 139–144.

Walker, S. The marble quarries of Proconnesos: isotopic evidence for the age of the quarries and for the lenos-sarcophagus carved at Rome, in: *Marmi Antichi: problemi d'impiego, di restauro e d'identificazione. Studi Miscellanei 26*, edited by P. Pensabene (Rome, 1985), 57–68.

Walker, S. *Catalogue of Roman Sarcophagi in the British Museum* (London, 1990).

Ward-Perkins, J. The imported sarcophagi of Roman Tyre. *Bulletin du Musée de Beyrouth* 22 (1969), 109–145.

Ward-Perkins, J. Nicomedia and the marble trade. *Papers of the British School at Rome* 48 (1980), 23–69.

Ward-Perkins, J. The marble trade and its organization: evidence from Nicomedia, in: *The Seaborne Commerce of Ancient Rome: Studies in Archaeology and History. Memoirs of the American Academy in Rome 36*, edited by J. D'Arms and E. C. Kopff (Rome, 1980), 325–336.

Ward-Perkins, J, and Throckmorton, P. The San Pietro Wreck. *Archaeology* 18 (1965), 201–209.

Wiegartz, H. *Kleinasiatische Säulensarkophage. Untersuchungen zum Sarkophagtypus und zu den figürlichen Darstellungen* (Berlin, 1965).

Wiegartz, H. Marmorhandel, Sarkophagherstellung und die Lokalisierung der kleinasiatischen Säulensarkophage, in: *Mansel'e Armağan/Mélanges Mansel*, 3 vols., edited by E. Akurgal and U. Bahadir Alkim (Ankara, 1974), 345–383.

Wilson, A. Machines, power and the ancient economy. *Journal of Roman Studies* 92 (2002), 1–32.

Wilson, A. Large-scale manufacturing, standardization, and trade, in: *The Oxford Handbook of Engineering and Technology in the Classical World*, edited by J. Oleson (Oxford, 2008), 393–417.

Wurch-Koželj, M. and Koželj, T. Roman quarries of apse-sarcophagi in Thasos of the second and third centuries, in: Y. Maniatis, N. Herz and Y. Basiakos (eds.), *The Study of Marble and Other Stones Used in Antiquity. Papers from the Third Meeting of ASMOSIA at 'Demokritos', the National Centre for Scientific Research, Paraskevi, near Athens, Greece, May 17–19, 1993* (London, 1995), 39–50.

5.
Multimethod Analyses of Roman Sarcophagi at the Museo Nazionale Romano, Rome

Frances Van Keuren, Donato Attanasio, John J. Herrmann, Jr., Norman Herz, L. Peter Gromet

Analytical Method

In the fall of 2007 and the spring of 2008, 27 marble chips from 20 sarcophagi at the Museo Nazionale Romano in the Baths of Diocletian, Rome (hereafter MNR), were analysed, in order to determine the provenances of their marbles.[1] (The Report is presented here as Appendix 1, with supporting graphs and tables, at the end of this article.) Dr. Donato Attanasio from the Istituto di Struttura della Materia, the Consiglio Nazionale delle Ricerche, Rome, first determined the colour and the maximum grain size (MGS) of each sample. He then conducted Electron Paramagnetic Resonance (EPR) analyses of the samples. Next, stable isotope analyses were carried out by Julia Cox at the Stable Isotope Laboratory of the University of Georgia Department of Geology, Athens, Georgia. Finally, Dr. Attanasio used the six resultant variables – the colour and MGS of the marble chips, the intensity and linewidth obtained from the EPR analyses, and the oxygen and carbon ratios obtained from the stable isotope analyses – to determine quarry assignments for the 20 sarcophagi. These assignments were achieved by running the data of the six variables through statistical commercial software (STATISTICA 7.1 and SPSS 13.0).

Process and Explanation of Analytical Techniques

The first step in the analyses of the 20 sarcophagi at the Museo Nazionale Romano was for Dr. Attanasio to chisel off small marble chips from the back surfaces of the chests and lids of the sarcophagi under investigation. He then took the samples to his laboratory.

1 All but one of the sarcophagi are in the Michelangelesque cloister, commonly referred to as the Chiostro Grande. The exception is a sarcophagus with Medea (Figure 5.3), located in Aula VI of the same museum.

To determine the colour of each marble sample, the surface of each chip was polished. Then a digital scan of this polished surface was taken at 300 or 600 dpi (dots per inch) resolution. Using a Kodak grey scale with the aid of Adobe Photoshop, the colour value of each pixel was measured on an 8-bit scale (black = 0, white = 255) and then used to obtain the average colour value of the sample.[2]

Then, to determine the maximum grain size of each chip, Dr. Attanasio treated the already polished surface for 30 seconds with dilute hydrochloric acid (HCl2N). The acid was applied to 'display the edges of the crystalline grains more clearly.'[3] The largest grains were then measured using 'a normal reflecting microscope.'[4]

Next, Dr. Attanasio detached part of the marble chip, about 30 mg., and finely ground it 'in an agate mortar and then weighed [it] within a normal quartz EPR tube (internal diameter 2.8–2.9 mm), to a precision of 0.1 mg.'[5]

Each sample was then placed in 'a cavity resonator placed at the centre of the field poles of an electromagnet ... which is connected to another two fundamental components of the spectrometer: the microwave source (usually a klystron) and a detector for measuring the obtained signals ... The sample within the cavity is irradiated with microwaves of a known constant frequency ... Scanning of the magnetic field then takes place and when the value of H_0 [the external magnetic field] reaches the resonance value ... absorption of energy by the sample occurs, the system goes into a state of imbalance and a signal that is presented as a spectrum reaches the detector.'[6] Dr. Attanasio explains that 'the resonance condition consists of irradiating the sample with electromagnetic waves of a suitable frequency such that a transition from the lowest to the highest level [of energy] is induced. This can be seen as a reversal from an antiparallel to a parallel orientation (spin-flip) and the change of the direction of rotation (spin) of the electron.'[7]

The spectrum that is obtained from inducing a resonance state in the sample is usually given in the form of what are called first derivative curves. They consist of a series of peaks and valleys, oriented along a central line. It is the spectrum of the element manganese (Mn^{2+}) that Dr. Attanasio examined. Mn^{2+} is a magnetic impurity that occurs in all marbles, but there are variations between quarries in 'the type and arrangement of atoms that are found around the manganese ions.' These variations 'depend on the particular type of material

2 Attanasio 2003, 99.
3 Attanasio 2003, 97.
4 Attanasio 2003, 97.
5 Attanasio 2003, 82.
6 Attanasio 2003, 62 and 79.
7 Attanasio 2003, 62.

and on its provenance.'[8] Two aspects of the Mn^{2+} are studied – the intensity or concentration of the manganese and the linewidth, or the temporal extent of the resonance condition. Table 1 in Dr. Attanasio's report in Appendix 1 gives the intensities and linewidths that were obtained for the 27 samples under investigation, and Graph 4 plots the logarithms of these intensities and linewidths.

The presence of manganese in marble goes back to the conditions of formation of marble's protolith, limestone. Nicholas E. Pingitore, Jr. explains what limestone is composed of, how it is lithified, and how manganese infiltrates it:

> Typically composed of the skeletal remnants of marine organisms,[9] most limestones are lithified by exposure to fresh water. This transition from carbonate sediment to limestone rock comes about through changes in texture, mineralogy, and chemistry of the sedimentary particles. Mineralogic stabilisation is accompanied by changes in minor and trace elements … [Manganese (Mn^{2+}) has] the proper charge and ionic radii to substitute freely for calcium in the calcite lattice.[10]

Subsequent to lithification, limestone is metamorphosed into marble, through heat and pressure. Both limestone and marble are most commonly composed of the mineral calcite (calcium carbonate). However, they can also be composed of the mineral dolomite (calcium-magnesium carbonate; see below for a discussion of dolomitic marble from Cape Vathy, Thasos).[11]

After determining the colour and MGS, and conducting the EPR analyses of parts of the 27 marble chips, Dr. Attanasio mailed what remained of the chips to the laboratory maintained by Julia Cox in Athens, Georgia. She then determined the stable isotopes of the samples.

The geological definition for isotopes is that they are atoms of the same element, which have both shared and different features. What is the same in isotopes is the number of positively-charged protons. Isotopes differ in their number of uncharged neutrons, and hence in their weights. The reason quarries can be differentiated by their stable isotope structures is that the limestone protoliths were formed under slightly different conditions. According to Scott Pike, 'the isotopic composition of a marble's limestone protolith is principally controlled by crystallisation temperature, chemical composition and the isotopic ratios of the water.'[12] When limestone protoliths are metamorphosed into

8 Attanasio 2003, 57, 60 and 81.

9 Other types of limestone were formed biogenically, i. e. with microorganisms, and chemically. Email from Norman Herz of October 22, 2008; and Herz 1988, 235–236.

10 Pingitore 1978, 799–800.

11 Herz and Garrison 1998, 200; Tykot et al. 2002, 189.

12 This quotation was supplied to me by Prof. Pike from his unpublished dissertation; Pike 2000. See also Herz 1988, 235–236.

marbles, the marbles preserve the isotopic structures of their protoliths. However, Norman Herz notes that when limestone is in the process of metamorphosis, there can be additional alterations to its isotopic structure. He observes that 'the higher the temperature [of metamorphosis] the lower the ^{18}O.'[13]

There are stable, i. e. non-radioactive, and unstable, i. e. radioactive isotopes. The stable isotopes that are analysed or counted in an isotopic analysis of a marble sample are Carbon 12 and Carbon 13, and Oxygen 16 and Oxygen 18. Carbon 12 has 6 protons and 6 neutrons, while Carbon 13 has 6 protons and 7 neutrons. Oxygen 16 has 8 protons and 8 neutrons, and Oxygen 18 has 8 protons and 10 neutrons. Carbon 12 and Oxygen 16, the lighter isotopes, are far more abundant in nature than Carbon 13 and Oxygen 18, the heavier isotopes.

Ms. Cox's first step in the stable isotope analyses was to prepare each sample. She drilled off a small quantity of marble dust from each chip. Less than 5 mg. of material are needed to conduct an isotopic analysis.[14] The second step in the analysis process was to dissolve the sample in acid. This converts the carbon and oxygen isotopes into molecules of carbon dioxide gas, or CO2. The carbon dioxide gas was then ionized, which involves the stripping of an electron from each molecule, and a resultant positive charge.

These ionized gas molecules were then accelerated towards a negative charge at the end of a tube within a mass spectrometer. The tube was magnetized. The magnet deflected or altered the course of the gas molecules. A molecule with light isotopes of carbon and/or oxygen was deflected more than a molecule with heavy isotopes of the same element(s). Collectors located at different positions at the end of the flight tube counted the molecules with the differing weights.[15] From the six different possible weights of the CO2 molecules, the types and numbers of isotopes were calculated. For example, a molecule with a weight of 44 would contain one Carbon 12 isotope and two Oxygen 16 isotopes.

The resultant counts of the carbon and oxygen isotopes allowed specific ratios to be determined. One ratio expressed the proportion of Carbon 13 versus Carbon 12 isotopes, and the other expressed the proportion of Oxygen 18 versus Oxygen 16 isotopes. These carbon and oxygen ratios from each sample were then related to the ratios of the same isotopes from a standard. A delta number expressed the difference in abundance of the heavy isotope in each sample, in relation to the abundance of that isotope in the standard. The delta number is like a percentage difference, except that it is expressed in parts per thousand rather than in parts per hundred.

13 Email of October 22, 2008.

14 Herz and Garrison 1998, 273.

15 Herz and Garrison 1998, 273.

Table 1 from Dr. Attanasio's report (in Appendix 1) provides the delta numbers that Ms. Cox obtained through her stable isotope analyses of the 27 samples, and Graphs 2–3 locate the points corresponding to these delta numbers. The vertical axis on the two graphs provides the location for the Carbon 13 number, and the horizontal axis supplies the location of the Oxygen 18 number.

Besides plotting the 27 samples, the two graphs include ellipses that indicate the distribution of the isotopic data for some of these ancient quarries – Afyon [Afy], Carrara [Ca], Ephesos (Kusini Tepe [Eph/KT], Belevi [Eph/BG], Aya Klikiri), Hymettos, Miletos, Paros (Marathi, Marathi lychnites, Chorodaki [Pa/Cho]), Pentelicon [Pe], Proconnesos [Pro], and Thasos calcitic.[16] Each ellipse incorporates the isotopic analysis results for multiple samples collected by Dr. Attanasio from that quarry. Altogether, his database contains 852 samples from the quarries listed.[17]

Dr. Attanasio calls the rounded fields for the quarries their probability ellipses. As he explains in his report, the closer to the centre of an ellipse a sample of unknown provenance is positioned, the more likely it is to come from the quarry represented by that ellipse (see Table 2 in Appendix 1 for the relative and absolute probabilities that the 27 samples have been correctly assigned to quarries). If there were no overlap of the ellipses for the quarries, secure assignments to quarries of samples of unknown provenances could be made on the basis of stable isotope analyses alone. However, as is immediately apparent from the two graphs, there is extensive overlap of the quarries' probability fields. For example, the field for Carrara lies completely inside the field for Proconnesos. Thus, neither quarry can be eliminated as a possible provenance for samples whose isotopic results fall inside both fields.

If the same samples that fall within both quarry fields are analysed in additional ways, discrimination between Carrara and Proconnesian marble can be achieved. For example, the manganese (Mn^{2+}) concentration or intensity of Proconnesian marble, as determined by EPR analyses, is much lower than that of Carrara marble (see the data for quarries at the end of Table 1). This difference in intensity results in an almost complete separation of the EPR fields for Carrara and Proconnesos that are plotted in Graph 4. Note that here all the samples in the Carrara field (see samples 11 and 12 from Figure 5.2) are located outside of the field for Proconnesos (see samples 26 and 27 from Figure 5.3). However, in Graph 4 there is still overlap between the fields for Pentelicon and

16 The quarries for which abbreviations are provided are those whose ellipses are included in Graphs 2–3. The quarries for which abbreviations are not provided were considered as possible provenances, but their ellipses are not shown in Graphs 2–3. For information on the periods of use of these quarries, see Attanasio 2003; and Attanasio et al. 2006.

17 Attanasio et al. 2006, 65, Table 2.2.

Afyon, which resulted in uncertainty of quarry assignment regarding samples 4–5 (Figure 5.4), and samples 13 and 14 (from the chest of Figure 5.1).

To continue the description of the analyses of the 27 samples, after Ms. Cox finished conducting the stable isotope analyses, she sent the delta numbers of the results to Dr. Attanasio. Using statistical commercial software (STATISTICA 7.1 and SPSS 13.0), he then gave different weights to the six experimental variables or discriminants that he now had for the 27 samples – the delta numbers for the Oxygen 18 and Carbon 13 isotopes, the MGS and colour of the samples, and the intensity and linewidth obtained from the EPR analyses. The purpose of the different weighting was to maximize the separation of the ellipses representing the quarry fields.

Three different formulas were used to determine three different discriminant coordinates for each sample. Discriminant coordinate 1 was the sum of the sample's intensity multiplied by 0.82, plus the delta number for Oxygen 18 multiplied by 0.64, plus minor contributions from other discriminants. Discriminant coordinate 2 was the maximum grain size multiplied by 0.88, plus the intensity multiplied by 0.53, plus minor contributions from other discriminants. Discriminant coordinate 3 was the delta number for Carbon 13 multiplied by 0.71, plus the delta number for Oxygen 18 multiplied by 0.63, plus much less contributions from other discriminants.

These three discriminant coordinates then became the vertical and horizontal axes for Graphs 5 and 6 in Dr. Attanasio's report, which plot the 27 samples and the most important quarry fields. As is evident from Graph 6, sample 14 now falls within the ellipse for Pentelicon and outside that of Afyon. Thus, the marble of the chest of MNR 128581 (Figure 5.1), from which samples 13 and 14 were taken, can be identified as Pentelic. However, sample 4 still falls within the ellipses for both Pentelicon and Afyon on Graphs 5 and 6, and sample 5 falls only within the ellipse for Afyon in Graphs 5 and 6. The micaceous inclusions in the Medea sarcophagus (Figure 5.4), from which both samples 4 and 5 were taken, demonstrates, though, that the marble for both samples must be Pentelic.

Summary of Analysis Results

Graph 1 in Dr. Attanasio's report summarises the final assignments to quarries that were made on the basis of the isotopic and EPR analyses, and the statistical analyses of the six experimental variables or discriminants. The chests of twenty sarcophagi from the Museo Nazionale Romano were analysed. Five of these sarcophagi had lids, which were also analysed. Thus, a total of 25 pieces were analysed. Fourteen of these pieces proved to be of Proconnesian marble. Twelve

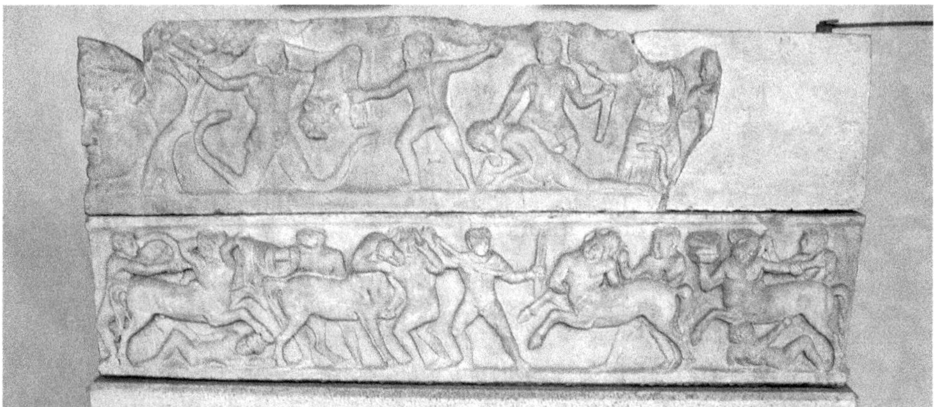

Figure 5.1: Roman child's sarcophagus from Pomezia, c. 140, with Gigantomachy on the lid and Centauromachy on the chest. Lid of Carrara marble and chest of Pentelic marble. MNR 128581 (samples 13–15). Photograph : Frances Van Keuren.

of these pieces are chests from sarcophagi whose lids have been lost.[18] The thirteenth and fourteenth pieces are a lid and chest from the same sarcophagus (samples 26 and 27 from Figure 5.3). Seven pieces were assigned to Carrara. All but one of these pieces consisted of chests and lids from three sarcophagi (e. g., samples 11 and 12 from Figure 5.2, and samples 21 and 22 from Figures 5.5–5.6). The seventh piece is the lid from a sarcophagus whose chest proved to be of Pentelic marble (sample 15 from Figure 5.1). Finally, four pieces were assigned to Pentelicon. Three of these pieces are chests for which the lids have been lost (e. g., samples 4 and 5 from Figure 5.4), and the fourth piece is the chest from the already-mentioned sarcophagus whose lid was identified as Carrara marble (samples 13 and 14 from Figure 5.1).

Sarcophagi Analysed

Carrara Marble

The seven samples that have been assigned to Carrara come from the lids and chests of three sarcophagi and the lid of a fourth sarcophagus (Figure 5.1). The earliest of the Carrara pieces is the lid from a child's sarcophagus, found in Pomezia in Latium, of c. 140 (Figure 5.1). The lid depicts a Gigantomachy and

18 In the case of MNR 124735, the sarcophagus was furnished with a flat slab of marble rather than a proper lid.

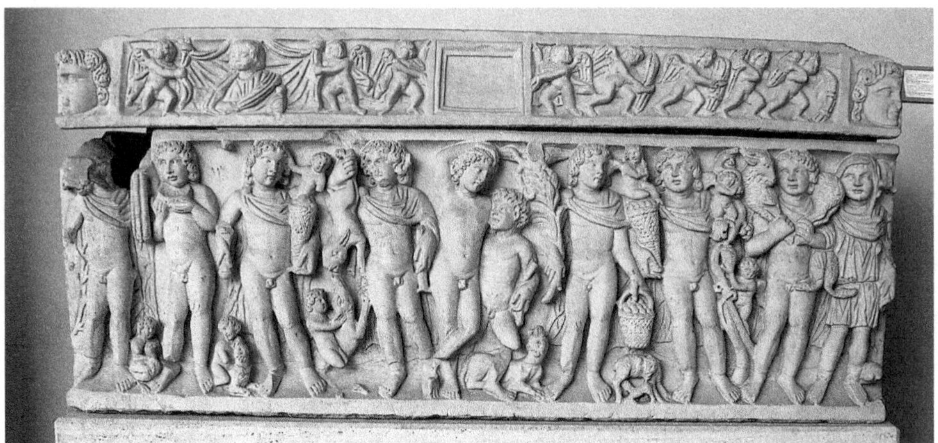

Figure 5.2: Roman sarcophagus of unknown provenance, c. 320, with Dionysos and four Seasons. Lid and chest of Carrara marble. MNR 407 (samples 11–12). Photograph: Frances Van Keuren.

the chest, assigned to Pentelicon, shows a Centauromachy.[19] The lid and chest of the next Carrara sarcophagus, a garland sarcophagus found in Vigna Casali, Rome, are dated c. 130–150. The chest has a pair of tragic masks above the left garland and a pair of comic masks above the right garland. On the lid are four reclining Seasons.[20]

There is a chronological gap between these sarcophagi from the early Antonine period and the next two sarcophagi from the first half of the fourth century. One, dated c. 320, shows Dionysus and a satyr in the centre of the chest, flanked by the four Seasons. The lid shows the female deceased, a blank funerary tablet, and eight Erotes, four of whom gather grain (Figure 5.2).[21] This sarcophagus, like the second sarcophagus from the fourth century, appears of be made of reused material, since its lower left corner was added in a separate piece. The chest of the second sarcophagus (Figures. 5.5–5.6), found in a burial chamber on the Via Decima in the Malpasso locality, Rome, and of coarser execution than Figure 5.2, has two strigillated panels that flank a bust of the deceased, a youth wearing a tunic and *pallium* and holding a scroll, enclosed in a

19 MNR 128581: samples 13, 14 and 15. Sapelli, in Giuliano 1981, 57–58; Koch and Sichtermann 1982, 147; Vian and Moore 1988, 243, no. 501, pl. 154; *ASR* XII,2, 170–171, no. 148, pls. 120–121; and Huskinson 1996, 27, no. 2.5.

20 MNR 121657: samples 2–3. Honroth 1971, 57–58, and 89, no. 107; Dayan and Musso, in Giuliano 1981, 144–146; *ASR* VI,2,1, 118, no. 61.

21 MNR 407: samples 11–12. Musso, in Giuliano 1981, 128–131; *ASR* IV, 4, 448, no. 256.

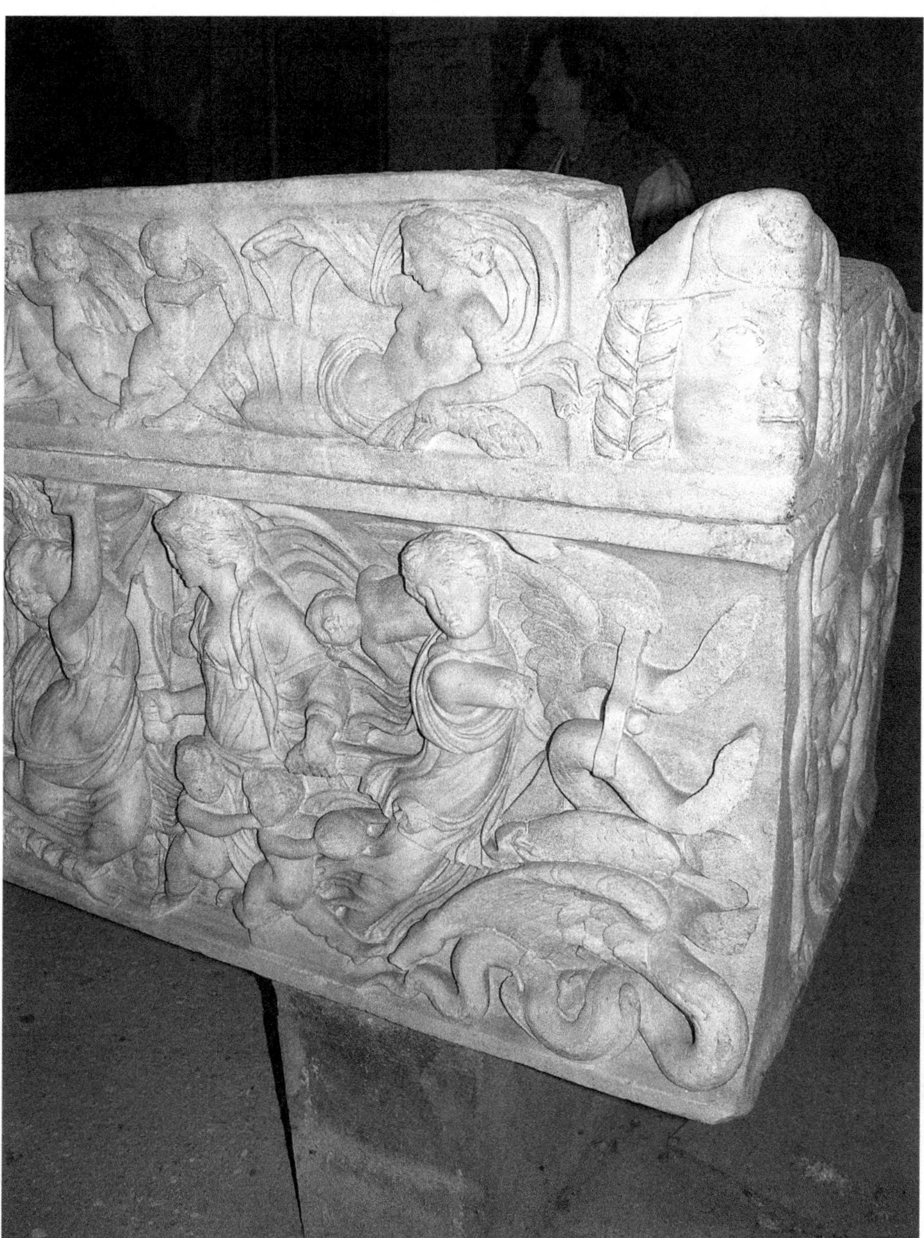

Figure 5.3: Detail of right front of Roman sarcophagus from Via di Porta Maggiore, Rome, c. 150–160, with story of Creusa and Medea. Lid and chest of Proconnesian marble. MNR 75248 (samples 26–27). Photograph: Frances Van Keuren.

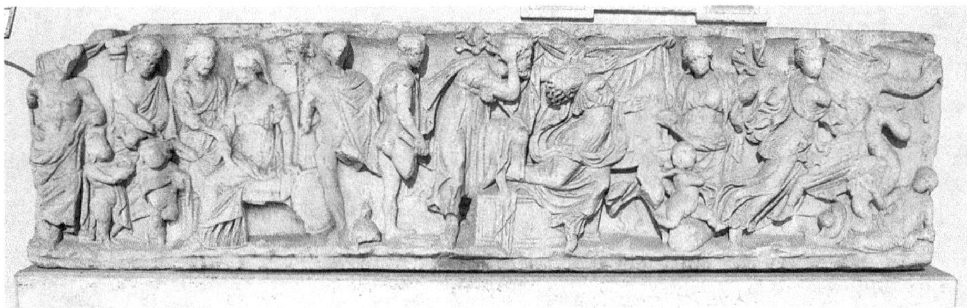

Figure 5.4: Roman sarcophagus dated c. 170, and known since the late sixteenth century, with the story of Creusa and Medea. Pentelic marble. MNR 222 (samples 4–5). Photograph: Frances Van Keuren.

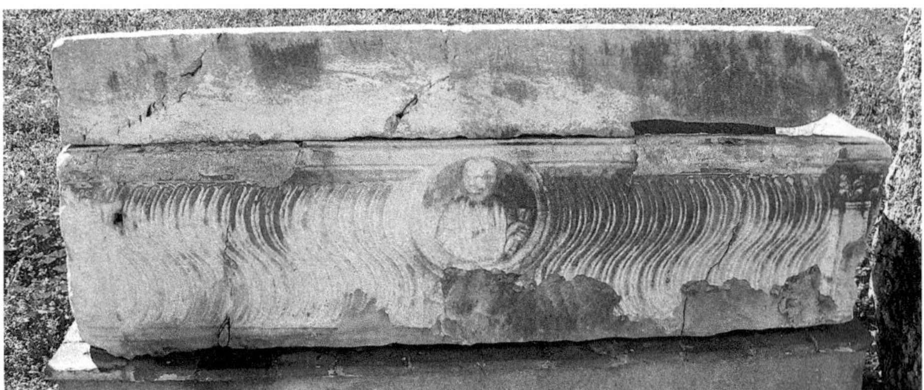

Figure 5.5: Roman sarcophagus from a burial chamber on the Via Decima, Rome, c. 300–350, with two strigillated panels that flank a bust of the deceased youth. Lid and chest of Carrara marble. MNR 115247 (samples 21–22). Photograph: Frances Van Keuren.

roundel, which evokes a shield (*clipeus*).[22] The undecorated lid is too deep for its chest and sawn, not chiselled. The chest of this sarcophagus, which appears to have been executed in the first half of the fourth century, may be a reworked block. The diagonal division and the stray holes on its back side strongly suggest reuse.[23]

22 MNR 115247: samples 21–22. Pietrogrande 1934, 166–168; Dayan, in Giuliano 1982, 79–80.

23 Email from John J. Herrmann, Jr. of October 31, 2008. For further discussion of these sarcophagi, see Herrmann, Appendix 2 below.

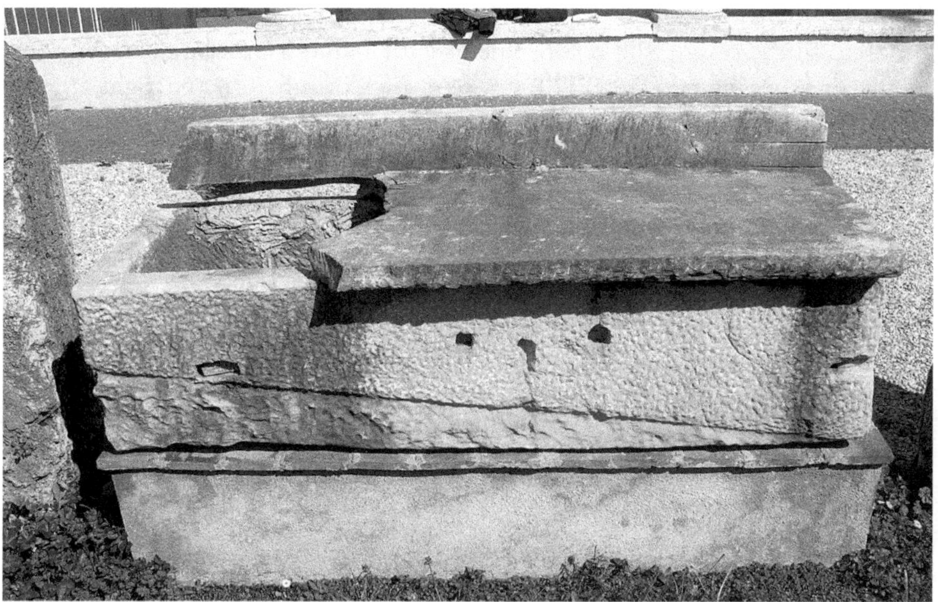

Figure 5.6: Back side of Figure 5.5 showing evidence of a previous use. Photograph: Frances Van Keuren.

Proconnesian Marble

Thirteen sarcophagi at the Museo Nazionale Romano proved to be made of Proconnesian marble. The sarcophagi range in date from the middle Antonine period, through the third century.

The first piece, a child's sarcophagus of c. 150, depicts Meleager and the Calydonian boar in the central columned niche, flanked on each side by a strigillated panel; on the far left, Atalanta stands with a hound, and on the far right is a second hero.[24]

The second sarcophagus was found in a funerary chamber on the Via di Porta Maggiore, Rome. The detail of the right front in Figure 5.3 clearly shows the grey banding that is characteristic of Proconnesian marble.[25] Dated c. 150–160, the sarcophagus illustrates the story of Creusa and Medea on the front of

24 MNR 56138: sample 8. *ASR* XII,6, 130–131, no. 144, pls. 120 and 122; Musso, in Giuliano 1981, 115–117; Woodford 1992, 422–423, no. 71, pl. 215; and Huskinson 1996, 28, no. 2.20.

25 Attanasio et al. 2006, 201; and Attanasio et al. 2008, 748.

the chest.[26] On the left, Creusa receives the fatal wedding gifts from Medea's children. In the centre, she is consumed by the flames from the poisoned robe, in the presence of her father, King Creon of Corinth. On the right, Medea contemplates killing her two sons by Jason, and then flies away with their bodies on her chariot drawn by two winged serpents. The lid shows four reclining Seasons.

The third middle Antonine sarcophagus, of unknown provenance, has an inscribed tablet on the centre of the chest with the name of Lucius Tuccius Corinthianus. On each side the tablet is upheld by a Nike flying above an overturned basket containing fruit on one side and flowers on the other.[27]

The next Proconnesian sarcophagus, dated to the late Antonine period, is of special interest because of its extensive paint traces. Found on the Via Lidia, Rome, it has an oak wreath in the centre of the chest enclosing the name of Ulpia Domina. A pair of Nikai supports the wreath, and beneath each one is a cornucopia. A winged genius with downturned torch stands on the far left and far right.[28]

A fragment of a sarcophagus from the late second century shows a draped reclining male, who leans on an animal that is probably a dog. Identified as Endymion, this figure was probably from the right corner of the front of a chest, as on a sarcophagus with the same theme in the Louvre.[29]

On a child's sarcophagus of c. 200 two Erotes hold up a shield inscribed with the name of Publius Flavius Alexander at the centre of the chest. Two Erotes on the left drag a goat to sacrifice, while two more Erotes on the right stand at an altar.[30]

Another sarcophagus dated c. 200 was for the burial of a girl. She is depicted in the centre of the chest inside a laurel wreath, which is supported by a pair of flying Erotes. On the far left and far right are Cupid and Psyche embracing.[31]

26 MNR 75248: samples 26–27. Schmidt 1968, 21, 45 note 4, pl. 32.2; Musso, in Giuliano 1985, 279–283; Berger-Doer 1992, 122, no. 5, 124, no. 21, pl. 54; and Gaggadis-Robin 1994, 12, no. 8, figs. 10–12.

27 MNR 72879: sample 9. Dayan, Musso and Friggeri, in Giuliano 1981, 104–105.

28 MNR 125891: sample 6. Dayan, Musso and Friggeri, in Giuliano 1981, 86–88.

29 MNR fragment without inventory number: sample 20. Sapelli, in Giuliano 1982, 72–73; and *ASR* XII,2, 159, no. 116, pl. 113.4. The Louvre sarcophagus, dated to the early third century, is in Baratte and Metzger 1985, 67–69, no. 23; and *ASR* XII,2, 117–118, no. 55, pl. 51.1. University of Georgia graduate student Maria Graffagnino found the iconographic parallel of the Louvre sarcophagus.

30 MNR 226119: sample 16. Dayan, Musso and Sabbatini Tumolesi, in Giuliano 1981, 48–49; and Huskinson 1996, 50, no. 6.32.

31 MNR sarcophagus without inventory number: sample 25. Musso, in Giuliano 1981, 98–99; Blanc and Gury 1986, 981, no. 202, pl. 692; Huskinson 1996, 53, no. 7.6, where the marble is identified as Carrara.

A sarcophagus dated c. 220 and found on the Via Casilina in Rome, shows a portrait bust of the deceased in a *clipeus*, which is held by two flying Genii. Beneath the *clipeus* are an eagle, Oceanus and Tellus, and on the far left and far right edges of the chest are groups of Cheiron instructing Achilles in the lyre.[32]

A very well preserved, round-ended chest, resembling a vat (*lenos*), was found in Tomb D on the Via Belluzzo, Rome. Although it has the size of an adult sarcophagus, the *lenos* contained the skeleton of a ten-year-old girl. It is decorated with strigillations and two *clipei* with busts of Helios and Selene, which both appear to have the face of the deceased.[33] In the excavation report, Rita Santolini dates the *lenos* to the first decades of the third century, but stylistically it resembles the 'Badminton Sarcophagus' in New York, a *lenos* that is itself difficult to date but which must be from the late Severan period or later.[34]

A fragmentary *lenos* featuring the musical contest between the satyr Marsyas and Apollo, and the subsequent flaying of Marsyas, is another sarcophagus that exhibits stylistic similarities to the 'Badminton Sarcophagus'. The part of the *lenos* that is preserved is the base and the lower part of the sculptured figures. It was found with parts of many other sarcophagi, in a dump close to the Trastevere station, Rome. Additional fragments that show the upper parts of figures from the musical contest and flaying, and that match the missing parts of the two scenes on the *lenos*, clearly come from its front and right sides. These matching fragments are located at the National Gallery in Oslo and the Metropolitan Museum of Art in New York.[35] All three portions have now been analysed, with results that exhibited unexpected variations.[36] These variations

32 MNR 124735: sample 10. Sapelli, in Giuliano 1981, 90–93; *ASR* XII,1, 195, no. 3.

33 Sample 1. Santolini 1986–87, 130–134; Gury 1994, 707, no. 1. University of Georgia graduate student Soon Bae Kim identified the closest iconographic parallel for the *lenos*, a funerary altar of Iulia Victorina from the late first century, which shows the deceased child both in the guise of Luna and Sol. See Letta 1988, 623, no. 454, pl. 384.

34 For the Badminton Sarcophagus, see note 70 below. In an email of December 7, 2008, John J. Herrmann Jr. noted these common features in the two *lenoi:* 'Smooth and rubbery [treatment]. Flowing hair curling around a drill hole. Identical hands around shaft of pole or thyrsus. Similar facial proportions – and simplified modelling … Generally simplified, easy stylisation.'

35 MNR *lenos* without inventory number: sample 23. Bartoli 1953, 1–2, fig. 1; McCann 1978, 79–84, no. 13; Sande 1981; Musso, in Giuliano 1982, 82–86, where the marble is identified as Carrara; Rawson 1987, 184–186, no. XX, figs. 5, 18 and 57. Mancini 1913, 117–118, who reported on the initial discovery of the *lenos*, wrote: 'Fra la terra di scarico si rinvennero in grande quantità resti di sarcofagi.'

36 The results of these additional analyses were presented in a poster at the IX International Conference ASMOSIA (Association for the Study of Marble and Other Stones in Antiquity): Interdisciplinary Studies on Ancient Stone, Tarragona, 8–13 June 2009. Entitled 'Isotopic, EPR and Petrographic Analyses of 20 Roman Sarcophagi at the Museo Nazionale Romano, Rome', the poster was co-authored by Frances Van Keuren,

may be due to the quarrying of the block for the *lenos* from the C-5 part of the Proconnesian quarries, where samples of large variability were collected.[37]

A sarcophagus with a funerary tablet bearing the name Aurelia Luciosa was found on the Via del Corso in Rome. The *tabula ansata* is flanked by two strigillated panels, and on the far left and right corners of the chest are Composite pilasters. The sarcophagus may have been produced in the third century.[38]

A sarcophagus from the Via Fezzan in Rome is difficult to date. According to Anna Maria Ramieri, the treatment of the two strigillated panels that flank the inscription tablet indicates that that the piece is one of the earliest examples of strigillated sarcophagi from the second century. Marina Bertinetti concludes that the inscription with the names of Lollia Valeria Maior and her husband Gaius Sicinius Olympius is later than the sarcophagus, i. e. from the third or fourth century. The latter scholar suggests, though, that the inscription may indicate a reuse of the sarcophagus in late antiquity.[39]

A fragment from the left corner of the front of a sarcophagus has not been dated, evidently due to the poor state of preservation of its surface. It depicts a nude male who moves to the right, while standing on tiptoe with his right leg advanced. He twists his torso back to the viewer's left, while raising a *syrinx* in his right hand. Over his left shoulder is an animal skin, and a panther bounds to the right at his feet. This figure was identified as Pan by Friedrich Matz, an identification which was followed by Anna Maria Ramieri.[40] However, the absence of goat legs on this figure and the uncertain nature of the flame-shaped protuberance over his forehead raise questions about his identity. Since he closely resembles a tiptoeing satyr with a *syrinx* on a *lenos* in Dresden, he seems more likely to be a satyr with a flame-shaped hair strand or ornament on a fillet.[41]

Julia Cox, Shelby Hipol, Donato Attanasio, John J. Herrmann, Jr., and Dorothy H. Abramitis. These analyses should also be published, in article form, in the conference volume.

37 Attanasio et al. 2008, 762–764; and email from Donato Attanasio of September 24, 2009.

38 MNR 524: sample 19. *CIL* 6.2, 1610, no. 13343; Ramieri and Bertinetti, in Giuliano 1982, 64–65.

39 MNR 126285: sample 18. Ramieri and Bertinetti, in Giuliano 1982, 62–64. The initial discovery of the sarcophagus is reported by Felletti Maj 1953, 234–235, fig. 1.

40 MNR 750: sample 17. *ASR* IV, 4, 482, no. 317; Ramieri, in Giuliano 1982, 107–108.

41 For the sarcophagus in Dresden, see *ASR* IV, 1, 159–161, no. 52, pl. 60. The satyr with the *syrinx* is Matz's figure type TH 61 (vol. 4, pt. 1, 44). Maria Graffagnino found this useful iconographic parallel.

Pentelic Marble

Three sarcophagi and the chest of a fourth were revealed to be of Pentelic marble. The earliest of the Pentelic pieces, a child's sarcophagus of c. 140, has already been discussed above, since the lid is of Carrara marble (see Figure 5.1). The chest, which shows a Centauromachy, is of Pentelic marble.[42] In spite of the difference of material, the lid and chest appear to have been carved by the same workshop.

A sarcophagus fragment, found at Ostia and dated c. 150–160, comes from the right corner of the front of a chest. The fragment is from a depiction of Pluto's rape of Proserpina. The horses from Pluto's chariot and the figure of Mercury who leads them to the Underworld are preserved, along with the thrown-back head, right arm and left foot of Proserpina, and the left thigh and knee of Pluto on his chariot.[43] There is also a second fragment believed to come from the same sarcophagus that shows the chariot with winged serpents belonging to Ceres. Although this fragment is reported to be in the Magazzini of the Museo Nazionale Romano, it could not be found for testing.[44]

Slightly later in date than the Proconnesian sarcophagus with the story of Creusa and Medea (Figure 5.3) is a Pentelic sarcophagus with the same theme (Figure 5.4).[45] On this second Medea sarcophagus, dated c. 170, the groupings of characters are arranged in a fashion very similar to the earlier example. Unfortunately, the surface of the Pentelic sarcophagus is very worn, evidently because it has been known since the sixteenth century, which makes stylistic comparison with the Proconnesian sarcophagus difficult. Nonetheless, the Pentelic sarcophagus appears to exhibit a flatter handling in the modelling of the figures and the drapery treatment, and it seems to rely on deeper drilling of details such as the pupils of the eyes. Thus, the two sarcophagi may well be the products of two different workshops, but they were clearly using common figural compositions, perhaps transmitted by means of copybooks with line drawings.

42 MNR 128581: samples 13, 14 and 15. Sapelli, in Giuliano 1981, 57–58; Sengelin 1997, 712, no. 404b, pl. 463; and Huskinson 1996, 27, no. 2.5.

43 MNR 654: sample 24. Visconti 1866, 325, pl. S.2 (engraving); *ASR* III, 3, 459–460, no. 360; Musso, in Giuliano 1982, 109–111.

44 Sichtermann 1974, 313–314, fig. 7; Blome 1978, 456. University of Georgia graduate student Katie Seefeldt researched this sarcophagus fragment and its iconographic parallels, which are listed in Angeli 1988, 901, nos. 126–134.

45 MNR 222: samples 4–5. Musso, in Giuliano 1981, 138–143; Berger-Doer 1992, 122, no. 7, pl. 53; Schmidt 1992, 393, no. 53, pl. 200; Gaggadis-Robin 1994, 17–18, no. 21, figs. 32–34. University of Georgia graduate student Chad Alligood researched the two Medea sarcophagi (Figures 5.3–5.4), and studied their iconographic similarities.

The latest Pentelic piece is a child's sarcophagus from Ostia, dated c. 280–300. In the centre of the chest is a portrait of an adult male in a *clipeus*, which was reworked from a portrait of a boy with a Horus lock. The *clipeus* is held up by a pair of standing Erotes, and beneath it is a cock fight. Two more Erotes with ducks and a rabbit stand on the far left and far right edges of the chest.[46]

Dolomitic Marble from Cape Vathy, Thasos

The genesis for undertaking the marble analyses reported in this article was the work on the sarcophagi at the Museo Nazionale Romano by John J. Herrmann, Jr., and Richard Newman. Using the definitive techniques of X-ray diffraction and the electron-beam microprobe, they determined that seven of the sarcophagi in the Chiostro Grande were made of dolomitic marble from the quarries on Cape Vathy, Thasos.[47] Dolomitic marble is composed almost entirely of the mineral dolomite, i. e. calcium-magnesium carbonate.[48] The attribution to Thasos was reinforced by the macroscopic characteristics of the marble (coarse grain and virtually unmarked white colour). The goal of the project whose results are presented in this article was to determine what calcitic marbles were attested in some of the additional sarcophagi in the Chiostro Grande, besides those of dolomitic marble.

Robert H. Tykot provides this explanation of X-ray diffraction and the electron-beam microprobe:

> These methods involve the measurement of characteristic wavelengths of electromagnetic radiation … absorbed or emitted when a sample is 'excited' (e. g. by bombardment with … X-rays, or electrons). A complex spectrum is produced in which peaks at certain wavelengths are characteristic of one or more elements, and the area under a peak (intensity) is proportional to the amount of that element present in the analyzed material.[49]

---

46 MNR 128086: sample 7. Schauenburg 1972, 512, note 53; Musso, in Giuliano 1981, 100–102; *ASR* V, 4, 197, no. 46; Blanc and Gury 1986, 982, no. 214; Huskinson 1996, 65, no. 9.29.

47 The analyses were conducted at the laboratory of the Museum of Fine Arts in Boston. See Herrmann and Newman 1995, 82; Herrmann and Newman 1999, 301; and Herrmann 1999, 57–58, 63, and 69. Another definitive technique for distinguishing calcitic from dolomitic marble is the application of dilute hydrochloric acid to a marble surface, chip or flakes. When there is no effervescence or fizzing, to use the layman's term, the marble must be dolomitic. When, on the other hand, there is effervescence, the marble must be calcitic.

48 Herz 1988, 236–237.

49 Tykot 2004, 410.

The seven sarcophagi from the Museo Nazionale Romano of dolomitic marble from Cape Vathy range in date from the Trajanic through the early Severan period.[50] The earliest one, found in Ostia and dated to the Trajanic period, belongs to a Greek artisan from Ephesus named Titus Flavius Trophimas. To the left of the inscription tablet, located on the centre of the chest, are depictions of Trophimas' two friends, who are shown practicing their crafts of shoemaking and rope making. Trophimas himself is shown to the right of the inscription tablet, in the role of an Isiac initiate.[51]

The second sarcophagus, found on the Via Aurelia in Rome and dated c. 120–150, contained the body of a ten-year-old girl named Flavia Sextiliane. The centre of the chest has the girl's name inscribed on a *clipeus* that is borne by a pair of flying Erotes. Additional Erotes stand with torches on the left and right edges of the chest, and the lid is decorated with more Erotes, some with arms.[52]

Two later sarcophagi of Antonine date depict Erotes making arms. One of the sarcophagi is from the Ponte Rotto in Rome, and the other has an unknown provenance. These sarcophagi share the motif of a shield in the centre of the chest, which is supported on the right by an Eros who stands with his head turned back and away from the shield.[53] The same motif can be found on a fragment of the Trajanic frieze from the temple of Venus Genetrix in Rome, which is believed to have served as a source of inspiration for all three sarcophagi from the Chiostro Grande that show Erotes with arms.[54]

Three Dionysiac dolomitic sarcophagi show a satyr and two maenads from Friedrich Matz's repertoire of Neo-Attic figure types. The survival of these Dionysiac types until the late Antonine and early Severan periods, when these sarcophagi are believed to have been produced, demonstrates the longevity of such figure types. Outline renderings of favourite Dionysiac figure types, kept in sarcophagus workshops, would be one possible means to preserve knowledge of such figure types over the centuries.

The first two Dionysiac sarcophagi appear to be contemporary, since they both have been dated c. 170–180. Each one was found in Rome and shows Dionysus in a chariot drawn by centaurs. One sarcophagus, found in the church of Sts. Nereus and Achilleus on the Via Appia, depicts the wine god discovering a sleeping Ariadne. The satyr directly to the viewer's right of Ariadne, who holds

50 For a fuller discussion of these sarcophagi, see Van Keuren and Gromet 2009, 198–203.

51 MNR 184: Dayan, Musso and Lombardi, in Giuliano 1981, 148–150. This sarcophagus could not be located in the Chiostro Grande in March, 2008.

52 MNR 128578: Dayan, Musso and Friggeri, in Giuliani 1981, 184–186; Huskinson 1996, 64 no. 9.23.

53 MNR 175 and 900: Dayan and Musso, in Giuliano 1981, 59–61 and 159–160; Blanc and Gury 1986, 1018 no. 541, pl. 715; Huskinson 1996, 42 and 49 nos. 6.27 and 6.29.

54 Floriani Squarciapino 1950, 109 ff.; Hesberg 1981, 1074–1075, fig. 13 (frieze fragment from the temple of Venus Genetrix).

a *lagobolon* in his left arm as he lunges to the right, is Matz's figure type TH 18.[55] The second Dionysiac sarcophagus, found on the Via Aurelia Antica, shows a rapidly-moving flute player in front of Dionysus' chariot. This maenad, who raises her arms high to play her instrument, belongs to Matz's type TH 36.[56]

On the last Dionysiac sarcophagus from the early Severan period, the wine god again rides in a chariot drawn by two centaurs. To the right of his chariot is an ecstatic maenad with billowing drapery who raises her tympanum high while throwing her head back. She is an example of Matz's Neo-Attic type TH 27.[57] Although this maenad strikes the tympanum rather than playing the double flute, she is very close in pose to the maenad of type TH 36 on the previous Dionysiac sarcophagus, which suggests that standard figure types could be altered to play slightly different roles.

Conclusion

The earliest sarcophagus from those at the Museo Nazionale Romano that have been analysed is from the Trajanic period, and is made of dolomitic marble from Thasos. Found in Ostia, the sarcophagus was made for a Greek artisan from Ephesus named Trophimas. This evidence suggests that immigrants like Trophimas may have introduced burial in marble sarcophagi in Rome's port city, a practice which then spread to the broader populace of Rome.

Pentelic marble was used in Rome for Imperial monuments of special significance in terms of their propagandistic content – for example, the Arch of Titus, and the Trajanic Frieze that was reused on the Arch of Constantine.[58] The emphasis on mythological content on all but one of the Pentelic sarcophagi suggests the erudition and hence the high social status of the families who purchased them. The earliest of the sarcophagi, dated c. 140, is a chest from a child's sarcophagus that is decorated with a Centauromachy (Figure 5.1). Two sarcophagi for adults, dated to the third quarter of the second century, feature Pluto's abduction of Proserpina and the tragic stories of Creusa and Medea (Figure 5.4). Only the latest Pentelic sarcophagus from the end of the third century, which has a re-cut head of the deceased, lacks a mythological storyline.

55 MNR 214: *ASR* IV, 3, 399–400, no. 225; Musso, in Giuliano 1981, 123–125; Gasparri 1986, 555, no. 191. For figure type TH 18, see *ASR* IV, 1, 25, no. TH 18.

56 MNR 128577: *ASR* IV, 2, 251–252, no. 108; Musso, in Giuliano 1981, 64–66. For figure type TH 36, see *ASR* IV, 1, 33, no. TH 36.

57 MNR without inventory no.: *ASR* IV, 2, 257–258, no. 117; Musso, in Giuliano 1981, 119–121. For figure type TH 27, see *ASR* IV, 1, 30, no. TH 27.

58 Amadori et al. 1998, 48–49.

Perhaps the most interesting discovery regarding the 20 sarcophagi at the Museo Nazionale Romano that were analysed for this study is the discontinuity in the use of Carrara marble. The lid of the just-mentioned child's sarcophagus (Figure 5.1) and the lid and chest of another sarcophagus, both dated to the early Antonine period (c. 130–150), were revealed to be of Carrara marble. No sarcophagus from the second half of the second century or the third century is made of this marble. The absence of Carrara sarcophagi from the late second century coincides with a marked decrease in the use of Carrara marble in the public buildings of second-century Rome.[59] The lack of third-century Carrara sarcophagi is consistent with Susan Walker's conclusion regarding the 'sharp decline in the use of Carrara marble for sarcophagi decorated at Rome in the third century AD.'[60] Note too that Carrara is not included in the list of quarries in Diocletian's Edict on Maximum Prices of 301.[61] However, two sarcophagi dated to the first half of the fourth century (see Figures 5.2 and 5.5–5.6) indicate that there was a revival in the use of Carrara marble in late antiquity. Multiple analysis methods have revealed that Carrara marble was also used in the Constantinian friezes and *clipei* from the Arch of Constantine.[62]

A renewed interest in Carrara marble during the fourth century is consistent with Walker's suggestion of 1988 that 'there is reason to suppose a limited revival of the use of Carrara in Constantinian Rome. It is not yet clear whether the revival concerned freshly quarried, stockpiled or reused blocks.'[63] In Appendix 2 at the end of this article, John J. Herrmann, Jr. suggests that both of the Carrara sarcophagi from the fourth century that were analysed (Figures 5.2 and 5.5–5.6) were made from reused materials, along with a large proportion of Early Christian sarcophagi from the Museo Pio Cristiano at the Vatican.

In her article of 1988, Walker accepted the theory that during the fourth century, the port for Carrara was an estuarine lake to the west of Luni, itself located to the southwest of Carrara on the Ligurian Sea. According to this theory, in the fourth century the port would have become overgrown with reeds and Luni itself damaged by flooding.[64] However, Paolo Fazzini and Marina Maffei proposed in 2000 that the Roman port for Luni may have been located instead in 'a sheltered fluvial inlet along a bend of the R. Magra, near its mouth.' They did not find evidence of extensive destruction of Luni until the second half of the seventh century, when there were three 'catastrophic flooding

59 Bruno et al. 2002, 298.

60 Walker 1988b, 187. See also Walker and Matthews 1988, 124.

61 For the list of quarries in this edict, see Lauffer 1971, 192–193, no. 33; Roueché 1989, 299–300.

62 Amadori et al. 1998, 49.

63 Walker 1988b, 189–190.

64 Walker 1988b, 190.

events.'[65] Thus, the reason for the decline in the use of Carrara marble for sarcophagi after 150 may not be the clogging up of the harbour of Luni.

A consideration of price may have led to the apparent preference during the late second and third centuries for the two marbles most strongly represented in our late Antonine and Severan test group. According to Diocletian's Edict of 301, Proconnesian marble was the cheapest and Thasian marble was only slightly more expensive, while marble from Afyon was far more expensive than both island marbles.[66] Of the 20 sarcophagi from the Museo Nazionale Romano that were analysed for this study, the majority, i. e. twelve chests and the lid and chest of a thirteenth sarcophagus (Figure 5.3), were revealed to be of the cheapest Proconnesian marble. This statistic supports Walker's observation that 'by eye it would appear that Proconnesian … became the most favoured Greek marble for metropolitan sarcophagi.'[67] Significantly, the earliest of the thirteen Proconnesian sarcophagi was produced c. 150 in the middle Antonine period, just after the second-century sequence of Carrara sarcophagi in the analysed group ended in the early Antonine period. Ten of the thirteen Proconnesian sarcophagi can be dated, on the basis of their figural decoration. Five fall in the second half of the second century. The popularity of Proconnesian marble in sarcophagi from 150–200 coincides chronologically with its first use in Rome for 'major public works.'[68]

It may be significant that Parian marble did not appear among our second century sarcophagi. Parian lychnites was certainly used for sculpture in Rome at that time,[69] but this traditionally high-status marble may well have been largely restricted to high-status projects, such as statuary. It may not, as this group of tests suggests, have only occasionally been used by workshops producing sarcophagi.

The five additional Proconnesian sarcophagi that can be dated were produced in the third century. Three belong to the first two decades of the third century, i. e. the Severan period. Two further Proconnesian sarcophagi may date either from the late Severan period or the time of the Soldier Emperors (235–280). Stylistically they compare rather closely to the famous 'Badminton Sarcophagus', which has recently been revealed to be of Parian Lychnites marble through multiple analysis techniques. This sarcophagus has been dated from c.

65 Fazzini and Maffei 2000. See also Bini, Chelli and Pappalardo 2006, for their study on the location of the coastline around Luni during Roman times.

66 Gnoli 1971, 14–16; and Dodge and Ward-Perkins 1972, 177–178.

67 Walker 1988a, 30.

68 Attanasio, Brilli and Bruno 2008, 752.

69 Herrmann et al. 2000, 258 and 260, fig. 11: Hadrianic head of Artemis from Grottaferrata. See also Pensabene et al. 2000: irregular Parian blocks with consular dates of 132, 153, 163, 164.

230 to as late as c. 270. The treatment of its back side shows that it is a reused entablature block.[70]

The period of the Soldier Emperors corresponds to a time of change – and perhaps crisis – in the Roman marble trade, as in Roman civilization generally. Symptomatic in the realm of marble is the disappearance of control marks with consular dates on marble blocks after the first decade of the third century.[71] Nonetheless, Diocletian's Edict on Maximum Prices, issued in 301, demonstrates that quarrying continued at some locations until the early fourth century, even if only for marble veneer.[72]

Production of sarcophagi continued at Rome through the time of the Soldier Emperors, as is shown by other famous sarcophagi of that time, such as the 'Ludovisi Battle Sarcophagus'[73] and the 'Sarcophagus of the Annona',[74] both of which have grey bands and appear to be Proconnesian marble. Three types of *lenoi* that were decorated with heads of lions and full figures of lions were produced during the third century. Susan Walker suggests that production of the third type, with full figures of lions that bring down prey, continued until the end of the third century. Isotopic analyses revealed that Proconnesian marble was used for the majority of the first two types, but for less than half of the third type.[75] Two additional *lenoi* of the third type have been tested, and one proved to be Proconnesian,[76] while the other was Pentelic.[77] The shipwreck off San Pietro on the Italian coast near Taranto, dated by its late Roman pottery to the first half of the third century, carried nine roughed-out examples of Walker's first type of *lenos* and three roughed-out examples belonging to her second or third type. Isotopic analyses demonstrated that all of them were of dolomitic Thasian marble.[78]

The standard practice for the production of Roman sarcophagi seems to have been to rough out the shape of the sarcophagus in the quarry.[79] This process involved the roughing out of the basic shape of each sarcophagus, and

70 McCann 1978, 94–106; and Bartman 1993. The recent analyses revealing the sarcophagus is of Parian Lychnites are being presented at the first symposium of the International Association of Roman Sarcophagi, Marburg, 2–8 October 2010.

71 Amadori et al. 1998, 52: 'dopo il primo decennio del III secolo non s'incontrano più nei blocchi grezzi delle cave le consuete numerazioni, sigle e nomi delle officine.'

72 Corcoran and DeLaine 1994.

73 De Angelis d'Ossat 2002, 218–221.

74 Andreae 1977, 304, fig. 597.

75 Walker 1985.

76 A Proconnesian *lenos* in Toledo of c. 240: Knudsen et al. 2002, 237, fig. 9.

77 A Pentelic *lenos* in Boston of c. 260–270 (MFAB 1975.359).: http://www.mfa.org/collections/search_art.asp?coll_keywords=1975 %2E359

78 Ward-Perkins and Throckmorton 1965; Walker 1985, 62–63; Alessio and Zaccaria 1997; Herrmann 1999, 63.

79 See Wurch-Kozelj and Kozelj 1995.

the removal of the interior of the chest, evidently in order to lighten the load during shipping.[80] Sarcophagi were sometimes the only type of marble cargo on Roman ships, as in the case of the San Pietro wreck, which contained dolomitic marble sarcophagi of rectangular shape as well as oval *lenoi.*[81] In other cases, as in the Torre Sgarrata wreck, roughed-out sarcophagi as well as un-worked marble blocks were shipped together.[82] However, in Rome's marble yards, roughed-out sarcophagi are not found with un-worked, evidently discarded blocks.[83] Ben Russell shared these observations:

> Like Clayton [Fant], I know of no blocks at Portus or Rome from which a sarcophagus could have been cut – but partly this might be because if any such blocks ever existed they would have been used up, probably in Late Antiquity. The shipwreck evidence is more conclusive – roughed-out blanks or finished pieces only.[84]

Once roughed-out sarcophagi reached Portus (northwest of Ostia) or Rome, they would have been transported to sculptural workshops, where they would have been given carved decoration. Bonanno Aravantinos proposes that in Ostia, such workshops were located near the cemeteries of Pianabella, Laurentina and the Via Ostiense, all located outside the city walls to the southeast.[85] The basis for this hypothesis was the discovery near these cemeteries of fragments of sarcophagi whose figural decoration is in various stages of execution, with tool marks still visible.[86] Alternatively, these fragments might instead be pieces of sarcophagi from tombs; i. e., they might be from sarcophagi that were purchased before they had received the finishing touches, and that

80 In an email of February 18, 2004 (her book will be forthcoming), Nusin Asgari reports these types of finds in the Proconnesian quarries: '(1) Roughed out sarc.-chest with 2 bosses on one long side (for the lion heads) – this type is the same as the Thasian quarry-*lenoi.* (2) Roughed out quarry-*lenoi* without any bosses [Walker 1985, *lenos* types 2 and 3]. (3) Roughed out quarry-blocks, large and small, in oval form, the interior of which have not as yet been hollowed out.'

81 Herrmann, 1999, 63. For drawings of the sarcophagi as they were found, see Ward-Perkins and Throckmorton 1965, 208–209; and Alessio and Zaccaria 1997, 215–216, figs. 2–3.

82 Throckmorton 1989, with drawing p. 269. Calia et al. 2009 and Gabellone et al. 2009 report that, according to isotopic and mineropetrographic analyses, the sarcophagi and the blocks are of two types of Thasian marble, dolomitic from Cape Vathy and calcitic from Cape Phanari.

83 For the marble yards of Portus and Rome, see Maischberger 1997; and Fant 2001.

84 Email communication of May 21, 2009. See also his article in this volume. It appears that sarcophagi of Dokimeian marble were shipped finished, except for portrait heads of the deceased. See Walker 1988a, 33; and Van Keuren and Gromet 2009, 196.

85 Aravantinos 2008, 149–152.

86 Ibid., 150–154, figs. 1–6.

were then pressed into service prematurely.[87] That sarcophagi, even imperfect ones, were in demand in Rome and vicinity is demonstrated by the extensive evidence regarding their reworking from previously-used examples and from blocks first used for other purposes.

Appendix 1
The marble provenance of 20 Sarcophagi (27 samples) from the Museo Nazionale Romano.

Donato Attanasio

The experimental results are given in Table 1. The chest 222 and the chest 128581 were resampled (samples 5 and 14, respectively) in order to confirm the analyses. Average quarry data for the most relevant quarries are included at he end of Table 1. The assignments, however, were carried out using a more extensive selection of possible provenance sites (see the full list of quarries below).

The assignment has been carried out using simultaneously 6 experimental variables[88]:

2 isotopic:	$\delta^{18}O$ (delta Oxygen 18)	$\delta^{13}C$ (delta Carbon 13)
2 petrographic:	MGS (Maximum Grain Size), Colour	
2 EPR (Electron Paramagnetic Resonance):	Intensity (=INTENS), Linewidth (=W)	

The site selection included 9 of the most likely quarry sites (15 groups, 852 samples):

Carrara, Hymettos, Pentelicon,
Paros (Marathi, Marathi lychnites, Chorodaki),
Thasos calcitic, Afyon (Bacakale, Röder II/V, Röder III/IV),
Ephesos (Kusini Tepe, Belevi, Aya Klikiri), Miletos, Proconnesos.

87 Ben Russell proposed such a premature use for another unfinished sarcophagus at the MNR, which had only received carved borders for the fronts of the chest and lid, along with the border for the clipeus portrait on the chest: email communication of May 21, 2009; and Musso, in Giuliano 1984, 246–247.

88 Separate isotopic/MGS or EPR/MGS assignments tend to misclassify Hymettos for Carrara or give uncertain Carrara provenances.

Table 1

No.	Label	Inv/Descr	$\delta^{18}O$	$\delta^{13}C$	dolom	Intens	W	Colour	MGS
1	1.26	Busts Selene, Helios	-2.02	1.89	0.0	0.041	0.627	195	1.10
2	2.14	121657, Chest	-1.70	1.94	0.0	0.424	0.588	193	0.45
3	3.13	121657, Lid	-2.02	2.17	0.0	0.574	0.627	225	0.45
4	4.12	222 chest	-4.72	2.71	0.0	9.84	0.854	204	0.65
5	08.4	222 chest bis	-4.72	2.55	0.0	1.385	0.587	198	1.0
6	5.4	125891, Ulpia Domina	-3.62	2.73	0.0	0.033	0.630	192	1.70
7	6.7	128086	-6.88	2.71	0.0	0.617	0.640	211	0.55
8	7.9	56138	-2.25	1.96	0.0	0.053	0.678	209	1.10
9	8.8	72879	-1.51	3.45	0.0	0.169	0.535	200	1.70
10	9.5	124735	-1.51	2.70	0.0	0.016	0.592	199	1.10
11	10.11	407, Lid	-1.72	2.01	0.0	0.589	0.612	215	0.40
12	11.10	407, Chest	-1.99	2.15	0.0	0.461	0.627	217	0.50
13	12.3	128581, chest	-13.25	1.47	0.0	1.912	0.534	212	0.30
14	08.3	128581 chest bis	-9.64	1.91	0.0	1.720	0.566	213	0.70
15	08.2	128581 lid	-1.89	2.10	0.0	0.617	0.680	214	0.55
16	13.1	226119	-2.41	3.06	0.0	0.027	0.601	188	1.60
17	14.23	750	-1.30	3.03	0.0	0.030	0.578	198	1.70
18	15.16	126285	-0.96	3.40	0.0	0.091	0.573	172	1.75
19	16.17	524	-1.74	3.17	0.0	0.041	0.668	224	1.40
20	17.18	Endymion, dog, erratic	-1.71	3.12	0.0	0.036	0.709	200	1.70
21	18.21	115247, Chest	-1.29	2.03	0.0	0.979	0.576	221	1.10
22	19.2	115247, Lid	-1.19	2.21	0.0	0.530	0.594	227	0.90
23	20.22	Lenos, Marsyas	-1.59	2.68	0.0	0.036	0.654	199	1.60
24	21.24	654	-4.71	2.81	0.17	3.814	0.734	202	0.90
25	08.1	Cupid Psyche pp. 98–99	-2.02	3.05	0.0	0.036	0.642	210	2.20
26	08.6	75248 chest	-2.34	3.27	0.0	0.020	0.587	195	1.70

Table 1 *(Continued)*

No.	Label	Inv/Descr	$\delta^{18}O$	$\delta^{13}C$	dolom	Intens	W	Colour	MGS
27	08.5	75248 lid	-2.26	3.05	0.0	0.027	0.736	177	1.70
	Ca		-1.89	2.11	0.01	0.685	0.634	211	0.80
	Afy		-4.32	1.80	0.00	2.425	0.539	193	0.86
	Hy		-2.17	2.20	0.03	0.142	0.460	182	0.69
	Pe		-7.00	2.63	0.003	2.263	0.582	229	0.96
	Pa/ Cho		-1.11	1.79	0.04	0.195	0.479	214	2.07
	Th		-0.73	2.98	0.006	1.308	0.557	201	3.84
	Pro		-1.80	2.51	0.06	0.064	0.514	197	1.93

Using the 6 variables mentioned above, the rate of discrimination for the 15 marble groups is 83.7 %, or 82.9 % after statistical validation. The results of the assignment for the 27 marble samples under investigation are summarized in Table 2 below:

Definitions of the probability parameters in Table 2

Relative (posterior) probability: This is the probability that the sample belongs to some group, assuming that it originates in any case from one of the groups in the selection. The threshold is 60 %. Low values indicate that the sample's assignment is in doubt between two or more groups.

Absolute (typical) probability: This is a distance dependent parameter measuring the absolute probability that the sample belongs to the chosen group or, in other words, is a typical representative of the group's properties. The threshold is 10 %, corresponding to samples on the edge of the 90 % probability ellipse. Low values indicate anomalous samples (outliers) or samples possibly not belonging to any group in the selection.

Distance: This is the distance of a point under consideration from the center of the ellipse that represents the probability field of a quarry. The central point of an ellipse expresses the average and hence most characteristic values of a quarry. The closer a point under consideration is to the center of an ellipse, the more likely it is to be made of the marble represented by the ellipse.

Table 2

	Sample	Description	Isotopes	Site1	Relative (posterior) probability	Absolute (typical) probability	Distance
1	1.26	Busts Selene, Helios	Ca	Pro	77	**52**	5.0
2	2.14	121657, Chest	Ca	Ca	91	**53**	5.1
3	3.13	121657, Lid	Ca	Ca	100	**47**	5.6
4	4.12	222 chest	Afy	Afy	56	**1**	17
5	08.4	222 chest bis	Afy	Afy	90	**75**	3.4
6	5.4	125891, Ulpia Domina	Pro	Pro	93	**88**	2.4
7	6.7	128086	Pe	Pe	98	**28**	7.5
8	7.9	56138	Hy	Pro	71	**32**	7
9	8.8	72879	Pro	Pro	39	**21**	8.4
10	9.5	124735	Pro	Pro	99	**53**	5.1
11	10.11	407, Lid	Ca	Ca	99	**33**	6.9
12	11.10	407, Chest	Ca	Ca	89	**77**	3.3
13	12.3	128581, chest	?	Pe	100	**0**	52
14	08.3	128581 chest bis	~Pe	Pe	100	**26**	7.8
15	08.2	128581 lid		Ca	100	**94**	1.8
16	13.1	226119	Pro	Pro	98	**96**	1.5
17	14.23	750	Pro	Pro	96	**96**	1.4
18	15.16	126285	Pro	Pro	94	**37**	6.5
19	16.17	524	Pro	Pro	96	**60**	4.6
20	17.18	Endym., dog, erratic	Pro	Pro	99	**59**	4.6
21	18.21	115247, Chest	Cho	Ca	93	**82**	2.9

Table 2 *(Continued)*

	Sample	Description	Isotopes	Site1	Relative (posterior) probability	Absolute (typical) probability	Distance
22	19.2	115247, Lid	Pro	Ca	97	**97**	1.3
23	20.22	Lenos, Marsyas	Pro	Pro	96	**90**	2.2
24	21.24	654	Afy	Afy	63	**14**	9.6
25	08.1	Cupid Pysche pp. 98–99	Pro	Pro	94	77	3.3
26	08.6	75248 chest	Pro	Pro	99	**85**	2.6
27	08.5	75248 lid	Pro	Pro	100	**22**	8.3

Comments:

25 different pieces were sampled and analysed. Two chests, however (nos. 4 and 13), needed to be verified and were resampled (samples 5 and 14). For this reason, Tables 1 and 2 contain data for 27 samples.

5 sarcophagi provided samples from both the chest and the lid (121657, 407, 128581, 115247, and 75248). 4 of them turned out to be made of the same marble (Carrara for 121657, 407, and 115247; Proconnesos for 75248). The last sarcophagus (128581), however, was manufactured using different marbles: Carrara for the lid and Pentelicon for the chest.

13 chest samples (1, 6, 8, 9, 10, 16, 17, 18, 19, 20, 23, 25, 26) and 1 lid sample (27) are very low in EPR intensity ($\leq$ 0.1) and medium (~ 1.1–1.7 mm) grained. In agreement with isotopes and other properties, they are all assigned to Proconnesos.

3 chest samples (2, 12, 21) and 4 lid samples (3, 11, 15, 22) exhibit medium EPR intensity (~0.5). The grain size is generally fine, although sample 18 has a MGS = 1.1 mm. In agreement with isotopes and other properties, they are all assigned to Carrara.

2 chest samples (7 and 13/14) are assigned as Pentelicon. Sample 13 shows an extremely negative $\delta^{18}O$ (-13.25). Resampling has given -9.64. The Pentelicon assignment has been confirmed and improved.

2 chest samples (4/5, 24) require some further comment. In statistical terms, the most probable provenance site is certainly Afyon in both cases. Pentelicon, however, represents a reasonable alternative, with the probability values being only slightly smaller. The presence in both marbles of numerous micaceous inclusions indicates unambiguously that Pentelicon is, in fact, the true

provenance of both samples. Note that in this case resampling and retesting of sample 4 (sample 5) was not helpful.

The final distribution of the 25 pieces (20 chests, 5 lids) is:

Proconnesos	13 chests	1 lid	14 total samples	56 %
Carrara	3 chests	4 lids	7 total samples	28 %
Pentelicon	4 chests	0 lids	4 total samples	16 %

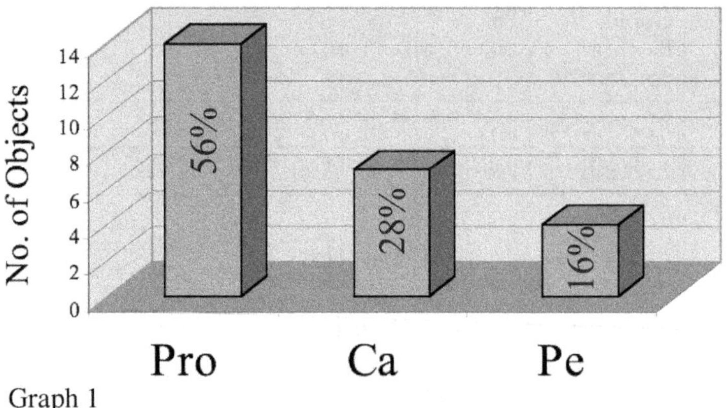

Graph 1

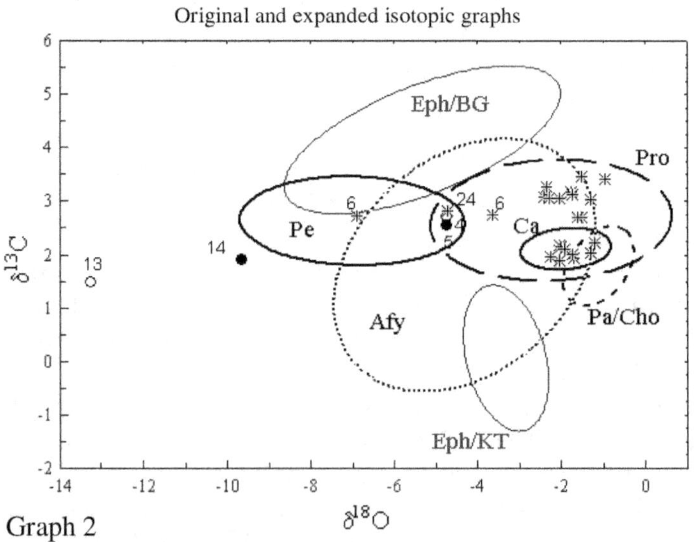

Graph 2

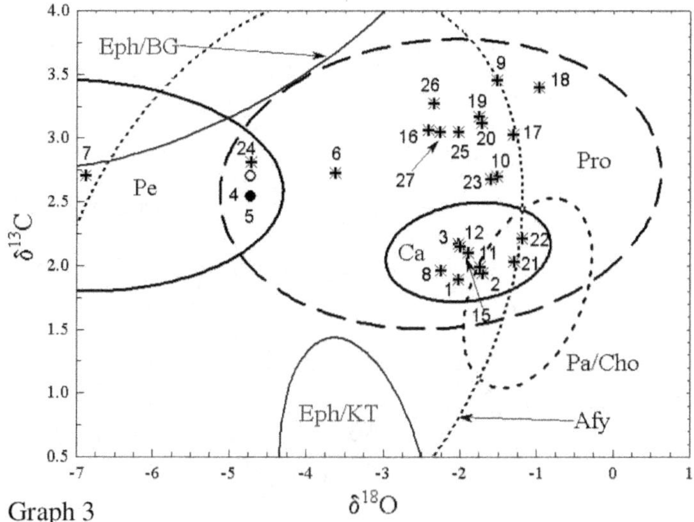

Graph 3

EPR log graph (intensity vs. line width)

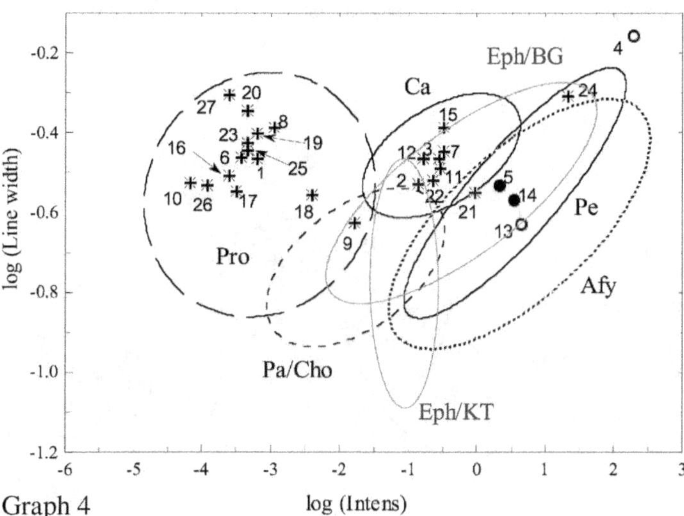

Graph 4

Statistical plots.
Discr.Coord. 1= 0.82 x Intensity + 0.64 x $\delta^{18}O$ + minor contributions
Discr.Coord. 2= 0.88 x MGS + 0.53 x Intensity + minor contributions
Discr.Coord. 3= 0.71 x $\delta^{13}C$ + 0.63 x $\delta^{18}O$ + minor contributions

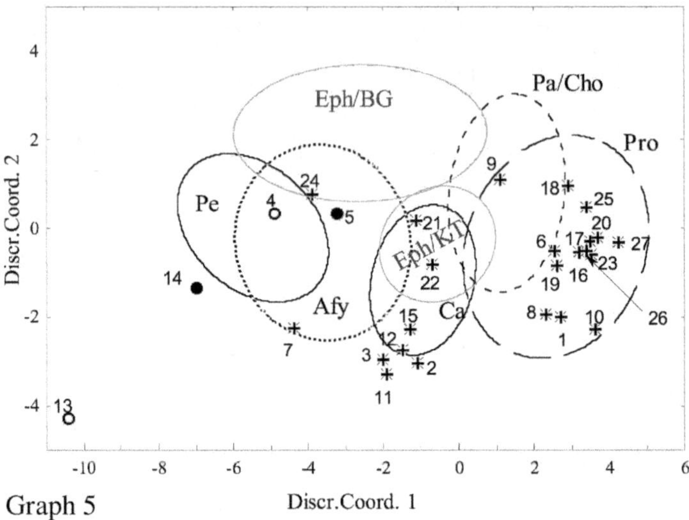

Graph 5

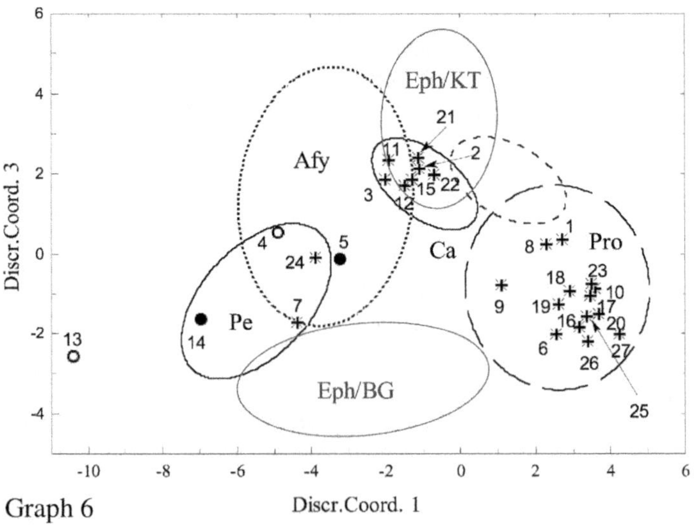

Graph 6

Appendix 2
Sarcophagi Made from Reused Architectural Blocks in the Fourth Century

John J. Herrmann, Jr.

This program of scientific testing in the Museo Nazionale Romano has identified Carrara marble in two sarcophagi of the fourth century. At least one of them seems to have been made from an old block previously employed for a different purpose. The back side of the Carrara marble strigillated sarcophagus with a bust of a youth in a *clipeus* has several features that seem in no way related to the funerary function of the piece (see Figures 5.5–5.6). A long diagonal line divides the backside into upper and lower fields that have different kinds of tool marks. The marks of a pointed chisel in the upper field are sharp and clear. The lower field, on the other hand, has an amorphous surface that suggests the passage of water. Peg holes in the upper field seem unrelated to any possible use as a sarcophagus. While no specific function for these features can be suggested, they make it clear that the block had gone through one or two previous phases of use before taking its present form.

The other fourth-century Carrara sarcophagus also has anomalous features that could well be due to reuse of a pre-existing block (Figure 5.2). On the lower part of its left end are two long, well patinated troughs for iron clamps. This ancient repair was intended to fasten a slab of marble along the lower front of the sarcophagus. It seems likely that this expedient was intended to compensate for an imperfection in the block – perhaps damage from a previous use.

Examination of the chests of Early Christian sarcophagi in the Vatican's Museo Pio Cristiano Lateranense makes it clear that at least some fourth-century sarcophagi were made of reused blocks originally intended for large public buildings.[89] A sarcophagus with the twelve Apostles[90] has a plain ovolo moulding along the lower edge of the back; such a profile betrays a former use or intended use as a cornice in a major colonnade. A column sarcophagus[91] has a plain ovolo and cavetto along its lower rear edge. Another column sarcophagus has a plain cyma reversa along the lower edge of its back.[92] Two more sarcophagi – a Crossing of the Red Sea[93] and a strigillated sarcophagus with an Orans[94] –

89 See also Herrmann 2009, 124.

90 *Rep.* I, cat. no. 65 (inv. 31521); Hourihane, system no. 000181933.

91 *Rep.* I, cat. no. 53 (inv. 31475); Hourihane, system no. 000102362.

92 *Rep.* I, cat. no. 52 (inv. 31489); Hourihane, system no. 000103395.

93 The mouldings are simple cavettos. *Rep.* I, cat. no. 64 (without new inventory number); Hourihane, system no. 000103943.

94 *Rep.* I, cat. no. 73 (inv. 31452); Hourihane, system no. 000102000.

have narrow architectural mouldings on their ends. All five of these blocks must also have come from dismantled or unfinished public buildings.[95] The marble of these chests has not been tested, but optically it seems to include both fine-grained white, grey-spotted marble and grey-banded coarser grained marble. Hence it is likely that buildings made of both Cararra and Proconnesian marble provided marble for the sarcophagi.

A frieze sarcophagus of Roman type in the Archaeological Museum, Split, Croatia also has an architectural moulding – a plain cyma recta and two fillets – along its lower rear edge, as pointed out by Guntram Koch.[96] The sarcophagus shows the Israelites crossing the Red Sea on its front, and three figures separated by strigillated panels on its reverse.[97] All the figural work dates from the late fourth century, and only the moulding reflects the block's previous architectural use.

It should be noted that all these mouldings are in concealed places on the sarcophagi. They appear on undecorated sides or backs of the chests and are not used decoratively themselves. When the mouldings appear on the short sides of the chests, they are simple, low, and hardly visible on the decorated front. Modern photographers tend to minimize them or avoid them altogether. All the mouldings are schematic; they are not finished as an egg-and-dart or as a Lesbian cymation.

The fact that private individuals could have access to these blocks connected with major public buildings is to some degree surprising from a legal point of view. Patrizio Pensabene has emphasized that imperial legislation in the fourth century tended to restrict private access to marble from public buildings. He has, however, suggested that some reused material could have come from deposits connected with unfinished buildings,[98] and this may well have been the source for the large blocks with unfinished mouldings used for these sarcophagi.

By themselves the five chests in the Museo Pio Cristiano with architectural mouldings represent a significant proportion of the 26 well-preserved sarcophagi in the collection. There are, in addition, various less conspicuous indications that marble was reused for other sarcophagi in the Museo Pio Cristiano. Seven other chests were put together from various pieces rather than carved from single blocks. The joints between pieces are sharp, straight cuts.[99]

95 The lid of a frieze sarcophagus also has a sima profile on its rear edge: *Rep.* I, cat. no. 6 (inv. 31509); Spinola 2000b; Hourihane, system no. 000102367.

96 We discussed the issue of fresh versus reused blocks at the Archaeological Museum, Split, on June 8, 2007.

97 *Rep.* II, cat. no. 146; Hourihane, system no. 000098149.

98 Pensabene, in Pensabene and Panella 1993–1994, 128–130.

99 *Rep.* I, cat. nos. 2 (inv. 31485); 7 (inv. 31440); 49 (inv. 31525); 61 (inv. 28591); 74 (inv. 31407); and 29 (inv. 31554); Hourihane, respectively, system nos. 000101953, 000102360, 000102608, 000102535, 000182033, and 000102188. The fourth

This kind of patchwork is not seen in sarcophagi from earlier centuries and again suggests that the blocks were salvaged marble rather than freshly quarried. As noted above, a Carrara marble sarcophagus in the Museo Nazionale Romano provides a discreet instance of this kind of piecing (Figure 5.2). Giandomenico Spinola has argued that a joint in one of the Vatican sarcophagi is due to considerations of display,[100] but other sarcophagi in the collection make it clear that the cuts are not modern, since the pieces to be attached are missing. This is particularly evident in the case of a strigillated sarcophagus with a learned lady at the centre and a shepherd at the right end; the sarcophagus lacks the figural panel at the left end that should have abutted the vertical edge of the left-hand panel of strigillations.[101]

Some of the remaining 14 sarcophagi in the Museo Pio Cristiano revealed other anomalies, such as different kinds of tooling on the back and sides. An alternation of pointed, flat, and claw chisels on the different sides might well be indications that the blocks were reused.

Several fourth-century chests, on the other hand, lacked any such anomalies and in all probability were sculpted from newly quarried blocks. Three massive sarcophagi stood out for their regularity of shape and consistency of workmanship: the 'Dogmatic' sarcophagus,[102] the 'Ludovisi' sarcophagus,[103] and a strigillated sarcophagus centred on the Denial of Peter.[104] They are prime candidates for being new production, and, it might be added, all three present the medium or coarse grain and dark grey stripes of Proconnesian marble. Several smaller sarcophagi, which also seemed to be Proconnesian marble, again lacked anomalies. The sarcophagi of Sabinus[105] and of Priscus[106] date from the fourth century. Four other apparently Proconnesian chests date from the second half of the third century or the beginning of the fourth: a child's strigillated sarcophagus,[107] a pastoral sarcophagus,[108] the sarcophagus from the Via Salaria,[109] and that of Aurelia Severa.[110]

---

sarcophagus is also Spinola 2000a. Also a sarcophagus with Seasons and an Orans, inv. 31425 (not in *Rep.* I).

100 Spinola 2000a.

101 *Rep.* I, cat. no. 74 (inv. 31407); Hourihane, system no. 000182033. In recent years the reconstructed left panel has been removed, revealing the smooth surface of the joint.

102 *Rep.* I, cat. no. 43 (inv. 31427); Hourihane, system no. 000101998.

103 *Rep.* I, cat. no. 86 (inv. 31408); Hourihane, system no. 000102544.

104 *Rep.* I, cat. no. 77 (inv. 31495); Hourihane, system no. 000102309.

105 *Rep.* I, cat. no. 6 (inv. 31509); Spinola 2000b; Hourihane, system no. 000102367.

106 inv. 31592; without figures.

107 inv. 31419; non-Christian.

108 *Rep.* I, cat. no. 32 (inv. 31465); Hourihane, system no. 000102370.

109 *Rep.* I, cat. no. 66 (inv. 31540); Hourihane, system no. 000099487.

110 inv. 30932; without figures.

A rapid review of the Vatican's collection of Christian sarcophagi then demonstrates that certainly some, and possibly a very substantial part of the collection and, by extension, of fourth century sarcophagi in Rome in general were made of previously quarried marble blocks. The phenomenon of scavenged marble is difficult to detect in most cases since the sculptors seem to have wanted to conceal anomalies, which apparently would have detracted from the ideological messages they wished to project. The reuse of blocks for sarcophagi in the fourth century is not entirely surprising, given that so much of the marble used in the architecture of the period in Rome was reused, but, as noted above, the availability of massive architectural blocks for private use represents something of a novelty. It is less surprising that some newly quarried marble blocks for sarcophagi would have come from the Proconnesos, the source of most of the marble for Constantinople, the new and rapidly expanding capital city of the Empire, and a great exporter to other parts of the Empire, including fourth-century Rome.[111] The question now remains, what portion of the Proconnesian marble sarcophagi at Rome was made of reused marble. Even more intriguing is the question of whether any of the marble from other quarries used for Roman sarcophagi in the fourth century was fresh production. In particular, activity in the quarries of Carrara (ancient Luna) remains a major unknown. Based on the sarcophagi in the Museo Pio Cristiano and the tested sarcophagi in the Museo Nazionale Romano, it seems possible that blocks for sarcophagi may not have been produced in Carrara during the fourth century.

Acknowledgements

Dr. Maria Antonietta Tomei, Director of the Museo Nazionale Romano in the Baths of Diocletian, most generously granted permission for samples to be taken from the 20 sarcophagi at her museum. Funding support for the analyses was provided by the Writing Intensive Fellows Program, the University of Georgia, and the Lamar Dodd School of Art, the University of Georgia. The Samuel H. Kress Foundation in New York provided funds for Prof. Frances Van Keuren and three of the four University of Georgia students who worked on the 20 sarcophagi in her fall 2007 seminar – Chad Alligood, Maria Graffagnino, Soon Bae Kim, and Katie Seefeldt – to travel to Rome in March 2008 and study and photograph the sarcophagi, and to meet with Dr. Donato Attanasio in his lab. These students' most significant contributions are recognised in the footnotes. Prof. Van Keuren's husband Lenny Valliere, chemist at Coca Cola in

111 For Proconnesian capitals and column shafts at Rome, see Pensabene 1973, cat. nos. 383–384; Herrmann 1988, pp. 94–96, 154, 180 (B), figs. 173, 176, 318–319; Kramer 1997; Pensabene, in Pensabene and Panella 1993–1994, p. 142; Pensabene et al. 1999.

Atlanta, provided invaluable help with the discussion of the analytical techniques in the first part of the article. Mary Emerson, Associate Lecturer at the Open University, Milton Keynes, England, looked at the sarcophagi at the Museo Nazionale Romano with Prof. Van Keuren, and offered many important insights. Finally, Dr. Janet Huskinson was most helpful, flexible and patient during the difficult preparation of this collaborative article.

Bibliography

Alessio, A. and Zaccaria, A. Nuove ricerche sul relitto di San Pietro in Bevanga (Manduria –Taranto), in: G. Volpe (ed.), *Atti del convegno nazionale di archeologia subacquea.* Anzio, 30–31 maggio e 1 giugno 1996 (Bari, 1997), 211–224.

Amadori, M. L., Lazzarini, L., Mariottini, M., Pecoraro, M. and Pensabene, P. Determinazione della provenienza dei marmi usati per alcuni monumenti antichi di Roma, in: *Marmi antichi II: Cave e tecnica di lavorazione, provenienze e distribuzione*, edited by P. Pensabene (Rome, 1998), 45–55.

Andreae, B. *The Art of Rome* (New York, 1977).

Angeli, S. de. Demeter/Ceres, in: *LIMC* vol. 4 (Zürich and Munich, 1988), 893–908.

Aravantinos, B. Sarcofagi di Ostia. *Archeologia Classica* 59, n.s. 9 (2008), 147–182.

Attanasio, D. *Ancient White Marbles: Analysis and Identification by Paramagnetic Resonance Spectroscopy* (Rome, 2003).

Attanasio, D., Brilli, M. and Ogle, N. *The Isotopic Signatures of Classical Marbles* (Rome, 2006).

Attanasio, D., Brilli, M. and Bruno, M. The Properties and Identification of Marble from Proconnesos (Marmara Island, Turkey): A New Database Including Isotopic, EPR and Petrographic Data. *Archaeometry* 50.5 (2008), 747–774.

Baratte, F. and Metzger, C. *Musée du Louvre: Catalogue des sarcophages en pierre d'époques romaine et paléochrétienne* (Paris, 1985).

Bartman, E. Carving the Badminton Sarcophagus. *Metropolitan Museum Journal* 28 (1993), 57–75.

Bartoli, A. Marsia e Apollo sul Palatino. *Bollettino d'Arte,* ser. 4, vol. 38 (1953), 1–8.

Berger-Doer, G. Kreousa II, in: *LIMC,* vol. 6 (Zürich and Munich, 1992), 120–127.

Bini, M., Chelli, A. and Pappalardo, M. Geomorfologia del territorio dell'antica Luni (La Spezia) per la ricostruzione del paesaggio costiero in età romana. *Atti della Società Toscana di Scienze Naturali residente in Pisa. Memorie.* Serie A, vol. 111 (2006), 57–66.

Blanc, N. and Gury, F. Eros/Amor, Cupido, in: *LIMC,* vol. 3 (Zürich and Munich, 1986), 952–1049.

Blome, P. Zum Umgestaltung griechischer Mythen in der römischen Sepulkralkunst. Alkestis-, Protesilaos- und Proserpinasarkophage. *Mitteilungen des Deutschen Archaeologischen Instituts. Roemische Abteilung* 85 (1978), 435–457.

Bruno, M., Cancelliere, S., Gorgoni, C., Lazzarini, L., Pallante, P. and Pesabene, P. Provenance and distribution of white marbles in temples and public buildings of Imperial Rome, in: J. J. Herrmann, Jr., N. Herz, and R. Newman (eds.), *ASMOSIA 5: Interdisciplinary Studies of Ancient Stone, Proceedings of the Fifth International Conference of the Association for the Study of Marble and Other Stones in Antiquity,* Museum of Fine Arts, Boston, June 1998 (London, 2002), 289–300.

Calia, A., Giannotta, M.T., Lazzarini, L. and Quarta, G. The Torre Sgarrata Wreck: Characterization and Provenance of White marble Artefacts in the Cargo, in: Y. Maniatis (ed.), *ASMOSIA VII: Actes du VIIe colloque international de l'ASMOSIA Thasos 15–20 septembre 2003,* Bulletin de Correspondance Hellénique Supplément 51 (Athens, 2009), 333–342.

Corcoran, S. and DeLaine, J. The unit measurement of marble in Diocletian's Prices Edict. *Journal of Roman Archaeology* 7 (1994), 263–273.

De Angelis d'Ossat, M. (ed.). *Scultura antica in Palazzo Altemps, Museo Nazionale Romano* (Milan, 2002).

Dodge, H. and Ward-Perkins, B. (eds.). *Marble in antiquity: collected papers of J. B. Ward-Perkins* (London, 1972).

Fant, J.C. Rome's marble yards. *Journal of Roman Archaeology* 14 (2001), 167–198.

Fazzini, P. and Maffei, M. The disappearance of the city of Luni. *Journal of Cultural Heritage* 1 (2000), 247–260.

Felletti Maj, B.M. Roma (Via Fezzan, Quartiere Nomentano). Rinvenimento di un sarcofago. *Notizie degli scavi di antichità* ser. 8, vol. 7 (1953), 234–235.

Floriani Squarciapino, M. Pannelli decorativi del tempio di Venere Genitrice. *Atti della Accademia Nazionale dei Lincei. Memorie* ser. 8, vol. 2 (1950), 61–118.

Gabellone, F., Giannotta, M.T. and Alessio, A. The Torre Sgarrata Wreck (South Italy): Marble Artefacts in the Cargo, in: Y. Maniatis (ed.), *ASMOSIA VII: Actes du VIIe colloque international de l'ASMOSIA Thasos 15–20 septembre 2003,* Bulletin de Correspondance Hellénique Supplément 51 (Athens, 2009), 319–331.

Gaggadis-Robin, V. *Jason et Médée sur les sarcophages d'époque impériale* (École Française de Rome, 1994), 'Collection de l'École Française de Rome' 191.

Gasparri, C. Dionysos/Bacchus, in: *LIMC,* vol. 3 (Zürich and Munich, 1986), 540–566.

Giuliano, A. (ed.). *Museo Nazionale Romano: Le Sculture,* vol. I.2 (Rome, 1981).

Giuliano, A. (ed.). *Museo Nazionale Romano: Le Sculture,* vol. I.3 (Rome, 1982).

Giuliano, A. (ed.). *Museo Nazionale Romano: Le Sculture,* vol. I.7.2 (Rome, 1984).

Giuliano, A. (ed.). *Museo Nazionale Romano: Le Sculture,* vol. I.8, part 1 (Rome, 1985).

Gnoli, R. *Marmora romana* (Rome, 1971).

Gury, F. Selene/Luna, in: *LIMC,* vol. 7 (Zürich and Munich, 1994), 706–715.

Herrmann, J., Jr. and Newman, R. The exportation of dolomitic sculptural marble from Thasos: evidence from Mediterranean and other collections, in: Y. Maniatis, N. Herz and Y. Basiakos (eds.), *ASMOSIA III Athens: Transactions of the 3rd International Symposium of the Association of the Study of Marble and Other Stones used in Antiquity,* Athens 17–19 May 1993 (London, 1995), 73–86.

Herrmann, J., Jr. and Newman, R. Dolomitic Marble from Thasos Near and Far: Macedonia, Ephesos and the Rhone, in: M. Schvoerer (ed.), *Archéomatériaux: Marbres et autres roches. ASMOSIA IV,* Bordeaux-Talence 9–13 octobre 1995 (London, 1999), 293–303.

Herrmann, J. J., Jr. *The Ionic Capital in Late Antique Rome* (Rome, 1988).

Herrmann, J. J., Jr. The Exportation of Dolomitic Marble from Thasos: A Short Overview, in: *Thasos: Matières premières et technologie de la préhistoire à nos jours, Actes du Colloque International 26–29/9/1995, Thasos, Liménaria* (Athens, 1999), 57–69.

Herrmann, J. J., Jr. Christian Sarcophagi of Reused Marble in the Vatican, in: *IX ASMOSIA International Conference: Interdisciplinary Studies on Ancient Stone, Tarragona, 8–13 June 2009* (Association for the Study of Marbles and Other Stones in Antiquity and Institut Catala d'Arqueologia Classica), 124.

Herrmann, J., Jr. Moens, L. and De Paepe, P. Some Identifications of Sculptures in Parian Marble in Boston, in: D.U. Schilardi and D. Katsonopoulou (eds.), *Paria Lithos: Parian Quarries, Marble and Workshops of Sculpture. Proceedings of the First International Conference on the Archaeology of Paros and Cyclades, Paros,* 2–5 October 1997 (Athens, 2000), 253–265.

Herz, N. Classical Marble Quarries of Thasos, in: *Antike Edel- und Buntmetallgewinnung auf Thasos*, edited by G.A. Wagner and G. Weisgerber (Bochum, 1988), 231–244.

Herz, N, and Garrison, E.G. *Geological Methods for Archaeology* (New York and Oxford, 1998).

Hesberg, H. von, Archäologische Denkmäler zu den römischen Göttergestalten. *Aufstieg und Niedergang der römischen Welt* II 17.2 (1981), 1032–1099.

Honroth, M. *Stadtrömische Girlanden: Ein Versuch zur Entwicklungsgeschichte römischer Ornamentik.* Sonderschriften hrsg. vom Österreichischen Archäologischen Institut in Wien, vol. 17. (Wien, 1971).

Hourihane, C. (director), *Index of Christian Art* (Princeton, ongoing, http://ica.princeton.edu/).

Huskinson, J. *Roman Children's Sarcophagi: Their Decoration and its Social Significance* (Oxford, 1996).

Knudsen, S.E., Craine, C. and Tykot, R.H. Analysis of classical marble sculptures in the Toledo Museum of Art, in: J. Herrmann, N. Herz, and R. Newman (eds.), *ASMOSIA 5: Interdisciplinary Studies of Ancient Stone, Proceedings of the Fifth International Conference of the Association for the Study of Marble and Other Stones in Antiquity*, Museum of Fine Arts, Boston, June 1998 (London, 2002), 231–239.

Koch, G. and Sichtermann, H. *Römische Sarkophage. Handbuch der Archäologie* (Munich, 1982).

Kramer, J. *Spätantike korinthische Säulenkapitelle in Rom* (Wiesbaden, 1997).

Lauffer, S. *Diokletians Preisedikt. Texte und Kommentare: Eine altertumswissenschaftliche Reihe*, vol. 5 (Berlin, 1971).

Letta, C. Helios/Sol, in: *LIMC*, vol. 4 (Zürich and Munich, 1988), 592–625.

Maischberger, M. *Marmor in Rom: Anlieferung, Lager- und Werkplätze in der Kaiserzeit.* Palilia, vol. 1 (Wiesbaden, 1997).

Mancini, G. *Roma.* Nuove scoperte di antichità in città e nel suburbio. *Notizie degli scavi di antichità* ser. 5, vol. 10 (1913), 116–120.

McCann, A.M. *Roman Sarcophagi in The Metropolitan Museum of Art* (New York, 1978).

Pensabene, P. *I capitelli (Scavi di Ostia* VII) (Rome, 1973).

Pensabene, P. and Panella, C. Reimpiego e progettazione architettonica nei monumenti tardo-antichi di Roma. *Rendiconti della Pontificia Accademia Romana di Archeologia* 66 (1993–1994), 111–283.

Pensabene, P., Semeraro, T., Lazzarini, L., Turi, B., and Soligo, M. The provenance of the marbles from the depository of the Temple of the *Fabri Navales* at Ostia, in: M. Schvoerer (ed.), *Archéomatériaux: Marbres et autres roches. ASMOSIA IV*, Bordeaux-Talence 9–13 octobre 1995 (London, 1999), 147–156.

Pensabene, P., Lazzarini, L., Soligo, M., Bruno, M., and Turi, B. The Parian Marble Blocks of the Fossa Traiana, in: D.U. Schilardi and D. Katsonopoulou (eds.), *Paria Lithos: Parian Quarries, Marble and Workshops of Sculpture. Proceedings of the First International Conference on the Archaeology of Paros and Cyclades*, Paros, 2–5 October 1997 (Athens, 2000), 527–536.

Pietrogrande, A.L. Roma. Reg. VI. Ruderi e sarcofagi scoperti sulla via di Decima. *Notizie degli scavi di antichità* ser. 6, vol. 10 (1934), 155–168.

Pike, S. *Archaeological Geology and Geochemistry of Pentelic Marble, Mount Pentelikon, Attica, Greece* (unpublished Diss., University of Georgia, 2000).

Pingitore, N.E. The Behavior of Zn^{2+} and Mn^{2+} during Carbonate Diagenesis: Theory and Applications. *Journal of Sedimentary Petrology* 48.3 (September 1978), 799–814.

Rawson, P.B. *The Myth of Marsyas in the Roman Visual Arts: An Iconographic Study.* BAR International Series 347 (Oxford, 1987).

Roueché, C., with contributions by J.M. Reynolds. *Aphrodisias in Late Antiquity: The Late Roman and Byzantine Inscriptions including Texts from the Excavations at Aphrodisas conducted by Kenan T. Erim.* Journal of Roman Studies Monograph 5 (London, 1989).

Sande, S. The Myth of Marsyas: Pieces of a Sculptural Jigsaw. *Metropolitan Museum Journal* 16 (1981), 55–73.

Santolini, R. Sarcofago a *lenòs* strigilato con *Helios* e *Selene* entro clipei. *Notizie degli scavi di antichità* ser. 8, vol. 40–41 (1986–87), 130–134.

Schauenburg, K. Ganymed und Hahnenkämpfe auf römischen Sarkophagen. *Archäologischer Anzeiger* (1972), 501–516.

Schmidt, M. *Der Basler Medeasarkophag; ein Meisterwerk spätantoninischer Kunst* (Tübingen, 1968).

Schmidt, M. Medeia, in: *LIMC,* vol. 6 (Zürich and Munich, 1992), 386–398.

Sengelin, T. Kentauroi et Kentaurides, in: *LIMC,* vol. 8 (Zürich and Munich, 1997), 671–721.

Sichtermann, H. Sarkophag-Miszellen: Fragmente. *Archäologischer Anzeiger* (1974), 308–323.

Spinola, G. cat. no. 48, in: *Pietro e Paolo: La storia, il culto, la memoria nei primi secoli,* edited by A. Donati (Milan, 2000a), 126 and 207–208.

Spinola, G., cat. no. 50, in: *Pietro e Paolo: La storia, il culto, la memoria nei primi secoli,* edited by A. Donati (Milan, 2000b), 129 and 208–210.

Throckmorton, P. The Ship of Torre Sgarrata, in: H. Tzalas (ed.), *Tropis I. 1st International Symposium on Ship Construction in Antiquity: proceedings* (Athens, 1989), 263–274.

Tykot, R.H., Herrmann, J.J., Jr., van der Merwe, N.J, Newman, R. and Allegretto, K.O. Thasian marble sculptures in European and American collections: isotopic and other analyses, in: J.J. Herrmann, Jr., N. Herz, and R. Newman (eds.), *ASMOSIA 5: Interdisciplinary Studies of Ancient Stone, Proceedings of the Fifth International Conference of the Association for the Study of Marble and Other Stones in Antiquity,* Museum of Fine Arts, Boston, June 1998 (London, 2002), 188–195.

Tykot, R.H. Scientific methods and applications to archaeological provenance studies, in: M. Martini, M. Milazzo and M. Piacentini (eds.), *Proceedings of the International School of Physics 'Enrico Fermi' Course CLIV* (Amsterdam, 2004), 407–432.

Van Keuren, F., with contributions by L. Peter Gromet. The Marbles of Three Mythological Sarcophagi at RISD and of Other Sarcophagi Found in Central Italy, in: *KOINE: Mediterranean Studies in Honor of R. Ross Holloway,* edited by D.B. Counts and A. Tuck (Oxford, 2009), 187–206.

Vian, F. and Moore, M.B. Gigantes, in: *LIMC,* vol. 4 (Zürich and Munich, 1988), 191–270.

Visconti, C.L. Delle pitture murali di tre sepolcri ostiensi discoperti nel MDCCCLXV. *Annali dell'Instituto di Corrispondenza Archeologica* 38 (1866), 292–325.

Walker, S. The Marble Quarries of Proconnesos: Isotopic Evidence for the Age of the Quarries and for *Lenos*-Sarcophagi Carved at Rome, in: *Marmi antichi: Problemi d'impiego, di restauro e d'identificazione*, edited by P. Pensabene (Rome, 1985), 57–65.

Walker, S. Aspects of Roman Funerary Art, in: *Image and Mystery in the Roman World: Three papers given in memory of Jocelyn Toynbee*, edited by J. Huskinson, M. Beard and J. Reynolds (Gloucester, 1988a), 23–36.

Walker, S. From West to East: Evidence for a Shift in the Balance of Trade in White Marbles, in: N. Herz and M. Waelkens (eds.), *Classical Marble: Geochemistry, Technology, Trade. Proceedings of the NATO Advanced Research Workshop on Marble in Ancient Greece and Rome: Geology, Quarries, Commerce, Artifacts.* Il Ciocco, Lucca, Italy. May 9–13, 1988. NATO ASI Series E: Applied Sciences, vol. 153 (Dordrecht, 1988b), 187–195.

Walker, S. and Matthews, K. Recent Work on Stable Isotope Analysis of White Marble at the British Museum, in: J.C. Fant (ed.), *Ancient Marble Quarrying and Trade: Papers from a Colloquium held at the Annual Meeting of the Archaeological Institute of America, San Antonio, Texas, December, 1986.* BAR International Series 453 (1988), 117–125.

Ward-Perkins, J.B. and Throckmorton, P. The San Pietro Wreck. *Archaeology* 18 (1965), 201–209.

Woodford, S. Meleagros, in: *LIMC,* vol. 6 (Zürich and Munich, 1992), 414–435.

Wurch-Kozelj, M. and Kozelj, T. Roman quarries of Apse-Sarcophagi in Thassos of the second and third centuries, in: Y. Maniatis, N. Herz and Y. Basiakos (eds.), *ASMOSIA III Athens: Transactions of the 3rd International Symposium of the Association of the Study of Marble and Other Stones used in Antiquity,* Athens 17–19 May 1993 (London, 1995), 39–47

6.
In the Guise of Gods and Heroes: Portrait Heads on Roman Mythological Sarcophagi

ZAHRA NEWBY

The Roman practice of adding portrait heads to the characters on mythological sarcophagi is well known. These faces with their individualised features and period hairstyles gaze out at us from the pages of handbooks and catalogues, giving a vivid impression of the way that Roman lives and deaths could be directly equated with the fates of mythological figures. Yet this very ubiquity begs a question: just how representative of the larger category of Roman mythological sarcophagi are the chests with portrait heads? The aim of this paper is to conduct a close analysis of mythological sarcophagi with portrait heads, to look at what the presence of portraits adds to the mythological scenes and to ask whether they should be seen as simply intensifying the message of a mythological scene or of altering and nuancing it in a particular way.

Despite the familiarity of sarcophagi with portrait heads, little analysis of these chests as a group has been done.[1] While readings of some individual pieces suggest that the addition of portrait heads sometimes refocused the meaning of a myth in surprising ways, the prevailing assumption among scholars seems to be that portrait features on sarcophagi merely reinforce the normal message of the mythological subject matter.[2] For many scholars, the portraits simply make explicit a message which may be more muted elsewhere. In Koortbojian's words 'all mythological sarcophagi assert analogies; the presence of the portrait features of the deceased merely intensifies and particularizes the monument's message'.[3]

Greater analysis of the sarcophagi with portrait heads might be expected from Henning Wrede's discussion of images assimilating individuals with particular gods. This discusses a number of mythological sarcophagi alongside statues or reliefs which show individuals in the dress of, or with the attributes of, divine figures.[4] However, Wrede's focus is necessarily selective, and depends on

1 For brief accounts see Fittschen 1970, 188, n. 64 f.; Schauenburg 1980, esp. 153–4; Koch-Sichtermann 1982, 607–14; Zanker and Ewald 2004, 45–50. On unfinished heads see also Andreae 1984 and Huskinson 1998.

2 Individual accounts: Blome 1992, 1062–5; Zanker 1999. Fittschen 1984 concentrates on the portraits as evidence for dating but also reveals a few unusual uses of the myths.

3 Koortbojian 1995, 18.

4 Wrede 1981, esp. 139–57.

his own reading of the meaning of the myths. Apart from scenes showing the deceased in the guise of a particular god (relatively rare on sarcophagi except in the cases of Selene and Mars), Wrede only includes mythological sarcophagi showing heroes when he reads the myth as one of apotheosis.[5] Rather than analysing what the addition of portrait heads adds to these sarcophagi, Wrede starts from the belief that they show prospective messages about a happy afterlife and does not examine how sarcophagi with portrait heads differ from those without.[6]

The messages of mythological imagery on sarcophagi have, however, been extensively debated for decades with views ranging from those which see the myths as allegories of apotheosis, expressing belief in the soul's continued survival after death, to interpretations of them as retrospective, commenting on the deceased's qualities and interests during life, or simply reflecting his tastes and education.[7] Recent scholarship stresses the multiple levels at which mythological sarcophagi could be interpreted, adding to the ranks of interpreters bereaved relatives seeking consolation for the sudden death of a loved-one, or the ante-mortem purchaser commissioning his or her own tomb.[8] Interpretations of the meaning of *portraits* on particular mythological figures often seem simply to reflect an individual scholar's view of what that particular myth meant in a funerary context.[9] Yet study of funerary inscriptions suggests a wide range of views about life and death, ranging from the bleak to the hopeful, suggesting that belief in immortality was, as Lattimore concluded, 'not widespread, nor clear, nor very strong'.[10] While some representations of myths were more violent, or conversely more idyllic, than others, the same imagery could in some circumstances provoke differing interpretations depending on the beliefs and hopes of those who viewed it. Close examination of some individual sarcophagi with portrait faces leads me to challenge the dominant assumption that they simply intensify the normative message of the mythological subject matter and, indeed, that one dominant reading of a myth always existed. Rather,

5 Wrede 1981, 5–6. Ariadne is included, Endymion not. For criticism of the subjective criteria applied, see Mottahedeh 1984.

6 Wrede 1981, 168–75.

7 The poles of the argument are represented by Cumont 1942 and Nock 1946, with modifications by other scholars. For discussion see Turcan 1978; Koch-Sichtermann 1982, 583–617; also Müller 1994, 139–70. The reviews by North 1983, Grassinger 1998, Ewald 1999 also comment on interpretation.

8 Zanker and Ewald 2004 especially stress the messages to the bereaved, sometimes underplaying the role of those who commissioned their tombs before death. For the importance of organising one's tomb during life see Trimalchio in Petronius, *Satyricon* 71 discussed by Whitehead 1993.

9 E.g. Engemann 1973, 28 on the self-evident interpretation of Ariadne and Endymion as symbols of apotheosis.

10 Lattimore 1942, 342.

I will argue that the addition of portrait features reflects an awareness of the multivalency of mythological imagery and the desire to authorise a particular interpretation of the myth, changing and particularising its meaning in interesting and important ways.

The frequency and distribution of portrait heads

Despite the frequency with which mythological sarcophagi with portrait heads are illustrated, they are not actually that common. Of around 1200 mythological sarcophagi of Roman production which survive, only about 70 include either portrait features or unfinished heads. Even taking into account the fact that a large proportion of the surviving sarcophagi are too fragmentary or damaged to tell whether portraits were originally present, this is a very small proportion. The distribution of portraits across different myths is also uneven, as can be seen in Table 1.[11]

While the small numbers involved mean that the statistics should be handled carefully, some features are immediately apparent. Firstly, a large number of mythological scenes never include portrait heads.[12] These include violent scenes such as the deaths of the Niobids and the abduction of the daughters of Leucippus, as well as scenes often taken to refer to the *virtus* of the deceased, such as Achilles on Scyros. On other myths, portrait heads are definitely the exception rather than the rule. This is especially true for the sarcophagi with the rape of Persephone and those showing Meleager, two of the most popular themes on sarcophagi but with very few examples of portrait heads. In other myths, portrait features are much more popular, as on sarcophagi showing Achilles and Penthesilea, or Mars approaching the sleeping Rhea Silvia. This last group of sarcophagi is a small one, and only emerges in the third century. It is, however, closely related to the scenes of Selene approaching the sleeping Endymion and Dionysus's discovery of the sleeping Ariadne. Both

11 The numbers here are based on the catalogues in *ASR*, updated with new discoveries as far as possible, and reflect my own opinion in those cases where the presence of portrait features is debated. The table is intended to give a general impression and does not claim to be exhaustive. I do not include sarcophagi where women are assimilated with the Muses or Aphrodite outside a specific mythological narrative context. There are a few one-off sarcophagi, such as those showing Protesilaos (discussed below) and Hylas (Zanker and Ewald 2004, 96–8: see also Birk, this volume) not included in these figures. I include here sarcophagi from Italian workshops which copy Roman metropolitan forms, but not sarcophagi from elsewhere in the Roman world. The addition of portrait heads to mythological figures is not generally found on the Attic or Asia Minor sarcophagi.

12 For surveys of mythological themes on Roman sarcophagi see Sichtermann-Koch 1975; Koch-Sichtermann 1982, 127–95; Zanker and Ewald 2004, 278–381.

Table 1: Portraits on Mythological Sarcophagi

Subject	No. of sarcophagus fronts where heads are visible (total)	No. with portrait heads/unfinished heads	%, where known, where heads have portraits or are unfinished
Achilles & Penthesilea	13 (24)	9	69 %
Adonis	12 (24)	1	8 %
Alcestis	6 (12)	2	33 %
Discovery of Ariadne	31 (34)	14	45 %
Endymion	55 (107)	17	31 %
Hercules Labours	12 (30)	3	25 %
Hippolytos	18 (35)	3	17 %
Mars & Rhea Silvia	3 (6)	3	100 %
Meleager	59 (136)	7	12 %
Pelops	5 (7)	1	20 %
Persephone	48 (80)	4	8 %

of these themes can also feature portrait heads, as we see on around half the Ariadne figures, and a third of Selene and Endymion figures. Other figures who sometimes gain portrait features are Alcestis, Heracles and Hippolytus.

The vast majority of these portraits (around 90 %) show hairstyles of the third century and it seems as though the period from 200–250 was the most popular time for portrait identifications. Indeed, in some groups of mythological sarcophagi almost all the third-century examples have portraits.[13] During the second century (at least until the Severan period) portraits are much less common. This is also true of sarcophagi with the Muses or Erotes, which present a generic mythological world rather than a specific mythological narrative. Apart from a couple of early exceptions, these do not receive portrait features until well into the third century.[14] On non-mythological sarcophagi the

13 Engemann 1973, 28, n. 124.

14 Exceptions: *ASR V, 2, 1*, no. 5 (a sarcophagus in Berlin showing a young girl among Erotes); Moretti 1975, no. 8 (G. P. Begni) = Wrede 1981, no. 239 (Sarcophagus from Cività Castellana showing the portrait of a boy on the figure of a Muse, not in *ASR* V,3).

taste for portraits seems to correspond to this general picture. Early examples of battle sarcophagi feature a series of separate combats without any individualisation of particular figures, only focusing on a central group around the turn of the third century when portrait features (or an unfinished head) begin to be added to the central figure.[15] Lion hunt sarcophagi almost always give portrait (or unfinished) features to the central figure, but only begin to emerge around 230, developing out of the mythological hunt sarcophagi.[16] Portraits appear rather earlier on the small group of '*Vita romana*' sarcophagi showing the deceased as general, magistrate and husband which emerge around 170.[17] Tondo portraits also begin to appear on Dionysiac and marine sarcophagi towards the end of the second century, filling with portrait faces shields or shells which had previously remained empty or bore simply an inscription.[18]

There seems to have been an increasing desire to include portraits on sarcophagi from the late second century onwards, though this ranged from images of the deceased on lids or shields, sometimes carried by mythological figures, to full identification of the deceased with a particular mythological character. Rather than seeing the addition of portraits to mythological sarcophagi as influenced by the display of narratives featuring the deceased on non-mythological sarcophagi the trend towards portraiture seems to occur on both mythological and non-mythological frieze sarcophagi roughly concurrently; in both it is erratic until the later second century and reaches its height in the third century, continuing even later on some sarcophagi types.

On some late sarcophagi, individual mythological figures could also be excerpted from their narrative contexts and represented with portrait heads. This can be seen on the Ariadne sarcophagi in Naples (from Auletta) and Copenhagen, as well as on the Endymion sarcophagus in the Palazzo Braschi and one in the British Museum where the central figure has been reworked from a female Ariadne figure to one showing Endymion.[19] When such figures are taken out of their narrative context the question arises as to whether we should still think of them as showing the deceased in the guise of Ariadne or Endymion, or rather simply as a representation of the deceased in eternal

Both are dated mid second century. For discussion of portraits on these groups see *ASR* V,2,1: 109–113 (Kranz) and *ASR V, 3:* 128–33 (Wegner).

15 Andreae 1956; Schäfer 1979, 357–8.

16 See Andreae *ASR* I, 2 for analysis of the group. One late exception to this is a sarcophagus in the Palazzo dei Conservatori, dated to c. 280, which seems instead to allude to the hunting spectacles of the arena; *ASR* I,2, no. 110.

17 Collected in *ASR* I,3 (Reinsberg). For a discussion of the meaning of the group see also Muth 2004.

18 *Vita Romana:* Tondo portraits: Matz 1971, see further *ASR* IV,4, 452–66 (Matz); *ASR* V,1 (Rumpf).

19 *ASR* IV,3, no. 229; Wrede 1981, cat.54 ; *ASR* XII,2, no. 102; Sichtermann 1966. See also Birk in this volume and Figure 7.5.

repose.[20] It raises the question of what importance should be given to the events of the myth itself, as opposed to the qualities and attributes embodied in the figure of the hero or heroine. These isolated figures share some characteristics with the representations of humans in the forms of gods in statues or reliefs. Wrede's discussion of these figures, which appear from the later first century, suggests that they were used to embody particular qualities such as beauty, chastity, or success in business; their significance linked to this one point of correspondence.[21] Similar figures also appear on sarcophagi where the deceased is shown in the guise of Venus or as one of the Muses, outside a narrative context.[22] Here we might see the identification as stressing the beauty or education of the figure. When identifications are made in the context of particular mythological narratives, however, the events of the myth open up a wider range of options about which qualities and values are being expressed.

Second-century Mythological Sarcophagi with Portraits: Loss, Virtue and Family Values

While the majority of mythological portrait sarcophagi date to the first half of the third century, the earliest examples go back to the mid second century.[23] The most famous example is the well-known Alcestis sarcophagus in the Vatican whose inscription provides us with important contextual information (Figure 6.1).[24] This informs us that Gaius Junius Euhodus, of the Palatina tribe, made the sarcophagus for himself and his wife, Metilia Acte. She was priestess of the Magna Mater in Ostia, while he served as five-yearly magistrate of the guild of carpenters in the 21st *lustrum*, 158–163.[25] The sarcophagus shows multiple heads with portrait features. The figure of Alcestis on her death-bed is given the features of an aging woman, with a hairstyle reminiscent of the early Antonine period, c. 140–150. Presumably this is the face of Metilia Acte herself. Behind this figure appear the heads of an old woman, also with an early Antonine

20 See the debate between Sichtermann 1966 esp. 82–7; ibid., *ASR* XII,2, 46–8 and Engemann 1973, 28–30; the literature is reviewed by Koortbojian 1995, 138–41.

21 Wrede 1981, 67–124.

22 Venus: e.g. clipeus portrait with deceased as crouching Venus, *ASR* V.1, no. 92; Zanker and Ewald 2004, 126–7, fig. 110. On Muses see Marrou 1938; Wrede 1981, 148–9.

23 On the fragment in Ostia showing Demeter with portrait head, dated to 140s, see below, n. 49. A Muse sarcophagus with the portrait of a boy from Cività Castellana is also early, c. 150; Moretti 1975, 259 f, no. 8 (G. P. Begni); Wrede 1981, 140–1, 285–6, no. 239.

24 *ASR* XII,1, no. 76. See also Wood 1978/1993; Zanker and Ewald 2004, 202–3, figs. 182–3; 298–30, no. 8.

25 *CIL* XIV.371. Dating of the *lustrum:* Fittschen 1984, 142, 160, n. 46; *ASR* XII,1, 111 (Grassinger).

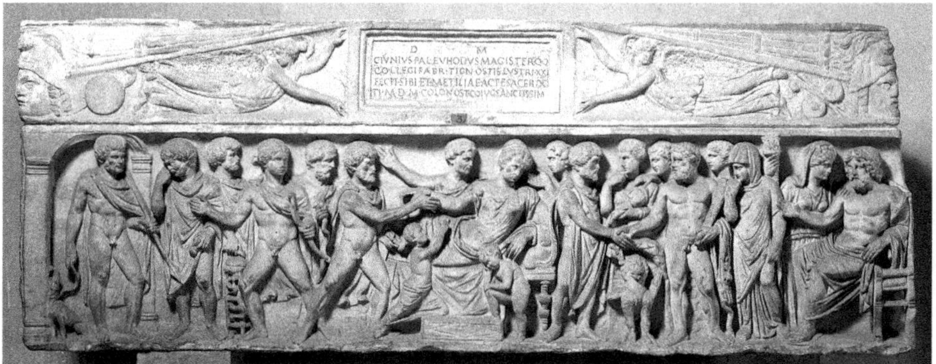

Figure 6.1: Alcestis sarcophagus, Vatican Museo Chiaramonti inv. 1195. Photo: Vatican Museums.

hairstyle, and of a younger woman with hair in the style of Faustina the younger, from c. 152. They may represent the features of members of Metilia and Euhodus' family. The figure of Admetus himself appears twice, approaching his wife's deathbed and clasping hands with Heracles. Both figures show portrait features with a hairstyle like that of the emperor Lucius Verus common from 160.[26] The figures of an old man in the deathbed scene, and some of the hunters to the left also appear to have portrait features, again evoking members of the couple's wider family.

As Klaus Fittschen has noted, the hairstyles shown here actually span a period of some twenty years, though there is no indication that the portraits were executed at different dates and all seem to be contemporary with the working of the sarcophagus.[27] Its date can be fixed to soon after 160 from the evidence of the inscription and Euhodus' portrait face. The fact that Metilia sports an earlier portrait type may be due to one of two factors: either she continued to wear a style which had already gone out of fashion, or she had, in fact, died some years earlier. If the latter, it is possible that she was initially buried in a simpler grave and it was only once Euhodus had gained increased wealth and prestige, notably in the form of his magistracy, that he decided to commission a new sarcophagus to commemorate them both. The presence of other family portraits on the sarcophagus need not necessarily mean that they had all died too, since they are not mentioned in the inscription, but it does draw attention to the wider family setting of the couple and suggests their grief

26 The hunter at the far left has also been seen as Euhodus because of his portrait features, but these differ markedly from the other two depictions: Blome 1978, 442–4; Zanker and Ewald 2004, 298; *ASR* XII,1, 125 (Grassinger). On the portraits see also Fittschen 1984, 141–3.

27 Fittchen 1984, 141–3.

at Metilia's death. Euhodus' membership of the Palatina tribe suggests that he was probably a freedman, a fact which may have motivated this display of extended family, an attribute denied to him while he was a slave.[28]

The sarcophagus is part of a smallish group of Alcestis sarcophagi which cluster in the second half of the second century.[29] The majority of these do not have portrait features but show the same general scene of the death of Alcestis in the centre while Admetus is shown with a group of his hunters to the left.[30] One in St Aignan, France, has a Greek inscription on the lid informing us that it was dedicated by a mother to her daughter; on others, such as the one in the Villa Albani, the stress is on grief at Alcestis' death, with figures showing gestures of distress.[31] Grave poetry shows that the figure of Alcestis could be used as the prime exemplum of a virtuous woman: a bilingual Greek and Latin inscription from Sardinia marks the grave of a woman named Pomptilla who is said to have prayed to die in place of her husband when he was suffering from an illness. Her subsequent death is taken as proof of her outstanding loyalty as a wife. In the Greek section of the inscription Pomptilla is explicitly compared with various Greek heroines who were renowned for their loyalty to their husbands – Penelope, Laodicea, Evadne and Alcestis.[32] The addition of portrait features on the Vatican sarcophagus particularises the myth and also allows a greater stress on Admetus/Euhodus who is shown as loving husband as well as, in his heroic nudity, as a vibrant and vigorous figure. His handshake with Hercules, at the right end of the sarcophagus, also acts as a symbol of concordia, a virtue which was also prized on sarcophagi with scenes of Roman life.[33]

In its presentation of a dying woman lying on a couch with her family gathered around, the iconography of the sarcophagus also echoes imagery found on non-mythological sarcophagi of the period. The '*vita privata*' sarcophagi and reliefs catalogued by Rita Amedick include examples of the deceased reclining on a *kline* which can feature quite detailed portraits, as on a *loculus* cover from Ostia where the woman's hairstyle suggests a date of c. 150.[34] Closer to the picture of grief shown on the Alcestis sarcophagi are the images of relatives grieving for the death of a child which appear on biographical sarcophagi of children.[35] These date from the Hadrianic period onwards and sometimes give reasonably precise features to the deceased or his/her parents, though elsewhere

28 On the Palatina tribe see Meiggs 1973, 190–1. It is also possible that some of the figures could have been fellow-*liberti* rather than family members.

29 Blome 1978, 435–45; *ASR* XII,1, 110–28 (Grassinger).

30 The chest in Genoa, *ASR* XII,1, no. 86, c. 200–210, also has a worn portrait head.

31 *ASR* XII,1, nos. 75, 77.

32 *IG* XIV.607; *CIL* X.7563/78; Peek 1955, 636–40, no. 2005, l. 22–31.

33 *ASR* XII,1, 127 (Grassinger).

34 *ASR* I,4, no. *176.

35 *ASR* I,4: 72–4 (Amedick).

the faces are more generic.[36] The sharing of visual types between mythological and non-mythological sarcophagi suggests the projection of Roman funerary values into a mythological world, perhaps as an extended poetic analogy expressing the virtues of the deceased. When portrait features are added these two worlds fuse together in a particular and powerful way.

In the grave inscription of Pomptilla she is compared not only to Alcestis, but also to Penelope, Evadne and Laodameia. Only the latter of these three appears on sarcophagi, in a one-off piece in the Vatican museum, dated to c. 170 (Figure 6.2).[37] It shows the story of Protesilaus in a series of scenes, starting from the left short side where the hero's departure for the Trojan War is shown. On the front he is shown disembarking from the boat at Troy whereupon he is immediately killed. While his corpse lies on the ground his ghost (the heavily draped figure) is led down to Hades by Hermes. In the adjoining scene, however, we see the hero again, restored to his youthful form, being led by Hermes back to his palace for a reunion with his wife.[38] This takes place in the centre of sarcophagus and is shown as a formal *dextrarum iunctio* in front of the doors of the palace. The figures of Protesilaus and Laodameia are assimilated to the poses of married couples on *vita humana* sarcophagi and both heads are unfinished.[39] To the right of this scene the rest of the myth is retold, with their figures reverting to idealised forms. Laodameia lies grieving on her bed; the similarity to deathbed scenes such as those of Alcestis, discussed above, foreshadows her imminent suicide. To the far right Protesilaus is led back down to Hades, which is defined on the right short side by the scenes of the torments of the sinners Tantalus, Ixion and Sisyphus.

Only one other version of this myth survives on sarcophagi, a piece in Naples Santa Chiara which has a different iconography, showing Protesilaus' return to Laodameia as she reclines on the ground.[40] The Vatican sarcophagus is thus a unique piece, probably designed as a special commission. This makes the unfinished state of the central portraits particularly interesting. The explanation sometimes offered for unfinished heads, that they were stock workshop pieces which never received the intended personalisation, clearly does not work for

36 The well-known biographical sarcophagus of a child in the Louvre gives quite precise features to the boy's mother, *ASR* I,4, no. 114, dated c. 150 (this does not include the death scene). For examples of possible portraits of the deceased see *ASR* I,4, nos. 60, 198 (later addition?) contra e.g. no. 2. The frequency and use of portraits on non-mythological sarcophagi would repay further study.

37 *ASR* III,3, no. 423; Zanker and Ewald 2004, 374–7, no. 35.

38 The story of Protesilaus is told by Apollodorus 3.30 and Lucian, *Dialogues of the Dead* 28 [23], 427.

39 On marriage sarcophagi see *ASR* I, 3 (Reinsberg).

40 *ASR* III,3, no. 422, Zanker and Ewald 2004, 101–2, fig. 85. The myth also appears on the Velletri sarcophagus, along with a number of other myths: Andreae 1963, 34–5.

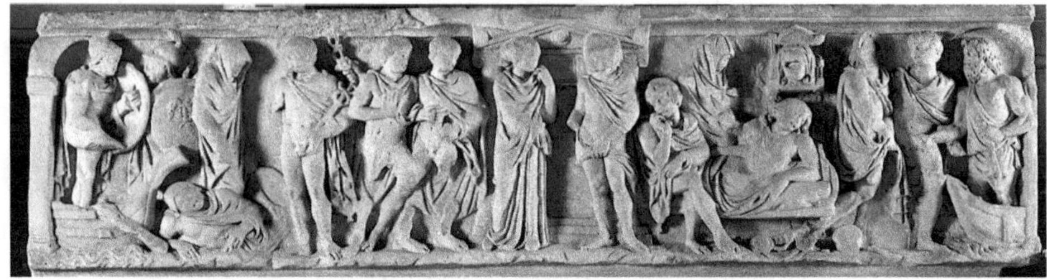

Figure 6.2: Protesilaus and Laodameia sarcophagus, Vatican Galleria dei Candelabri inv. 2465. Photograph: Vatican Museums.

what must have been an individual commission.[41] On close examination it is also evident that the two faces do not show the same extent of a lack of finish. While the head of Protesilaus is left as a large undistinguished block of circular stone, that of Laodameia has been more finely worked with the result that we can see the impression of her features and the clear outline of her chin and hair. She appears to wear her hair in a large, low, bun on the back of the neck, in a style similar to that favoured by Faustina the Younger in the 160s.[42] Other unfinished heads on sarcophagi show a similar range in the state of the heads, from blocks of roughly hewn marble, as for example on an Ariadne sarcophagus in Moscow, to blurred but recognisable outlines of faces such as that on the Ariadne sarcophagus of Maconiana Severiana, now in the J. Paul Getty Museum (see below, Figure 6.4).[43]

The usual interpretation of the Protesilaus sarcophagus is that it was made by a grieving wife for her predeceased husband, as would befit the course of the myth.[44] Yet if this sarcophagus did commemorate a dead husband, why was the portrait of the dead man left so obviously unfinished? The fact that on this sarcophagus one head is more finished than the other leads me to interpret it not as a tomb for a dead husband, but one for a dead wife. This would explain why the head of Laodameia is more highly finished than that of Protesilaus, where the head is left as a mere block, possibly for portrait features to be added at a later date. Andreae has suggested that some heads were deliberately left unfinished as a form of aspirational statement about the dead, often on sarcophagi for children.[45] The sketchy nature of Laodameia's face here might express the wish to imagine a reunion beyond the grave, rather than the certainly of such a union. Without the evidence of an inscription to help with

41 See Koch and Sichtermann 1982, 610–14; Andreae 1984 and Huskinson 1998 for fuller discussions of unfinished heads.

42 Fittschen 1982, 55–63 (types 7 and 8).

43 Moscow: *ASR* IV,1, no. 47. Getty: previously Hever Castle, *ASR* IV,3, no. 214.

44 Zanker and Ewald 2004, 99–100, 377.

45 Andreae 1984, 114–18, 125.

interpretation we cannot know for certain who the sarcophagus was designed to hold and who commissioned it. However, the differing states of the portraits do, to me, suggest a monument to a dead woman rather than a man, even if it was eventually designed to hold them both.

This is certainly in conflict with the order of events in the myth where Protesilaus died first. However, in grave poetry references to Laodameia often appear in contexts where the death of a loyal and loving wife is lamented by her still-living husband.[46] We can read the sarcophagus as an extended consolation to the bereaved along the lines of the following: 'Even in myth great lovers were separated by death, think of Protesilaus and Laodameia. Just as loyal and faithful a wife was X; so great a love has been sundered'. The placement of Laodameia and Protesilaus in the pose of a Roman married couple evokes the formal public union of this couple during life, while also extending the hope or desire for a reunion in the afterlife.

There are a couple of other examples of portraits on funerary art from this period. One is a relief in Venice archaeological museum which probably served as a slab covering a burial. Fittschen has convincingly interpreted it as showing the myth of Cleobis and Biton (as famously told in Herodotus, *Histories* 1.33). The figures of Cleobis and Biton are given portrait features, while their mother shows the hairstyle of the younger Faustina, suggesting a date in the 160s.[47] It would appear to commemorate the tomb of two sons, set up by their mother. Again, we can see this as a form of visual consolation. Grave poetry and inscriptions often feature the theme that those the gods love die young as well as the idea that those who meet an untimely death will be whisked away to dwell with the gods in the heavens.[48] The imagery of this relief asserts a similar message in visual form, offering the hope that the boys will be received into a happy afterlife, while stressing both their *pietas* towards their mother and the gods and the love shared between the family, who are shown embracing at the far right of the scene.

These early examples of portrait sarcophagi from the 160s show the flexibility of mythological narratives and the desire of relatives to use myth to express messages about themselves and their loved-ones.[49] As well as expressing

46 E.g. Peek 1955, 189, no. 727; 636–40, no. 2005; 688–9, no. 1737a.

47 Fittschen 1970; Sperti 1988, 142–51, no. 43. See also Zanker and Ewald 2004, 216–17, fig. 195.

48 Lattimore 1942, 39–42, 259.

49 A fragment in Ostia showing a female figure in a chariot with portrait features is often identified as the portrait of a bereaved mother assimilated to Demeter searching for Persephone (Zanker and Ewald 2004, 94, 270, n. 45 with further bibliography; see also Blome 1978, 453–5 recognising the problems of iconography discussed here). While the figure resembles the Demeter on Persephone sarcophagi (e.g. *ASR* III,3, no. 372) she is here accompanied by a second female figure holding a flaming torch, elsewhere an

the desire for consolation and the qualities sought in a wife or child (love, *pietas*, loyalty) they also show the cultural frame of reference of the deceased and their families, the widespread tendency to turn towards mythological analogies to express the truths of human life. In the process, they also proudly assert the educational level of these families, which seem to encompass both freedmen and higher status families.[50]

The sarcophagus of Metilia Acte is part of a series of Alcestis sarcophagi. On the chest in St. Aignan the addition of an inscription identifying the deceased as a daughter suggests that the myth may have been read as a symbol of the grief caused by a sudden loss.[51] The addition of portraits to the Vatican chest draws out different aspects of the myth. It allows the sarcophagus to become not just a celebration of the wifely perfection of Metilia herself, but also a proud statement of the status of Junius Euhodus whose magistracy is mentioned in the inscription, and who is shown in the mythological scenes as a loving husband, vigorous figure, and welcoming host. His place within a wide family, something which he as a freedman would have particularly valued, is also expressed by the numerous portraits of the figures around Metilia's deathbed.

These sarcophagi come from a period when the genre of sarcophagus art was still developing, and a number of chests were created as one-off commissions.[52] At the same time, marriage and magistrate sarcophagi with portraits began to appear.[53] It was a period of experimentation, showing the desire to use this new form of funerary decoration to express the qualities valued in human life via the time-honoured analogies of myth. Portrait heads are relatively rare here, but when added they act in a similar way to inscriptions. They can extend the message of the myth and stress particular aspects, such as Admetus' manly virtue, or Laodameia's loyalty, as well as familial grief. Portraits and inscriptions do not just add specificity, they also direct us to the elements of the myth which are seen as particularly important for the commemoration of a particular individual, perhaps suggesting a desire to control the messages offered by this new form of funerary imagery. After this initial period of experimentation, however, the addition of portrait heads to mythological scenes largely disappears again until the Severan period.

attribute of Persephone. If Persephone too is shown here this is unlikely to be a fragment from a Rape of Persephone sarcophagus and may instead assimilate the deceased to Demeter to convey ideas of her fecundity, as in some funerary statues, Wrede 1981, 213–19.

50 The question of social status is too complex to discuss here. Freedmen are particularly well-represented in all areas of funerary art (see Mouritsen 2005 with further references) but there is also evidence of senatorial families commissioning mythological sarcophagi, e.g. *ASR* IV,1, no. 26; *ASR* IV,3, no. 214.

51 *ASR* XII,1, no. 75.

52 E.g. the so-called Peleus and Thetis sarcophagus, Müller 1994.

53 *ASR* I,4 (Amedick).

Portraits on Later Mythological Sarcophagi

The majority of portraits on later mythological sarcophagi are found on sarcophagi with three themes: the discovery of Ariadne, Selene's visit to the sleeping Endymion, and Mars approaching the sleeping Rhea Silvia. These share a number of compositional similarities as can be seen from the combination of the myths of Selene/Endymion and Mars/Rhea Silvia on a sarcophagus in the Vatican (below, Figure 6.6) and in the reworking of an Ariadne-type figure to serve as a male Endymion on a sarcophagus in the British Museum.[54] However, a careful analysis of the use of portrait features suggests that the messages these scenes conveyed could vary substantially.

Ariadne

Sarcophagi showing the discovery of Ariadne by Dionysus form a sub-set of the much larger group of Dionysiac sarcophagi which generally show the god and his followers in scenes of revelry and triumph.[55] The prominence of the group varies greatly. While it is sometimes placed in the centre, it is often only one element in a much larger scene of Dionysiac worship and revelry.[56] On some pieces the addition of portrait features help to draw attention to the scene. A sarcophagus once on the Paris art market shows the discovery scene prominently placed in the centre but surrounded by figures of dancing maenads and, at the far right, a scene of sacrifice.[57] Here the figure of Ariadne seems to have portrait features. Her hair is parted in the middle and falls over her ears, with shoulder locks, in a manner similar to portraits of the younger Faustina and Lucilla, and her eyes are open.[58]

On the majority of the sarcophagi with portraits, however, Ariadne is not given a prominent position in the centre of the sarcophagus. Indeed, on a group of vat-shaped sarcophagi showing the Triumph of Dionysus, she is often relegated to a side position underneath a lion's head.[59] An example in Blenheim shows the drunken Dionysus standing in the centre of the sarcophagus,

54 *ASR* III,1, no. 92; *ASR* XII,2, 54 f. (Sichtermann); Koortbojian 1995, 135–8.

55 *ASR* IV,3, 360–404, *ASR* IV,1 (Matz).

56 For an example where it is more prominent, without portrait features, see *ASR* IV,3, no. 225; Engemann 1973, 28, n. 123.

57 *ASR* IV,3, no. 317.

58 Scholars have been reticent about calling this a portrait, though Matz (*ASR* IV,3, 389) noted the late Antonine hairstyle. Engemann 1973, 28, n. 122 denies a portrait on the grounds of the shoulder locks, but these are found elsewhere.

59 On the group see *ASR* IV,1, 146–56.

surrounded by his entourage.[60] The sleeping Ariadne (without a portrait head) lies to the right, beneath a lion's head, and is mirrored on the left side by the reclining figure of Heracles. Rather than seeing this primarily as a representation of the union of Dionysus and Ariadne, we should probably see her here instead as simply one more attribute of the god himself. Yet on some sarcophagi of a similar type Ariadne is indeed given portrait features. An example in Bolsena, dated to the early Severan period, shows on the front Dionysus standing between Hercules and a satyr.[61] A maenad rushes off to the right. Even further to the right the sleeping Ariadne appears beneath the lion's head boss, her body following the curve of the sarcophagus around the right end. Compositionally she is the pendant to a reclining figure of Tellus or Gaia on the left, who holds a cornucopia. The visual stress of the image is upon Dionysus, and his proud and confident pose. Yet Ariadne here is given portrait features, only really visible when we look at the sarcophagus from the right end when we see that she wears a hairstyle of the late Antonine/early Severan period. The portrait head might have been included to make the identification between the deceased and Ariadne clearer, on a design which did not really concentrate on her. It is also possible that the setting of the sarcophagus in the tomb privileged this viewpoint, particularly if it was displayed on the right wall of a tomb and approached from the right side. The addition of portrait features here can be read as a conscious effort to make a connection between deceased and mythological figure, on a visual type which did not, in itself, readily accommodate this.

A couple of other examples appear on fragments in Oslo and Paris. On both the figure of Ariadne is again pushed to the right, curved, end of the sarcophagus. On the fragment in Oslo she has portrait features, while on the piece in the Louvre the face is unfinished.[62] While Ariadne is here identified with the deceased, the composition of these sarcophagi as a whole did not stress the discovery of Ariadne by Dionysus and their ensuing union, but rather her place as part of the Dionysiac realm. Rather than supporting the interpretation of these sarcophagi as a sign of the apotheosis of the deceased through divine union with the god, here the dead woman is shown lying in a state of blissful sleep amidst a Dionysiac realm, perhaps offering a consolatory message to her bereaved relatives.[63]

60 *ASR* IV,1, no. 45.
61 *ASR* IV,1, no. 46.
62 Oslo: *ASR* IV,1, no. 46a; see also L'Orange 1962, 41–2. Louvre: *ASR* IV,1, no. 49.
63 On apotheosis see Engemann 1973, 28; Wrede 1981, 142–5.

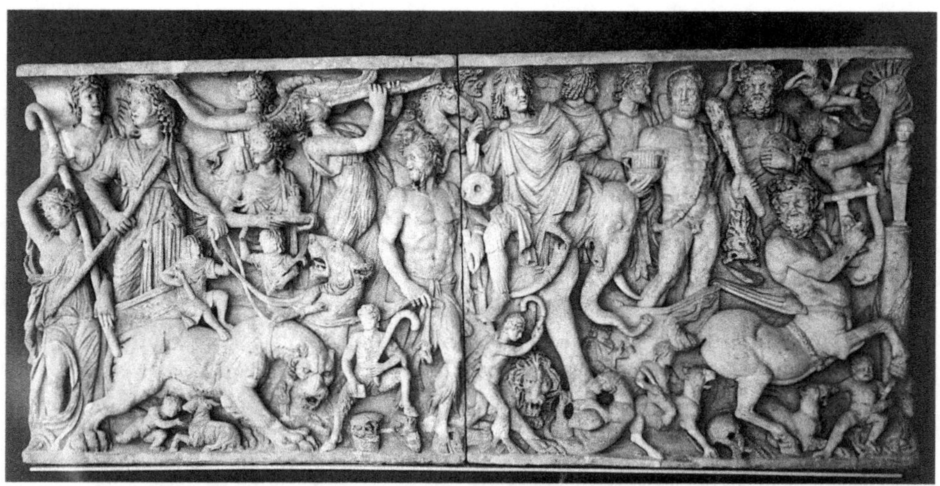

Figure 6.3: Dionysiac Triumph sarcophagus, Woburn Abbey.
Photograph: © Forschungsarchiv für römische Plastik Köln, neg. no. 1112.14.

Another sarcophagus which places the deceased in the Dionysiac realm via the use of portrait features is the unusual piece in Woburn Abbey (Figure 6.3).[64] This shows a densely packed scene of Dionysiac triumph with the god himself appearing in a chariot drawn by tigers at the left edge. To the right of the relief appears another chariot, this time drawn by centaurs and holding the figure of Hercules who appears naked except for a wreath and his lionskin, and holding his club and a wine *krater.* Unlike the drunken figures of Hercules which appear on some other Dionysiac sarcophagi, he is shown as an imposing figure. He wears a portrait head with hair and beard of the early third century. The deceased is thus placed into a context of Dionysiac feasting and revelry but assimilated with the powerful god Hercules, rather than the more effete Dionysus. Dionysus seems to have been generally an inappropriate figure to identify an adult male with, although a couple of examples do exist.[65] Here, the figure of Hercules offered a powerful, virile, model which also allowed for the male deceased to be shown as part of the Dionysiac realm.

Other Dionysiac sarcophagi stress the union of Ariadne and the god more clearly. On a vat-shaped sarcophagus in Moscow the figure of Ariadne is moved

64 *ASR* IV,2, no. 100, Matz dates it to Caracalla's reign; Angelicoussis 1992, 75–8, no. 78 (220–230); Zanker and Ewald 2004, 161, fig. 146 (c. 240).

65 The figure of the drunken Dionysus is given a portrait head on a strigillated sarcophagus in the Praetextatus catacombs: Wrede 1981, 155, 263, no. 181; Zanker and Ewald 2004, 160, fig. 145. A sarcophagus in the Museo Nazionale Romano which shows Dionysus and Ariadne enthroned may also have unfinished portrait features: Zanker and Ewald 2004, 164, fig. 150.

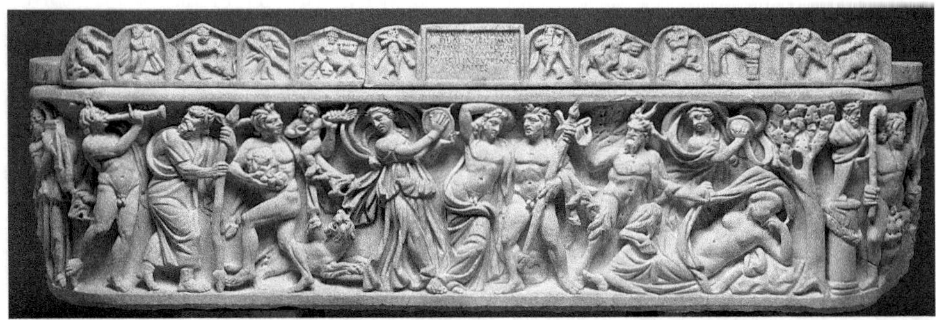

Figure 6.4: Sarcophagus of Maconiana Severiana showing the Discovery of Ariadne. The J. Paul Getty Museum, Villa Collection, Malibu, California. No. 83.AA.275 (Sarcophagus and Lid, Marble 210–220 AD, artist unknown). Photograph: museum.

closer to the god, to the left of the lion head boss. She has her head left as an unworked block to receive portrait features, though these were never completed.[66] Other examples are rectangular in shape and seem to belong in the mid-to-late Severan period. A sarcophagus in the Palazzo Borghese in Rome shows Dionysus descending from his centaur chariot to approach the sleeping Ariadne, who lies with one breast bared, and has a portrait and Severan hairstyle.[67] Another piece in the Hermitage Museum has a figure of Ariadne with a portrait and hairstyle of the late Severan period.[68] Two other pieces show unfinished heads. On the sarcophagus of Maconiana Severiana, the daughter of a senatorial couple, the head of Ariadne is left sketched out without a complete portrait (Figure 6.4).[69] Given the care and cost spent on the sarcophagus it seems likely that this was a deliberate decision on the part of her parents, possibly to express their hope that she was now in the Dionysiac realm, and perhaps that she might meet in the afterlife the husband who had been denied her in life. The unfinished portrait might allude to the girl's own untimely death, and the incompleteness of her life, whose natural progression to marriage and womanhood could now only be completed beyond the grave.[70]

A second sarcophagus on which the portrait was left unfinished is a chest in the Louvre, found with a companion piece showing Selene and Endymion in a tomb in Bordeaux.[71] The sarcophagus seems to have been designed for a couple. The figure of Ariadne has her face unfinished, but with the outline of the hair

66 *ASR* IV,1, no. 47.

67 *ASR* IV,3, no. 223.

68 *ASR* IV,3, no. 212; Matz suggests that the sarcophagus was carved earlier and the portrait added to an unfinished head at the time of use.

69 *ASR* IV,3, no. 214; Andreae 1984, 114; Walker 1990 discusses the sarcophagus in depth, including the difficulties of dating.

70 Andreae 1984, 114; Huskinson 1998, 144.

71 *ASR* III,1, no. 72; Zanker and Ewald 2004, 108–9, figs. 91–2.

drawn in. On the lid a male figure wearing a toga is also left with his face unfinished. The sarcophagus would thus seem to have been designed for a couple where the woman died first. By representing her as Ariadne her bereaved husband might have wanted to stress her beauty and desirability, through her nudity, and his hopes that she rest at peace in the afterlife. He himself is represented as a Roman citizen through the formal pose on the lid. The reasons for these portraits remaining unfinished are deeply obscure. The piece would have been an expensive commission and seems deliberately designed to belong with its companion Endymion piece where the portraits also remain unfinished. The space for the dedicatory inscription on the lid is also left blank. It may be that there was a deliberate decision made to leave the portraits unfinished, though it is harder to explain why a realistic portrait such as that on the lid would have been neglected. Perhaps this is a case of a sudden change of plan or circumstances; the man himself may have died before he was able to see through the completion of the sarcophagus and his heirs failed to carry it through.[72]

Endymion

The companion piece to the Louvre Ariadne sarcophagus shows the myth of Endymion.[73] The central figures of Selene and Endymion are shown against a background which is packed with figures; shepherds, goats and personifications fill every inch of space. Selene and Endymion are marked out by their size, which is shared by only a few other figures, and especially by the unfinished heads which are roughed out enough to tell the general outlines of the hairstyles. The space on the lid for an inscription is left bare. While we assume that a specific couple is commemorated here, their identity and features remain obscure to us.

This sarcophagus is one of a number which show portrait features or the provision for them on both Endymion and Selene.[74] The aim of these sarcophagi seems to be to draw a clear comparison between Selene and Endymion and the love between a married couple. The addition of portrait

72 Robert (*ASR* III,1, 86) notes that the sarcophagi were found piled on top of one another, apparently in a fourth-century context, which might suggest reuse. While the imagery suggests that they were designed for couples, only one skeleton was found inside each – a female skeleton in the Ariadne sarcophagus and a male one inside the Endymion sarcophagus. Robert had suggested that they were made for the husband and wife of one couple but Wrede 1981, 265–66, no. 185 notes that the shape of the hairstyle on Selene is different from that on Ariadne. Perhaps they were initially designed for two couples of the same family.

73 *ASR* XII,2, no. 72.

74 *ASR* XII,2, nos. 56, 73, 76, 77 (see Vighi 1935, 246), 92, 93, 95.

features to the mythological characters may be aimed at tying down the interpretation of the myth. Discussions of the funerary symbolism of this myth have ranged widely, from stressing the use of sleep as an analogy to death – the sleeping Endymion thus represents the dead person buried within – to seeing the myth as a complex metaphor for the apotheosis of the soul after death, as proposed by Franz Cumont.[75]

Koortbojian discerns a number of different messages in the myth suggesting that the central scene embodies the deceased's encounter with the divine while the bucolic scenes which surround the main image suggest a pastoral oasis of peaceful meditation.[76] On this reading Endymion represents the deceased man, perhaps presented in a consolatory way where sleep is compared to death and the dead shown residing in an idyllic bucolic setting. However, Koortbojian also draws attention to suggestions that it is through sleep that people communicate with supernatural forces – both with the gods and with the dead. According to this interpretation Endymion would not be dead, but the bereaved party, and the visitation of Selene compared to the dead wife's appearance in her husband's dreams.[77] On the sarcophagi where Selene and Endymion are given portrait features which are also idealised, for example through the addition of shoulder locks to Selene's image, the message could be seen as one of aspiration rather than faith, a statement by which the bereaved husband expresses his hope of seeing his dead wife in his dreams, or of a final reunification after death.[78] Such hopes are expressed in some funerary inscriptions; in one from Rome a wife prays to see her dead husband in her dreams and hopes that she will soon join him in death.[79]

When portraits are added to both figures, the stress seems to be on the assimilation of the couple's love to that of Selene and Endymion, rather than to Endymion's apotheosis or happy afterlife. If Endymion alone is shown, however, the message might be a stronger assertion of a faith in a happy afterlife. There are a number of fragments where Endymion has a portrait head, or his features unfinished in preparation for one; in many cases, however, we are lacking the figure of Selene and thus cannot tell whether she too might have been designed to have a portrait.[80] On one striking example, however, we find the figure of Endymion alone: a sarcophagus in the Palazzo Braschi in Rome where Endymion is shown with his eyes open and with portrait features, in the

75 Cumont 1942; Sichtermann (*ASR* XII,2, 41–53) discusses the symbolism of the myth.
76 Koortbojian 1995, 73–84, esp. 83.
77 Koortbojian 1995, 106–111.
78 Shoulder locks appear on *ASR* XII,2, nos. 93 and 95.
79 *CIL* VI,18817, discussed and translated by Koortbojian 1995, 108.
80 *ASR* XII,2, nos. 49, 85, 90.

company of the figures of Eros, the drunken Dionysus and Mars and Venus.[81] His pose clearly associates him with the figure of Endymion, but the mythological narrative is lacking – perhaps here we have a much stronger statement that the deceased was as beautiful as Endymion and is now at peace in the company of the gods.[82] The beauty of these dead men is sometimes stressed by their nakedness, as is their erotic allure. Here, perhaps, we have a figure who died before he had a chance to marry, whose vitality and desirability are stressed and proclaimed to make him the equal even of those beloved by the gods.[83]

One thing that is striking on the Endymion sarcophagi is that while human males are assimilated to heroes, as we see elsewhere on sarcophagi, the women are identified with a goddess. This is rare on other types of sarcophagi, though it does appear on grave statues in the round.[84] On many sarcophagi it is Selene, rather than Endymion, who occupies the central position. On an impressive sarcophagus in Woburn Abbey the goddess is given the portrait features of a mature woman who wears her hair in the style of the 250s (Figure 6.5).[85] Endymion's head, however, is left unfinished, though in the sketched-out technique which characterises other sarcophagi where there seems to have been a deliberate decision to leave the head unfinished.

The concentration on Selene here suggests that the sarcophagus was either commissioned by, or primarily designed for, a woman. However, it is unlikely that it was commissioned by a still-living husband for his dead wife. The impression of Endymion's portrait face is rather more youthful than that of the woman and shows no signs of the beard usually worn by mature men. If the sarcophagus was commissioned by the woman before her death, he may represent a husband who had died young, or possibly even her son. Mother-son relationships seem to be alluded to on other mythological sarcophagi, even when the myths concerned dealt with sexual relationships between men and women. The Theseus sarcophagus in Cliveden gives the abandoned Ariadne features which are much older than those on the figure of Theseus, suggesting that she may be identified with the mother of the deceased buried within, seventeen-year-old Artemidorus, whose features appear on the figures of Theseus.[86] The sarcophagus of Hippolytus in the Museo Nazionale Romano turns the scene of Phaedra's illicit love for her stepson into a scene of grief by a mother for her dead son, whose education is stressed by the fact that the letter he

81 *ASR* XII,2, no. 102.

82 On this sarcophagus see Sichtermann 1966; Koortbojian 1995, 135–41.

83 Cf. the sarcophagus of Maconiana Severiana, discussed above.

84 Wrede 1981, 67–139.

85 *ASR* XII,2, no. 94; Wrede 1981, 267, no. 189 (250–260); Angelicoussis 1992, 85–8, no. 65 (250).

86 *ASR* III,3, no. 430; Blome 1992, 1062–5.

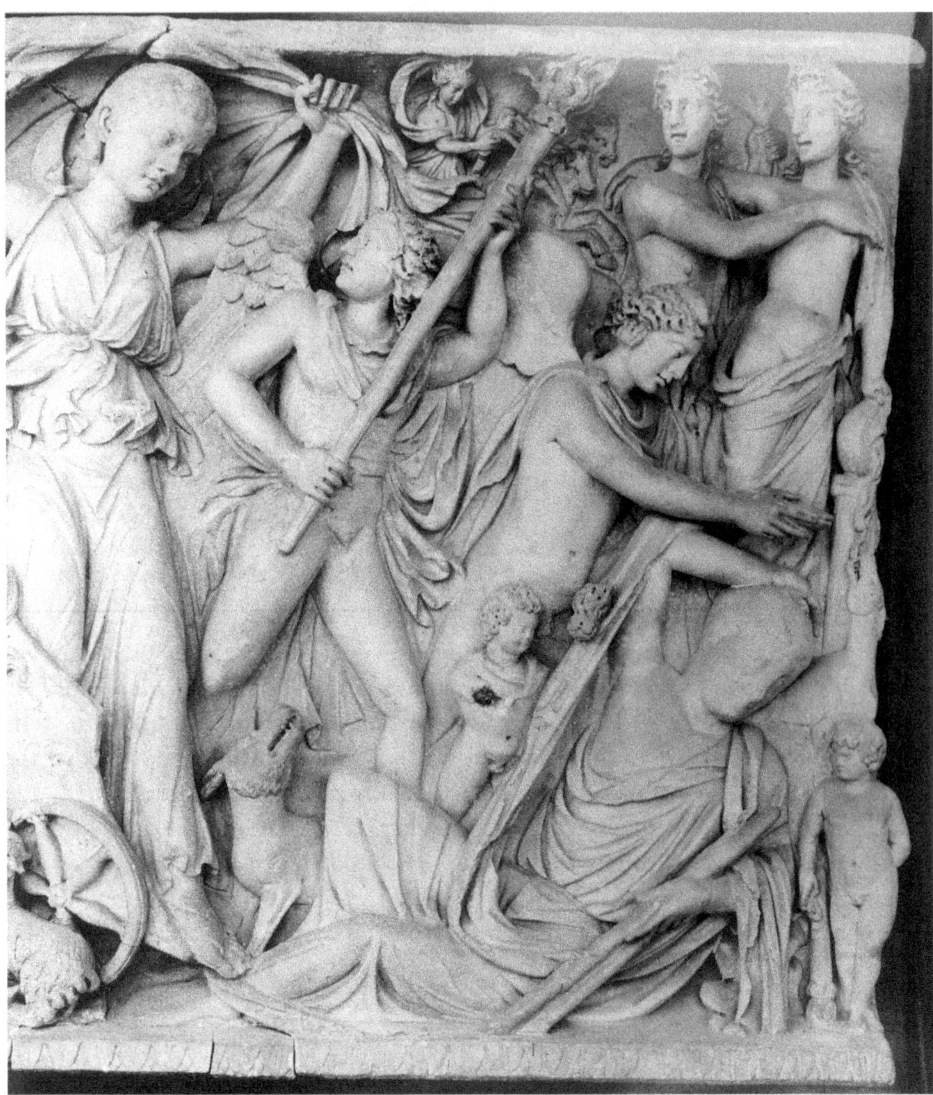

Figure 6.5: Selene and Endymion sarcophagus, Woburn Abbey; detail. Photograph: © Forschungsarchiv für römische Plastik Köln, neg. no. 1134/2.

carries is portrayed as a diptych.[87] On the Woburn Abbey sarcophagus we could be dealing with the expression of the hope that mother and son will be reunited in death. It is impossible to tell whether this was a commission before her death by a woman whose son (or husband) had already died, or by a still living son whose representation in the form of the sleeper Endymion alludes to his

87 Zanker 1999.

sightings of his mother in his dreams. In either case, the mismatch in the portraits suggests a separation in the circumstances of the two figures, and the expression of a hope for reunification rather than the certainty of resurrection.

It is important to remember that when inscriptional evidence is provided it often reveals a use of sarcophagi imagery which is contrary to that we would expect. On an Endymion sarcophagus in New York the inscription and portrait on the lid reveal the sarcophagus to have been chosen not to commemorate the death of a young man, but rather as a dedication by a woman to her dead mother.[88] Like the personalising inscriptions, portrait heads too could help to give a new twist to a mythological analogy, selecting from a range of interpretative options the one which was particularly desired by the commissioner. The great popularity of the Endymion myth as a theme for sarcophagi might well have been precisely its flexibility and range of meanings: sleep as a metaphor for death, the hope of a happy slumber in an idyllic realm, the belief that the youthful beauty of the deceased ought to bring them divine salvation, or the hope for marital reunion beyond the grave. All of these interpretations, and more, were available for selection and stress by changing the details of dress and portrait features.

Mars and Rhea Silvia

Whereas Ariadne sarcophagi seem to celebrate the beauty and desirability of a deceased woman and to express the hope that she will find peace within the Dionysiac joys of the afterlife, the Selene and Endymion sarcophagi could commemorate either a deceased man alone, or both partners in a couple, celebrating their hopes for reunion and their enduring love. The celebration of marital love also provides the theme for the small group of Mars and Rhea Silvia sarcophagi, which are closely linked to the sarcophagi of Selene and Endymion. In this myth the roles are reversed with the male taking the active role. Where we can tell, all the monumental representations of the scene seem to have portrait features, all dating to the first half of the third century.[89]

A sarcophagus in the Vatican represents the myths of Rhea Silvia and Endymion side by side, with portrait heads on the figures of Mars and Rhea

88 *ASR* XII,2, no. 80. It has been suggested that this is an example of reuse of a earlier sarcophagus. See also the sarcophagus dedicated to Gerontia in the Capitoline Museum, *ASR* XII.2, no. 27. In either case, the mythological imagery might still have had some resonance.

89 The two exceptions are sarcophagi where the couple appear as one motif among a number of scenes: *ASR* III,2, no. 192 (columnar sarcophagus), di Mino and Bertinetti 1990, 89–92, no. 67 (A. Bedini, *clipeus* sarcophagus).

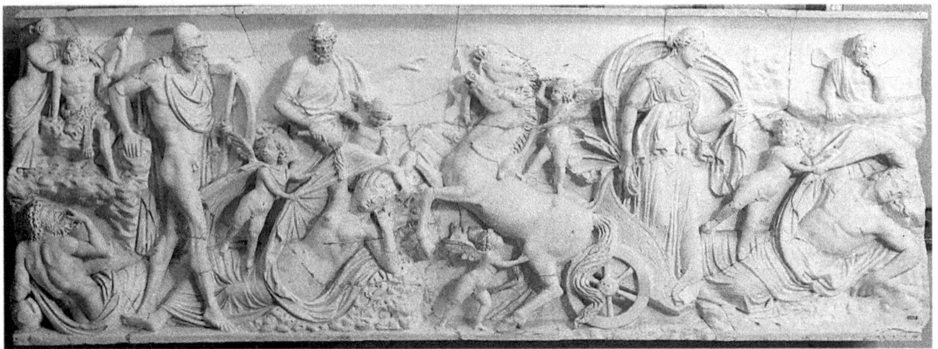

Figure 6.6: Mars and Rhea Silvia Sarcophagus, Vatican Museo Gregoriano Profano inv. 9558. Photograph: DAIR 74.535.

Silvia (Figure 6.6).[90] Fittschen has noted that whereas Rhea Silvia wears a hairstyle of the early Severan period (Figure 6.7), the face of Mars is reminiscent of the period of Caracalla, some 10–15 years later (Figure 6.8).[91] The female portrait is marked by its youthfulness, while that of Mars is older, with lines across the forehead. It seems likely that the sarcophagus was commissioned by a man while still alive to commemorate himself and a wife who had died some ten years before. Her portrait may have been completed following a death mask or portrait bust, and her remains transferred to the new coffin. The man's devotion to his wife even after years without her is expressed by his decision to commission a sarcophagus commemorating them both, and perhaps expresses his hope for a reunion in the afterlife. She seems to lie in a trancelike, timeless state, with eyes which are open but unseeing, her nakedness expressing her nubile beauty (Figure 6.7). The man's portrayal in the form of the active war god heroises him and draws attention to his own virtues and vigour as well as to his love for his wife. Whether the figures of Selene and Endymion also had portrait features on this sarcophagus is unknown because both heads are restored. However, it seems unlikely. The second couple may have been added to provide another mythological analogy for the love of the couple, and because of the typological similarities between the two situations. The general message of the imagery might be reconstructed as follows: 'I, as vigorous as Mars, hope to be reunited with my beautiful wife who lies sleeping in the afterlife, just as Mars was united with Rhea Silvia, and Selene with Endymion.'

The second example where the heads of both protagonists are preserved is a sarcophagus in Palazzo Mattei in Rome which sets the central figures against a

90 *ASR* XII,2, no. 99.

91 Fittschen 1984, 160, n. 47a. He suggests that the sarcophagus style also dates to the period of Caracalla.

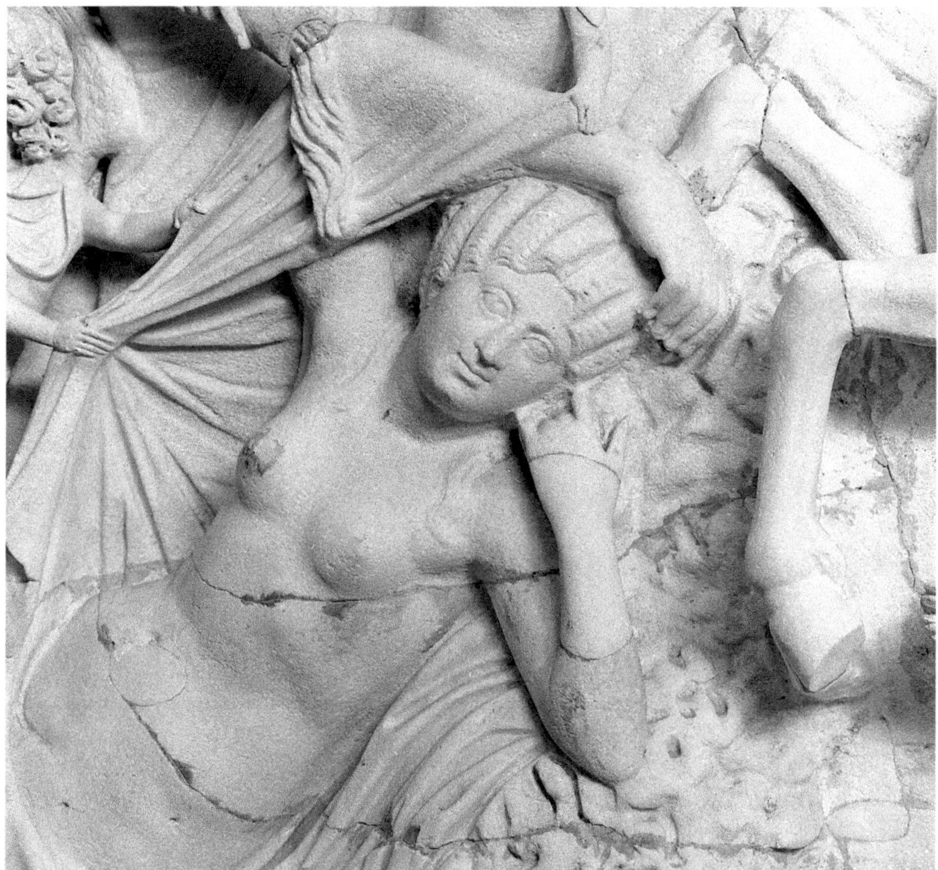

Figure 6.7: Mars and Rhea Silvia Sarcophagus, detail. Photograph: DAIR 74.539.

background of subsidiary personifications (Figure 6.9).[92] Here too, Fittschen suggests that the portrait types represent different periods. He dates the hairstyle of the woman to the border between the early and mid Severan period, whereas he sees in the portrait of the man features of the period 240–250. He concludes that the sarcophagus dates to the latter period.[93] However, other evidence suggests that the sarcophagus dates to the late 220s. The hairstyle worn by Rhea Silvia is similar to those worn by Julia Mameaea and Orbiana (respectively the mother and wife of Alexander Severus) and the short beard and moustache worn by the figure of Mars have parallels in the portraiture of Alexander Severus

92 *ASR* III,2, no. 188; Guerrini 1982, no. 61. Another sarcophagus in the Palazzo Mattei (*ASR* III,2, no. 190; Guerrini 1982, no. 60) has the lower half, including the figure of Rhea Silvia, restored.

93 Fittschen 1984, 149.

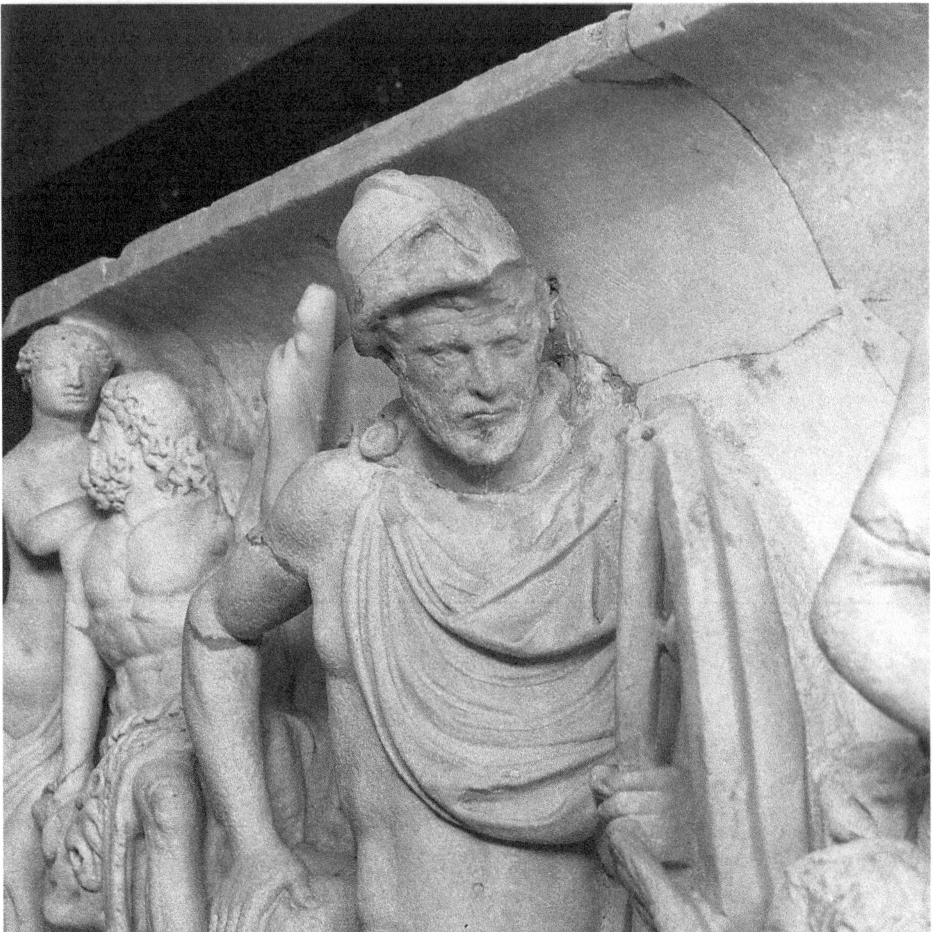

Figure 6.8: Mars and Rhea Silvia Sarcophagus, detail. Photograph: DAIR 74.540.

himself.[94] There is no obvious difference in ages between the two figures and it seems safest to assume that they do represent a married couple, though perhaps here too the wife died first and the sarcophagus was commissioned by her husband to commemorate them both.

This sarcophagus front has been linked with two short sides in the Vatican, one of which shows the discovery of the twins Romulus and Remus being suckled by the she-wolf. Unlike the majority of mythological scenes found on

94 Guerrini 1982, 215. Orbiana was wife of Alexander Severus between 225–227. A coin portrait of Alexander wearing a short beard and moustache is dated to 228: Wiggers and Wegner 1971, 179, pl. 45e (*Sesterce* 515). The evidence thus supports a date in the late 220s for the sarcophagus.

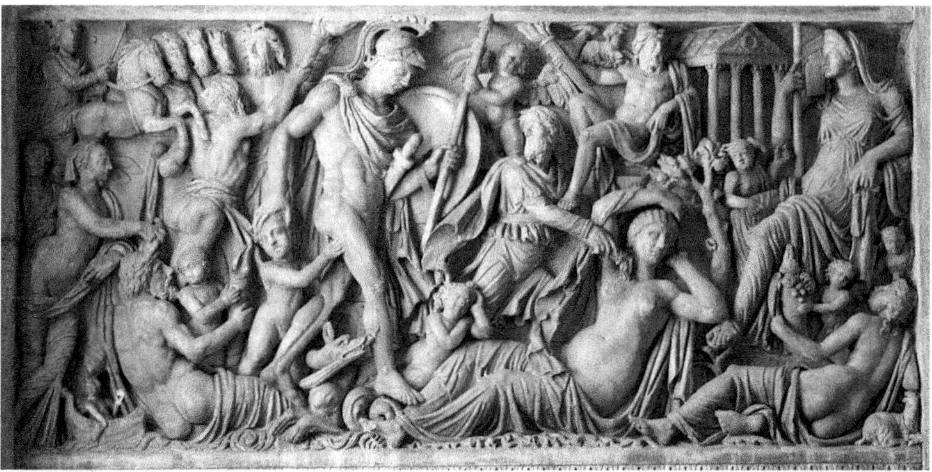

Figure 6.9: Mars and Rhea Silvia Sarcophagus, Palazzo Mattei, Rome. Photograph: author.

sarcophagi, this one relates specifically to the history of Rome. The derivation of the type perhaps emerges from a desire to identify both partners of a couple with a mythological couple, and to show the male taking the active role. Scenes of Dionysus and Ariadne were unsatisfactory to express this because Dionysus was an inappropriate god with whom to identify a male Roman citizen. Mars, however, could express the martial vigour of the dead husband, while Rhea Silvia could express the wife's desires and hopes to be reunited with her husband in the afterlife. The use of a myth central to Roman identity might also have given an added resonance to these sarcophagi, representing the deceased couple in the guise of the very founders of the Roman race.[95]

Achilles and Penthesilea

The mutual love between a couple is the central message of another group of sarcophagi where both male and female protagonists commonly receive portrait features. The group of Achilles and Penthesilea sarcophagi emerges around the start of the third century from a group of battle sarcophagi showing the Amazonomachy.[96] Here, however, the stress is changed from the presentation in the central group of a Greek warrior holding the corpse of an Amazon, to the representation of Achilles supporting the slumped body of the Amazon queen. The size of the figures relative to the background figures is also increased to

95 Cf. statues of couples as Mars and Venus, Wrede 1981, 133–5. Another sarcophagus on a Roman mythological theme is the Aeneas and Dido sarcophagus in the Museo Nazionale Romano, *ASR* XII,1, no. 68.

96 *ASR* XII,1, 179–87 (Grassinger).

draw attention to them. The early examples of the type do not seem to have portrait features, though one early-third-century sarcophagus in the Palazzo Borghese has unfinished heads.[97] From around 220 until 250, though, portrait heads become standard for this type.[98] While both husband and wife were celebrated in these sarcophagi, the type seems to stress the love and virtue of the man rather than that of the woman.[99] Through his assimilation to the martial hero Achilles he is shown as a warrior, while his love and support for his wife are expressed through his embrace of her slumped body.[100] What it meant for a wife to be likened to Penthesilea is less clear; perhaps it is primarily the fact of her death which is important here rather than any specific virtues which she is seen to embody.

Masculine virtues: courage, heroism and marital devotion

The Achilles and Penthesilea sarcophagi offer two sorts of messages. Like the chests celebrating Endymion and Selene and Mars and Rhea Silvia they use portrait heads to allude to the happy union between husband and wife. At the same time the presentation of this couple on a battlefield also stresses the martial vigour of the man. The rise of this group of sarcophagi coincides with changes in the closely related group of battle sarcophagi, as well as with the new development of hunt sarcophagi. While both of these groups are usually discussed separately from the mythological sarcophagi, they actually share a number of similarities with them in their use of portraits to project the deceased into the midst of narratives of courage and heroism.

The battle sarcophagi form a small group which developed from around 160/170 and have often been associated with the contemporary wars against the Sarmatians and Marcomanni.[101] The earliest sarcophagi show a series of separate combats against Gallic opponents, but around 190 the depictions change to focus instead on one huge battle showing Roman soldiers attacking barbarians, with a focus on a central group of a mounted general. This development from

97 *ASR* XII,1, 119.

98 There are five sarcophagi where portraits are present (*ASR* XII,1, nos.125 (much restored), 127, 131, 137, 138) and four where the portraits seem to have been left unfinished (*ASR* XII,1, nos. 119, 130 (the current portraits are restorations, probably from unfinished bosses), 140, 141). These include sarcophagi from Campanian workshops in addition to Roman ones.

99 Fittschen 1984, 143–49, 160, n. 52 argues that a sarcophagus in the Vatican Belvedere has portraits of different dates, perhaps showing a man and his mother, but this dating is rejected by Grassinger, *ASR* XII,1, no. 127 in favour of one for both portraits in the 230s.

100 *ASR* XII,1, no. 122 shows a general on a *sella castrensis* on the side, also stressing military virtues; Achilles is not given a portrait here.

101 Andreae 1956; Koch and Sichtermann 1982, 90–2.

separate scenes of battle to a centralised group is closely parallel to the changes in Amazonomachy scenes, discussed above. Here, too, the central figure was increasingly identified with the deceased buried within through the addition of a portrait face. This remains unfinished on the late Antonine Portanaccio sarcophagi but is clearly visible on other examples of the type, most famously on the latest known example, the Great Ludovisi Sarcophagus in Rome.[102] While the iconography of these sarcophagi has often been taken as evidence that they served as the tombs of men of senatorial rank, in many cases this cannot be proven.[103] The addition of portraits serve to link the deceased with the courageous actions of a general, but the representations are heavily idealised, differing from the reality of a battlefield and strongly influenced by imperial iconography.[104] Thus they can be read as imaginative versions of battle and military prowess into which the deceased is projected through the addition of his portrait features to the victorious general.

A similar trend can be seen on hunting sarcophagi. Until the late Severan period mythological hunt sarcophagi never receive portrait features, a surprising fact if portraits are thought simply to intensify the normative reading of mythological imagery on sarcophagi. We might have expected to find portraits in a range of mythological scenes which offered analogies for the virtues of the deceased buried within, such as those showing Hercules, Meleager or Adonis. Yet only a few of these show portraits.[105] The Meleager sarcophagi are particularly striking. The story of Meleager and the Calydonian boar hunt is a popular theme on sarcophagi from the middle of the second century until well into the third century. However, only a very few third-century examples show portrait heads on the figure of Meleager. The earliest is a sarcophagus dated to the 220s or 230s. It shows Meleager on foot attacking the Calydonian boar and wearing the portrait features of a young man, similar to portraits of Alexander Severus.[106] Another two examples come from later in the third century.[107] All three overlap chronologically with the emergence of a new category of non-

102 Portonaccio: Rome, Museo Nazionale Romano inv. 112327; Giuliano 1979–1995 I, 8, 1: 177–88 (L. Musso). Great Ludovisi sarcophagus: Rome, Museo Nazionale Romano inv. 8574; Giuliano 1979–1995 I, 5: 56–67 (L. de Lachenal). For discussion of the type and particularly the unusual version in the Borghese collection see Schäfer 1979.

103 For the link with senatorial families see esp. Wrede 2001, 16, 21–4.

104 Schäfer 1979, 357.

105 Hercules: *ASR* III,1, no. 103 (Wrede 1981, no. 137, Jongste 1992, no. F6,); no. 107 (Wrede 1981, no. 136, Jongste 1992, no. F5); no. 110 (Jongste 1992, no. F9); all third century. On Adonis see below.

106 *ASR* XII,6, no. 26.

107 *ASR* XII,6, nos. 30, 152. Koch 1984, 27–9 also notes the later addition of a portrait head to a reused Antonine Meleager sarcophagus. See also *ASR* XII,6, nos. 62, 74 for portraits on figures of children.

mythological hunting sarcophagi where the protagonists regularly wear realistic portraits.[108]

B. Andreae's analysis of these hunt sarcophagi shows that they developed from the iconography of mythological hunt sarcophagi. The link is shown most clearly on the 'Lepri-Gallo' sarcophagus, dating probably to the 220s.[109] This is a hybrid between a *vita humana* and mythological sarcophagus. The right half of the sarcophagus shows a hero on horseback hunting a boar, a scene taken from the iconography of Hippolytus sarcophagi. Unusually, the hero wears portrait features.[110] To the left, however, the customary scene of his departure from Phaedra is replaced instead with a scene which shows the deceased man in human form. Instead of the dress of a mythological hero he wears the costume of a professional *venator* and is shown taking his leave from a female figure who also wears portrait features, presumably those of his wife. As Andreae noted, the iconography here is not taken from the departure scene on Hippolytus sarcophagi, which showed Hippolytus' rejection of Phaedra and her advances, but rather has parallels with the departure of Adonis from Aphrodite and with the representation of couples on marriage sarcophagi.[111] Thus the tenderness and pathos of the man's departure from his wife is stressed.

The wife here appears in the guise of a female huntress, usually identified as the goddess Artemis/Diana, an appropriate patron goddess for the hunter. However, she also has similarities with the figures of Atalanta which appear on Meleager sarcophagi. The pose of the couple, especially the woman's gesture and the direction of her gaze, are closely paralleled on the central scene of a strigillated sarcophagus in Wilton House.[112] This shows a naked hero making a sacrifice while a female huntress stands behind him touching his shoulder and looking towards him. The boar's head at his feet suggests that he is intended to represent Meleager, and that the woman is Atalanta. Both figures wear roughed-out portrait faces, clear enough to see the impression of eyes, mouth and hair, but without a final finish. The suggestion seems to be that this is a couple who are assimilated in death to the lovers Meleager and Atalanta.

On the hunt sarcophagi the mounted hunter is the central figure, his active pose stressing his courage and victory. His face usually wears portrait features or is roughed out to receive them. Yet on a number of sarcophagi the addition of portrait features to one of the female figures in the scene also indicates the moral support which he receives from his wife. A few of these figures are dressed as

108 *ASR* I,2 (Andreae) gives a full analysis. See further below.

109 *ASR* III,2, 218–19, no. 179; Andreae *ASR* I,2, 18–21.

110 Hippolytus sarcophagi rarely show portraits, for one later example on the figure of Hippolytus in the hunt, see *ASR* III,2, 205–6, no. 165.

111 *ASR* I,2, 19.

112 *ASR* XII,6 , no. 147, mid-third-century.

huntresses and identified as the goddess Artemis/Diana, as on the Lepri-Gallo sarcophagus and a chest in Barcelona.[113] More commonly, though, the figure wears a helmet and carries a shield and is interpreted as a personification of Virtus.[114] She is shown playing an active role in the hunt, offering support to the male hunter.

As we have seen, the messages of love, marital support and male courage which these sarcophagi express are also shared by some of the mythological sarcophagi. Both use portraits to draw out particular messages and values from the representations of idealised hunts and battles. While scholarship tends to treat these groups of sarcophagi separately, dividing them into 'mythological' and 'real life', the hunt sarcophagi discussed by Andreae are by no means realistic depictions of everyday life. The victim here is usually a lion, the hunting of which was reserved for emperors or shows in the amphitheatre, while the presence of symbolic figures such as that of Virtus also elevates the tone. This is a heroic and aspirational realm, presenting the deceased as a victor and celebrating his courage, prowess and vitality, perhaps even likening him to famous figures of the past, such as Alexander the Great. The sarcophagus asserts that the deceased was the sort of man to do great deeds but does not actually recount the real details of his history. Where Virtus wears portrait features the sarcophagus also shows us the support this man had from a wife who was always behind him or at his side, offering support.

Andreae suggests that the move away from mythological hunt sarcophagi allows for a change in the emphasis of the myth – whereas the great heroes Meleager, Adonis and Hippolytus all met early deaths despite their greatness, and thus could have acted as consoling examples to the bereaved, these instead assert the focus on victory and strength. Andreae sees this victory as one over death itself, here embodied by the lion.[115] Whether such a strong message of apotheosis was intended remains, I think, debateable. Yet these sarcophagi certainly do assert powerful messages about what the deceased was like. The imagery chosen, while not drawn from the canonical stories of classical mythology, was just as 'mythologising' as those, in the sense that it asserts an aspirational and symbolic meaning rather than being a literal depiction. The few examples of portrait heads added to hunting figures on mythological scenes must be read alongside the non-mythological hunt sarcophagi; they suggest the

113 *ASR* I,2 21–24, no. 8.

114 E.g. Andreae *ASR* I,2 1980, 46–49, 157–8, no.75 (in Reims, the portraits seem to have been added later); 57–59, no. 86 (Praetextatus catacombs); 43–45, 162–63, no. 104 (Capitoline Museum Rome, unfinished portrait on Virtus); 106, 171, no. 162 (Via de' Condotti, Rome, heads of both Virtus and hunter are unfinished); 66–68, 184–5, no. 247 (Vienna, heads of both Virtus and hunter roughed out but unfinished). See also Wrede 1981, 323–5, nos. 339–344.

115 *ASR* I,2, 134–6.

desire here too to stress the positive side of the myth, asserting the hero's (and this deceased's) victory and prowess, rather than drawing attention to the death awaiting him.[116] On both mythological and non-mythological battle and hunt sarcophagi the presence of portraits serves to parachute the deceased into an idealised realm, endowing his achievements with a glow of heroic endeavour.

The precise placement of the portraits can also be used to particularise the message. Only a few Hippolytus sarcophagi show portrait features. One of these, a sarcophagus in Capua, shows Hippolytus in the hunt scene with a portrait, the sarcophagus drawing attention to the deceased's courage.[117] In others, however, the provision for portrait features suggests a different emphasis on the myth's significance. A sarcophagus in the Villa Doria Pamphili shows the usual depiction of the Hippolytus myth, with Hippolytus in the hunt to the right and his departure from Phaedra to the left. Hippolytus' head in the departure scene appears to have been left unfinished, but with the outlines of a portrait roughed out.[118] The identification which is suggested with the deceased thus draws our attention to the departure of the hero, rather than to his prowess in hunting. The stress on departure is particularly clear on another, well-known sarcophagus in the Museo Nazionale Romano which changes the usual Hippolytus iconography to focus, instead, on the departure of the youth.[119] The scene combines the departure of Hippolytus from Phaedra with a scene of the news of his death being brought to Theseus at the right hand end. Changes are made to the usual depiction: roughed-out portraits are given to the figures of Phaedra and Hippolytus and the young hero stands prominently in the centre of the relief, holding a diptych. The events of the mythological narrative are thrust into the background as the image stresses instead a mother's sorrow at the loss of a youth full of such potential.[120]

We might argue that the mythological content of this sarcophagus has been entirely ousted by its use as a message about parental love and loss. Yet the mythological subject is still present and presumably important. Rather than seeing this as an example of *Entmythologierung* ('demythologisation'), I would instead argue that the portraits and other iconographical changes direct the viewer to a particular interpretation of the myth, one which asserts that the young man buried here was as youthful, beautiful, educated and skilled in

116 They are especially close to the small group of boar-hunt sarcophagi, discussed by Andreae *ASR* I,2, 108–110.

117 *ASR* III,2, no. 165.

118 *ASR* III,2, no.166; Sichtermann and Koch 1975, 35, no. 28. The crucial central section of the sarcophagus is now missing but from old photographs it looks as though the head was at least roughed out. See also Calza 1977, 154–5, no. 182; pls. 114a and b show the former and current state of the sarcophagus.

119 MNR inv. 112444.

120 Zanker 1999; also Zanker and Ewald 2004, 328–9, no. 17.

hunting as Hippolytus. Like that hero he met an early death, and was mourned by his parents just as extensively as Hippolytus was by Theseus. The addition of a sketched-out portrait to Phaedra might suggest that the woman shown here is also dead, perhaps even that it was her grief for her lost son which led to her death, just as Phaedra's grief over her love for Hippolytus led ultimately to hers. The particulars of the myth – that Phaedra's was an unholy, incestuous love, and that she committed suicide after contriving her step-son's death – are irrelevant; what matters is the depths of emotion the tale evokes, and its ability to show how great a loss has been endured.

Portraits of Persephone – reading against the grain

So far we have looked at a number of sarcophagi which feature portraits or unfinished heads. These could work in one of a number of ways. At the most prosaic level they help to draw out an aspect of the scene which might otherwise be lost, as on the figures of Ariadne on the Dionysiac sarcophagi in Bolsena and Oslo. In some cases they seem to have intensified a 'normal' reading of the scene, as for example on sarcophagi with Achilles and Penthesilea where portrait heads are the norm and presumably reflect the great love between the couple represented. On others, such as the Ariadne, Endymion and Rhea Silvia sarcophagi, they could perhaps help to stress one particular aspect of the myth – the hoped-for happy sleep of the deceased in the Dionysiac realm, where Ariadne alone is given portrait features, or the love between the deceased couple, on sarcophagi where both Selene and Endymion are given portraits. On others, as we have seen above, the addition of portraits could help to direct our attention to one particular part of a myth. When portraits were given to the hero in the hunt scene they suggest the deceased's heroism, comparable to that of Meleager or Hippolytus. However, if portraits were intended for the hero in the departure scene the stress changes to focus on the grief of the bereaved at the loss of the deceased. The atypical addition of portrait features to figures on Persephone sarcophagi similarly shows their ability to draw out less prominent features of the myth and redirect the funerary message.

The rape of Persephone is one of the most popular images in funerary art. Appearing as far back as the fourth century BC Macedonian tombs at Vergina, in Roman art it appears not just on sarcophagi but also in mosaics and paintings which adorned tombs.[121] It even appears on funerary urns and altars, which otherwise generally avoid mythological scenes.[122] Yet it is largely lacking in domestic art. While other myths appear in a variety of contexts, this one had a

121 Lindner 1984.

122 Davies 1986; Sinn 1987, 80–81; Boschung 1987, 51–2.

predominantly funereal tone. This is not surprising; the abrupt hastening down to the underworld of a beautiful maiden in the prime of life was an obvious metaphor for the pain and violence of untimely death. That the myth was commonly understood in such a way can be seen from a few scattered inscriptions. The reliefs of the Flavian Tomb of the Haterii included a fragmentary representation of the Rape of Persephone. A separate inscription identifying the daughters of the houses, Hateria Magna and Hateria Quintilla, as '*virgines raptae*' suggests that the myth provided an analogy for their untimely deaths, the marriage with Death perhaps taking the place of a mortal marriage.[123] A similar linkage appears later in the fourth-century Tomb of Vibia on the Via Appia where a painting of the rape is accompanied by an inscription reading '*Abreptio Vibies et discensio*', 'the snatching and going down [to Hades] of Vibia'.[124] Yet the myth could be used to express the violence of the death of any person, not just young girls. Some of the funerary urns with representations of the myth do commemorate women, such as that for Saenia Longina.[125] However, others could commemorate couples, men or male children.[126] Even when these ash chests and altars commemorate women, they never make the link between Persephone and the deceased explicit through the use of portrait heads.

This flexibility of the myth as a metaphor for untimely death probably determined its use on sarcophagi where it is one of the most popular mythological themes, surviving in around 90 examples dating from the earliest sarcophagi well into the third century. Only a few of these, however, show portrait faces. On two sarcophagi the addition of portraits is found in the flower-picking scene and serves to redirect the emphasis of the scene. Both are quite heavily worn and dating is difficult. A sarcophagus in Messina shows the abduction of Persephone by Hades at the right, and Demeter on her serpent chariot at the left.[127] In between we see Persephone kneeling in a meadow as Hades approaches her (Figure 6.10). Her face is worn but it clearly shows a Severan hairstyle with central parting and exposed ears. Such styles were worn in the mid Severan period, for example by the wives of Elagabalus, and continued in fashion until the 240s. The hair here does not appear to be tightly waved and is quite similar to a head in Copenhagen, identified as that of Julia Mamaea and dated to c. 230.[128] The face of Persephone in the chariot scene is lost, but from

123 Wrede 1978, 425–8; idem 1981, 298, no. 272.

124 Lindner 1984, 59–60, no. 53; Wrede 1981, 300, no. 276.

125 Sinn 1987, no. 668; CIL VI.2570

126 Boschung 1987, nos. 821, 780, 781, 820; Wrede 1981, no. 16.

127 *ASR* III,3, no. 399; Mastelloni 1992, 75–9, no. 3.

128 Ny Carlsberg Glyptotek inv. 1416; Johansen 1995, 66–7, no. 23. Wrede 1981, 296–7, no. 266 dates the sarcophagus to 210–220; Koch and Sichtermann 1982, 177 to 230–240; Lindner 1984, 68–9, no. 78 to 225–250.

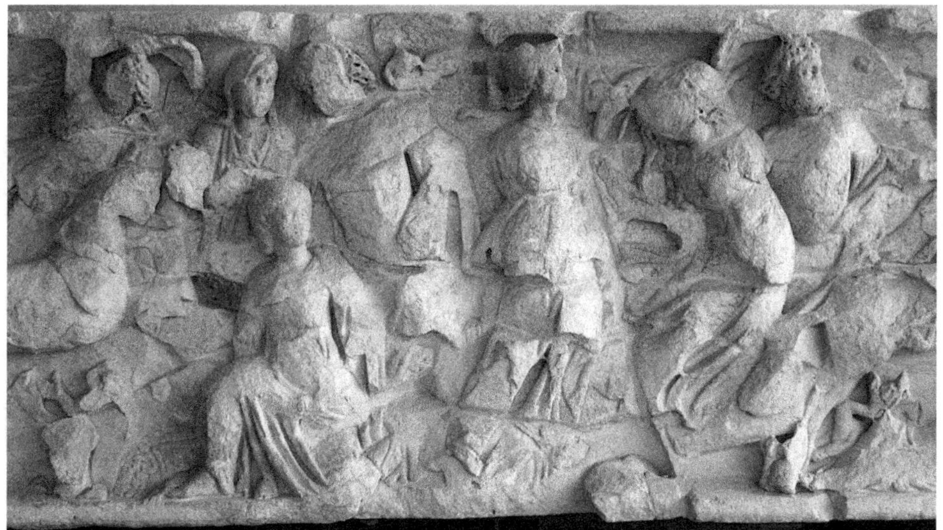

Figure 6.10: Persephone Sarcophagus, Messina; detail. Photograph: author.

the flowing locks which survive it seems clear that she did not have a portrait face; neither does Hades in either of his appearances. Rather than drawing a link between the death of the woman buried here and the violent untimely abduction of Persephone, the addition of portrait features instead draws our attention to the meeting between Persephone and Hades in the meadow. Venus leans towards Hades conspiratorially, as if drawing his attention to the girl. Persephone's dress slips from her right shoulder, a hint of her sexual attractiveness. The addition of portrait features to this scene draws attention to the beauty and attractiveness of Persephone and the deceased who is assimilated to her.

Another sarcophagus in the Palazzo Giustiniani in Rome also adds portrait features to the myth of Persephone (Figure 6.11).[129] In the flower-picking scene Hades is given the features of a bearded, short-haired man, similar in style to many portrait heads of the mid third century.[130] The face of Persephone here is very damaged but examination of the sarcophagus suggests that it too had a portrait face, though the hairstyle is simpler than the usual Severan styles. The hair is drawn back from the face in separate strands, as on the other figure of Persephone in the abduction scene. The incisions for the corners of the eyes can be clearly seen, showing that the face was not left unfinished, as had been

129 *ASR* III,3, no. 390.

130 Wrede 1981, 296, no. 265 dates it to c. 240; Koch and Sichtermann 1982, 177 to 230–240.

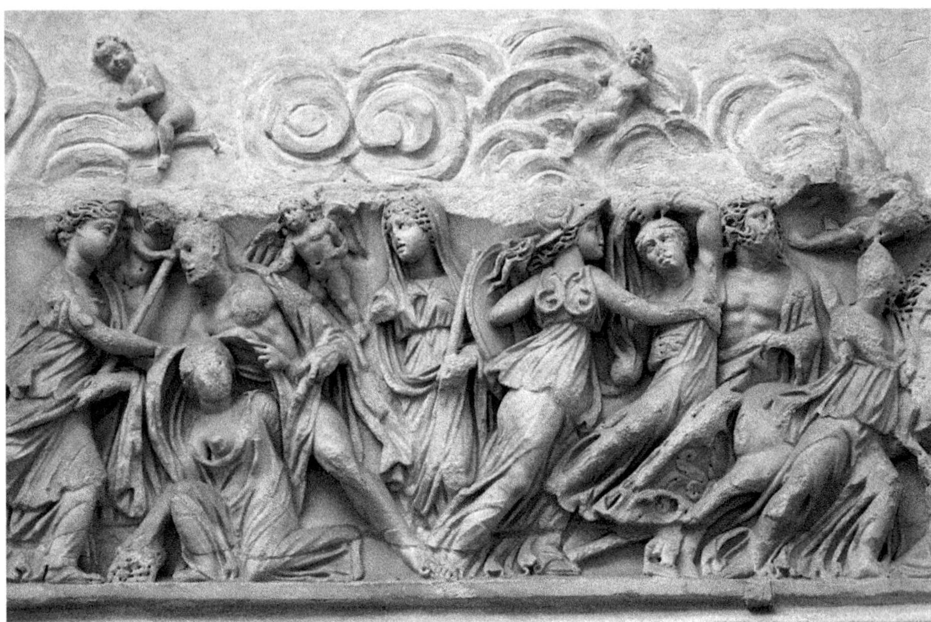

Figure 6.11: Persephone Sarcophagus, Palazzo Giustiniani, Rome. Photograph: author.

claimed by Robert.[131] The face of Persephone in the abduction scene is also clearly characterised as a portrait by the careful chiselling of the hair, in contrast to the roughly drilled locks which appear on other figures. Here, however, Hades appears without a portrait face.

The addition of portrait features alters the usual focus of the myth. As in the Messina sarcophagus the attraction felt by Hades for Persephone is stressed in the flower-picking scene, where the figure of Venus rushes forwards to unveil the girl. Her sexual attractiveness is also highlighted by the slipping drapery on her right shoulder. The addition of portrait features serves to underline the beauty of the deceased woman, and the sexual union between her and her husband. In the abduction scene she looks back as she is torn away, perhaps an indication of the grief which her death evokes and her unwillingness to leave mortal life.

The use of portraits on these two sarcophagi suggests a widening of the messages of the myth, which is partly achieved by the inclusion of the flower-picking scene, not always shown on sarcophagi.[132] Persephone's beauty and desirability are stressed, while the equation of Hades with her husband on the Palazzo Giustiniani sarcophagus adds an additional layer of meaning, prompting

131 *ASR* III,3, 475; also Wrede 1981, 296, no. 265. Contra see also Zanker and Ewald 2004, 94.

132 See Koch and Sichtermann 1982, 175–9 on the development of the type.

us to think about the deceased's life and marriage, and not just the fact of her death. On a third sarcophagus the addition of a portrait head gives a surprisingly positive spin to the myth. This is the famous chest in the Capitoline Museum.[133] Here the other elements of the myth are pushed to the sides to allow the central space to be dominated by the representation of Persephone in Hades' chariot. Rather than appearing as a prone figure slumped in his arms, she is shown as if seated upright. Her upper torso is completely naked, stressing her beauty, and she is given portrait features. She looks steadily to the right, in the direction of travel. The overwhelming impression here is of a welcoming of death, an anticipation of the Underworld she is being taken towards. Perhaps the deceased wishes to suggest that she had no fear of death, or that she was looking forward to being reunited with her loved ones in the afterlife.

In its confident, almost triumphal, tone this sarcophagus can be likened to one showing the myth of Adonis in the Vatican, the only example of this myth I have found where portrait features are present.[134] The iconography of this sarcophagus also differs from other Adonis sarcophagi. Rather than showing the wounded Adonis lying in Aphrodite's arms at one end of the relief, here the couple are prominently seated in the centre of the relief. A servant cleaning Adonis' leg refers to the wound he sustained in the hunt, but his erect authoritative pose makes it appear of minor importance. Both Adonis and Aphrodite are given portrait features, probably those of a young married couple. She gazes lovingly towards him, while he looks out towards the viewer. The clear sense is one of triumph, reunification in death and even heroisation. These two sarcophagi are some of the clearest examples we have of a different attitude towards death, not as an object of fear, but approached with the firm confidence that life and love could continue even beyond the grave.[135]

All three of the Persephone sarcophagi mentioned above show that the addition of portrait features changes the normal reading of the myth, turning a consolation for untimely death into a message about the beauty of the deceased, or a positive message about the afterlife. There is one other sarcophagus, however, where the figure of the abducted Persephone is unusually given portrait features. This is a fragment which was previously in the Villa Gentili but has since disappeared, probably into a private collection.[136] An old photograph shows that it portrayed Hades grasping the figure of Persephone on

133 *ASR* III,3, no. 392; Zanker and Ewald 2004, 93–4, fig. 77, 370–2, no. 33.

134 *ASR* XII,1, no. 65; discussed by Koortbojian 1995, 50–3; Zanker and Ewald 2004, 210–1, figs 189–90; 290–2, no. 5. See also, however, the sarcophagus in Berlin which pairs scenes from a *vita privata* sarcophagus with Adonis hunting; *ASR* XII,1, no. 59; Brilliant 1992.

135 See Newby 2007, 245–7.

136 *ASR* III,3, no. 380.

his chariot.[137] She is show in the usual unwilling pose but, strikingly, has a hairstyle which identifies her face as being a portrait. Her hair seems to have been parted in the middle and lies low on her neck before being drawn up into a bun. Her ears are clearly visible. Similar portrait types appear on heads of Octacilia Severa, Tranquillina and Etruscilla in the 240s though it could also be earlier.[138] The stress here is on Persephone's violent abduction to Hades and its identification with the fate of the deceased. If the sarcophagus does belong to the 240s it might explain the presence of portrait features here to stress what we have seen above was usually the normative reading of the myth. Against a backdrop where Persephone sarcophagi begin to have been used to stress other aspects of the myth (as in the three examples mentioned above) perhaps the client here wanted to reinforce their own, more negative, reading – that it was a harsh and violent death which had ripped their loved one out of the world of the living.

Conclusions

This analysis of a number of mythological sarcophagi suggests that the decision to add portrait features did not simply reflect a desire to intensify the evident message of the imagery. Rather, when a range of possibilities for interpretation existed it helped to privilege a particular reading, or even to give a new twist to the usual use. It could also help to draw attention to the central mythological figure when the composition threatened to become overrun by subsidiary figures. In many ways the portraits act as the visual equivalent to inscriptions, which are relatively rare on sarcophagi. They provide extra information and help to focus the message of the mythological imagery. Yet this concentration on the link between hero or heroine and the deceased does not necessarily limit the imagery of the sarcophagus to one message alone. While a particular aspect of the analogy is drawn out through the assimilation, the rest of the narrative context of the myth might still extend the message, provoking verbalised comparisons such as those we find in consolatory poetry. Portrait features also act in flexible ways, sometimes deviating away from the usual iconography of the myth. While the precise messages of many of these sarcophagi must remain obscure to us, they attest to the continued flexibility and multivalency of mythological imagery in the funerary sphere and its possibilities for the expression of human values, hopes and beliefs.

137 Koch 1976, 109–10, no. 24, fig. 24.

138 Wegner 1979, 51–62, 78–82.

Acknowledgements

I would like to thank the following for their help during the preparation of this paper: Chris Gravett of Woburn Abbey for providing photographs; Maria Pia Malvezzi of the British School at Rome for arranging access to palazzi in Rome; the owners of the Palazzi Mattei and Giustiniani for allowing access to study and photograph the sarcophagi and Dott.ssa Maria Amalia Mastelloni for access to the Persephone sarcophagus in Messina. Other museums and organisations are credited in the list of figures. Initial research on this topic was carried out during a trip to Rome funded by a British Academy small grant. The research was completed and written up during a period of research leave funded by the University of Warwick and the AHRC Research Leave scheme. I am grateful to all these institutions for their support.

Bibliography

Andreae, B. *Motivgeschichtliche Untersuchungen zu den römischen Schlachtsarkophagen* (Berlin, 1956).

Andreae, B. *Studien zur römischen Grabkunst* (Heidelberg, 1963).

Andreae, B. Bossierte Porträts auf römischen Sarkophagen – ein ungelöstes Problem, in: B. Andreae (ed.), *Symposium über die antiken Sarkophage, Pisa 5.–12. September 1982* (Marburger Winckelmann-Programm, 1984), 109–128.

Angelicoussis, E. *The Woburn Abbey Collection of Classical Antiquities. Monumenta Artis Romanae XX* (Mainz am Rhein, 1992).

Blome, P. Zur Umgestaltung griechische Mythen in der römischen Sepulkralkunst. Alkestis – Protesilaus- und Proserpinasarkophage. *Mitteilungen des Deutschen Archäologischen Instituts, Römische Abteilung* 85(1978), 435–457.

Blome, P. Funerärsymbolische Collagen auf mythologischen Sarkophagreliefs. *Studi Italiani di Filologia Classica* 10.2 (1992), 1061–1073.

Boschung, D. *Antike Grabaltäre aus den Nekropolen Roms.* Acta Bernensia 10 (Bern, 1987).

Brilliant, R. Roman Myth/Greek Myth: Reciprocity and Appropriation on a Roman Sarcophagus in Berlin, in: *Studi Italiani di Filologia Classica* 10.2 (1992), 1030–1045. Reprinted in: *Commentaries on Roman Art: Selected Studies,* edited by R. Brilliant (London, 1994), 423–438.

Calza, R. (ed.). *Antichità di Villa Doria Pamphilj* (Rome, 1977).

Cumont, F. *Recherches sur le symbolisme funéraire des romains* (Paris, 1942).

Davies, G. The rape of Proserpina on Roman grave altars and ash chests. Shadow 3.2 (1986), 51–60.

di Mino, M. R. and Bertinetti, M. (eds.). *Archeologia a Roma. La material e la tecnica nell'arte antica* (Rome, 1990).

Ewald, B. Death and Myth. New Books on Roman Sarcophagi. *American Journal of Archaeology* 103 (1999), 344–348.

Engemann, J. *Untersuchungen zur Sepulkralsymbolik der späteren römischen Kaiserzeit* (Jahrbuch für Antike und Christentum Ergänzungsband 2) (Münster, 1973).

Fejfer, J. *Roman portraits in context.* (Berlin, 2008).
Fittschen, K. Zum Kleobis und Biton-Relief in Venedig. *Jahrbuch des Deutschen Archäologischen Instituts* 85 (1970), 171–193.
Fittschen, K. *Die Bildnistypen der Faustina minor und die Fecunditas Augustae* (Göttingen, 1982).
Fittschen, K. Über Sarkophage mit Porträts verschiedener Personen, in: B. Andreae (ed.), *Symposium über die antiken Sarkophage, Pisa 5.–12. September 1982* (Marburger Winckelmann-Programm, 1984), 129–161.
Giuliano, A. *Museo Nazionale Romano. Le Sculture.* 12 vols (Rome, 1979–1995).
Grassinger, D. Mythen auf römischen Sarkophagen. *Journal of Roman Archaeology* 11 (1998), 554–556.
Guerrini, L. *Palazzo Mattei di Giove. Le Antichità* (Rome, 1982).
Huskinson, J. 'Unfinished Portrait heads' on later Roman sarcophagi: some new perspectives. *Papers of the British School at Rome* 66 (1998), 129–168.
Johansen, F. *Roman Portraits III. Ny Carlsberg Glyptotek* (Copenhagen, 1995).
Jongste, P. F. B. *The Twelve Labours of Hercules on Roman Sarcophagi* (Rome, 1992).
Koch, G. Verschollene mythologische Sarkophage. Ein archäologischer Steckbrief. *Archäologischer Anzeiger* 1976, 101–110.
Koch, G. and Sichtermann, H. *Römische Sarkophage. Handbuch der Archäologie* (Munich, 1982).
Koortbojian, M. *Myth, Meaning and Memory on Roman Sarcophagi* (Berkeley, Los Angeles and London, 1995).
L'Orange, H. P. Eros psychophoros et sarcophages romains. *Institutum Romanum Norvegiae. Acta ad Archaeologiam et artium historiam pertinentia* 1 (1962), 41–48.
Lattimore, R. *Themes in Greek and Latin Epitaphs* (Urbana, 1942).
Lindner, R. *Der Raub der Persephone in der antiken Kunst* (Würzburg, 1984).
Marrou, H.-I. *ΜΟΥΣΙΚΟΣ ΑΝΗΡ. Étude sur les scènes de la vie intellectuelle figurant sur les monuments funéraires romains* (Grenoble, 1938).
Mastelloni, M. A. Sarcofagi romani del Museo Regionale di Messina. *Quaderni dell'attività didattica del Museo Regionale Messina* 2 (1992), 57–91.
Matz, F. Stufen der Sepulkralsymbolik in der Kaiserzeit, in: Symposium über die antiken Sarkophagreliefs, edited by H. Wiegartz et al. *Archäologischer Anzeiger* 86 (1971), 86–122 at 102–116.
Meiggs, R. *Roman Ostia* (Oxford, 1973).
Moretti, M. *Nuove scoperte e acquisizioni nell' Etruria Meridionale* (Exhibition Catalogue, Villa Giulia). (Rome, 1975).
Mottahedeh, P. E. Review of Wrede 1981. *American Journal of Archaeology* 88 (1984), 95–96.
Mouritsen, H. Freedmen and Decurions: Epitaphs and Social History in Imperial Italy. *Journal of Roman Studies* 95 (2005), 38–63.
Müller, F. G. J. M. *Iconological Studies in Roman Art I: The So-Called Peleus and Thetis Sarcophagus in the Villa Albani* (Amsterdam, 1994).
Muth, S. Drei statt vier. Zur Deutung der Feldherrnsarkophage. *Archäologischer Anzeiger* (2004), 263–273.
Newby, Z. Art at the crossroads? Themes and style in Severan art, in: *Severan Culture*, edited by S. Swain, S. Harrison and J. Elsner (Cambridge, 2007), 201–249.
Nock, A. D. Sarcophagi and Symbolism. *American Journal of Archaeology* 50 (1946), 140–170.
North, J. A. These he cannot take. *Journal of Roman Studies* 73 (1983), 169–174.
Peek, W. *Griechische Vers-Inschriften* (Berlin, 1955).

Schäfer, T. Zum Schlachtsarkophag Borghese. *Mélanges de l'École française de Rome, Antiquité* 91 (1979), 355–382.

Schauenburg, K. Porträts auf römischen Sarkophagen, in: *Eikones. Studien zum griechischen und römischen Bildnis. Hans Jucker zum sechzigsten Geburtstag gewidmet (Zwölftes Beiheft zur Halbjahresschrift Antike Kunst)* (Bern, 1980), 153–159.

Sichtermann, H. *Späte Endymion-Sarkophage. Methodisches zur Interpretation* (Baden-Baden, 1966).

Sichtermann, H and Koch, G. *Griechische Mythen auf römischen Sarkophagen* (Tübingen, 1975).

Sinn, F. *Stadtrömische Marmorurnen (Beiträge zur Erschließung hellenistischer und kaiserzeitlichen Skulptur und Architektur 8)* (Mainz am Rhein, 1987).

Sperti, L. *Rilievi Greci e Romani de Museo Archeologico di Venezia* (Rome, 1988).

Turcan, R. Les sarcophages romains et le problème du symbolisme funéraire. *Aufstieg und Niedergang des Römischen Welt* 16.2 (1978), 1700–1735.

Vighi, R. Cesano di Roma. Rinvenimento di sarcofago romano e dei resti di una capella medioevale. *Notizie degli scavi di antichità* 1935, 244–247.

Walker, S. The sarcophagus of Maconiana Severiana, in: *Roman Funerary Monuments in the J. Paul Getty Museum I. Occasional Papers on Antiquities 6* (Malibu, 1990), 83–94.

Wegner, M. *Das römische Herrscherbild III.3. Gordianus III bis Carinus* (Berlin, 1979).

Whitehead, J. The 'Cena Trimalchionis' and biographical narration in Roman middle-class art, in: *Narrative and Event in Ancient Art*, edited by P. J. Holliday (Cambridge, 1993), 229–325.

Wiggers, H. B. and Wegner, M. *Das Römische Herrscherbild III.1* (Berlin, 1971).

Wood, S. Alcestis on Roman Sarcophagi. *America Journal of Archaeology* 82 (1978), 499–510. Reprinted with postscript in: *Roman Art in Context. An Anthology*, edited by E. D'Ambra (New Jersey, 1993), 84–103.

Wrede, H. Die Ausstattung stadrömische Grabtempel und der Übergang zur Körperbestatung. *Mitteilungen des Deutschen Archäologischen Instituts, Römische Abteilung* 85 (1978), 411–433.

Wrede, H. *Consecration in Formam Deorum: Vergöttlichen Privatpersonen in der römischen Kaiserzeit* (Mainz, 1981).

Wrede, H. *Senatorische Sarkophage Roms. Der Beitrag des Senatorienstandes zur römischen Kunst der hohen und späten Kaiserzeit.* Monumenta Artis Romanae 29 (Mainz am Rhein, 2001).

Zanker, P. and Ewald, B. C. *Mit Mythen leben. Die Bilderwelt der römischen Sarkophage* (Munich, 2004).

Zanker, P. Phädras Trauer und Hippolytos' Bildung: zu einem Sarkophag im Thermenmuseum, in: *Im Spiegel des Mythos. Bilderwelt und Lebenswelt.* Palilia 6, edited by F. de Angelis and S. Muth (Wiesbaden, 1999), 131–142.

7.
Man or Woman? Cross-gendering and Individuality on Third Century Roman Sarcophagi

Stine Birk

When it comes to the representation of ordinary men and women on Roman sarcophagi of the second and third century the iconographic repertoire tends to be repetitive and conventional, reflecting the shared ideals of contemporary society and communal values. Individuality is rarely expressed through sarcophagus imagery, so that when unusual or distinctive images appear they can be taken to offer a rare insight into the specific wishes or concerns of particular people. One such example is the cross-gendered figure, created by applying a male or female portrait to a body of the opposite sex. I shall argue that these images were a product of the choice of individuals and, as used on sarcophagi, they reveal the fluidity of gender categories in contemporary Roman society.

The normal interpretation of cross-gendered images is that they are the unintentional results of the production process involved in carving sarcophagi.[1] Because of their repertoire of repetitive motifs sarcophagi are usually thought to be prefabricated products that were purchased from stock. According to this explanation the mismatched combination of head and body occurred because the purchaser had to take what was available when a sarcophagus was needed. The workshop would have only a limited number of sarcophagi with a predesigned motif from which the patron could choose.[2] So, as one of the final steps in the carving process, probably at purchase, a portrait of the dead was added to one of the protagonists in the decoration that had already been sculpted: it was during this process that a male body could be equipped with a female portrait, or vice versa. Even so, we cannot know for sure when portraits were added to the figures, since both the identity of the patron and the exact time-scale of the purchase remain uncertain.

1 Koch and Sichtermann 1982, 610; Koch 1990, especially 65–66.

2 It has, for example, been estimated that around 50 different myths were represented on sarcophagus reliefs (Koch and Sichtermann 1982. For an overview of the popularity of myths on Roman sarcophagi, see Zanker 2005). However, when we are talking about sarcophagi with figures individualised through the application of a portrait only, the number of different myths used comes down to 15.

The identity of the patron is often not revealed directly (though sometimes a name or title is stated in an inscription on the lid) but may be suggested by the portraits carved on the relief. The patron may be either the person who bought the coffin for him or herself, or a relative of the deceased. In the latter case we can be fairly certain that the commission of a sarcophagus was a family matter, since imagery and inscriptions on sarcophagi both refer to social relationships within families.[3] I suggest however, that, with the exception of children's sarcophagi, the patron of a cross-gendered sarcophagus was the person who was going to be buried in the coffin. Cross-gendered figures on sarcophagi can therefore be seen as rare examples of individual wishes that are revealed in the otherwise standardised iconography of sarcophagi. However, it should be noted that whether the sarcophagus was purchased before or after the death, and whoever its patron might have been, the important issue for this discussion is that the intention of the cross-gendered image was to negotiate the *post mortem* identity of the deceased.

Sarcophagus imagery is normally centred on one, or at most two individuals; and it is primarily their identities which are constructed through the portrait figures. This happens independently of whether the choice of motif was made by the deceased themselves or by the family. In broad terms, it can therefore be said that one sarcophagus is equated with one particular person (or in some cases two), which is why I consider sarcophagus imagery to be an expression of self-representation. However, the family could, by purchasing a sarcophagus for a deceased relative, construct an identity that in the end also reflected back on the family itself; so in such cases the choice of motif is not a matter of the individual self-representation of the deceased, but of the family. Both scenarios and types of patrons are likely, and both kinds of self-representation can be found within the vast corpus of sarcophagi.

In purchasing a sarcophagus, therefore, someone had at some point made a conscious choice about its motifs. The lavish quality of sarcophagus decoration suggests that the sculpted reliefs were supposed to be gazed at, either during the funerary ritual or, as is known from various tomb buildings, afterwards when the coffin had been displayed inside the tomb. A motif that was not socially acceptable would, therefore, not have been chosen, and if the prefabricated decoration of the coffin was inappropriate it could be changed. Thus, the final appearance of the decoration can be seen as a deliberate choice of the patron.

3 As in the image popular on sarcophagi of a medallion with the bust of a man and a woman, which presumably shows a married couple, e.g. the inscription on a strigillated sarcophagus, stating that the sarcophagus was given by a man to his wife (*ASR* I, 4, cat 186). Other kinds of family relations are found, e.g. on children's sarcophagi, where the patron most often appears to be a parent (e.g. *ASR* IV, 3, cat. 214) or grandparent (Østergaard 1996, cat. 48).

So, to return to the question of how cross-gendered images came about, there is compelling evidence that they were deliberately made. Certain sarcophagi clearly show that the sculptor chose such a representation, even when there were other options. A graphic example occurs on a sarcophagus showing a pair of busts – male and female – framed by a conch (Figure 7.1).[4] The heads of these were roughed out in preparation for the later addition of portraits, but only one was ever finished, that of a woman which was added to the bust in male clothing. By taking the male bust as a basis for her portrait when the female one was also available, the dead woman commemorated here has deliberately displayed herself in a male sphere. In the present discussion it is of little importance whether the woman chose the image for herself or whether it was chosen for her: in both cases, the option remained of using the female bust with the roughly carved head. Whoever commissioned it, the piece still clearly shows that a woman's identity could be constructed by using metaphors that traditionally belonged to a masculine world.

Other evidence, of a more practical nature, also suggests that some cross-gendered images were deliberately chosen. For it is obvious that even drastically re-cutting a figure from one sex into another did not pose a major problem to Roman craftsmen. This is clear from a sarcophagus now in the Huntington Library and Art Gallery in San Marino, California (Figure 7.2) where a female figure was re-worked to represent a man.[5] The dress has been shortened, and cutting marks still visible around the male portrait reveal that the original hair-style was female (though probably only roughly carved). The coffin may have been reused for a secondary burial of a man, and the figure was therefore re-carved to suit the need of this man; or it may have been the only coffin of its kind available in the workshop, and the figure was altered as it did not suit the need of the new patron. But the sarcophagi to be discussed in this article did not involve such a radical makeover as found on the Huntington sarcophagus. On these the addition of a portrait to a body of the opposite gender was chosen, as I will argue, because the figure thereby created possessed virtues that the deceased wanted to emphasise in his or her commemoration.

The cross-gendered figures on sarcophagi raise important new opportunities for gender analysis, and strengthen ideas explored in recent studies that Roman gender should be viewed as a spectrum – rather than a polar, male/female dichotomy – in the search for individual self-definition.[6] As Eric Varner has

4 Rome, Museo Nazionale Romano, inv. 196637.

5 Koch 1990.

6 See for example the study of Bassler 2008, 52 on the problem of Christian self-definition, where she says: 'Each human body comprised male and female aspects, and depending on the relative strength of these aspects each individual would be located at a specific point along the male-female axis.' Her discussion is concerned with first century

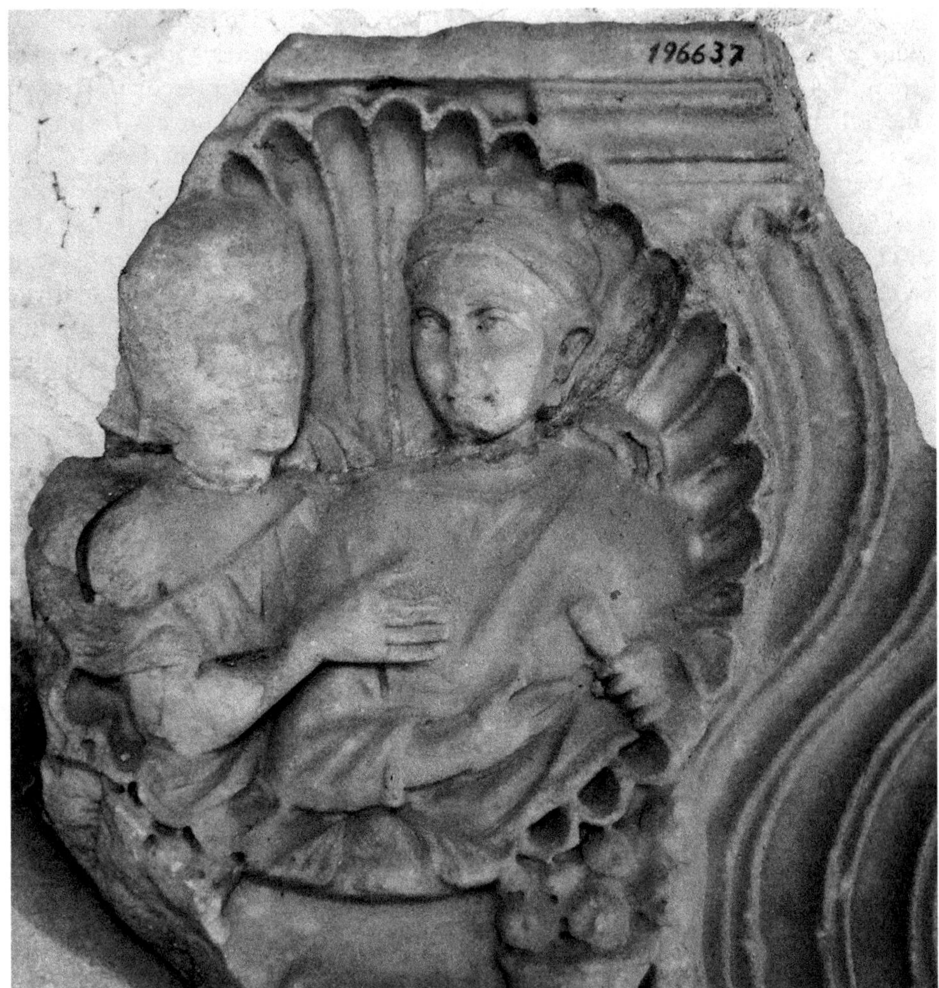

Figure 7.1: Museo Nazionale Romano delle Terme inv. 196637. Photograph: Stine Birk, by permission of the museum

shown, even the Emperor could align himself visually with female deities through the use of portraits, despite the obvious difference in gender.[7] By showing this, Varner makes us aware that in various media of Roman art the repertoire of figures used for portrait identities was not centred on binary oppositions; and applying this to the study of sarcophagi opens new possibilities of interpretation in regard to gender roles and self-definition. For the fact that

self-definition but she extends her argument to encompass the third century as well (55–56). See also Bartman 2002.

7 Varner 2008, 188.

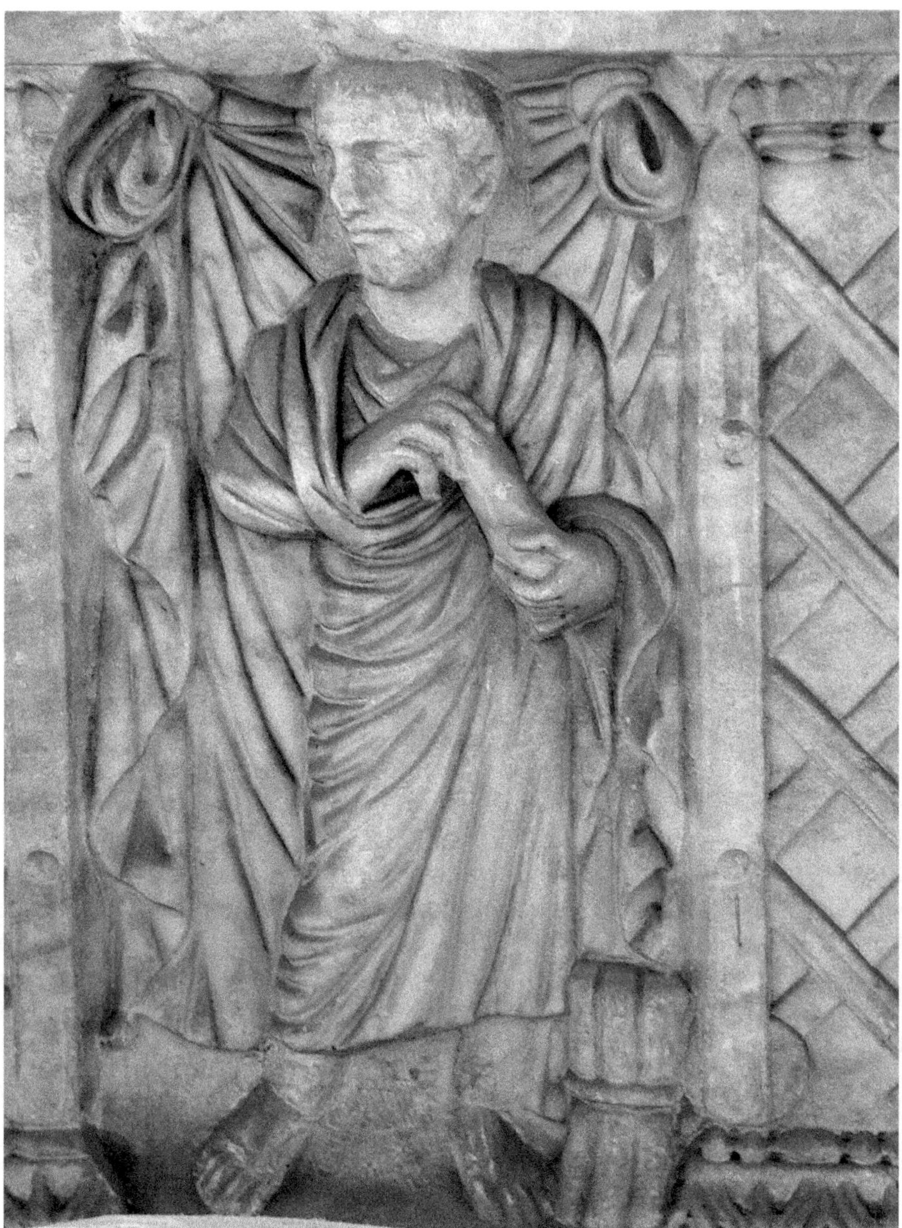

Figure 7.2: The man on the central relief has been recarved from a female figure. The rough tool marks on the feet show that the figure originally wore a long dress (*palla*) and shoes instead of sandals. Around the head the outline of a roughly carved area is evidence that the original figure was meant to have a female hairstyle. The Henry E. Huntington Library and Art Gallery, inv. 22.6, San Marino, California.
Photograph: Troels Myrup Kristensen, by permission of the museum.

cross-gendered images were carved on sarcophagus reliefs meant to commemorate the identities and idealised virtues of the dead shows that such images were socially acceptable. Through them we are reminded of the instability of gender categories, and can explore the role of these categories in the construction of identity.

Social Identity and Commemoration on Roman Sarcophagi

The production of sarcophagi in Rome was extensive and the choice of imagery available for personal commemoration multiple, although always within the limits of convention. On more than 650 surviving sarcophagi, the deceased is represented as one of the main characters in an episode from mythology or the 'ideal' human life; or a portrait bust, enclosed in a medallion or framed by a *parapetasma*, is carved alongside scenes alluding to (an idealised) everyday life or a mythological narrative.[8] Images on Roman sarcophagi should be understood as analogies of human situations, such as love and desperate grief, and also of essential aspects of the life of men and women, such as their mutual relationship and the different roles they take in different social contexts.[9] They therefore reflect social norms and ideals, and rarely illustrate professional activities or actual lived experiences.

Since the imagery of myth surrounds their portraits on the sarcophagi, the dead are directly associated with it and with the social ideals it expresses. This means that sarcophagi can be extremely informative about what virtues were considered socially desirable, either by the dead themselves or by the relatives who determined their commemoration. Furthermore, the conventional iconography of sarcophagus reliefs, so widely used amongst middle and upper class Romans at the time, shows how collective social ideals tended to dictate the popularity of a motif. Although the relative uniformity of this imagery can make it hard to discover anything about the 'individual', it also means that any deviations from the norm – such as the cross-gendered images – offer potential opportunities for further insights into a particular 'person', and into his or her characteristics and desires.

8 Birk 2009. (This unpublished PhD dissertation includes a catalogue of most of the surviving sarcophagi with portrait figures from the third century. It considers the appearance and meaning of these figures in regard to issues such as gender roles and individuality, and gives a special emphasis on how ideal identities are used in the construction of memory.)

9 For sarcophagus imagery as reflections of human situations, see Zanker and Ewald 2004. On myths on sarcophagus reliefs as analogies, see Koortbojian 1995, 9.

Looking at portrait representations of men and women in the vast corpus of sarcophagi it is possible to identify a number of regular assignations of gender categories and roles (some of which are, of course, obvious). Men are usually portrayed as magistrates,[10] hunters,[11] mythological heroes,[12] and, in the intellectual sphere, as philosophers and poets.[13] Female portraits are often given to mythological characters associated with physical beauty such as Rhea Silvia or Ariadne, and to human figures whose femininity is often emphasised by their off-the-shoulder drapery, which imitates images of Venus.[14] Another common female figure type is the veiled woman, who appears, for instance, in nursing scenes and in scenes where she is often paired with a man, such as the *dextrarum iunctio*[15] or with a learned man; the main symbolic value of these representations is probably devotion or *pietas.*[16]

Over time, the motifs and repertoire of figures on sarcophagi changed, some disappearing while others came into vogue.[17] For instance, during the third century there was an increasing tendency to represent women as 'learned' women characterised by a scroll, which became more frequent than female images that emphasised physical beauty and devotion. The popularity of this type of the 'learned woman' may suggest that the ideals of the female had changed, and that in the late third century women were part of the intellectual scene and were on a more or less equal footing to men – in terms of funerary imagery at least.[18] But when cross-gendered images of such subjects occur (that is to say, when the portrait consisted of a female head carved on to the body of a 'learned' man', as opposed to the homogenous image just mentioned), it is not sufficient to explain them as the unintended result of the production process of

10 Wrede 2001; *ASR* I, 3, 154–69.

11 For examples of hunters individualised through the use of a portrait see, *ASR* I, 2, cat. 8, 41, 28, 32, 59, 60, 65, 75, 101, 78, 104, 112, 125, 126, 128, 131, 150, 179, 180, 188, 192, 193, 204, 235, 240, 241, 246, 247; Blome 1998; Calza 1977, 225

12 For examples of heroes individualised through the use of a portrait see, *ASR* XII, 2, cat. 65 (Adonis); *ASR* XII, 1, cat. 119, 125, 127, 131 (Achilles); *ASR* IV, 2, cat. 100 and *ASR* III, 1, cat. 103 (Hercules); *ASR* III, 3, cat. 180 (Mars).

13 Including *togatus* which often is juxtaposed with veiled women, as exemplified by a strigillated sarcophagus with a seated man and a woman (Ewald 1999a, cat. E 17). For examples of learned men individualised through the use of a portrait see, Ewald 1999a, cat. D 6, D 8, A 10, G 3, E 23; *ASR* I, 3, cat. 8.

14 For examples see, *ASR* IV, 1, cat. 46, 47, 49 and *ASR* IV, 3, cat. 214, 222 (Ariadne); *ASR* III, 2, cat. 180 (Rhea Silvia); *ASR* V, 2, 2, cat. 121, 176, 197; *ASR* I, 4, cat. 186 (naked shoulder and/or veil).

15 For examples of the veiled women see, *ASR* I, 3, cat. 6, 22, 23, 25, 35, 138; *ASR* I, 4, cat. 273.

16 *ASR* I, 3, 152–4.

17 Ewald 2005, 56.

18 Huskinson 1999; 2002.

sarcophagi, where uniform, repetitive imagery was encouraged by the needs of prefabrication.[19]

Interpreting the Body on Roman Sarcophagi

The body is the visual expression of a person. Combined with the way we dress, the body functions as a means of non-verbal communication that signals social concepts and constructions such as class, age, and importantly for this article, gender, where our views traditionally depend on the visual appearance of the body.[20] Representations of the body on sarcophagi made by Roman craftsmen for Roman customers are therefore informative about an individual's construction of self and identity, and, in this case, about how gender was perceived, lived, and tolerated.

Even before we get to identifying or interpreting a figure on a relief or a statue we register certain things about its body – whether it is male or female, naked or dressed, or young or old, for example. The face is also important. Figures on sarcophagi were provided with a generic or roughly carved head, or with an individualised portrait. Such portraits strengthen the idea that a direct, conscious choice of self-representation was made, whereby the dead are identified in terms of the particular symbolic values attached to the body.

Yet despite the centrality of these issues and the fact that these reliefs are filled with all kinds of bodily representations, the body is not often discussed in studies of sarcophagi. Even when it is (and particularly in the case of mythological scenes), discussions usually take the appearance of the bodies for granted.[21] The general attitude towards the body-type chosen to represent the deceased is that it is determined by the subject-matter of the image. A good example is a recent study of the Hylas relief, later used as architectural decoration in the inner court of Palazzo Mattei in Rome (Figure 7. 3), which I shall discuss in greater detail below. In this image one of the nymphs abducting Hylas has a boy's portrait, yet no comment has been made on this cross-gendering. Instead, the figure of the boy-nymph has been seen as the result of a practical arrangement that made it possible for every member of the family to be included as a protagonist in the scene.[22] Yet this argument could be turned

19 For discussion of cross-gendered images as an outcome of mass-production, see Huskinson 2002, 25–26; Koch 1990, 64–6.

20 Lee 2000, 114–115; Sørensen 2006, 117–119; Meskell 2000, 14.

21 On myths on sarcophagi generally, see Zanker and Ewald 2004; Koortbojian 1995; Ewald 1999b. On *vita romana* and other motifs such as philosopher and muses, see *ASR* I, 3; Ewald 1999a.

22 Zanker and Ewald 2004, 97. The frontal relief of the sarcophagus is now built into a wall in the courtyard of Palazzo Mattei, Rome.

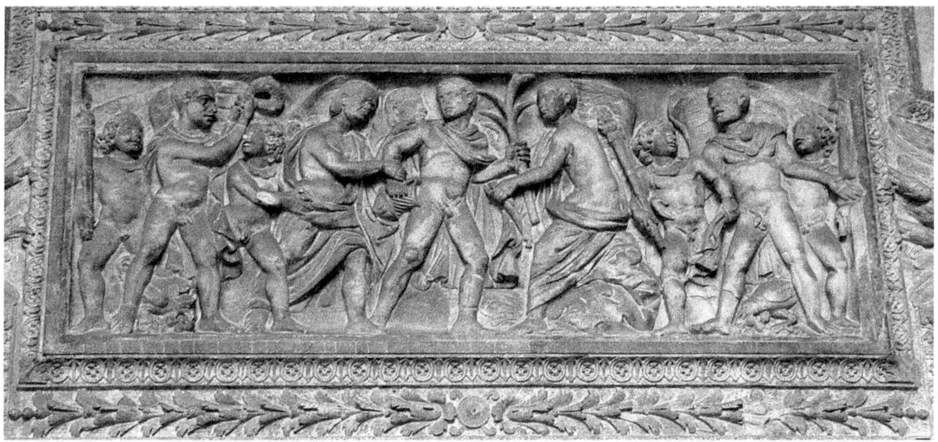

Figure 7.3: Hylas is being abducted by two nymphs. One of the nymphs is shown as an elderly woman whereas the other is a boy. Palazzo Mattei, Rome.
Photograph: Troels Myrup Kristensen

around, to claim that the motif may have been chosen specifically because it allowed the dead boy to be associated with a female body and the particular qualities it implied. How this would work out will be examined more closely in the next section.

Seen in this light, cross-gendered images, such as this, have an effect on our understanding of gender and gender relations in the Roman world. This assumption is further strengthened by the fact that, as argued by Laqueur, in antiquity the body was imagined as a single sex, meaning that the female body possessed all the same elements as the male but placed in the wrong places.[23] The two genders were then one sex, and in medical terms this meant that the degree to which individuals had the characteristics of a man or woman depended on their relative bodily heat. As a consequence gender was not seen as a fixed binary construction, which means that the boundary between male and female was one of degree and not of kind. This ancient attitude towards the body suggests that our own perception of gender distinctions in antiquity should be more flexible, since it opens up the possibility of viewing gender as something relative and moveable. Thus, an individual's gender might be defined according to the relative strength of male and female aspects, and could even change in the course of life according to context, situation, social relations or personal experiences.

23 Laqueur 1990, 25–62.

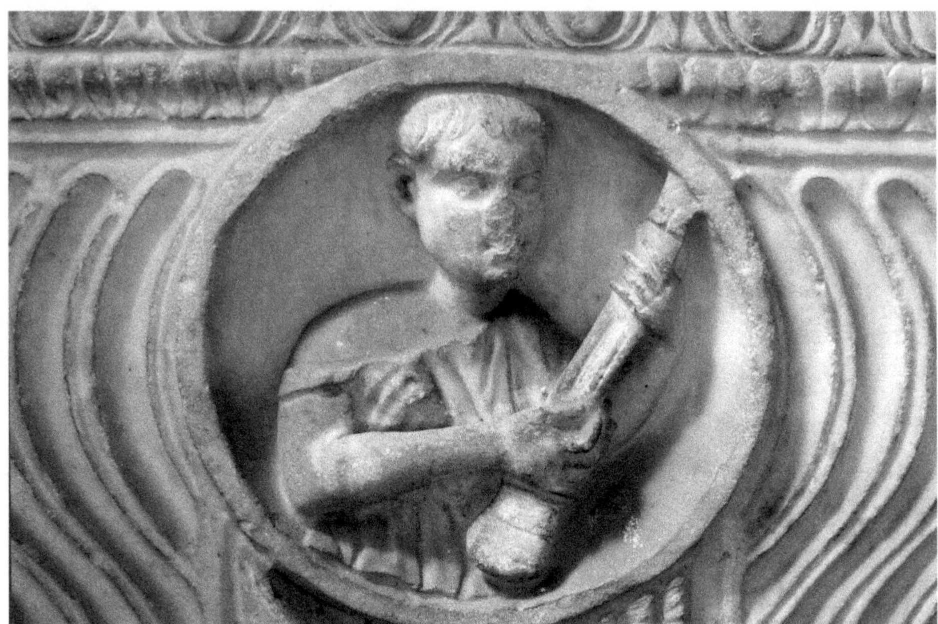

Figure 7.4: A boy is represented in drapery that slips off his shoulder, and holding an instrument. The drapery makes an allusion to Venus whereas the instrument shows him as skilled in music. His musical abilities associate him with the world of the muses. Ny Carlsberg Glyptotek inv. 854, Copenhagen.
Photograph: Stine Birk, by permission of the museum.

Cross-gendered Bodies on Roman Sarcophagi

Of the various kinds of cross-gendered images to appear, the most common consists of a male portrait applied to a female body. Sometimes this body is unambiguously presented with female features, such as curvy contours and breasts visible beneath a long dress, and sometimes even with one shoulder exposed in an allusion to the iconography of Venus (Figure 7.4).[24] At other times it may simply be the case that a male body is represented in such a way that it appears almost womanly (Figure 7.5).[25]

24 Copenhagen, Ny Carlsberg Glyptotek, inv. 854. Østergaard 1996, cat. 56.

25 British Museum, inv. GR 1947.7–14.8; Walker 1990, cat. 43. The 'womanly' male body is a not wholly unfamiliar phenomenon within Roman visual culture, e.g. male gods like Dionysos or Priapos and young men as Narcissus and Hermaphroditos all show a great deal of femininity both in their behaviour and physical appearance: Cain 1997; Oehmke 2004; Oehmke 2007. The masculine hero Hercules also became female when he changed clothes with Omphale (before they participated in a ritual honouring Bacchus): Ovid, *Fasti* II 283–358. Kampen 1996b, 242.

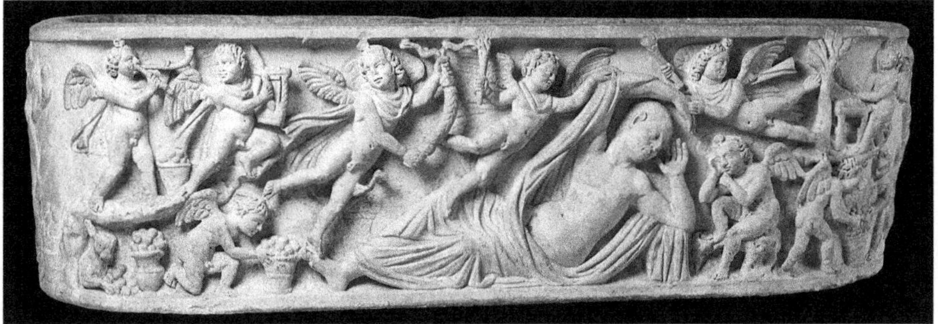

Figure 7.5: An effeminate representation of a man. The Endymion figure was probably re-carved from a sleeping Ariadne. British Museum inv. GR 1947.7–14.8. Photograph: By permission of the museum.

An example of such a feminised male figure appears on a sarcophagus now in Palermo Cathedral (Figure 7.6).[26] The relief shows the nine Muses and the figures of two boys, who are represented rather differently. These may depict two brothers, or perhaps the same person twice over, with each figure embodying a specific gender role. Such dual representations of the same individual are not uncommon in Roman art where two figures portraying the same person but in different ways, either in the same statue group or on the same relief, can emphasise distinct aspects of the person's life and virtues.[27] On the Palermo sarcophagus the young man on the right end is shown as a male seated philosopher: the scroll is his link to the world of learning, and the muses are his inspiration. In contrast, the young man on the left is represented by the image of a muse: the long dress, exposed shoulder, shapely breasts, and lyre firmly link him with feminine qualities.[28] These two figures do not invite any categorisation according to sexual orientation; we cannot explain this choice of crossed male and female iconography by their relationship with the other portrait figures on the reliefs, nor can we at this stage draw any general

26 Palermo, Cathedral. *ASR* V, 3, cat. 68; Ewald 1999a, cat. A 13.

27 Hallett 2005, 212–15.

28 The gender of the portrait has been disputed. As one of the first commentators, Wegner pointed out that the portrait was re-cut from female to male (*ASR* V, 3, cat. 68). Fittschen 1972, 490 also thought that the portrait was of a boy, but later (1992) claimed it was of a very young girl. But there are various problems with this line of argument, e. g. to support his claim that portraits of young girls can look like boys, he cited the sarcophagus from Civitá Castellana, to be discussed in detail below. In this a skeleton of a boy of about 12 years was found (Moretti 1975, 261), and there is a general agreement that the relief represents a 'boy muse' (Ewald 1999a, cat. H 2; Wrede 1981, 140, cat. 239). In his discussion, Fittschen also mistakenly emphasises the sex of the child instead of acknowledging the ambiguous gender categories in the representation of very small children.

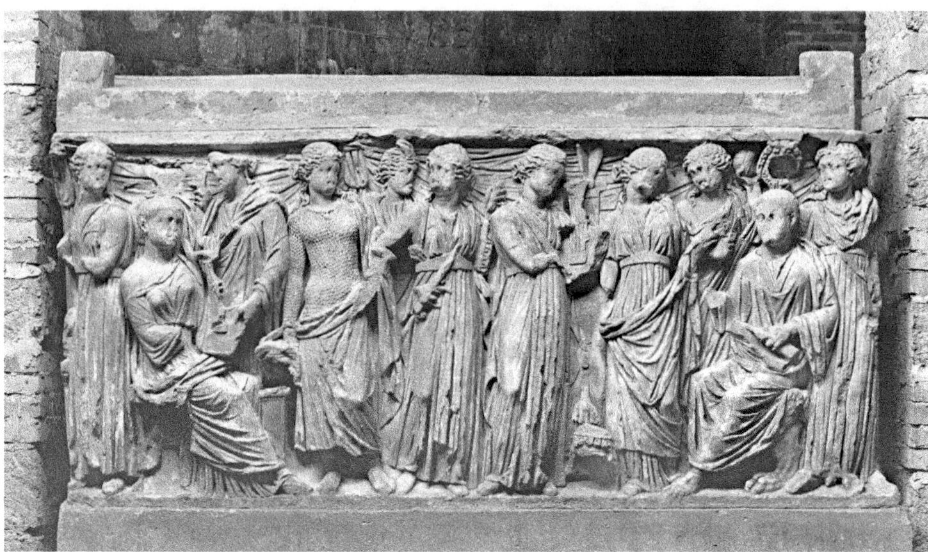

Figure 7.6: Two brothers (or maybe it is the same boy shown twice) are shown in the sphere of the nine Muses. The boy on the right is represented in off the shoulder drapery, following the iconography of Venus. Cathedral, Palermo. Photograph: DAIR 1971.0681

conclusion from them about gender categories. But their age may be an important factor since it does seem that age can play a significant role in the choice of cross-gendered figures and, as I will also show later, androgyny seems to have been more easily permissible for boys than for adults.[29] I will return to the issue of cross-gendering and age below.

Not only boys could take on signifiers of femininity: men too could be represented in this way. A strigillated sarcophagus in the Capitoline Museums shows a typical pair of figures engaged in intellectual activity.[30] In the left corner panel is a 'learned woman',[31] and in the right the usual male pendant, a philosopher. But despite the femininity of the woman's body, both figures have male portrait features. The similarity of the two portraits makes it likely that it is

29 For cross-gender on funerary reliefs as expressions of a sexual relationship, see Clarke 2003, 215–9 and Varner 2008, 194. On sexual ambivalence in antiquity, see also Brisson 2002.

30 Capitoline Museums, Palazzo dei Conservatori, Scala II, 15, inv. 821; Ewald 1999a, cat. F 18.

31 Huskinson 1999; 2002. Another representation of a man carved with the body of a muse is found on the so called 'Plotinus sarcophagus'. The figure on the right of the central group has a female body and wears a long garment. The head is of a bearded man. The muse originally intended was transformed into a philosopher-like figure. Unlike the other cross-gendered sarcophagi treated in this article this figure does not have a portrait.

the same person who has been depicted twice.[32] If so, then the man has chosen to represent himself by means of two different figure-types, both of which promote him as an intellectual although one has an obviously female body, with clearly curvaceous lines and breasts. It seems as if this choice of appearance was intentional since it would have been easy to rework the body to make it look more masculine, or, alternatively, not to finish the head with male portrait features (after all, it was very common on Roman sarcophagi to leave the head roughly prepared). But none of these options was followed. So presumably the man wanted to represent two different aspects of himself; one relating to male skills and the other to female qualities. There is a possibility that the lower part of the figure has been re-cut as the relief is low and the dress of an unusual type; if that was done, the purpose might have been to shorten the dress. But that is not certain – and even if the dress was shortened, there is still the question of why no effort was made to conceal the hips and breasts in order to make the figure appear less explicitly feminine.

Another feminine, almost sensual, representation of a man is found on the sarcophagus in the British Museum (Figure 7.5). The man has a portrait that enables us to date the sarcophagus to the first part of the third century.[33] He is represented as Endymion; but originally, before some minor re-cutting, the figure must have been a sleeping Ariadne.[34] The graceful femininity of the body is still apparent, especially in the round belly and slender waist.

Many pragmatic explanations can be found to account for such representations, especially where they involve some re-carving (a process that is often fraught with complicated questions); yet even so they do not change the fact that the resulting cross-gendered images were socially acceptable, and tolerated even on commemorative monuments.

All these examples show how gender categories were unstable and could be varied without transgressing the boundaries of what was socially acceptable for displays of self-representation.[35] They also show how the same portrait features applied to figures of different sex could display different sides of a person's identity. This raises some important questions about how differences between the sexes are interpreted, and about what that means for the understanding of gender.[36] But at this stage I would like to emphasise one general conclusion: that is, whatever their primary motivation, such cross-gendered figures were obviously acceptable to Roman society. It was not a moral outrage for a man

32 Ewald 1999a, 192.

33 Walker 1990, cat. 43.

34 The breasts were cut down and a penis was inserted to make him male. For discussion, see *ASR* XII, 2, 54–5.

35 Montserrat 2000.

36 Gilchrist 1999, 13.

to be depicted with a feminine body, even on monuments like these made to commemorate the dead and their social virtues.

Femininity and 'Suspect Men' in Roman Society

Archaeological literature has generally tended to view male iconography as the more privileged and power-laden, and to see the female as a metaphor of weakness. But this evaluation seems to be challenged by the evidence from antiquity. Since there are more examples of cross-gendered images with a male portrait head on a female body than there are examples of female portraits on a male body, men who assumed female physical attributes in this way cannot be seen as 'suspect'; nor should, as an opposition to suspect, the term 'virtuous' be used to describe women when they take on male attributes.[37] That way of thinking is part of a feminist mindset that talks about gender and gender roles in term of hierarchy and power relations.[38] I find it more helpful to consider that boys and men, as well as women and girls, selected their iconography, or that the imagery was chosen for them, because they wanted to express specific virtues and skills that were traditionally associated with the other sex. This view does not imply that the choice of iconography inevitably made a person more 'virtuous' or 'suspect'; but rather that the individuals concerned have chosen to mix gendered iconography in order to construct their own particular visual and social identity.[39]

In iconography, men could take on feminine signs, not only through the physical characteristics of the body (as discussed in the last section) but also by means of attributes. For instance, a relief in the Vatican includes two possible cross-gendered figures of men, of which one alludes to the iconography of

37 Kampen 1996a, 18 explicitly uses the term 'suspect' about men with female attributes and 'virtuous' about women with male attributes. Also, Montserrat (2000, 159–61) for the female as the lowest ranking in a gender hierarchy dominated by power relations; individuals with male bodies and suggestions of femininity (including hermaphrodites or other kind of third gender) slipped several points down the scale towards *femaleness.*

38 See Gilchrist 1999, 2–3.

39 An example of how male bias has affected the interpretation of sarcophagi is provided by an image which commemorates a man through wool-working scenes (Malibu, Getty Villa, inv. 86.AA.701 Koch 1988, 24–7). He has been described as a businessman engaged with the production of wool (Koch 1988, 26; and Amedick in *ASR* I, 4, 116, cf. no. 68). But if the wool-workers and the protagonist had been women, then the interpretation would probably have been limited to household duties since wool-working was traditionally thought to be a female virtue (Kampen 1996a, 22; Dixon 2001, 117). This illustrates the obvious risk of making gender-stereotypical assumptions – seeing the wool-work for women as a domestic ideal, but for a man as an indication of larger enterprises outside the house.

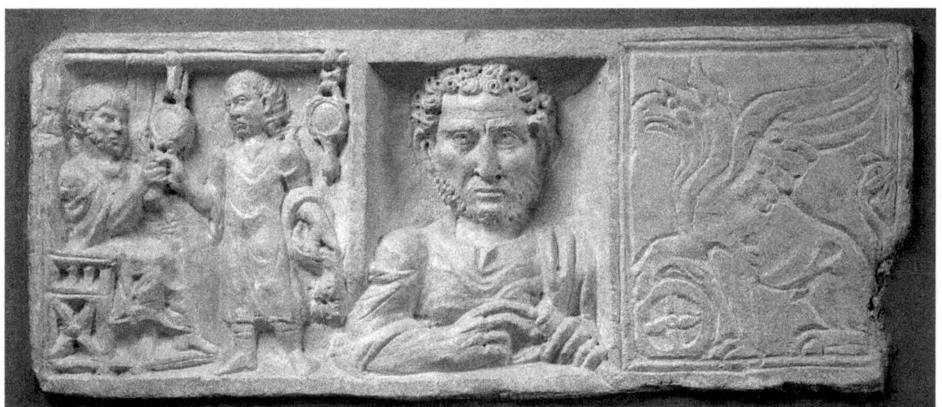

Figure 7.7: The central panel shows a female bust with a portrait of a bearded man. Loculus plate. Rome, Musei Vaticani, Museo Gregoriano Profano inv. 9517. Photograph: DAIR 1936.0639.

Venus through drapery which exposes a shoulder, while the other is associated with the female world by means of a mirror (Figure 7.7).[40] (In the Roman world the mirror was an object associated with women and femininity, and men who used mirrors were considered effeminate).[41] The whole relief is separated into three panels: in the centre is the bust of the man with the Venus-style drapery, on the left the scene with figures and a mirror, and on the right a griffin. The portrait bust in the central panel is of a middle-aged man with curly hair and a beard. He holds a scroll in his hands, which are strong, large and masculine. But in comparison his shoulders seem slightly too small, while the outline of breasts is visible beneath the dress and his drapery has slipped from his shoulder. It is not possible that the bust was re-carved from female to male, since that would have meant enlarging the female hands, so all in all, the most likely conclusion is that this figure was originally carved as a cross-gendered image.

The left panel of this relief depicts a seated man with what appears to be a scroll in his left hand. He stretches his right hand forward and grabs the hand of another man standing in front of him. This man is dressed in a *tunica* with sleeves with a *stola* around his left arm. Two mirrors and a curtain hang from a rod in the background; and it looks as if the seated man grasps one of the mirrors, perhaps to give it to the other. The heads of the two figures have been carved with male portrait features, although the face of the standing man has been re-carved from a portrait of a woman with long loose hair to portray a short haired man. Traces of the woman's locks are still visible on the man's

40 Vatican Museum, Museo Gregoriano Profano, inv. 9517; this was once thought to be from a sarcophagus but is now believed to be a *loculus* plate.

41 Sinn 1991, 48.

shoulders, and the *stola* and the mirror add to his appearance of femininity. This scene has been variously interpreted as depicting a shop, or a cult, or a *dextrarum iunctio,*[42] but several questions remain to be answered. Why did this woman (whose original portrait was re-cut as the man's) have long hair in the first place? Roman women always wore their hair up, and I know of no other example where portrait figures have loose hair. On the other hand servants, captives, and grieving women were depicted with long, loose hair, as was Eve in early Christian art (as a sinner in opposition to the modest and pious Mary, who is represented on sarcophagi with her hair tucked away under a veil).[43]

Another explanation of the long hair might be that this is an image of an actor, which might also explain why the figure wears a *stola.*[44] Yet most actors were men, while this figure seems originally to have been a woman, and, unlike most other images of actors, it also has portrait features. A useful comparison may be with the depiction of actors on the grave relief of a boy named Flavius where they are engaged in a drama about the Muses, perhaps staged for his funeral.[45] These do not have portrait features but are cross-gendered since four of them are dressed as Muses – two wear long robes belted just below the breast; one has a mask with a full beard that contrasts with his feminine dress and long, curly wig; and the fourth, also with a full-length robe, could be Calliope, the muse of epic poetry, or possibly a poet. (Flavius himself is represented with a scroll like a poet or some other learned figure, but he also wears a *bulla*, which shows that he was still a child.)[46] The Ostia *loculus* relief lacks any reference to the theatre (even in the minimal form of a mask or some other theatre prop) which is yet another reason for rejecting a theatrical explanation. A more positive suggestion is that, its images might be intended to represent one and the

---

42 Sinn 1991, cat. 21; *ASR* I, 4, cat. 285.

43 An example of the first is the servant with a cup behind the *pandurium* playing woman on the sarcophagus of Caecilius Vallianus: Rome, Museo Gregoriano Profano (see below). For the grieving woman found on a deathbed see a sarcophagus from the Louvre: Inv. Ma 319. *ASR* I, 4, cat. 115. For young women with loose hair e.g. on *Ara Pacis:* Polaschek 1972, 147.

44 For cross-gendering of actors see also a statuette from Rome which has been interpreted as a representation of an actor (Savarese 2007, 79). The generic face is round and soft like the face of a woman (or young man), and the hair is piled up. The figure is veiled, and wears a *pallia*, and long dress, through which the telling outline of the body can be seen. What appeared to be a woman, is now shown as a man. The breast is flat, the waist unemphasised. The torso appears to be somewhat quadrilateral and no effort has been made to conceal the genitals. On the contrary the rather pronounced outline of the male organ is being emphasised by the tight-fitting garment. The sculpture shows a female character performed by a male actor.

45 Rome, Museo della Villa Doria Pamphilj, inv. 162. Calza 1977, cat. 137; Savarese 2007, 104.

46 On the *bulla*, see Harlow and Laurence 2002, 40, 67.

same man by the two different figures – the man standing with a mirror, and the man whose portrait has been carved on the bust; in both cases, an effort seems to have been made to represent the man with female attributes. If so this relief is the most explicit example of a person whose gender is not couched in the binary gender categories.

Four sarcophagi – two for adults and two for boys – decorated with deathbed scenes further strengthen the fact that it could be acceptable to add male portraits to female bodies.[47] These show the deceased reclining on a bed surrounded by various attendants; on the two sarcophagi made for adults, these are servants waiting at the deathbed, while on the two made for boys they are mourners. The two dead men wear long dresses, with outlines of breasts visible underneath. On one sarcophagus the man lifts his arm above his head in a graceful gesture, emphasising the intrinsic femininity of the figure. On the other the man is depicted with a female body surrounded by 'soft domestic qualities',[48] symbolised, for instance, by the children playing beneath the couch (Figure 7.8). This lid of this sarcophagus bears an inscription saying that it belonged to P. Caecilius Vallianus, a 63-year old military man.[49] From a modern perspective it is almost impossible not to be intrigued as to why this military man chose to depict himself on his funeral monument in this way, as a reclining figure with a female body. As for the two boys, they are shown on their deathbed wearing robes that expose their shoulders as a sign of feminine beauty, and in the company of the nine muses who cluster around them. This allusion to literary and musical abilities connects these two examples with other sarcophagi that depict boys as muses – a theme that has been interpreted as referring to the life course of a child (see below).

Two more examples that strengthen the claim that feminine attributes could be used for male iconography without making the men 'suspect' are two sarcophagi dedicated to adolescents. One is a sarcophagus dedicated to a youth aged 17 years, four months and 21 days.[50] He was of equestrian rank and was commemorated by his father. Yet his portrait was carved on a female bust with *palla* and breasts, showing that this very masculine background did not prevent the use of a female body for his self-representation. The other example is a Season sarcophagus in the Vatican, where the portrait features suggest that the

47 Adults: Musei Vaticani, Museo Gregoriano Profano, inv. 9538/9539 (*ASR* I, 4, cat. 286) and Carrara (*ASR* I, 4, pl. 4,5). Boys: Museo Nazionale Romano delle Terme, inv. 535 and Stuttgart, Württembergisches Landesmuseum, inv. Arch 6318.

48 Huskinson 1996, 26.

49 Whether the lid belongs to the sarcophagus or not has been discussed, but the argument that variation in the size of the lid compared to the chest is not enough to reject the possibility that the two pieces belong together (since this is relatively common for Roman sarcophagi).

50 Museo Nazionale Romano inv. 113227. Guiliano 1985, 234–37; Ewald 1999a, cat. I 1.

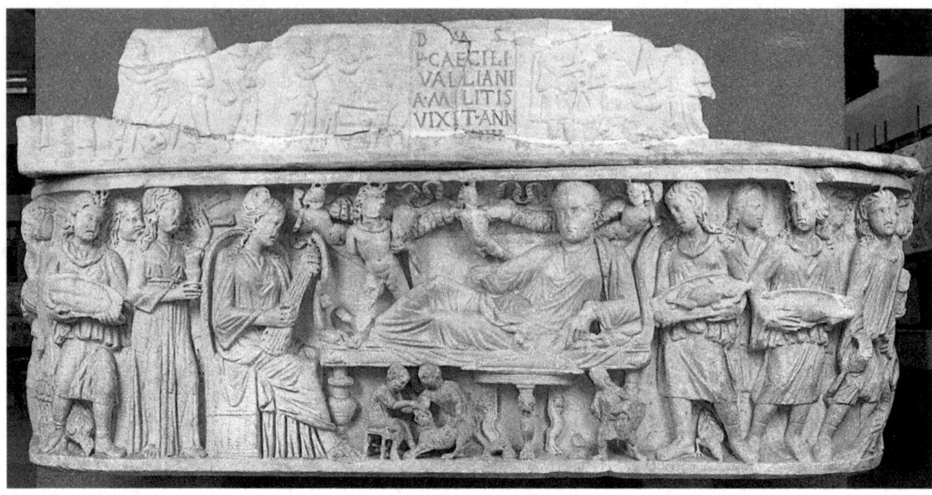

Figure 7.8: The reclining man is shown with a female body with breasts, and with drapery that slips off one shoulder. Rome, Musei Vaticani, Museo Gregoriano Profano inv. 9538/ 9539. Photograph: DAIR 1990.0413.

subject is an adolescent.[51] This portrait is carved on the body of a 'learned woman' (as revealed by the figure's curving outline and long dress).

Femininity taken on by male characters is also found among mythological figures such as Narcissus, or gods such as Apollo and Dionysus who also crossed the line between the two sexes.[52] They assumed many female characteristics in both their behaviour and iconography. Yet even so, their figures continued to be used as a basis for images commemorating young men whose personal portraits were added. For example, a sarcophagus, now at Hearst Castle, shows Apollo among the muses (Figure 7.9).[53] The long dress covering most of the feet, the curves of the body, and the emphatic waist make his figure appear effeminate, while the lyre which he holds is often shown played by women on 'intellectual' sarcophagi (while men have a scroll), and by muses in other scenes.[54] Yet combined with this rather effeminate representation of Apollo is the realistic portrait of a young man.

From all these examples it may be deduced that the feminine possessed its own specific virtues, which could be combined with masculinity – even within a

51 Vatican Museum, Cortile Ottagono 879: *ASR* V, 4, no.90; Koch 1990, 65–7; Fittschen 1992, note 20.

52 Seneca describes Dionysus as someone who was not ashamed to act with femininity: *Hercules Furens*, 472–6.

53 Hearst Castle, California, inv 529-9-414.

54 Examples are *ASR* V, 3, cat. 25, 47, 48, 68 (here Figure 7.3); *ASR* V, 3, 80, 138, 160, 162, 184, 188, 193.

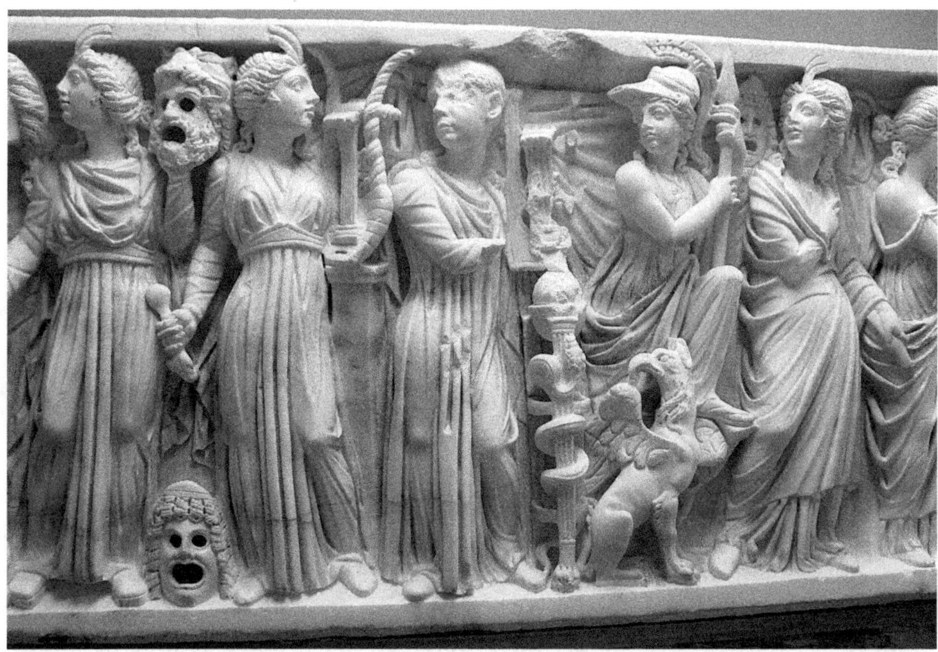

Figure 7.9: Apollo among the Muses. He is shown with a slender waist and a long dress, and his posture recalls representations of the Muses. Hearst Castle inv. 529-9-414. Photograph: Stine Birk. Published by permission of Hearst Castle®/California State Parks.

male body – without crossing the bounds of acceptability. They all show that, in a third century funerary context, to be depicted with feminine physical characteristics made neither boys nor men 'suspect' characters.

Unstable Bodies: Women and Male Iconography

The use of the word 'suspect' to designate men with feminine attributes illustrates a tendency in archaeological interpretation to see the feminine as secondary to the masculine.[55] But the concept of gender in the Roman world was not only about being either male or female; it varied according to period, social class, age, status, and ethnicity.[56] Literary evidence has established a picture of elite Roman ideals which is often reflected in the figural representations of sarcophagi – though sometimes rather differently. But some do not appear at all: good examples are images of wool-working and of the woman as mother and wife, both of which are well known metaphors for the

55 For this attitude towards Roman men using female iconography, see note 37.
56 Clarke 1998, 278–79; Montserrat 2000, 164.

conduct of an ideal woman.[57] It is therefore important not to see Roman women as a static, uniform category: wool-working seems to originate as an ideal in literary sources of the first century BC and first century AD, and does therefore not reflect attitudes towards women in the third century.[58] The ideal woman as a mother is another image that appears only very rarely on sarcophagi of this date.[59] This is striking, as sarcophagi are supposed to convey the ideal identity of the deceased. The value of sarcophagus imagery as evidence for the perception of gender, sex and femininity is therefore high, since visually it illustrates contemporary ideals different from those which appear in literary sources, and suggests that in third century Rome the 'learned woman' takes precedence over all other types of female ideals. So, to get a more nuanced picture of third century gender ideals overall, the literary sources, most often written by men, need to be supplemented with evidence from the archaeological record, where, at least in the case of sarcophagi, women's voices are also present.

Representations of women dressed in male clothing and involved in what are usually considered to be socially important male activities can help us to new ways of seeing gender. They make illuminating contrasts with the uniform imagery of female social identity that prevail on Roman sarcophagi, and offer glimpses of individuality at the micro-level of the specific commemorations. Two examples occur on lion hunt sarcophagi of the canonical type, one of which is now at Nieborow, Poland, and the other (fragmentary) at S. Sebastiano in Rome; on both of these the central hunter has feminine features and hairstyle, rather than a male portrait (Figure 7.10).[60] On the Nieborow sarcophagus this 'huntress' is clearly accompanied by *Virtus* (and this was probably also the case on the other example, where traces of her spear may be seen across the huntress's gesticulating arm). The masculine qualities which *Virtus* personifies are reinforced by the 'male' environment of the episode, with the attacking lion, and the hunters with their horses and dogs. Yet there is no doubt about the femininity of the 'huntresses'. Although the face of the figure on the Nieborow sarcophagus is carved without much refinement, it has a small mouth and chin and round cheeks. The arrangement of her hair is also clear:

57 For wool-working as a female ideal, see for example Lovén 1998; Dixon 2001, 117, 119–22; Allison 2006, 5, 7.

58 An example of a study where Roman women are seen as a universal category is Lovén 1998. She emphasis wool-working as a female ideal in general. On women's virtues, deeds, and roles in Roman society based on written evidence from the first century BC and into the second century AD, see Shelton 1988/1989, 291–306.

59 For the ideal of Roman womanhood as closely tied to the women's role in the family, see Kampen 1996a, especially p. 13; Clark 1993, 13–21, 94–5.

60 Both sarcophagi date to the late third century. Nieborow Castle, Arcadia, inv. Nb 2723, Poland; Mikocki 1995, cat. 58; Rome, S. Sebastiano ASR I, 2, cat. 150; Huskinson 2002, 26. On the canonical type of lion hunt sarcophagi, see *ASR* I, 2.

combed from the forehead and backwards into locks, and wound in plaits from the neck, it represents a popular third century fashion for women.[61]

That these two sarcophagi were carved with the same image of a female hunter, and in the same period, makes it unlikely that this was the unintentional outcome of some craftsman's action. Rather, the women who chose this image have deliberately shown themselves within a male environment in order to illustrate specific components of their identity. After all, if they had wanted a female role model, they could have chosen a mythological figure such as Diana or Artemis or the personification of *Virtus* herself (present on both sarcophagi), who would have proved a perfect vehicle for them to signal their strength as a woman. But instead, these women chose to express themselves through the body of a man and through male iconography. It is the male *virtus* in the primary role of the huntsman that was their ideal, and their own biological sex seems to have been no hindrance to the use of this iconography.

These visual examples of bodily representation, as a means of constructing female identity, seem to be related to ideas expressed by the Neoplatonic philosopher Porphyry (c. 234 – c. 305) when he wrote that in order for a woman to become a philosopher, she should banish from her soul everything womanly, as if she were enclosed in the body of a man.[62] Porphyry's statement is of course a metaphor, and the images of the female huntresses can be seen as a visual equivalent. In these representations the women were literally enclosed in a body of a man, and they have become huntsmen, with all the strength and virtues that this role implies. By representing themselves in this guise these women associated themselves with particular virtues that they held personally important, even though these were generally regarded in society as characterising men.

This pattern can be illustrated by further examples where female portraits were added to male figures. For instance on a strigillated sarcophagus, which has a scene of a lion killing a deer at each corner, the central bust has a female portrait carved on a male body.[63] On another example a woman is represented as a *togatus* bust.[64] Both these female portraits were probably created by re-carving of a bust that originally was intended for a man. These representations should be seen in the light of the popular motif of the 'learned woman'; its frequent use

61 Bergmann 1977, 180–200, cf. end of third century hairstyles.

62 Rousseau 1995, 118. The idea is also commonly found in early Christian writing, see Bassler 2008, 53–7.

63 Tarragona, Museu Paleocristiano, inv. MNAT (P) 53. See *ASR* VI, 1, cat. 365. Cf. similar sarcophagus Rome, Museo Nazionale Romano Rome, inv. 124745, also with female head on a bust identified as male (Sapelli in Giuliano 1985, cat. 1,1).

64 *ASR* V, 4, cat. 60 (Tutzing, season sarcophagus).

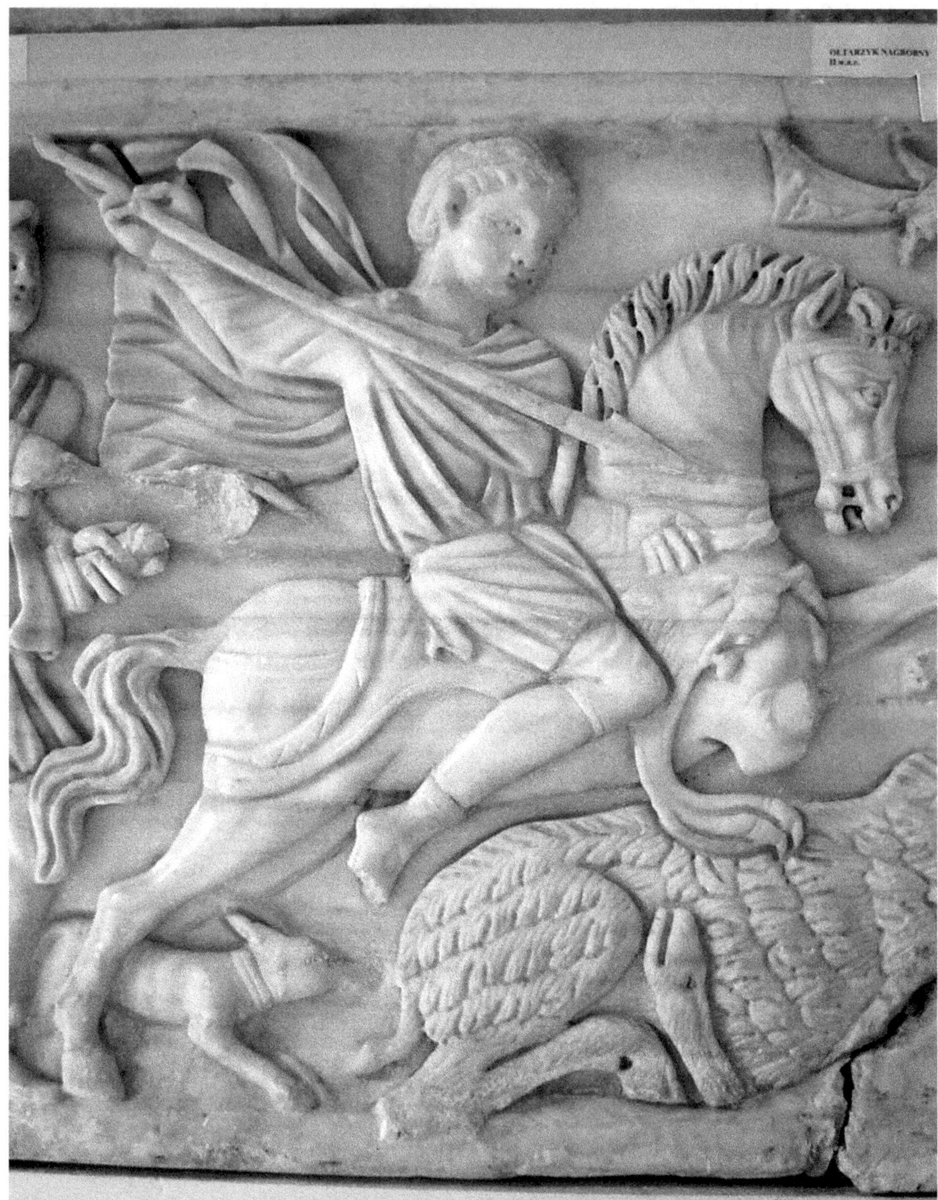

Figure 7.10: On this relief the lion hunter is depicted with a female hairstyle, with the hair combed backwards from the forehead and plaits fastened around her head. Nieborow inv. NB 2723 MNW, Arcadia, Poland. Photograph: Stine Birk.

on sarcophagi resulted in the occurrence of more or less generic 'learned' bodies, which would explain the appearance of these figures.

If there may be some doubt as to whether cross-gendered bodies were deliberately chosen in these last two cases of 'learned women', the choice appears explicit on two other sarcophagi which have female portraits on male bodies. The imagery of these sarcophagi offered the possibility of applying the female portrait to a female body, but both the deceased women used the male figure as the basis for her self-representation. The first example has already been mentioned briefly (Figure 7.1): it shows a central conch with busts prepared for both a male and a female portrait.[65] Generally such a pair is interpreted as a married couple, and on such sarcophagi the male bust usually has a scroll, while the woman often puts one arm around his neck and the other on his chest. Through the scroll and gestures, each figure possesses its own qualities, but the composition also expresses a hierarchy of gender roles since it looks as if the woman wants to demonstrate her support for her husband. On this example, the male figure, and not the female, has been chosen to represent the woman. By taking on the qualities that were intended for a male figure, the deceased woman is making an explicit statement. Perhaps she intended to show that she held priority of rank (which was usually symbolised by the man posed in front of his supportive wife), or that she possessed the intellectual knowledge represented by the learned figure with the scroll. But whatever the intentions behind the choice, it seems clear that using a Venus-like female figure type did not appeal to this woman.

The other example occurs on a strigillated sarcophagus of the popular 'five panel' design (whereby three figured scenes are separated by two panels of fluting).[66] The centre shows a philosopher seated reading to a Muse, the left panel a 'learned woman', and the right a standing philosopher. The seated philosopher is carved with a portrait head of a woman, unmistakeable because of her hairstyle.[67] Confirmation that it was an explicit choice of cross-gendering comes from the fact that the 'learned woman' on the left panel was left with a roughly carved head while the standing philosopher on the right panel was finished, again with female portrait features. So, if cross-gendering was not socially acceptable the female learned figure would have been chosen for self-representation instead of the figures of the two male philosophers.

---

65 See note 4 above.

66 Ostia, Museo, inv. 48277. It was found in a hypogeum together with two other sarcophagi with portrait figures, Baldassarre 1991/92.

67 Another example representing a female philosopher is a strigillated sarcophagus from Palazzo Lazzaroni, Rome (*ASR* V, 4, Cat. 181). On women and intellectuality in third century, see Huskinson 1999; 2002.

Boys will be Boys? Age and the Instability of Gender

The majority of all cross-gendered images are of boys, and are likely to represent a relationship between age and gender connected with the life course of a child. This is particularly interesting for current debates since the individual and the life course have recently received much scholarly attention, as have Roman childhood and the representation of children.[68]

These deceased boys are often represented with the Muses. Sometimes they are actually portrayed as one of the nine, wearing her appropriate dress and attributes and flanked by the other eight, in the frieze composition typical of the Muse sarcophagi which were so popular in the third century.[69] Similar representations of boys dressed like Muses or 'learned women' also occur on sarcophagi, which have portraits set in a central medallion or in front of a *parapetasma*, and evoke ideas of intellectual culture.[70] The high percentage of cross-gendered images which depict a boy or youth as a Muse or some other intellectual female figure suggests that greater gender flexibility was allowed in the representation of children than of adults. It is known from other societies that the sex of a child was perceived as neither male nor female, but undefined, until fixed by the occurrence of a certain 'rite de passage', or by a socially significant relationship such as marriage or childbirth. Images of children on sarcophagi show how this progression was possible in Roman society too.[71] Some visual representations of very small children in Roman funerary art do not make a clear distinction between boys and girls, as can be seen on a sarcophagus commemorating two babies, where their round and fleshy faces makes it hard to distinguish their sex; this ambivalence may have been intentional.[72] This suggests that these cross-gendered images of boy-Muses may be seen as representing some relationship between gender and a particular stage in an individual's life course – which in this case is shown by the presence of the Muses to be a formative stage connected with education and learning.[73]

A Muse sarcophagus from the second century, now in Cività Castellana, is a very early example of sarcophagi that have a figure with portrait features.[74] It too

---

68 Huskinson 1996; Dimas 1998; Harlow and Laurence 2002; Rawson 2003; Backe-Dahmen 2003; 2008; Huskinson 2005 and 2007; Sigismund-Nielsen 2007; Cohen and Rutter 2007.

69 *ASR* V, 3; Huskinson 1996, 38–40; 2007, 336.

70 Examples of both types will be provided below.

71 Strathern 1992, 66; Sørensen 2006, 119

72 Koch and Sichtermann 1982, ill. 297. Another example of this is a sarcophagus lid with a reclining child with a female body and a portrait of a boy. Museo Capitolini, inv. 329. Sichtermann and Koch 1975, cat. 68, plate 165.

73 Gilchrist 2004, 142–160; Huskinson 2005, 102.

74 Cività Castellana, Forte Sangallo, inv. 59646.

has a cross-gendered image of a boy dressed like a Muse, and we know from the skeleton found in it, that the sex of the deceased corresponded to the sex of the portrait.[75] The boy holds a lyre – normally the attribute of Terpsichore or Erato – and is placed among the other eight Muses, so that visually he has become one of the nine muses; his body is quite feminine, with clearly visible breasts. This is a very direct way of projecting the virtues of the Muses on to the boy.[76]

On at least another three sarcophagi a dead boy is shown accepted into the company of the Muses. One shows him as the central figure in their gathering, with four Muses on each side of him, and a mask placed on a pedestal at his feet.[77] Yet even though this time he is actually depicted as a male philosopher, he may still be regarded as a 'stand in' for the ninth Muse or, in symbolic terms, he has become the ninth Muse. This shows yet again that the boy-Muses should not be seen as 'effeminate' representations, but as embodying the special virtues and characteristics of the intellectual life which transcend human gender.

The second example that further emphasises the instability of gender in the sphere of the Muses is a sarcophagus that is now known only through a drawing in the Dal Pozzo-Albani volumes.[78] Nine figures are displayed, under five arches. It appears to have been important for the craftsman to accommodate this number (synonymous to the nine Muses) as he had to compromise the symmetry of the composition to do so, so that the second arch contains only one figure instead of the normal two. All of the figures represent Muses apart from the male poet with portrait features which dominates the centre. Although it is difficult to decide from the drawing whether this is a boy or a man, he has been described on the sarcophagus as a *young* poet.[79]

Apart from the sarcophagi already discussed (Figures 7.4 and 7.6) a third and last example of a boy-poet among eight Muses is a sarcophagus in Verona.[80] The portrait, though badly damaged, is of a boy. His hair has an unusual appearance, rendered by horizontal lines, but this time he has the characteristics of the Muse Calliope, with his hips twisted in a sinuous pose. Here again he takes the place of the ninth Muse – even though he does not have the identifying feathers on his head – and he embodies her virtues.

Other sarcophagi use cross-gendered images of children to make more general points about age. A *clipeus* sarcophagus of a boy aged one year and 30 days, dedicated by his parents to their 'most sweet' son is an example of how the

75 Moretti 1975, 261; Huskinson 1996, cat. 5.1; Wrede 1981, cat. 239. Fittschen 1972 argues that the portrait is of a girl, see note 28 above.
76 Huskinson 2007, 336; Wrede 1981, 140–41.
77 Naples, Museo Archeologico Nazionale, inv. 205250. See ASR V, 3, cat. 23.
78 Vermeule 1960, cat. 14, fig. 14.
79 *ASR* V, 3, 91.
80 Museo Maffeiano, Verona, *ASR* V, 3, cat. 227.

same iconography could be used for both sexes to show that the child had not reached puberty.[81] The boy's portrait has been applied to a female bust with breasts. This sarcophagus can be dated to the end of the third century because of the hair carved straight across the top of the forehead.[82] Another example of the acceptability of boys' portraits on female bodies is found in what is probably a representation of a father and a son on a strigillated sarcophagus.[83] This was decorated with a central medallion containing a male and a female bust, but the male bust is carved with a portrait of a man whereas the female is carved with what seems to be a portrait of a boy. As already described, such representations of a couple in a medallion were usually intended for a man and wife, and show the woman putting her arm around the man. But in this particular case it is the man who supports the female bust by putting her in front of the composition and leaning his arm on her shoulder. This change of iconography, combined with the fact that the female bust has the portrait head of a child, shows that the social role of children of such young age was different from that of adolescents and adults; and the iconography explicitly tells us that the child died so young that it was still under the protection of its father.

Another two sarcophagi, this time with Christian motifs, show how the use of female bodies did not affect the idealised aspect of a boy's commemoration. One is a boy's portrait carved on to a female bust in a medallion; in the other case the portrait is applied to a female *orans* figure.[84] None of the examples mentioned has been interpreted as representing a girl, but that this imagery of sex-gender relations could be turned the other way around is illustrated by a sarcophagus without an individualised figure.[85] Octavia Paulina was six years, four months and five days when she died, and was represented on her sarcophagus as a victorious girl athlete, using imagery of male athletic contests. In the centre of the relief she is depicted in triumph, crowning herself with a wreath with one hand and holding a palm branch in the other. On the left end of the relief she is seen with two boys pouring oil on her body, while on the right end she is shown wrestling with girls among boys. This image of a girl who fights and competes is unusual on sarcophagi, and must be read as a conscious way of illustrating particular aspects of her life and personality, as well as the

81 London, British Museum, inv. GR 1896.6–19.5. See Walker 1990, cat. 36; Huskinson 1996, cat. 9.36.

82 Walker 1990, cat. 36.

83 Rome, Palazzo Corsetti-Podocatari, *ASR* VI, 1, cat. 97.

84 Rome, Capitoline Museum, Sala II, inv. 70. See *Rep.* I, cat. 811. The sarcophagus with a boy's portrait carved on the bust of a female Orans is in Liebieghaus, inv. 1505, see Bol 1983, cat. 96.

85 ASR I, 4, cat. 67; Huskinson 2007, 338. A sarcophagus with a dedication to Publia Aelia Proba depicts the girl with a very 'boyish' look. That she is a girl is shown by the plait piled up from her forehead and pulled backwards: Stuart Jones 1968, 78–9.

sense of triumph that her father Octavius wanted to convey in her commemoration.

Yet further testimony that changing gender was less problematic for pre-adult figures can be found in the Hylas sarcophagus, briefly discussed above (Figure 7.3). As we saw, the scene depicts the abduction of Hylas by the nymphs, and Hercules and the Argonaut Polyphemus who are searching for him. Hylas and the nymph on his right have preserved their original portraits (the rest are modern restorations).[86] Hylas has the portrait of a middle-aged man resembling Gallienus. The nymph has the portrait features, not of a girl as would have been appropriate to the body, but of a boy with short hair and a soft, round face: the near-naked female body was obviously no deterrent to the addition of a male portrait.[87] The cross-gendered appearance of this figure is likely to be connected with the young age of the boy who had probably not survived to attain the toga of manhood, *toga virilis*, which could mean that his gender, in terms of social roles, could still be at a formative stage.[88] Because of the differences in age of the man represented as Hylas and the boy-nymph it is possibly one of the very rare examples of a representation of a parent and a child, and it may illustrate some particular virtue divined through their mutual relationship.

Just as the representation of boys as muses could be explained by their particular stage of personal and cultural development[89] so too these other cross-gendered images of children might be concerned with their age or place in the life course, as in terms of rites of passage for example.[90] If so, they may be evidence for the claim that people could be thought of as crossing from one gender to another at certain points in life.[91]

Conclusion

To look for a single explanation, such as sexuality or social status, of the occurrence of cross-gendered images is fruitless. Instead, each case needs to be considered on its own terms. Common to them all is the individual's decision to use a cross-gendered image to evoke specific virtues. As a consequence, the images become visual examples of how gender and identity could be

86 The relief was once thought to represent a family, but close examination shows that, for example, the faces of Hercules and Polyphemus are modern, connected with an extensive restoration of the reliefs from Palazzo Mattei in the 16th century.

87 Zanker and Ewald 2004, 97.

88 On the *toga virilis*, see Harlow and Laurence 2002, 67–9.

89 Huskinson 1999, 195.

90 Gilchrist 1999, 94–100

91 Fowler 2004, 44.

constructed. Here the cross-gendered figures are interpreted as expressions of individuality, but the fact that such images were tolerated on funerary memorials broadens the argument to include some wider social values. For their use on commemorative monuments, where ideal identities are constructed, explicitly shows that this was a socially acceptable way of expressing virtues. With their cross-gendered imagery, these sarcophagi are thus an informative source for understanding the way gender was lived and perceived in Roman society, and they show that it was neither fixed nor stable: age had an impact on gender roles as well as qualities, appearance, occupation, virtues and skills.[92]

In his book on representations of lovemaking in the Roman world John R. Clarke argued that 'in matters of sex – the Romans were not at all like us.'[93] This idea should stretch to our perception of gender roles as well. The spectrum of gender roles from which the Romans could draw both actions and identity was, as shown here, broader than the usual male/female dichotomy. I will not suggest the existence of a third gender category in Roman society, as has been done in the study of other cultures, but according to the cross-gendered images on sarcophagi, gender roles could vary according to the activity performed (a point illustrated by the female lion hunters, for instance), or through the knowledge gained (as seen when boys represented muses).[94] These cross-gendered images seem to be a reasonable basis for suggesting that gender categories in Roman society should be seen as flexible and as offering many possibilities for constructing identity.[95] Furthermore, they show that the female had virtue in itself, and that by taking on attributes of women, men did not become 'suspect'.[96] Instead, the concept of gender becomes a process of interpreting the body, of giving it cultural form,[97] and in this way masculinity could be applied to a female body, as well as femininity to a male.[98] This way of perceiving genders brings us near to understanding what is illustrated visually on the sarcophagi discussed here. Cross-gendering does not cancel out the categories male and female, but instead creates a situation in which the dead could evoke

92 Herdt 1994.

93 Clarke 1998, 275.

94 For studies in 'third gender' see Fowler 2004, 44; Joyce 2004, 88; Gilchrist 1999, 59–64. For both historical and anthropological studies in third genders, see Herdt 1994.

95 Also biology speaks against this categorisation into either male or female, as both hormones and genetic sex vary greatly, Gilchrist 1999, 57–8, Meskell 1999, 73.

96 See also Varner 2008 for feminine features in the representation of men in Roman imperial art. A portrait statue of a man from Tunis shows that this was an attitude that reached further than Rome. The man is represented with the iconography of the female personification of Tyche. Bianchi Bandinelli 1971, 218, fig. 202.

97 Butler 1986, 36.

98 Butler 1990, 6.

specific qualities or virtues for their commemoration and present themselves to society in their own personal terms.

Bibliography

Allison, P. M. Mapping for Gender. Interpreting Artefact Distribution inside 1st- and 2nd-Century A.D. Forts in Roman Germany. *Archaeological Dialogues* 13.1 (2006), 1–20.

Backe-Dahmen, A. *Innocentissima aetas römische Kindheit im Spiegel literarischer, rechtlicher und archäologischer Quellen des 1. bis 4. Jahrhunderts n. Chr.* (Mainz, 2003).

Backe-Dahmen, A. *Die Welt der Kinder in der Antike* (Mainz, 2008).

Baldassarre, I. Tre sarcofagi figurati della tomba 34 dell Isola Sacra. *Studi Miscellanei* 30 (1991/92), 305–22.

Bartman, E. Eros's Flame: Images of sexy Boys in Roman Ideal Sculpture, in: *The Ancient Art of Emulation: Studies in Artistic Originality and Tradition from the Present to Classical Antiquity*, edited by E.K. Gazda (Memoirs of the American Academy in Rome, 2002), 249–271.

Bassler, J. M. The Problem of Self-Definition: What Self and Whose Definition? in: *Redefining First-Century Jewish and Christian Identities: Essays in Honor of Ed Parish Sanders.* Christianity and Judaism in Antiquity Series, Vol. 16, edited by F. E. Udoh (Paris, 2008), 42–66.

Bergmann, M. Studien zum römischen Porträt des 3. Jahrhunderts n. Chr. *Antiquitas 3* (Bonn, 1977).

Bianchi Bandinelli, R. *Rome: The late Empire, Roman Art, A.D. 200–400* (New York, 1971).

Birk, S. *Reading Roman Sarcophagi, Identity, Commemoration and Production.* (Unpublished PhD dissertation, Aarhus University, 2009).

Blome, P. Der Löwenjagdsarkophag Ludwig im Antikenmuseum Basel, in: *Sarkophagstudien 1. Akten des Symposium "125 Jahre Sarkophag-corpus"*, edited by G. Koch (Mainz, 1998), 1–6.

Bol, P. C. *Bildwerke aus Stein und aus Stuck von archaischer Zeit bis zur Spätantike* (Melsungen, 1983).

Brisson, L. *Sexual Ambivalence: Androgyny and Hermaphroditism in Graeco-Roman Antiquity* (Berkeley, 2002).

Butler, J. Sex and Gender in Simone de Beauvoir's Second Sex. *Yale French Studies 72* (1986), 35–49.

Butler, J. *Gender Trouble: Feminism and the Subversion of Identity* (London, 1990).

Cain, H.-U. Dionysos "Die Locken lang, ein halbes Weib? ..." Euripides Sonderausstellung Museum für Abgüsse Klassischer Bildwerke München (Munich, 1997).

Calza, R. *Antichità di Villa Doria Pamphilj* (Rome, 1977).

Clark, G. *Women in Late Antiquity: Pagan and Christian Life-Styles* (Oxford, 1993).

Clarke, J. *Looking at lovemaking. Constructions of sexuality in Roman art, 100 B.C.-A.D. 250* (Berkeley, 1998).

Clarke, J. *Art in the lives of ordinary Romans: visual representation and non-elite viewers in Italy, 100 B.C.-A.D. 315* (Berkeley, 2003).

Cohen, A. and Rutter, J. B. *Constructions of childhood in ancient Greece and Italy* (Princeton, 2007).

Dimas, S. *Untersuchungen zur Themenwahl und Bildgestaltung auf römischen Kindersarkophagen* (Münster, 1998).

Dixon, S. *Reading Roman women: sources, genres, and real life* (London, 2001).

Ewald, B. C. *Der Philosoph als Leitbild: Ikonographische Untersuchungen an römischen Sarkophagreliefs* (Mainz, 1999a).

Ewald, B. C. Review Article: Death and Myth: New Books on Roman Sarcophagi. *American Journal of Archaeology* 103 (1999b), 344–348.

Ewald, B. C. Rollenbilder und Geschlechterverhältnis in der römischen Grabkunst. Archäologische Anmerkungen zur Geschichte der Sexualität, in: *Neue Fragen, neuen Antworten. Antike Kunst als Thema der Gender Studies*, edited by N. Sojc (Berlin, 2005), 55–73

Fittschen, K. Review of Max Wegner, Die Musensarkophage. *Gnomon* 44 (1972), 486–504.

Fittschen, K. Mädchen, nicht Knaben, zwei Kinderbüsten in Cleveland und Wellesley. *Römische Mitteilungen* 99 (1992), 301–305.

Fowler, C. *The Archaeology of Personhood.* (London, 2004).

Gilchrist, R. *Gender and Archaeology: Contesting the Past* (London, 1999).

Gilchrist, R. Archaeology and the Life Course: A Time and Age for Gender, in: *A Companion to Social Archaeology*, edited by L. Meskell and R. W. Preucel (Oxford, 2004), 142–160.

Giuliano, A. *Museo Nazionale Romano, Le Sculture I,8,1* (Rome, 1985).

Harlow, M. and Laurence, R. *Growing up and growing old in Ancient Rome: a life course approach* (London and New York, 2002).

Hallett, C. H. *The Roman Nude. Heroic Portrait Statuary 200 B.C – A.D 300* (Oxford, 2005).

Herdt, G. *Third sex, third gender: beyond sexual dimorphism in culture and history* (New York, 1994).

Huskinson, J. *Roman Children's Sarcophagi: Their Decoration and its Social Significance* (Oxford, 1996).

Huskinson, J. Women and Learning – Gender and Identity in Scenes of Intellectual Life on Late Roman Sarcophagi, in: *Constructing Identities in Late Antiquity*, edited by R. Miles (New York, 1999), 190–213.

Huskinson, J. Representing Women on Roman Sarcophagi, in: *The Material Culture of Sex, Procreation, and Marriage in Premodern Europe*, edited by A. L. McClanan and K. R. Encarnación (New York, 2002), 11–31.

Huskinson, J. Disappearing Children? Children in Roman Funerary Art of the First to the Fourth Century AD, in: *Hoping for Continuity. Childhood, Education and Death in Antiquity and the Middle Ages*, edited by K. Mustakallio, J. Hanska, H.-L. Sainio and V. Voulanto (Rome, 2005), 91–104.

Huskinson, J. Constructing Childhood on Roman Funerary Memorials, in: *Constructions of Childhood in ancient Greece and Italy*, Hesperia supplement 41, edited by A. Cohen and J. Rutter (American School of Classical Studies at Athens, 2007), 323–338.

Joyce, R. Embodied Subjectivity: Gender, Femininity, Masculinity, Sexuality, in: *A Companion to Social Archaeology*, edited by L. Meskell and R. W. Preucel (Oxford, 2004), 82–95.

Kampen, N. B. Gender Theory in Roman Art, in: *I Claudia: Women in Ancient Rome*, edited by D. E. E. Kleiner and S. B. Matheson (Yale, 1996a), 14–25.

Kampen, N. B. Omphale and the Instability of Gender, in: *Sexuality in Ancient Art: Near East, Egypt, Greece and Italy*, edited by N. B. Kampen (Cambridge and New York, 1996b), 233–46.

Koch, G. *Roman funerary sculpture: catalogue of the collections.* (Malibu, 1988).

Koch, G. Ein dekorativer Sarkophag mit Scherengitter in der Henry E. Huntington Library and Art Gallery, San Marino, in: *Roman Funerary Monuments in the J. Paul Getty Museum, vol 1.* Occasional Papers in Antiquities 6, edited by G. Koch and M. True (Malibu, 1990).

Koch, G. and Sichtermann, H. *Römische Sarkophage* (Munich, 1982).

Koortbojian, M. *Myth, meaning, and memory on Roman sarcophagi* (Berkeley, 1995).

Laqueur, T. W. *Making sex: body and gender from the Greeks to Freud* (Harvard, 1990).

Lee, M. M. Deciphering Gender in Minoan Dress, in: *Reading the Body, Representations and Remains in the Archaeological Record*, edited by A. E. Rautman (Philadelphia, 2000), 111–123.

Lovén, L. L. LANAM FECIT – Wool Working and Female Virtue, in: L. L. Lovén and A. Strömberg (eds.), *Aspects of Women in Antiquity: Proceedings of the First Nordic Symposium on Women's Lives in Antiquity*, Göteborg 12–15 June 1997 (Jonsered, 1998), 85–95.

Meskell, L. *Archaeologies of social life: age, sex, class et cetera in ancient Egypt* (Oxford, 1999).

Meskell, L. Writing the body in Archaeology, in: *Reading the Body, Representations and Remains in the Archaeological Record*, edited by A. E. Rautman (Philadelphia, 2000), 13–21.

Mikocki, T. Collection de la Princesse Radziwill: les monuments antiques et antiquisants d'Arcadie et du Château de Nieborów. *Archiwum filologiczne* 52 (Wroclaw, 1995). 118–19.

Montserrat, D. Reading gender in the Roman world, in: *Experiencing Rome, Culture Identity and Power in the Roman Empire*, edited by J. Huskinson (London, 2000), 153–182.

Moretti, M. *Nuove scoperte e acquisizioni nell'Etruria Merdionale.* (Rome, 1975).

Oehmke, S. *Das Weib im Manne: Hermaphroditos in der griechisch-römischen Antike* (Berlin, 2004).

Oehmke, S. Halbmann oder Supermann? Bemerkungen zum effeminierten Priapos. In: *Geschlechterdefinitionen und Geschlechtergrenzen in der Antike*, edited by E. Hartmann, U. Hartmann and K. Pietzner (Stuttgart, 2007), 263–76.

Østergaard, J. S. *Romersk kejsertid: Katalog: Ny Carlsberg Glyptotek* (København, 1996).

Polaschek, K. Studien zu einem Frauenkopf im Landesmuseum Trier und zur weiblichen Haartracht der iulisch-claudischen Zeit. *Trierer Zeitschriften für Geschichte und Kunst des Trierer Landes und seiner Nachbargebiete* 35 (Trier, 1972), 141–210.

Rawson, B. *Children and childhood in Roman Italy* (Oxford, 2003).

Rousseau, P. Learned Women and the Development of a Christian Culture in Late Antiquity. *Symbolae Osloenses* 70 (1995), 116–147.

Savarese, N. *In scaena: il teatro di Roma antica* (Milano, 2007).

Sichtermann, H. And G.Koch, *Griechische Mythen auf römischen Sarkophagen* (Tübingen, 1975).

Sigismund-Nielsen, H. Collegia: A new way for understanding the Roman family. *Hephaistos: Kritische Zeitschrift zur Theorie und Praxis der Archäologie* 24 (2006), 201–213.

Sigismund-Nielsen, H. Children for profit and pleasure in: *Age and Ageing in the Roman Empire*, Journal of Roman Archaeology Supplementary Series n. 65, edited by M. Harlow and R. Laurence (Portsmouth R.I, 2007), 37–54.

Sinn, F. *Museo Gregoriano Profano ex Lateranense, Katalog der Skulpturen* (Mainz, 1991).

Shelton, J.-A. *As the Romans did: a source book in Roman social history* (second edition). (Oxford, 1988/1998).

Strathern, M. *Reproducing the Future: Anthropology, Kinship and the New Reproductive Technologies.* (London, 1992).

Stuart Jones, H. *A catalogue of the ancient sculptures preserved in the municipal collections of Rome: the sculptures of the Palazzo dei Conservatori* (Rome, 1968).

Sørensen, M. L. S. *Gender, Things, and Material Culture*, in: *Handbook of Gender in Archaeology*, edited by S. M. Nelson (Oxford, 2006), 105–135.

Varner, E. Transcending Gender: Assimilation, Identity, and Roman Imperial Portraits, in: *Role Models in the Roman World, Identity and Assimilation*, edited by I. L. Hansen and S. Bell (Ann Arbor, 2008), 185–205.

Vermeule, C. C. The Del Pozzo-Albani drawings of classical antiquities in the British Museum. *Transactions of the American Philosophical Society, New Series* 5, Fol 12. nr. 14 (1960), 9.

Walker, S. *Catalogue of Roman sarcophagi in the British Museum* (London, 1990).

Wrede, H. *Consecratio in formam deorum: vergöttlichte Privatpersonen in der römischen Kaiserzeit* (Mainz, 1981).

Wrede, H. *Senatorische Sarkophage Roms: der Beitrag des Senatorenstandes zur römischen Kunst der hohen und späten Kaiserzeit* (Mainz, 2001).

Zanker, P. and Ewald, B. C. *Mit Mythen Leben: Die Bildwerk Der Römischen Sarkophage* (Munich, 2004).

Zanker, P. Ikonographie und Mentalität. Zur Veränderung mythologischer Bildthemen auf den kaiserzeitlichen Sarkophagen aus der Stadt Rom, in: R. Neudecker and P. Zanker (eds.), *Lebenswelten. Bilder und Räume in der römischen Kaiserzeit. Symposium am 24. und 25. Januar 2002 zum Abschluss des von der Gerda Henkel Stiftung geförderten Forschungsprogramms Stadtkultur in der Kaiserzeit 16. Palilia* (2005), 243–51.

8.
Myth and Visual Narrative in the Second Sophistic – a Comparative Approach: Notes on an Attic Hippolytos Sarcophagus in Agrigento

Björn C. Ewald

I.

In the decorated marble sarcophagi, produced in the Roman Empire during the second and third centuries, death became the occasion for significant private expenditure which bears characteristics of what has been called 'abjection'.[1] Where we might see decay and decomposition, the rotting corpse, we are greeted by a visual feast of immaculate and immortal marble bodies (Figure 8.1 a-d). The sarcophagus itself in its materiality – the wealth of figures and the richness of its narrative, the splendour of its painting and gilding – becomes a redemption for death and decay, and a principle means in the fight against the threat of oblivion. The making of the sarcophagus can thus be understood as a pious act of substitution in which the integrity of the body is symbolically reinstated. To use a mythological simile that seems fitting to a discussion of sarcophagi depicting the Hippolytos myth, this is much like the way in which Theseus piously pieces together the mangled portions of his son's dismembered body – *corpus fingit* – in the horrific last scene of Seneca's *Phaedra.* In this play, the integrity of the corpse is regarded as a prerequisite for proper mourning (1261): *quam magna lacrimis pars adhuc nostris abest.* A later Christian tradition would go the opposite way, reminding us of decay and decomposition in a memento mori that consciously pairs abjection with sublimation and catharsis in its artful representation of withering flesh.[2] This, of course, implies the creation of a new paradox around life and death, and the promise of a very different exchange of bodies[3] – but that is another story.

It is not by accident that the emergence of richly decorated sarcophagi during the second century takes place at a time in which concerns about the body intensify, and in which the body becomes a main conduit for discourses

1 Kristeva 1982, 1–18.
2 Ariès 1981, 353–395; *Zum Sterben schön* 2006.
3 Walker Bynum 1995, 1–58.

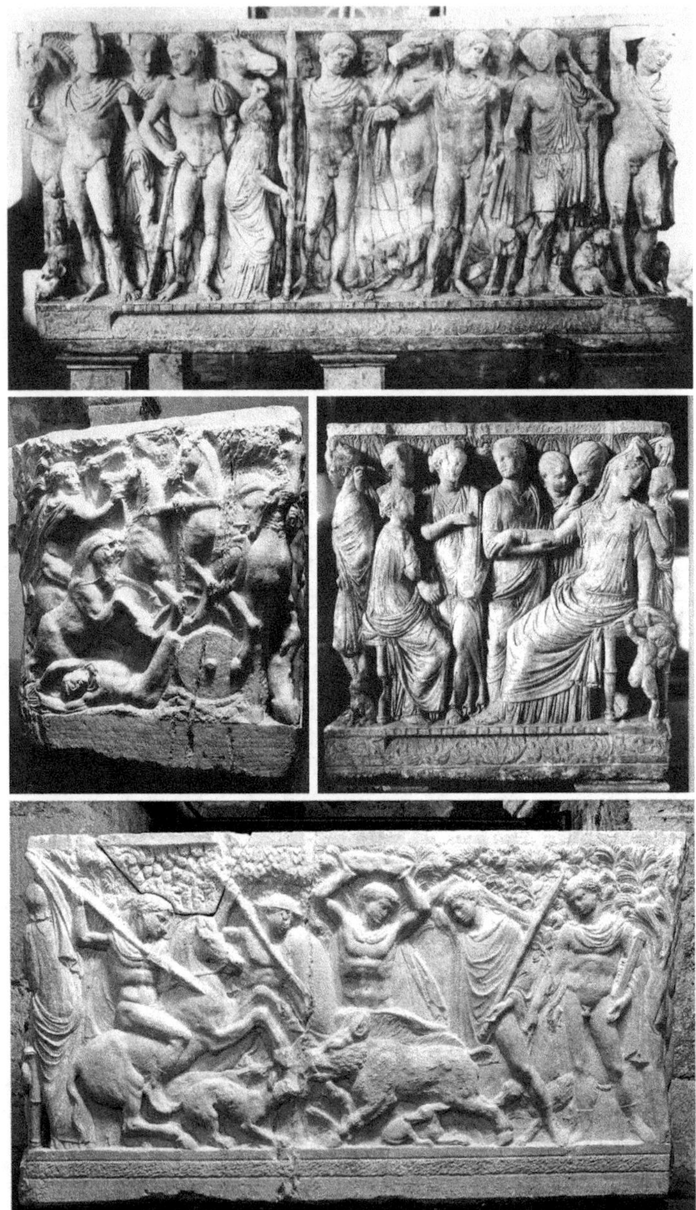

Figure 8.1 a-d: Attic Hippolytos Sarcophagus in Agrigento, San Nicola. 3rd Cent. A.D.
a) Front: Hippolytos with his hunting companions and the nurse.
Photograph: DAIR 72.619.
b) Left small side: Chariot crash of Hippolytos. Photograph: DAIR 71.854.
c) Right small side: The love sick Phaedra and her servants in the *gynaeconitis*.
Photograph: DAIR 56.860.
d) Back: Boar hunt of Hippolytos and his companions. Photograph: DAIR 71.856.

about the self.[4] Among the male, urban elites of the empire, the body could be experienced as a source of anxiety, as an object of self-observation and self-examination, but also as the centre of a new economy of pleasures. The body became the focal point of new forms of attention, new 'techniques of the self' (concerning, for example, dietetics and sexual behaviour), and also functioned as the principal locus for the experience of the unity of the self.[5] In this environment, the challenge of death and decay must have been experienced with particular intensity and must have become particularly 'visceral'. And it generated new, strong responses: acts of image-making and substitution that (re-)present both the deceased and his or her relatives in new symbolic bodies – immortal, heroic and perfect.[6]

The rapidly increasing popularity of lavish marble sarcophagi, carved with figured reliefs, also implied an unprecedented proliferation of narratives of the self. With the sarcophagi of the second and third centuries, death becomes the occasion and opportunity for visual storytelling on a grand scale – storytelling that is no longer a privilege of the hero, aristocrat or emperor, but in the private or semi-private realm of the tomb, an option for anyone who could afford it. We should not forget that for many a patron, the marble reliefs on a sarcophagus must have been the only lasting narratives produced about them, the only images ever made of them, and the only memories of them with aspirations to permanence. This upsurge of interest in recounting the virtues of oneself and loved ones occurs, not accidententally, in a period that sees an increase in the quantity and diversity of biographical and autobiographical literature (or rather, its ancient correlates), which was pervaded by elements of the *encomium.*[7]

On the sarcophagi the matrix for these narratives about the dead, their surviving relatives and their relationships is provided by Greek and (more rarely) Roman myth. Shifting the account of life and death beyond the threshold of *vita humana* into myth deliberately removed it from the realm of daily life and inserted it into a symbolic order which, in the process, was itself reaffirmed as a valid frame of reference for the interpretation of human existence. It is only within this symbolic order that the simple circumstances of life and death, in

4 Foucault 1986, 99–143.
5 Ewald 2008a, 291.
6 This is, admittedly, not the standard account of the 'transition from cremation to inhumation'. However, cf. Zanker and Ewald 2004, 28; Alexandridis 2005; Ewald 2005. For the various archaeological and historical approaches to the issue of the change in burial customs and the emergence of sarcophagi, see F. Sinn in: Koch and Sichtermann 1982, 27–30; Morris 1992, 31–69; Hopkins 1983; Müller 1994, 139–170. Also Heinzelmann 2001 (with further references); Flämig 2007, 89–91; Davies in this volume.
7 Whitmarsh 2005,74–85.

themselves inexplicable and arbitrary, are invested with intelligibility, consistency, and coherence. The imagery exchanges, as Hans Belting has put it in a different context, the 'catastrophe of death' for a 'definition of death' (and, one may add, of life); and in this process, the contingent biological facts of life and death are socially and culturally charged.[8] Of course, the relatively formulaic character of the mythological emplotment we encounter on the sarcophagi, with its praise of the deceased's qualities and virtues, had the effect of erasing the very individuality it was meant to preserve. Every form of 'narrative identity' produces a strained relationship between 'the coherence conferred by emplotment' and the 'discordance' and 'contingencies' of the narrated life.[9] On the sarcophagi, this gap was particularly wide: the relative closeness or distance between the deceased and/or patron of the sarcophagus on the one hand and the mythological exempla (including protagonists and basic storyline) on the other must have varied considerably from case to case (for example in terms of age, gender, the manner of death).[10] For the patrons of such sarcophagi, all this was not an issue. For them, the beauty and the value of mythical emplotment lay precisely in what causes us unease: while *they* placed particular emphasis on the fictionalization of events, actions and lives lived, *we* come to the sarcophagi with a contrary understanding of death and biography as an 'unmasking' and revelation of 'true self'. On the sarcophagi, death does not serve as an opportunity to portray the deceased as he or she 'had really been', but it rather triggers acts of fictional 'doubling'[11] that locate the truth of the self in the – often inherently transgressive – fantasies of myth. This capacity to fictionalize carried a whole range of positive connotations in itself. It was deeply rooted in elite education and its rhetorical exercises, which required swift changes between widely differing, fictive subject positions.[12] It also characterized the world of the Greek novel with its fantastic settings and surprising events, and the poetic pastimes of the Graeco-Roman elites.

The forms of mythical emplotment and role play we encounter on the sarcophagi rest on some further preconditions. First, it required a recognition of the cultural authority of Greek myth and a willingness to employ a mythological idiom as a means of dramatising the act of 'speaking about oneself'. The success of the mythological idiom also depended on the existence of a distinct and

8 Belting 2000, 140.
9 Ricoeur 2005, 100–101.
10 Precisely for this reason, inscription-based examinations which investigate the relationship between the themes of sarcophagi and their patrons, will never arrive at definitive or conclusive results – however useful they may be individually in illuminating the micro-history surrounding the processes of ordering, making, transporting and displaying sarcophagi.
11 Iser 1993; Žižek 1997.
12 Gleason 1995, xx–xxvi.

clearly demarcated 'space' – in the double sense of the concrete 'Bildraum'[13] of the tomb and of a corresponding set of mental coordinates – in which the sensuousness and intense corporeality of this visual language, which included male/female nudity and sometimes extreme portrayals of suffering and passion,[14] were given a positive connotation.

Finally, the routine character of the mythological role play we encounter on the sarcophagi suggests a considerable facility in the application of mythological imagery to individual's self-images of their own lives. What we see on the sarcophagi is unthinkable without what had been happening on the wall-paintings of houses in Pompeii and elsewhere a century earlier. The dense mythological imagery on these Roman walls had long offered itself for embedded experiences and self-exploration and had provided a mirror (often distorting) for the viewer's personal dreams and desires, fears and passions, and body image. The Roman sarcophagi depend to a great extent on these pre-existing modes of living with and responding to mythological images.[15]

However, the underlying myths (which were mostly Greek) did not survive their direct use as raw material for the fictionalised biographies of well-to-do patrons without sustaining some casualties. To the modern eye, the marriage of Greek myth with Roman biography is not always a happy one. Among the first casualties in the Roman re-coding of the mythological material are precisely the concerns that had been central to the treatment of those myths in the classical period. These include the conflicts arising from the discrepancies in status between gods, heroes and mortals (on the sarcophagi, portrait identifications are found in all three categories, flattening out the differences between them), the conflict between *nomos* and *physis*, and the tension between the collective demands of the *polis* and the moral demands of the individual. It is difficult not to measure the Roman adaptations against the original polysemy of the Greek tragedies whose performances on stage often stand at the beginning of the visual tradition on which the sarcophagus workshops fed: on the Roman sarcophagi,

13 Zanker 2000.

14 Its 'Engramme leidenschaftlicher Erfahrung', according to Warburg 2000, 4. I am thinking here in particular of scenes of suffering and pathos (which occupied a central role in Warburg's Mnemosyne Atlas), such as the suicide of Meleager's mother Altheia, the killing of the Niobids, or the slow bleeding to death of Adonis – in short, the visual equivalent of what Roland Barthes, in his visionary treatment of 'Tacitus and the funerary baroque', once called 'le tourment d'une finalité dans la profusion,' Barthes 1964, 111. I return to the issue in a forthcoming work.

15 The role and function of mythological imagery in the domestic sphere, as well as responses to such images and their role in the formation of subjectivities, has been explored from various perspectives in recent years. See, in particular, Bergmann 1994; Bergmann 1996; Fredrick 1995; Koloski-Ostrow 1997; Muth 1998; Fredrick 2002; Platt 2002; Zanker 2002, 112–132; Valladares 2005; Lorenz 2006; Elsner 2007. Non vidi: Lorenz 2008.

the great collective attempts to come to terms with the basic conflicts of human existence in the classical polis have been turned into highly individualised narratives about Roman freedmen, military officers, and so on.

In making use of formalist approaches to the analysis of narrative, developed in the context of literary theory and film semiotics, one might say that Roman appropriations of Greek myths on the sarcophagi are characterised by a marked tension between the underlying mythological narratives (in all their variability) on the one hand (the '*fabula*') and the '*syuzhet*' (or 'discourse manifestation') on the other.[16] The latter can be understood 'as the artistic organisation, or 'deformation', of the causal-chronological order of events'[17] at the level of its appropriation, that is, the re-editing and re-patterning of the mythological material in the sarcophagus workshops in different regions of the Roman Empire. The mythological plot, in other words, is always overlaid with a variety of discourses (for example, about love and death, or gender) that define the conditions of its possibility. Even though myth remains ultimately irreducible to these discourses, and is never fully eclipsed by them (for else there would be no point in employing a mythological idiom in the first place), it is these discourses that usually bring myth into being on the sarcophagi. What is important to note, however, – and this is the main concern of my contribution – is that the same myths can be refracted through different prisms of intelligibility in different sarcophagus workshops, most notably the ones in Rome and in Athens, where the greatest number of mythological sarcophagi were produced. The objective of this paper is to demonstrate how the same myths are in different cases constructed within a different cultural matrix. I will focus on so-called Attic sarcophagi (i. e. sarcophagi produced in an Athenian workshop during the second and third centuries, but widely exported to other parts of the Mediterranean[18]), and subject them to a comparative analysis with their Roman

16 Stam et al. 1992, 69–75. Without being able to address the issue in any depth here, it should at least be noted that *fabula* or storyline on the one hand, and *syuzhet* on the other, are not irreconcilable opposites, but rather are interconnected, and contaminate one another, in multiple ways. Archaeologists thus also speak, not quite correctly, of a 're-telling' of myth, and emphasise myth's unlimited malleability; however, on examples such as the one discussed here, the re-arrangement of myth does not result in an image of any pronounced narrative interest.

17 Stam et al. 1992, 71.

18 On so-called Attic sarcophagi, which constitute the largest body of sculpture known from Roman Athens, see Koch and Sichtermann 1982, 366–475 (fundamental and most comprehensive treatment); Koch 1993, 97–112; *ASR* IX,1. Also Ward Perkins 1956; Wiegartz 1975; Linant de Bellefonds 1985; Koch 1988; Rudolf 1989; Rudolf 1992. Much material can also be found in a number of edited volumes (such as Koch 1993b). While these (and other) studies provide the indispensable material basis for any further engagement with such monuments, and often provide excellent documentation, they remain entirely within the classificatory systems and paradigms of "Sarkophagfor-

counterparts depicting the same myths. Such a close reading from a comparative perspective can yield immediate insights into modes of self-fashioning available to wealthy customers in various parts of the empire, which co-existed but were significantly different.

My starting point and principal example is a once famous Attic sarcophagus in Agrigento.[19] The front side shows Hippolytos with his hunting companions in a highly static composition that places particular emphasis on the paradigmatic representation of the male body in varying postures (Figure 8.1 a). The figures' perfect physiques, as well as the expensive horses and hunting dogs, leave no doubt about the elevated social standing of the hero and his companions and their function as aristocratic role models. Hippolytos himself (and so the entire scene's grounding in myth) is recognisable only through the letter he holds in his left hand and his proximity to the bent nurse who has the letter's container in her left hand. On the right end of the sarcophagus (Figure 8.1 c) we see the lovesick Phaedra with her servants, and on the left end, Hippolytos' chariot crash (Figure 8.1 b). The back shows a generic boar hunt that further develops the hunting theme on the front (Figure 8.1 d); in analogy to other examples of the type, Hippolytos is probably the hunter on horseback in the left-hand side of the frieze.

The scene on the front which shows Hippolytos and his hunting companions in the presence of the nurse has no obvious place within the known visual or literary traditions of the Hippolytos myth, in particular the tragic versions by Euripides and Seneca.[20] In the extant Euripidean tragedy, Hippolytos does indeed address his companions towards the end of his conversation with Theseus (Eur. *Hipp.* 1098), but this takes place long after the nurse has communicated Phaedra's proposal to the hero. In the prelude to Seneca's tragedy (*Phaedra* 1–84), Hippolytos appears together with his hunting companions and leaves for the hunt at the end of the scene, but this occurs long before his encounter with the nurse (*Phaedra* 431–588), which is followed by his meeting with Phaedra herself (*Phaedra* 589–718). So if we look for parallels for such a parataxis of naked or half-naked male bodies in various postures, we find them not in the literary tradition or even in representations of the Hippolytos myth in other artistic genres, but rather in gatherings of athletes on

schung" and are at times hard to digest for the uninitiated. For a (preliminary) attempt at a broader historical and contextual interpretation of Attic sarcophagi, see Ewald 2004. For recent discussions of specific contexts, see Perry 2001; Cormack 2004; Flämig 2007, 81–84 and passim.

19 *ASR* III,2, 178–181 no. 152; *ASR* IX,1, 148 no. 47.

20 See *LIMC* V, 1, 1990, 445–464 pls. 315–325 s. v. Hippolytos (P. Linant de Bellefonds); Lewerentz 1995, 113–116. Little is known about Euripides' first Hippolytos tragedy, as well as Sophocles' *Phaedra*, and their relation with the visual tradition.

fourth-century BC reliefs, or in classical statue groups such as the Daochos monument in Delphi, or even on some of the ephebic stelai from Roman Athens (Figure 8.2).[21] The composition as a whole seems to be an original invention of a sarcophagus workshop in early-third-century Athens.

II.

A little over two hundred years ago, the sarcophagus in Agrigento, now half forgotten even by specialists, was a celebrated work of art. When Johann Wolfgang von Goethe visited the cathedral in Agrigento (Girgenti) on his 'Italienische Reise' in April 1787, he praised the Hippolytos sarcophagus in the highest terms in a famous entry in his travel journal.[22] Goethe writes: 'I have never seen a bas-relief as wonderful or as well preserved. If I am not mistaken, it is an example of Greek art from its most graceful period.'[23] Goethe also captures the essence of the image on the front side very well by noting: 'The artist's main concern was to portray beautiful young men. In order that the eye should concentrate its attention on them, he has made the old nurse very small, almost a dwarf.'[24] The 'beautiful youths' he noted are indeed the proper subject of the sarcophagus relief in question.

Goethe was certainly not the first to praise the sarcophagus. Johann Joachim Winckelmann had described it briefly and correctly identified its subject matter in his *monumenti antichi inediti* of 1767 (p. 137). A few years later it was discussed in a detailed and insightful way by Johann Hermann von Riedesel – a close friend of Winckelmann – in his 'Reise durch Sicilien und Großgriechenland' (an account of a trip he undertook in 1767).[25] Independently of Winckelmann, Riedesel also correctly identified the general subject matter and praised the sarcophagus as 'one of the most excellent, and perhaps the most beautiful basso relievo's (*sic*) of antiquity which has been preserved in marble to

21 *Mind and Body* 1989, 182 no. 72; Newby 2005, 171–172 fig. 6,1. The single figures on the Hippolytos sarcophagus in Agrigento are, as has long been noted (*ASR* IX,1, 114) heroizing stock figures of Greek sculpture workshops of the imperial period. For example, the youth on the left margin of the Attic Hippolytos sarcophagus in St. Petersburg (*ASR* IX,1, 154 no. 64 fig. 90,1) is a mirror image of the statue of Podaleirios from the baths in Dion (Pandermalis 1997, 39). See also Ewald 2004, 263.

22 Goethe 1992, 336; Rodenwaldt 1940; 1942, 9–10.

23 Goethe 1962, 265: 'Mich dünkt von halberhabener Arbeit nichts herrlichers gesehen zu haben, zugleich vollkommen erhalten. Es soll mir einstweilen als ein Beispiel der anmutigsten Zeit griechischer Kunst gelten.'

24 Ibid., 265: 'Hier war die Hauptabsicht, schöne Jünglinge darzustellen, deswegen auch die Alte, ganz klein und zwergenhaft, als ein Nebenwerk das nicht stören soll dazwischen gebildet ist.'

25 Riedesel 1771; 1773.

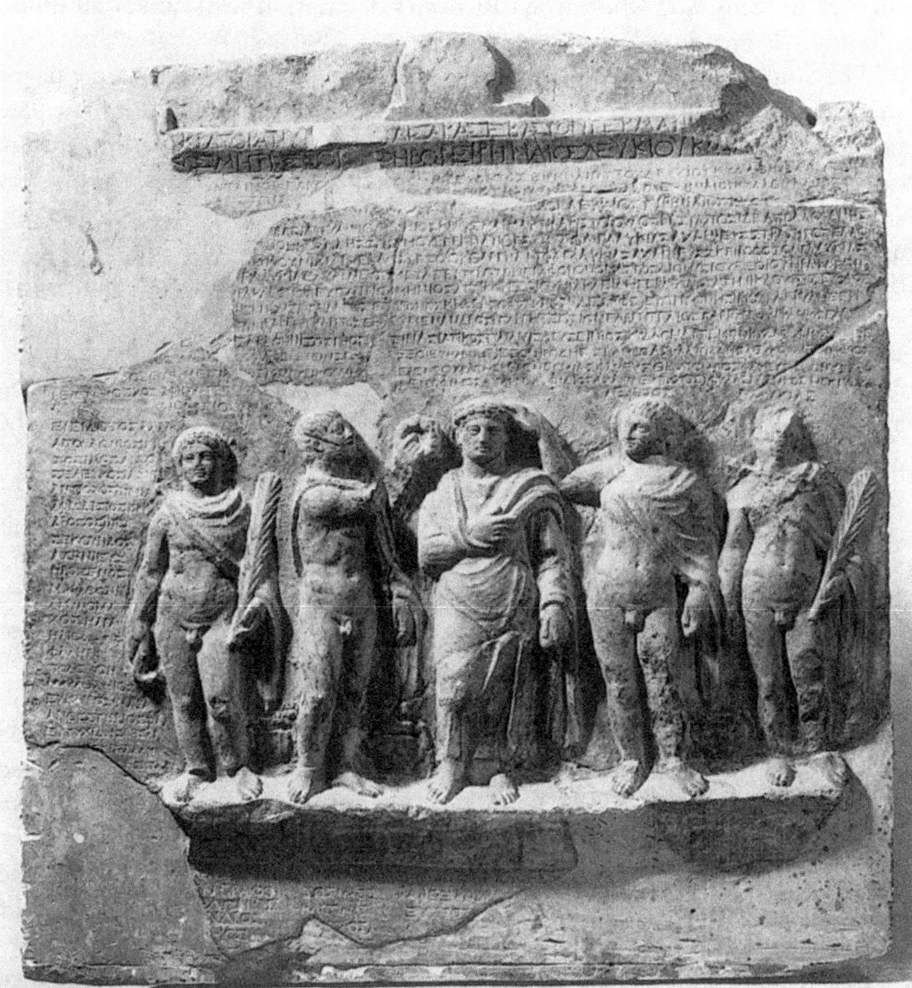

Figure 8.2: Fragment of an ephebic relief from the Trajanic period, showing the *cosmetes* in the center, flanked by his two sons who crown him, and two other ephebes. Athens, National Museum Inv. 1469. (after Zahra Newby, *Greek Athletics in the Roman World,* Oxford, Oxford University Press, 2005, p. 172 fig. 6.1)

our times.' He especially extolled the figure of Phaedra on the left end as 'one of the most beautiful female forms which art can imitate; the profile of the face is as perfect and harmonious, as a mortal can imagine.'[26] Consequently, an engraving (by Salomon Geßner) of the lovesick Phaedra and her servants came to decorate the title page of the German edition of Riedesel's work (Figure 8.3). Riedesel's description provided the pretext for Goethe, who followed his

26 Riedesel 1773, 26–27.

footsteps in Sicily, and who carried Riedesel's description with him at all times, as he himself mentions.[27]

The authority of Riedesel's and Goethe's views made the sarcophagus famous, and it figures in virtually every description of Sicily from the late eighteenth and nineteenth century. In 1861, for example, Ferdinand Gregorovius – himself a representative of a rather impassioned and poetic direction in German nineteenth century scholarship – calls the Hippolytos sarcophagus 'the most precious treasure' in the otherwise 'miserable city' of Girgenti.[28] Like Riedesel, Gregorovius dedicates his warmest praise to the Phaedra relief, which he finds 'the climax and soul of the whole, a relief of the highest beauty and gracefulness.' He recognises the sarcophagus as 'the copy of a Greek masterwork, made by the hand of a Roman artist;' and because of the well known 'predilection of the Sicilian Greeks for Euripides' he concludes that the sarcophagus was, more precisely, 'a Sicilian work of art.'[29]

Only a few decades later, the German photographer Wilhelm von Gloeden – 'the archetypal gay Victorian'[30] – arranged five Sicilian youths for one of his pictures in a manner that betrays the influence of the sarcophagus in Agrigento (Figure 8.4). In the arrangements of his *tableaux vivants,* von Gloeden often drew inspiration from famous statues and paintings. In Sicily, where he settled in 1887 and where homosexual relationships were not threatened with draconian prison sentences as they were in Germany, von Gloeden found his 'ideal Arcadia'.[31] Gloeden himself writes of his stay: 'The Greek forms appealed to me, as did the bronze-hued descendants of the old Hellenes, and I attempted to resurrect the old, classical life in pictures.'[32] In order to turn the Sicilian peasants and fishermen, who served as his models, into Grecian ephebes, Gloeden rubbed them down with 'an emulsion of fresh milk, olive oil, and glycerine.'[33] Of course, Gloeden's photographs, which already provoked ironic comment during his lifetime, were anything but a 'resurrection of classic life.' By translating the relaxed stances of the late classical, athletic figure types used

27 Osterkamp 1987; Salmeri 2001, 69.

28 Gregorovius 1861, 222–225: the 'herrlichsten Schatz' in the otherwise 'elenden Stadt' of Girgenti.

29 Ibid., 222–225: 'Gipfel und Seele des Ganzen, ein Relief von der höchsten Schönheit und Anmut;' 'Copie eines griechischen Meisterwerks, von römischer Künstlerhand gefertigt;' 'Vorliebe der sicilianischen Griechen für den Euripides;' and 'ein Werk sicilianischer Kunst.'

30 Waugh 2002, 636.

31 Pohlmann 1998, 6; my translation.

32 Ibid., 14: 'Die griechischen Formen reizten mich, ebenso das Bronzekolorit der Nachkommen der alten Hellenen, und ich versuchte es, das alte klassische Leben im Bilde wiederauferstehen zu lassen.'

33 Ibid., 15.

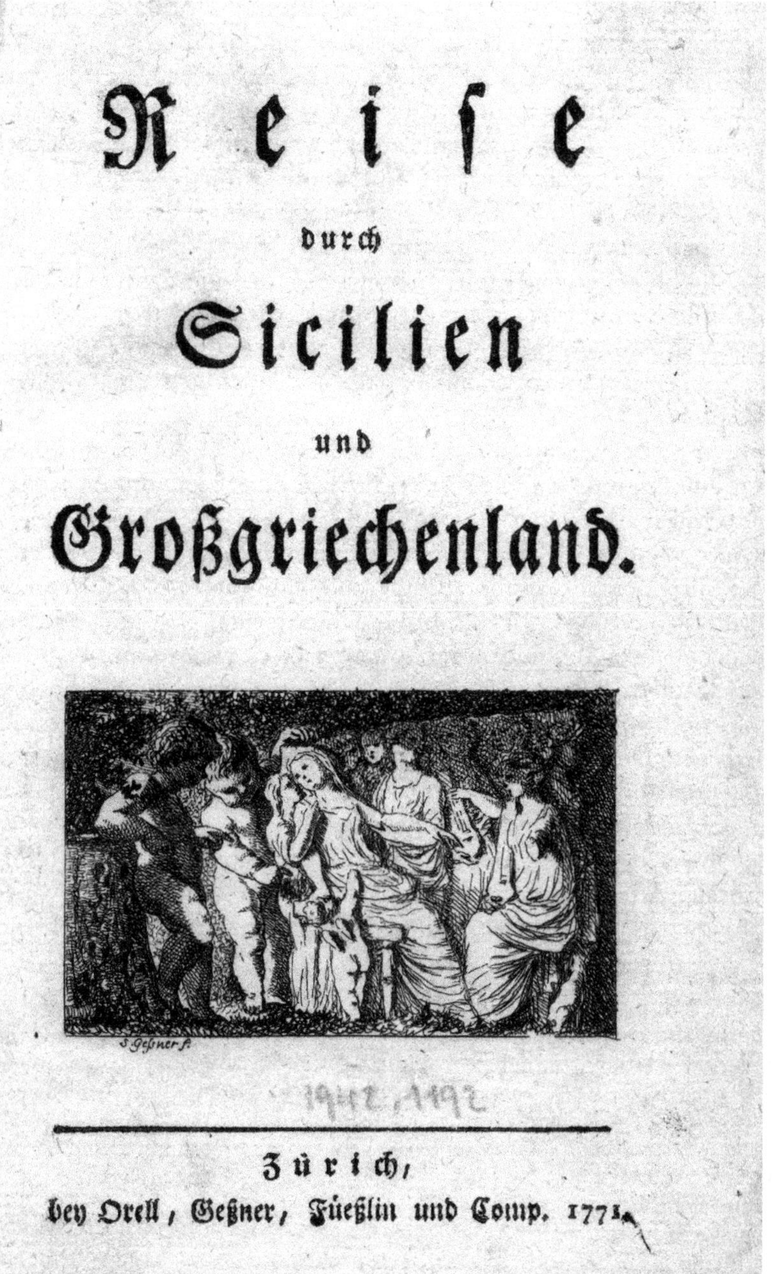

Reise
durch
Sicilien
und
Großgriechenland.

S. Geßner f.

Zürich,
bey Orell, Geßner, Füeßlin und Comp. 1771.

Figure 8.3: *Frontispiece* of Riedesel 1771, with engraving of the lovesick Phaedra on the right small side of the Hippolytos Sarcophagus in Agrigento. (Reproduction: Daniela Gauss).

on the sarcophagus into the 'soft, passive accessibility'[34] of the adolescent objects of desire of Victorian 'gay culture', Gloeden's photographs expose precisely the gap that separates the modern figure of the homosexual from the homosocial Greek culture he attempts (but of course fails) to resurrect.[35] Gloeden's pictures can be situated within what Foucault termed the "reverse' discourse' on homosexuality that emerged in the nineteenth century: homosexuality beginning 'to speak on its own behalf', and demanding that its "legitimacy' or 'naturality' be acknowledged.'[36] In von Gloeden's case, this 'naturality' takes the shape of a highly mannered emulation of an art on whose universal recognition he could still count. But be this as it may, with regard to the Hippolytos sarcophagus in Agrigento, eighteenth- and nineteenth-century travellers had a much better perception of the ephebophile aesthetics of the main relief than all later interpreters.[37]

It would be interesting to trace the history of reception of this sarcophagus further, to understand when and how what had once been praised as perhaps the most beautiful marble relief known from antiquity, and what had served as an important focal point of German philhellenism, ultimately came to be regarded as the late product of a dying culture, and how pieces like this subsequently slipped almost completely off the scholarly agenda. Without addressing the issue in detail here, I would point to two factors which were decisive in this process of scholarly 'forgetting'. One was scholarly 'progress' and the nineteenth-century *dispositif* of 'evolution', 'development' and 'historicisation' itself, which correlated with a refinement of taxonomies and stylistic methods, and an increasing availability of photographs. In the 1870s it was generally accepted that sarcophagi of this kind were neither 'classical' Greek works nor Roman copies of them, but were produced by artisans in Roman Greece. Shortly after 1900, Roman Athens was finally established as the home of the workshops of Attic sarcophagi.[38] As a result, the sarcophagus in Agrigento could no longer

34 Waugh 2002, 636.

35 Compare also the comments by Roland Barthes in von Gloeden 1978, 11: 'These little Greek gods (already contradicted by their darkness) have dirty peasant's hands, badly cured fingernails, worn out and dirty feet; their foreskins are swollen and well in evidence, no longer stylized, that is, pointed and smaller: they are uncircumsised, this is all one sees: the Baron's photographs are at the same time sublime and anatomic.'

36 Foucault 1978, 101.

37 See also Potts 1994, 113–144.

38 Koch and Sichtermann 1982, 366 (with further references). Richard Payne Knight had, as early as 1777, already compared the sarcophagus in Agrigento with an Attic sarcophagus in Rome (then believed to be that of Julia Mammaea and Alexander Severus) and concluded: "Eigentlich sollte man es für römisch ansprechen, und es mag die Asche eines Konsuls oder Prätors unter den Kaisern enthalten haben." (Goethe 1985, 584. Also Rodenwaldt 1940, 600–601; Salmeri 2002, 67 with fn. 28; 70). Painter and Whitehouse 1990; *ASR* IX,1, 136 no. 24 pl. 44,1.

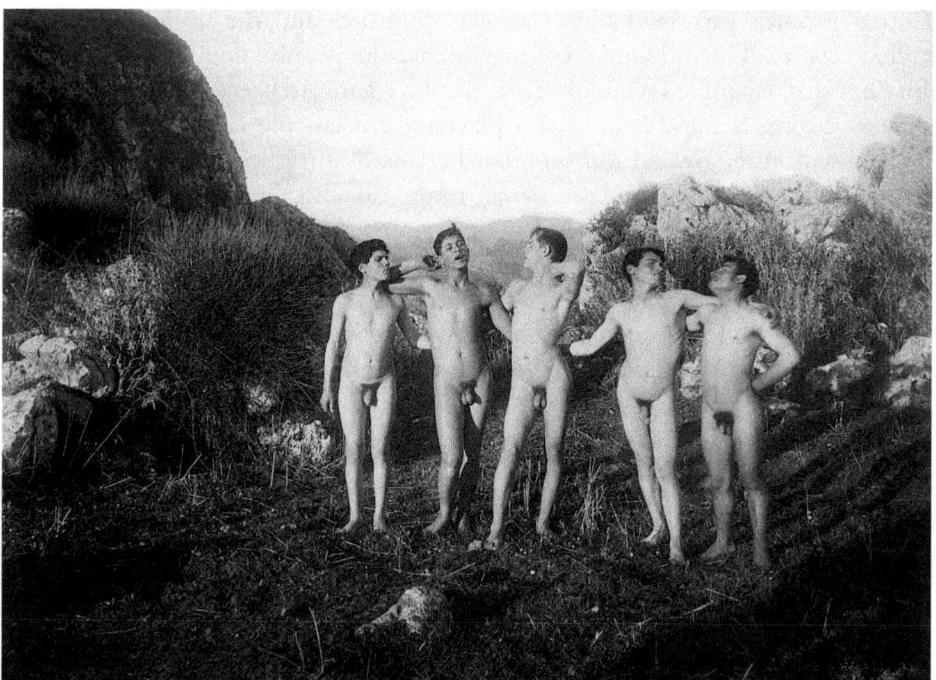

Figure 8.4: Wilhelm von Gloeden, Sicilian Youths, 1890–1900. Fotomuseum Winterthur, Switzerland. Alinari/Art Resource, New York.

serve as a reference point for German philhellenism, but inevitably had to become part of the story of the decline of Greece and Greek art under Roman rule. It is this story that dominates even in the most recent (and otherwise excellent) scholarly discussion of the piece, which points out the compositional 'deficits' and narrative shortcomings of such works.[39]

Another reason for the declining interest in the Agrigento sarcophagus lies in the profound change in the tastes and aesthetic interests of viewers in the early twentieth century. The lowered heads and tired gestures of almost all figures in its reliefs – originally a sign of modesty (*aidos;* cf. Dio Chrys. 21.13) and *sophrosyne* in the male figures, and in the case of Phaedra, of despair and pain – exuded a sentiment that resonated strongly with eighteenth- and nineteenth-century observers. But in the early twentieth century there emerged a new heroic and military ideal of the body from the spirit of Nietzsche[40] and *Lebensphilosophie.* With the resulting 'vitalist' reinvention of Greek art history by its most prominent practitioners during the 1920s,[41] archaeological interests

39 *ASR* IX,1, 120.
40 Pohlmann 1998, 23.
41 Marchand 1996, 312–340.

shifted towards early and high classical sculptures and the upright figures of archaic *kouroi.* The influential German archaeologist, philologist and poet Ernst Buschor for example, who directed the German Archaeological Institute at Athens during the 1920s and who played a crucial role in the rediscovery of archaic sculpture, greeted the *kouroi* as heralds of a fresher, healthier and more heroic humanity.[42] About the same time, on the Roman front, Gerhard Rodenwaldt was much concerned with defining the Romanness of Roman art within a dualistic theory that pitches supposedly genuine Roman art forms (equated with an indigenous ethnic element that constitutes the raw, positive life force without which no culture can survive) against the refining and civilizing, but also weakening Hellenic element.[43] In such an environment, enthusiasm for the Agrigento sarcophagus (itself a Greek work of art from the Roman Imperial period, and thus ill positioned in such highly charged methodological gambit) had to cool off, and Goethe's praise of the sarcophagus became a source of embarrassment in German archaeology – how could the great poet have been so wrong? Indeed, Rodenwaldt himself raises the question of how Goethe could have possibly dedicated such warm words of praise to works of art that are 'late and minor.'[44] Interestingly, in the early twentieth century, the reception of the Hippolytos sarcophagus in Agrigento and that of Gloeden's fin-de-siècle photographs run in parallel. Gloeden's photographs, however, have experienced a remarkable renaissance since the 1960s and 1970s as a result of the sexual revolution and gay movement, so that forty years after their distribution had been banned in fascist Italy, they came to attract critics like Roland Barthes and to inspire artists like Andy Warhol, Joseph Beuys and Robert Mapplethorpe.[45] The same can hardly be said of the sarcophagi. Today, very few archaeologists will encounter pieces such as the sarcophagus in Agrigento during their training, and fewer still regard them as suitable topics for research.

III.

The best way of understanding the specific character of the transformation of the Hippolytos myth on the Agrigento sarcophagus is to employ a comparative approach, that is, to juxtapose a close reading of the Attic examples with one of

42 Compare the decisively Nietzschean terminology in his praise of 6th century BC *kouroi* as a species of ancient 'Übermenschen' (Buschor 1950, 5): '…das Haupt ohne Drehung und Neigung, (…) Gestalten von ungebrochenem Leben, von tadelloser Schönheit und Brauchbarkeit (…).'

43 Brendel 1979, 119–121; Rodenwaldt 1935; 1939.

44 Rodenwaldt 1940, 600; Rodenwaldt 1942, 9–10.

45 von Gloeden 1978; Pohlmann 1998; 24.

the Roman pieces.[46] So, to provide a reference point for a closer analysis of the Attic sarcophagi depicting Hippolytos and Phaedra, I shall begin with a brief account of how the myth was told on Roman metropolitan sarcophagi. Within the traditional typology of Roman sarcophagus studies this is the main group of Hippolytos sarcophagi which extends from around 180 to 240, and is thus contemporary with most of the Attic sarcophagi depicting the same theme.[47] Since the Roman metropolitan Hippolytos sarcophagi have received various scholarly treatments in recent years,[48] I will keep my discussion short and limit myself to aspects that are relevant in the present context.

The Roman Hippolytos sarcophagi belonging to this main group are usually decorated on three sides. The front shows two scenes in the manner of a continuous narrative (Figure 8.5 a): Hippolytos' farewell to Phaedra on the left and the boar hunt on the right. The left-hand scene, which shows the encounter between Phaedra and Hippolytos at the moment in which the hero is confronted with the indecent proposal conveyed by the nurse, is an invention of the visual arts which is not found in either the Euripidean nor the Senecan tragedy.[49] The direct combination of Phaedra and Hippolytos most likely serves, as Paul Zanker demonstrated a few years ago, to represent a heroic hunter taking his leave of a female lover.[50] This reading of the scene as a departure (*profectio*) is supported by the gesture of Hippolytos' hand, which is understood as a rejection of the proposal made by the nurse but which is also found in a very similar form in the figure of Domitian departing for a military campaign on the Cancelleria Relief A.[51] The pain and despair of the love sick Phaedra are thus re-interpreted as grief at Hippolytos' departure.[52] On a further and higher level of allegory – and one that would be in perfect accordance with the funeral context

46 Use of the comparative method, though in different ways, has occasionally been made in the study of mythological imagery, including sarcophagi. Examples include Giuliani 1989; Zanker 1992; Muth 1998; Ewald 2004.

47 Koch and Sichtermann 1982, 150–151; *ASR* IX,1, 73–92.

48 Lewerentz 1995; Zanker 1999; Zanker and Ewald 2004, 98–99; 325–329.

49 In Euripides' *Hippolytos* the nurse acts on her own initiative, and the initial scene with the proposal made to Hippolytos by the nurse was apparently not performed on stage – what the audience sees is Phaedra's horrified reaction as she listens in on the nurse and Hippolytos (555–600), who then enter the stage together (601–668), where Hippolytos rejects the offer, ordering the nurse not to touch him (606). At that moment, Phaedra has apparently already rushed off to commit suicide (as suggested by 599; however, she appears briefly on stage one more time before killing herself: 680–731). In Seneca's *Phaedra*, Hippolytos and his stepmother meet in private, as is explicitly mentioned (599–600); towards the end of their conversation, Phaedra throws herself down at his knees, and Hippolytos almost slits her throat in a sacrifice to Diana.

50 Zanker 1999.

51 Zanker-Ewald 2004, 327; Hannestad 1988, 135 fig. 85.

52 Zanker 1999, 137.

– the tormented heroine probably also served as an allegory for the pain of a mother or wife at the loss of her son or husband.[53] All this did of course obscure central elements of the underlying mythical plot. But the validity of this interpretation is confirmed by the close formal and structural parallels with the telling of other myths on Roman sarcophagi, such as the stories of Venus and Adonis and Bellerophon and Stheneboia.[54] These are, just like the Hippolytos sarcophagi, organized as a continuous narrative in two or three scenes (though not necessarily organized in chronological sequence), with the departure for the hunt serving as a starting point.

The hunting scene on the right half of the front seems to have been invented by the Roman workshops in particular for the sarcophagi. For the representation of the hunting Hippolytos, the sculptors of Roman sarcophagi adapted an imperial image, of the emperor proving his manly virtue, but also his extraordinary status and his power to civilise through his actions in the hunt.[55] The hunting Hadrian in the tondi on the Arch of Constantine provides the best examples (Figure 8.6). The personification of *virtus*, who accompanies Hippolytos on the sarcophagi and encourages him to kill the boar, is also derived from imperial representations. Its adaptation to private funerary monuments shows how much emperor and elites belonged to the same 'community of values' during the second century.[56] But on the sarcophagi the nudity of Hippolytos translates the imperial scheme into the mythological and

53 Despite a long tradition of investigation into sepulchral symbolism, a tradition which took its most extreme form in Cumont's *Recherches sur le symbolisme funéraire des Romains* (1942) and which is now merely of interest for the history of scholarship, there has (since the perceptive remarks by Nock 1946) been very little discussion of just what degree of allegory was even intended on sarcophagi and in what ways the images on sarcophagi point beyond themselves to secondary and tertiary meanings (with the exception of Giuliani 1989, 38–39, who, within the framework of Quintilian's rhetorical precepts, recognises in the mythological sarcophagus imagery a form of *allegoria apertis permixta*). The allegories or mythological similes appear in general to remain at a rather low level of abstraction: an archway for the transition from virgin to bride and life to death on the Leukippides sarcophagi (Zanker and Ewald 2004, 332–336), for example, or allegories for the horrors of death (Niobids) and for guilt and despair (Altheia on Meleager sarcophagi). In any event, they do not approach the level of abstraction evident in the myth-allegories already cultivated in philosophical circles in antiquity. The question is also of general relevance for the understanding of the long transition from polysemic, quasi deconstructive modes of representation to the hieratic compositions of late antiquity described by Elsner 1995.

54 Zanker 1999, 137; Zanker and Ewald 2004, 288–294; 301–304.

55 Lewerentz 1995, 123. On the rich connotations of the hunt in a Roman context, which go beyond the simple manifestation of *virtus* (Rodenwaldt 1935), see the various contributions in Martini 2000.

56 Mayer 2002; Wrede 2001.

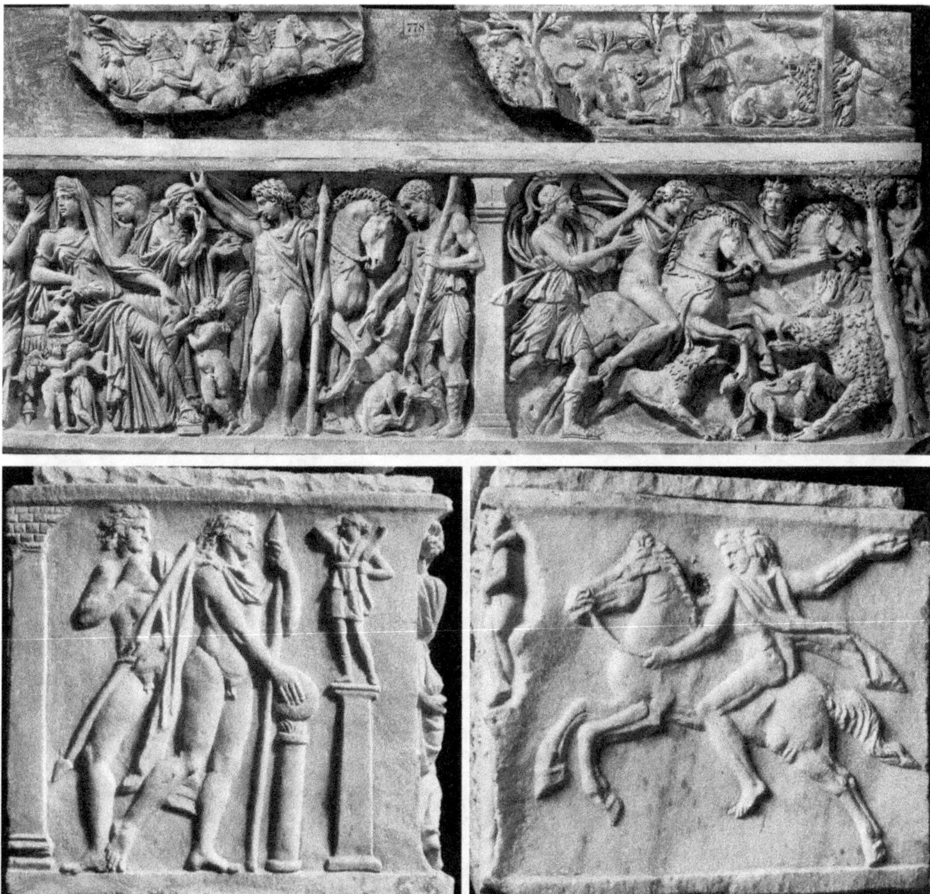

Figure 8.5 a-b: Roman metropolitan Hippolytos sarcophagus in Rome, Musei Vaticani. 2nd cent. A.D. Front: Phaedra and Hippolytos (left) and Hippolytos on the boar hunt (right). Photograph:DAIR 71.1099. left small side: Hippolytos pours a libation in front of a statue of Artemis. After Zanker-Ewald, 2004.

heroic realm.[57] It also suggests an eroticisation of the image of the hunter and the hunt itself that is evident too in literary sources such as Phaedra's *epistula* to Hippolytos in Ovid's *Heroides* (4), or in Seneca's *Phaedra*, when the heroine even fantasises about chasing wild beasts herself, and 'hurling stiff javelins' with her

57 For Roman nudity as characteristic of the hero, see Hallett 2005, with Ewald 2008a. For a semiology of Roman nudity, see Cordier 2005.

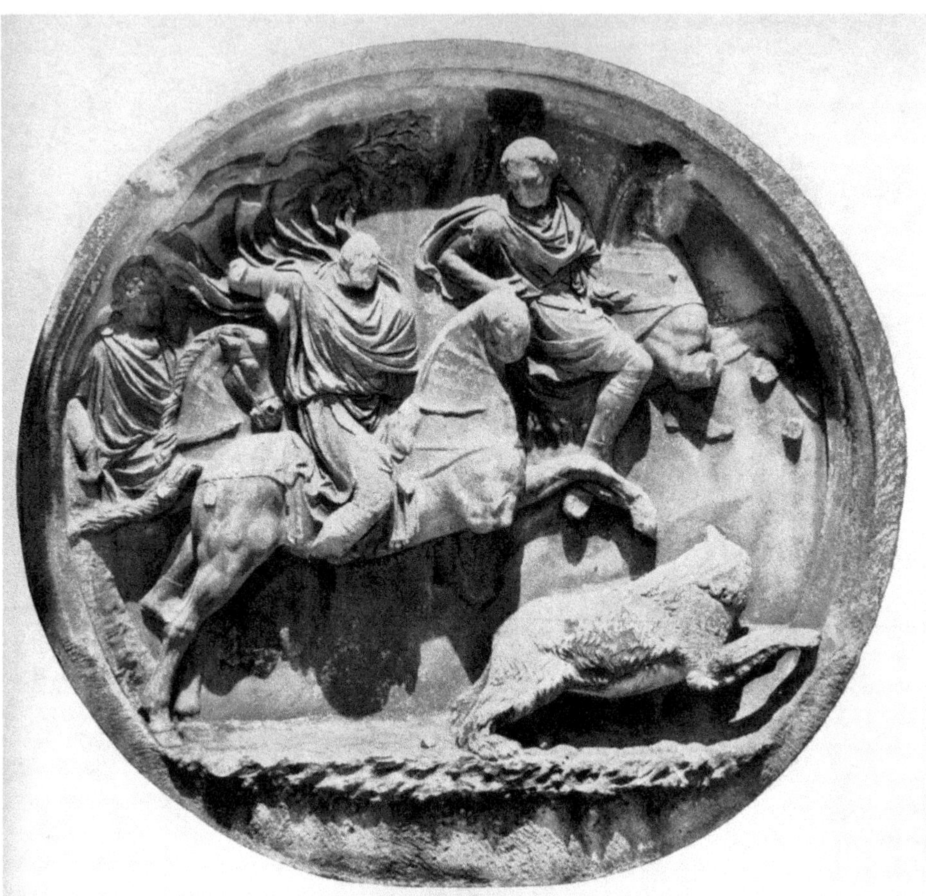

Figure 8.6: Rome, Arch of Constantine. Hadrianic Tondo with the emperor on a boar hunt. After Rodenwaldt 1927, 633.

'soft hand'.[58] Hippolytos' nudity thus serves as a means for making Phaedra's desire plausible to an ancient viewer.

The scenes on the ends and lids of such sarcophagi usually develop the theme of the hunt further. A scene commonly used on the sides shows Hippolytos offering a sacrifice to a small statue of Artemis (Figure 8.5 b). One may be inclined to understand this, within the framework of the Euripidean tragedy, as an illustration of the hero's one-sided worship of Artemis – which, with all its consequences, was a central motif and driving force of the

58 Sen. *Phaed.* 111: (…) *et rigida molli gaesa iaculari manu* (Edited and translated by John G. Fitch; Loeb Classical Library 62, Cambridge MA 2002). On 'eroticisation' of the hunt, ibid. 441.

Euripidean tragedy. But here again, the visual correspondence with an imperial mode of representation suggests otherwise; the emperor's sacrifice to Diana on another Hadrianic tondo from the Arch of Constantine provides the closest match (Figure 8.7). Within a Roman horizon of reception, the scene of sacrifice thus could be read as evoking yet another quality (*pietas*) that was meant to reflect on the virtue of the deceased.[59] This is important as it illustrates a general characteristic of the Roman re-coding of this mythological material: Roman appropriations take the edge off myths and empty them of precisely the tragic content that is essential to their classical elaboration. Or, more precisely: Roman art relocates the process of semiosis to the surface level of the image and the latter's new function within a system of visual communication that was fundamentally alien to its original content.

Overall, then, on the Roman sarcophagi the highly complex story of the tragic love of a passionate heroine for her stepson, which ends with the death of both, is restructured into a simple narrative about a loving woman's farewell to a pious and handsome hunter. Within this narrative, the male role is defined by the key virtue of *virtus*, complemented by *pietas*. The transformation of the Hippolytos myth on Roman sarcophagi is thus characterised by a peculiarity, even an apparent paradox, which characterises the use of myth on many (though not all) Roman sarcophagi. On the one hand, an elaborate mythical language serves to visualise psychological states (such as the love and pain of Phaedra) as well as physical qualities (such as the beauty of the heroic hunter Hippolytos) for which there were no genuinely Roman iconographic formulas available within the 'semantic system' of Roman art.[60] On the other hand, the Greek myths are refracted and refocused through the lens of an all too familiar and relatively stable system of Roman *virtutes*. This system greatly reduced the myths' inherent complexity and polysemy, but made them more intelligible and palatable for a Roman understanding which tended to perceive and filter events, actors and actions through a set of abstract concepts, rather than understand them from the perspective of the human body and its intrinsic capabilities and limitations, as had been the case in Greek art.[61] But then it is only the modern scholar's gaze which notices such conceptual inconsistencies and fractures within the visual narratives on Roman sarcophagi, the cracks and fissures that traverse

59 Lewerentz 1995, 122–24. This assumption is confirmed by the differing literary tradition. At the beginning of the Euripidean tragedy (Hipp. *Eur.* 73–87), Hippolytos does indeed offer a 'plaited garland … from a virgin meadow' to Artemis, but this has little to do with the sacrifice shown on the sarcophagi.

60 Hölscher 2004.

61 The abstract basic structure of Roman art was already understood very clearly by G. Rodenwaldt 1935; 1939. However, the issue was only fully explored by T. Hölscher in various influential works 1980; 2004. For the somatocentrism of Greek art as expression of a 'Kultur des unmittelbaren Handelns', see Hölscher 1998.

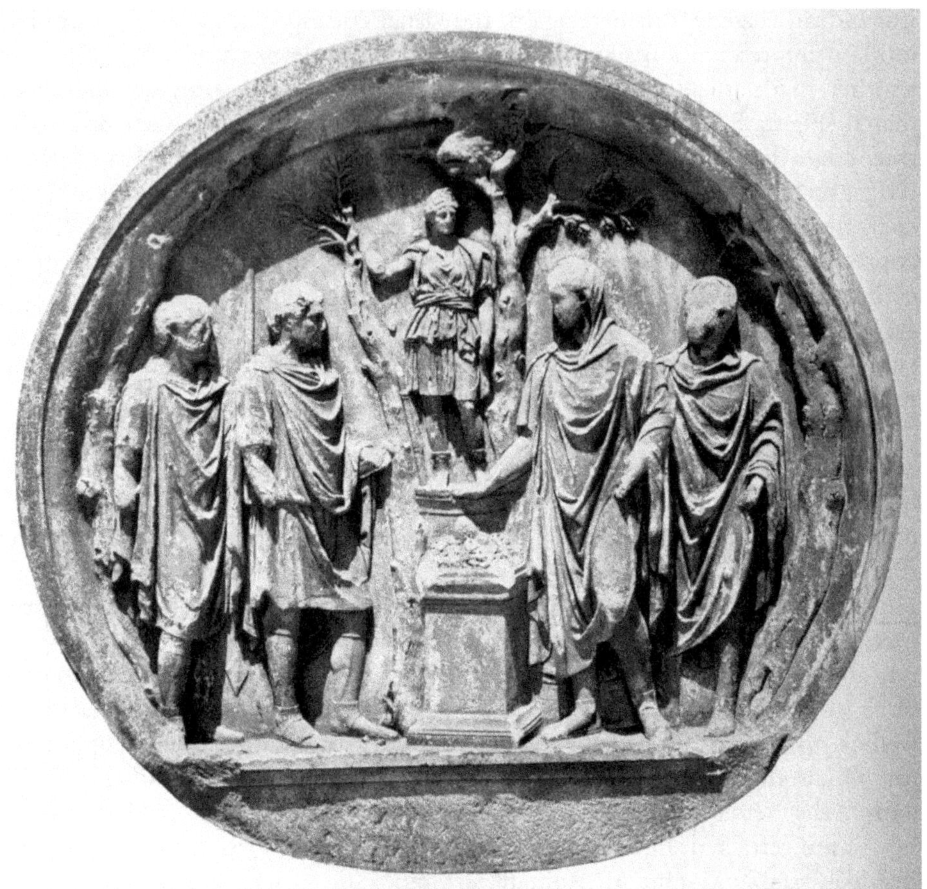

Figure 8.7: Rome, Arch of Constantine. Hadrianic Tondo with the emperor sacrificing to a statue of Artemis. After Rodenwaldt 1927, 632.

them, as well as the different realms (Greek myth, Roman imperial art) from which the iconographic elements and patterns are taken. For most Roman viewers, these heterogeneous elements must have merged into a seamless, frictionless whole: on the allegorical level, Greek myth and Roman imperial myth have become interchangeable, and the latter is treated as 'just another mythology'.

With this in mind I now turn to the Attic Hippolytos sarcophagi. Apart from obvious differences which I discuss shortly, they share a few general characteristics with their Roman counterparts that should be noted. For instance, they presuppose the same positive understanding of the two mythical protagonists as role models and exempla for the physical qualities and virtues (in the case of Hippolytos) and emotional states (in the case of Phaedra) of the patrons of the sarcophagi, although the figures of Phaedra and Hippolytos are never given portrait heads.[62] And it is safe to assume that mythological sarcophagi of this kind were often commissioned by the surviving partner upon the death of her or his companion (or possibly also by parents for their deceased son[63]), and often accommodated two corpses. For the Attic sarcophagi, at least, this assumption is confirmed by the fact that the third-century *kline* lids often show a reclining couple, equipped with portrait heads.

Despite differences in the selection of scenes, Attic and Roman sarcophagi have a further common point in their representation of the Hippolytos myth: both suppress certain elements or turning points in the narrative (even some which had made memorable scenes on stage). Examples include Phaedra's suicide, the display of her body and Theseus' lament over it (Eur. *Hipp.* 776–855), Theseus' discovery of the message which includes Phaedra's false accusation of Hippolytos (856–880), Theseus cursing his son (882–898) and then arguing with him (899–1103), Artemis' revelation of the truth to Theseus (1283–1341), and the encounter between Theseus, Artemis and the dying Hippolytos (1342–1439). While the Attic examples do show the fatal chariot crash of Hippolytos (Figure 8.1 b), his later death in the palace is not represented (1440–1466). Also missing is the scene from Seneca's *Phaedra* in which a desperate Theseus tries to piece together the limbs of his son's body, and neither Attic nor Roman sarcophagi depict narratives about Hippolytos's subsequent fate, which were developed by post-Euripidean authors, in particular the story of how Asklepios' resuscitated Hippolytos at the request of Artemis.[64] The absence of these is of interest insofar as it shows that the potential for formulating positive perspectives or hopes for the afterlife, inherent in the myth itself, was not realised in the images. In fact, on the Attic sarcophagi, the visual narrative finds explicit closure in the scene of Hippolytos' chariot crash (Figure 8.1 b).

Themes central to the tragedians' versions of the myth are likewise blended out of the imagery of both Roman metropolitan and Attic sarcophagi. These include the key Euripidean motif of the impotence of a human who has become nothing more than the plaything of conflicting divine forces (personified by Aphrodite and Artemis), the idea of the individual as victim of his own exaggerated moral claims[65], and, in Seneca's version of the myth, the antagonism between urban luxury and vice on the one hand and the solitary but virtuous

62 On the lack of portrait identifications of Roman patrons and their relatives with mythological figures on Attic sarcophagi, which seems to indicate, among other things, different demarcations between individual and collective, see Ewald 2004, 250.

63 Zanker 1999.

64 The main sources here are Verg. *Aen.* 7, 767–769; Paus. 2, 27, 4; Apollod. 3, 10, 3; Ov. *Heroid.* 15, 533–534. See Lewerentz 1995, 113–116.

65 Holzhausen 1995, 34, 39.

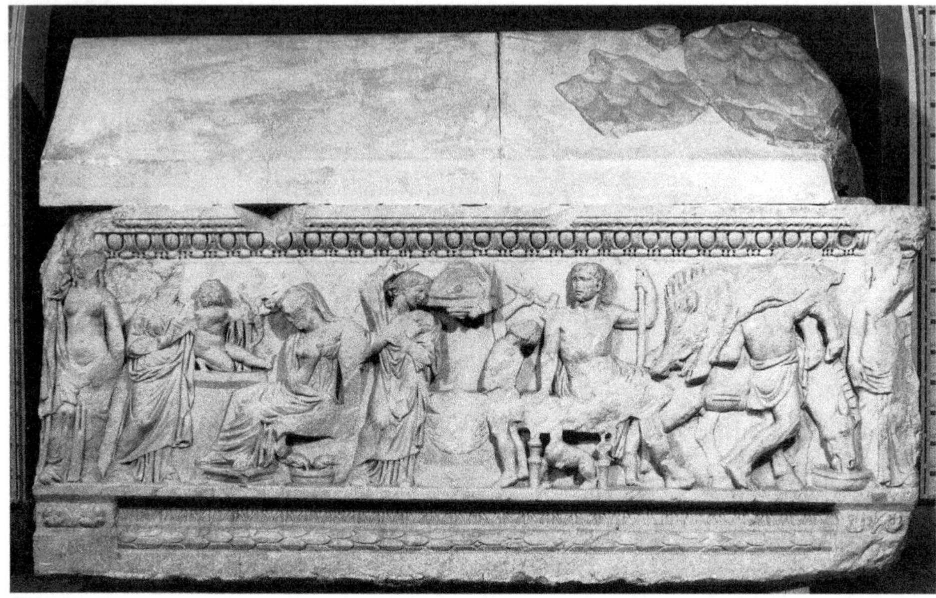

Figure 8.8: Beirut, National Museum Inv. 447. Attic Hippolytos sarcophagus showing Phaedra and Hippolytos seated, and in the center the shrine of Artemis. 2nd cent. A.D. After *ASR* IX, 1, 1, pl. 76,1.

existence of the hunter on the other. Furthermore, the motif of Hippolytos as a 'failed ephebe' who refuses to complete the transition to manhood and married life, and thus to an existence as a responsible citizen of the *polis*, has no role on the sarcophagi.[66] The same holds true for Phaedra's 'crime of loving a member of her own close kin group' and her 'wanting to commit adultery within the home'[67]: as we have already seen, the adaptations of the mythical material by the Roman and Athenian sarcophagus workshops could, without hesitation, translate the relation between Hippolytos and his stepmother Phaedra into that of a married couple, or of mother and son.[68]

Yet, the representation of the Hippolytos myth on Attic sarcophagi differs greatly from that found on their Roman counterparts. What emerges from the Attic rendering of the myth is the absence of the Roman grid of intelligibility (centred, as we have seen, around certain key virtues and abstract concepts) as a function that organises and re-patterns the visual narrative, and the existence of an alternative and specifically Greek set of cultural coordinates within which the mythical narratives are constructed. Interestingly, abstract personifications such

66 Mitchell-Boyask 1999.

67 Sissa 2008, 19.

68 Zanker 1999.

as *virtus*, *Concordia*, *honos* or *pietas*, so common on Roman sarcophagi (Figure 8.5 a), are missing entirely from the Attic examples.

In contrast to the Roman Hippolytos sarcophagi of the main group (Figure 8. 5 a-b), which do not show a significant development between the second and third centuries, the Attic sarcophagi of the second and third centuries form two distinct and very different sets. The earlier group, represented primarily by two examples in Beirut (Figure 8.8; from Tyre) and Istanbul, shows two scenes on the front side which are not to be read as a continuous narrative but rather as descriptions of contrary male and female role models of the heroic hunter and the loving female respectively.[69] Framed by caryatids on the corners of the front, we see Hippolytos and Phaedra seated back to back at the shrine of Artemis. In the centre of the frieze, a little servant with a hammer fixes the antlers of a stag to a small shrine. The antlers must mean a trophy dedicated by Hippolytos to his patron goddess Artemis, as was customary among hunters throughout antiquity. The servant is observed by the seated Hippolytos, who leans casually on a lance in a pose reminiscent of the figure of Dionysos on the Parthenon east frieze. To the right, a servant is unloading an enormous boar from a watering mule.

The left part of the frieze is occupied by the seated Phaedra and two standing female figures. Phaedra's posture, with lowered head and raised right hand, reveals the tormented state of her soul. Her left hand is supported by the nurse who stands behind her and makes an exclamatory gesture. The image leaves no doubt that Phaedra's desperate state is caused by Aphrodite, who stands in front of her and instructs a little Eros where to shoot his arrow.

Although this early group shows Hippolytos and Phaedra together on the front, they have nothing else in common with either the contemporary Roman pieces or the later Attic Hippolytos sarcophagi of the third century. In fact, the whole composition seems to be without parallels and must have been created specifically for the Attic sarcophagi. Its particular value apparently lay in the presentation of the opposing male and female universes of values and 'fantasmic' roles[70] – the loving female, consumed by her passion, and the pious hunter, resting after his pursuits – which are here juxtaposed with such abrupt clarity. The fact that both Phaedra and Hippolytos are seated, and that the available image space is divided equally among them, points to a gender symmetry or 'balance', in spite of the strict segregation of the two realms. This relative (that is, compositional and spatial) gender balance is not to be found on the later Attic Hippolytos sarcophagi, at least not within the mythological realm. A further value of this early iconography may have resided in the

69 *ASR* IX,1, 73–77; 112–118. I am not discussing here the small sides of these sarcophagi.

70 On the notion of fantasy, see Žižek 1997.

meanings evoked by the garlanded altar and shrine of Artemis which is placed exactly in the centre of the composition. This offered generic connotations of sacred worship that must have been welcome at the tomb which, after all, was a place of pious duties towards the deceased, as well as a semantically charged sphere conceptualised as a *heroon.*[71] It is no longer possible to say whether the representation of Hippolytos at the shrine of Artemis also involved concrete reference to a classical painting or a specific Attic sanctuary dedicated to Artemis.

In the early third century, this second-century composition was abandoned in favour of the highly static formula which is found on the Agrigento sarcophagus depicting Hippolytos and his hunting companions (Figure 8.1 a). Although these third-century Attic sarcophagi have very little in common with their second-century predecessors, they do maintain one characteristic – the relatively strict separation between the male and the female realms, with each of the mythical protagonists shown in his or her own distinctive environment. This symbolic division of male and female worlds is further reinforced by the removal of Phaedra and her cortège from the front of the sarcophagus to one of its small sides (Figure 8.1 c).[72] The sarcophagus' original polychromy – probably a rose-brown for Hippolytos and his companions and a much paler tone for Phaedra and her female servants – would have contributed to the gendered differences between the (warm, dry) male and (cool, moist) female bodies. Likewise, the poses and gestures of the protagonists convey clear gender distinctions, including the different concepts of male/female action and agency that such body language communicates: the naked hunter Hippolytos is shown in a relaxed, but erect stance, in an outdoor setting, while the richly dressed Phaedra appears seated in her woman's chamber, attended by female servants who try to lift her limp arm. The sarcophagus' artists did not have to look far for the scheme of the woman in pain: they found it in Attic funerary *stelai* of the fourth

71 Cormack 2004; Ewald 2008a.

72 Cf. Wiegartz 1975, 203. In a variant of this group, the hunting party does not take up the entire space available on the front side of the sarcophagus but rather is combined with the Phaedra group, which, however, is now pushed towards one of the edges of the image. Thus, here too the visual field is no longer divided equally among the protagonists; and the female sphere is, as it were, marginalised. However, this group, in particular in an example in Beirut (Linant de Bellefonds 1990, 460–461; *ASR* IX,1, 84–86 no. 57 pl. 84, 1), differs from the examples discussed here, such as the sarcophagus in Agrigento, in its emphasis on the hetero-erotic aspect: the gazes of the protagonists meet at the moment in which the old nurse unveils Phaedra; the little Eros with the torch symbolises the burning desire which takes possession of Phaedra at this very moment. The gesture of unveiling is here reinterpreted in a remarkable manner: the expression of extreme passion and emotional turmoil in Euripides (Eurip. *Hipp.* 201–201; 245. 250) has morphed into a self-conscious, almost coquettish self-presentation which could even be read in the sense of a marriage gesture.

century BC and in marble *lekythoi* depicting women in childbirth, as could be seen in the Kerameikos and other cemeteries throughout Attica (Figure 8.9).[73] On the sarcophagus relief two maidservants try to cure Phaedra's pain by playing string instruments (*panduria*), at the same time evoking the idea of a distinguished and musical household.[74]

The separation between male and female in the symbolic configuration of space is a particular characteristic of the Attic sarcophagi; the Roman sarcophagi, by contrast, have no scene where Phaedra appears separately in the *gynaeconitis* without Hippolytos. Instead, as we have seen, they place particular emphasis on the direct encounter between the two. It is tempting to draw parallels here between the sarcophagi and the different symbolic configurations of space in the Greek and the Roman house. Roman authors such as Cornelius Nepos (*vitae praef.* 6–7) and Vitruvius (6,7,1–5) are sensitive to differing symbolic social and spatial practices east and west, and tend to frame them in terms of a strict Greek-Roman dichotomy, regardless of the much more complex and varied reality in both the Greek and the Roman house.[75] For Vitruvius, the Greek house is, as Wallace-Hadrill notes, 'shaped around a radical distinction between men's and women's areas, a distinction which makes no sense to the Italian, (and) which is posited on divergent social convention, above all the Greek taboo on attendance by respectable female members of the household at the men's *symposia* (...)'.[76] But the segregation between male and female realms can be understood not only in terms of Greek versus Roman, but also as the re-enactment of a distinctly classical system: in the fourth century, Xenophon (*oec.* 9,5) presupposes a strict segregation of male and female areas of the house (*andronitis* and *gynaeconitis*), and it has been argued that the classical house was, to a certain degree, built around such distinctions.[77]

The – literal – marginalisation of Phaedra, and of the female sphere more generally, in the principal mythological reliefs of third-century Attic sarcophagi is in sharp contrast with the complementary characterisation of non-mythological women as it occurs on the *kline* lids that were usually combined with such caskets (Figure 8.10). These representations of men and women on the lid (one of whom must have usually been the patron of the sarcophagus, who had dedicated it to the deceased partner) offer a virtual counter-image to what we see in the mythological reliefs on the casket. The *kline* lids are

73 Demand 1994, 124; 161 pl. 6; Vedder 1988; Catoni 2005.

74 On the role of music (and education) in the definition of the female sphere, see Hemelrijk 1999, 81–84; also Friedlaender 1934, 236–237. For the ideal in funerary art, see Ewald 1999, 121–134.

75 Wallace-Hadrill 1996.

76 Ibid., 106.

77 Ibid., 107; cf. Ault and Nevett 2005, 161–163.

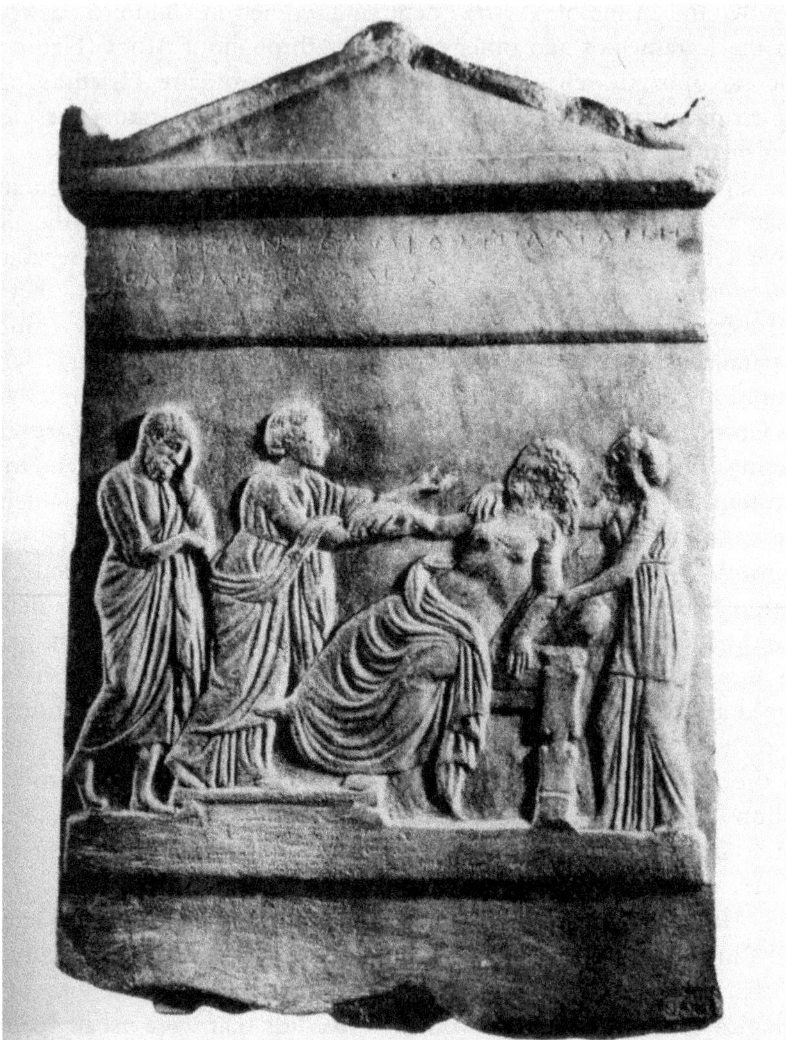

Figure 8.9: Athens, National Museum Inv. 749. Grave Stele for Plangon and Tolmides. From Oropos. 4th cent. B.C. Inst. Neg. Athen NM 417.

characterised by shared space and near gender symmetry as far as the couple's reclining poses are concerned; gestures such as the man's hand on his wife's shoulder further emphasise the affectionate nature of their relationship. Gender distinctions are made only by means of attributes, with the man holding an open scroll, while the woman grasps a swathe of her garment or a garland with one hand and holds a pomegranate or rests her head on her other. The man is thus praised for his literary cultivation, the woman for the generic qualities of modesty and *sophrosyne.* The richly decorated mattresses and soft pillows, on

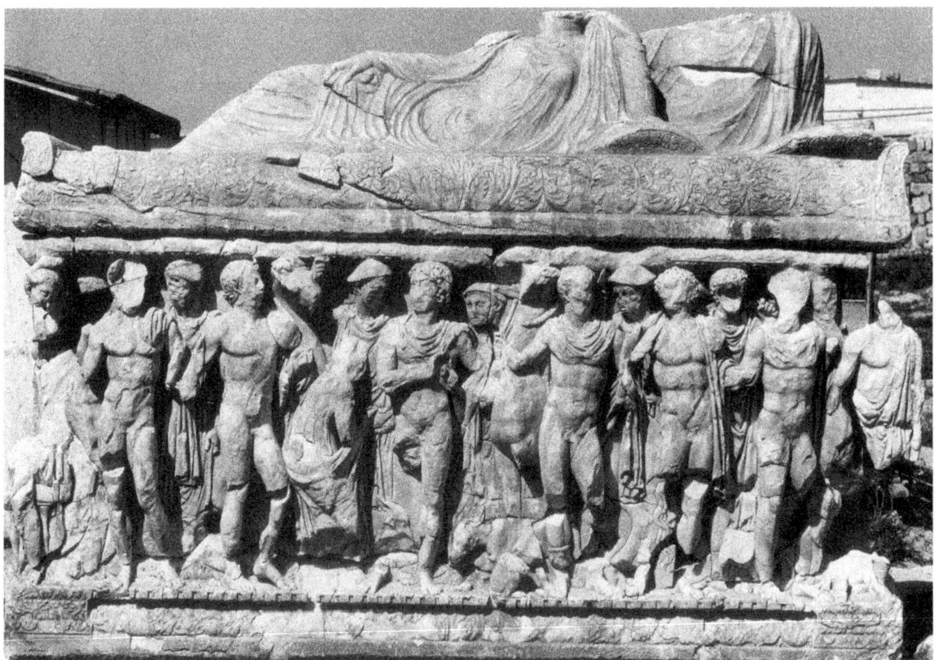

Figure 8.10: Tyre, Necropolis Inv. 330. Attic sarcophagus showing Hippolytos with his hunting companions and servants as he receives the letter from the nurse (cf. 8.1a). The kline lid shows a reclining couple. 3rd cent. A.D. After *ASR* IX, 1, 1, pl. 88, 4

which both partners balance their left arms, underscore the theme of domestic luxury and elevated social status.

Such *kline* lids, in other words, say much more about the perception of women and of contemporary elite women's roles in the Greek East during the period in question than do the mythological reliefs on the bodies of these sarcophagi. It is well documented that during the second and third centuries elite women had access to high religious and civic offices (if not to proper magistracies), commanded their own property and capital, functioned as public benefactors and patrons of elaborate tombs, and received high civic honours in return.[78]

One could say that – if looked at as a whole – the sarcophagus' iconography is characterised by a marked friction between the space of myth and memory in its reliefs on the one hand and that of the social values of the contemporary *Lebenswelt* in its *kline* portraits on the other. While the representation of the couple on the *kline* lid minimises gender differences, the mythological reliefs on the sarcophagus deliberately use gender to produce a cultural anachronism which perfectly evokes the retrospective ideology and general *habitus* of the

78 Van Bremen 1996; Cormack 2004, 133–143.

Second Sophistic, and which also emphasises how the tomb stands outside ordinary time and place through its conceptualisation as an heroon.[79] The sarcophagus itself participates in the collapse of the horizon of time that characterises the particular 'Bildraum' of the tomb.

Scholars of the literary culture of the Second Sophistic and its principles of 'atticism' and 'language purity' have long been aware of the breaks and contradictions on various levels – gender being one of them – that were caused by the use of ancient idioms, and the relentless attempt to 'frame the present in the terms of the past'. Simon Swain notes that 'a language purism like atticism, which was so closely linked to social and political control by the male elite and which depended for its existence on an educational system dominated by men, cannot have failed to reinforce division of the sexes.'[80] It seems that the iconography of the sarcophagi tries to come to terms with these issues through a composite mode of representation that downplays the discrepancies and incompatibilities between the two cultural codes. This, in turn, suggests that the Second Sophistic, while indeed very much a male affair in the register of the symbolic, did not necessarily lead to a reinforcement of gender inequalities on all levels.

The remaining small side and the back of these Hippolytos sarcophagi depict the hunt of Hippolytos or the transport of the prey following the hunt, as well as the hero's chariot crash (Figure 8.1 b).[81] On the left end of the example in Agrigento, we see Hippolytos lying on the ground with the runaway team of horses, which a companion tries to restrain, above him, the head of the bull sent by Poseidon is visible at the upper edge of the image. The chariot crash places the object's praise of Hippolytos' beauty and manliness in the context of death: the image of the heroic hunter in the blossom of his youth is contrasted with an image of his tragic and early demise. The death scene demonstrates that, although Attic sarcophagi are generally lacking in the forms of continuous narrative found in Rome, a basic narrative sequence is nonetheless intended: the sarcophagi construct an ideal biography of male beauty, virtue and premature death which might be compared with funeral orations or obituaries like Dio's *Melancomas.*

'Death' on Attic sarcophagi is almost always a male, heroic affair. Unlike their Roman counterparts, the Attic examples hardly ever show the deaths of women or children.[82] This again accords with 'atticism' and the self-conscious employment of an outdated frame of reference in the cultural domain of Roman Athens. Yet, within the visual system of Attic sarcophagi, the accidental

79 Cormack 2004; Ewald 2008a.
80 Swain 1996, 413.
81 On the small sides of Attic Hippolytos sarcophagi, see *ASR* IX,1, 83–92; 115–118.
82 Ewald 2004, 240–241.

death of Hippolytos is unusual insofar as it is the only death that is not a *kalos thanatos* in battle or the result of an injury suffered in war. The hero's fatal chariot crash apparently had sufficient heroic connotations to be deemed worthy of representation, if only on the ends or the back of sarcophagi. This must have to do with the fact that chariot racing was an aristocratic sport with high stakes; it was not uncommon for the wealthy owners of horses and chariots to perform as charioteers themselves.[83] A contemporary viewer would have been able to make connections between Hippolytos' accident and what could be witnessed in the hippodrome, including the frequent crashes in chariot races. The visual correspondences between Hippolytos' accident and the deadly chariot crashes of Phaeton and Oinomaos, as well as the *naufragium* on Roman circus sarcophagi, prove the legitimacy of the connection with chariot racing, and demonstrate how the chariot crash of Hippolytos – regardless of the specific mythological context – could be understood as a common allegory of death.[84]

Before I return to the question of the overall meaning of such compositions, I want to take a very brief look at the Attic sarcophagi depicting the discovery of Achilles on Scyros. Here we have a different myth, but also an iconographic development that runs exactly parallel – and is without doubt homologous – to that found on the Attic Hippolytos sarcophagi.

The Attic Achilles sarcophagi of the second century present a dynamic composition which consists of three separate figure groups[85] (Figure 8.11): in a position slightly off-centre we see Achilles in female clothing, dynamically moving in the direction of his fellow warriors. He has just revealed his identity by grabbing a shield and a lance. Deidameia is shown either kneeling before him, as on the example in St. Petersburg illustrated here, or running beside him, trying to hold him back. To the right, Deidameia's sisters are working wool, to the left is a group of Greeks, including Odysseus. The whole composition thematises the revelation of male beauty and virtue, as well as the different male and female domains and spheres of action, in a manner similar to that of the early Hippolytos sarcophagi (Figure 8. 8). Through the figure of Deidameia, the scene also represents Deidameia's desire for the hero, as well as the violent separation of the lovers.[86]

83 Scanlon 2002, 309–322.

84 On the connection with the death of Phaeton, see *ASR* III,2, 181; *ASR* IX,1, 116–117. On Oinomaos' chariot crash, see Zanker and Ewald 2004, 364–367. On the *naufragium* on Roman sarcophagi, see Scanlon 2002, 314–318.

85 *ASR* IX,1, 26–30; Raeck 1992, 134–6.

86 On the aspect of Deidameia's desire: Muth 1998, 165. On the aspect of the violent separation of the lovers: Amedick 1998; *ASR* XII,2, 201–203; also Zanker and Ewald 2004, 280–282 (with further references). On an interesting variation of the episode on an Attic sarcophagus in London (*ASR* IX,1, 131–132 no. 17 pl. 32, 1), Deidameia is shown in the scheme used for the lovesick Phaedra, in order to visualize her longing for

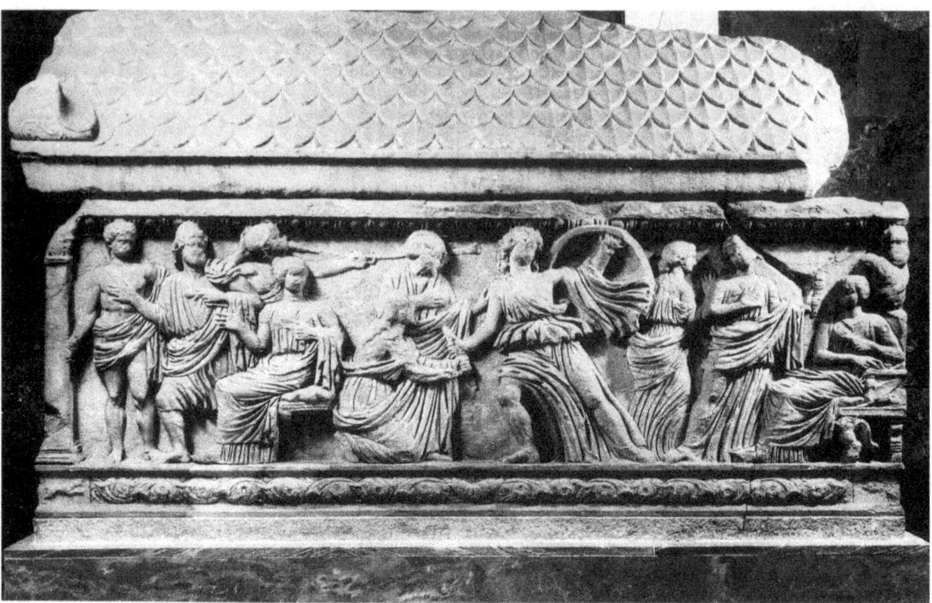

Figure 8.11: St. Petersburg, Ermitage Inv. A 1026. Attic sarcophagus showing Achilles on Scyros. 2nd cent. A.D. After *ASR* IX, 1, 1, pl. 26, 1.

In the late second or early third century, this dynamic composition was abandoned in favour of one showing two bearded men seated opposite each other at both ends of the front, gazing at the youths in the centre of the frieze (Figure 8.12–13); they are commonly identified as Lycomedes (left) and Agamemnon (right).[87] In comparison with the earlier composition, the theme of Deidameia's desire, and more generally any reference to the female realm, is underplayed, or eliminated altogether. For instance, on the examples in the Louvre and the Musei Capitolini, only three or two females remain, while on another example in Tyre (Figure 8.13) not a single female figure appears on the front.[88] Obviously, this transformation points in the same direction as the contemporary Hippolytos sarcophagi (Figures 8.1 a and 8. 10), and is governed by the same interest on the part of viewers. The naked Achilles appears, like Hippolytos, as a member of a group of coevals in a highly static composition in which nothing is left of the transitory character of the Scyros episode on second-century sarcophagi. As in the case of the Hippolytos sarcophagi, this development occurs independently of the rendering of the same myth at

Achilles. On the Scyros episode in other media, see also Raeck 1992; Muth 1998, 151–193; Trimble 2002; Russenberger 2002.

87 *ASR* IX,1, 43–49.

88 Louvre and Musei Capitolini: *ASR* IX,1, 43 no. 21 pl. 43, 3; 44–45 no. 24 pl. 44, 1. Tyre: *ASR* IX,1, 45–46 no. 42 pl. 52,1.

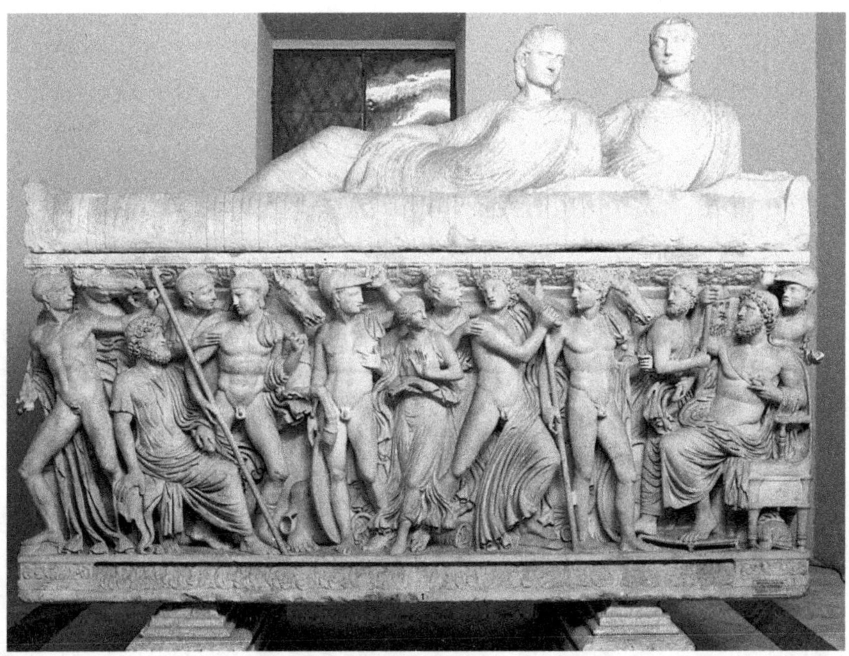

Figure 8.12: Rome, Musei Capitolini Inv. 218. From a tomb in Rome, Monte del Grano. Attic sarcophagus showing Achilles on Scyros. The *kline* lid shows a reclining couple. 3rd cent. A.D. After *ASR* IX, 1, 1, pl. 44, 1.

Rome, where no substantial changes can be observed during the same period. Instead, on the Roman sarcophagi the aspect of hetero-erotic love receives much greater emphasis than on the Attic examples, as is clear from the great number of erotes that can swarm around Deidameia and Achilles, as on a metropolitan example in the Louvre.[89]

How can we conceptualise these changes within the typological development of Attic sarcophagi, and what was the specific value of the new iconographies? Since there was no reason to abandon the old iconographic schemes in the first place, the new compositions should not be seen (as they usually are) as a symptom of decline or lack of artistic imagination. Rather, they must be the result of deliberate choice and reflect a genuine interest on the side of artists and patrons, who understood such compositions as an improvement in the visual rendering of both myths, even though they came at the price of a significant obscuring of the internal narrative logic of the underlying stories. The source of this interest is obvious: the multiplication of the figures of naked youths on both the Hippolytos and the Achilles sarcophagi, and in particular the addition of male viewers on the latter (who change the scopic regime within the

89 Muth 1998, 164–168; *ASR* XII,2, 201 no. 21 pl. 17, 1.

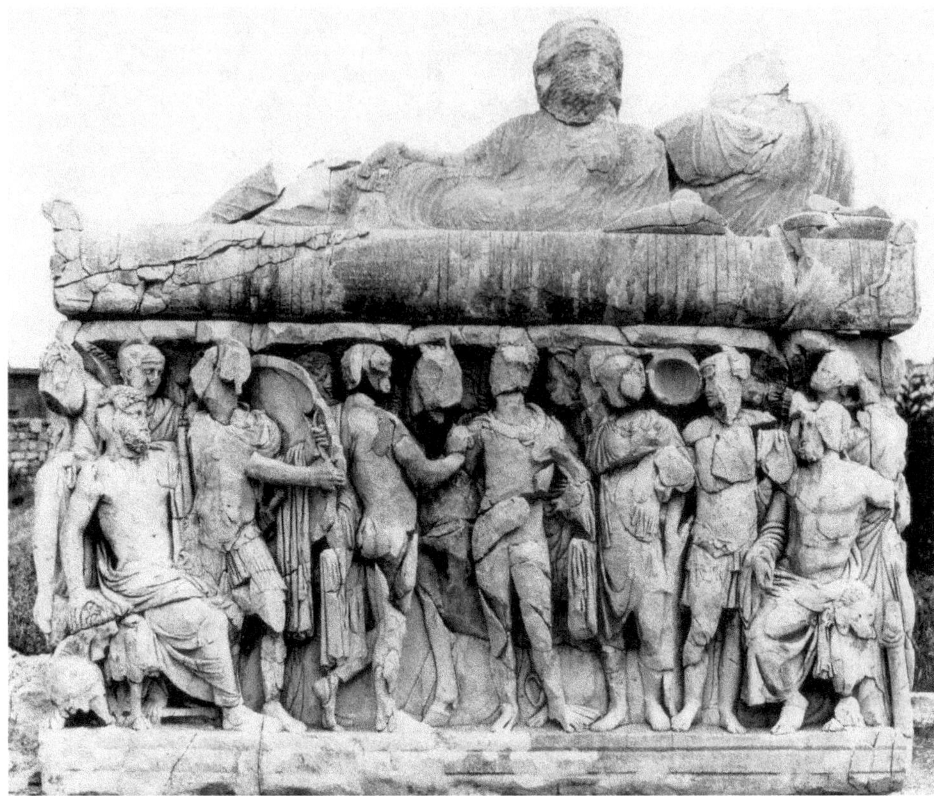

Figure 8.13: Tyre, Necropolis Inv. 328/329. Attic sarcophagus depicting Achilles on Scyros. The *kline* lid shows a reclining couple with unfinished portrait heads. 3rd cent. A.D. After *ASR* IX, 1, 1, pl. 52, 1.

image entirely), leaves no doubt that these reliefs are about the naked male body as the object of the male gaze – that is, they are about male desire, and not about the male body as the object of female viewers and female desire (as is always the case on Roman sarcophagi, and is after all the drive of at least the Hippolytos myth and Phaedra's love). On the Achilles example in Tyre (Figure 8.13), and also on some of the Hippolytos sarcophagi, one of the youths even presents his firm buttocks as an erotic signal to the viewer.[90] The scheme of older male viewers and handsome young men presenting themselves, attempts to re-enact the 'homo-social visual economy'[91] of the classical period – a culture of 'showing and viewing'[92] which had focused on the figure of the young athlete or ephebe.[93]

90 *ASR* IX,1 152 no. 57 pl. 84,1; 154 no. 64 pl. 89, 2.
91 Stähli 2001, 208.
92 Sennett 1994, 32–50.

By reaffirming a 'classical' scopic relationship, the sarcophagus images answer directly to concerns such as those raised by Dio (21) in his discourse 'on beauty', in which the current decline of Greece is linked to the disappearance of handsome young men, and the proper ways of viewing, desiring and praising them. (By the way, the ephebic *stelai* mentioned above, Figures 8. 2 and 8.14, which were set up by the ephebes in honour of the *cosmetes* for a particular year, show a comparable interaction between mature, bearded men and younger men dressed in chlamydes;[94]but, in comparison with the sarcophagi, 'active' and 'passive' are reversed in these monuments – the *cosmetes* stands still while the ephebes crown him). With regard to the usual identification of the patron of the sarcophagus, shown on the *kline* lid above the main casket, with the mythological protagonist depicted in the main relief, such compositions set in motion a complex and highly narcissistic economy of desire: Achilles and Hippolytos are, at the same time, the desired object and – as mythological avatars of the sarcophagus' patron – the desiring subject.[95] The libidinal mechanics of such images are quite different from (and more complex than) that of von Gloeden's Victorian photographs (Figure 8.4), which cast the spectator clearly (though not consistently) in the role of the gay subject who takes his scopic pleasure.[96]

The hetero-erotic discourse, which is suppressed or blended out in the main reliefs of these sarcophagi, is given a highly representative, even monumental form on the *kline* lids. Such non-mythological iconographies, though heavily typified (so-called *vita humana* scenes are not *a priori* less fictional than the mythological ones, and do not provide a more immediate or privileged access to ancient realities than do the literary sources), are rooted in various realities of their time – a heightened status for women, a re-valuation of the private realm as a suitable object for representation, and the spread of a new ideal of conjugality defined by mutual affection and sentiment.[97] Numerous texts from

93 On scopophilia and athletic nudity in Roman Greece, see Goldhill 2001, 1–4 and 183; Ewald 2004, 242–247; Koenig 2005, 97–147 (with further references).

94 On the ephebic stelai from Roman Athens, see Lattanzi 1968; Rhomiopoulou 1997; Newby 2005, 168–201 (the examples given here on pp. 171–172 and 174–176).

95 For the alternative identifications offered by the figures of the seated men, which in individual cases may have been seen to refer to the deceased's social role (for example, as a gymnasiarch), see Ewald 2004, 245–247, and in a forthcoming book on the Attic sarcophagi. On the problematic identification of these figures as Lycomedes and Agamemnon, and the genealogy of the motif, see Koortbojian 1998, 560 and 563.

96 Waugh 2002.

97 For a, broadly speaking, Foucauldian approach to the representation of both mythological and non-mythological couples on Roman metropolitan sarcophagi, see Zanker 1995, 267–289; Muth 1998, 300–310 (overlooked in Ewald 2004, 250–253); Zanker 2003; Ewald 2005; *ASR* I,3.

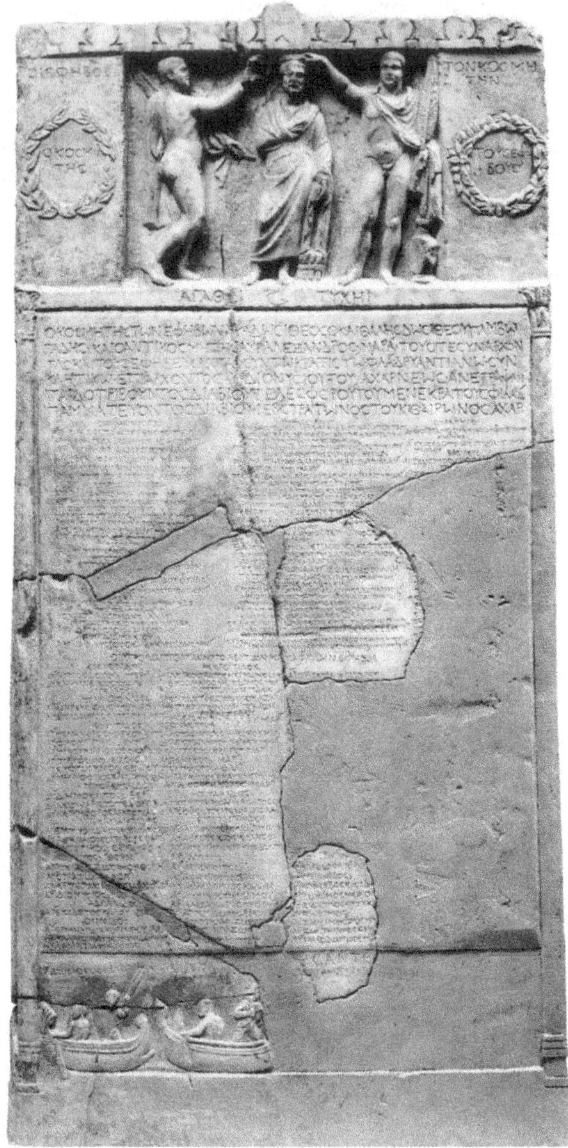

Figure 8.14: Athens, National Museum Inv. 1465. Ephebic relief with the *cosmetes* in the centre, being crowned by two ephebes. A.D. 212/213. After Rhomiopoulou 1997, p. 49.

the imperial period suggest that for a couple to recline together commonly 'announce(d) a licit, proprietary sexual connection'.[98]

98 Roller 2006, 121; see also Stein-Hölkeskamp 2005, 73–86 (on the possible impact of the new conjugal ideal on the *convivium*). Dunbabin 2003, 122–125 notes, quite

Interestingly, these *kline* lids, which replace the older second-century roof shaped lids without sculptural decoration, come into fashion in the later second century, shortly before the iconographic change within the main reliefs of Attic sarcophagi, that I have been describing, takes place. This near-synchronicity between the introduction of the *kline* lid and the iconographic transformations in the main relief shows that the emergence of the new iconography for the married couple is directly related to the cultivation of a decisively homo-erotic aesthetic on the body of the sarcophagus.

If seen as a whole, the sarcophagi offer a visual program which provides a direct insight into the complex mindset of the (male) elites of the second and third centuries in the Eastern part of the Empire: they attempt to combine the nostalgic self-image of a (Classical) homo-social and agonistic society, centred around the naked male body with all its erotic and moral implications, with the contemporary re-valuation of conjugal relationships and an increased importance of the private realm. The question of the two kinds of love and how to integrate them – the 'Hellenic' love for boys or ephebes on the one hand and conjugal love on the other – was, as Foucault has shown, a crucial question in the Greek literature of the time.[99] The shifting geometrics of power under the empire had forced male elites to redefine a whole set of personal, familial and social relations – with their spouses, their children and their own bodies. In this context, the matrimonial relationship becomes 'the most active focus for defining a stylistics of moral life', and it becomes the template for a new unitary conception of *eros*. The traditional Hellenic love for boys, on the other hand, undergoes 'a kind of philosophical 'disinvestment"; and reflection on it in the Greek literature of the imperial period loses 'some of its intensity, its seriousness, its vitality, if not its topicality. (...) It participates in the reactivation of classical culture, but in a dull way.'[100]

One of Foucault's witnesses for the proposed shift, alongside Lucian's *Erotes*, is Plutarch's 'dialogue on love'[101] and this dialogue is also of the greatest interest in the context of the sarcophagi discussed here. For it activates the same semantic field of the hunt, athletics, epheby, homoeroticism and marriage which provides the coordinates for the visual narratives on the late Attic Hippolytos and Achilles sarcophagi. Bacchon – the main character and central focus of the dialogue – is desired both by the elderly men of Thespiae and by Ismenodora, a widow who has been charged with finding a younger woman to be Bacchon's

rightly, for the *kline* lids that they lack a 'direct reference to a meal', as well as the emphasis placed on 'representative display and luxury.'

99 Foucault 1986, 189–232. This is not the place for engaging with the various responses of classical scholars to the third volume of the *History of Sexuality*. For a recent survey of the state of affairs, with further references, see Skinner 2005, 242–247; 269–275.

100 Foucault 1986, 189–192.

101 Ibid., 193–210.

wife. Desired equally by men and women and simply called 'the beautiful one' (*kalos*), Bacchon is an aristocratic ideal, an *ephebos* and hunter who spends his time in the *gymnasium* and the *palaestra*. Effectively Bacchon is confronted with the choice between his familiar life with his hunting companions (*synkynegoi*) and his usual admirers at the *palaestra* on the one hand, and the security of a marriage to a wealthy, but older, woman on the other. In this difficult situation he turns to his older cousin and one of his *erastai* for counsel, who, in turn, are divided in their opinion, and this disagreement becomes the driving force of the subsequent conversation. In the end, as we may expect in Plutarch, marriage rules. But the dialogue as a whole articulates a series of questions and problems which also characterise the later Achilles and Hippolytos sarcophagi; and it is extremely helpful in describing the *syuzhet* or 'discourse manifestation' (see above) which likewise also structures the visual narratives on the sarcophagi.

But it is important to note that the sarcophagi do not simply address the same issues as Plutarch's dialogue. Rather, they re-organise and re-configure the same issues in a very specific manner. Whereas in Plutarch, for instance, pederasty and marriage feature as opposites (in spite of the entire discourse on the transcending power of Eros), the 'programme' of the later Hippolytos and Achilles sarcophagi seeks to evoke the two types of love in a composite and synthetic way. In doing so, it gives ample room to a highly mannered and classically stylised homoeroticism. This homoeroticism may have been, above all, a cultural trope at the time (and Foucault dismisses Maximus of Tyre's speeches about the right kind of male love for precisely this reason) – but one that was obviously essential in the definition of a Greek 'cultural identity'. However, unlike the conjugal relationship, which is expressed through poses and gestures, the 'homoerotic' relation remains a purely scopic and 'aesthetic' one, and it plays out in the open, in the community with other men.

Another advantage of the new compositions lay in their capacity to express a composite concept of *paideia* that encompassed literary education as well as physical excellence and corporeal perfection. The open scroll in the hand of the sarcophagus patron reclining on the *kline* lid, as well as the – at times monumental[102] – bundles of scrolls that sometimes appear next to him, allude to his literary education. The precise scope of this literary cultivation cannot, of course, be determined further on the basis of the representations on the sarcophagi alone; the general reference is probably to those texts that had gained a certain canonicity in the Second Sophistic, but can in particular cases also be a play on the performative presentation of the deceased's own literary work and poems.[103] In any case, the scroll (and the type of education for which it stands) is usually presented as an attribute of the deceased man, whereas the woman

102 See the examples in Goette 1991; Rhomiopoulou 1997, no. 120.
103 Stein-Hölkeskamp 2005, 232–246.

holds a hand garland and, sometimes, a pomegranate.[104] On the other hand, the nude mythical heroes in the main reliefs of Attic sarcophagi serve as a means of praising the tomb owner's *kalokagathia* – the perfect physique that denotes moral excellence and manliness. For, despite their lack of portrait features, and the obvious differences to him in age and physique, they must have usually been implicitly identified with the sarcophagus patron.[105] A number of recent works on Greek athletics under the Roman empire have made abundantly clear that athleticism and the idea of physical excellence continued to play a crucial and defining role in the self-image and self-presentation of local elites in the Greek east of the Roman empire, and that there was anything but a decline in athletics and physical education during the imperial period.[106] Moreover, the perfectly trained body could become a signifier of moral excellence, manliness and self-control, of *sophrosyne*, *enkrateia*, *eupsychia*, *andreia* (and *euandreia*) – as both honorific inscriptions and texts such as Lucian's *Anacharsis* and in particular Dio's *Melancomas* (e.g. 14) demonstrate.[107] The static compositions of the late Attic sarcophagi, devoid of any and all action, and the choice of late classical stances and sparing gestures, must be related to the intense moral and philosophical investments in corporeality and athletics that took place during the period. The success of a new ideal of restraint and self-control would have engendered a new interest on the part of viewers, and the sarcophagi themselves

104 There are, however, some remarkable exceptions to this strict gendering of literary *paideia:* on the *kline* lid belonging to a monumental sarcophagus from Asia Minor in Sardis, we see the deceased Claudia Antonia Sabina (herself a woman of high rank) together with her daughter; in her left hand she holds the scroll otherwise only held by men (Cormack 2004, 284–287 fig. 177). Likewise, on the Roman examples, women often hold bookrolls, perform oratory gestures and can even be shown reading: Ewald 1999, 126; Huskinson 1999.

105 Of particular interest for the understanding of this discrepancy (and why it was not conceived as a problem) is a passage in Dio's *Melancomas* (29,5, translation J.E. Cohoon), in which male beauty is conceptualised, in a pseudo-platonic manner, as a quality that transcends the bearer and his actual age: 'But when it is a question of perfect and true beauty, it would be surprising if anyone ever possessed it as this man did. For he had it in his whole body and always to the same degree, both before he reached years of manhood and afterward; and he would never have lived long enough, even if he had reached an extreme old age, to have dimmed his beauty.' It also seems relevant in this context that the famous Greek beauty contests (*euandriai*) could include competitions for older men: Crowther 1985.

106 Van Nijf 2001, 320–329; Van Nijf 2003; Van Nijf 2004; Koenig 2005; Newby 2005.

107 Van Nijf 2003. See also Ewald 2004, 244; Koenig 2005, 97–157; Newby 2005, 141–167; 229–271, and the contributions in Kah and Scholz 2004.

would have played a role in the reproduction and transmission of a relaxed, yet controlled and sophisticated elite corporeal *habitus.*[108]

The concept of *paideia* evoked on the Attic sarcophagi thus differs from that found on the Roman examples, where – in particular after the early third century – the male deceased are portrayed wrapped in the *pallium* (*himation*), with bookroll in hand and surrounded by philosophical counsellors.[109] While on the Roman sarcophagi, the praise of 'education' and learning places particular emphasis on spiritual advice, and marks a beginning of the problematisation of nudity and a general turning away from the visual discourse that was centred on the human body, the Attic examples never give up their somatocentric mode of representation.[110] In their relentless adherence to the naked male body as an axiom for the representation of different myths, the Attic sarcophagi participate in the active revival of an outdated (although universally understood) frame of reference by which prestige and honours were bestowed according to physical perfection, ability and beauty, rather than through dress and symbols of rank, or proximity to the emperor.[111] All of this need not be understood as a conscious rejection of Roman social and power relations (and in fact, the athletic festivals in the Greek East were often associated with the imperial family). But it is worth noting in this context that on the Attic sarcophagi – in contrast to the Roman examples – we do not find explicit references to the position of the patron of the sarcophagus within the Roman social hierarchy, or indeed hardly any scenes which fall under the *vita humana* rubric.[112]

The connection between the sarcophagi and a dual, composite concept of *paideia* proposed here finds confirmation on the small side of an Attic Hippolytos sarcophagus in Apollonia, Libya (Figure 8.15).[113] While the Hippolytos sarcophagi usually remain within the paradigm of the hunt, here we see a naked youth, very likely Hippolytos himself, with a discus in his left hand; he is flanked by another athlete and a female figure (Phaedra?). The herm in the background and the vessel in front of him firmly situate the scene within the realm of the *gymnasium* and *palaestra.* This not only confirms the connection made here, but also demonstrates how interchangeable hunt and athletic training (and, one might add, warfare) continued to be in the construction of manliness in the imperial period.[114] In sum, the sarcophagi strongly support

108 For the 'body language' of the late classical models, see Fehr 1979, 16–24; also Tanner 2006, 121. For sophistic self-fashioning, and the importance of bodily habitus in the Second Sophistic, see Gleason 1995.

109 Zanker 1995, 267–289; Ewald 1999.

110 Ewald 2005.

111 Foucault 1986.

112 Ewald 2004, 247–250.

113 *ASR* IX,1, 149 no. 49 pl. 108, 2.

114 Barringer 2001; Martini 2000.

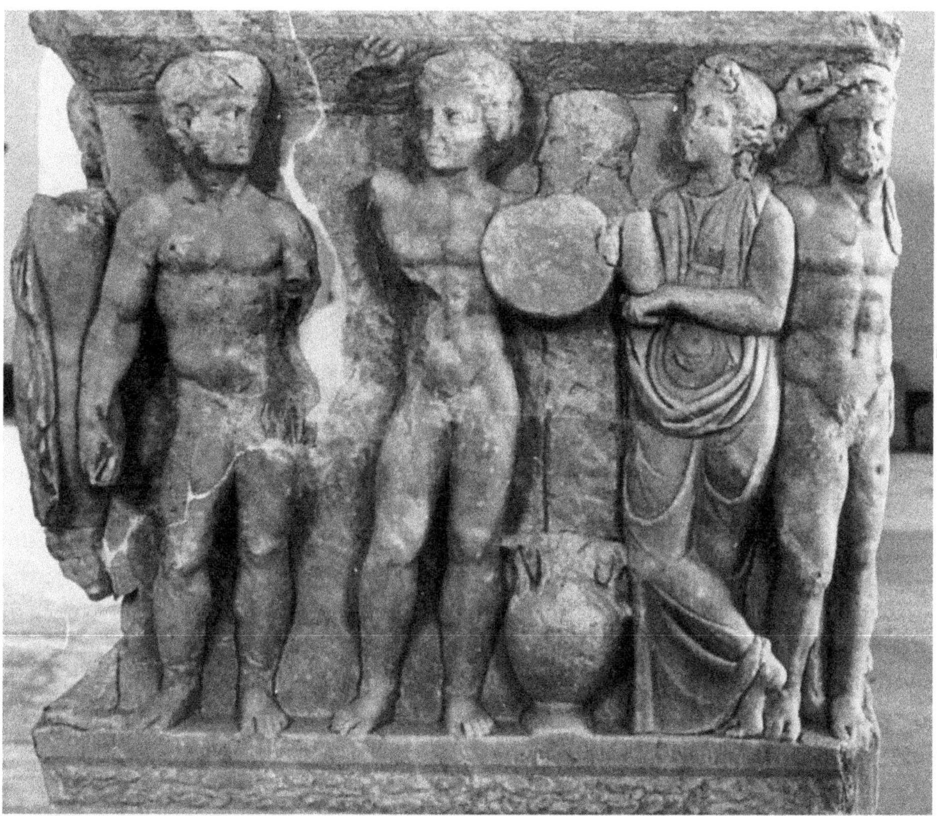

Figure 8.15: Apollonia (Libya), Museum. Right small side of an Attic Hippolytos sarcophagus showing Hippolytos as athlete with discus in hand. 3rd cent. A.D. After *ASR* IX, 1, 1, pl. 108, 2.

recent claims that the physical aspects of Greek *paideia* should never be underestimated in favour of its rhetorical and literary components.

The late Hippolytos (and, in part, Achilles) sarcophagi put particular value on the characterisation of the mythical protagonist as a member of a group of young men of the same age, among whose ranks the hero is only given minimal emphasis (Figures 8.1 a; 8.10; and 8.13). This points to a decidedly horizontal social organisation of young men through different age groups. On the most basic level, the upbringing of young men in groups, together with their age-mates, was a hallmark and a distinctive characteristic of Greek education and cultural identity. Dio Chrysostom (21, 4–6) for example, contrasts it with the upbringing of young boys by women and older eunuchs among the Persians, and the 'unnatural' forms of desire and social conduct – such as intercourse of boys with their mothers – that this breeds. More specifically, one could refer to Athenian epheby – which in the late Hellenistic and Roman periods continued to exist as an elitist educational institution – as a possible means of understanding this phenomenon. This is not to claim that the images on the sarcophagi can be explained simply in terms of a proven relationship to the socio-cultural reality of their time. Instead, it suggests that they and the institution of epheby are two cultural forms particularly suited to illuminate one another, and that the links between them must have been particularly strong.[115] At the beginning of their one-year training, the ephebes were organised into groups (*systremmata*) of varying sizes and put under the direction of a trainer. Their experience of ephebic education must have been characterised significantly by male bonding, camaraderie and a corporate spirit: the ephebes referred to each other as *adelphos* and *philos*, and the ephebic oath included a vow 'not to desert the comrade at whose side I stand.'[116] Even years after they had trained and studied together, former ephebes could still 'refer to each other as *synephebi*.'[117] Alongside the group aspect just discussed, other characteristics of the images – which will not be analysed in further detail here – find an echo in the institution and rituals of epheby: the *chlamys*, for example, worn by the youths (ephebes were characterised as 'chlamys wearers', *chlamydephoroi*[118]); the horses and the paradigm of the hunt; the sometimes fetishistic presentation of weapons; Achilles' cross-dressing and the scene of him taking up the shield and lance.[119] Greek epheby constitutes, in short, a space of cultural resonances within which these images in the eastern regions of the Empire, and in Athens itself in particular, were received.

Just how important it was to belong to a specific age group is also attested by the fact that this was regularly mentioned in inscriptions on the tombs of young men. In a funerary inscription from Ephesos, for example, quoted here in the translation by O. Van Nijf, the age group of the young Symmachos, who had died at 21, is evoked not only once, but twice:

"My father Herodes begot me, my mother Ammion bore (me), to whom I left sadness, having died. Three times seven years I had completed when I went to Hades, unmarried, without child, by name I was called Symmachos, *whom my age group of fellow ephebes* (synephebon) *mourned*, because I had to leave *techne* and *sophia* behind. I left the house of my parents empty, and I left behind

115 Ewald 2004, 242–247.

116 Pelekidis 1962, 110–113; Burckhardt 1996, 57–63. On Greek epheby in Hellenistic and Roman times, see Lattanzi 1968; *Der Neue Pauly* 3, 1997, 1071–1076 s.v. Ephebeia (H.-J. Gehrke); Albanidis 2000; Newby 2005, 169–201; and various contributions in Kah and Scholz 2004.

117 Albanidis 2000, 16.

118 Mitchell-Boyask 1999, 62–63 with fn. 20 (in reference to Theoc. 15,6 and IGRom 4,360.25).

119 Ewald 2004, 242–247.

things that I worshipped: the *gymnasion*, *techne*, and *the age group with whom I grew up....*"[120]

IV.

One could argue against the close reading of the Hippolytos sarcophagi given here that it puts a lot of pressure on the details of iconography. Yet, the results obtained on the micro-level of iconography are reflected on the macro-level of the overall distribution of themes on Attic sarcophagi.[121] The marginalisation of the female realm in the mythological reliefs of Attic sarcophagi, for example, is matched by the virtual absence of the kind of 'love myths' commonly found on the Roman examples, such as Selene and Endymion, Venus and Adonis, etc. Nonetheless, one must be careful when making generalisations from the results obtained here not to collapse 'forms of art' into 'forms of life', or to resort to cultural essentialism. What I have described is merely a specific visual discourse that emerged at a particular moment within a particular *Bildraum*. Other artistic genres, such as mosaics from Roman Greece, do not show a parallel development; in fact, an examination of Greek Achilles mosaics from the imperial period has yielded results that might seem to contradict the ones presented here.[122] But it is perhaps, after all, no accident that the discourse I have attempted to disentangle emerges in the specific context of the tomb rather than in the house: at the tomb, death's potential to disrupt the chain of cultural transmission, to collapse the symbolic order and to reveal its 'objective frailty'[123] was felt with particular urgency. As a result, the tomb, more than the house, was the place where a culture's basic tenets had to be constantly reaffirmed: in the Greek East, tombs were privileged spaces of social, not only individual, memory. Whoever entered them entered, quite literally, the world of heroes.

---

120 Van Nijf 2004, 214; my italics.

121 Ewald 2004.

122 Muth 1998, 184, notes that on the third and fourth century mosaics showing Achilles on Scyros, the hetero-erotic aspect of the myth (the love of Deidameia and the other daughters of Lycomedes for Achilles) is particularly emphasised. For the reasons mentioned above, I have doubts about short circuiting art forms and corresponding 'Mentalitätsunterschiede(n)', and the far reaching conclusions drawn from iconographic differences in the representations of the Achilles myth in East and West: if one were to approach the sarcophagi in the same manner (briefly mentioned there on p. 168 fn. 629), one would have to arrive at the opposite conclusions. For the methodological issues involved (such as the co-existence of seemingly contradictory discourses), see Foucault 1972, 3–39;149–165.

123 Kristeva 1982, 70.

Acknowledgements

I would like to thank Janet Huskinson and Jaś Elsner for their invitation to publish in this volume, their hospitality at Corpus Christi College, Oxford, and the open forum for discussion provided at the conference in 2006. I also wish to thank Dr. Ulrich Pohlmann (Munich) and Prof. Giovanni Salmeri (Pisa) for information on W. von Gloeden and the reception of the Hippolytos sarcophagus in Agrigento respectively. Versions of this contribution were given as a talk at the Scuola Normale Superiore in Pisa in 2005, and in the Department of Classics at the University of Chicago in 2007, and I have benefited from discussions there.

Bibliography

Albanidis, E. The Ephebia in the Ancient Hellenic World and its Role in the Making of Masculinity, in: *Making European Masculinities. Sport, Europe, Gender. The European Sports History Review* 2, edited by J. A. Mangan (London, 2000), 4–23.

Alexandridis, A. Individualisierung, Homogenisierung und Angst vor Vergänglichkeit. Weibliche Grab- und Ehrenstatuen der späten Republik und frühen Kaiserzeit, in: *Neue Fragen – neue Antworten*, edited by N. Sojc (Berlin, 2005), 111–124.

Amedick, R. Achilleus auf Skyros. Die Eikones des jüngeren Philostrat und die Ikonographie römischer Sarkophage. *Akten des Symposiums '125 Jahre Sarkophag-Corpus', Sarkophag-Studien 1* (Mainz, 1998), 52–60.

Ariès, P. *The Hour of Our Death* (New York, 1981).

Ault, B. A. and Nevett, L. C. (eds.). *Ancient Greek Houses and Households. Chronological, Regional, and Social Diversity* (Philadelphia, 2005).

Barringer, J. *The Hunt in Ancient Greece* (Baltimore, 2001).

Barthes, R. *Essais critiques* (Paris, 1964).

Belting, H. Aus dem Schatten des Todes. Bild und Körper in den Anfängen, in: *Der Tod in den Weltkulturen und Weltreligionen*, edited by C. von Barloewen (Frankfurt, 2000), 120–176.

Bergmann, B. The Roman House as Memory Theater: The House of the Tragic Poet in Pompeii. *Art Bulletin* 76 (1994), 225–256.

Bergmann, B. The pregnant moment: Tragic wives in the Roman interior, in: *Sexuality in Ancient Art*, edited by N. B. Kampen (Cambridge, 1996), 199–218.

Bremen, R. Van. *The Limits of Participation: Women and Civic Life in the Greek East in the Hellenistic and Roman Periods* (Amsterdam, 1996).

Brendel, O. J. *Prolegomena to the Study of Roman Art* (New Haven and London, 1979).

Burckhardt, L. A. *Bürger und Soldaten. Historia Einzelschriften* 101 (Stuttgart, 1996).

Buschor, E. *Frühgriechische Jünglinge* (Munich, 1950).

Cantoni, M. B. Le regole del vivere, le regole del morire: su alcuni stele attiche per donne morte di parto. *Revue archéologique*, 39 (2005) 27–53.

Cordier, P. *Nudités Romaines. Un problème d'histoire et d'anthropologie* (Paris, 2005).

Cormack, S. *The Space of Death in Roman Asia Minor. Wiener Forschungen zur Archäologie 6* (Vienna, 2004).

Crowther, N.B. Male 'Beauty' Contests in Greece. The Euandria and Euexia. *Antiquité classique.* 54 (1985) 285–291.
Demand, N. *Birth, Death and Motherhood in Classical Greece* (Baltimore and London, 1994).
Dunbabin, K. M. D. *The Roman Banquet. Images of Conviviality* (Cambridge, 2003).
Elsner, J. *Art and the Roman Viewer: The Transformation of Art from Paganism to Christianity* (Cambridge, 1995).
Elsner, J. *Roman Eyes. Visuality and Subjectivity in Art and Text* (Princeton and Oxford, 2007).
Ewald, B. C. Men, Muscle and Myth. Attic Sarcophagi in the Cultural Context of the Second Sophistic, in: *Paideia. The World of the Second Sophistic*, edited by B. Borg (Berlin, 2004), 229–275.
Ewald, B. C. Rollenbilder und Geschlechterverhältnis in der römischen Grabkunst, in: *Neue Fragen – neue Antworten*, edited by N. Sojc (Berlin, 2005), 55–73.
Ewald, B. C. Review of C.H. Hallett, The Roman Nude: Heroic Portrait Statuary 200 B.C.–A.D. 300. *Art Bulletin* 90. 2 (2008), 286–292.
Ewald, B. C. The Tomb as Heterotopia (Foucault's "hétérotopies"): Heroization, Ritual and Funerary Art in Roman Asia Minor (Review of Cormack 2004). *Journal of Roman Archaeology* 21 (2008), 624–634.
Fehr, B. *Bewegungsweisen und Verhaltensideale. Physiognomische Deutungsmöglichkeiten der Bewegungsdarstellung an griechischen Statuen des 5. und 4. Jhs. v. Chr.* (Bad Bramstedt, 1979).
Flämig, C., *Grabarchitektur der römischen Kaiserzeit in Griechenland.*(Rahden, 2007).
Fredrick, D. Beyond the Atrium to Ariadne: Erotic Painting and Visual Pleasure in the Roman House. *Classical Antiquity* 14 (1995), 266–288.
Fredrick, D. *The Roman Gaze: Vision, Power, and the Body* (Baltimore, 2002).
Friedlaender, L. *Sittengeschichte Roms* (Vienna, 1934).
Foucault, M. *The Archaeology of Knowledge* (New York, 1972).
Foucault, M. *The History of Sexuality I. Introduction* (New York, 1978).
Foucault, M. *The History of Sexuality III. The Care of the Self* (New York, 1986).
Giuliani, L. Achill-Sarkophage in Ost und West: Genese einer Ikonographie. *Jahrbuch der Berliner Museen* 31 (1989), 25–39.
Gleason, M. *Making Men. Sophists and Self-Presentation in Ancient Rome* (Princeton, New Jersey, 1995).
Gloeden, W. von. *Interventi di Joseph Beuys, Michelangelo Pistoletto, Andy Warhol* (Napoli, 1978).
Goethe, J.W. *Italian Journey.* Translated by W.H.Auden and E. Mayer (Harmondsworth, 1962).
Goethe, J. W. Philipp Hackert, in: *Kunsttheoretische Schriften und Übersetzungen. Schriften zur bildenden Kunst* I (Leipzig, 1985).
Goethe, J. W. *Italienische Reise. In Zusammenarbeit mit Christof Toenes herausgegeben von Andreas Beyer und Norbert Miller* (Munich, 1992).
Goette, H. R. Attische Klinen-Riefelsarkophage. *Athenische Mitteilungen* 106 (1991), 315–330.
Goldhill, S. The Erotic Eye. Visual Stimulation and Cultural Conflict, in: *Being Greek under Rome. Cultural Identity, the Second Sophistic and the Development of Empire*, edited by S. Goldhill (Cambridge, 2001), 154–194.
Gregorovius, F. *Siciliana. Wanderungen in Neapel und Sicilien* (Leipzig, 1861).
Hallett, C. H. *The Roman Nude: Heroic Portrait Statuary 200 B.C.–A.D. 300* (Oxford, 2005).

Hannestad, N. *Roman Art and Imperial Policy* (Aarhus, 1988).
Heinzelmann, M. (ed.). *Römischer Bestattungsbrauch und Beigabensitte in Rom, Norditalien und den Nordwestprovinzen von der späten Republik bis in die Kaiserzeit, Palilia* 8 (Wiesbaden, 2001).
Hemelrijk, E. A. *Matrona Docta. Educated Women in the Roman Élite from Cornelia to Julia Domna* (London and New York, 1999).
Hölscher, T. Die Geschichtsauffassung in der römischen Repräsentationskunst. *Jahrbuch des Deutschen Archäologischen Instituts* 95 (1980), 265–321.
Hölscher, T. *Aus der Frühzeit der Griechen: Körper-Räume-Mythen* (Tübingen, 1998).
Hölscher, T. *The Language of Images in Roman Art* (Cambridge, 2004).
Holzhausen, J. Eros und Aidos in Phaidras Monolog. *Akademie der Wissenschaften und der Literatur Mainz. Abhandlungen der Geistes- und sozialwissenschaftlichen Klasse* 1995, Nr. 1 (Stuttgart, 1995).
Hopkins, K. *Death and Renewal* (Cambridge, 1983).
Huskinson, J. Women and Learning. Gender and Identity in Scenes of Intellectual Life on Late Roman Sarcophagi, in: *Constructing Identities in Late Antiquity*, edited by R. Miles (London, 1999).
Iser, W. The Fictive and the Imaginary. Charting Literary Anthropology. (Baltimore,1993).
Kah, D. and P Scholz (eds). *Das Hellenistische Gynasion* (Berlin, 2004)
Koch, G. and Sichtermann, H. *Römische Sarkophage* (Munich, 1982).
Koch, G. Zum Klassizismus auf attischen Sarkophagen des 2. und 3. Jhs. n. Chr. *Praktika tou XII diethnous synedriou klasikes archaiologias*, vol. 3 (Athens, 1983 [1988]), 155–160.
Koch, G. *Sarkophage der römischen Kaiserzeit* (Darmstadt, 1993).
Koch, G. (ed.). *Grabeskunst der römischen Kaiserzeit* (Mainz, 1993).
Koenig, J. *Athletics and Literature in the Roman Empire* (Cambridge, 2005).
Koloski-Ostrow, A. Violent Stages in Two Pompeian Houses: Imperial Taste, Aristocratic Response and Messages of Male Control, in: *Naked Truths: Women, Sexuality, and Gender in Classical Art and Archaeology*, edited by A. Koloski-Ostrow and C. Lyons (London, 1997), 243–266.
Koortbojian, M. Review of Rogge 1995 in: *Bonner Jahrbücher* 198,1998, 557–564.
Kristeva, J. *Powers of Horror. An Essay on Abjection* (New York, 1982).
Lattanzi, E. *I Ritratti dei Cosmeti nel Museo Nazionale di Atene* (Roma, 1968).
Lewerentz, A. Zur Sepulkralsymbolik des Hippolytosmythos auf römischen Sarkophagen. *Boreas* 18 (1995), 111–130.
Linant de Bellefonds, P. *Sarcophages attiques de la nécropole de Tyr. Une étude iconographique* (Paris, 1985).
Lorenz, K. Zur Quadratur des Sofabildes, in: *Lebenswelten: Bilder und Räume in der römischen Stadt der Kaiserzeit, Palilia* 16, edited by R. Neudecker and P. Zanker (Wiesbaden, 2006), 205–221.
Lorenz, K. *Bilder machen Räume: Mythenbilder in pompeianischen Häusern* (Berlin, 2008).
Marchand, S. L. *Down from Olympus. Archaeology and Philhellenism in Germany, 1750–1970* (Princeton, 1996).
Martini, W. (ed.). *Die Jagd der Eliten in den Erinnerungskulturen von der Antike bis in die frühe Neuzeit* (Göttingen, 2000).
Mayer, E. *Rom is dort wo der Kaiser ist* (Mainz, 2002).
Mind and Body. Athletic Contests in Ancient Greece. National Archaeological Museum 15th May 1989–15th January 1990. Exhibition Catalogue (Athens, 1989).

Mitchell-Boyask, R. Euripides' Hippolytus and the Trials of Manhood (The Ephebia?), in: *Rites of Passage in Ancient Greece: Literature, Religion, Society*, edited by M. Padilla (Chicago, 1999), 47–63.

Morris, I. *Death Ritual and Social Structure in Classical Antiquity* (Cambridge, 1992).

Müller, F. G. J. M. The *So-Called Peleus and Thetis Sarcophagus in the Villa Albani* (Amsterdam, 1994).

Muth, S. *Leben im Raum – Erleben von Raum* (Heidelberg, 1998).

Newby, Z. *Greek Athletics in the Roman World: Victory and Virtue* (Oxford, 2005).

Nijf, O. Van. Local Heroes: Athletics, Festivals and Elite Self-Fashioning in the Roman East, in: *Being Greek under Rome. Cultural Identity, the Second Sophistic and the Development of Empire*, edited by S. Goldhill (Cambridge, 2001), 306–334.

Nijf, O. Van. Athletics, Andreia and the Askêsis-Culture in the Roman East, in: *Andreia. Studies in Manliness and Courage in Classical Antiquity*, edited by R. M. Rosen and I. Sluiter (Leiden and Boston, 2003), 263–286.

Nijf, O. Van. Athletics and *paideia:* Festivals and Physical Education in the World of the Second Sophistic, in: *Paideia: The World of the Second Sophistic*, edited by B. Borg (Berlin and New York, 2004), 203–228.

Nock, A. D. Sarcophagi and Symbolism. *American Journal of Archaeology* 50 (1946), 140–170.

Osterkamp, E. J. H. von Riedesel. La guida di Goethe in Sicilia, in: *Un paese indicibilmente bello. Il Viaggo in Italia di Goethe e il mito della Sicilia*, edited by A. Meier (Palermo, 1987) 194–213.

Painter, K. and Whitehouse D. The History of the Portland Vase, *Journal of Glass Studies* 32, 1990, 24–84.

Pandermalis, D. *Dion. The Archaeological Site and the Museum* (Athens, 1997).

Pélékidis, C. *Histoire de l'éphébie attique des origines à 31 avant Jésus-Christ* (Paris, 1962).

Perry, E. Iconography and the Dynamics of Patronage. A Sarcophagus from the Family of Herodes Atticus. *Hesperia* 70 (2001), 461–492.

Platt, V. Viewing, Desiring, Believing: Confronting the Divine in a Pompeian House. *Art History* 25 (2002), 87–112.

Pohlmann, U. *Wilhelm von Gloeden: Taormina* (Munich, Paris and London,1998).

Potts, A. *Flesh and the Ideal. Winckelmann and the Origins of Art History* (New Haven and London, 1994).

Raeck, W. *Modernisierte Mythen. Zum Umgang der Spätantike mit klassischen Bildthemen* (Stuttgart, 1992).

Rhomiopoulou, K. *Ellenoromaika glypta tou Ethnikou Archaiologikou Mouseiou* (Athens, 1997).

Ricoeur, P. *The Course of Recognition* (Harvard, 2005).

Riedesel, J. H. von. *Reise durch Sicilien und Großgriechenland* (Zürich, 1771).

Riedesel, J. H. von. *Travels through Sicily and that Part of Italy formerly called Magna Graecia. Translated from the German by J. R. Forster* (London, 1773).

Rodenwaldt, G. *Über den Stilwandel in der antoninischen Kunst., Abhandlungen der Berliner Akademie der Wissenschaften* Nr. 3 (Berlin, 1935).

Rodenwaldt, G. *Die Kunst der Antike. Hellas und Rom* (Berlin, 1927).

Rodenwaldt, G. The Transition to Late-Classical Art, in: *The Cambridge Ancient History XII. The Imperial Crisis and Recovery A.D. 193–324*, edited by S. A. Cook, F. A. Adcock, M. P. Charlesworth, and N. H. Baynes (Cambridge, 1939), 544–570.

Rodenwaldt, G. Archäologische Gesellschaft zu Berlin. Sitzung am 22. Januar 1940. *Jahrbuch des Deutschen Archäologischen Instituts* 55 (1940), 599–608.

Rodenwaldt, G. *Goethes Besuch im Museum Maffeianum zu Verona. 102. Winckelmannsprogramm der Archäologischen Gesellschaft zu Berlin* (Berlin, 1942).

Rudolf, E. *Attische Sarkophage aus Ephesos. Österreichische Akademie der Wissenschaften, Philosophisch-Historische Klasse, Denkschriften* 209 (Vienna, 1989).

Rudolf, E. *Der Sarkophag des Quintus Aemilius Aristides. Österreichische Akademie der Wissenschaften, Philosophisch-Historische Klasse, Denkschriften* 230 (Vienna, 1992).

Russenberger, C. Achill im Wohnraum der Kaiserzeit: Liebhaber, Krieger, Musterknabe. *Historische Abhandlungen des Seminars der Universität Bern* 18 (2002), 53–73.

Salmeri, G. La Sicilia nei libri di viaggio del Settecento tra letteratura e riscoperta della grecità. *Analecta Romana Instituti Danici* 28 (2001), 65–82.

Scanlon, T. F. *Eros and Greek Athletics* (Oxford, 2002).

Sennett, R. *Flesh and Stone. The Body and the City in Western Civilization* (New York and London, 2003).

Sissa, G. *Sex and Sensuality in the Ancient World* (New Haven and London, 2008).

Skinner, M. B. *Sexuality in Greek and Roman Culture* (Malden, MA, 2005).

Stam, R. and Burgoyne, R. and Flitterman-Lewis, S. *New Vocabularies in Film Semiotics. Structuralism, Post-Structuralism and Beyond* (London and New York, 1992).

Stähli, A. Der Körper, das Begehren, die Bilder, in: *Konstruktionen von Wirklichkeit*, edited by R. von den Hoff and S. Schmidt (Stuttgart, 2001), 197–209.

Swain, S. *Hellenism and Empire. Language, Classicism, and Power in the Greek World, AD 50–250* (Oxford, 1996).

Tanner, J. *The Invention of Art History in Ancient Greece* (Cambridge, 2006).

Trimble, J. F. Greek Myth, Gender, and Social Structure in a Roman House: Two Paintings of Achilles at Pompeii, in: *The Ancient Art of Emulation*, edited by E. K. Gazda (Michigan, 2002), 225–248.

Valladares, H. The Lover as Model Viewer: Gendered Dynamics in Propertius I.3, in: *Gendered Dynamics in Latin Love Poetry*, edited by R. Ancona and E. Greene (Baltimore, 2005), 206–242.

Vedder, U. Frauentod-Kriegertod im Spiegel der attischen Grabkunst des 4. Jhs. v. Chr. *Athenische Mitteilungen* 103 (1988), 161–191.

Wallace-Hadrill, A. Engendering the Roman House, in: *I Claudia. Women in Ancient Rome*, edited by D. Kleiner and S. Matheson (Austin, 1996), 104–115.

Walker Bynum, C. *The Resurrection of the Body in Western Christianity, 200–1336* (New York, 1995).

Warburg, A. *Der Bildatlas Mnemosyne*, edited by M. Warnke and C. Brink, in: *Gesammelte Schriften. Studienausgabe* Abt. II, Bd. II,1, edited by H. Bredekamp et al. (Berlin, 2000).

Ward-Perkins, J. B. The Hippolytus Sarcophagus from Trinquetaille. *Journal of Roman Studies* 46 (1956), 10–16.

Waugh, T. The Third Body. Patterns in the Construction of the Subject in Gay Male Narrative Film, in: *The Visual Culture Reader* (Second Edition), edited by N. Mirzoeff (London and New York, 2002), 636–653.

Whitmarsh, T. *The Second Sophistic* (Oxford, 2005)

Wiegartz, H. Kaiserzeitliche Relief – Sarkophage in der Nikolaoskirche, in: *Myra. Eine lykische Metropole in antiker und byzantinischer Zeit. Istanbulder Forschungen* 30, edited by J. Borchardt (1975), 161–251.

Winckelmann, J. J. *Monumenti antichi inediti* II (1767).

Wrede, H. *Senatorische Sarkophage Roms* (Mainz, 2001).

Zanker, P. Bürgerliche Selbstdarstellung am Grab im römischen Kaiserreich, in: *Die Römische Stadt im 2. Jh. n. Chr.*, *Xantener Berichte* 2, edited by H.-J. Schalles, H.von Hesberg and P. Zanker (1992), 339–358.

Zanker, P. *The Mask of Socrates. The Image of the Intellectual in Antiquity* (Berkeley, 1995).

Zanker, P. Bild-Räume und Betrachter im kaiserzeitlichen Rom, in: *Klassische Archäologie. Eine Einführung*, edited by A.H. Borbein, T. Hölscher and P. Zanker (Darmstadt, 2000), 205–226.

Zanker, P. *Un'arte per l'impero. Funzione e intenzione delle immagini nel mondo romano. A cura di Eugenio Polito* (Milan, 2002).

Zanker, P. Die mythologischen Sarkophagreliefs als Ausdruck eines neuen Gefühlskultes. Reden im Superlativ, in: *Sinn (in) der Antike*, edited by K.-J. Hölkeskamp et al. (Mainz, 2003) 335–355.

Zanker, P. and Ewald, B. C. *Mit Mythen leben. Die Bilderwelt der römischen Sarkophage* (München, 2004).

Žižek, S. *The Plague of Fantasies* (London and New York, 1997).

Zum Sterben schön. Alter, Totentanz und Sterbekunst von 1500 bis heute. Edited by A. von Hülsen-Esch and H. Westermann-Angerhausen in Zusammenarbeit mit Stefanie Knöll. Exhibition Catalogue. (Köln and Düsseldorf, 2006).

9. Image in Distress? The death of Meleager on Roman sarcophagi

Katharina Lorenz

The recent interest in Roman mythological sarcophagi has been fuelled by their potential to throw light on the ideas and ideals that governed Roman social life and behaviour. In particular, sarcophagi offer genuine insight into Roman approaches to Greek myths as a device for producing meanings related to the context of death, to rituals at the tomb, and to strategies of commemoration in general.[1] This perspective has been opened by moving away from approaches prevalent in the later nineteenth and most of the twentieth century, which concentrated on matters of iconography, the relationship between depicted scenes and literary or philosophical texts, and on how the reliefs on Roman sarcophagi could be used to provide insight into the Greek originals which they allegedly copied.[2]

The most pressing current questions for our understanding of mythological sarcophagi include asking how life and particular lives may be plotted not only against the narratives of myth but particularly against myths borrowed from a different culture: to what extent do mythological reliefs on sarcophagi represent a miraculous or supernatural narrative and to what extent can they be understood as representing or reflecting on the *everyday?* Can one establish the general devices by which either of these two areas of signification is generated within Roman images or signalled for Roman viewers, and can one trace the ways these characteristics play out in any one image? Can certain periods of production or themes within mythological imagery in Roman culture be distinguished by the way in which this relationship between the mythological and the everyday is defined or re-enacted?

Ruth Bielfeldt has recently demonstrated that one answer previously given to these questions, an answer opting for historical development as explanation,

1 Relevant studies include: Blome 1978; Giuliani 1989; Brilliant 1992; Grassinger 1994; Koortbojian 1995; Zanker 1999; Ewald 2004; Zanker and Ewald 2004; Bielfeldt 2005. The earliest work in this vein: Rodenwaldt 1935; Schefold 1961. See also Junker 2006 on the emergence of the genre and Ewald 2004 and Zanker 2005 on the distribution of mythological topics across the different periods of its use.

2 For recent overviews on sarcophagus scholarship, past and present: Koch and Sichtermann 1982, 6–20; Zanker and Ewald 2004, 24–27; Bielfeldt 2005, 16–22.

can no longer be sustained: in her study of the Orestes sarcophagi of the second century she demonstrated that even in the Hadrianic and Antonine periods myth is used as a paradigm, and thus refuted Peter Blome's hypothesis that a development can be traced from the sarcophagi of the earlier second century as purely enacting a classicistic revival of Greek myths to those of the late second and third century as being devoted to what he labels an *interpretatio Romana*, as geared towards an allegorical reading.[3]

In emphasising the connection between the mythological and the *everyday*, Bielfeldt pursues a line of enquiry first explored by Luca Giuliani who labelled the balance between elements pertaining to the world of factual or lived reality and to that of figurative imagery as an *allegoria apertis permixta.* Here Giuliani followed Quintillian's description of a similar device in rhetoric, in the *Institutio Oratoria:* 'Oratory often has use for allegory of this kind, but rarely in a pure state, for it is generally combined with words used literally. (...) The mixed form is always the commonest [in Cicero]: 'I thought that Milo would always have other storms and squalls to weather. I mean in the troubled waves of our public assemblies.' If he had not added 'of our public assemblies' it would have been a pure allegory; as it is, he has given us a mixture. In this type, we get both splendour from the imported words and intelligibility from those used literally.'[4]

The Quintilian passage vouches for the existence of this line of thought in Roman imperial discourse. But Bielfeldt puts the sarcophagi reliefs at the centre of a still wider discourse about the nature of the *image.* She argues against the explanatory models still current and popular in sarcophagus scholarship that stress *abstracted reading* or *visualised rhetoric,* because of their inability to account fully for the combined, intertwined transmission of myth and *interpretatio Romana* on any one Roman sarcophagus, in no matter what period.[5] In their stead, she introduces a model in which both allegorical paradigm and mythological narrative join forces in order to generate a narrative that is located within the actual myth as well as pointing beyond it.[6] In this proposal, Bielfeldt's discussion leads directly to some of the more prominent black holes of art historical scholarship – questions of the nature and character

3 Bielfeldt 2005, 20–22, 329–332; Blome 1992, 1071–1072.

4 Quintilian 8, 6, 47–48: *Habet usum talis allegoriae frequenter oratio, sed raro totius, plerumque apertis permixta est. (...) Illud commixtum frequentissimum: 'equidem ceteras tempestates et procellas in illis dumtaxat fluctibus contionum semper Miloni putavi esse subeundas.' Nisi adiecisset 'dumtaxat contionum', esset allegoria: nunc eam miscuit. Quo in genere et species ex arcessitis verbis venit et intellectus ex propriis* (transl. Russell 2001). Giuliani 1989, 38–39; cf. Bielfeldt 2005, esp. 277 nr. 810. Zanker refers to this phenomenon as an act of bridge-building for the viewer: Zanker and Ewald 2004, 69.

5 Bielfeldt 2005, 22. For concepts of *abstracted reading:* Koortbojian 1995, 9–15; Zanker and Ewald 2004, 52–54.

6 Bielfeld 2005, 277–278; 329–332.

of *the image*, of what *the image* is and what it wants.[7] And it touches upon the perennial dispute of *image* versus *text*, on the question of whether an image is descriptive or narrative, or whether it fluctuates between the two concepts, thus negating their heuristic value with regard to the realm of the visual.

Bielfeldt's findings raise a further set of questions with regard to the share of each of the two components – myth and *interpretatio Romana* – in generating visual narrative. In the following, my aim is to break up Bielfeldt's synthesis once more in order to explore how mythological narrative and paradigmatic content are balanced on the sarcophagi to form the distinct narrative voice of a sarcophagus relief. By addressing one particular sarcophagus and by comparing it to sarcophagi with similar decorations and to earlier representations of the particular myth depicted, I want to keep my sample set articulate while at the same time maintaining suitably wide axes of enquiry so as to tackle the Romans' appropriation of the *image* in the funerary realm in general.

The sarcophagus I choose, a piece now in Paris, presents events from the myth of Meleager.[8] This story is frequently told throughout the ancient world,[9] and it gains particular popularity on Roman sarcophagi from the early Antonine period onwards: it provides the storyline for about two hundred sarcophagi still extant today, the largest group of mythological sarcophagi devoted to one hero.[10] Meleager's story unfolds around the hunt for the Calydonian boar. One strand has him fall in love with Atalanta during the hunt.[11] He presents her with the animal's hide and infuriates his uncles whom Meleager kills in the ensuing quarrel. As revenge for this transgression against her brothers, Althaia, Meleager's mother, burns the log, which served as a token for his life, on a pyre, and he dies of a fever in his bed. Another narrative strand of the mythological nexus of Meleager stories does not include the love theme but in the aftermath of the hunt has Meleager being killed in the attempt to conquer Pleuron.[12]

A range of events from these narratives is selected for depiction: the most substantial group of sarcophagi – about seventy examples from workshops in Rome, ten found in the Western provinces and twenty-five from Attic

7 See Mitchell 2005, 28–56, esp. 48–56; cf. also Mitchell 1986, 95–115, extracting this position from his discussion of Lessing's Laocoon.
8 Paris, Musée du Louvre, Inv. Ma 539; see below note 16 (8).
9 *LIMC* VI 1992, s.v. *Meleagros* (Susan Woodford), esp. 433–436.
10 *ASR* III, 2, 221–311; Koch 1973; *ASR* XII,6, 6; Fittschen 1975; Brilliant 1986 145–165.
11 Ovid *Met.* 8, 267–546.
12 Homer *Iliad* 9, 529–599; Bacchylide*s*. 5,76–175; *Soph. mel.* (TrGF IV, 345–347); Apollodoros. 1,8,3; Paus. 10, 31, 3–4.

workshops[13] – focus on the hunt for the Calydonian boar. In these cases, Meleager kills the monstrous boar amidst a choice team of heroes. Sarcophagi from workshops in Rome also feature other episodes, including a meal made from the boar, now roasted, which appears on fifteen sarcophagus lids.[14] A second group of thirty-eight sarcophagi concentrate on the recovery of Meleager's body as part of the Pleuron episode on the main relief;[15] while a third group of ten sarcophagi display Meleager on his death-bed together with Atalanta, with six further fragments indicating that this episode was more popular than is reflected by the remaining corpus.[16]

---

13 *ASR* XII,6, 85–106, 138–148; *LIMC* VI, 1992, s.v. *Meleagros* (Susan Woodford) no. 110–130.

14 *ASR* XII,6, 125–129.

15 *ASR* XII,6, 106–118; *LIMC* VI, 1992, s.v. *Meleagros* no. 144–149.

16 *ASR* XII,6, 38–47. The sarcophagi belonging to this group:
(1) Ostia, Museo Archeologico 101; from Ostia. 160. L 1.37 H 0.40 D 0.36. *ASR* III, 2, no. 282 fig. 575; *ASR* XII,6, no. 112 pl. 96a; *LIMC* VI, 1992, s.v. *Meleagros* no. 150. (Figure 9.5).
(2) Paris, Musée du Louvre Ma 654. 160. *ASR* III, 2, no. 279 pl. 93; *ASR* XII,6, no. 113 pl. 95a. (Figure 9.1).
(3) Rome, Villa Albani, Galleria del Canopo. 170. L 1.89 H 0.43. *ASR* III, 2, no. 278 pl. 92; *ASR* XII,6, no. 114, fig. 8; *LIMC* VI, 1992, s.v. *Meleagros* no. 153.
(4) Rome, Museo Capitolino 623. 170. L 1.95 H 0.385. *ASR* III, 2, no. 281 pl. 93; *ASR* XII,6, no. 120 pl. 96c. 98–101; *LIMC* VI, 1992, s.v. *Meleagros* no. 151. (Figure 9.6).
(5) Milan, Torno Collection. 170/80. L 2.20 H 0.65. *ASR* III,2, no. 282 pl. 93; *ASR* XII,6, no. 117 pl. 102a; *LIMC* VI, 1992, s.v. *Meleagros* no. 152.
(6) Rome, Studio Canova. 180. L 0.48 H 0.55. *ASR* III, 2, no. 280 pl. 92; *ASR* XII,6, no. 115 pl. 95b.
(7) Wilton House, Wiltshire, from Rome. 180. L 2.15 H 0.65. *ASR* III, 2, no. 275 pl. 89; *ASR* XII,6, no. 122 pl. 103a,104. 105. 113 e. f; *LIMC* VI, 1992, s.v. *Meleagros* no. 154.
(8) Paris, Musée du Louvre, Inv. Ma 539. 190. L 2.05 H 0.74 D 0.98. *ASR* III, 2, no. 277 pl. 91; *ASR* XII,6, 38–47, 120–1, no. 116, pl. 103b. 106–11. 113a.b; Baratte-Metzger 1985, 97–99 no. 37; *LIMC* VI, 1992, s.v. *Meleagros* no. 155; Zanker and Ewald 2004, 68–75; 351–352 fig. 44. 51. 62.
(9) Castel Gandolfo, Villa Barberini, once Vatican. Around 230. L 2.06 H 0.47. *ASR* III, 2, no. 276 pl. 90; *ASR* XII,6, no. 121 pl. 96d. 112. (Figure 9.7).
(10) Florence, Museo Archeologico 1911. *ASR* XII,6, no. 118 pl. 102b.c; *LIMC* VI, 1992, s.v. *Meleagros* no. 156.
(11) Rome, S. Giovanni in Laterano. *ASR* XII,6, no. 123.
(12) Rome, Palazzo Giustiniani, lost. *ASR* XII,6, no. 124 pl. 113 g.
(13) Side panel, lost, once Rome, Villa Borghese. *ASR* III, 2, no. 225b pl. 77; *ASR* XII,6, no. 125 fig. 9.
(14) Side panels, Vatican. *ASR* XII,6, no. 126 pl. 113c.d.
(15) Ostia. *ASR* XII,6, no. 196. 197.
(16) Lost, once Rome,Villa Strozzi. *ASR* XII,6, no. 65 pl. 79 g;
(17) Lost. 170/80. *ASR* XII,6, no. 119 pl. 96b.

These last two episodes – in contrast to the other events from the story, such as the boar killing – highlight the sarcophagus' funerary function through its mythical subject-matter and thus place it directly in the centre of the contested ground between *the mythological* and *the everyday.* Sarcophagi that display these episodes represent a quintessential *image in distress*, torn between providing an allegorical layer of mythical reflection and documenting real-life situations. And they do so by playing out the funerary theme not outside the human realm, as do the hunting sarcophagi where death is observed as being dealt to animals, but within the human realm proper.

The depictions of these two mythological episodes are constructed in clear homology to the experiential framework within which the reliefs were to be viewed: that of death. Each of them puts particular emphasis on funerary practices, mourning and laying-out of the dead body, thus facilitating an *interpretatio Romana* by reflecting in a mythological frame what scholars have called the theme of *Vita Romana*, an idealised version of Roman everyday life.[17] The relief on the Paris sarcophagus is an example of the third group showing Meleager on his death-bed. And it is this focus on funerary activities, that reflect the actual function of the sarcophagus in its decoration, which renders the Paris coffin an excellent object of study to explore the balancing of mythological narrative and paradigmatic content.

Moreover, the sarcophagus is dated to 190, towards the end of the forty-year period in which this particular episode was popular, just after the peak of the popularity of mythological sarcophagi around 160, a time which marks the watershed between classicistic revival and *interpretatio Romana,* according to Blome's postulate. This era is characterised by a varied output of mythological themes in the funerary sphere, just before a decline in interest and a marked streamlining of the visual repertoire can be observed.[18] The iconography of the hunt for the Calydonian boar has a much longer life span which reaches from the middle of the second century to the very end of the third.[19] The Paris image of Meleager on his death-bed serves then as a good visual example for a period in which the appropriation of myth is particularly diverse and wide-spread, but which at the same time heralds the end of the most intensive use of myths on sarcophagi.

17 cf. *ASR* I, 3.
18 Zanker and Ewald 2004, esp. 245–247.
19 *ASR* XII,6, 81.

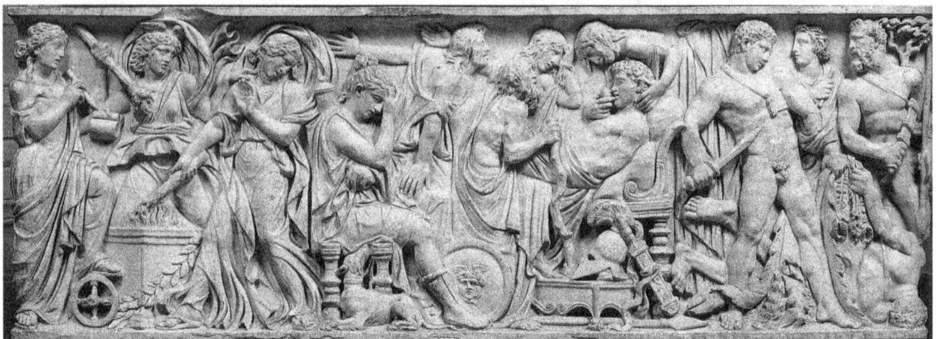

Figure 9.1: Meleager death-bed sarcophagus. Paris, Musée du Louvre MA 654. Photograph: Munich, Museum für Abgüsse Klassischer Bildwerke, Photothek.

Closing in on myth: an issue of image and text

The Meleager sarcophagus in the Louvre (Figure 9.1) features thirteen characters on the front, arranged in a larger central group and two smaller ones to its sides: in the centre, Meleager appears on his death-bed, surrounded by family members and by Atalanta; on the right, Meleager fights his uncles; and on the left, Meleager's mother, Althaia, is depicted at an altar, accompanied by two figures who bear traits of the Moirai and the Erinyes.[20]

One step towards assessing the casket's design and the ways in which it conveys the myth is to compare it with the most prominent account of the story, provided by Ovid in his *Metamorphoses*, largely borrowed it is thought from a no-longer extant tragedy by Euripides.[21] In Ovid, after the killing of the Calydonian boar Meleager courts Atalanta with the hide, but when this is seized by his uncles, Plexippus and Toxeus, he slaughters them in his rage; their sister Althaia, distraught with grief for her brothers and in revenge determined his fate by casting the brand into the fire, at which point Meleager succumbs to fever and dies.

The sarcophagus and Ovid's account share a range of similarities: the relief carving features Althaia burning a piece of wood; also, Meleager is depicted on his deathbed, surrounded by mourning attendants; and there is an argument involving a boar hide on display which seems to have fatal results. And yet, a close inspection also uncovers several differences between the account in the text and what is on display on the sarcophagus, and these differences seem to be anything but accidental.

Firstly, the frieze does not showcase the same narrative sequencing that structures the text: whether one tries to 'read' the sequence from left to right, or

20 Paris, Musée du Louvre; see above note 16 (8).

21 Ovid *Met.* 8, 267–546.

from right to left, there remain constant inconsistencies in comparison to the sequence in Ovid. Starting from the left, we first encounter the scene of Althaia and two other women around the altar. Meleager's mother puts the log in the fire and so seals her son's fate. This is the perfect prequel for what is then to follow further to the right: the depiction of Meleager's death amidst his family.

After that, however, the sequence as prefigured by the text, and a chronological unfolding of the myth, is broken: the third scene on the relief shows the killing of the Thestiadai, which is visualised as if in progress, with one uncle fighting against Meleager and the other already dead on the ground, still clinging to the boar's hide in Meleager's hands. This episode presents the cause of the scene on the far left and thus must have taken place before it. At the same time, if we attempt to 'read' the frieze from right to left, the killing of the uncles does indeed precede Meleager's funeral and is one of its causes. But the transition from the death-bed scene to Althaia at the altar, which is the immediate cause of Meleager's death, also constitutes a divergence from the narrative sequence of Ovid's text and the myth as diachronically related.

Secondly, the relief features a range of objects which are not attested in any textual versions of the myth: Althaia burns the log not in a pyre but on an altar which gives the procedure a more institutionalised, Roman, religious flavour. And in the scene of the fight against the Thestiadai, Meleager is about to attack them with a sword. According to Ovid, this attack took place with a spear. Given that Meleager is a hunter and the murder happens at the scene of the hunt, in an act of unreflective fury on Meleager's part, a spear is in fact the more plausible weapon. Yet, it is only the uncle still standing who carries a spear along with his sword. This deviation with regard to equipment recurs in the central scene where next to Meleager's bed, alongside the spear, appear a shield with a gorgon's head, a helmet and a sword.

Packaging myth: Meleager and Atalanta

In the second step of this enquiry, I will assess the discrepancies that emerge from the comparison of text and image. What is of particular interest is the way in which Meleager's attributes, which might be thought *descriptive* elements within the imagery, impact on the *narrative* on display. The weapons depicted around Meleager are more characteristic of a warrior than of a hunter. But since they appear on a range of other reliefs from the death-bed group,[22] they can be taken as a defining visual attribute for Meleager in the scenes of his death. These

22 Ostia, Museo Archeologico 101; see above note 16 (1); Rome, Museo Capitolino 623; see above note 16 (4); Milan, Torno Collection see above note 16 (5); Wilton House, Wiltshire; see above note 16 (7).

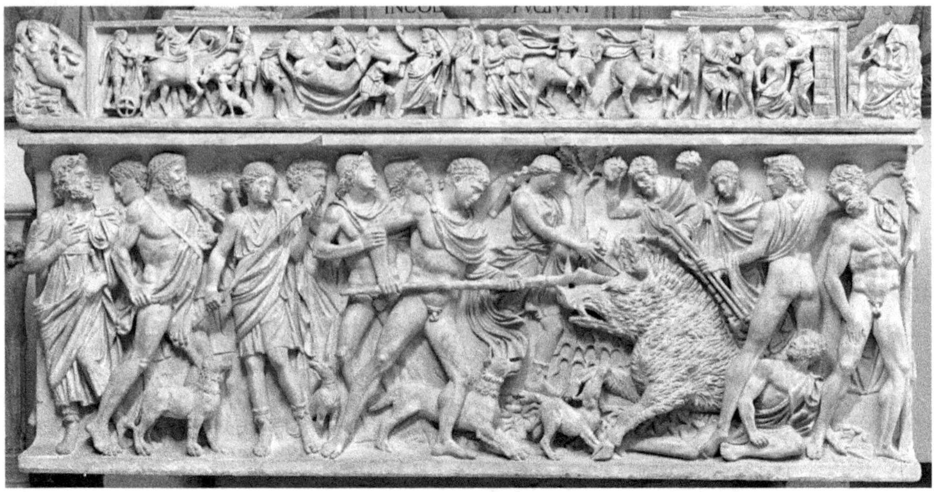

Figure 9.2: Calydonian hunt sarcophagus. Rome, Palazzo Doria.
Photograph: DAIR 1971.1474.

attributes distinguish the group of sarcophagi showing Meleager's death from other depictions of the hero: on the sarcophagi that depict the Calydonian hunt in full action Meleager is never shown using any weapon other than his spear, and never even wears a sword strap around his upper body (Figure 9.2).[23] The same is true for all his fellow hunters.[24]

The only scenes which feature Meleager with the weapons of a warrior are the images of the battle of Pleuron, a version of the Meleager story which is used in Homer's *Iliad* to lure Achilles back into battle.[25] It tells how after the hunt for the Calydonian Boar, Artemis' wrath has still not abated, and she incites a quarrel over the spoils of the hunt between the Aitolians based at Calydon and the Curetes from Pleuron. In the resulting war, Meleager kills his

23 The only exception is a relief in St. Peter in Rome: Rome, S. Pietro in Vaticano. H 0.70 L 2.06 D 0.60. 180/90. *ASR* XII,6, no. 146 pl. 121.

24 An exception form two bearded characters which appear in many of those hunting sarcophagi classified as the main group of the Calydonian boar hunt by Guntram Koch, for example the one in Palazzo Doria (Rome, Palazzo Doria. ca. 180/90. L 2.47 H 0.94 D 1.10. *ASR* III, 2, no. 231 pl. 79; *ASR* XII,6, no. 8 pl. 13c.): Carl Robert interpreted the one on the left who carries a double axe into the hunt as the death demon Orcus: *ASR* III, 2, 273–275; *ASR* XII,6, 8; Bernard Andreae suggested Ankaios / Hercules, *ASR* XII,6, 8.

25 Homer *Iliad*. 9, 529–599. Robert in *ASR* III, 2, 275–276 who presumes the version without Atalanta to be older than the other one; *ASR* XII,6, 29; LIMC VI.1, 1992, s.v. *Meleagros* 414–415. For example: Rome, Vatican, Museo Gregoriano Profano 3098. L 0.665 H 0.28. Mid-Antonine period. *ASR* III, 2, 284 pl. 94; *ASR* XII,6, 113 no. 85 pl. 80c; Rome, Villa Doria Pamphili. L 2.05 H 0.70. 190/200. *ASR* III, 2, 283 pl. 94. *ASR* XII,6, no. 84 pl. 89a.

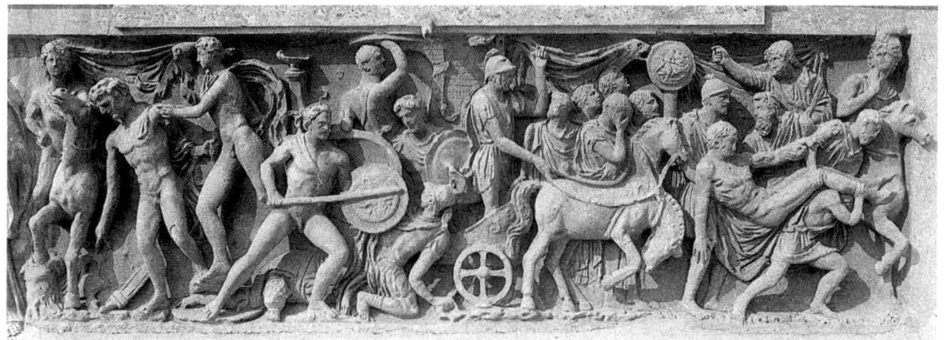

Figure 9.3: Meleager recovery sarcophagus. Rome, Villa Doria Pamphili. Photograph: DAIR 8336.

uncles. The curse his mother subsequently puts on him makes him avoid further fighting, but when his city is threatened, he enters the battle again and is then killed by Apollo.[26]

With regard to these visual treatments of the Pleuron episode, the choice of armour on the death-bed sarcophagus in Paris could be seen as pointing towards that particular strand of the myth in which Meleager excels as a soldier. And indeed, this seems to be the focus of the so-called 'recovery sarcophagi' which feature the Pleuron episode (as on a relief now in the Villa Doria Pamphili (Figure 9.3).[27] But what still needs to be explained is why one would want to employ one mythological recension of the Meleager story in the context of a quite different mythological narrative. Within a death-bed scene in which Atalanta features prominently, the sarcophagus alludes to the attack on Pleuron and Meleager's subsequent death in a version of the myth which is characterised by her absence.

One explanation is that the formal template for the scenes of Meleager's death did not come primarily from versions of the Pleuron episode but from those of the death of Patroclus.[28] In a process Michael Koortbojian has labelled '*intermingling*',[29] a composition featuring different stages in the life of a warrior

26 According to the versions in the Minyas and Hesiod: Paus 10, 31.3. Bacchylides has Althaia burn the log and thus cause his death: Bacchylides 5, 138–150. Apollodoros also mentions that she then kills herself: Apollod. 1,8.3.

27 For the sarcophagus see above note 15. On the relief, the hero's hunting prowess is alluded to by the decoration on a shield that shows him advancing against the boar.

28 Giuliani 1989, 35–37. The argument is based on: Berlin, Antikenmuseum 1982.1. L 2.01 H 0.55 D 0.48. 160. Koch 1983; Giuliani 1989; *ASR* XII, 1. As comparison: Ostia, Museum. L 2.01 H 0.557 D 0.485. 160. Gallina 1993; *ASR* XII, 1, 204–205 no. 27 pl. 28–31; Zanker and Ewald 2004, 283–285. Figure 2.1.

29 Koortbojian 1995, 58–59. For similar strategies in the shaping of different stages of life for the Orestes iconography see Bielfeldt 2005, 265–270.

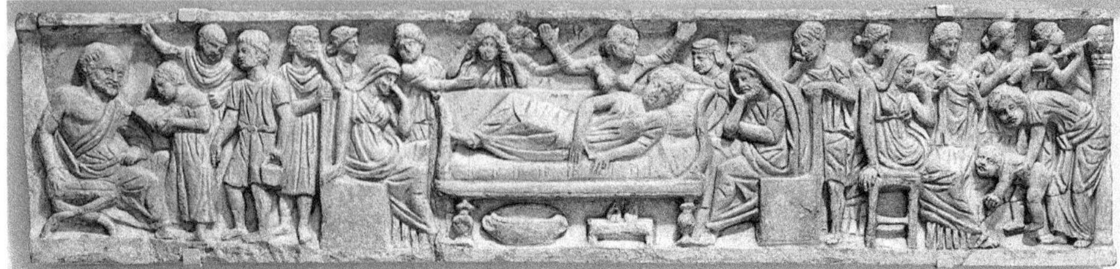

Figure 9.4: Death-bed sarcophagus. Paris, Musée du Louvre MA 319. Photograph: Museum (L59).

is appropriated for the death-bed scenes and as a visual template for the story of Meleager, a myth which principally deals with a hunter. The result, the mixture of the hunt and warfare directed towards generating a strong impression of the deceased's *virtus*, can best be compared to the content of the *Vita Romana* lion hunt sarcophagi which become popular from the middle of the third century.[30] But the presentation on the death-bed also ties in with another visual tradition – the depiction of female children or mothers on the death-bed, surrounded by their family, a topic particularly popular on *Vita Romana* sarcophagi of the mid-Antonine period (Figure 9.4).[31] In their combination, these different visual layers allude to various stages in the life of the hero, thus turning the frieze also into a biographical representation.[32]

But the blend of two central areas of Roman male virtue, the hunt and war, within a family context opens up another question: why choose the theme of Meleager to present the different life stages of a courageous fighter amidst his family, when he is a mythological hero with a relationship to his family that is ambiguous, to say the least? One might want to see in this an example of the Romans' great ability to select certain convenient elements of a story without taking too much notice of the potential conflict with the underlying myth that

30 *ASR* I, 2, 42–48; Andreae 1985; cf. the earliest lion hunt sarcophagus in Paris: Paris, Louvre 1808; from the Borghese Collection. L 2.28 H 0.58. 230–240. ASR I 2, 65 pl. 1.3; Rodenwaldt 1936, 96–97 pl. 1,3; *ASR* I, 2, no. 65 pl. 24–30; Koch and Sichtermann 1982, 93–94 pl. 82; and: Rome, Palazzo Mattei II. L 2.14 H 1.33. 250. *ASR* I, 2, no. 133 pl. 13,1; 14,3–9; 16,1–5.

31 Toynbee 1971/1982, 44 fig. 10; *ASR* I,4, 72–73; Huskinson 1996, 95–99, 101–104; George 2000, 202–205; Dimas 1998. For example: Paris, Louvre Ma 319; from Rome, Collection Della Valle. First quarter third century. L 157 H 38 T 7. *ASR* I,4, no. 115 pl. 56, 1.2. I am using the term *Vita Romana* here in line with Reinsberg's study (*ASR* I,3), in order to highlight these scenes, not as documents of how life in the real looked but as another form of cultural construct.

32 On biographical sarcophagi: Geyer 1978; Kampen 1981; Whitehead 1986. Reinsberg in *ASR* I, 3, 170–173 with a critical discussion of the notion of biographical depiction. For similar strategies in the depiction of Orestes on sarcophagi see Bielfeldt 2005, 265–270.

might be implied.[33] But in the case of the Paris sarcophagus, another explanation is possible. The story of Meleager offers a feature that is not provided by other mythological narratives which could serve aspects of military *virtus* and family relations much better; this is the provision of a loving and equally formidable female consort, Atalanta, who in the imperial period is employed as a metaphor for a physically beautiful and loyal wife.[34] Hence the heroic and military implications of the Pleuron recensions of Meleager's death are necessarily intermingled with the personal qualities of the love-narrative of Meleager's desire, which centres on Atalanta.

In contrast to Meleager who appears with attributes that signal different meanings and intimations, the presentation of Atalanta is consistent within all the different groups of sarcophagi devoted to episodes from the story of Meleager: she appears in the guise of the goddess Artemis.

This close connection to the outdoors might then explain the piece of rock visible on the Paris sarcophagus between her leg and the stool on which she sits – a rather surprising element given that the scene is set indoors.[35] The importance of Atalanta is emphasised further by another feature: she is the tallest figure on the frieze. If she stood up, she would burst through the upper edge of the relief; in this, she is only matched by the figure of Meleager fighting on the far right who – if standing properly upright – would have a similar effect. Yet, Atalanta does not appear at the physical centre of the relief. That is marked by the shield adorned with the gorgon's head, which leans behind her right leg. But because she interacts so closely with this reference point, and literally frames it, she becomes the extended centre of the frieze, once more directing the focus towards the right of the relief.

A further feature clearly emphasises Atalanta's role in this scene, something unmatched by the other characters on the frieze. This is the way her face is shown: she is depicted as struck by grief, burying her face in her right hand. This is visualised through a rather odd, unnatural motif: she covers the left part of her face with her right hand. This awkward gesture means that the viewers of the sarcophagus have an excellent snapshot of her face, which would not have been offered if she had – more naturally – covered the right side of her face as she does on some of the other sarcophagi in this group:[36] in the Paris

33 Paul Zanker has demonstrated this in his study on the depiction of Hippolytus on Roman sarcophagi: Zanker 1999; see also Bielfeldt 2005, 25–27, 278 for similar problems with regard to the figure of Orestes.

34 *CIL* VI, 379 65. Hesberg and Tonn 1983, 185; Zanker and Ewald 2004, 72–74.

35 For an interpretation of the rock as a mistake by the artist who copied from a model book: *ASR* XII,6, 39–40, 121; Ewald, in Zanker and Ewald 2004, 352.

36 On the two early pieces in Ostia and Milan, Atalanta covers her face completely: Ostia, Museo Archeologico 101; see above note 16 (1); Milan, Torno Collection see above note 16 (5).

sarcophagus the shielding arm works almost like a frame, highlighting her facial features.

In short, the figure of Atalanta is here designed to attract the gaze, a function underlined by the fact that her dog is also looking up towards her and that the shield with the gorgoneion, the epitome of gaze-attracting devices, is positioned directly next to her.[37] Atalanta herself, however, is not actively seeking to establish contact. The way in which she shuts herself off from the action on the frieze opens her to the audience. She is not simply a figure which can offer consolation to a mourning female viewer, which is how she has been principally interpreted.[38] Rather, she functions as a gateway into the image as a whole, and the fact that she is taller than the space provided for by the relief is only another supporting element of her relation to the sphere outside the image.

One final feature underlines Atalanta's central role in the frieze: she occupies the topmost layer of the relief sculpture, the one closest to the world of the viewers. Towards the right, she dominates a hierarchy of layers of relief that reaches down to the fighting uncle on the very right. He is partly covered by the body of his dead brother, in front of which Meleager is positioned, thus dominating the relief arrangement of this scene. In the central scene, in which Atalanta presents the dominating figure, Meleager's bed overlaps the fighting Meleager, thus positioning the death-bed scene hierarchically above that on the right and turning Atalanta into the figure controlling the whole frieze towards her right. Towards the left of Atalanta, the arrangement is less clear-cut. The huntress overlaps in parts with Althaia, but not wholly: they appear to share a relief plane, and this could explain the need for the deeply drilled, vertical ridge that separates their garments from each other. And while the figure with the torch is located on a plane further to the rear, the Moira on the far left could once more occupy the same relief layer as Althaia and Atalanta.

Personalising myth: Atalanta as a trigger for modular narrative

The staggered arrangement that characterises the frieze in parts supports a modular system of representation, which is facilitated by the sarcophagus' existence as a material object. The result is a very specific take on the story: Atalanta serves as the hook for the construction of this visual and thematic system, based on the compositional emphasis her figure receives. Appropriating Atalanta as a gateway figure and as narrative voice has an important effect on viewing the sarcophagus. She provides a distinctly female perspective on

37 On the Gorgo as shield-device Howe 1954. On the meaning of gorgoneia more generally: Mack 2002, esp. 575–576, 596–598; Hedreen 2007, 221–227.

38 Zanker and Ewald 2004, 68–75, esp. 69–70.

Meleager's life, and on the display of male virtues; and it is this which explains the appropriation of a range of different visual templates in order to present this particular myth. In the *conclamatio* scene around the death-bed, this function of Atalanta does not change the basic descriptive content: a young man, associated with the trade of war and the hunt by means of his weapons, is dying. It is a death which occurs prematurely, to judge by the grief of old and young who surround him.[39] This could be understood as a straightforward *allegoria apertis permixta*, an addition of elements which directly refer to the reality existing outside the image – of bereavement and a corpse newly buried inside the sarcophagus – in order to aid the understanding of the myth. But Atalanta adds two further layers of meaning: firstly, she triggers our understanding that this is not a *Vita Romana* scene but a mythological one. She is the only figure in the *conclamatio* scene characterised by features which locate her outside the normal – her hunting attire, the rock and the dog at her feet, and the gorgon-shield. With this baggage of narrative detail, she vouches for the mythological pedigree of the rest of the scene.

And yet, because she has become part of this descriptive setting and also sports features – her hair and the stool on which she sits – that belong to the sphere of the normal, the differentiation between the mythological sphere and the *everyday* world is blurred. Viewers are invited into the picture by a mythological character, who clearly marks the scene as one located in the mythological world of dreams and wishes; but what they are to encounter with the help of her gateway figure is actually not that different from the real world outside the image. Atalanta's presence both creates the grounds for a mythological interpretation, while at the same time it also questions its very existence since the myth reflects the actualities of real-life mourning.

Secondly, with Atalanta as starting point for the experience of the central scene, the grief of the whole extended family – of siblings, nurse and teacher – which takes up most of the space in that scene, is clearly channelled and subordinated to the sorrow of the wife and lover. Her exposed position highlights that – while death is a family affair and orchestrated by poignant collective grief – the real, perennial grief, so intense that it cannot be part of the general mourning, is that of the faithful partner.

39 cf. *conclamatio* scenes on sarcophagi depicting the *Vita Romana: ASR* I,4, 72–74, 79–81; George 2000, 202–205. For example: Child's sarcophagus, Agrigento, Museo Regionale. 120–130. L 90 H 39 T 41. *ASR* I,4, no. 2 pl. 53.1–3. Child's sarcophagus, London, British Museum GR 1805.7–3.144; from Rome, Palazzo Capranica. Mid-Antonine period. L 105 H 36. *ASR* I,4, no. 60 pl. 70, 2.4. Sarcophagus, Rome, Museo Torlonia 414; from Via Portuense. Around 200. L 157 H 36. *ASR* I,4, no. 198 pl. 54, 1–3. Sarcophagus, Paris, Louvre Ma 319; from Rome, Collection Della Valle. First quarter third century. L 157 H 38 T 7. *ASR* I,4, no. 115 pl. 56, 1.2.

Atalanta's impact as a focalising figure for the scene on the right is even greater. Experienced through her perspective, Meleager's fight is removed from the potential ethical ambivalence that the killing of family members and the merciless treatment of the dead could convey. Meleager is not an over-emotionalised hero, blinded by love and acting in the heat of the moment, nor is he simply a select image of generic virtue and fighting prowess. From this viewpoint, Meleager is the man who protects the claims of his lover and wife, and fights for them with all his might. He is turned into a visual *exemplum* of deep and unconditional marital love.

Yet, taking Atalanta's point of view in this way also has a destabilising effect on the categories of the narrative and the descriptive,[40] and on the clear differentiation of what belongs to the myth and what is part of an *allegoria apertis permixta*. On the one hand, the towering size of Atalanta in the central scene and of Meleager in the scene on the right, and the elements of the *non-normal* mythology which characterise them (such as Atalanta's attire and, in the case of Meleager, the arrangement around a boar hide and a dead body), establish clear links between them across the two scenes. They support each other in their mythological roles and provide a narrative framework for the *conclamatio* scene around the death-bed which otherwise veers towards the non-mythological. These two presentations of Atalanta and Meleager have the potential to turn description into mythological narrative, and to elevate the suffering on display to a heroic level.

On the other hand, as the fighting Meleager on the right becomes a model of virtue through the perspective of Atalanta, he is turned into a descriptive attribute for what is displayed in the centre of the frieze, the mourning of a formidable fighter. He is exploited specifically in this way to explain the state of sorrow in which Atalanta is depicted, that is because she was loyally devoted to her partner who went so far as killing members of his own family to secure her claim to the boar's hide. In this way, Meleager's mythological pedigree is once more dissolved in order to be used as an explanation for the depth of grief felt by the huntress and by the extended family. And within this context, the fact that Meleager is marching forward not with a spear – as one would expect in an unplanned assault by a hunter, and as indeed Ovid reports it – but with a sword, the Romans' close combat weapon of choice, only supports the *normative* function of his character.

Atalanta's appearance, which is compositionally closely linked to the fighting Meleager on the far right, also revives the scene where she is present at the fight that is depicted on the earliest version of Meleager's death on Roman

40 These categories are here employed as defined by Luca Giuliani: Giuliani 2003, 35, 283, 285–86 (*narrative*); 36, 222–24 (*descriptive*).

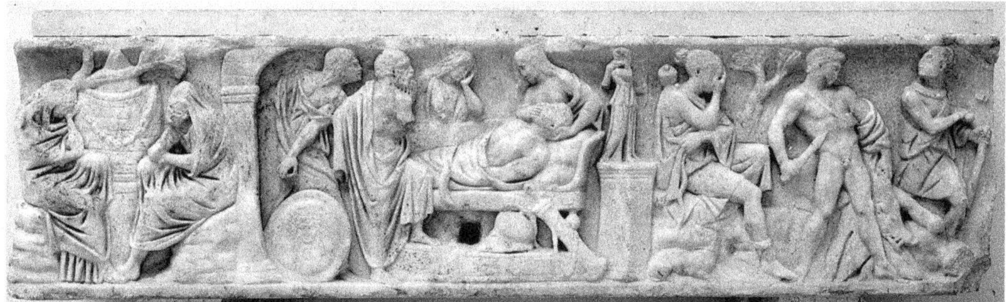

Figure 9.5: Meleager death-bed sarcophagus. Ostia, Museo Archeologico 101. Photograph: DAIR 1967.1068.

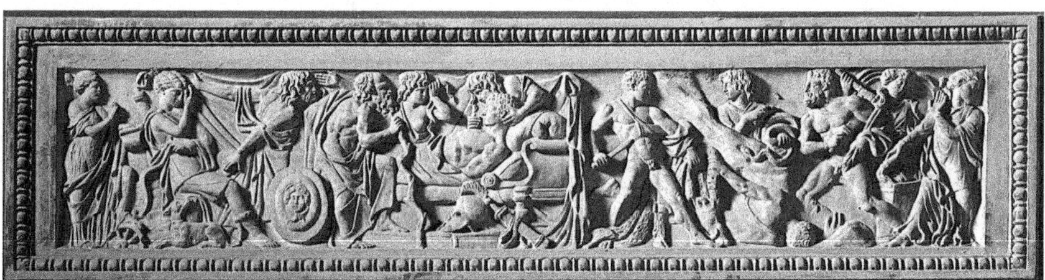

Figure 9.6: Meleager death-bed sarcophagus. Rome, Museo Capitolino 623. Photograph: DAIR 3160.

sarcophagi (Figure 9.5).[41] And it also bears reference to the scene of the loving get-together between Meleager and Atalanta that can be found on the sarcophagus depicting the Calydonian hunt in Museo Capitolino.[42] In this context, then, the puzzling remnant of rock under Atalanta's foot, earlier interpreted as a marker for her relation to the outdoors, could also be taken as an indication that the huntress is functionalised in a two-fold way. Not only is she the gateway for the external viewers to connect with the relief, but she also links two different stages of the mythological narrative – the love between the two hunters as manifested in Meleager's fight against his uncles on the one hand and his death on the other – relating them to female emotion as point of reference. With this doubled metaleptic function[43] (that is the crossing of the threshold between viewers and picture and between different stages of narrative) the figure of Atalanta turns what is labelled the *Death of Meleager* into a tableau of female sorrow, contemplating both its causes and its results (cf. the death bed sarcophagus in the Museo Capitolino (Figure 9.6)).

41 Ostia, Museo Archeologico 101; see above note 16 (1); Rome, Palazzo Doria; see above no. 16.

42 Rome, Museo Capitolino 822: *ASR* XII, 6, no. 12, pl. 17d.

43 For metalepsis as a phenomenon of visual narrative cf. Lorenz 2007.

For the scene on the left, the huntress as a gateway figure is of minor importance, not least reflected in the fact that she shares a relief plane on the sarcophagus with Althaia. Like Atalanta, all the characters in this scene are marked as belonging to a sphere outside the normal by the attributes they carry and the actions they perform with them. Of particular interest are the two women towards the left, one with the torch, the other holding a book and standing on a wheel: together with the figure on the far right who stands between Meleager and the uncle, they form what one could call a group of Fates, the Greek *Moirai*, but a group in which the individual members are also charged with attributes that normally characterise Nemesis (the torch) or the Furies (the scourge held by the figure on the very right).[44] The three are linked with each other by a particular stylistic feature, in the drilling of their hair. The effects of light and shade which this creates, generate an expressive appearance, and set them off from the rest of the cast of figures.

As a threesome, these women serve as a set of those demons Althaia also turns to in Ovid's account of the myth: 'Behold, o triple goddesses of vengeance, you three well-wishers, behold these rites of fury. I avenge an evil deed, commit another. A death for a death, a crime for a crime, and a trouble added multiplied!'[45] So, while individually bearing the more specific attributes related to Nemesis and the Furies, which herald fate and revenge, collectively they add another layer of discourse into the depiction that is concerned with the different stages of life as expressed by the Fates or *Moirai*, on the level of abstract allegory. And their presence again establishes an iconographic link to *Vita Romana* biographical sarcophagi,[46] where the *Moirai* can be found particularly in scenes around a child's death-bed.[47]

The scene on the left with its mixture of allegorically and mythologically charged figures matches the significative quality of the scene on the right, and both provide a framework for the central *conclamatio* scene which on its own leans towards the representation of a human life (as opposed to mythological) event. And yet, even though Atalanta's impact on the left scene is reduced, her figure still introduces some instability around the categories of narrative and descriptive, even in this part of the imagery. With Althaia and Atalanta on the same relief plane, both depicted in poses of distress – the former outwardly trying to fend off fate, the latter inwardly grappling with it – the focus is

44 Moirai: *LIMC* VI, 1992, s.v. *Moirai* (Stefano De Angeli); Brendel 1936, 76–95. Nemesis: *LIMC* V,I 1992, s.v. *Nemesis* (Pavlina Karanastassi, Federico Rausa).

45 Ovid *Met.* 8,481–484: '*'Poenarum' que 'deae triplices, furialibus' inquit 'Eumenides, sacris vultus advertite vestros. Ulciscor facioque nefas. Mors morte pianda est, in scelus addendum scelus est, in funera funus.*' (trans. Humphries 1955).

46 *LIMC* VI, 1992, s.v. *Moirai* no. 38–44.

47 For example: Paris, Louvre Ma 319, see above note 31. On the symbolic value of the globe in these scenes: Brendel 1936, 92–95.

directed towards an intimation of female attitudes of piety. The pair become a visual sign of the mourning of sons, brothers and husbands, and of sacrificing on their behalf.[48]

In this context, another difference from Ovid's text gains heuristic value: Althaia burns the log that seals the fate of her son not on a pyre, as reported by the poet, but on an altar, decorated with garlands to show that it is a proper Roman altar ready for the performance of sacrifice. This reference to Roman religious realia pushes Althaia out of the sphere of myth and into the realm of normative everyday life, as someone performing a Roman sacrifice; and so it supports a descriptive function for Althaia that is also confirmed by the comparative analogy with the figure of Atalanta.

Thus, in linking the two figures, the line between narrative and descriptive is once more blurred, and the figures of Atalanta and Althaia fulfil a combined *mythological* and *everyday* function: the joint presence of the huntress and the Roman altar means that Althaia appears not only as the grief-struck mother, blinded by anger and incited by the Moira-Nemesis to seal the fate of her son. Rather, she can become a mother desperate to fight off the evil powers by fulfilling her religious duties in sacrifice. As Bielfeldt has argued, this ambivalence in Althaia's figure is also conveyed through her twisted pose – a posture nicely reflecting her inner turmoil as stressed in Ovid's *Metamorphoses.*[49] And yet, the personification on the left, together with the figure with the scourge on the far right (who are the calmest characters in the scene) signal that all these attempts are futile, both in the narrative realm of myth and the descriptive realm of life: things will go according to what is written in the Moira's book of fate, towering over the wheel of life.

All in all, then, Atalanta's function on the frieze appears two-fold: her figure delivers a descriptive visual image of the state of mourning, and this is enriched by the two scenes towards the right, which showcases the qualities of the lover she has lost. In this way, the scene on the far right, which was originally a narrative image, can also be turned into a scene of allegorical paradigm for the sphere of *Vita Romana.* At the same time, she also serves as the root and cause of the events which unfold towards the right and this makes her an element of narrative: she provides the narrative voice to guide the viewer through these events, first the death, and then the events which lead to this death. And she can have the same ambivalent narrative-cum-descriptive power in relation to the

48 cf. Ovid *Met.* 4, 488–490 where Althaia announces the *officium* she fulfils for the *manes* of her brothers by burning the log.

49 Bielfeldt 2005, 133–134. Ovid *Met.* 8, 462–468: 'She tried to toss the log on, and four times held back her hand. Mother and sister duelled, each name conflicting, in her heart, with the other. (...) One moment she looked menacing, in the next all mild and pitiful.' (trans. Humphries 1955).

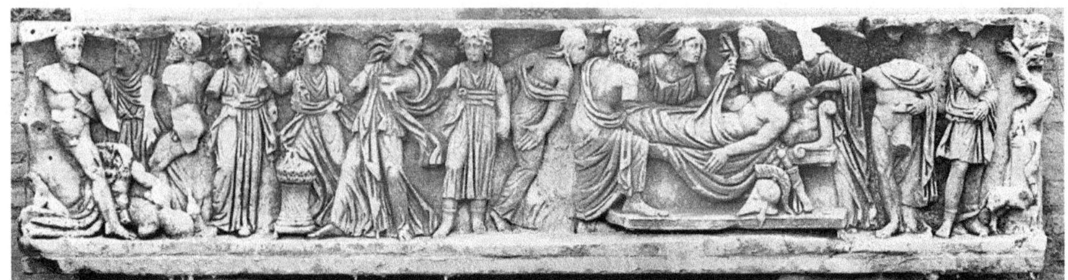

Figure 9.7: Meleager death-bed sarcophagus. Castel Gandolfo, Villa Barberini. Photograph: DAIR 1970.4136.

figure of Althaia, providing the reason for her state, while at the same time offering a parallel visual of mourning. The only figures on the frieze which are not exposed to shifting narrative and descriptive values are the *Moirai.* While everything else on the frieze is up for debate, they provide a constant frame of reference, which tells of an unchanging direction leading to the ultimate fate, which is death.

Meleager and Atalanta in Roman art: a lateral narrative

The narrative structure of the Paris sarcophagus – and particularly Atalanta's role in it – can be specified further by comparing it to other versions of the death of Meleager on sarcophagi, and to depictions outside the funerary sphere on the walls of Pompeian houses which feature Meleager and Atalanta, from about a century earlier. On all the extant sarcophagi, the composition consists of three modular scenes, except for the one in Castel Gandolfo where there are four (Figure 9.7).[50]

On the earliest sarcophagus of the group, the casket in Ostia, a *Vita Romana* scene is combined with the depiction of the death-bed, and of Atalanta present at the fight of Meleager against one of the Thestiadai (Figure 9.5).[51] From right to left, the relief tells Meleager's story, starting from the quarrel, which is clearly marked out as a mythological event by the attributes given to the characters. Following this, in the centre of the relief, is the scene around Meleager's death-bed, but in the absence of Atalanta it lacks any mythological marker: only the shield with gorgoneion signals that here might be more at stake in the scene than just the death of a formidable fighter, mourned by his siblings, nurse and teacher. The relief ends on the far left with a *normal* visual image of grieving, the depiction of a veiled man and woman mourning in front of a tomb. So, on this early piece, the mythological is already gradually traced back into the realm of

50 Castel Gandolfo, Villa Barberini; see above note 16 (9).

51 Ostia, Museo Archeologico 101; see above note 16 (1).

the normal. Formally, however, the relief is arranged in such a way that the scene at the tomb is not the end-point but the very gateway into the picture, since it is placed on the topmost layer of the relief. From there, the frieze develops to the right, step-by-step immersing itself ever more into the mythological sphere while regressing in narrative time.

The Ostia relief thus presents an actual *allegoria apertis permixta:* it feeds on *Vita Romana* scenes in order to channel the meaning of the mythological elements. And this, in return, means that the *mythological* and the *everyday* are approached on the relief as separate entities; another of the early reliefs presents a similar scene.[52] In contrast, on the later Paris sarcophagus layers of the *mythological* and the *everyday* are merged into a single, homogeneous visual language in order to showcase different forms of female sorrow.

On the later sarcophagi, any reference to the real-life funerary sphere has disappeared. Instead, an allegorical layer of meaning is introduced with the appearance of a *Moira* to show that the image's meaning resides in the sphere outside the picture, as happens, on a sarcophagus in Milan.[53] Here, the *Moira* is depicted on the topmost layer of the relief on the far left, with her left leg on the wheel of fortune, and writing into her book. She has commanding presence in relation to the figure of the mourning Atalanta, who is here characterised as being outdoors, sitting on a rock in front of a statue of Artemis.[54]

In the death-bed scene further to the right the depiction once more leaves the realm of the narrative, only to give way to another mythological image, of Meleager's fight. Thus, the death-bed scene appears enclosed by a mythological framework similar to that on the Paris sarcophagus. But the experience of this particular arrangement is directed not by a mythological figure (such as Atalanta), but by a figure – an allegory of fate – that operates outside both the real and the mythological spheres while having resonances in each. The figure serves as an *allegoria apertis permixta* personified, and so can facilitate a gradual transition from one sphere to the other.

Another option which leads towards the imagery on the Paris sarcophagus is explored on the relief of a sarcophagus in the Capitoline Museum (Figure 9.6).[55] Here too, the *Moira* with her book opens the scene on the far left, once more dominating the topmost relief plane; and again she is succeeded by Atalanta. But although the huntress sits on a rock, there are no other signs of an outdoors setting, such as a statue of Artemis. Instead, Atalanta turns her face

52 Rome, Villa Albani, Galleria del Canopo; see above note 16 (3).

53 Milan, Torno Collection; see above note 16 (5).

54 A similar combination of Moira and Atalanta in the outdoors can be found on the sarcophagus in the Villa Albani which also shows a scene in front of a tomb: Rome, Villa Albani, Galleria del Canopo; see above note 16 (3).

55 Rome, Museo Capitolino 623; see above note 16 (4).

openly towards the viewers of the relief, and she is screened by a parapetasma that serves as a background for the death-bed scene as a whole. By making her part of the death-bed scene, the differentiation between the *Vita Romana* presentation of death and the mythological episodes around Meleager's life is abolished on this relief and replaced by the theme of the grieving wife. And while feeding on elements which characterise an *allegoria apertis permixta*, the result of this combination is of a rather different quality: it does not use elements of the everyday in order to facilitate an understanding of the *mythological* and the abstract on display. Rather, by merging these elements visually, it generates a virtual sphere located outside these categories. In this it is helped by the modular composition which does not present the episodes in their actual sequence as a consecutive narrative would require.[56]

The focus on Meleager and Atalanta as a couple, and in particular on Atalanta as eminent part of the relationship on the sarcophagi, is not an entirely new focalization of the myth in Roman art. It is an approach similar to the one which can be found in the nine frescoes from the walls of Pompeian houses which feature the two Calydonian hunters (Figures 9.8 and 9.9).[57] These Pompeian depictions are solely focused on the encounter between Meleager and Atalanta after the successful hunt gathered around the dead boar,[58] in what Wulf Raeck has referred to as *conversation pictures*,[59] and which bear similarity to the depiction of the two on some of the column sarcophagi.[60]

In the Pompeian versions, Meleager is always seated, and Atalanta stands next to him, equipped with her usual weapons, the spears and her bow. Meleager is generally characterised with sword and spear.[61] Comparison with other mythological wall-paintings shows that the sword is employed as an

56 Two sarcophagi in this group continue the consecutive arrangement of the Ostia casket: Wilton House, Wiltshire; see above note 16 (7); Castel Gandolfo, Villa Barberini; see above note 16 (9).

57 Lorenz 2008, 55–83 for a detailed discussion; cf. also *LIMC* II, 1984, s.v. *Atalanta* (John Boardman); *LIMC* V,I 1992, s.v. *Meleagros* (Susan Woodford); Raeck 1992, 71–76; Muth 1998, 216–217.

58 The only exception is: Naples, Museo Archeologico Nazionale 8980. From Pompeii, Casa del Centauro (VI 9,3). Third Style. Lorenz 2008, 67–70.

59 Raeck 1992, 78–80.

60 For example: Rome, S. Pietro in Vaticano. H 0.70 L 2.06 D 0.60. 180/90. *ASR* XII,6, no. 146 pl. 121. And similarly on an Attic and an Attic-inspired sarcophagus: Chicago, Alsdorf Foundation, from Antiocheia Orontes. L 1.20 H 0.95. First half third century. *ASR* XII,6, no. 168 pl. 133a. Autun, Musée Rolin no. 66, from Arles. H 0.85 L 2.25 D 0.86. Third century. *ASR* III, 2, 219 pl. 72; *ASR* XII,6, 136–137 no. 159 pl. 133b.

61 cf. fresco from the Casa delle Danzatrici (Pompeii VI 2,22). Fourth Style. *PPM* IV 238–239 fig. 18–19; Lorenz 2008, 56–60 fig. 5. In the Villa Imperiale, the sword is his only weapon: Pompeii, Villa Imperiale, *cubiculum* (B). Third Style. Schefold 1957, 292; Lorenz 2008, 60–64, fig. 6.

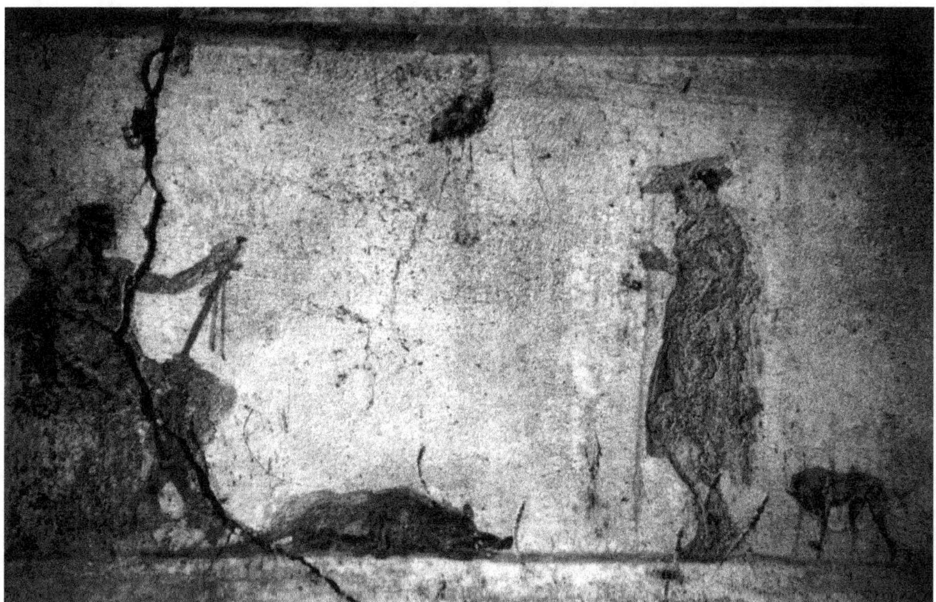

Figure 9.8: Meleager and Atalanta. Pompeii, Villa Imperiale. Photograph: author.

attribute in order to add a layer of military *virtus* to Meleager, elevating him out of the context of the ordinary hunter and into the role of a manly warrior.[62] This is the same strategy which can be observed later on the sarcophagi.

Another key characteristic of the Pompeian versions is that the couple are displayed in a symmetrical relationship in which they both have equally active roles, and this is indicated by their position towards each other, as well as by their weapons. Not all mythological couples on the Pompeian walls are displayed in such a symmetrical way – some are asymmetrical in favour of the male, some in favour of the female partner.[63] And yet, with Atalanta always presented as standing, she is the partner who has the ability to alter the relationship between the two.

The final characteristic of the Pompeian frescoes is that while Meleager is depicted in a similar way on both the walls and the sarcophagi, the iconographical range for the figure of Atalanta is wider in Pompeii than on the sarcophagi. Her presentation can either lean towards that of Artemis, the goddess of the hunt, or towards Aphrodite, the goddess of love: like Artemis, she can appear as competent and active huntress, depicted in the outdoors

62 Lorenz 2008, 246–247.
63 Lorenz 2008, 246–249.

(Figure 9.8);[64] or she can be depicted as sensual and attractive woman, for example in frescoes in the Casa della Venere in Conchiglia (Figure 9.9) and the Casa della Danzatrici. Then, she is also shown with clear markers of civilization in the background, either the interior of a house or the facades of a temple. Essentially, this means that her character can be charged with different characteristics of *pulchritudo*, and with different shades of beauty – on the one hand a dynamic, but chaste fitness, on the other an elaborate sensuality. And frequently, a mix of the two appears.

In the Pompeian images, the male hero is not depicted as the central figure to whom Atalanta's depiction defers. Rather, she is the character who facilitates the encounter. But in the scenes of the Calydonian hunt on the sarcophagi and mosaics, Atalanta is turned once more into an exotic element amidst the large group of hunting comrades. On those monuments, Meleager forms the distinct centre of attention and action, and Atalanta appears as his trustworthy consort. Thus, the coherent presentation of the two heroes on the Pompeian walls gives way to a conception of the story which puts a clear focus on the male protagonist throughout the second and third century.

In this sense, the presentation of Meleager and Atalanta on the sarcophagi of the death-bed group appears to be much closer to the conception of the mythological protagonists on the Pompeian walls than to those on the 'Calydonian hunt' sarcophagi. But they also differ from the frescoes in the way in which they facilitate the figure of Atalanta; and this is precisely what heralds a change in the use of myth that distinguishes the appearances of the myth in first century domestic settings from those found in funerary contexts of the second century. On the Pompeian frescoes, the shifts in the representation of Atalanta demonstrate a certain uneasiness and fluidity about the ways in which myth can be appropriated to the world outside the picture.[65]

But on the death-bed sarcophagi such unease does not exist. Instead, a blend of multiple layers of meaning leads the viewer into a virtual sphere which feeds on the everyday, the mythological and a more generic form of the allegorical, all at the same time. The discursive engagement with the status of myth so characteristic of the Pompeian frescoes has been solved, and has been turned into an almost pervasive use of myth. The mobility between the different spheres of reality and fiction that characterises the framework of reception for which the relief is intended is proved by two particular features – Atalanta's role as gateway-figure, which aids the understanding of a scene taken from the *Vita*

64 For example: Villa Imperiale: see above no. 61. Pompeii, House Regio VII 15,3. 45x47. Third Style. Schefold 1957, 207; *PPM* VII 772 fig. 9; Lorenz 2008, 56–60 fig. 4. Casa della Venere in Conchiglia (Pompeii II 3,3). 32x37. Fourth Style. *PPM* III 166 fig. 82; Lorenz 2008, 64–66 fig. 9. Casa delle Danzatrici: see above no. 61.

65 Lorenz 2008, 250–258.

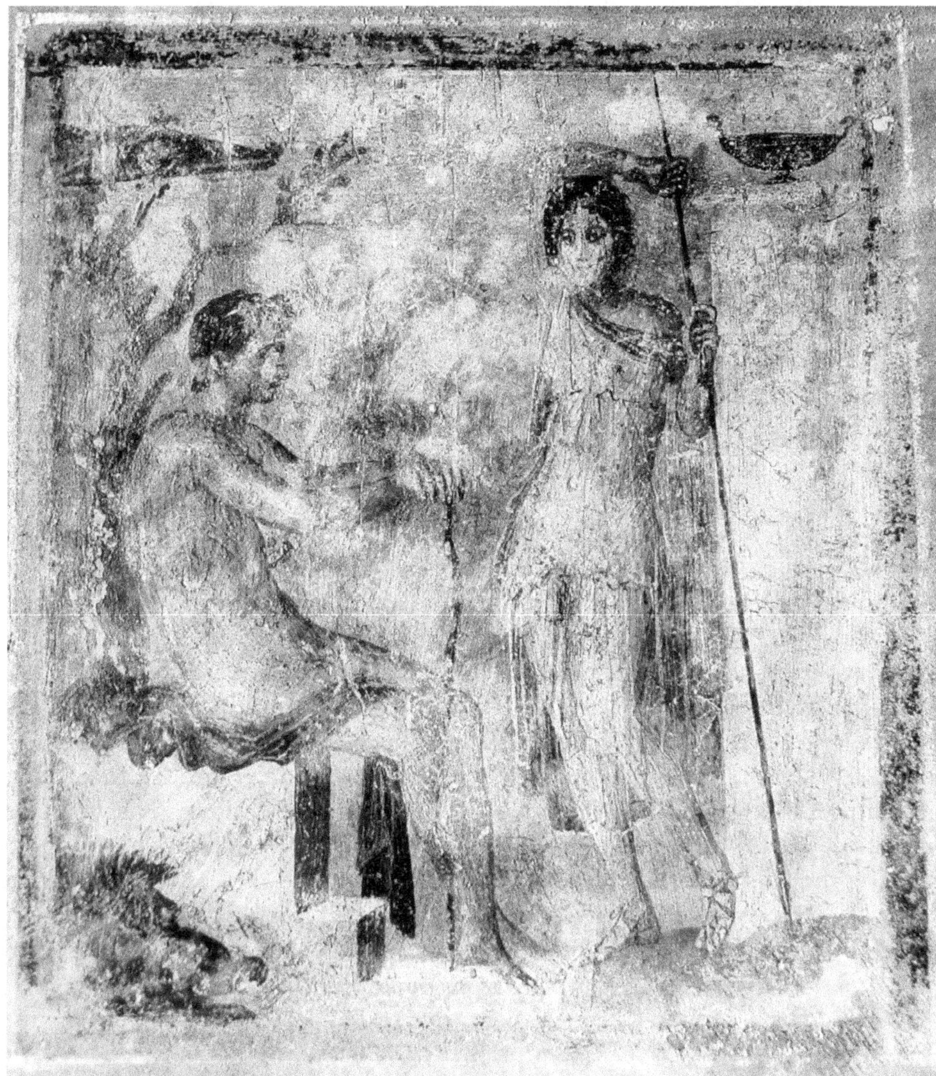

Figure 9.9: Meleager and Atalanta. Pompeii, Casa della Venere in Conchiglia (II 3,3). Photograph: DAIR 57.879.

Romana repertoire but using the visual template of another myth, and the selective use of the *Moirai*-cum-*Erinyes*-cum-Nemesis figures. The relief demonstrates a familiarity with, and an interest, in the sphere of the virtual that is not even matched by the scenes of the Calydonian hunt which are much more strongly based within the realm of myth.

Distress dissolved: life, death, and myth

The Paris sarcophagus stands out from the other versions of the death of Meleager produced in the last quarter of the second and the early third century in the way in which it functionalises Atalanta as an intermediary for viewers of the sarcophagus and as a narrative voice for the experience it chooses to represent. Some other reliefs, especially the sarcophagus in the Capitoline Museum, use similar strategies, but the Paris sarcophagus develops these more fully and presents them within a particularly well-balanced, organic composition.

The Paris sarcophagus also explores the interfaces between mythological and everyday content and the permeability of these categories, as it moves away from the rhetorical concept of the *allegoria apertis permixta*; and this journey is primarily linked to the figure of Atalanta. In this respect, the sarcophagus continues some strategies of reception aesthetics which can already be found about a century earlier in representations of the story of Meleager and Atalanta on the walls of Pompeii. There, in the Casa della Venere in Conchiglia, for example, it is also Atalanta who – with a period face and contemporary clothing – makes direct advances to the viewers, turning from a mythological into a descriptive character (Figure 9.9).[66] But in contrast to representations like that in Pompeii and on some of the other sarcophagi, on the Paris sarcophagus the mythological and everyday spheres are combined not just to trigger a discourse about each other, but also to generate a new narrative force: through the eyes of Atalanta, the mythological story is personalised in its entirety. The modular narrative structure does not merely offer points of identification for those outside the image. Rather, it allows them to immerse themselves fully in its mythological world, generating a type of mediated reality that is very different from the juxtaposition of mythological and everyday on sarcophagi like the one in Ostia.

This means that the narrative voice constructed around Atalanta is not just testimony to the strategies of selection that characterise the Romans' use of myth in which certain elements from individual myths are employed while others are discarded in order to generate distinct Roman messages;[67] nor does it merely represent a move from classicising symbolism to an *interpretatio Romana* which Peter Blome attests for the late-Antonine period,[68] and against which Bielfeldt convincingly argued;[69] but it is not simply a mixture of myth and allegorical

66 Lorenz 2008, 63–66.

67 see Zanker 1999; Zanker and Ewald 2004, 247–266; cf. also Giuliani 1989; Koortbojian 1995, 120–126; Bielfeldt 2005, esp. 321–328.

68 Blome 1992, 1071–1072.

69 Bielfeldt 2005, 22.

paradigm either. The Paris sarcophagus is clearly concerned with the allegorical and emotional content which mythological scenes are capable of transmitting. Thus it is designed around the assumption that its viewers are willing and able to engage in acts of abstracted reading, to select specific aspects of mythological knowledge while ignoring others in order to make sense of this particular representation and grasp its allegorical meanings. But the significance of the sarcophagus does not stop there: it is not just a reference to something else in an iconological sense, it does not just present a case of Greek myths emulated in order to generate and transmit behavioural ideals and allegorical messages related to the context of death and religious rites at the tomb, nor does it only present a paradigmatic narrative. Instead it offers a pervasive narrative experience that feeds off the specific characteristic of its two constitutive components, the mythological and the everyday. As such, it immerses the viewers and invites them to a reading of the myth – through the eyes of Atalanta – very different from the known textual versions of the story, while at the same time, by means of the modular setup, the individual scenes can constantly generate their own narrative scenarios, adding to, or counter-acting Atalanta's perspective.

These different voices are facilitated by the material carrier, the sarcophagus, which provides them with narrative space, but at the same time also determines and frames their workings through its funerary function. Turned into a narrative engine, the Paris sarcophagus demonstrates that a multitude of perspectives and the ambivalence between the descriptive and the narrative do not cause any kind of breakdown in the way pictures may direct their viewers, which is usually regarded as a crucial problem of visual narrative.[70] On the contrary: on the Paris sarcophagus, these elements facilitate the great potential of visual narrative. The scenes on this coffin demonstrate that descriptive and narrative elements can be both immanent in one and the same visual form, waiting for the viewers to unlock their workings, providing them with a story, and at the same time also with a counter-reading of it.

These strategies of modular, shuffled narrative, breaking with a linear pattern of story-telling, are a brilliant means of enticing the complexities out of a story, by inviting the viewer to re-visit and re-think previous assumptions about the development of the story-line. But it is also notable that these multilayered strategies are not extended to all the figures depicted, thus facilitating a particularly subtle transmission. The *Moirai*, who belong to an allegorical realm somewhere between the spheres of the mythological narrative and everyday life, are not affected by multiple interpretations: their meaning and their role on the frieze remains unchanged in that they point to the inescapability of fate and the inevitability of death. This quality is also manifest

70 cf. Mitchell 1986, 95–115 and his discussion of Lessing; also: Giuliani 2003, 21–37.

on the side panels of the Paris sarcophagus which show two Sphinxes striding towards the frontal frieze. Together the *Moirai* and the Sphinxes have an apotropaic significance that is matched by the gorgon-shield in the centre of the front, and they provide a robust and clearly shaped framework that enfolds the mythologically-articulated world of female sorrow and grieving.

The Paris sarcophagus might be said to feature a two-way system of transmitting its meanings: a framework constituted by the side panels and the *Moirai* corroborates a direct message about the power of death that is already inherent in (or generic to) the sarcophagus as an object, while the rest of the frieze confronts its viewers with a paradigmatic narrative, immersing them in a discourse that stands at the interface of myth and *Vita Romana*. In combining these two forms of transmission, the selection of allegories and ideals forms only one element within a vibrant set of significations, while the key to the images on these monuments seems to lie in their strategies of packaging the different spheres of meaning and explanation. In contrast to earlier forms of combining elements of myth and *Vita Romana* that are found in Roman imperial art, on the walls of Pompeii, and on other sarcophagi, reliefs like the Paris sarcophagus no longer represent a simple or straightforward state of distress. Nor do they show any uncertainty about whether they want to showcase the consoling world of mythological fantasy to make real life more bearable, or to offer affirmative ideals that give guidance to the grieving. Depictions like the relief of the Paris sarcophagus want to be all of these things, while playing their constitutive elements against each other. This is why these reliefs are designed to absorb their viewers into the pictorial sphere, with the certainty of death provided as the only framework to delimit this process of immersion.

The vitality and interest of such images in an intense discourse between the different categories of virtuality, and in the power and versatility of visual narrative, starts earlier than the stylistic changes which can be observed on the sarcophagi of the late-Antonine period at the end of the second century,[71] but they highlight once more the search for new ways to develop visual expression that took place in these decades.[72] This particular set of qualities was lost in the course of the third century, when more explicit and less discursive forms of representation came to be of interest on the sarcophagi – an interest which quite swiftly led to the abandonment of mythological stories altogether.

71 Rodenwaldt 1935.

72 Wegner 1931, 61–62,167–174; Rodenwaldt 1935, 1944/45, 84–86. For a recent overview: Newby 2007.

Bibliography

Andreae, B. *Die Symbolik der Löwenjagd* (Opladen, 1985).

Bielfeldt, R. *Orestes auf römischen Sarkophagen* (Berlin, 2005).

Blome, P. Zur Umgestaltung griechischer Mythen in der römischen Sepulkralkunst. Alkestis-, Protesilaos- und Proserpinasarkophage. *Mitteilungen des Deutschen Archäologischen Instituts. Abteilung Rom* 85 (1978),435–457.

Blome, P. Funerärsymbolische Collagen auf mythologischen Sarkophagreliefs. *Studi italiani di filologia classica* 10 (1992), 1061–1073.

Brendel, O. Symbolik der Kugel. Archäologische Untersuchungen zur Geschichte der älteren griechischen Philosophie. *Mitteilungen des Deutschen Archäologischen Instituts, Abteilung Rom* 51 (1936), 1–95.

Brilliant, R. *Visual Narratives. Storytelling in Etruscan and Roman Art* (Ithaca and New York, 1986).

Brilliant, R. Roman Myth/Greek Myth: Reciprocity and Appropriation on a Roman Sarcophagus in Berlin, in: *Studi Italiani di Filologia Classica* 10.2 (1992), 1030–1045.

Dimas, S. *Untersuchungen zur Themenwahl und Bildgestaltung auf römischen Kindersarkophagen* (Münster, 1998).

Ewald, B.-C. Men, muscle and myth. Attic sarcophagi in the context of the Second Sophistic, in: *Paideia. The world of the second sophistic*, edited by B. Borg (Berlin, 2004), 229–267.

Fittschen, K. *Meleager Sarkophag* (Frankfurt, 1975).

Gallina, A. Il sarcofago di Pianabella. *Archeologia Laziale* 11 (1993), 149–154.

George, M. Family and *familia* on Roman biographical sarcophagi. *Mitteilungen des Deutschen Archäologischen Instituts, Abteilung Rom* 107 (2000), 191–207.

Geyer, A. Ikonographische Bemerkungen zum Neapler Brüdersarkophag. *Jahrbuch des Instituts* 93 (1978), 369–393.

Giuliani, L. Achill-Sarkophage in Ost und West: Genese einer Ikonographie. *Jahrbuch der Berliner Museen* 31 (1989), 25–39.

Giuliani, L. *Bild und Mythos* (Munich, 2003).

Grassinger, D. The meanings of myth on Roman sarcophagi, in: *Myth and Allusion. Meanings and Uses of Myth in Ancient Greek and Roman Society* (Boston, 1994), 91–107.

Hesberg-Tonn, B. *Coniunx Carissima* (Cologne, 1983).

Howe, T.P. The origin and function of the Gorgo head. *American Journal of Archaeology* 58 (1954), 134–149.

Huskinson, J. *Roman Children's Sarcophagi. Their decoration and its social significance* (Oxford, 1996).

Junker, K. Römische mythologische Sarkophage. Zur Entstehung eines Denkmaltyps. *Mitteilungen des Deutschen Archäologischen Instituts. Abteilung Rom* 112 (2006), 163–188.

Kampen, N. Biographical narration and Roman funerary art. *American Journal of Archaeology* 85 (1981), 47–58.

Koch, G. Verschollene Meleagersarkophage. *Archäologischer Anzeiger* (1973), 287–293.

Koch, G. Nachlese zu den Meleagersarkophagen. *Archäologischer Anzeiger* (1975b), 530–552.

Koch, G. Der Achillsarkophag in Berlin. *Jahrbuch der Berliner Museen* 25 (1983), 5–25.

Koch, G. and Sichtermann, H. *Römische Sarkophage. Handbuch der Archäologie* (Munich, 1982).

Koortbojian, M. *Myth, Meaning and Memory on Roman Sarcophagi* (Berkeley, Los Angeles and London, 1995).

Lorenz, K. The anatomy of metalepsis. Visuality turns around on late fifth-century pots, in: *Debating the Athenian Cultural Revolution. Art, literature, philosophy, and politics 430–380 B.C.*, edited by R. Osborne (Cambridge, 2007), 116–143.

Lorenz, K. *Bilder machen Räume. Mythenbilder strukturieren pompeianische Häuser* (Berlin, 2008).

Mitchell, W.J.T. *Iconology* (Chicago, 1986).

Muth, S. *Erleben von Raum – Leben im Raum* (Heidelberg, 1998).

Newby, Z. Art at the crossroads? Themes and style in Severan art, in: *Severan Culture*, edited by S. Swain, S. Harrison and J. Elsner (Cambridge, 2007), 201–249.

Raeck, W. *Modernisierte Mythen* (Stuttgart, 1992).

Schefold, K. *Die Wände Pompejis* (Berlin, 1957).

Toynbee, J. M. C. *Death and Burial in the Roman World* (London and Southampton, 1971 and 1982).

Whitehead, J.K. *Biography and Formula in Roman Sarcophagi* (Ph.D Yale, 1984).

Zanker, P. and Ewald, B. C. *Mit Mythen leben. Die Bilderwelt der römischen Sarkophage* (Munich, 2004).

Zanker, P. Phädras Trauer und Hippolytos' Bildung: zu einem Sarkophag im Thermenmuseum, in: *Im Spiegel des Mythos. Bilderwelt und Lebenswelt. Palilia* 6, edited by F. de Angelis and S. Muth (Wiesbaden, 1999), 131–142.

Zanker, P. Ikonographie und Mentalität. Zur Veränderung mythologischer Bildthemen auf den kaiserzeitlichen Sarkophagen aus der Stadt Rom, in: R. Neudecker and P. Zanker (eds.), *Lebenswelten. Bilder und Räume in der römischen Kaiserzeit. Symposium am 24. und 25. Januar 2002 zum Abschluss des von der Gerda Henkel Stiftung geförderten Forschungsprogramms Stadtkultur in der Kaiserzeit. Palilia 16* (Wiesbaden, 2005), 243–51.

10.
Borrowed Verse and Broken Narrative: Agency, Identity, and the (Bethesda) Sarcophagus of Bassa

Dennis Trout

Sometime in the late fourth century, a young woman named Bassa was laid to rest in the Catacomb of Praetextatus near the Appian Way, roughly two kilometres outside Rome's Aurelian walls. Bassa's marble sarcophagus – ravaged and scattered in time by vandalism and landslide but reassembled in the early twentieth century (Figure 10.1) – now stands in the handbooks as an (anomalous) example of the so-called Bethesda type.[1] Thirteen other representatives of this sarcophagus group are currently known and each of these thirteen, as far as can be determined, presents the same five New Testament scenes in the same order.[2] In every case, as illustrated by well-preserved examples from the Vatican cemetery and the Cathedral of Tarragona (figs. 2 and 3),[3] a central tableau arranged in two registers portrays (at least in its upper half) an episode from the Gospel of John in which Jesus heals a paralytic at Jerusalem's pool of Bethesda (Jn 5.1–9). On either side of this central panel appear four other standard scenes, two on each side, and these also reference

1 On the catacomb see Spera 2004 and Spera 2006. More than thirty fragments of Bassa's sarcophagus were collected throughout Praetextatus in the late nineteenth and early twentieth centuries. Because this catacomb was significantly disturbed by ancient depredations as well as subsequent landslides and looting, it is now impossible to determine with any certainty Bassa's original burial spot within the complex, though the recorded find spots make regions D and F in the NW sector of the catacomb likely: for a synopsis see Mazzei 2004, 112–113. J. Wilpert published the sarcophagus first in 1932, 294; tab. 207 no. 1. For more recent presentations see *Rep.*I, 229–30, taf. 85, no. 556; Nicoletti 1981,14–16, no. 4; and Koch 2000, 314, List 4, group 1.3, no. 29, Anm. 4. Einzugs-Sarkophage (Bethesda-Sarkophage). The fragments are now on display at the Catacomb of Praetextatus (*non vidi*); only the front panel survives: see Mazzei 2004, 111. A version of this paper was presented at the Eighth Biennial Shifting Frontiers in Late Antiquity Conference, Bloomington, Indiana, 2–5 April 2009. I would like to thank the Center for the Arts and Humanities at The University of Missouri for generous financial support and Jaś Elsner and Carl P. E. Springer for thoughtful suggestions.

2 On the order of the scenes: Simon 1938, 205; Nicoletti 1981, 1. Nicoletti 1981, 3 identifies fourteen Bethesda sarcophagi (including Bassa's) but fragments represent the majority; see also Koch 2000, 314–15 for the same number.

3 Vatican: *Rep.* I, 59–60, taf. 20, no. 63; Nicoletti 1981, 7–9, no. 1. Tarragona: Sotomayor 1975, 213–219, no. 38; Nicoletti 1981, 9–12, no. 2.

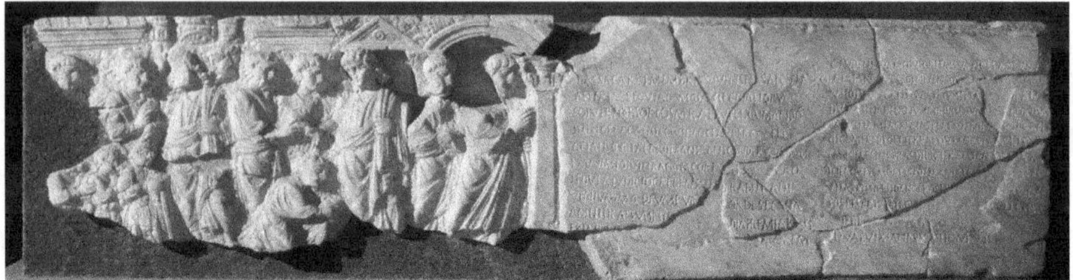

Figure 10.1: Rome, Museo cristiano delle catacombe di Pretestato. The sarcophagus of Bassa. Photograph: Foto Archivio, P.C.A.S.

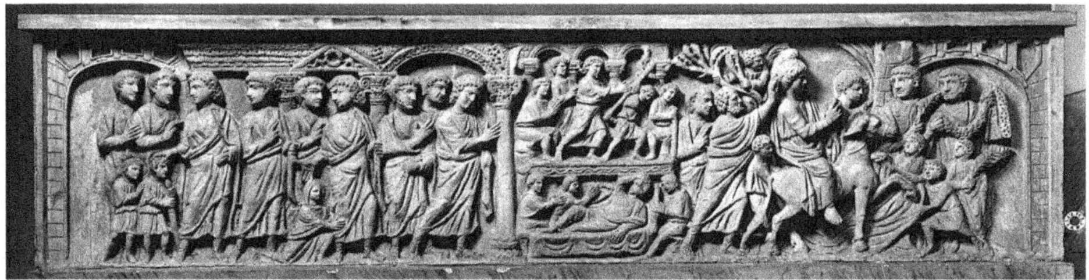

Figure 10.2: Città del Vaticano, Museo Pio Cristiano. Bethesda sarcophagus (Art Resource)

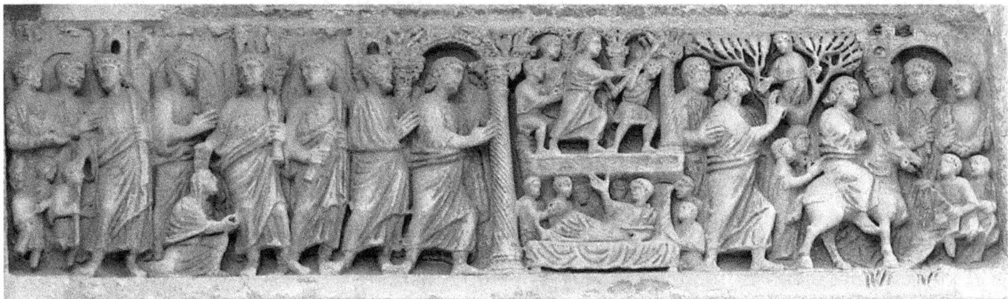

Figure 10.3: Tarragona, Cathedral. Bethesda sarcophagus (courtesy of J.Elsner)

gospel events (two scenes of wonder working, Zacchaeus in the sycamore tree, and Jesus' final entry into Jerusalem).

In the unique case of Bassa's sarcophagus a verse epitaph (*ICUR* 5.14076), sampling expressions found elsewhere and disrupting the type's figural flow, occupies the front panel's entire right half, replacing not only the Bethesda type's final two scenes (Zacchaeus and Jesus' entry) but also its central eponymous panel. Though easily dismissed as awkward and inept, the idiosyncratic design of Bassa's sarcophagus may rather testify to the ingenuity with which several otherwise unknown Romans – Bassa, her husband, Gaudentius, and the artisans of one city workshop – manipulated ideas and art forms in order to fashion and express social identity in late ancient Rome.[4] From this perspective, Bassa's sculpted and inscribed coffin is both a striking 'index' of social agency in this age of cultural transformation and an eloquent witness to the less sensational ideological negotiations undergirding the genesis and evolution of late antique *Roma Christiana.*[5] The following discussion begins with the text of Bassa's epitaph, moves on to consider her sarcophagus' Bethesda imagery, and concludes with a synthetic reading of her compelling memorial.

The Epitaph

Of the more than thirty fragments of Bassa's sarcophagus recovered from the debris of Praetextatus' subterranean galleries, eleven preserve her epitaph – nearly entire (figs. 4 and 5).[6] The text, which is original to the design and not retrofit onto a previously sculpted and erased surface,[7] is arranged in two columns each of ten hexameter lines.[8] A *chi-rho*, which also serves as the last word of the first line, is prominent between the two columns. Above the first line on the left are the traces of the same line in red paint. Below the last line on the right are the date of Bassa's deposition – one day before the *calends* of a missing month – and her age – twenty-

4 Our Bassa and Gaudentius cannot otherwise be identified nor can their social rank be determined with any certainty. That they were of at least moderate wealth is evident. Dresken-Weiland 2004, 150 suggested that the presence of a metrical epitaph points to an 'ambiente senatorio' for the couple but versification may just as well indicate social or literary aspirations among those of lower rank. See for example the verse epitaph of Celerinus, just a presbyter, cited below. Similarly for *acrosticha* (as is Bassa's epitaph); Sanders 1991, 200 sees the acrostic epitaph as a form favoured by the 'classes moyennes' including ecclesiastics. Furthermore, Dresken-Weiland's sample of 310 inscribed early Christian sarcophagi from Rome yields only sixty-nine of sure 'ceti elevati' (forty-six of which are senatorial) and otherwise includes soldiers, a *casarius* (cottager), and a *grammaticus.* Nomenclature is also of little help. Gaudentii appear across the Italian social spectrum as represented, for example, by clerical office holders; see e.g., Pietri and Pietri 1999, 887–892, 'Gaudentius 2–10,' from *fossor* to bishop. Bassae, the indices of *ICUR* reveal, are (surprisingly) rare: but see *ILCV* 2799 (a *virgo*); *ILCV* 3878 (apparently an agnomen), neither of high social rank; and *CLE* 1058, the verse epitaph of an earlier Bassa, whom '*Pluto rapuit . . . ad infera templa.*'

5 Gell 1998, especially 12–21, supplying a rationale for viewing Bassa's sarcophagus as an artefactual index of social agency. Mazzei 2004, 113, too, recognised as much, seeing in the incorporation of the epitaph 'un ingerenza particolarmente volitiva da parte del committente.'

6 Wilpert 1932 knew nine fragments of Bassa's epitaph. A tenth fragment, the end of lines 3–6 of column B, was added by E. Josi in 1935, who then re-published the text at Josi 1935, 12–13. In 1947 A. Ferrua identified an eleventh fragment of the inscription, the end of the final line of column A, before publishing the epitaph in 1971 as *ICUR* 5.14076. See Mazzei 2004, 115 for confirmation after restoration.

7 Nicoletti 1981, 16; Mazzei 2004, 113.

8 Bassa's epitaph is thus one of a group of 'circa 350' Christian metrical funerary inscriptions from Rome; see Carletti 1998, 61.

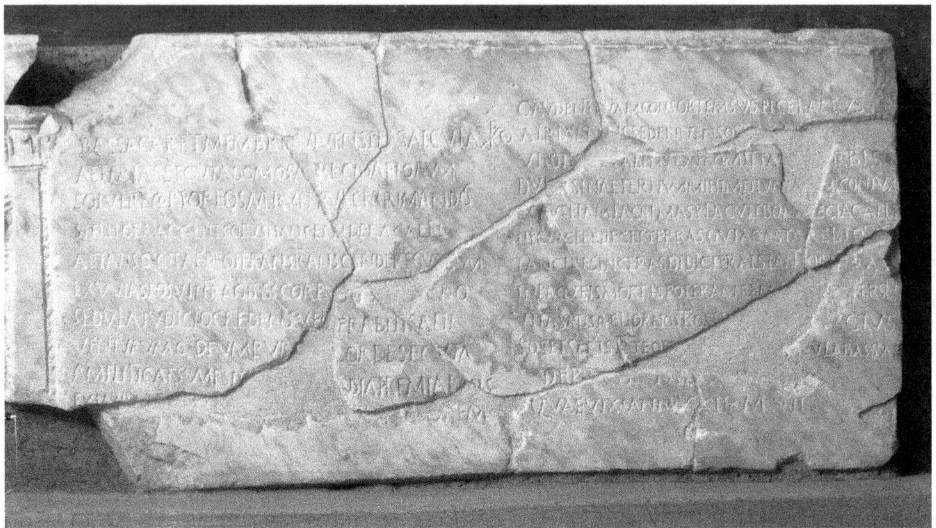

Figure 10.4: The Sarcophagus of Bassa: Epitaph. Photograph: Foto Archivio, P.C.A.S.

two years and seven months. The poem is an acrostic, a bit of panache that appears to have been popular among fourth-century Christians at Rome.[9] The first letters of each line spell out *Bassae suae* (on the left) and *Gaudentius* (on the right), that is, 'to his Bassa, Gaudentius.'

The right-hand column (A) envisions Bassa's disembodied ascent from her tomb to a lucent home in a starry heaven:

[B]assa caret m[emb]ris
Bassa caret membris vivens per saecula Xpo
Aeterias secuta domos ac regna piorum
Solvere corporeos meruit pulcerrima nodos;
Stelliger accepit polus hanc et sidera caeli
Aetatisq(ue) citae properans transcendere cursum
Exuvias posuit fragiles corpusq(ue) s[epu]lcro;
Sedula iudicio credens venerabilis Al[t]i
Venturumq(ue) deum puro [cum] corde secuta
Amplificae sumpsit [sibi gau]dia premia lucis
Eximium [. . . . . . umq]ue [de]corem.[10]

9 Of the eighty-six acrostic *carmina Latina epigraphica* (including *ICUR* 5.14076) counted by Sanders 1991, 193–197, forty are considered 'pagan' and forty-six Christian while only one of the former, but twelve of the latter, can be dated to the fourth century.

10 *ICUR* 5.14076. Line 2: for *aetheria/as/is/um* as the opening word in ten Vergilian lines see Warwick 1975, 34. Line 4: cf. Statius, *Thebaid* 12.565, '*stelligeri iubar omne poli*;

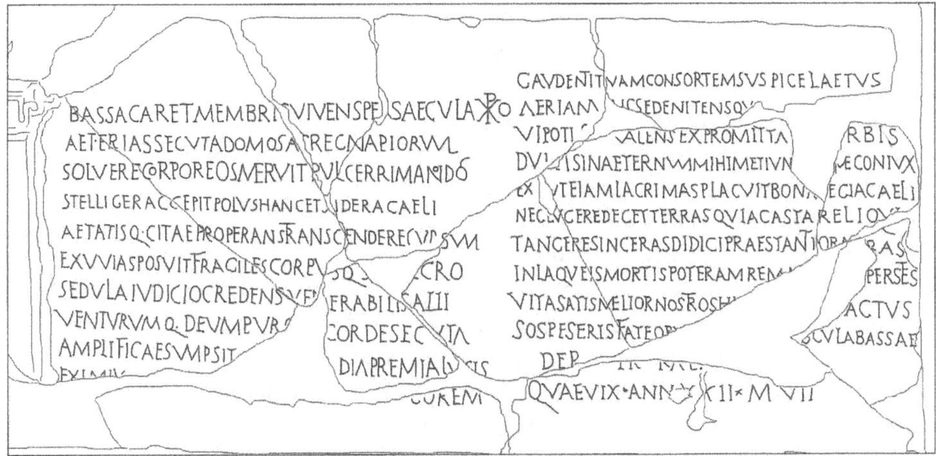

Figure 10.5: The Sarcophagus of Bassa: Epitaph, apograph by B. Mazzei.
Photograph: Foto Archivio, P.C.A.S.

Bassa is free of her limbs, living through the ages in Christ.
Pursuing an ethereal home and the kingdoms of the pious,
most beautiful, she deserved to loose the knots of the flesh.
Star-bearing heaven and the stars of the sky have received her
and hastening to move through the course of swift passing life,
she has placed her fragile husk and body in the tomb.
Worthy of respect, steadfastly trusting in the judgment of the high God,
and attending with pure heart the God who will come,
she has taken to herself the pleasures (and) rewards of the boundless light
distinguished . . . . . . and beautiful.

The left hand column (B) consoles Gaudentius, in part through an address from Bassa herself, who speaks to her husband from heaven's court with the promise of their future reunion:

Gaudenti tuam consortem suspice laetus
Aeria nunc sede nitens qu[ae. . .
Vi potiore valens expromit ta[lia ve]rbis:
Dul[c]is in aeternum mihimet iun[tissi]me coniux

sidera caeli' at Ver. *Aen.* 1.259 (Aeneas' place of reward as promised to Venus by Jupiter), *Geo.* 2.1, and *Geo.* 4.58. Line 5: cf. Ver. *Aen.* 6.313, '*transmittere cursum.*' Line 7. *Altus* for God is unusual, as Ferrua noted; the superlative, *Altissimus*, is known: cf. Ps 91.2; Dan 4.21. Line 8: for the frequent appearance of *secuta/ae/i/um/us* in this position in the Vergilian hexameter see Warwick 1975, 769–770. For other poetic echoes see below.

Ex[c]ute iam lacrimas, placuit bona [r]egia caeli;
Nec lugere decet terras quia casta reliqu[i];
Tangere sinceras didici praestantior a[u]ras;
In laqueis mortis poteram rema[nere su]perstes;
Vita satis melior nostros hi[c . . . . . .]actus;
Sospes eris fateor v[. . . . . o]scula Bassae.
dep(osita) pr(idie) kal(endas) . . . .
quae vix(it) ann(os) XXII m(enses) VII

Gaudentius, happily look up at your wife,
who shining brightly now in her lofty abode . . .
prevailing with renewed strength, utters such things in words:
'Sweet husband, most closely bound to me forever,
drive off your tears, the noble court of heaven is pleasant,
and it is not fitting to weep because I, a virtuous woman, have abandoned earth;
More pre-eminent I have learned how to take hold of the pure upper air;
in the snares of death I was able to remain alive;
A much better life . . .
You will be saved, I confess . . . the kisses of Bassa.'

Bassa's epitaph generally adheres to the standards of quantity and prosody inherited from the poetry of the past and common to the *carmina epigraphica* of the later fourth century.[11] Nor are the verses without their charm. The acrostic aligns her poem not only with the literary aspirations of a number of other fourth-century epitaphs but also, in effect, with the kind of cultural pretensions already displayed in the prodigiously laborious *carmina figurata* of Optatianus Porfyrius or still to come, for example, in the sixth-century verses of Venantius Fortunatus.[12] This cleverness and effort variously leave their mark in word play and arrangement. The poem begins and ends with Bassa's name while Gaudentius stands at mid-point as the first word of the second column (as hers is of the first) – and thus the first letter in each column reads as the first letter of each name both horizontally and vertically. Furthermore, the *gaudia* of A9 anticipate the naming of Gaudentius just two lines later, much as the heavenly 'pleasures' embraced by Bassa are prelude to her reception of her husband in the

11 There are no elisions. In A2 the first syllable of *secuta* must be lengthened, although at A8 the same syllable is properly scanned as short. At B1 we should expect *laete* for *laetus*, that is, a vocative in agreement with *Gaudenti* not a nominative, but such a deviation is otherwise known in contemporary inscriptions. Finally, and in the same line, the first syllable of *tuam* also has to be lengthened.

12 See above note 9 with Levitan 1985 and Graver 1993.

regia caeli. If the poem's final line did indeed read '*Sospes eris fateor u[enies et ad o]scula Bassae* (You will be saved, I confess, and will come to the kisses of Bassa)' – as Antonio Ferrua suggested – then word play may also have ended the epitaph: *Bassae*, juxtaposed with *oscula* as the final two words of the poem, may have evoked for some readers the poetic but rare *basia* (kisses), punning upon her name but also reinforcing the conjugally erotic tenor of the piece.[13] There are, of course, echoes of Vergil, direct or otherwise, while alliteration and end rhyme decorate several lines, further testifying to the care lavished on composition.[14]

Especially striking, however, is the vigour with which Bassa lays claim to a specifically astral afterlife. Celestial imagery cascades from the poem – *aeterias domos, premia lucis, aeria sede,* and *sinceras auras* – but is brilliantly concentrated in the *stelliger polus* and *sidera caeli* that surround Bassa (*hanc*) in the fourth line of the first column – or better, amid which Bassa rests just before the line's *caesura.* Yet if Bassa's enthusiasm for the stars appears unusually strong, it is hardly unique. Bassa's eminently noble contemporary, Petronius Probus (whose sepulchral poem manifestly puns upon his name) was interred at St. Peter's but nevertheless, his lengthy verse epitaph proclaimed, lived on to possess the stars (*vivit et astra tenet*).[15] Rather less exalted in life but no less grand in his designs was the otherwise unknown presbyter, Celerinus, who abandoned his body at S. Agnese in order to rejoice among those same stars (*qui gaudet in astris*).[16] In this company the eighty-six year old *inlustris femina,* Decentia, vouches for the notion's continuing appeal a century on: *sidera me retinent,* declared her epitaph. The stars possess me! *ad vitam redii.*[17]

The sources of this poignant astral longing are distant, though earlier at Rome the sublime heights reached out for by such late ancient Christians as Bassa and Probus were reserved for civic benefactors of heroic stature and, eventually, emperors. In the second century BCE Quintus Ennius, in an

13 Ferrua at *ICUR* 5.14076, noting that Josi's *[per cuncta sae]culae Bassae* violated both the marble and the meter. The potential word play, pointed out to me Carl P. E. Springer, further favours the supplement.

14 On Vergil see above note 10 and below. A3 is nicely alliterative; A8 offers a series of *–um* endings.

15 *CIL* 6.1 1876, 389 *ad* nos. 1751–1756 = *CLE* 1897, 1347 = *ILCV* 1924–1931, 63 = *ICUR* 2 1935, 4219. Probus died about 390. See *PLRE* 1 1971, 736–740, 'Probus 5,' and Trout 2001, 157–176.

16 *CLE* 668 = *ILCV* 1129 = ICUR 8.20798: *Praesbyter hic situs est Celerinus nomine dic[tus], / corporeos rumpens nexus qui gaudet in astris.* From S. Agnese on the Via Nomentana with a consular date of 381. See Pietri and Pietri 1999, 426, 'Celerinus 1;' Rüpke and Glock 2008, 606, 'Celerinus 3'. For his sister, Aemiliana, interred in the same catacomb, see *ILCV* 1129n = ICUR 8.20878.

17 *CLE* 1363 = *ILCV* 217a: *sidera me retinent … ad vitam redii. Quae vixit annos p(lus) m(inus) LXXVI.* Early sixth century? See *PLRE* 2 1980, 348, 'Decentia'.

epigram penned as a pseudo-epitaph for Scipio Africanus, had already opened 'heaven's great gate' and the 'regions of the heavenly gods' to the victor over Hannibal: 'If it is permissible for anyone to ascend to the regions of the heaven-dwelling gods,' Scipio's 'epitaph' boasted, 'Heaven's great gate lies open to me alone.'[18] The appealing notion would, of course, find its worthy echo in Cicero's reflections on service to the *res publica.*[19] But the conceit of celestial reward granted for special merit and *virtus* exercised on behalf of the state, finds its early apogee in the language used by the Augustan poets to describe the apotheosis of Caesar or forecast the heavenly prize awaiting Augustus himself.[20] It is especially telling, of course, that the concept found manifold expression in the one text, Vergil's *Aeneid,* whose influence over fourth-century ways of thinking (and writing poetry) is virtually incalculable.[21] It was, for example, through displays of manliness, Apollo informed the epic's young Iulus (9.641), that men might reach the stars: 'A blessing on your new *virtus,* boy, *sic itur ad astra.*' So, too, Jupiter would remind Juno that Aeneas (as Indiges) was owed to the heavens and would be raised to the stars (*ad sidera tolli*) by the Fates (12.794–95). Even the manly Dido knew as much: *fama,* she proclaimed, was her sole pathway *ad sidera.*[22]

It was more likely the burgeoning cult of the martyrs, however, rather than the late antique cultivation of Vergil, that most immediately inspired and shaped the imagery of many late fourth- and early fifth-century private epitaphs intent upon charting a course to the astral zone. Here there is only time to draw attention to the singular influence of the *elogia* of Damasus, bishop of Rome from 366 to 384, both upon the character of Bassa's epitaph itself and also more generally upon the late-fourth-century resurgence of the epigraphic habit and revitalisation of the *carmen epigraphicum* at Rome.[23] Throughout the Roman suburbs, in proximity to the tombs of the city's early Christian heroes, Damasus installed dozens of elegantly inscribed marble tablets celebrating (however vaguely) in Vergilian inspired verse the *res gestae* of martyrs whose sepulchers' (like Bassa's) retained only *corpora* and *membra* and whose *animae* (like hers)

---

18 Courtney 1993, 40–42, 'Ennius 44': *si fas endo plagas caelestum ascendere cuiquam, / mi soli caeli maxima porta patet.*

19 Cicero, *De re publica* 6.15–29 (the *Somnium Scipionis*): *ea vita via est in caelum* (6.16).

20 On the numismatic and poetic evidence for Octavian/Augustus' appropriation of the *sidus Iulium* see Gurval 1997.

21 See, for example, MacCormack 1998; McGill 2005; Green 2006 and the essays in Rees 2004 and Scourfield 2007.

22 *Aen.* 4.322–323: … *qua sola sidera adibam, / fama prior.*

23 On the central role of Damasus' verse *elogia* and epitaphs in this regard see Carletti 2001, 335, 347, 380.

had shot heavenward.[24] At the Catacomb of San Callisto, on the Via Appia, not far from Bassa's resting place, revered tombs – Damasus had proclaimed – preserved the 'bodies' of a 'throng of the pious' though the 'palace of heaven' had snatched up their spirits.[25] In the same neighbourhood, at the Basilica Apostolorum (and in lines and phrases that reappeared on Bassa's sarcophagus) Peter and Paul followed Christ *per astra* to reach the *aetherios sinus regnaque piorum*, where Damasus hailed them as Rome's *nova sidera* – as once Vergil had cast Octavian (not yet Augustus) as Rome's 'new star'.[26]

Indeed, no text better illustrates the drift of concepts and language from the 'official' commemorative *elogia* of the martyrs to the graves of ordinary Romans than Bassa's epitaph. The debts are manifest in expression alone. The phrase *regna piorum*, for example, which ends the second line of the first column of Bassa's epitaph, had earlier appeared in Damasus' *elogium* for Hippolytus on the Via Tiburtina (35.4) while the variant *regnaque piorum* concludes a line in four other Damasan *elogia* (25.4, 43.5, 39.8), one of which is the *elogium* for Peter and Paul installed at the Basilica Apostolorum (20.5). The collocations *aetheriam domum*, *aetherias domus*, and *deum venturum*, which are apparently echoed in lines two and eight of the first column of Bassa's epitaph, each appear once in a Damasan poem (43.5, 25.2, and 39.2 respectively) while the Virgilian tag *regia caeli*, which ends line five of the second column, appears in the same position in four Damasan martyrial *elogia*, as well as in his epitaph for his sister Irene (16.3, 25.2, 39.4, 47.3; 11.11 [Irene]).[27] A number of these *elogia*, it is worth noting, as well as Irene's epitaph, were installed in complexes in the general vicinity of the Catacomb of Praetextatus.

But one Damasan *elogium* was, in fact, on display quite close to hand. In the area of the so-called *spelunca magna* of the same catacomb complex, that of Praetextatus, that would receive Bassa's sarcophagus, Damasus had installed a text honouring the martyrs Felicissimus and Agapitus. Three pieces of the

24 E.g. Curran 2000, 148–155; Trout 2005, 298–315, both with bibliography. On Damasus' poetics and the role of Vergil therein see Fontaine 1981, 111–125, but especially 119–122; Fontaine 1986, 115–145.

25 Ferrua 1942, 16.1–3: *Hic congesta iacet quaeris si turba piorum. / corpora sanctorum retinent veneranda sepulcra. / sublimes animas rapuit sibi regia caeli.* All further references are to Ferrua's edition. On line 16.3 note the echoes of Ver. *Aen.* 5.254–255: *quem (Ganymede) praepes ab Ida / sublimem pedibus rapuit Iovis armiger uncis*; 6.719–720: *putandum est / sublimis animas iterumque ad terra reverti / corpora?*; and 7.210: *regia caeli.*

26 Damasus, 20. 4–7: *sanguinis ob meritum Xpumq(ue) per astra secuti / aetherios petiere sinus regnaque piorum: / Roma suos potius meruit defendere cives. / Haec Damasus vestras referat nova sidera laudes.* Ver. *Geo.* 1.32: *anne novum tardis sidus te mensibus addas.* On the imagery of early imperial apotheosis see Gurval 1997, and Gradel 2002, 291–320, with stars on coins commemorating *divus* Augustus (fig. 12.1 A) and *diva* Faustina Maior (fig. 12.3 J). On a Damasan jab at the Dioscuri see Trout 2005, 304–305.

27 Ver. *Aen.* 7.210 (on the apotheosis of Dardanus): *aurea nunc solio stellantis regia caeli.*

original marble tablet were discovered in 1927 in the pavement of S. Nicola dei Cesarini, which in 1132 had been built into Temple A of the Largo Argentina complex. The full text, however, had long been known from a late antique copy.[28]

Aspice, et hic tumulus retinet caelestia membra
Sanctorum subito rapuit quos regia caeli.
Hi crucis invictae comites pariterq(ue) ministri
Rectoris sancti meritumq(ue) fidemq(ue) secuti
Aetherias petiere domos regnaq(ue) piorum.
Unica in his gaudet Romanae gloria plebis
Quod duce tunc Xysto Xpi meruere triumphos.
Felicissimo et Agapeto martyrib(us) Damasus episc(opus) fecit.

Behold! This tomb, too, preserves the celestial limbs
of saints whom suddenly the palace of heaven snatched up.
These, at once comrades and attendants of the unconquered cross,
imitating both the merit and the faith of (their) holy bishop,
won an ethereal home and the realms of the pious.
The singular glory of the Roman people rejoices in them
because with Sixtus at that time as their leader they gained Christ's triumphs.
For Felicissimus and Agapitus, the holy martyrs, Damasus the bishop made (this).

Regia caeli and *secuti* appear in this *elogium* with the same semantic value and in the same metrical position as they do in Bassa's epitaph but, most tellingly, line five of Damasus' epigram for Felicissimus and Agapitus must be the inspiration for the second line of the first column of Bassa's epitaph: Damasus' *aetherias petiere domos regnaq(ue) piorum* has become in the hands of the author of Bassa's epitaph *aeterias secuta domos ac regna piorum.*[29] A bit of clumsiness in the adaptation, requiring the lengthening of the normally short first syllable of

28 Damasus, 25. For the details see Ferrua 1942, 152–156. There were at least two other Damasan *elogia* in the same general area: 24 (Januarius) and 27 (Quirinus?). Fragments of another (26) point to a third. For the debate on the exact location of the *memoria* of Felicissimus and Agapitus see Tolotti 1977, 82–87; Spera 2004, 192–205, and Spera 2006, 257.

29 Already noted by Wilpert 1932, 294 and Ferrua 1942, 154. For a similar construction note Damasus 39.5: *aeternam petiere domum regnaque piorum*, for the martyrs Felix and Philip at the catacomb of Priscilla.

secuta, only highlights the dependency.[30] In short, if all we now possessed were a pilgrim's copy of Bassa's epitaph, we would be happy to draw from such evidence further conclusions about the influence of Damasus' monumental *elogia* on the literary and imaginative sensibilities of Rome's everyday Christians – and remark how easily commemorative strategies and poetic language leaked from martyr cult to private tombs in late fourth-century Rome, opening the starry heavens to some whose claims upon the ethereal realm arose neither from the kind of bloody self-sacrifice made by the martyrs nor the lofty social rank of a *consularis* such as Petronius Probus but from their professed enactment of less spectacular religious and conjugal ideals.[31]

The Visual Imagery

Bassa's epitaph, however, is also a predominant component of a visual field (Figure 10.1). And although, the relatively rough and uneven finish accorded to the sculpted images may be evidence of priority given to the inscribed text,[32] it is especially the monument's unusual melding of poetic language and figural images that establishes it as striking testimony to the complex mechanisms of agency and identity in late ancient Rome. As previously noted, all other representatives of the Bethesda group (see Figures 10. 2 and 10.3) apparently reproduce the same sequence of scenes.[33] Not only the particular images,

30 See above note 11. In line eight of the same column, however, *secuta*, in the Damasan position at the line's end, scans properly.

31 Carletti 1998, 51–53, on such language of merit as *castus/a* and the preference for *coniunx.*

32 On the apparently incomplete aspects of the sculpted relief, unpolished and without drillings, see Nicoletti 1981, 16 and Mazzei 2004, 113–114.

33 Art historians concerned with the classification, chronology, workshops, and style of Christian sarcophagi have variously assessed the Bethesda type. Lawrence 1927, 23–24 initiated debate by construing the Bethesda type as a subset of the city-gate type (itself, in her view, a subset of the columnar type) and dating the city-gate group to the later fourth century, a dating now generally accepted on stylistic grounds. But Lawrence also argued that the city-gate type was a continuation of 'Asiatic' traditions of iconography, style, and ornament, though allowing that the Bethesda subset represented, in her view, a 'mixed' form, incorporating elements of the western 'frieze' tradition. In a subsequent study, Lawrence 1932, 103–185 further identified the workshops of southern Gaul, perhaps staffed by eastern craftsmen, as the medium through which such 'Asiatic' influences (along with unfinished columnar sarcophagi) reached Rome. See esp., 121–122, for her assignment of both Red Sea type and Bethesda type sarcophagi, including the Tarragona (Nicoletti 1981, no. 2; Koch, 2000, 315, no. 38) and Vatican (*Rep.* I, no. 63) examples illustrated here (figs. 2 and 3) to a Gallic atelier (she was not yet aware of Bassa's sarcophagus). Scholarly opinion, however, now favours a Roman origin for the Bethesda type and identifies Roman workshops as the certain source of the two examples from

therefore, but also the regularity of their order must have determined how some ancient viewers read the Bethesda type – and thus responded to its manipulation by the patrons who commissioned and the artisans who carved Bassa's sarcophagus. A brief discussion of the general type's scenes is, therefore, in order.

The group's central, emblematic scene is universally understood to reference (at least in its upper register) a healing miracle recounted only in the Gospel of John (5.1–9):

> Some time later, Jesus went up to Jerusalem for one of the Jewish festivals. Now at the Sheep Gate in Jerusalem there is a pool whose Hebrew name is Bethesda. It has five colonnades and in them lay a great number of sick people, blind, lame, and paralysed. Among them was a man who had been crippled for thirty-eight years. Jesus saw him lying there, and knowing that he had been ill a long time he asked him, 'Do you want to get well?' 'Sir,' he replied, 'I have no one to put me in the pool when the water is disturbed; while I am getting there, someone else steps into the pool before me.' Jesus answered, 'Stand up, take your bed and walk.' The man recovered instantly; he took up his bed and began to walk.[34]

Most often the Bethesda type's depiction of this episode is seen to unfold in a serial narrative that moves from the lower to the upper register of the central tableau and embraces the figure of Christ just to the left of this tableau.[35] In the lower half, the cripple lies on his pallet, waiting to be carried into the pool's healing waters, and gestures towards the approaching figure of Christ; in the upper half, he has apparently fulfilled Christ's command, 'Stand up, take your bed and walk'.[36] Fidelity to the details of John's account – the colonnade above and wavy water lines on the horizontal divider – leave no doubt that the Bethesda episode is represented in the upper register.[37] In 1985, however, Françoise Monfrin, echoing an observation of Manuel Sotomayor, noted the striking differences in the design of the bed and especially the clothing of the sick man portrayed in the two registers. Sotomayor had explained the contrast

Rome (Bassa's and the Vatican sarcophagus) and perhaps for the Spanish and North African Bethesda examples, while recognising that the fragmentary Gallic examples were most likely locally carved; see the summary at Nicoletti 1981, 4–6, 79–90, and the scheme of Koch 2000, 298–302, who classifies the Bethesda type as 'die Einzugs-Sarkophage (Bethesda-Sarkophage)' and makes it a subset of the single frieze type ('Einzonige Fries-Sarkophage') of the 'valentiniansch-theodosianischen Zeit'.

34 Translation: *The Oxford Study Bible* (New York, 1992). The episode is unusually detailed by New Testament standards and may target the healing cult of Asclepius; see Knipp 1998, 151–153.

35 E.g. Wilpert 1932, 293; Nicoletti 1981, 64–66; Knipp 1998, 149–52.

36 Jn 5.8: *surge tolle grabattum tuum et ambula.* All biblical citations (despite the possible anachronism) are from the *Biblia Sacra Iuxta Vulgatam Versionem* (Stuttgart, 1994). Knipp 1998, 143–149 offers detailed description.

37 See Minasi 2000, 242 on the rarity of representations that clearly distinguish the healing at Bethesda from the healing of the paralytic at Capernaum recorded in the synoptic gospels (Mt 9.1–8; Mk 2.3–12; Lk 5.5.18–16).

between the tunic and *pallium* of the main figure in the lower register and the simpler sleeveless (*exomis*) tunic of the paralytic in the upper register as a double reference to the same Bethesda episode, which he thought was portrayed descriptively above but typologically below, where the reclining figure's more ornate dress was intended to suggest the regeneration of baptism.[38] Monfrin, however, argued that the contrast between the upper and lower 'paralytic' made problematic any identification of them as representations of the same individual at two stages of the Bethesda miracle narrative. Moreover, Monfrin suggested that the lower scene was iconographically reminiscent of a *prothesis* or *conclamatio*, the lamentation over the dead or dying, and represented a different healing episode from that shown in the upper register. He argued, therefore, on iconographic, scriptural, exegetical, and liturgical grounds, that the most likely scriptural source for the lower scene was Christ's healing (at Capernaum) of the servant of the centurion, which appears in Matthew (8.5–13) and Luke (7.1–10) and was at times conflated with John's account (4.43–54) of Christ's healing of the son of the royal official, an episode set in Galilee immediately prior to John's account of the healing at Bethesda.[39] Despite persistent argument for the unity of the two scenes, Monfrin's critique has raised significant and unresolved questions about the identification of the lower register of the central tableau.[40] What that critique does not deny, however, and what must have been evident to all ancient viewers, is that both registers, upper and lower, unambiguously advertised Christ's salvific power.

Christ's power to heal miraculously is equally on display in the two scenes to the left of the central panel. On the far left Christ restores the sight of two (or three) blind men in a scene often equated with a Gospel episode set at Jericho, though other scriptural candidates are possible and certainty is unlikely, even perhaps unnecessary.[41] Between this scene and the central scene appears a woman kneeling before Christ, who holds his right hand over or atop her head. On the basis of the posture and gestures of the woman and the figure of Christ, it has seemed preferable to see here a representation of the haemorrhaging woman cured by touching Christ's clothing.[42] To be sure other candidates have been proposed: the suppliant Canaanite or Phoenician woman of Matthew

38 Sotomayor 1975, 217–218.

39 Monfrin 1985, 979–1020.

40 Nicoletti 1981, 65–66, had responded to Sotomayor; as would Knipp 1998, 155–160 but without notice of Monfrin.

41 Mt 20.29–34, the only New Testament text that offers a double healing. See Simon 1938, 206 and Nicoletti 1981, 40–46, with discussion of sources and comparanda. For the possibilities see also Ranucii 2000, 200. On entertaining ambiguity see Monfrin 1985, 999–1000. Note that the Tarragona sarcophagus and Bassa's portray three blind figures; see Nicoletti 1981, 9–10, 14–15.

42 Matt 9.20–22; Mk. 5.25–34; Lk 8.43–48 with Nicoletti 1981, 47–52.

15.22 and Mark 7.25,[43] and Mary, the sister of Lazarus, whose appeal before Christ is known from John 11.32.[44] In any case, many ancient viewers, even if similarly uncertain, should nonetheless have understood this supplication scene, buttressed by incontestable scenes of healing to its left and right, as another display of Christ's curative powers. To the right of the central tableau unfold two further easily identified New Testament scenes. The first portrays Luke's account (19.2–8) of the calling of the tax-collector Zacchaeus, perched in the sycamore tree from which he hoped to catch sight of Jesus as he passed through Jericho en route to Jerusalem.[45] The final scene then illustrated Christ's (triumphal) entry into Jerusalem itself, seated upon a donkey and greeted with shouts of Hosanna and the waving of palm branches.[46]

Typically the identification of scenes, especially the first two on the left, has responded to assumptions or arguments about the overall meaning and message of the Bethesda type. And this, too, understandably has provoked various reflections. M. Simon in 1938, for example, and more recently Galit Noga-Banai, intrigued by the architectural detail of the central scenario and the unusually regular sequencing of the other images, have keyed the type's message to a pilgrim's or reader's experience and understanding of Holy Land topography.[47] Other interpretations, less closely bound to material *realia*, have drawn attention to contemporary catechetical instruction and exegetical strategies that loaded the episode of the waters of Bethesda with baptismal overtones.[48] But in a funerary context, as Monfrin also stressed,[49] many viewers must naturally have read the progression from easily allegorised scenes of healing to the resurrection alluded to by Christ's Jerusalem advent as a narrative of divine power and salvation that had profound implications for their own eternal welfare.[50] That is, the extraordinary momentum of narrative and design that draws the viewer forward through the miracle series to the threshold of

43 Wilpert 1932, 293; Monfrin 1985, 999–1000.

44 Simon 1938, 213–215.

45 Nicoletti 1981, 69–71, distinguished here (by the repetition of the figure of Christ) from the entry scene itself, in which Zacchaeus had been included when previously represented.

46 Nicoletti 1981, 72–73; Mathews 1999, 27–28 on the popularity of the scene on western sarcophagi.

47 Simon 1938, 200–223; Noga-Binai 2007, 107–123.

48 See, for example, the discussions at Monfrin 1985, 984 and 994–995, who sees the baptismal typology as overly subtle; Knipp 1998, 155–158; and Noga-Binai 2007, 112–113.

49 Monfrin 1985, 997–999.

50 On the importance of 'social context' to the construction of meaning see Elsner 1995, 249–287.

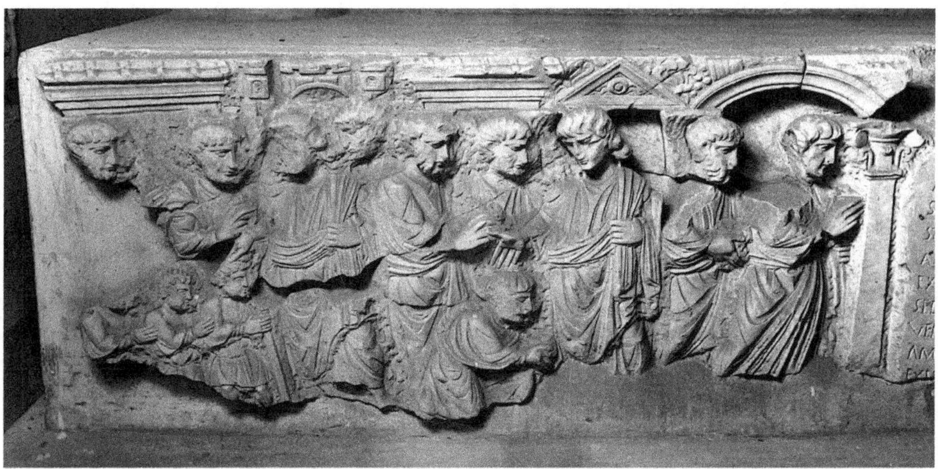

Figure 10.6: The Sarcophagus of Bassa, left front. Photograph: DAIR 1963.1123 (Sansaini).

Christ's victory ovcr dcath also implics thc dcccascd's journcy toward thc everlasting reward guaranteed by that Gospel narrative.[51]

It is, then, this particular narrative thrust, with all its promise, that the design of Bassa's sarcophagus seems so artlessly to suspend (Figures 10.1 and 10.6), portraying the healing of the blind men (apparently numbering three not two), the kneeling woman, and even Christ approaching the Bethesda Pool, but replacing the anticipated visual climax with the epitaph's verbal display.[52] But just how clumsy or cavalier is this monument?

Agency and Identity

We may never know more about Bassa than her epitaph tells. She died young and lamented, at twenty-two probably not a new bride for Roman girls, pagan and Christian, typically first married in their late teens.[53] Perhaps the

51 Simon 1938, 208–209 and Nicoletti 1981, 35–40, concerning the narrative thrust of the Bethesda design comparable to that of the Red Sea type.

52 Wilpert 1932, 294: a 'strano combiamento'; Nicoletti 1981, 16: 'L'interruzione ... è senza dubbio estranea allo spirito che informa l'arte cristiana'.

53 Nordberg 1963, 66–68: 'the most usual age at which women in Rome got married was between 15 and 18 years,' though the statistical average of his group (125 women) was 20.4 years of age; Carletti 1977, 39–51: with an average of 20.3 but with half of his examples (90 of 187) falling between 14 and 18 years of age (40–41); Shaw 1987, 30–46: 'late teens' (43).

complications of childbirth were to blame.[54] In any case, her age put her in good company: Henric Nordberg's 1963 study of Christian epitaphs yielded an average female life span for the commemorated dead of exactly twenty-two years (22.0).[55] Bassa also joins the ranks of girls and very young women who disproportionately populate Rome's funerary epigraphy[56] – an imbalance most likely reflecting the propensity of men to commemorate wives and daughters for the benefit of male public culture. It follows, then, that Gaudentius probably conducted Bassa's last rites, commissioned her monument, and, as the acrostic also suggests (*Bassae suae . . . Gaudentius*), composed her epitaph. After all, as Éric Rebillard has convincingly argued, the burial and commemoration of Christians was still very much a family affair, immune from the strictures of ecclesiastical control.[57]

But the readers of Bassa's epitaph were also viewers and we should try to put ourselves in the place of those who by intent or coincidence, in the course of funerary rites or annual commemorations and banquets for the dead, may have paused to consider the message(s) of Bassa's memorial.[58] It is often postulated, as it has been, for example, by Richard Brilliant, Michael Koortbojian, and Jas' Elsner, that the abbreviated scenes on second-century mythological sarcophagi might act as metonymous tableaux, inviting viewers, through analogy and allegory, to identify the deceased with the stories of Meleager or Achilles or Endymion displayed on their coffins.[59] Fourth-century 'private' art at Rome

54 Carroll 2006, 153–154.

55 Nordberg 1963, 38–40, based on 1254 Christian epitaphs of Roman women (ranging from the third to the sixth century).

56 E.g. Shaw 1987, 34–35; Dresken-Weiland 2004, 149–153, calculating that 32 % of 310 early Christian Roman sarcophagi from the last third of third century to the end of the fourth were utilised for the burial of women as opposed to 30.6 % for men (reversing the trend she observes for earlier pagan sarcophagi).

57 Rebillard 2003, 143–160 and surveyed at Rebillard 2009, 220–230.

58 The viewing context of all such monuments is difficult to establish, a problem compounded in this case by uncertainty on the original location of Bassa's sarcophagus, though placement in a *cubiculum*, visible to passersby as well as family, may be likely. See, e. g. Fiocchi Nicolai, in Fiocchi Nicolai, Bisconti, and Mazzoleni 2002, 44–46. For more on funerary rites and the regularity of annual commemorative rituals and banquets (*refrigeria*) in this age see Krautheimer 1960, 31–33; Marinone 2000, 71–80, noting (75) the difficulty of reconstructing these rites in the adverse conditions of the catacombs; Bisconti, Fiocchi Nicolai, et al. 2001, 63–96; and Jensen 2008, 107–143.

59 Brilliant 1984, 124–165, esp. 150 (on the 'metonymous order established by the Roman artists in their creation of a doubly referential system of causality, applicable to the bios of Meleager and to the life of the deceased') and 164 (where artists and patrons collaborate in the construction and reading of a 'metonymous tableau' and linear narrative ceases to govern the composition of the visual program). Koortbojian 1995, 1–22, with emphasis on analogical and symbolic associations between the myths and the life of the deceased; Elsner 1998, 149–54.

should have been no less susceptible to readings that connected patrons with the narrative and figural imagery they commissioned or deployed. For instance, the interplay of domestic scenes, mythological imagery, and Christian exhortation on the luxurious Casket of Proiecta encouraged viewers not only to reconcile 'complex and even contradictory discourses' but also to imagine and eroticise 'Proiecta's' uxorial life.[60] Similarly, the juxtaposed Biblical tableaux and conventional (not to say pagan) imagery of the sarcophagus of the noble neophyte Junius Bassus (Figure 11.1) – 'loftier' in death than he had been even as Urban Prefect in 359 – in dialogue with his coffin's Christian epitaph and 'classicising' verse *elogium*, suggestively linked Bassus both to his aristocratic forebears and to an alternate nobility of witness – especially the Roman Peter and Paul – that included a magisterial Christ figure.[61] In this regard, his sarcophagus' fecund symbolic and allegorical enticements surely seduced ancient viewers no less successfully than they have modern art historians.[62]

Might, then, some Roman viewers – adept consumers of visual imagery – have made more of Bassa's ensemble than a hodge-podge of broken narrative and borrowed verse?[63] Certainly the patchwork quality of the sarcophagus, with its bricolage quality and Damasan *spolia*, conforms to an 'aesthetic of appropriation' widely evident in such diverse fourth-century monuments as the Arch of Constantine and the Vergilian cento, wherein Roman eyes, it seems, were readier to recognise thematic unity than the stylistic or generic incongruities that have distracted some modern art historians.[64] Moreover, the juxtaposition of images and words in Bassa's sarcophagus is surely not as jarring as it first appears. The stranded figure of Christ, who gestures toward, even leans into, the *tabula* of the epitaph, surely encourages the viewer to understand Bassa's ascension to the 'ethereal home' of the saints as yet another miracle

60 Shelton 1981, with Elsner 1995, 251–258, 266 ('a highly sophisticated parallelism between patron and goddess') and especially Elsner 2003b, 22–36, quote 32. Shelton 1981, 31 considered the casket and the inscription contemporary; as Elsner 2003b, 22 points out, a 'later owner' could have added the inscription.

61 For the similar rhetoric of Constantine's mausoleum/Church of the Holy Apostles see Elsner 2000, 159–162.

62 Malbon 1990, e.g., 134, 152–53, with discussion of earlier studies 22–38; and more recently Elsner 2003a, 82–86 and Suzawa 2008, 99–116. Peter and Paul are prominent in their arrest scenes and in a *traditio legis* tableau where they flank an enthroned Christ, who also appears in a Jerusalem entry scene and his own arrest scene. For the 'classicising elegiacs' (289) of the *elogium* see Cameron 2002, 288–292, emending the final distich to '*[cedite sublimes] spirantum cedite honores, / [celsius (loftier) est culmen] mors quod huic tribuit*'.

63 A good example of interpretive sophistication among 'ordinary' Romans at Clarke 2003, 215–219: 'double entendre' in an Ostian sarcophagus.

64 Clark and Hatch 1981; Elsner 2000, quote 176; McGill 2005, with Kinney 1997, 139–140, on the challenge presented to modern observers by ancient theomorphic portraits.

performed by Christ. Wonders once worked – sight restored and health renewed – vouched for by scripture and easily seen as metaphor – thus justify Bassa's assurance to Gaudentius (and others temporarily left behind): from 'death's snares' you, too, will be saved (*sospes eris*). Perhaps some were even prepared to see Bassa's untimely death glossed metonymically in the trials of those rescued here by Christ's touch and presence, particularly in the image of the kneeling woman (the sole female present in the Bethesda type), to whom Jesus said 'Your faith has healed you (*fides tua te salvam fecit*)'.[65] In any case, like them, as her epitaph proclaimed, she 'trusted in God' and followed Christ with a 'pure heart'.[66] Similarly Christ's restoration of sight to the blind men finds an echo in Bassa's plea that Gaudentius should look up (*suspice*) to see a scene of salvation and eternal life that was veiled to eyes not touched in some way by Christ's power. Despite the shift in idiom, then – from figural to textual – these and other themes might well seem to link the two halves of Bassa's sarcophagus, making her astral victory but another chapter in the coffin's narrative of spiritual healing and salvation.

Such connections, present on the surface, would not have been hard to imagine. But just as Bassa's epitaph cites a Damasan poem installed elsewhere in the same catacomb – eliding the years that separated Theodosian Rome from the ancient city of the martyrs while also fashioning Bassa as a new kind of witness – might not her sarcophagus also allude to its other intertext? Did some who came upon Bassa's sarcophagus sense the presence of the 'missing' scenes? The healing at Bethesda, the calling of Zacchaeus, and Christ's triumphal procession would then bleed through the words to resituate Bassa's celestial immortality against the background of those long-ago events that had spawned Rome's newest history. To such eyes, Christ of the Bethesdan pool and the palm frond acclamations might have been visible in the epitaph's prominent (and easily recognisable) christo-gram, through which Bassa would live forever (*vivens per secula Xpo*).[67] Zacchaeus, told by Luke's Jesus, 'today this house has been saved,' prefigures the salvation of Bassa and her house, swept now into Jesus' universalising proclamation, 'For the Son of Man has come to seek and save what was lost (*perierat*),' – which also might mean, of course, what has died (*pereo*). Indeed, the foundations of Bassa's vaunted *regna piorum* and *regia caeli* had been set in place by the crucifixion and resurrection that are the narrative

65 Mt 9.21–22: '*Si tetigero tantum vestimentum eius, salva ero.*' *Et Iesus conversus et videns eam dixit:* '*Confide, filia; fides tua te salvam fecit.*' If not adequate on its own to explain Gaudentius' (or Bassa's) choice of a Bethesda type for his wife's memorial, the presence of the kneeling woman may have cemented its appeal.

66 Compare A8, '*venturumq(ue) deum puro [cum] corde secutā*', with Mt 20.34 (on the two blind men at Jericho): '*et confestim viderunt et secuti sunt eum*'.

67 Carletti 1998, 53–54 on the high frequency (10 %) of the christo-gram in Roman funerary epigraphy.

fulfillment of Christ's Jerusalem advent and the implicit dénouement of the Bethesdan imagery.

It would be foolhardy to push such notions too far, to demand a particular set of correlations between the words of Bassa's epitaph and the elements of the Bethesda narrative that her verses have replaced. It may not be irresponsible, however, to think that from this sarcophagus' mix of words, images, and allusions ancient viewers were also tempted to construct meanings that transcended what would have been possible on the basis of the inscribed text or sculpted images alone. Moreover, both the idiosyncrasy of the coffin's design and the bravado of its verse epitaph suggest that Bassa, Gaudentius, and the artisans of some Roman atelier expected viewers to see/read this memorial in some fashion against a background of merit and reward that receded past Rome's martyrial horizons, so recently illuminated by the *elogia* of Damasus, to the even more distant age of wonders worked by the living Christ on the eve of his own resurrection (and perhaps to the equally ancient astral claims of divinised heroes and emperors).

In other words, Bassa's monument has a no less powerful claim than Proiecta's casket or Junius Bassus's sarcophagus to document a purposeful manipulation of the still fluid signs and symbols that embodied 'religion' in this age. As a less exalted participant in the visual revolution that Jas' Elsner has called the 'deep Christian project of fostering a cohesive sense of identity related to Scripture,' then, Bassa's sarcophagus reflects the efforts of middling Romans to (re-)invent themselves by manipulating a scriptural, poetic, and visual vocabulary that rose to prominence along the cultural front of the post-Constantinian decades.[68] In Bassa's case, episcopally sponsored classicising poetry and art forms made legible through singular and seriatim standardisation were borrowed and bent to the novel expression of personal and social identity. Cumulatively such endeavors might forge the loyalties that allowed Christianity to weather the disputes, schisms, and sectarian violence that often seem to dominate the story of *Roma Christiana.* Singularly they reveal the array of voices that continually shaped and re-shaped that Christianity.

Bibliography

Bisconti, F., Fiocchi Nicolai, V. et al. Riti e corredi funerari, in: *Christiana loca: Lo spazio cristiano nella Roma del primo millennio 2,* edited by L. Pani Ermini (Rome, 2001), 63–96.

Brilliant, R. Mythological Sarcophagi: Proleptic Visions, in: *Visual Narratives: Storytelling in Etruscan and Roman Art,* by R. Brilliant (Ithaca and London, 1984), 124–165.

68 Elsner 1995, 247–287, quote 251.

Cameron, A. The Funeral of Junius Bassus. *Zeitschrift für Papyrologie und Epigraphik* 139 (2002), 288–292.
Carletti, C. Aspetti biometrici del matrimonio nelle iscrizioni cristiane di Roma. *Augustinianum* 17 (1977), 39–51.
Carletti, C. 'Un mondo nuovo.' Epigrafia funeraria dei cristiani a Roma in età postcostantiniana. *Vetera Christianorum* 35 (1998), 39–67.
Carletti, C. Dalla 'pratica aperta' alla 'pratica chiusa': produzione epigrafica a Roma tra V e VIII secolo, in: *Roma nell'alto medioevo* (Spoleto, 2001), 325–392.
Carroll, M. *Spirits of the Dead: Roman Funerary Commemoration in Western Europe* (Oxford and New York, 2006).
Clark E. and Hatch, D. *The Golden Bough, The Oaken Cross: The Virgilian Cento of Faltonia Betitia Proba* (California, 1981).
Clarke, J. R. *Art in the Lives of Ordinary Romans: Visual Representation and Non-Elite Viewers in Italy, 100 B.C.-A.D. 315* (Berkeley, Los Angeles, and London, 2003).
Courtney, E. *The Fragmentary Latin Poets* (Oxford, 1993).
Curran, J. *Pagan City and Christian Capital: Rome in the Fourth Century* (Oxford, 2000).
Dresken-Weiland, J. Ricerche sui committenti e destinatari dei sarcofagi paleocristiani a Roma, in: F. Bisconti and H. Brandenburg (eds.), *Sarcofagi tardoantichi, paleocristiani e altomedievali: Atti della giornata tematica dei Seminari di Archeologia Cristiana (École Française de Rome-8 Maggio 2002)* (Vatican City, 2004), 149–153.
Elsner, J. *Art and the Roman Viewer: The Transformation of Art from the Pagan World to Christianity* (Cambridge, 1995).
Elsner, J. *Imperial Rome and Christian Triumph: The Art of the Roman Empire AD 100–450* (Oxford and New York, 1998).
Elsner, J. From the Culture of *spolia* to the Cult of Relics: The Arch of Constantine and the Genesis of Late Antique Forms. *Papers of the British School at Rome* 68 (2000), 149–184.
Elsner, J. Inventing Christian Rome: The Role of Early Christian Art, in: *Rome the Cosmopolis*, edited by C. Edwards and G. Woolf (Cambridge, 2003a), 71–99.
Elsner, J. Visualizing Women in Late Antique Rome: The Projecta Casket, in: *Through a Glass Brightly: Studies in Byzantine and Medieval Art and Archaeology Presented to David Buckton*, edited by C. Entwistle (Oxford, 2003b), 22–36.
Ferrua, A. *Epigrammata Damasiana* (Vatican City, 1942).
Ferrua, A. *Inscriptiones Christianae Urbis Romae. Vol. 5* (Vatican City, 1971).
Fiocchi Nicolai, V., Bisconti, F. and Mazzoleni, D. *The Christian Catacombs of Rome: History, Decoration, Inscriptions* (second edition) (Regensburg, 2002).
Fontaine, J. *Naissance de la poésie dans l'occident chrétien* (Paris, 1981).
Fontaine, J. Damase poète Théodosien: L'imaginaire poétique des epigrammata, in: *Saecularia Damasiana: Atti del convegno internazionale per il XVI centenario della morte di papa Damaso I* (Vatican City, 1986), 115–145.
Garver, M. *Quaelibet Audendi:* Fortunatus and the Acrostic. *TAPA* 123 (1993), 219–245.
Gell, A. *Art and Agency: An Anthropological Theory* (Oxford, 1998).
Gradel, I. *Emperor Worship and Roman Religion* (Oxford, 2002).
Green, R. P. H. *Latin Epics of the New Testament: Juvencus, Sedulius, Arator* (Oxford and New York, 2006).
Gurval, R. Caesar's Comet: The Politics and Poetics of an Augustan Myth. *Memoirs of the American Academy in Rome* 42 (1997), 39–71.

Jensen, R. M. Dining with the Dead: From the *Mensa* to the Altar in Christian Late Antiquity, in: *Commemorating the Dead: Texts and Artifacts in Context*, edited by L. Brink and D. Green (Berlin and New York, 2008), 107–143.

Josi, E. Note sul cimitero di Pretestato III: La sistemazione del materiale epigrafico nel cimitero di Pretestato. *Rivista di archeologia cristiana* 12 (1935), 7–18.

Kinney, D. *Spolia, Damnatio* and *Renovatio Memoriae. Memoirs of the American Academy in Rome* 42 (1997), 117–148.

Knipp, D. *'Christus Medicus' in der frühchristlichen Sarkophagskulptur: Ikonographische Studien der sepulkralkunst des späten vierten Jahrhunderts* (Leiden, Boston, and Köln, 1998).

Koch, G. *Frühchristliche Sarkophage* (Munich, 2000).

Koortbojian, M. *Myth, Meaning, and Memory on Roman Sarcophagi* (Berkeley, Los Angeles, and London, 1995).

Krautheimer, R. Mensa-Coemeterium-Martyrium. *Cahier archéologiques fin de l'antiquité et moyen âge* 11 (1960), 15–40.

Lawrence, M. City-Gate Sarcophagi. *The Art Bulletin* 10 (1927), 1–45.

Lawrence, M. Columnar Sarcophagi in the Latin West: Ateliers, Chronology, Style. *The Art Bulletin* 14 (1932), 103–185.

Levitan, W. Dancing at the End of the Rope: Optatian Porfyry and the Field of Roman Verse. *Transactions of the American Philological Association* 115 (1985), 245–269.

MacCormack, S. *The Shadows of Poetry: Vergil in the Mind of Augustine* (Berkeley, Los Angeles, and London, 1998).

Malbon, E. S. *The Iconography of the Sarcophagus of Junius Bassus* (Princeton, 1990).

Marinone, M. I riti funerari, in: *Christiana loca: Lo spazio cristiano nella Roma del primo millennio 1*, edited by L. Pani Ermini (Rome, 2000), 71–80.

Mathews, T. F. *The Clash of the Gods: A Reinterpretation of Early Christian Art. Revised and Expanded Edition* (Princeton and Oxford, 1999).

Mazzei, B. A proposito del sarcofago di Bethesda delle catacombe di Pretestato, in: F. Bisconti and H. Brandenburg (eds.), *Sarcofagi tardoantichi, paleocristiani e altomedievali: Atti della giornata tematica dei Seminari di Archeologia Cristiana (École Française de Rome-8 Maggio 2002)* (Vatican City, 2004), 111–130.

McGill, S. *Virgil Recomposed: The Mythological and Secular Centos in Antiquity* (Oxford and New York, 2005).

Minasi, M. Paralitico, in: *Temi di iconografia paleocristiana*, edited by F. Bisconti (Vatican City, 2000), 241–243.

Monfrin, F. La guérison du serviteur (*Jn* 4,43–54): Une nouvelle interprétation des sarcophages de Bethesda. *Mélanges de l'École Française de Rome. Antiquité* 97 (1985), 979–1020.

Nicoletti, A. *I sarcofagi di Bethesda* (Milan, 1981).

Noga-Banai, G. *Loca Sancta* and the Bethesda Sarcophagi, in: *Salute e guarigione nella tarda antichità. Atti della giornata tematica dei Seminari di Archeologia Cristiana*, edited by H. Brandenburg, S. Heid, and C. Markschies (Vatican City, 2007), 107–123.

Nordberg, H. *Biometrical Notes: The Information on Ancient Christian Inscriptions from Rome Concerning the Duration of Life and the Dates of Birth and Death.* Acta Instituti Romani Finlandiae 2.2. (Helsinki, 1963).

Pietri, C. and Pietri, L. (eds.). *Prosopographie chrétienne du Bas-Empire 2: Prosopographie de l'Italie chrétienne* (Rome, 1999–2000).

Ranucci, C. Guarigione del cieco, in: *Temi di iconografia paleocristiana*, edited by F. Bisconti (Vatican City, 2000), 200.

Rebillard, É. *Religion et sépulture: L'Église, les vivants et les morts dans l'Antiquité tardive* (Paris, 2003).

Rebillard, É. The Church, the Living, and the Dead, in: *A Companion to Late Antiquity*, edited by P. Rousseau (Malden and Oxford, 2009), 220–230.

Rees, R. (ed.). *'Romane memento': Vergil in the Fourth Century* (London, 2004).

Rüpke, J. and Glock, A. *Fasti Sacerdotum: A Prosopography of Pagan, Jewish, and Christian Religious Officials in the City of Rome, 300 BC to AD 499*, translated by D. Richardson (Oxford and New York, 2008).

Sanders, G. *Lapides memores. Païens et chrétiens face à la mort: Le témoignage de l'épigraphie funéraire latine*, edited by A. Donati, D. Pikhaus, and M. van Uytfanghe (Faenza, 1991).

Scourfield, J. H. D. (ed.). *Text and Culture in Late Antiquity: Inheritance, Authority, and Change* (Swansea, 2007).

Shelton, K. *The Esquiline Treasure* (London, 1981).

Simon, M. Sur l'origine des sarcophages chrétiens du type Béthesda. *École Française de Rome: Mélanges d'archéologie et d'histoire* 55 (1938), 200–223.

Shaw, B. The Age of Roman Girls at Marriage: Some Reconsiderations. *Journal of Roman Studies* 77 (1987), 30–46.

Sotomayor, M. *Sarcofagos romano-cristianos de España: Estudios iconográfico* (Granada, 1975).

Spera, L. Praetextati, Coemeterium, in: *Lexicon Topographicum Urbis Romae: Suburbium.* Vol. 4, edited by A. La Regina (Rome, 2006), 250–261.

Spera, L. *Il complesso di Pretestato sulla Via Appia: Storia topografica e monumentale di un insediamento funerario paleocristiano nel suburbio di Roma. Roma Sotterranea Cristiana 12* (Vatican City, 2004).

Suzawa, Y. *The Genesis of Early Christian Art: Syncretic Juxtaposition in the Roman World.* BAR International Series 1892 (Oxford, 2008).

Tolotti, F. Ricera dei luoghi venerati nella spelunca magna di Pretestato. *Rivista di archeologia cristiana* 53 (1977), 7–102.

Trout, D. The Verse Epitaph(s) of Petronius Probus: Competitive Commemoration in Late-Fourth-Century Rome. *New England Classical Journal* 28 (2001), 157–176.

Trout, D. Damasus and the Invention of Early Christian Rome, in: *The Cultural Turn in Late Ancient Studies: Gender, Asceticism, and Historiography*, edited by D. B. Martin and P. Cox Miller (Durham, 2005), 298–315.

Warwick, H. H. *A Vergil Concordance* (Minneapolis, 1975).

Wilpert, J. *I sarcofagi cristiani antichi Vol. 2* (Vatican City, 1932).

11.
Image and Rhetoric in Early Christian Sarcophagi: Reflections on Jesus' Trial

JAŚ ELSNER

Introduction: Art and Rhetoric

Roman art is strikingly rhetorical.[1] In particular, sarcophagi – with their highly distinctive and restricted spatial field for visual representation and the relatively narrow range of formal devices employed to decorate them – are strongly so.[2] By formal devices I mean the repertoire of compositional elements that make up sarcophagi,[3] the repetition of iconographic types (whose differences and specific identities may depend on no more than a single attribute being present or absent, or the juxtaposition with another scene) and the particular (relatively restricted) range of treatments of the carved surface.[4] The relatively limited range of formal elements, combined with a marked creativity and variation in their deployment, creates what is simultaneously an interrelated corpus of copious material (both pagan and Christian) and one in which many figurative images allude (at different levels) to narratives that may range from myth and oral tradition to scriptural texts. But each item claims rhetorical specificity and difference from the others through its employment (including its position, thematic juxtaposition, formal and technical treatment) by contrast with other standard elements.

Since the era of Roman sarcophagi (at its heyday between roughly 100 and 400) coincides so closely with what is called the Second Sophistic, the great

---

1 A point at the heart of Meyer 2007.

2 For some general discussion of formal matters (not in relation to rhetoric), see Koch and Sichtermann, 1982, 62–84 and Koch, 2000, 29–64.

3 For instance, lids with separate scenes and a central block for an inscription, tondi with representations of the deceased, framing choices like colonnades with varieties of entablature, the use of unusual spaces created by such framing – such as, the spandrels of an arch – and so on.

4 Such treatments include the shallower relief of end panels by comparison with fronts, the different choices of abstract decoration such as strigillation (curving to the left or the right) or conch-shaped patterning and so forth, or the fluting or strigillating of columns in colonnades, and the willingness to alternate such patterning with figural decoration.

flowering of Greek rhetorical education and performance in Roman culture, and then the rise of Christian rhetorical culture in the fourth century, it is hardly surprising that parallels between visual and literary rhetoric have been drawn.[5] In this paper, concentrating on later Roman sarcophagi with Christian themes, I want to emphasise one aspect of the rhetorical nature of Christian sarcophagi – namely, their powerful investment in issues of apology and polemic. Two things need to be stressed at the outset. First, this is only one aspect of Christian sarcophagi and it is an arena in which they differ in certain respects from the pagan (or, perhaps better, pre-Christian) sarcophagi that preceded them, since no other set of sarcophagus iconographies has the same confessional insistence or makes similar claims to an overt religious sectarian identity, unless one were to grant much stronger cultic meanings to the large corpus of sarcophagi with Dionysiac themes than has become popular in recent years.[6] Second, by focusing on apology and polemic, I turn to a central issue in Christian culture – especially in the many pamphlets written by Christians against pagans and against each other – whose inflections in literary discourse are clearly modulated differently from how they operate in visual imagery. But, whether in texts or in art, the edge of both polemic and apology is highly dependent on a series of rhetorical tropes such as *synkrisis* (comparison), encomium and panegyric (both forms of praise), *psogos* (invective), *topos* (the amplification of faults or virtues), and *antirrêsis* (the contradiction of another's argument), which all have notable theoretical literatures in the many rhetorical handbooks used in ancient education which survive from our period.[7] Apology and polemic were at the heart of how people were trained to think and to express themselves, and so it is hardly surprising to find such qualities invested and reflected in the art of the early Church.

---

5 For instance, Müller 1994, 139–70; Zanker and Ewald 2004, 110–115.

6 The current consensus (of Dionysiac imagery as a 'Glücksvision') is perhaps best represented by Zanker and Ewald 2004, 135–67 by contrast with the earlier and much more religious interpretations of Turcan 1966, 368–632.

7 All these technical terms within rhetoric and their specific associations with arguments of praise or blame (hence apology or polemic) are to be found in our earliest such handbook, the *Progymnasmata* of Aelius Theon from the first century (ed. M. Patillon and G. Bolognesi, Paris, 1997 and tr. Kennedy, 2003, 1–72). Most are repeated with some elaboration in the later *progymnasmata* collected in Spengel, 1854–6 and translated in Kennedy, 2003. Likewise, Menander Rhetor, the works attributed to whom belong to the late third or early fourth century, divides all epideictic oratory into encomiastic (*enkomiastikous*) or invective (*psetikous*), which are respectively to do with praise (*epainos)* and blame (*psogos*): 331.1–15 (the opening of Book 1, ed. and tr. D. Russell and N. Wilson, *Menander Rhetor*, Oxford, 1981).

Apology and Polemic in Early Christian Sarcophagi: The Case of the Trial of Jesus

> Our Saviour and Lord Jesus Christ was silent when false witnesses spoke against him, and answered nothing when he was accused; he was convinced that all his life and actions among the Jews were better than any speech in refutation of the false witnesses and superior to any words that he might say in reply to the accusations... It might well cause amazement among those with moderate intellectual powers that a man who was accused and charged falsely did not defend himself and prove himself not guilty of any of the charges, although he could have done so.[8]

So begins Origen's great defence of the faith, *Contra Celsum*, written in about 248. Of course, there is a certain knowing elegance in the irony that Origen (c. 185–255) begins his eight book refutation of the false accusations against Christianity made by Celsus with reference to the Saviour's silence in the face of false witness.[9] But there is also a substantial point, which Origen makes by citing the Gospels of Matthew and Mark,[10] in the scandal – from the pagan point of view – of Jesus's silence at the moment when a wise man of the world of ancient philosophy, sophistic rhetoric or polytheism (a Socrates, an Apuleius, an Apollonius) would have delivered a brilliant and lengthy speech of apology.[11] Indeed, insofar as pagan assaults on Jesus have survived (preserved by the excerpts of, and ripostes to, them in apologetics like Origen's), Jesus' meekness was one obvious and direct target.[12] As the great pagan apologist and Neo-Platonist, Porphyry of Tyre (234 – c.305) wrote sometime between 270 and 300:

> How is it that Christ uttered nothing worthy of a wise and divine man either when brought before the High Priest or before the governor, when he could have instructed the bystanders and made them better people? Why instead did he tolerate being hit with a reed, spat on, crowned with thorns, and not act like Apollonius, who spoke freely to the emperor Domitian and then vanished from the royal

8 Origen, *Contra Celsum*, praef. 1–2, translated by Henry Chadwick. For a historian's discussion of the Gospel account of the trial (something very different from early Christian and pagan interpretations of the Gospels and from Origen's employment of them), see Millar 1990.

9 On Jesus' silence in *Contra Celsum*, see Frede 1999, 136, 143–5, and Perrone 2005, 105–111.

10 The key texts are Matt. 26. 59–63 and 27.11–25; Mark 15, 2–15; Luke 23.1–25. Origen explicitly quotes Matt. 26. 59–63 and 27.11–14.

11 See Frede 1999, 144: 'There was no apologia – let alone a triumphant, self-assertive one. This the pagans found impossible to understand, unacceptable and ignominious.' Further on this topic and its place in the development of Christian notions of uniqueness, see Elsner 2009.

12 As in Celsus' attack in Origen, *Contra Celsum* II.33–5 and 67–8; and probably in Hierocles's attack on Jesus by contrast with Apollonius of Tyana to judge by Eusebius's comments in his *Contra Hieroclem* 38.

> chamber to appear a few hours later very clearly in the city of Dicaearchia, now called Puteoli? As for Christ, even if he had to suffer in accordance with God's commands, still he did not have to undergo his suffering without speaking freely. He could have pronounced some words of goodness and wisdom to Pilate, his judge, and not be insulted like some commoner from the street corner.[13]

This fragment, among the many cited and refuted by Macarius of Magnesia in his *Apocriticus* written in the later fourth century,[14] indicates the scandal of Jesus' silence to be still a live issue well beyond the Peace of the Church and into the Theodosian era.

My point in opening with this polemic is to foreground the charged and not purely Scriptural basis of at least one particular theme in the iconography of early Christian art. Just as certain topics in Christian imagery may be taken to have an implicit polemical intent against paganism (notably the refusal of the three Hebrews, later put into the fiery furnace, to worship an idol),[15] so others – such as the representations of the miracles and not least the trial of Jesus – may be said to offer an apologetic edge that justifies and elevates Christianity above its ancient religious competitors as the (one) true religion. In this sense, early Christian art is much closer to the world of polemic and apology which characterises most early Christian writing, both before Constantine's conversion and in the century after his death, than has usually been assumed. The representations of Christ before Pilate, many of which date from between Porphyry's late pagan attack on the Christians and Macarius' refutation of Porphyry (indeed most of them cluster within the later fourth century), cannot be said to portray the theme that made this subject so controversial in the polemical and apologetic literature – namely, Jesus' silence. Indeed, how can silence be unambiguously represented in visual form? Nonetheless these images may be taken to make a special emphasis of his trial, and consequently to use it as the basis of a visual claim for Christian primacy. It is impossible to say how many of those who saw such images knew also of the fierce literary polemic on the same Scriptural theme, with which Origen chose to open his *Contra Celsum*,

13 Porphyry *Adversus Christianos* fr. 63 in von Harnack 1916, no. 1, 84–5 (also in von Harnack 1911, 32) and in Goulet 2003, 72–3. The translation here is after Jones 2006, 139–41. On Porphyry's *Adversus Christianos*, see Riedweg 2005, with extensive bibliography at 188–98.

14 For discussion of Macarius and a date of about 375 for his text, see Goulet 2003, vol. 1, 48–65, esp. 65.

15 Most famously perhaps in the fourth century Adelfia sarcophagus in Syracuse (lower register, far left side) – see *Rep.* II, 20, pp. 8–10. See also *Rep* I. 28, pp. 24–6 and *Rep* I. 160, pp. 100–101 (both from lids); *Rep* II. 10, pp. 3–4; *Rep*, II. 63, pp. 20–21; *Rep.* III, 32, p. 16; *Rep.* III, 38, pp. 24–5; *Rep.* III, 41, pp. 28–9; *Rep.* III, 42, pp. 29–31 (the image here is lost and hypothetically restored to a unique position at the right of the upper tier); *Rep.* III, 118, pp. 72–4 (on the left side); *Rep.* III, 438, p. 205 (a fragment). See e.g. Carletti 1975, pp. 64–87 and Wegner 1980.

but it is hard to imagine that any who did would not have found their responses to the visual rendition enriched.

The case for the significance of the theme of Christ's trial lies in the number of sarcophagi which depict the topic and the emphasis they give it.[16] Invariably the trial is placed in a privileged position at the far right of the sarcophagus front – that is, the end point of a narrative reading, if one reads the images from left to right as in a text (see Figures 11.1 and 11.2).[17] The scene functions as an end point not only through position, in relation to its placement on the plane of a sarcophagus front or lid, but it serves also as an end to the story of Christ's life and mission in the sense that the trial is used as a metonym for the entire Passion narrative.[18] The trial depiction often stands for the Passion – either alone (in the majority of cases) or alongside one other scene from what would later become the Passion-cycle, such as the entry into Jerusalem or the washing of the feet.[19] Interestingly, in that the scene – whether as metonym for the

16 The surviving examples (excluding quite a few small fragments) are *Rep.* I, 28, pp. 24–6; *Rep.* I, 45, pp. 43–5 ('the Two Brothers' sarcophagus, where Pilate washes his hands but Jesus does not appear); *Rep.* I, 49, pp. 48–9; *Rep.* I, 57, pp. 54–5 (fragmentary); *Rep.* I, 58, p. 56; *Rep.* I, 189, pp. 119–20; *Rep.* I, 667, p. 268; *Rep.* I, 677, pp. 274–7; *Rep.* I. 679, pp. 278–9 (the sarcophagus of Pius II); *Rep.* I, 680, pp. 279–83 (the Junius Bassus sarcophagus of 359 from the Vatican); *Rep.* III, 41, pp. 28–9; *Rep.* III, 42, pp. 29–31 (the much damaged Servanne sarcophagus – here the trial of Christ is exceptionally placed at the centre of the lower tier); *Rep.* III, 53, pp. 39–40; *Rep.* III, 291, pp. 143–4; *Rep.* III, 412, pp. 191–2; *Rep.* III, 416, pp. 194–5 (lost but known from a seventeenth century drawing); *Rep.* III, 452, p. 210 (fragmentary); *Rep.* III, 453, pp. 210–11 (fragmentary but known from an eighteenth century drawing); *Rep.* III, 498, pp. 235–6 (the so-called sarcophagus of Mary Magdalene); *Rep.* III, 512, p. 245 (fragmentary); *Rep.* III, 646, pp. 296–7 (fragmentary). To this list (from the volumes of *Rep.* I-III) must be added Saggiorato 1968, no. 14, pp. 46–7 (a lost columnar sarcophagus from Narbonne known in a seventeenth century drawing) and no. 17, pp. 56–7 (a fifth-century example now in Milan). For some discussion, see e.g. ibid 88–93; Aixalà 1994; Koch 2000, 179; Hourihane 2009, 68–83 and the list of examples in his Appendix A, 375–81.

17 The only exception to this placement is the restored example of *Rep.* III, 42 in Arles. See the handy scheme in Table 1 of von Campenhausen 1929, after 85.

18 See Saggiorato 1968, 81–88 and Schiller 1972, 64. On the Passion sarcophagi generally, see von Campenhausen 1929; Gerke 1940a; Schrenk 1995, 35–51.

19 The Trial and entry into Jerusalem: *Rep.* I, 28 and 680; the Trial and washing of the feet: *Rep.* I, 58 and 679; *Rep.* III, 53 and 412. On the washing of the feet, see Giess 1962, 43–7, 95–6; Hourihane 2009, 76–80. On the entry into Jerusalem, see Dinkler 1970, 17–27. There are two exceptions: *Rep.* III, 41, which offers an entire Passion cycle in its lower zone, and *Rep.* I, 49, a fourth century columnar sarcophagus from the Domitilla Catacomb, known in the older literature as 'Lateran 171'. This has a central scene of the cross with chi-rho and sleeping soldiers flanked by Jesus with the crown of thorns and the carrying of the cross (by Simon of Cyrene?) to the left and the two trial images to the right; see Campenhausen 1929, 67–8 and Gerke 1940a, 71–5.

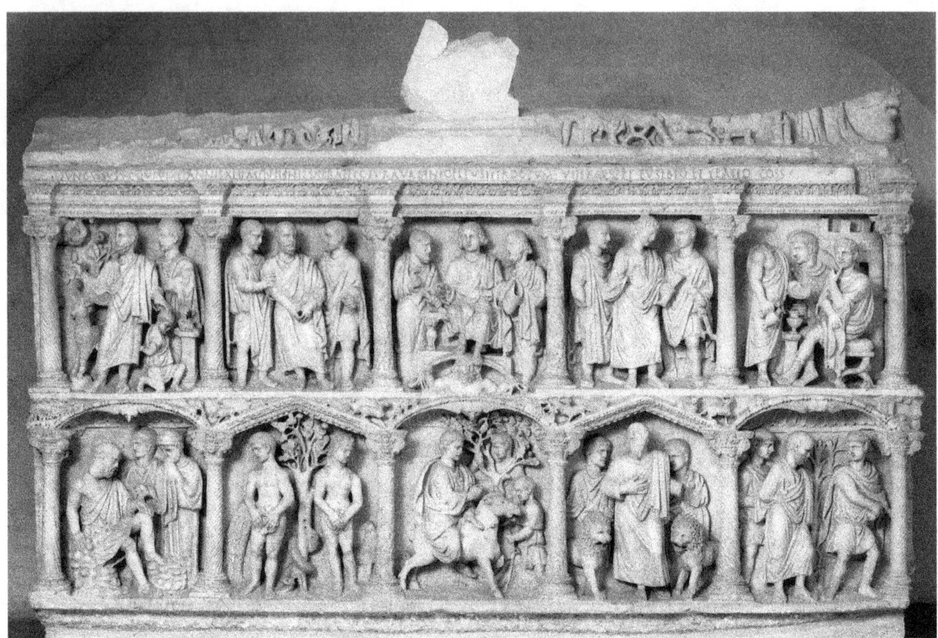

Figure 11.1: The Sarcophagus of Junius Bassus, dated by inscription to 359 AD and found in the Vatican. Now in St Peter's. The trial of Christ before Pilate appears in the top two intercolumniations to the far right. Photograph: Conway Library, Courtauld Institute of Art, negative A24/276.

Passion or as Origenic evocation of Christ's exceptional silence – is an end also in the sense of a triumphant apology for Christianity, it contrasts specifically with the regular (almost invariable) positional deployment of the polemical three Hebrews scene, which is almost always at the left end of a sarcophagus.[20] Effectively, the polemical and apologetic tendencies of iconographic types have a rhetorical placement visually in early Christian art as the opening and closing of arguments conducted through pictorial space. In a now almost wholly lost sarcophagus from the Vatican, known from Antonio Bosio's seventeenth century engraving (Figure 11.2), the Hebrews theme opens the visual argument at the top left (on the lid) and the trial of Jesus closes it on the bottom right (on the main base).[21] Likewise, in a two-tier frieze sarcophagus from Arles, Pilate washes his hands (though Jesus does not appear) at the far right of the upper register of the main coffin while the three Hebrews scene is depicted at the far left of the lower register.[22]

20 The one exception to a far-left place in the three Hebrews iconography is (again) *Rep.* III, 42, where the subject is hypothetically restored.

21 *Rep.* I, 28, pp. 24–6.

22 *Rep.* III, 41, pp. 28–9.

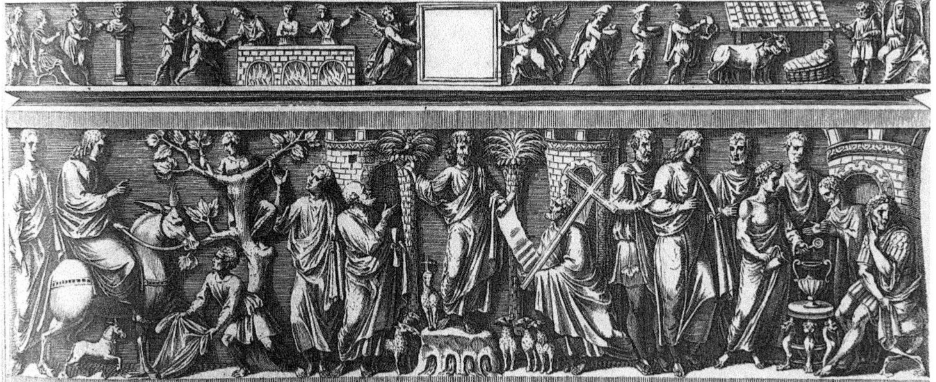

Figure 11.2: A now lost sarcophagus from the Vatican cemetery, probably last third of the fourth century. Lid: the Hebrews before Nebuchadnezzar, the Hebrews in the fiery furnace and the Epiphany; main front: the Entry to Jerusalem, Christ between Peter and Paul and the Trial before Pilate. Photograph: from Antonio Bosio, *Roma Sotterranea*, Rome 1632, p. 63.

In the case of columnar sarcophagi – the most common type by far to include the scene – the trial of Jesus has the unusual distinction of being the one iconographic type to operate across the demarcation of a column, occupying the two intercolumniations at a sarcophagus' right end (and in the case of double register sarcophagi at the right of the upper tier, see Figures 11.1, 11.3 and 11.4).[23] The expansion of an important scene across two intercolumniations in early Christian art is rare but not unique to this theme – Moses' crossing of the Red Sea occupied two intercolumniations in the highly influential mid-to-late fourth century frescoes of Old Testament narratives in Old St Peter's and, perhaps consequently, the full face of several late fourth century early Christian frieze sarcophagi.[24] This expanded visual space for the trial of Christ is echoed on the lid of the Brescia Casket, a very high-quality ivory box (perhaps a pyxis for Eucharistic bread or possibly a reliquary) from the later fourth century. There, an abbreviated Passion cycle in two bands, which excludes any typological Old Testament imagery (such as it appears in the iconography on the

23 The columnar examples are *Rep.* I, 49; *Rep.* I, 57; *Rep.* I, 58; *Rep.* I, 189; *Rep.* I,677; *Rep.* I, 680; *Rep.* III, 53; *Rep.* III, 291; *Rep.* III, 412; *Rep.* III, 416; *Rep.* III, 452; *Rep.* III, 498; *Rep.* III, 512; *Rep.* III, 646. Of these 14 examples, only *Rep.* I, 679 and *Rep.* III, 53 have the trial scene within a single intercolumniation; all others extend the subject across two. See Lawrence 1932, 103–85, esp. 109.

24 Our principal source for the Old St Peter's frescoes is Grimaldi 1972, 140 with discussion by Kessler 2002, 9, 53, 76–7, 98–9. Note that the Red Sea theme is reproduced in the fifteenth century cycle of mural copies of the St Peter's cycle in the Oratory of the Annunicata in Cori (ibid. 54, 101 and plate 3.9). On the Red Sea sarcophagi, see Rizzardi 1970.

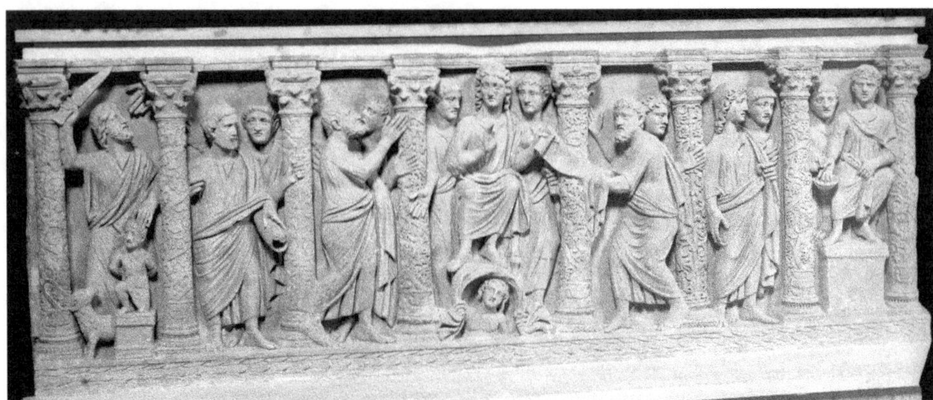

Figure 11.3: 'Lateran 174' – sarcophagus from the Vatican cemetery, third quarter of the fourth century AD. In the intercolumniations from left to right: the sacrifice of Isaac, Peter and an attendant, Paul turning to Christ in the centre, Christ enthroned, Peter receiving the Law, Christ arrested and Pilate washing his hands. Photograph: DAIR 1933.0151.

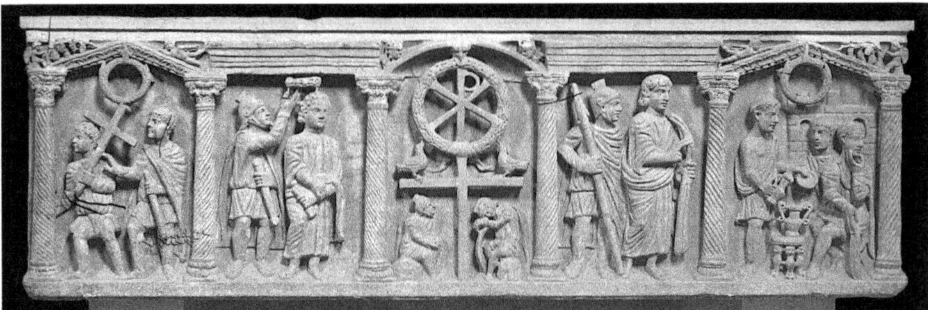

Figure 11.4: 'Lateran 171' – sarcophagus from the vicinity of the catacomb of Domitilla, dated to about 350 AD. Now in the Vatican Museum. In the intercolumniations from left to right: Simon of Cyrene carrying the Cross, Christ crowned with the crown of thorns, the *crux invicta* with soldiers beneath, Christ arrested and Pilate washing his hands. Photograph: DAIR. 1933.0155 (Brügner).

casket's four sides), has Jesus in the garden of Gethsemane, his arrest and Peter's denial on the upper level and the two trials of Jesus – before Caiaphas and Pilate – placed side by side as the culminating images of the Passion in the lower band.[25]

25 On the Brescia Casket, see Volbach 1976 (o.v. 1916), no. 107, 77–8; Kollwitz 1933; Delbrueck 1952; Watson 1981, 283–98; Tkacz 2002; Elsner 2008, 21–38, esp. 31–3. On the trial of Jesus on the casket in relation to some of its very complex visual typologies, see Tkacz 2002, 28–30, 76–9, 82–3.

As late as the sixth century, the trial of Christ retains exceptional visual importance in the two full-page miniatures devoted to the theme in the Rossano Gospels (fol 8r and fol 8v) where the trial appears to be the culmination of a visual narrative depicting the Passion and some parables.[26] This pictorial cycle draws on events from the four Gospels and seems to have served as a prefatory visual frontispiece to the text of all four.[27] Oddly, neither image represents Pilate washing his hands and it has been supposed that a third page depicting this event has been lost.[28] Two other manuscripts, the Syriac Rabbula Gospels of 586 and the Latin Gospels of St Augustine (made in Italy in the sixth century), include images of the trial within a larger Passion cycle but without special emphasis.[29] Likewise, the two scenes of Christ before Caiaphas and Pilate survive as small panels from the fifth century wooden doors of the church of Santa Sabina in Rome, where they figured within a substantive Passion cycle.[30] It is worth noting that the theme appears to be entirely absent from the other major category of early Christian art besides sarcophagi, namely catacomb painting, as well as from our surviving ivories other than the Brescia Casket.[31] Again, the trial is rare, though not unknown, in surviving or textually attested early Christian monumental church decoration.[32] From this swift iconographic

26 See Cavallo, Gribomont and Loerke 1987, 109–114 on the pictorial cycle and 145–54 on these miniatures; also Loerke 1961, 171–95; Kessler 2007, esp. 162–4; Hourihane 2009, 47. These identify both miniatures as representing the trial of Jesus before Pilate, while Lowden 1999, 19 says the second (fol. 8v.) is the trial before Herod. The disagreement is interesting but irrelevant for my purposes here. The manuscript is in Greek and probably from the east.

27 See Lowden 1999, 18–21.

28 There are now nine prefatory folios surviving out of what originally may have been as many as twenty (see Cavallo, Gribomont and Loerke 1987, 113). For the postulation of a third trial miniature, see Loerke 1961, 175–6.

29 The Rabbula Gospels read from right to left (as normal in Syriac), and the trial before Pilate (fol. 12 b) is part of a life and Passion cycle rendered as marginal illustrations to the Canon tables. Pilate faces Christ here and does not wash his hands. However, the Rabbula illustrator reserves the climax of the Passion cycle for full page miniatures of the Crucifixion and Resurrection, the Ascension, Christ enthroned and the Pentecost. See Cecchelli, Furlani and Salmi 1959, 66–7. The Gospels of St Augustine include the trial before Pilate as one of 12 small scenes in the Passion cycle miniature (fol. 125r, alongside the arraignment before Caiaphas) which begins with the entry into Jerusalem and ends with the carrying of the cross. See Wormald 1954, 1 for date and captions to plates v and vi.

30 See Jeremias 1980, 56–7, 58–9.

31 Pilate washing his hands appears in one of the small ivory panels from an early fifth century box now in the British Museum, to the left of a scene that includes both the carrying of the cross and Peter's denial. See Volbach 1976, no. 116, 82.

32 The trial before Pilate appears, as well as the arraignment of Christ before Caiaphas, in the sixth century mosaic cycle devoted to the Passion to the western end of the southern wall above the clerestory of Sant' Apollinare Nuovo in Ravenna. See Deichmann 1974,

survey we may say that the trial scene has a climactic and significant place in Passion narratives of the fourth century (although it does not occur in every medium of early Christian art in that period) and exceptionally after that in the Rossano Codex. Otherwise, if the scene is included at all, it is as one among many and not used climactically.

The Trial Scene in Fourth Century Sarcophagi

In discussing the employment of the trial scene on sarcophagi of the second half of the fourth century, one might isolate two principal uses. First, when the theme appears as the sole narrative image from the Passion alongside images evoking the martyrdoms of the two principal apostolic Roman saints – Peter or Paul, or both. Second, when the scene occurs in a group of images that focus on narratives from within the Passion cycle.[33] In both these cases, the meekness of Jesus – as emphasised by Origen and of a kind that caused incomprehension to apologists of traditional culture like Porphyry – stands as a paradigm, a model for his martyred successors and a contrast to other kinds of authority, notably the temporal power of the Roman state as embodied in Pilate within the trial scene. Silence as such may not be at issue here, but that characteristic rejection of all that the state and the culture stands for through a striking form of non-violent and non-verbal resistance – which Jesus' silence certainly came to mean to both pagan and Christian writers – is certainly at stake.

Let us begin with the incorporation of the trial in what may be termed a Roman martyrdom context. A series of sarcophagi – of which the most famous is that of Junius Bassus from 359 (Figure 11.1) – emphasise the martyrdoms of Peter and Paul alongside that of Jesus. All have Christ between two apostles, probably Peter and Paul, in the centre, or the image of the *crux invicta* flanked by two soldiers (one awake and one sleeping)[34] with the two trial intercolumniations to the right. On the left are a variety of scenes including the arrest or martyrdom of Peter or Paul (or both).[35] The images which appear

175, 176–7, 186–7. It is attested also in Choricius' description of the sixth century mosaics at the church of St Sergius in Gaza, see Choricius *Laudatio Marciani* I.74.

33 I do not follow the categories established by von Campenhausen 1929, and largely accepted with minor adaptations by Gerke 1940a, and Sotomayor 1962, 101–113.

34 *Crux invicta* at the centre: *Rep.* I, 667; *Rep.* III, 412, 416, 498. On the early Christian iconography of Peter, see Sotomayor 1962; on Paul, see Dassmann 1982, and Cooper 2005, 41–87 with bibliography.

35 The examples are (with scenes read from left to right): *Rep.* I, 57, originally found in the Vatican and now much cut down showing the arrest of an apostle, identified as Paul by von Campenhausen 1929, 58 and Gerke 1940a, 76; *Rep.* I, 58, which has the washing of the feet alongside Peter carrying his cross; *Rep.* I.189, from the San Sebastiano complex in Rome, a very early cult centre for both Peter and Paul, which shows both the

in addition to those that specifically allude to the martyr narratives of Peter and Paul include Christ washing Peter's feet, the stoning of Paul at Lystra (arguably an ante-type to his martyrdom), Christ appearing before Paul and the Sacrifice of Isaac. To this group might be added one further sarcophagus, known as Lateran 174 (Figure 11.3), which shows – in addition to Christ between saints and the trial – the sacrifice of Isaac and Peter with an attendant (which may be a rather triumphant rendition of his arrest), as well as a range of Petrine imagery on the two ends.[36] Of the non-martyrdom scenes, all but the Sacrifice of Isaac may be said to represent significant moments in the life-cycles of their respective apostles. The Isaac scene, by contrast, employs typology to give an Old Testament prototype for the sacrifice of Christ as epitomised in the trial scene.[37] Interestingly, a number of these objects are known to have come from the sites in Rome that specifically venerated Peter and Paul,[38] implying iconographic allusion to local cult.[39] Clearly in this usage, the trial scene is the largest single narrative theme overlapping two intercolumniations in all the examples that are columnar. It always occupies the right side of the coffin, with the martyr images to the left. Rhetorically, the trial serves both as the model imitated by the martyrdoms of Peter and Paul (especially in the images where Peter bears his own cross,[40] or where the arrest of Peter visually mirrors the arrest of Christ before Pilate)[41] and as scriptural authorisation for those martyrdoms as themselves an exemplary witness to the Christian salvific dispensation. Indeed, the fact that (in a left to right reading of these sarcophagi) the trial scene is always the last image, appears to support an interpretation of its rhetorical use as validation and mimetic archetype for the Petrine and Pauline passions rather than offering any sense of chronological patterning.

---

martyrdom of Paul and Peter carrying his cross; *Rep.* I, 667, a frieze sarcophagus from the cemetery of St Valentino with the martyrdom of Paul and Peter carrying his cross; *Rep.* I, 680, the Bassus sarcophagus found at the Vatican, which is exceptional in having two tiers of intercolumniations with the sacrifice of Isaac and the arrest of Peter at the left side of the upper tier and the martyrdom of Paul below Pilate at the right of the lower tier; *Rep.* III, 291 from Marseilles with Christ before Paul and the stoning of Paul at Lystra; *Rep.* III, 412 from Nimes, with the washing of Peter's feet alongside Peter carrying his cross; *Rep.* III, 416 which is lost but had the martyrdom of Paul and the arrest of Peter; *Rep.* III, 498 with the martyrdom of Paul and the arrest of Peter.

36 *Rep.* I, 677.

37 See e.g. Malbon 1990, 43–7 with earlier bibliography. Note that the Two Brothers sarcophagus (*Rep.* I, 45) pairs the Sacrifice of Isaac with Pilate washing his hands to the right of the upper tier beside the portrait medallion.

38 *Rep.* I, 57, 189, 677, 680.

39 See Elsner 2003, esp. 89–94.

40 *Rep.* I, 58, 189, 667; *Rep.* III, 412.

41 *Rep.* I, 680; *Rep.* III, 416, 498. Generally on the arrest of Peter, see Sotomayor 1962, 63–7.

Between the two wings of these sarcophagi with their insistence on Christ's Passion in Jerusalem and the post-scriptural passions of his senior apostles in Rome itself, are images of either Christ between Peter and Paul or of the *crux invicta* with the soldiers beneath. In the former group, there are a number of themes.[42] Christ may appear with a jewelled cross, and with the waters and trees of paradise surrounding him and his chosen apostles.[43] He may appear as teacher, seated or standing before two or more disciples.[44] He may appear in cosmic majesty seated over a personification of the earth and handing his law to Peter and Paul (Figures 11.1 and 11.3).[45] But in all these cases, the central scene effectively unites the temporal distinctions between the two sides (that is the priority of Christ's Passion and its emulation by the later martyrdoms) by placing Jesus *together* with his chosen apostles in an image that simultaneously evokes eternity and the handing down of spiritual authority through Peter and Paul. The movement of such images outside the places of cult directly dedicated to Peter and Paul effectively implies a further transfer of Episcopal authority through the blessing of their imagery to other sites valorised by their presence in Rome and in distant Gaul. It is worth noting that in many of these sarcophagi there is a deliberate differentiation in the facial type used for Jesus between the Pilate scene and the central glorification of Christ.[46] In the Pilate scene, Jesus is always beardless – emphasising his youth and perhaps the meekness which pagan polemicists found so unnerving. In the central scene, he is usually bearded and often elevated or enlarged,[47] and when beardless (as in the Bassus sarcophagus or Lateran 174, Figures 11.1 and 11.3) he is otherwise elevated, for instance by being enthroned over the world or carrying a jewelled cross.[48] At the very least this deliberate contrast between the meek Jesus of the trial and the triumphant Christ of the central scene – especially in the examples of Jesus enthroned over the world – calls into question recent attempts to deny any appropriation of imperial (as well as other kinds of) authority to the image of

42 For a survey of Christ types, see Gerke 1948.

43 *Rep.* I, 57.

44 *Rep.* I, 58, 189; *Rep.* III, 291 (on this last, 'the Sarcophagus of the Companions of St Maurice', see Drocourt-Dubrueil 1989, 19–25).

45 *Rep.* I, 677, 680. On the *traditio legis*, see Davis-Weyer 1961, esp. 7–15, which includes *Rep.* I, 58 as an example of this iconography at p. 10; Sotomayor 1962, 125–52; Hellemo 1989, 64–89; and most recently Cooper 2005, 67–87 with further bibliography.

46 For discussion and detailed illustration, see Gerke 1948. More recent accounts include Jensen 2000, 113–120, and Jensen 2005, 142–59.

47 Bearded: *Rep.* I, 28, 58, 189; *Rep.* III, 53.

48 Otherwise elevated: *Rep.* I, 57, 677, 680; *Rep.* III, 291.

Jesus in early Christian art.[49] The glorification of the cross, with its magnificent appropriation of the martyr crown around a chi-rho above the cross itself alludes both to the Crucifixion, with the soldier to the left of the cross typically looking up awake, and to the Resurrection, with the soldier to the right of the cross typically asleep. It effectively underlines the martyrdom dynamic of the sarcophagi in which it appears, nuancing the implications away from questions of ecclesiastical authority to those of martyrdom and cult.[50]

Among the sarcophagi, the coffin of Junius Bassus (Figure 11.1) calls for special attention since its two-tier programme of intercolumnar images (with yet a third tier of smaller-scale scenes with actors in the form of lambs that fill the spandrels of the arches that frame the lower register) is so much more extensive than the other examples. A long and still inconclusive discussion has raged since 1900 about how exactly to interpret the mass of potential iconographic and typological connections in a satisfactory, which is to say theologically coherent, manner.[51] Suffice it to say that no agreement has been reached or is likely to be. But it is interesting that while the upper tier closely resembles the iconography of Lateran 174 (with the Sacrifice of Isaac and the arrest of Peter to the left, the *traditio legis* at the centre with Christ enthroned over the earth, and the two trial intercolumniations to the right, Figure 11.3),[52] the lower tier of the Bassus sarcophagus includes a series of scenes that appear either in the other sarcophagi of the trial or in other sarcophagi with a strong emphasis on the martyrdoms of the Roman apostles. These are (to the lower right) the martyrdom of Paul,[53] (in the centre) the entry into Jerusalem,[54] (to the far left) the distress of Job.[55] Interspersed between these images, flanking the entry into Jerusalem, are two characteristic typological scenes of the Fall (with Adam, Eve, the Serpent and behind them sheaves and a lamb alluding to the Sacrifice of Cain and Abel) to the left, and of the Resurrection, in Daniel in the Lions' Den to the right. The Old Testament scenes thus evoke the Resurrection (Daniel), the Fall (Adam and

49 I have in mind T. Mathews, *The Clash of Gods*, Princeton, 1999 (revised edition), 3–22, with the reviews (of the original edition) by Kinney 1994, and Brown 1995, 499–502. Jensen 2000, 98–103 follows Mathews but is restrained and judicious.

50 On the *crux invicta* on sarcophagi (focussing on Lateran 171, *Rep.* I, 49), see Hellemo 1989, 98–100.

51 See de Waal 1900; Gerke 1936; Schefold 1939; Gaertner 1968; Malbon 1990; Tkacz 2002, 191–3.

52 See e.g. Malbon 1990, 32.

53 Also on *Rep.* I, 189, 777; *Rep.* III, 416, 498.

54 Also on *Rep.* I, 28.

55 Also on *Rep.* I, 61, a tree sarcophagus originally from St Paul's outside the Walls in Rome, with from left to right Sacrifice of Cain and Abel, the arrest of Peter, the *crux invicta*, the martyrdom of Paul and the distress of Job; and *Rep.* I, 215, a now fragmentary tree sarcophagus from San Sebastiano (also a cult site of Peter and Paul) with same iconography as I, 61.

Eve), Sacrifice (Isaac) and the testing of a saintly figure by God (Job).[56] Rather than looking for an overarching intellectual, aesthetic or theological harmony in the orchestration of these images, it may be wiser to see them as including as full an account as possible of all the options (iconographic but also rhetorical) within the fourth-century sarcophagus tradition that evoked and commented upon the triple martyrdoms of Christ, Peter and Paul as well as invoking their collective triumph.

Given the significance of this particular sarcophagus as the tomb of the City Prefect, its size and the inclusive nature of its iconographic mix – especially if one adds the six spandrel scenes which show the Hebrews in the fiery furnace, Moses (or Peter) striking the rock, Christ's miracle of the loaves, the Baptism, Moses (or Peter) receiving the law and the Raising of Lazarus (with all figures rendered as lambs) – one might argue that its aim is for a kind of visual totality within the highly reductive frame of a sarcophagus' shape and form, rather than for an ordered or clearly assimilable set of meanings. This Christian totality needs to be set beside the highly traditional scenes of the lid (insofar as the iconography of a very damaged artefact is recoverable), the inscriptions and the seasonal imagery of the ends.[57] The Bassus sarcophagus appears to be attempting to evoke not only a fullness in its Christian images but to situate or frame that within as full an account of traditional Roman 'daily life' and 'passing time' imagery (both themes typical of Roman funerary art) as was possible in an object of its size and shape.[58]

My second group of sarcophagi including the trial of Jesus have fronts with centres of the same kind as the first group, but with images all drawn from within the Scriptural cycle of the Passion.[59] That is, to the left side one or two Christological images are selectively offered to counterpoint against the trial. *Rep.* I, 28 (Figure11. 2) – a lost sarcophagus known from Antonio Bosio's engraving – put the entrance to Jerusalem to the left, playing on a contrast between Jesus' earthly triumph (which is particularly marked in the adventus

56 For discussion of these typologies, which I adduce loosely and not with reductive precision, see Malbon 1990, 42–7, 54–68. On the image of Job prefiguring the martyrs, see Dassmann 1973, 273–9.

57 On the lid, see Himmelmann 1973, 15–28; Daltrop 1978–80; Wischmeyer 1982, 23–36. On the verse inscription see Cameron 2002, correcting the fundamental errors in Malbon 1990, 114–6. On the ends, see Malbon 1990, 99–103 and Elsner 2000, esp. 272–5.

58 For some reflections on the theme of time in the Bassus sarcophagus, see Elsner 2003, 82–7, 89 and on the framing of its Christianity within secularizing and traditional imagery, see Elsner 2008, esp. 26–31.

59 They are *Rep.* I, 28, 49, 679 and *Rep.* III, 53.

scene of the lower centre in the Bassus sarcophagus)[60] and his meekness and humiliation in the trial by Pilate. Two other schemes – one shared by sarcophagi in Rome and Arles and the other on a unique sarcophagus in Rome – are of particular interest and complexity.

The sarcophagus, which once stood behind the high altar of the church of St-Honorat-les-Alyscamps in Arles, is one of the most impressive, coherent and complex of all surviving early Christian sculptural monuments (Figure 11.5).[61] Its iconography is closely replicated by an unfinished coffin in the Vatican subsequently re-employed for the burial of the fifteenth-century Pope Pius II (Figure 11.6).[62] It has a bearded Christ at the centre towering above the flat entablature of the colonnade in which he stands, flanked in the arcades to either side by two apostles. Christ hands the law to Peter, who carries a jewelled cross in reference to both Jesus' Passion and his own, to the immediate right, and holds his hand in blessing over Paul to the immediate left. The apostles behind Peter and Paul are not identifiable but carry palm branches. Lambs appear to either side of Jesus and immediately beneath the figures of Peter and Paul. In the arcade to the far right is the scene of the trial – this time relegated to a single intercolumniation where Jesus stands before Pilate who washes his hands. To the far left, Jesus washes Peter's feet, with the apostle enthroned in a parallel posture to Pilate.[63]

The imagery of water is insistent and brilliantly deployed. In the centre Christ stands in Paradise with the four rivers flowing from a rock on which his feet rest. To the far right, Pilate washes his hands with a low three-legged table and a fancy wash-stand beneath him and an attendant carrying jug and patera (Figure11.7). To the far left, Christ washes Peter's feet with a simple bowl in place of Pilate's elaborate lion-legged table and wash stand (Figure 11.8). The dynamic moves from Jesus doing the washing of feet, via Christ standing over the waters of Paradise, to Pilate washing his hands. In the now fragmentary ends, scenes of the Baptism of Jesus on the right and Peter striking water from the rock (an apocryphal legend particularly popular in catacomb painting for which a source appears not to have been identified yet)[64] on the left have been restored. Despite the loss of the figures of Christ and John the Baptist on the

60 See e.g. Malbon 1990, 53–4 with bibliography. Mathews 1999, 27–30, despite a discussion of the entry into Jerusalem which is important to his anti-imperial thesis, fails notably to account for the Bassus sarcophagus at any stage.

61 *Rep.* III, 53, 39–40 – a particularly acute entry by C. Christern-Briesenick. See also Klauser 1966, no. 16, 72–77; Saggiorato 1968, no.30, 78–80; Spier 2007, no. 64, 242–3.

62 *Rep.* I, 679.

63 On this parallelism (which occurs on a number of surviving sarcophagi), see Hourihane 2009, 76–80.

64 See Malbon 1990, 78–9 with bibliography in the notes.

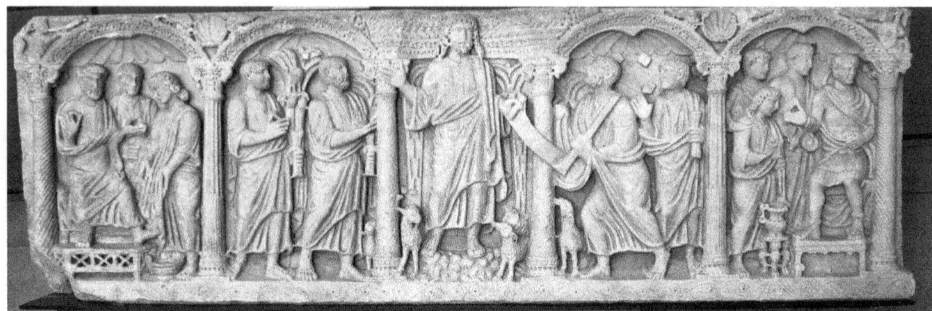

Figure 11.5: Sarcophagus from St Honorat-les-Alyscamps, in Arles, last third of the fourth century AD. Now in the Arles Museum. In the intercolumniations from left to right: Christ washing Peter's feet, two apostles of which the one on the right is probably Paul, Christ on the rock of paradise with lambs and four rivers flowing, two apostles of which Peter stands to the left and receives the Law, Christ before Pilate. Photograph: J. Elsner.

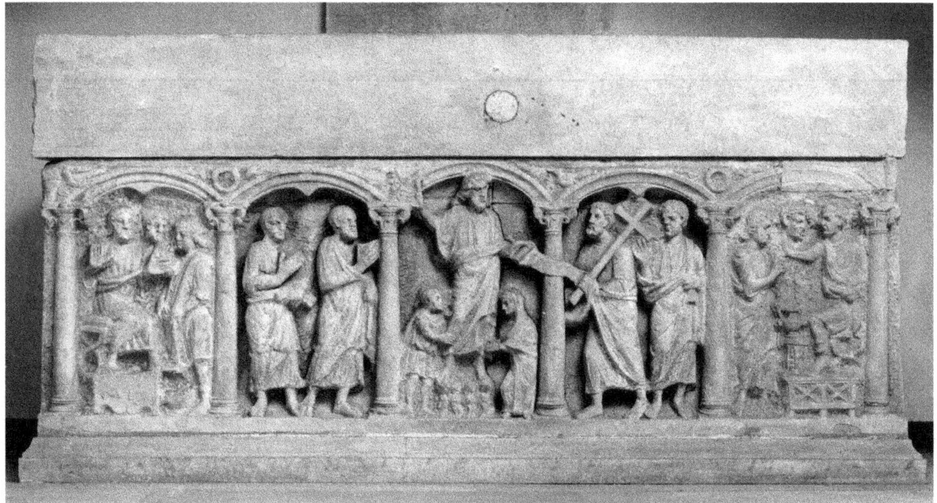

Figure 11.6: Unfinished sarcophagus from Rome, last quarter of the third century AD, reused in the fifteenth century in the Grotte Vaticane for the burial of Pope Pius II. In the intercolumniations from left to right: Christ washing Peter's feet, two apostles of which the one on the right is probably Paul, Christ on the rock of paradise with male and female worshippers and four rivers flowing, two apostles of which Peter stands to the left and receives the Law, Christ before Pilate. Photograph: Conway Library, Courtauld Institute of Art, negative A74/290.

right and of St Peter on the left, this is likely to be correct, as the iconography is parallel to the sides of another sarcophagus from Alyscamps now in the Arles Museum of roughly the same date and probable Roman provenance.[65] But what

65 *Rep.* III, 49, 35–6, with Saggiorato 1968, 72–8.

cannot be certain is whether the miracle maker at the rock is Peter or Moses functioning as his ante-type, or indeed a figure that could stand for both.[66] However, whatever precise interpretation one were to put on the sides, there is no doubt that the water imagery of the front flows into them in the form of the liturgically central and scripturally sanctioned waters of Baptism and the waters of miracle. If the figure conducting the miracle is Peter, then his own command over the waters is directly related to the rock imagery of the waters of Paradise on which Jesus stands in the centre and the washing of his own feet by Jesus to the left of the front. If Peter's striking of water from the rock is at all an allusion to his baptism of Cornelius (*Acts* 10. 44–8), then the imagery of the left side emulates and fulfils the Baptism of Jesus himself on the right. Likewise, Jesus' command over the waters – both in the central scene where they flow from beneath his feet and the washing of Peter's feet, where their flow is through his hands – is related to his baptismal chrism at the right end. The active nature of Christ's and Peter's relations with water in all the scenes of the front and ends other than the trial, where Pilate does the washing, is a superb visual device for emphasising the trial as the denial of pagan Rome's authority over the Saviour through his silence, as indicated visually by his having nothing to do with the water motif in that scene.

The contrast of Jesus and Pilate is pointed – with the two squeezed into a single arch (Figure 11.7). Pilate sits like a late Roman emperor in military dress with a jewelled diadem on his head.[67] He gestures flamboyantly – the hand he is about to wash filling the middle of the visual field in the intercolumniation. Jesus, clean-shaven by contrast with his image at the centre, almost bows before him, the epitome of the meekness and the spiritual rather than temporal authority which the trial supremely encapsulates. Yet the other key counterpoint is between the trial scene and the washing of the feet (Figure 11.8). There Peter sits in a posture that mirrors Pilate, although in tunic and pallium, gesturing not just with one hand but with both – and with his left hand occupying the centre of the scene in direct parallel with Pilate's right. Again Jesus is meek – standing, lower than the seated Peter, performing the ultimate obeisance in washing his disciple's feet. The juxtaposition of authorities is not between Pilate and Christ but between Pilate and Peter – the temporal representative of imperial paganism and the spiritual representative of Episcopal tradition, the former washing

66 See Saggiorato 1968, 79 and – in the context of the Bassus sarcophagus' lamb scene of the same subject – Malbon 1990, 78–82. Generally on the water miracle, see Sotomayor 1962, 57–63.

67 A good parallel for the military uniform (from diadem down to sandaled boots) is the image of the emperor Honorius in the ivory Probus diptych now in Aosta, dated to 406 – which may be roughly contemporary with *Rep.* III, 53 (if we date it as late as 400) and certainly no more than 20 years after the sarcophagus was carved. See Delbrueck 1929, no. 1, pp. 84–7; Volbach 1976, no. 1, pp.29–30; Kiilerich 1993, 65–7.

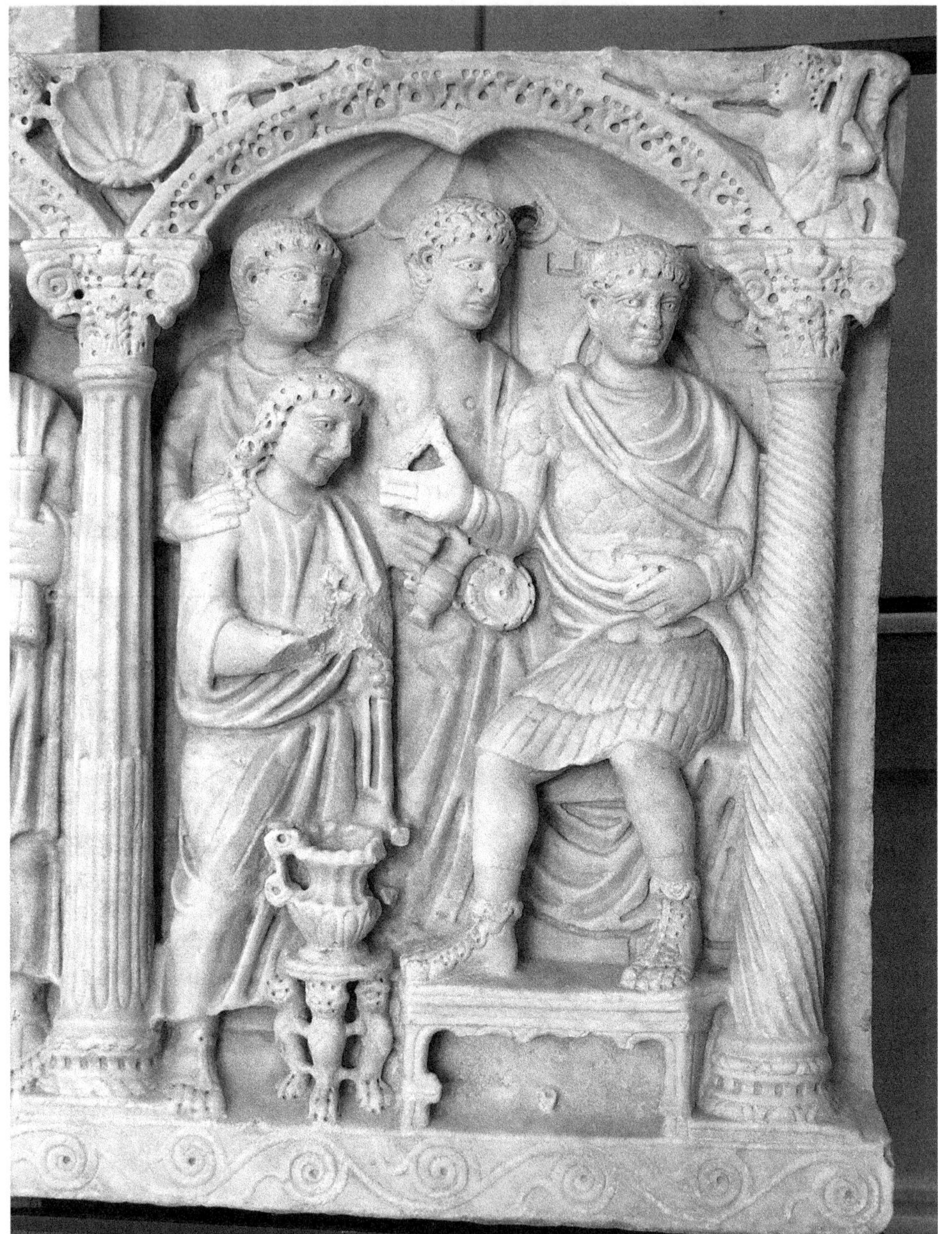

Figure 11.7: Detail of figure 5: last intercolumniation from the left: Christ before Pilate. Photograph: J. Elsner.

himself in rejection of Jesus and the latter anointed by Jesus as his successor through the washing of his feet. In each case, the meekness of Jesus is both the counterpoint to their respective authorities and the attitude which not only

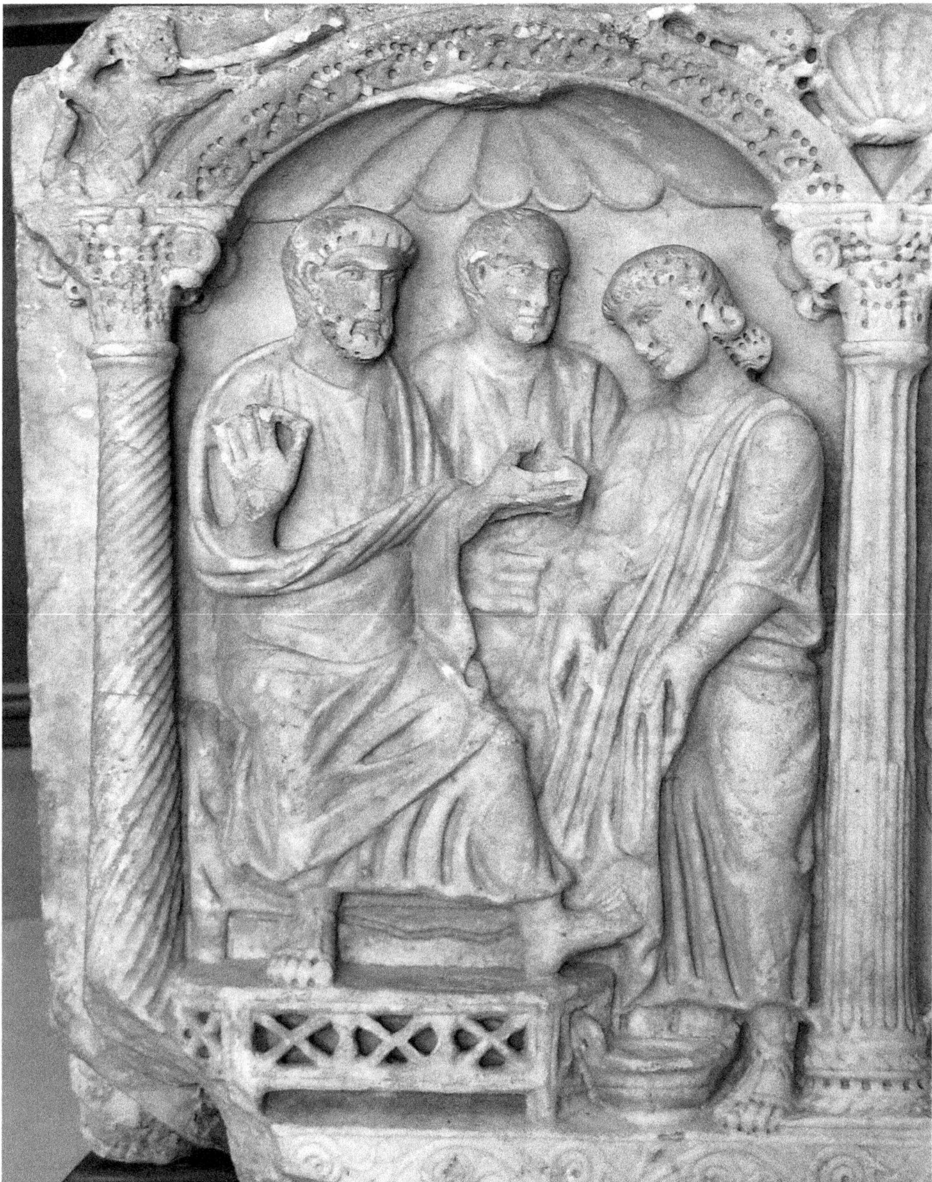

Figure 11.8: Detail of figure 5: first intercolumniation from the left: Jesus washes the feet of St Peter. Photograph: J. Elsner.

establishes that authority in the case of Peter, but also undermines its force with an authority, defined by Jesus' meekness, of a different order and nature from that displayed by both Peter and Pilate.

Against both these forms of authority stands the great central Jesus (Figure 11.5) – bearded, enlarged, bursting out of the architectural frame that incorporates all the other figures and scenes, no longer the meek figure of the left and right, but the triumphant Christ by virtue of whom Peter holds his episcopacy and the authority of a non-Christian empire (for which Pilate stands) is overturned.[68] The eschatological implication may be reinforced by the small figures in the arch spandrels at the far left and right sides of the front, which show tritons blowing trumpets and perhaps hint at the ending of days. The sea and dolphin imagery of the remaining spandrels again emphasises the water imagery which pervades this iconography and orchestrates its argument.

The other particularly striking scheme where the trial appears in a wholly Passion context is that of the sarcophagus known as Lateran 171, now in the Vatican Museums (Figure 11.4).[69] Here, uniquely, the trial of Christ – although in its usual place in the two intercolumniations (out of five) to the right of the main face – is the *first* depicted event of the Passion cycle, taken chronologically. In the centre is the *crux invicta,* which – whether read as a symbolic version of the Resurrection (given the martyr-crown, Chi-rho and sleeping soldier to the right) or of the Crucifixion (given the large central cross and the gesturing soldier to the left) – is the last chronological scene in the pictorial cycle.[70] To the immediate left of the *crux invicta* is a unique image of Christ being crowned with the crown of thorns,[71] and to the far left, Simon of Cyrene carries the cross to Calvary.[72] The architectural framing of the five niches has the two outer intercolumniations topped with pointed gables in the centre of which have been restored round wreaths.[73] These wreaths, immediately above and touching the cross carried by Simon to the left and above Pilate washing his hands to the right, are smaller versions of the great martyr-crown encircling Chi-rho of the central niche, with its large curved arch. As in the far left niche, in the centre the top of the cross touches the wreath (to create the characteristic *crux invicta* form). This dynamic of patterning matters because it picks up the motif of the crown of thorns in the second intercolumniation from the left, where Christ, who holds a scroll, is crowned by a Roman soldier holding a sword.

68 How Mathews 1999, 140 manages to make this image 'feminine', 'a figure who is both and old man and a woman' is entirely beyond me.

69 *Rep.* I, 49, where it is dated to the mid fourth century. See also the discussions of Gerke 1940a, 71–5; Saggiorato 1968, 20–3, 81–93; G. Spinola in Ensoli and La Rocca 2000, no. 306, 604–5; Spier 2007, no. 46, 219–20.

70 See Hellemo 1989, 98–100 on this scene.

71 See the discussion of Gerke 1948, 31–4.

72 So far as I know, this is a unique depiction of this scene.

73 The best guide to restorations and still the best available photograph is in Wilpert 1929, vol. I, tav 146 (where restorations are circled by a fine white line).

The crown of thorns scene – narratologically, the most extreme moment of Jesus' humiliation and the ultimate parodic inversion of his divine kingship – takes the meekness theme (usually epitomised by the trial images) to its extreme. But it is in fact portrayed with very little sense of humiliation: Jesus stands facing centre right and apparently untroubled while the soldier gently places the crown on his head. Given the insistent suggestion of martyr-crowns in the rest of the sarcophagus' imagery, the crown of thorns here may double up as a martyr-crown, a symbol of Jesus' triumph as supreme martyr. This scene with its level entablature and two figures of a Roman soldier to the left and Christ to the right, both facing rightwards, seems deliberately close to the imagery of the fourth niche which shows Jesus before Pilate. There, Christ's hand is in the gesture of blessing rather than holding a scroll, while the soldier (in very similar kit to his comrade in the crown of thorns image) holds a lance. But the flat entablature, two figures facing right with Jesus in front, and dress of both figures, are all parallel. If the scene before Pilate is the epitome of meekness, then the crowning with thorns is both the development of meekness to a still more extreme point and simultaneously its counterpoint as the proleptic embodiment of Jesus' triumph.

Interestingly, within the complex set of entablature choices that frame these intercolumniations, the narrative images are very simple with no background or context. The only exception to this is the last niche on the right with Pilate washing his hands, where the governor not only has an elegant lion-legged table and wash-stand, but appears to be seated in front of a large military building made from stone-blocks with crenellations and arched windows. It is as if only in the Roman-governor's scene is public, social and civic space allowed to intrude, while the remaining images operate at a more abstract or universal level – the salvation that lies beyond Pilate's washing of hands.[74] While this sarcophagus keeps carefully to Passion-centred iconography, its deployment and placement of scenes entirely disrupts any urge to a narrative or chronological reading. Rather, the imagery works from the centre outwards to the two images with Jesus that immediately flank it (all figures in both scenes facing to the right) and then to the far niches with Simon of Cyrene (on the left) striding with the cross leftwards out of the pictorial space, and Pilate (on the right) gazing rightwards away from the pictorial scene and both images of Jesus that turn towards him. These two outer images, especially when contrasted with the

74 The proliferation of furniture, toilet accoutrements and a castle-type building in the background is in fact common in the iconography of the Pilate scene (see e.g. *Rep.* I, 28; *Rep.* I, 680; *Rep.* III, 41; *Rep.* III, 53; *Rep.* III, 416; *Rep.* III, 453: I cite only examples where all these elements appear). However in all cases but Lateran 171, other scenes on the sarcophagus have background elements that socialise the imagery which are eschewed here.

two scenes including Jesus next to them, have an emphasis on surrogacy. Simon carries the cross in place of Christ, as his surrogate, while Pilate washes his hands as if this can absolve him of responsibility for his judgement. Pilate's hand-washing is also a kind of surrogacy, in place of his failure to free Jesus and as testament to the weakness of his authority (to do as he would wish) at precisely the point where his power is most directly enacted.

I have been arguing that the iconographic complexity of these sarcophagi cannot be fully accounted for without grasping some element of the simultaneously apologetic and polemical edge of the trial scene. Whether taken as a pictorial cue to the bigger exegetic problem of Jesus' silence, or interpreted more strictly visually, the scene both affirms Christian triumph and undermines traditional Roman power. The repeated iconography presents a confrontation of two kinds of authority in which the temporal one that does the judging, and will after all put the Saviour to death, is nonetheless depicted at the apogee of its weakness with Pilate in the concessive act of washing his hands to show that even he does not concur with the judgment he is himself perforce in the act of passing. By contrast, Jesus – although flanked by soldiers as a condemned prisoner at the first stage of his humiliation – stands making no concession at the outset of a path that will take him through public flogging and crucifixion to the triumph of Resurrection. The image of the trial – and indeed the total iconographic scheme of these sarcophagi – speaks simultaneously for an assertion of Christian supremacy in the form of the Saviour and an implicit denigration of pre-Christian Roman imperialism in the figure of Pilate. In the case of the most complex examples, such as the sarcophagus from Arles, Jesus stands in contrast with more than one form of earthly power – Peter's ecclesiastical authority which is visually shown to depend upon Christ's washing of his feet – and Pilate's judgment.

Visual Turns in the Rhetorical Image

We have seen something of the complex ways that the trial scene stands both apologetically for Christian triumph and polemically against pagan imperial authority. By way of conclusion, let us return briefly to a primarily *polemical* image, the scene of the three Hebrews refusing to worship the 'image of gold whose height was three cubits and the breadth thereof six cubits' which Nebuchadnezzar set up in the plain of Dura (see Figures 11.2 and 11.9).[75] The polemical potential of this scene against paganism is clear. In the case of the sarcophagi, by making the idol on its column (whether represented as a portrait bust or a painted panel) look as if it were the imperial image, the specific

75 Daniel 3.1–18.

targeting of that polemic against the pagan imperial state (with Nebuchadnezzar effectively standing for the Roman emperor) is an effective visual turn to make the polemic more pointed. But what is striking is the iconographic appropriation of the form of this scene to a quite different narrative, from which it can hardly be distinguished save by virtue of the other images juxtaposed against it. This is the theme of the three Magi (who are usually portrayed like the three Hebrews in Persian dress and Phrygian caps) before Herod (e.g. Figure 11.10), who is always accompanied by an idol, like Nebuchadnezzar, before they go on their way to find the Christ child.[76] Juxtaposed against images of the epiphany (that is, the Magi before the Virgin and Child), the theme must in this case refer to the Magi rather than the three Hebrews, or potentially to both with the Hebrews doubling up as the Magi like whom they look.[77]

In many ways this is a relatively simple switch, a case of the typical iconographic promiscuity that allows the Endymion type of Roman mythological sarcophagi to become Jonah in early Christian sarcophagi,[78] and indeed allows Ariadne to turn into Endymion (and back again) in non-Christian funerary sculpture.[79] But it also has a rhetorical role. It shifts the polemical edge from an undermining of Roman hegemonic culture, and specifically paganism, to an attack on idolatry in pre-Christian Jewish culture that is made explicitly by Herod's placement in relation to a graven image. What was once, and powerfully, part of the Jewish case against the polytheistic pagan environment (and accepted as such in early Christian art) now becomes part of the Christian case against Judaism, brilliantly effected by the sleight of hand that simply translates the iconography of one scene into that of another. There is no argument involved here, no justification of what has happened. Rather, the

76 Matthew 2.7. Spectacular examples include the great fourth century sarcophagi in the cathedrals of Tolentino and Ancona, as well as the so-called Stilicho sarcophagus at Sant' Ambrogio in Milan, respectively *Rep.* II, 148, 52–4 (right end of the main coffin); *Rep.* II, 149, 54–6 (right end of the main coffin); *Rep.* II, 150, 56–8 (left front of the lid). See also *Rep.* III, 492, 228–9 (a lid fragment) and the lid of a lost sarcophagus found in Trier and subsequently in Luxembourg in Gerke 1949, 13, 31–4 and illustrated from a drawing at taf. 3, abb. 5. For discussion, see Carletti 1975, 107–112 (also 83–7).

77 Indeed, given the significant placement of the epiphany beneath the main tondo at the bottom of the Adelfia sarcophagus (*Rep.* II.20), one does rather doubt the insistence of interpreters on the identification of the three Hebrews as the sole iconographic subject of the image at the left end of the bottom tier, since it could equally represent the Magi before Herod. See for example *Rep.* II, 20, 9, Carletti 1975, 71–2 or Sgarlata 1998, 23. Likewise, the scene on the lower tier of the right end of the St Trophime sarcophagus is usually seen as the three Hebrews (e.g. *Rep.* III, 118, 73 and Benoit 1954, no. 45, 48) but if read against the epiphany on the upper tier of the left end, then it could also be interpreted as the Magi before Herod.

78 See esp. Gerke 1940b, 120–9; also Mathews 1999, 30–3.

79 On Endymion and Ariadne, see e.g. Koortbojian 1995, 95–8, 135–40, with bibliography.

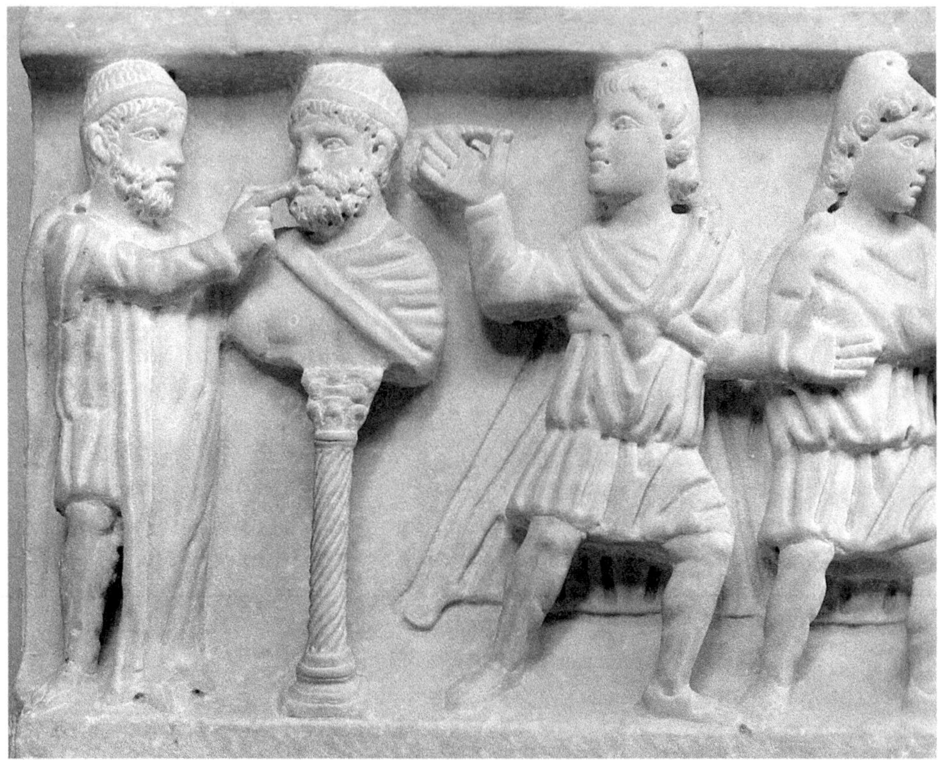

Figure 11.9: Detail from the left side of the lower register of the Adelfia sarcophagus from the Catacomb of San Giovanni in Syracuse, second quarter of the fourth century. Now in the Museo Archeologico Regionale P. Orsi in Syracuse. Nebuchadnezzar orders the Hebrews to worship his idol. Photograph: DAIR 1971.0863 (Singer).

argument is all in the rhetorical implications of the act of using the iconographic type of three Hebrews for the scene of the Magi before Herod. These are that the Christian dispensation will now rise in triumph over both the pagan Roman imperial origins and the Jewish ethnic and scriptural roots out of which jointly Christianity emerged. Moreover the consonance of imperial/royal portrait with that of the idol (Nebuchadnezzar looking just like his image of gold, in e.g. Figure 11.9, or Herod looking like his idol, something even more directly clear in the Tolentino sarcophagus than in Figure 11.10) implies not only a culture of idolatrous self-worship in the precursors of Christianity which the Incarnation of God has overturned but also a fundamental parallelism of pagan cult and Judaism by contrast with the triumphant and salvific new faith.[80]

80 Further on ways in which early Christians used material culture and iconography rhetorically to affirm religious transformation from and triumph over ancestral origins, see Elsner 2008, and Elsner forthcoming.

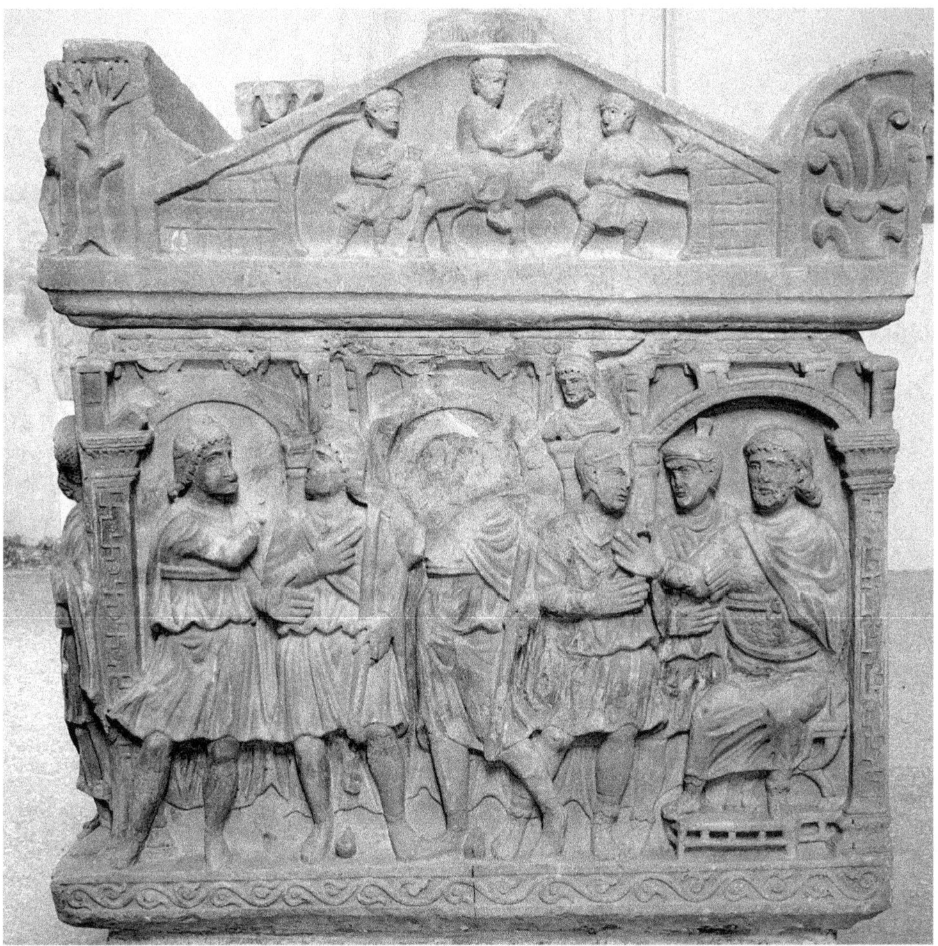

Figure 11.10: Sarcophagus of Flavius Gorgonius, Ancona Cathedral, late fourth century AD, right side. The Magi before Herod with an idol on a pillar.
Photograph: DAIR 1960.1416 (Boehringer).

Acknowledgements

This paper was first written as the Roberts Lecture, given at Dickinson College in 2008. I am particularly grateful to all who were involved, especially to Marc Mastrangelo, who invited me, and to Peter Struck, who responded. As ever, my co-editor has been characteristically generous and incisive in her comments.

Bibliography

Aixalà, J.M. i. La escena 'Pro Tribunali', Jesus ante Pilatos, en los sarcofagos de Pasion, in: *Historian Pictura Refert: Miscellanea in onore di padre Alejandro Resio Veganzones O.F.M.* (Vatican City, 1994), 1–14.

Benoit, F. *Sarcophages paléochrétiens d'Arles et de Marseille* (Paris, 1954).

Brown, P. Review of T. Mathews, *'The Clash of Gods.' Art Bulletin* 77 (1995) 499–502.

Cameron, A. The Funeral of Junius Bassus. *Zeitschrift für Papyrologie und Epigraphie* 139 (2002), 288–292.

von Campenhausen, H. Die Passionssarkophage: Zur Geschichte eines Altchristlichen Bildkresises. *Marburger Jahrbuch für Kunstwissenschaft* 5 (1929), 39–85.

Carletti, C. *I tre Ebrei di Babilonia nell' arte cristiana antica, Quaderni di Vetera Christianorum 9.* (Rome, 1975).

Cavallo, G., Gribomont, J. and Loerke, W. *Codex Purpureus Rossanensis* (Rome and Graz, 1987).

Cecchelli, C., Furlani, G. and Salmi, M. *The Rabbula Gospels* (Olten and Lausanne, 1959).

Cooper, S. A. *Marius Victorinus' Commentary on Galatians* (Oxford, 2005).

Daltrop, G. Anpassung eines Relieffragmentes an den Deckel des Iunius Bassus Sarkophags. *Rendiconti della Pontificia Accademia di Archeologia* 51–2 (1978–80), 157–170.

Dassmann, E. *Sündenvergebung durch Taufe, Buße und Märtyrerfürbitte in den Zeugnissen frühchristlicher Frömmigkeit und Kunst* (Münster, 1973).

Dassmann, E. *Paulus in frühchristlicher Frömmigkeit und Kunst* (Opladen, 1982).

Davis-Weyer, C. Die Traditio-Legis-Bild und seine Nachfolge. *Münchner Jahrbuch der Bildenden Kunst* 12 (1961), 7–45.

Deichmann, F. W. *Ravenna: Haupstadt der Spätantiken Abendlandes, Kommentar I* (Wiesbaden, 1974).

Delbrueck, R. *Die Consulardiptychen und der Verwandte Denkmäler* (Berlin, 1929).

Delbrueck, R. *Probleme der Lipsanothek in Brescia* (Bonn, 1952).

Dinkler, E. *Der Einzug in Jerusalem* (Opladen, 1970).

Drocourt-Dubrueil, G. *Saint Victor de Marseille: Art funéraire et prière des morts aux temps paléochrétiens (IVe-Ve siècles)* (Marseilles, 1989).

Elsner, J. Making Myth Visual: The *Horae* of Philostratus and the Dance of the text. *Römische Mitteilungen* 107 (2000), 253–276.

Elsner, J. Inventing Christian Rome: The Role of Early Christian Art, in: *Rome the Cosmopolis,* edited by C. Edwards and G. Woolf (Cambridge, 2003), 71–99.

Elsner, J. Historical Context and the Objects We Study: Three Boxes from Late Roman Italy. *Journal of the Warburg and Courtauld Institutes* 71 (2008), 21–38.

Elsner, J. Beyond Compare: Pagan Saint and Christian God in Late Antiquity. *Critical Inquiry* 35 (Spring 2009), 655–683.

Elsner, J. 'Pharoah's Army Got Drownded': Some Reflections on Jewish Narrative and Christian Meaning in Late Antiquity, in: *The Image of the Jew in Christian Art,* edited by H. Kessler and D. Nirenberg (Philadephia, forthcoming).

Ensoli, S. and La Rocca, E. (eds.). *Aurea Roma. Dalla città pagana alla città cristiana* (Rome, 2000).

Frede, M. Origen's Treatise *Against Celsus,* in: *Apologetics in the Roman Empire,* edited by M. Edwards, M. Goodman and S.Price (Oxford, 1999), 131–55.

Gaertner, J. Zur Deutung des Junius-Bassus-Sarkophages. *Jahrbuch des Deutschen Archäologischen Instituts* 83 (1968), 240–264.

Gerke, F. *Der Sarkophag des Junius Bassus* (Berlin, 1936).

Gerke, F. *Die Zeitbestimmung der Passionssarkophage* (Berlin, 1940a).

Gerke, F. *Die Christlichen Sarkophage der vorkonstantinische Zeit* (Berlin, 1940b).

Gerke, F. *Christus in der spätantiken Plastik* (Mainz, 1948).

Gerke, F. *Die Trierer Agricius-sarkophag* (Trier, 1949).

Giess, H. *Die Darstellung der Fusswaschung Christi in den Kunstwerken des 4–12 Jahrhunderts* (Rome, 1962).

Goulet, R. (ed.). Macarios de Magnésie. *Le Monogénès: edition critique et traduction française* vol. 2 (Paris, 2003).

Grimaldi, G. *Descrizione della basilica antica di S. Pietro in Vaticano* (ed. R. Niggl) (Vatican, 1972).

von Harnack, A. *Kritik des Neuen Testaments von einen Griechischen Philosophen des 3 Jahrhunderts* (Leipzig, 1911).

von Harnack, A. *Porphyrius, Gegen die Christen, Abhandlungen der Königlichen Preussischen Akademie der Wissenschaften, Philosophisch-Historische Klasse* (Berlin, 1916).

Hellemo, G. *Adventus Domini: Eschatological Thought in Fourth Century Apses and Catecheses* (Leiden, 1989).

Himmelmann, N. *Typologische Untersuchungen an Römischen Sarkophagreliefs des 3 und 4 Jahrhunderts n. Chr.* (Mainz, 1973).

Hourihane, C. *Pontius Pilate, Anti-Semitism and the Passion in Medieval Art* (Princeton, 2009).

Jensen, R. *Understanding Early Christian Art* (London, 2000).

Jensen, R. *Face to Face: Portraits of the Divine in Early Christianity.* (Minneapolis, 2005).

Jeremias, G. *Die Holztur der Basilika S. Sabina in Rom* (Tubingen, 1980).

Jones, C. P. *Philostratus, Apollonius of Tyana,* Loeb edition, volume 3 (Cambridge Mass., 2006).

Kennedy, G. *Progymnasmata: Greek Textbooks of Prose Composition and Rhetoric* (Atlanta, 2003).

Kessler, H. *Old St Peter's and Church Decoration in Medieval Italy* (Spoleto, 2002).

Kessler, H. The Word Made Flesh in Early Decorated Bibles, in: *Picturing the Bible: The Earliest Christian Art,* edited by J. Spier (New Haven, 2007), 141–168.

Kiilerich, B. *Late Fourth-Century Classicism in the Plastic Arts* (Odense, 1993).

Kinney, D. Review of T. Mathews, *The Clash of Gods. Studies in Iconography* 16 (1994), 237–242.

Klauser, T. *Frühchristliche Sarkophage in Bild und Word* (Olten, 1966).

Koch, G. *Frühchristliche Sarkophage* (Munich, 2000).

Koch, G. and Sichtermann, H. *Römische Sarkophage* (Munich, 1982).

Kollwitz, J. *Die Lipsanothek von Brescia* (Berlin, 1933).

Koortbojian, M. *Myth, Meaning and Memory on Roman Sarcophagi* (Berkeley, 1995).

Lawrence, M. Columnar Sarcophagi in the Latin West. *Art Bulletin* 14 (1932), 103–185.

Loerke, W. The Miniatures of the Trial in the Rossano Gospels. *Art Bulletin* 43 (1961), 171–195.

Lowden, J. The Beginnings of Biblical Illustration, in: *Imaging the Early Medieval Bible,* edited by J. Williams (Philadelphia, 1999), 9–59.

Malbon, E. *The Iconography of the Sarcophagus of Junius Bassus* (Princeton, 1990).

Mathews, T. *The Clash of Gods* (Princeton, 1999).

Meyer, M. *Rome et la naissance de l'art Européen* (Paris, 2007).
Millar, F. Reflections on the Trial of Jesus, in: *A Tribute to Geza Vermes: Essays on Jewish and Christian Literature and History, Journal for the Study of the Old Testament suppl. 100*, edited by P. Davies and R. White (Sheffield, 1990), 355–381.
Müller, F. *The So-Called Peleus and Thetis Sarcophagus in the Villa Albani* (Amsterdam, 1994).
Perrone, L. Fra silenzio e parola: Dall' apologia alla testimonianza del Cristianesimo nel *Contro Celso* di Origene, in: *L'apologétique chrétienne Gréco-Latine à l'époque prénicénienne (Entretiens sur l'antiquité classique de Fondation Hardt 51)*, edited by A. Wlosok and F. Paschoud (Geneva, 2005), 102–149.
Riedweg, C. Porphyrios über Christus und die Christen: *De philosophia ex oraculis haurienda* und *Adversus Chrsitianos*, in: *L'apologétique chrétienne Gréco-Latine à l'époque prénicénienne (Entretiens sur l'antiquité classique de Fondation Hardt 51)*, edited by A. Wlosok and F. Paschoud (Geneva, 2005), 151–203.
Rizzardi, C. *I sarcofagi paleocristiani con rappresentazione del passagio del Mar Rosso.* (Faenza, 1970).
Saggiorato, A. *I sarcofagi paelocristiani con scene di Passione* (Bologna, 1968).
Schefold, K. Altchristliche Bilderzyklen: Bassussarkophag und Santa Maria Maggiore. *Rivista di Archeologia Cristiana* 16 (1939), 289–316.
Schiller, G. *The Iconography of Christian Art* (London, 1972).
Schrenk, S. *Typos und Antitypos in der frühchristlichen Kunst* (Munster, 1995).
Sgarlata, M. Il Sarcofago di Adelfia, in: *ET LUX FUIT: Le catacombe e il sarcofago di Adelfia* (Palermo, 1998), 15–34.
Sotomayor, M. *S. Pedro en la iconografia paleocristiana* (Granada, 1962).
Spengel, L. *Rhetores Graeci*, (3 vols.) (Leipzig, 1854–6).
Spier, J. (ed.). *Picturing the Bible: The Earliest Christian Art* (New Haven, 2007).
Turcan, R. *Les sarcophages romains à representations dionysiaques (Bibliothèque des Écoles françaises d' Athènes et de Rome 210)* (Paris, 1966).
Tkacz, C. B. *The Key to the Brescia Casket* (Notre Dame, 2002).
Volbach, W. F. *Elfenarbeiten der Spätantike und des frühen Mittelalters* (Mainz, 1976).
de Waal, A. *Der Sarkophag des Junius Bassus* (Rome, 1900).
Watson, C. The program of the Brescia Casket. *Gesta* 20 (1981), 283–298.
Wegner, M. Das Nabuchodonosar-Bild, das Bild im Bild, in: *Pietas: Festschrift für Bernhard Kötting (Jahrbuch für Antike und Christentum Ergänzungsband 8)*, edited by E. Dassmann and K. S. Frank (Munster, 1980), 528–538.
Wilpert, G. *I sarcofagi cristiani antichi* (Rome, 1929).
Wischmeyer, W. *Die Tafeldeckel der christlichen Sarkophage konstantinischer Zeit in Rom* (Rome, 1982).
Wlosok, A. and Paschoud, F. (eds.). *L' apologétique chrétienne Gréco-Latine à l'époque prénicénienne (Entretiens sur l'antiquité classique de Fondation Hardt 51)* (Geneva, 2005).
Wormald, F. *The Miniatures in the Gospels of St Augustine* (Cambridge, 1954).
Zanker, P. and Ewald, B. *Mit Mythen leben: Die Bilderwelt der römischen Sarkophage* (Munich, 2004).

12.
'Houses of the dead'? Columnar sarcophagi as 'micro-architecture'

Edmund Thomas

At the end of the twentieth century architects across the world sought to bring architecture closer to humanity. 'Micro-architecture' in the form of shelters, street furniture, and inhabitable sculptures, designed as places of retreat or isolation, stimulated creative design.[1] Simultaneously, medieval art historians considered how a 'micro-architecture' of religious ornaments and furnishings, reproducing small buildings in miniature, had enabled individual viewers to identify more deeply with heavenly ideals.[2] Small-scale, sacred architectural forms – reliquaries, censers, screens, stalls, pulpits, fonts and baldachins – triggered emotional responses and offered spiritual refuge.[3] As François Bucher claimed, a quarter of a century earlier, these 'fluidly superimposed systems of decoration', combining 'formal bravado with theological complexity in a small space' and offering 'dazzling structural dexterity' and geometric complexity, were exemplars of Gothic style that sheltered the mysteries of Christianity.[4] Based on an aesthetic vocabulary taken from monumental archetypes, they acquired, through the innovative designs of architects seeking new fields for experimentation, sophisticated forms transcending those larger structures and became almost the *raison d'être* of the buildings housing them. Modern and medieval manifestations of micro-architecture differ in scale, but both make statements about relationships between ideal and real space, between body and soul, between different genres of architecture, and between architecture and the human body.

Classical antiquity knew ample instances of such 'micro-architecture', but their religious or philosophical significance has yet to receive similar investigation. Studies, for example, of the small ash urn from Chiusi (Figure 12.1) have focused instead on its potential as a literal representation of an Etruscan house and its use to historians as evidence for larger structures.[5] Yet,

1 *Micro-architectures* 2000, 29.
2 Boldrick and Fehrmann 2000; *Homes for the Soul* 2000.
3 Bucher 1976.
4 Bucher 1976, 83.
5 Prayon 1986, 193, fig. V.36. On the Chiusi urn, similar 'models', and prehistoric precedents: Staccioli 1969; Massari and Setti 2000.

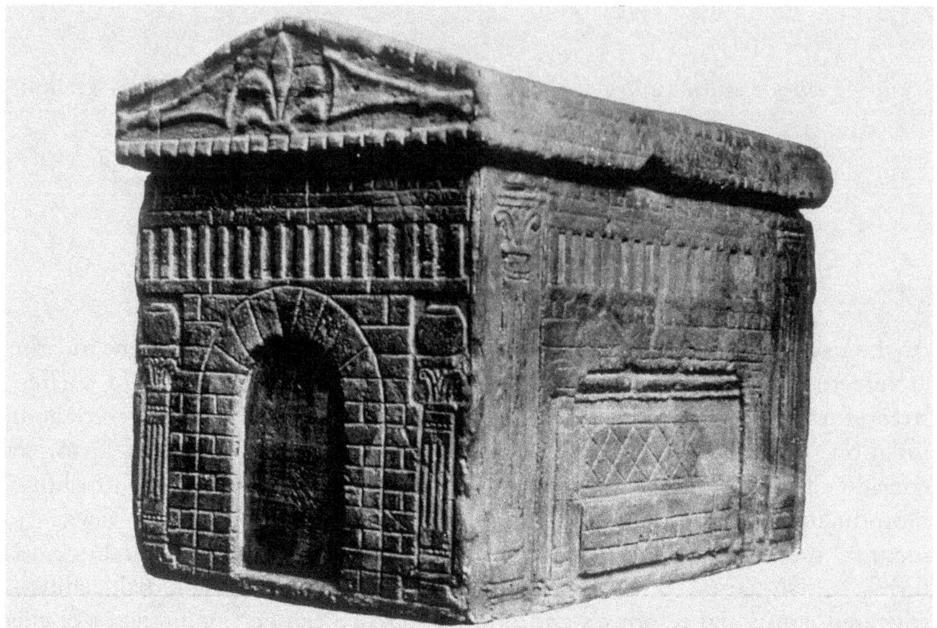

Figure 12.1: House urn from Chiusi. Museo Archeologico, Florence. Photograph: Museum.

unlike the marble or limestone models from Ostia and Niha, which replicate a building's plan accurately and in the latter case with measurements inscribed, Etruscan models have no precise reference to actual buildings.[6] Their features suggest only symbolic aspects of architecture, bestowing a spiritual or emotional quality on the ashes of the deceased.[7]

With the heavy recent emphasis on the pictorial content of sarcophagus reliefs it is easy to forget that Roman sarcophagi are also architectonic structures. Through their funerary purpose they answered emotional needs like medieval micro-architecture, and accordingly some early forms of the latter incorporated ancient Roman sarcophagi.[8] With column sarcophagi this architectural aspect is particularly evident. They are sometimes seen as curiosities, a minor chapter in the history of Roman sculpture.[9] Yet it is misleading to see them as wholly separate. In the subjects of their reliefs column sarcophagi cross boundaries, encompassing almost every theme and even abstract strigillations. This study, therefore, investigates a widespread phenomenon: the desire to place figures or scenes in columnar contexts and to create a semblance of architecture in a

6 For Ostia and Niha, see Wilson Jones 2000, 54–56, figs. 3.9–10.
7 Mansuelli 1970a.
8 See below, pp. 425–426.
9 Koch and Sichtermann 1982, 76–80, 503–507.

physically restricted space. It reveals much about Roman perceptions of architectural space and the human body.

Rather than being interpreted in terms of what they literally represent, column sarcophagi should be understood as offering a set of iconic architectural features derived from built contexts that gave them symbolic and emotional potency. Those features had particular force because of the relation between body and soul in Roman views of the afterlife and the widely-held idea that the funerary monument was the resting-place of the soul. They represent above all an architecture of the exterior. The actual recreation of interior space is almost unknown, the extraordinary exception being the sarcophagus from Simpelveld, where even the interior furnishings are carved in micro-relief on the inner face of the chest.[10] The latter may imply a different mortuary culture from elsewhere in the Roman Empire. Yet even there the inner carvings present the outsides of buildings too, producing a remarkable conflation of interior and exterior space. In most cases of micro-architecture, the object alludes only to exterior public space, highlighting the significance of ornament and form.

Reading column sarcophagi

At the start of the twentieth century column sarcophagi entered wider art-historical narratives. In 1899 the Berlin Museums acquired a relief apparently representing Christ and two Apostles and recut from one side of a column sarcophagus, from the district of Samatya (Psamathia) in Istanbul.[11] The now famous Psamathia Relief (Figure 12.2) influenced both the Russian art historian Dimitri Ainalov and the Austrian-Silesian scholar Josef Strzygowski, almost simultaneously, but apparently independently, in forming their historic accounts of the origins of later Roman art and culture.[12] For Ainalov, the resemblance of this fragment in its architectural decoration to sarcophagi from Asia Minor helped to support his theory of the 'Hellenistic foundations' of Byzantine art; for Strzygowski, the addition of a number of examples in Italian collections strengthened the case for the Asiatic in the argument 'Orient oder Rom?'. That very year, in 1901, the magnificent Sidamara sarcophagus, discovered a quarter of a century earlier, was brought from Cappadocia for display in the Imperial

10 Leiden, Rijksmuseum van Oudheden, I, 130/12.1; Holwerda 1933.

11 Effenberger 1990, 79.

12 Ainalov 1901, 160–164, and 1961, 216; Strzygowski 1901 (opposed to Riegl 1901: see Elsner 2002).

Ottoman Museum in Istanbul.[13] In the next year, in what remains the only full-length study of the structure and ornamentation of Roman sarcophagi, Walter Altmann cited the 'unzweifelhaft italisch' Melfi sarcophagus (Figures 12.10 and 12.11), found in 1856, as evidence of the western origin of column sarcophagi.[14] But the argument of the 'orientalists' gathered momentum. Further discoveries were made, and a distinct group of Asiatic column sarcophagi, unified above all by their architectural ornament, became established.[15] Studying the sarcophagus of Claudia Antonia Sabina found at Sardis in 1913, Charles Morey produced their first extensive classification, distinguishing eastern examples, including Melfi, from western 'imitations';[16] Marion Lawrence refined understanding of the western versions, considering them much later derivatives of Asiatic works;[17] Hans Wiegartz systematically classified the Asiatic, separating a main group from variant works produced in regional centres such as Aphrodisias and Nicaea;[18] and Marc Waelkens attributed that group to workshops at the marble quarries of Docimeion in Phrygia.[19] The lavish ornament of the Asiatic forms now appeared pre-eminent. The outputs of western workshops were dismissed as a secondary artistic phenomenon based on imitation of the virtuoso creations of sculptors in Asia Minor.

The chronology of column sarcophagi established by Morey and Lawrence on the basis of the style of their portrait heads and the manner of their architectural ornament was refined by Wiegartz to place Asiatic sarcophagi at the forefront of development. He put the first instance from Torre Nova around 145, preceding any western examples by some forty-five years.[20] But, if some sarcophagi from western workshops seem to imitate Docimian types, many look wholly independent, and as a whole the western column sarcophagi are formally more diverse and numerically more abundant.[21] After Peter Kranz re-dated some western examples to the 160s and Waelkens re-dated the Torre Nova sarcophagus to 150/155, it emerged that Docimian column sarcophagi lasted barely a century, from *c.* 150 to *c.* 260, whereas the western versions generally

13 Shapley 1923, 72 describes how it took months to transport it there, requiring the construction of special vehicles to bring it to the railway, where it was loaded onto two carriages.

14 Altmann 1902, 55.

15 Morey 1924, 22–25.

16 Morey 1924, 29–59.

17 Lawrence 1932.

18 Wiegartz 1965, 16 f., 50; cf. Morey 1924, 77 (Nicaea); Rodenwaldt 1933; Işik 1984 (Aphrodisias).

19 Waelkens 1982, 105–123.

20 Wiegartz 1965, 43 f., and 19, making the seasons sarcophagus in the Villa Savoia at *c.* 190 'one of the earliest Roman imitations.'

21 Koch and Sichtermann 1982, 76–80, with fig. 3 at 78 f.

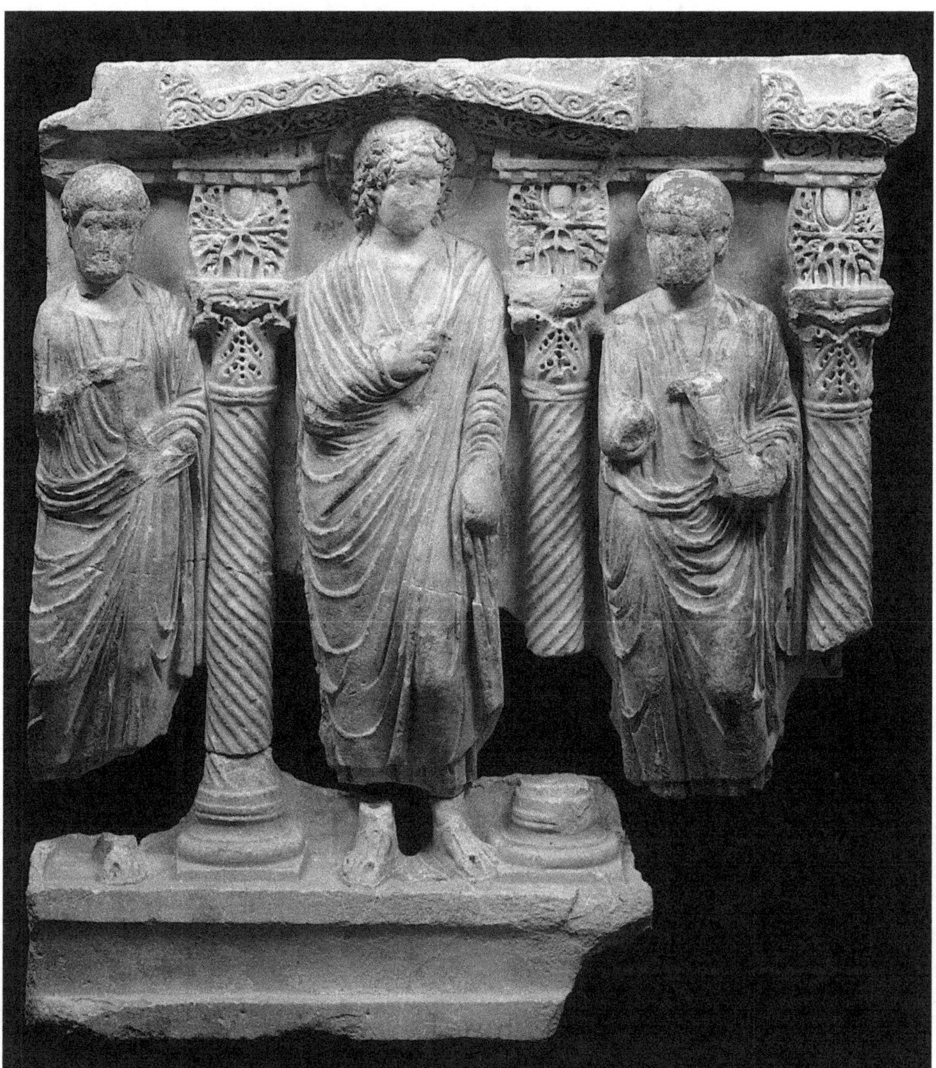

Figure 12.2: Reworked fragment of a marble sarcophagus relief from Psamathia, Istanbul. Antike Sammlungen, Berlin. Photograph: Museum.

regarded as derivative had earlier, Italic precedents, originated in their definitive form soon after the Docimian instances, and endured over a century longer.[22] Kranz argued that it was not Asiatic but earlier Roman traditions of funerary art which influenced the aedicular structure of western column sarcophagi. It even seemed possible that the design of Asiatic instances was partly derived from western prototypes, not *vice versa.*

22 Kranz 1978, 354 f.

Assessing the relationship of Asiatic column sarcophagi with western versions, Guntram Koch[23] suggested two possibilities: first, what he regarded as the unlikelier scenario, that older traditions were followed in Rome during the 160s with individual column sarcophagi made to order, and for that reason from *c.* 155–160 similar column sarcophagi were imported from Asia Minor in relatively large numbers; or, second, that the few early column sarcophagi made in Rome were imitations of the numerous grander, highly valued imports, using simpler means and indigenous forms, and followed by 'western' versions repeatedly copying Asiatic forms.[24] In assuming that one or other artistic tradition must have been the stimulus for this funerary practice, Koch adopts a position which not only echoes the old 'Orient oder Rom?' debate, but also envisages the workshop at the centre of and primarily responsible for artistic change. However, although Waelkens has conclusively identified the marble and sculptors as Asiatic, important issues are still raised by Gerhard Rodenwaldt's suggestion, despite its ethnocentric formulation, that the spur for what he called the 'Hellenising' manner of the sarcophagi 'lay not in the "Greekness" of the Hellenic world, but in the drive of Romans to absorb classical models.'[25] The character of the Asiatic column sarcophagi as works to order, rather than for stock, suggests that the model of classical architecture that they present was conceived not only by the artists, but by their patrons.[26]

There has still been no extensive study since Altmann of the architectural structure of Roman sarcophagi and its culural implications.[27] But, as for other periods, their extravagant and distinctive architectural ornament is instructive as a 'cultural form'.[28] Created at the height of the Second Sophistic, column sarcophagi offer a key to debates about Greek and Roman 'identity' in Italy and the Greek East during the second and third centuries.[29] Even in the East, the few known names of the deceased belong to families of the Roman hierarchy.[30] It will be argued here that it was the choice of Roman patrons, in both Italy and the East, in seeking an appropriate form of burial and commemoration for themselves and their families, which lay behind and motivated both the importation of column sarcophagi from Asia Minor and the creation of similar

23 Koch 1982, 171.

24 E.g. the Riccardi wedding sarcophagus in Florence and Velletri sarcophagus (Koch 1980, nos. 8 and 10).

25 Rodenwaldt 1933, 40.

26 Koch 2000.

27 Altmann 1902. But, for one region, see Gabelmann 1977.

28 Hesberg 1990.

29 Borg 2004.

30 E.g. Claudia Antonia Sabina at Sardis, Domitius Iulianus at Perge, Claudius Severinus at Aizanoi, and the asiarch Euethios Pyrrhon at Laodicea: on these instances, see further below.

forms at Rome and elsewhere, and that their decision about what was appropriate was determined by their interests in architecture as a symbolic form. As with houses, socio-cultural factors can be considered more important than environmental or technical ones in determining the form of 'micro-buildings' on sarcophagi.[31] Such architecture was no mere setting or background, but an important element of the 'visual world' of Roman funerary space, which is reflected in the close relationship between figures and columnar frames.[32] Patrons' architectural preferences were influenced not only by a leaning towards classicism and their Italic traditions, but by the character and symbolic discourse of contemporary public architecture. The impetus for the phenomenon of column sarcophagi lay in the tastes of Italian patrons of the Antonine age for both Roman forms and Greek *paideia.*

It is often said that column sarcophagi represent temples or *heröa* for the dead. The temple analogy is already evident in the Polyxena sarcophagus from Gümüşçay (*c.* 520–500 B.C.), with its lid imitating a tiled roof and prominent Ionic mouldings.[33] The contribution of columns to enhance this model is illustrated by the well-known fourth-century B.C. 'Mourning Women Sarcophagus' from the Royal Cemetery at Sidon.[34] Its Ionic pediments and colonnades seem explicitly constructed in the form of a temple, prostyle *in antis*; its Attic ornament mimics works like the Erechtheum; the ladies, whether Muses or individuals of the royal court, seem to stand within its peripteral colonnade.[35] That simulated architecture would have acquired added force if installed on a colonnaded tomb comparable in form if not in size to the Mausoleum at Halicarnassus.[36] But few, if any, aedicular sarcophagi of the imperial period have the literal equivalence to real architecture to which that work pretends. On the first Docimian column sarcophagi with temple-like pitched roof and antefixes the image of a temple is manifest, but the sides are not conventional temple walls. Some have a continuous frieze to the full height of the walls; others a colonnade with alternate projections and recessions more reminiscent of a portico than a peripteros; others again an arcade. Later forms lose the pitched roof altogether.

A second, equally common answer is that the building evoked by column sarcophagi is the house of the dead, as the presence of the tomb door might confirm. However, as has been observed of tomb buildings interpreted in this

31 Rapoport 1969, 46–82.

32 On sarcophagi images as a *Bilderwelt*, cf. Zanker and Ewald 2004.

33 Sevinç 1996, especially figs. 6 and 8.

34 Istanbul, Archaeological Museum, inv. 368. Palagia 2000, 178 fig. 3. Fleischer 1983, 40–44 discusses the architectural possibilities, deciding in favour of a heröon.

35 Ibid., 66–72.

36 Borchhardt 1984, 45–50, with 58 fig. 10.

way, the pitched 'roofs' of early sarcophagus lids are not characteristic of Roman houses.[37] Yet there were other ways to evoke the variegated domestic architecture of the Roman world, and this interpretation may be more plausible for earlier ash urns. However, the majority of column sarcophagi made in western and eastern workshops from the later second to the fourth century evoke not private houses, but public buildings. The 'normal type' of Docimian origin shows similarities to theatres, simulating a *scaenae frons* and sometimes the *pulpitum* below. It also recalls aedicular architecture more generally, of libraries, fountains, and baths. In the west the representation of arcades on sarcophagi has been compared to contemporary street architecture.[38] In these cases the symbol is communicated above all by the columnar structure.

The role of the architectural frame in relation to the figures and myths of Roman column sarcophagi is a reflection of the importance of columnar orders in Roman self-representation, itself a development of the analogy between human and column. Visual or verbal analogies, between the capital and the head, fluting and clothing, bases and shoes, tie the two together.[39] But, in addition, columns represent the principle of support, an image of human strength: the theories of Vitruvius; the use of Caryatids, telamons, and other support figures; the load-bearing heroism of Hercules and Aeneas; and the Christian idea of the Apostles as 'columns' of the Church all testify to the idea of man as a column bearing weight and meaning.[40] On sarcophagi columns establish scale, often a colossal one implied by the elevation of the deceased to a superhuman level, when figures break the human scale implied by the height of an entablature; but they are also markers and interchangeable with human figures. For Romans the visual language of classical architecture was, like other *ornamenta*, a mark of rank (*discrimen*), used to distinguish different social groups.[41] As *decor*, columns both provided adornment and were seen as appropriate and necessary indicators of status.[42] Their use in Roman houses is well known, from colossal pilasters framing doorways to atria, peristyles and painted orders.[43]

The placement of column sarcophagi figures on pedestals mirrors the essential dialogue between columns and portrait statues in Roman public buildings. It is well-known how Roman oratorical handbooks considered such

37 Wallace-Hadrill 2008, 42 f.
38 Weidhaas 1968.
39 Rykwert 1996, 27–67.
40 Hearn 1981, 210.
41 Gros 2006, 394; Onians 1988, 29; Gros 1995, 28.
42 Horn-Oncken 1967, 92–117; cf. Vitr. *De Arch.* 6.5.2 (with the political term *maiestas: OLD*, s.v., 1 c, and s.v. *decor*, 1, 3); ibid. 1.2.5.
43 Hales 2003, 103, fig. 27, and 122–138; cf. Pliny, *NH* 17.1 (Crassus); Cic. *Q. Fr.* 3.1.1.

framing of images as an effective mnemonic device.[44] The practice was plainest in theatres, where the columnar structure of scene buildings created a framework within which the audience could view the symbolic images dominating the stage and structure and interpret the relationships between them.[45] Statues of exaggerated size fill the intercolumniations of what, on the Haterii relief of buildings, can only be the Colosseum.[46] In the sanctuary of Palatine Apollo fifty statues of Danaids stood between the columns of the portico.[47] During the second century this mode of presenting statues to a public audience became characteristic of the architecture of Asia Minor. As the Library of Celsus sheltered allegorical images of its founder's virtues in the columned niches of its aedicular façade, so the gate court of Plancia Magna in Perge appeared like a *scaenae frons*, with statues on pedestals between freestanding columns and projecting entablature.[48]

Tombs too had an audience to address, and funerary art created memorable images.[49] On funeral stelae and larger monuments images of the deceased appear between columns, highlighting their rank through markers of clothing and columns.[50] Aedicular tombs were widespread in Italian funerary architecture of the late Republic and early Empire. With togate statues set high up between columns, they expressed not 'personal deification' but social status.[51] Similar schemes were applied to tombs across the Empire.[52] Sometimes the support metaphor is explicit. The portrait statues of the 'Tower of the Scipios' at Tarragona are enclosed under a flat-arched aedicule on the upper storey, while the cornice below is visually sustained by support figures on pedestals; in 'Mausoleum B' at Sabratha the Ionic columns below frame a tomb door, as on sarcophagi, while Egyptian-looking support figures leaning outwards from the

44 *Rhet. Her.* 3.16–24; Preisshofen and Zanker 1970–71.

45 Spectacularly, Aemilius Scaurus: Pliny, *NH* 36.189; Sear 2006, 55 f. For Augustan examples: Gros 1987, 338–343.

46 Castagnoli 1941; Stewart 2003, 123 sees 'a city of statues'; cf. Smith 2003, 70 fig. 125.

47 Propertius 2.31.3–4; Ovid, *Tristia* 3.1.61–2. Cf. Quenemoen 2006, 241, with reconstruction.

48 Mansel 1956, 105 f.

49 Epitaphs: Lattimore 1962; Carroll 2006, 126–150; buildings: Thomas 2007a, 183 f.; Wallace-Hadrill 2008, 50–52.

50 E.g. funerary stele from the Via Praenestina (*c.* 75–50 B.C.): La Regina 1998, 25 fig.; tomb of Sulpicii Platorini: Silvestrini 1987.

51 Of many examples: Sarsina, tomb of Murcius Obulaccus: Aurigemma 1963; Rufus monument: Ortalli 1991. Aquileia, 'great mausoleum': Mirabella Roberti 1997. Pompeii, tomb of the Istacidii: Kockel 1983. Capua, 'La Conocchia': Quilici and Quilici Gigli 2005. *Pace* Wrede 1981, 91, and Stewart 2003, 99–108, especially 102.

52 Glanum: Gros 1986; Beaucaire: Roth-Congès 1987. Cologne, tomb of Poblicius: Precht 1975; column monuments: Mylius 1925, pl. XI; Kähler 1934. Syria: Tchalenko 1953–58, i, 37 n. 2, pl. LXII.4–6; 122, 141, pls. XLIV, CLXXI.2; 190 f., pls. LXI, LXII.6, LXXXV.3.

upper storey remind viewers of the comparability of the column and the human figure.[53] At Sádaba the Atilii tomb shows the potential of column sarcophagi to be enlarged: a façade of five arched and pedimented niches framed by pilasters carved with trailing plants, garlands hanging between them.[54] In another case inscribed verses spell out the complementarity of statues and columns 'hanging in equal measure' (*pariter pendere*).[55]

Pillars of Hercules

Exploitation of marble quarries, their developing schools of sculpture, and the distribution of their products brought micro-architecture into its own. Columnar framing was used on ash chests;[56] sarcophagi, already formed as small monuments with Doric friezes,[57] were now modelled on buildings.[58] From the second century the architectural tendency of Roman funerary sculpture became more pronounced. Corner columns and pilasters appeared increasingly on ash chests, sometimes replaced by spiralling plant supports, and sometimes with a little bust in a conch shell below the inscription frame.[59] A micro-architectural equivalent to Pliny's *stibadium*, shaded with vines propped by *cipollino* columns, is a house urn once in the Sambon Collection in Paris, which has not only a replica tiled roof, but make-believe tendrils spreading over the walls.[60] The urn of Publius Volumnius Violens at Perugia seems, like the Chiusi urn before it, to evoke a temple, with Corinthian pilasters at the corners, a simulated tiled roof, lion's head water-spouts, sphinx acroteria, medusa's head in

53 Tarragona: Hauschild et al. 1966; Garner 1982; Gros 1996–2001, ii, 416 fig. 492. Sabratha: Di Vita 1976.

54 Menéndez Pidal 1970.

55 Cillium, monument of the Flavii: *CLE* 1552 = *CIL* VIII 213, lines 46–48; Thomas 2007a, 199.

56 E.g. Celadus, *dispensator* of Claudius: Rome, Capitoline Museum: Stuart Jones, no. 35; Q. Fulvius Priscus, scribe of the curule aediles: La Regina 2005, 84 fig.; cf. Vatican 9815/16 and an urn in the Palazzo Farnese.

57 E.g. Scipio Barbatus, and Peducaea Hilara, Modena: Koch and Sichtermann 1982, 37, 282, pls. 2, 300.

58 E.g. Rome, Museo Nazionale di Villa Giulia. Gasparri 1972 (suggesting early Augustan date); Koch and Sichtermann 1982, 40, pl. 11. The 'Arcadian' figures in the arcades are unparalleled.

59 E.g. Vatican 9813/14; Rome, MNR 121649 (ivy-draped pilasters with Ionic capitals: De Luca 1976, 119 no. 64, pl. 101); Mazara del Vallo, Sicily, Cathedral, with tendril pilasters and Corinthian capitals, sphinxes on pilasters, and *dextrarum iunctio* below: Koch and Sichtermann 1982, pls. 39, 41.

60 Now lost. Giuliano 1979, 243 no. 153; Koch and Sichtermann 1982, pl. 16; cf. Pliny, *Ep.* 5.6.36.

the tympanon, double doors, and an inscription on the architrave.[61] In northern Italy aedicular tombs were replaced by open-air sarcophagi with simulated tiled roofs, corner acroteria, and images of the dead under arches in columnar frames.[62]

At Ephesus, the sarcophagus of Celsus, in the vault below the library in his memory, presents a dialogue between vessel and building. The medusa head in the pediment of the sarcophagus replicates the figures in the pediments on the library's façade. Its front face lacks columns, but its arrangement of winged figures holding garlands, like those hanging from columns at Sádaba, mimics a columnar structure and rhythm; the corner figures look like caryatids.[63] For Wiegartz, the architectural mouldings of the cornice make this sarcophagus one of several precursors of column sarcophagi.[64] Some had lids steeply angled like pitched roofs, most strikingly a sarcophagus from Aydın-Tralles, which, with a circular boss in the pediment and elaborate mouldings, looks like a temple without columns.[65]

On an 'underworld sarcophagus' from Ephesus the architectural implications of the form are developed further.[66] Again the pediment end of the lid carries a round boss in the tympanum, but now its sloping sides are worked to imitate tiled roofs. On the short side an arch is framed by pilasters, from which a figure emerges, while others sit or stand along the long faces. This main level is supported visually by a smaller frieze along the podium, on which *amorini* holding garlands appear to support the cornice above their heads. This 'micro-building' has three levels of perception: the lid and pediments suggest a temple; the main register seems to represent the house of the dead, with open door on the short side and waiting figures along the front; the lowest level with supporting cupids hints at a theatre *pulpitum*, a locus for sculpture.[67] The style shows Attic influence, but the conception, with unworked rear, betrays the probable Roman patronage.

It was a small step from these temple-like chests to the addition of a columnar frame on examples belonging to the 'Torre Nova group'. The earliest

61 Haynes 2000, 382 fig. 298, with traditional interpretation as representing a house, but the architectural ornament and bucrania with garlands on the side walls suggest rather a temple; cf. Wallace-Hadrill 2008, 48.

62 Gabelmann 1977, 201 f.

63 Theuer 1953, 43–46, figs. 88–92.

64 Wiegartz 1965, 41.

65 Istanbul, Archeological Museum, inv. 449; Wiegartz 1965, 178 no. 21, pl. 11b-c.

66 Istanbul, Archeological Museum, inv. 2768; Wiegartz 1965, 40 f., 179 no. 36, pl. 14b; Andreae 1963, pl. 34.

67 Retzleff 2007.

known instance may be Afyon A, from Dinar-Apameia, dated to *c.* 150.[68] This sarcophagus showing the Labours of Hercules between half-columns was intended for an adult; in the surviving fragment the Cretan bull bound by Hercules extends a leg over the adjacent column. But this architectural archetype was favoured for children's sarcophagi. The child's sarcophagus after which the group is named, from a villa at Torre Nova on the Via Labicana (Rome B, *c.* 150–55), presents a theatrical setting in a temple frame.[69] On the front, the initiation of Hercules is framed by columns;[70] the figures stand on a raised stage, suggested by the high moulding above the Lesbian cymation, and appear in movement as if in a play; the curtains behind Dionysus on the right also suggest a set. The rear face contains a composed scene of mourning women between Corinthian pilasters, which develops the poses of the 'Mourning Women Sarcophagus' into a range of rectilinear postures of exaggerated classicism. On each side, figures balance architecture: on the far right of the front face, Hecate, in the low relief of the probably Attic model, almost vanishes into the wall like a pilaster on the inner side of the column; on the rear, a lady to the right stands upright like the column beside her, while to the left a seated figure rests her foot against the column base. This theatrical and architectural composition is reinforced by the ornament, which resembles contemporary theatre architecture in Asia Minor.[71]

Other children's sarcophagi of the 150s and 160s use the same format to present small-scale performances of Hercules' Labours by Cupids and Niobids.[72] The dialogue between bodies and columns is a frequent motif. On a chest in Richmond, Virginia (*c.* 150–160), Cupids prop each other up playfully between erect columns;[73] on Rome H (*c.* 165), perhaps an ostothek, one holds up a bearded companion between plain pilasters, while another raises a mask beside the pilaster capital, demonstrating the man-column analogy.[74] On a sarcophagus from Side a Cupid supports his staggering companion;[75] there are simulated tiled roof, lion's head antefixes, and shield with medusa's head in the

---

68 Buckler *et al.* 1939, 139 no. 413 pl. 73; Wiegartz 1965, 143; Waelkens 1982, 51 no. 1 for the date. (References to column sarcophagi here and below – e.g. as 'Rome A' – follow Wiegartz and Waelkens.)

69 Morey 1924, 44–46, figs. 75–78; Waelkens 1982, 51 f.; Wiegartz 1965, 62 f. and 168.

70 Wiegartz 1965, 58 f.

71 Morey 1924, 45; Waelkens 1982, 123.

72 Antalya L (*c.* 155): Wiegartz 1965, pl. 28; Beirut C (*c.* 160–165): Cumont 1929.

73 Waelkens 1982, 53 f. no. 10, pl. 15.1–4.

74 Palazzo Mattei. Rodenwaldt 1938, figs. 13–16, sees an allusion to Simias's 'Wings'; the provenance given as the Curia Hostilia (Ficoroni 1744) presumably follows the 18th-century toponym referring to the Caelian hill. Once thought modern because of the bearded cupid, it is confirmed as Antonine by Waelkens 1982, 54 no. 13.

75 Wiegartz 1965, 177 no. 9; Waelkens 1982, 61 no. 6 (Side E1); Mansel 1956, 75–78, fig. 31, with implausibly late date, and 1958, 226 f. figs. 34–35.

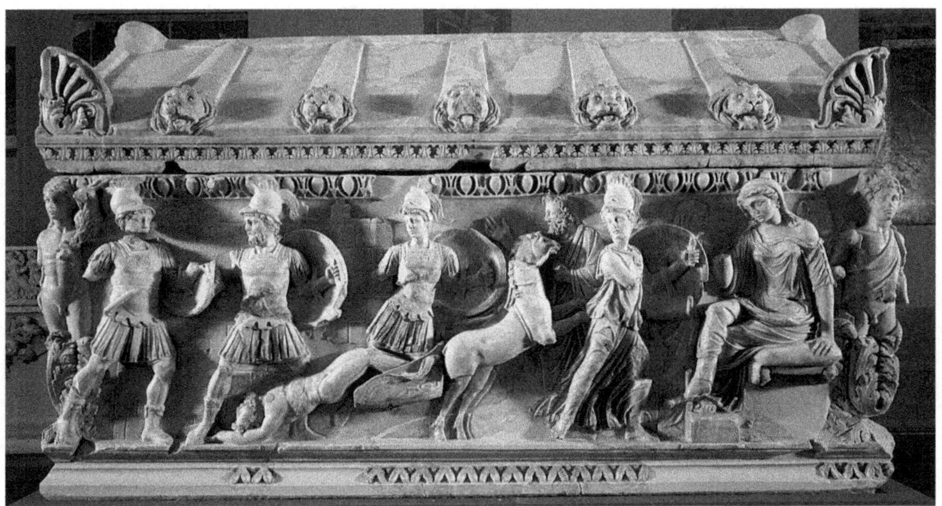

Figure 12.3: Sarcophagus from Rome, reconstructed from fragments. Museum of Art, Rhode Island School of Design, Providence, Museum Appropriation Fund, Inv. 21.074. Photograph by Erik Gould, courtesy of the Museum of Art, Rhode Island School of Design, Providence, Rhode Island.

pediment, but no columns, only winged victories at the corners. The reassembled fragments of a sarcophagus from Rome, now in Providence, Rhode Island (*c.* 155–160), present pediments, acroteria, lion's head water-spouts, cornice of acanthus leaves, and an egg-and-dart moulding above the figured friezes, but, instead of columns, a figure at each corner emerges from acanthus leaves as from a decorated column base.[76] The figured scenes embody physical strength: on the front, young men frame a scene of Achilles towing Hector's body before the walls of Troy (Figure 12.3); on the sides, two boxers square up to one another, and a youth lifts a rock as a leopard attacks his companion; on the rear, a bearded man looks on as cupids with hounds fight a lion and panther.[77]

The temple form of the 'Torre Nova' sarcophagi is starkly demonstrated by a reused chest in Ancona, stripped of its reliefs by Christians and converted by crosses inscribed on its walls and roof into a micro-architectural church.[78] Four Corinthian, spirally-fluted columns at the corners support a pitched roof with triangular pediments, acroteria, heavy raking cornices, and a central boss in the tympanon. The original effect can be inferred from the recently discovered

76 Waelkens 1982, 33 notes the resemblance of the lower cymation moulding to western forms; cf. Weickert 1913, fig. 14. For such *Schmuckbasen*, especially in Flavian Rome: Wegner 1966; Schreiter 1995.

77 Waelkens 1982, pls. 9.1–2.

78 Wiegartz 1965, 144, pl. 26.

sarcophagus of Claudius Severinus and his wife Berenice at Aizanoi (*c.* 160).[79] The deceased was probably the *archineōkoros* Lucius Claudius Severinus involved in the construction of an aqueduct at Aizanoi.[80] The semblance of roof, acroteria, and pediments supported by freestanding spirally-fluted columns, one at each corner, and the tetrastyle façade on the short left side give the idea of a miniature temple; even the doorway has inclined jambs, heavy upper mouldings and consoles like temple doors in the Roman East.[81] On the short left side, the 'temple' front, two winged Cupid sentries on pedestals seem to sleep between the columns, their heads drooping beside the capitals, their feet grazing the lower shaft. Even on the other sides, depicting an Amazonomachy, the human-column analogy is not absent. Beside the left-hand column of the front is the helmeted female mannequin of a trophy whose head matches the capital in size and proportions; her face is aligned with the lower acanthus leaves, the helmet with the florid volutes above.

Waelkens's re-dating of several early column sarcophagi shows that, rather than being an evolutionary precursor of later forms as Wiegartz argued, the so-called 'Torre Nova group' must have developed more or less contemporaneously with fully colonnaded or arcaded examples and frieze sarcophagi like the one in Providence. At least as early as Afyon A, a sarcophagus in the British Museum also showing the Labours of Hercules innovatively reshapes the conventional temple image (Figure 12.4).[82] The agile representations of the hero are set in a colonnade of spirally-fluted columns, the entablature alternately projecting and receding; and with a composite form of capital consisting of a row of stylised, lotus-like leaves below volutes of almost equal height. This arrangement of alternately concave and convex pedestals, corresponding to the ressauts of the entablature, seems to correct the less organised setting of almost identical figures in an almost fully preserved example from the east necropolis at Perge; here the lid presents the pitched, tiled roof of a temple, complete with acroteria and lion's head water-spouts.[83] The short side shows the door flanked by Attis figures on pedestals in Phrygian caps like support figures, and a medusa's head in the pediment above.[84] In Afyon B, a slightly later example using the same structure to show the Labours, the figures' heads cross the entablature mouldings, indicating the superhuman scale of Hercules and his feats; the entablature

79 Türktüzün 1993, especially 519–525, figs. 3–8.

80 Levick 1988, no. 10. This project, which Severinus either oversaw (restoring ἐργεπιστατήσαντος) or (partly) financed, may have included the restoration of a bath-gymnasium, as Mitchell 1993, i, 214 n. 112.

81 Famously at Baalbek, but also, more locally, the Temple of Zeus at Aizanoi.

82 BM Sculpture 2301, dated before 150: Waelkens 1982, 71.

83 Antalya, Archaeological Museum, inv. 1004. Wiegartz 1965, 147 (Antalya M), pl. 28a; Özoral 1977, figs. 1, 13; Waelkens 1982, 71. Length 2.50 m.

84 For the 'support figures', compare the 'Tower of the Scipios', above.

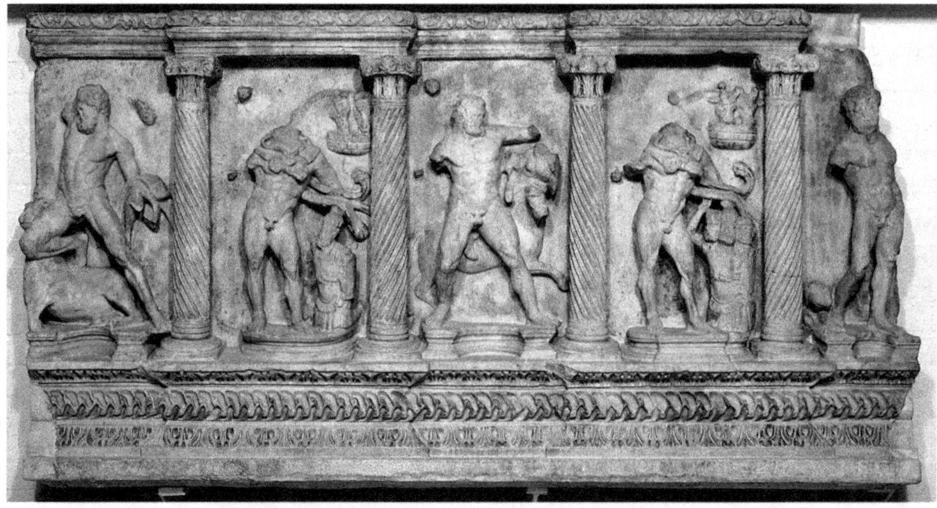

Figure 12.4: London B, fragment of the front face of a sarcophagus. British Museum, London, Sculpture 2301. Photograph: © The Trustees of the British Museum

breaks into an arch to enclose the hero's head.[85] Combining columns with heroic statuary, this architecture of ressauts borrows from the architecture of civic display to heighten the emotionality of the funerary idea. On Rome G (*c.* 160) a static set of Hercules figures is juxtaposed with dancing Bacchants and other Dionysiac figures. These staccato rhythms of entablature alternately forward and back, with spirally-fluted columns on pedestals, provided a 'baroque' effect derived from Trajanic and Hadrianic public buildings like the Library of Celsus and the Agora Gate at Miletus.[86]

The appearance of Hercules on so many early column sarcophagi is owed to the hero's suitability as a symbol of physical strength. Progenitor of the first columnar order (of the Dorian Heracleidae), he was also portrayed in columnar surrounds.[87] In the Antonine era these columnar frames acquired spiral flutes like those on the sarcophagi.[88] But Hercules also exemplified the principle of architectural support himself, having reputedly shouldered the heavens in his final labour like Atlas, as established in mythology and visualised in the famous

85 Buckler et al. 1933, no. 363 pl. 71; Wiegartz 1965, 143; Waelkens 1982, 74 no. 23, dating to *c.* 165; Apameia-Dinar in Lawrence 1951, 153 f., fig. 42.

86 Rome, Palazzo Mattei. Lawrence 1951, 154 f., fig. 43 ('Rome N'); Waelkens 1982, 73 no. 12. Sagalassus, theatre: Vandeput 1997, 107–112, pl. 59 (*c.* 180–200, or possibly earlier due to contrast with early Severan ornament). Miletus: Strocka 1981; Alföldy 1998.

87 Rykwert 1996, 143; Boardman 1990, 801 f. nos. 1368–1380.

88 Chapot 1907, 75 and 113 n. 3, citing Reinach 1904, 22 no. 143, from the Balkans; cf. also a Hercules sarcophagus from Apameia-Dinar: Lawrence 1951, 153 f., fig. 42.

metope at Olympia, a landmark of Antonine taste.[89] The story is not shown on sarcophagi, but, in a Roman twist, a sarcophagus from the colony of Pisidian Antioch shows Aeneas bearing Anchises extending up to the upper cornice.[90]

The connection between Hercules and spirally-fluted columns is drawn out on an inventive little monument on the high plain 18 km north-west of Antalya, which forms a built complement to the micro-architecture of sarcophagi. Some ninety years ago remains were recorded at this site near the Selçuk monument of Evdir Han once identified with Lagon/Lagbe in Pamphylia.[91] Still unexcavated, its Roman phases are poorly known; but it has the appearance of a sacred site, crossed by canals lined on both sides with richly decorated porticoes and altars.[92] Near the centre were observed the remnants of a small prostyle tetrastyle temple. Its façade was reconstructed with an arched lintel and four spirally-fluted columns on pedestals carved with scenes from the Herculean Labours.[93]

Following the re-location of Lagon elsewhere, this site is now believed to be the bishopric Eudokias settled by the Termessians in the later Roman period.[94] Interestingly, the central opening of the scene building at Termessus is also framed by two spirally-fluted columns.[95] In the central bay of the scene building at Suessa Aurunca, two similar columns of *giallo antico*, flanked by vertically fluted columns of *pavonazzetto*, framed a baroque statue of the benefactress Matidia Minor as Aura in grey-black Göktepe marble.[96] In earlier Italian designs spirally-fluted columns added a theatrical or 'Egyptian' quality to micro-architecture and larger buildings.[97] But in the Antonine age they came into their

89 Apollodorus 2.5.11; Boardman *et al.* 1990, nos. 2685, 2687 (S. Italian vases, mid-5th century and *c.* 380 B.C.) and 2767 (intaglio). Olympia, Temple of Zeus, Metope 10: Ashmole and Yalouris 1967, pl. 88; Boardman *et al.* 1990, no. 2683. For the importance of Olympia and its sculptures for Pausanias, see de Angelis 1991–92, 106, 252 f.

90 Ankara D (*c.* 160): Lawrence 1951, 152 f., fig. 41. Cf. contemporary coins: Mattingly 1940, 36 no. 237, pl. 6.5 (gold); 203 no. 1264; 207 no. 1292, pl. 30.5 (bronzes).

91 Moretti 1921, following the former identification by Spratt and Forbes 1847, i.2, 228 with the δῆμος Λαγβέων attested on an inscription (Ramsay 1888, 16 gives the ancient name as Lagbon). This location persists in archaeological literature (Benson 1959, 260; Webb 1996, 17). For correct identification, see below.

92 Stillwell 1976, s.v. 'Lagon (Evdir Han)' (U. Serdaroğlu).

93 Moretti 1921, 140.

94 French 1994, 87.

95 Lánckoronski 1890–92, ii, 95 fig. 53, 97 fig. 55, pl. XI; Chapot 1907, 124 f., fig. 155.

96 For the rebuilding after 138: Chausson 2008; the central bay of the second storey is dated by its Proconnesian capitals to the Antonine period: Cascella 2002.

97 Micro-architecture: Apulian vase painting: Romanelli 1928, IVd r, pl. 8: 2, 3, 5; Campanian wall-painting: Schefold 1952, 176, pl. 37; Campana plaques: Rome, MNR (Kranz 1978, pl. 161.2), and the similar BM Terracotta D 633 (GR 1805.7–3.317). Larger-scale: Verona, Arch of the Gavii and 'Porta dei Borsari': Blake 1959, 74, 143 f. (with first-century date, but others call the latter Hadrianic, and its rebuilding

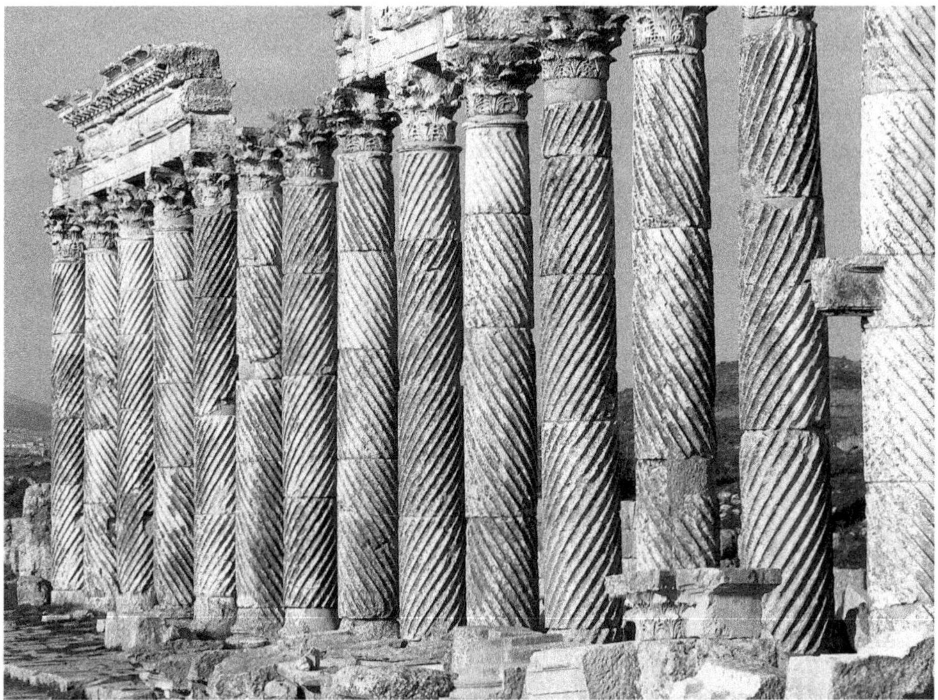

Figure 12.5: Columns of the Cardo Maximus, Apamea.
Photograph: M. Disdero, February 2005.

own: adorning scene buildings;[98] demarcating temple gateways;[99] framing divine images on eastern coins of the second and third centuries; and, complete with bronze statues of the Antonine emperors on brackets protruding from some column shafts, characterising an entire stretch of the colonnaded Cardo Maximus at Apamea (Figure 12.5) opposite the entrance to the Antonine agora and the Tycheion building, with one or more Atlas figures crouching on its podium.[100]

An extreme and highly original attempt to associate Hercules with the concept of architectural support, also using spirally-fluted columns, is the remarkable Velletri sarcophagus (Figures 12.6 and 12.7), which is now thought

---

inscription is of 265); Florence, sanctuary of Isis: Banchelli 2009; Tivoli, Hadrian's Villa, 'Antinoeion': Mari and Sgambaro 2007, 86 f., fig. 13 (also in *giallo antico*); and generally: Fano Santi 1993.

98 Fragments from the Theatre and the Odeion of Herodes Atticus at Athens: Benson 1959, 260, 264 f. (Athens M1–2, Athens K); and from the theatres at Curium and Sabratha: Benson 1956, 386.

99 E.g. Athens, Olympieion; Aphrodisias, Temple of Aphrodite.

100 Chapot 1907, figs. 129–149; Balty 1981, 64–75.

to have been made not in the late Antonine age as first thought, but in the 150s, the experimental phase of the earliest Asiatic column sarcophagi, if not earlier.[101] The contemporary architectural context of Rome and Greece helps to understand both the choice of themes and the work's extraordinary construction.[102] Some details reflect a theatre context: the snake-foot giant in the central tympanon of the left side (Figure 12.6) recalls a frieze of Pentelic marble from the theatre at Catania.[103] The bases of the spirally-fluted columns recall ancient Ionic tradition; the Ionic capitals, differing from the Corinthian or composite capitals of column sarcophagi, recall the 'Mourning Women Sarcophagus'; the palmettes echo classical Attic stelae. If these elements hail from the work's Attic style, the sarcophagus also shows Roman influence. The garlands extended along the roof by Cupids point to a Roman funerary tradition visible on the sarcophagus of Celsus and another at Corinth.[104] The profile and decoration of base and lid, with a succession of anthemion, Ionic cyma, and dentils, look distinctively 'Roman'; the victories killing bulls and lions attacking bulls, which appear in the left side pediment and as acroteria of two of the aedicules of the front, are paralleled on two garland sarcophagi from the tomb of Herodes Atticus at Cephisia.[105] The elaborate raking cornices of the pediments are reminiscent of the terracotta ornament of temple-tombs in Antonine Rome; the cultivated use of support figures alludes to contemporary architectural fashion: caryatids at Hadrian's Villa and Herodes Atticus's Triopion; telamons from the second-century stage of the Theatre of Dionysus.[106] The bull's heads at the corners evoke earlier Roman architecture.[107] The ornament as a whole suggests that blend of neo-Attic style and urban

101 Bartoccini's date of *c.* 190–193 was lowered to *c.* 200 by Lawrence 1965, 222, but backdated to *c.* 140 by Bernard Andreae (Andreae 1963, 25, and 2005, 32, figs.). Pensabene and Mesolella 2005, 67 suggest a date shortly after 150; Galli 2005, 76 assumes *c.* 150–175.

102 The Labours theme is depicted in reliefs from the theatre at Corinth, dated to the 2nd quarter of the second century: Sturgeon 1977, 95–114, pls. 67–83; cf. Sturgeon 2004. The idea may have been taken from the theatre at Delphi, where a late-Hellenistic frieze of the Labours was re-used in the late first century (Lévêque 1951, 247–263; Sturgeon 1978) or under Nero (Weir 1999). See also Sturgeon 2006.

103 Pensabene 1996–97, 63 fig. 51.

104 Koch and Sichtermann 1982, 227.

105 Pensabene and Mesolella 2005, 69.

106 Schmidt 1982, 99 f., 106 f., 123–127.

107 Telamons: Pensabene and Mesolella 2005, 65, cf. Pompeii, Forum Baths and Covered Theatre. Bull's heads: Pompeii, House of the Cryptoporticus, room 20 ('Diaeta'/ 'Southeast Triclinium'), S. wall, facing nude support figures: Maiuri 1933; Beyen 1938, 99–106, 432, figs. 33–36, 213b.

Roman taste which characterised the sacred landscape of Antonine rural estates.[108]

What kind of building is envisioned here is much disputed. For some, it is the 'palace of Hades', as the central figures on the main long side and the multiple doors suggest; if so, it is also clear that this palace is a creation of stage architecture and almost a parody of grand works. For others, it is a heröon for the dead, in the manner of Asiatic column sarcophagi. But, unlike the latter, it is striking that only six of the structural elements are columns, none of them on the main face. The majority of the supports are human or animal figures. The crouching telamons on the lowest level stand not at the corners as on the podia of some column sarcophagi,[109] but centrally, four along each long side carrying the two aedicules and two at the middle of each short side; the bull's heads are enormous relative to the figures around them and structurally equivalent to the corner caryatids above. The main entablature, projecting forward and back, is carried by caryatids, apart from the columns carrying the corner aedicules and the door-frames at the centre of the sides. Even the divine figures in the pediments share in the metaphor. Centrally, above Hades and Persephone enthroned and highlighted by Hades' staff, Caelus spreads a canvas perfectly within a segmental pediment to signify the vault of heaven carried by Atlas, encapsulating its etymological associations and the symbolic links between the simulated theatre stage and the audience of family mourners encircling the work.[110] On the lid, cupids carry garlands

The support metaphor recurs in the images between the supports across the sarcophagus's three storeys, which are thematically linked as often in Antonine art.[111] As on contemporary Asiatic sarcophagi, the back and sides of the central tier celebrate the Labours in a linear order reflecting the conventional narrative (Figure 12.7). The figures below highlight the final task, in which Hercules supported the heavens: the Hesperides pick apples from their tree; beside them, Sisyphus shouldering a rock recalls Atlas with his burden; a column-like mast stands at the middle of Charon's ferry. The last, hopeless figures carry nothing: Tantalus, upright in a stream of water with open, empty palms; and the Danaids, failed water-carriers. The front face is unified by the central figures of Hades and Persephone. At the lowest level chariots show the story of Persephone; on the main level the enthroned pair are flanked by the mythic couples Protesilaus and Laodamia and Admetus and Alcestis, a chiastic structure

108 For more on the Dionysiac landscape intimated here, especially the βουκόλοι, see Galli 2005, 81–90.

109 Compare also the sarcophagus in Palazzo Fiano, Rome: Wiegartz 1965, 179 no. 35, pl. 12a-b; Sapelli 1993; Bonanno Aravantinos 2005, 44 f. figs. 2–3.

110 For *cavus/caelum*, see Deschamps 1979; for *scaena/sphaera*, see Poulle 1999, 262.

111 Newby 2002, 131.

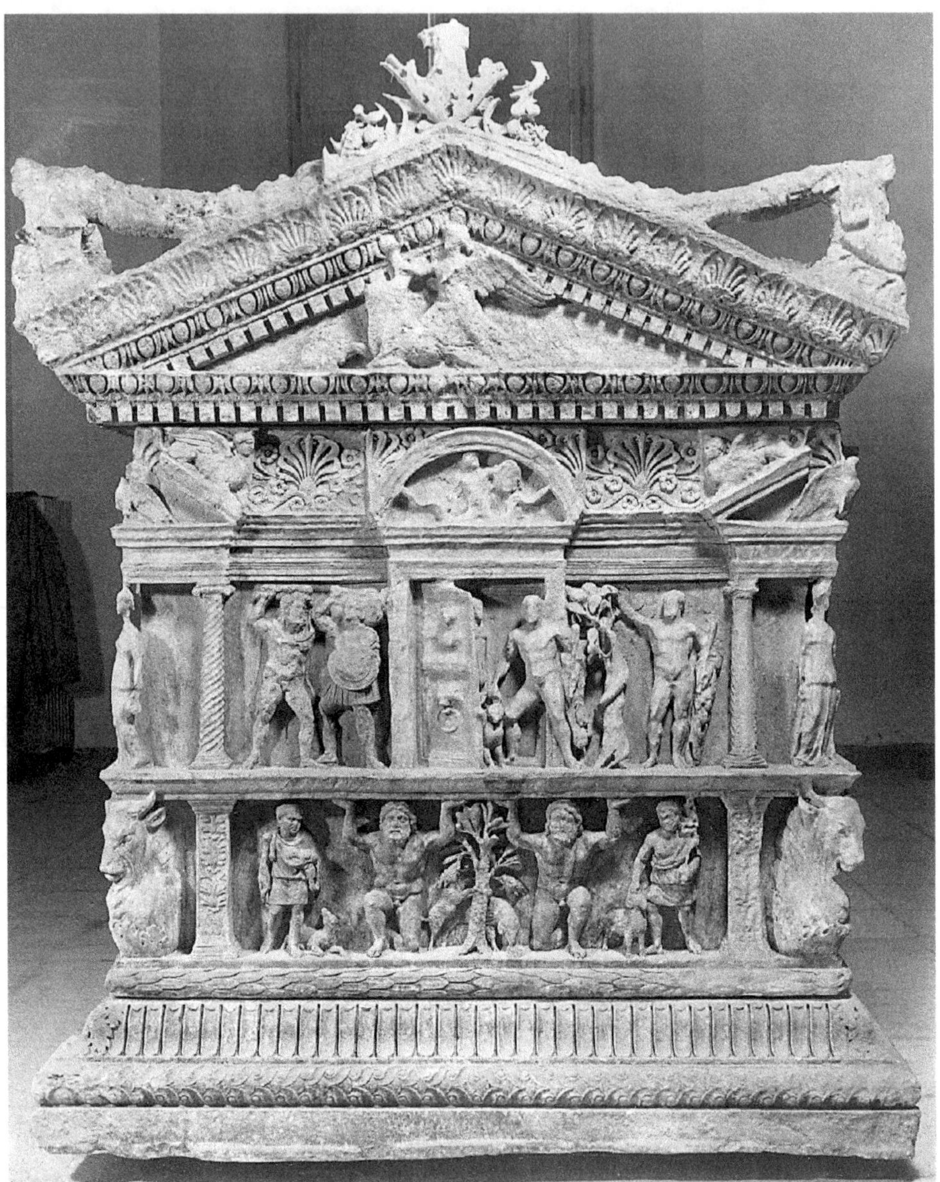

Figure 12.6: Velletri sarcophagus, left side. Museo Civico, Velletri. Photograph: DAIR 63.41.

playing on entry to and departure from the hidden interior of the sarcophagus, which taunts viewers about their own relative position; the lowest register shows Minerva, Diana and Tellus, arching his cloak to form the vault of the chthonic

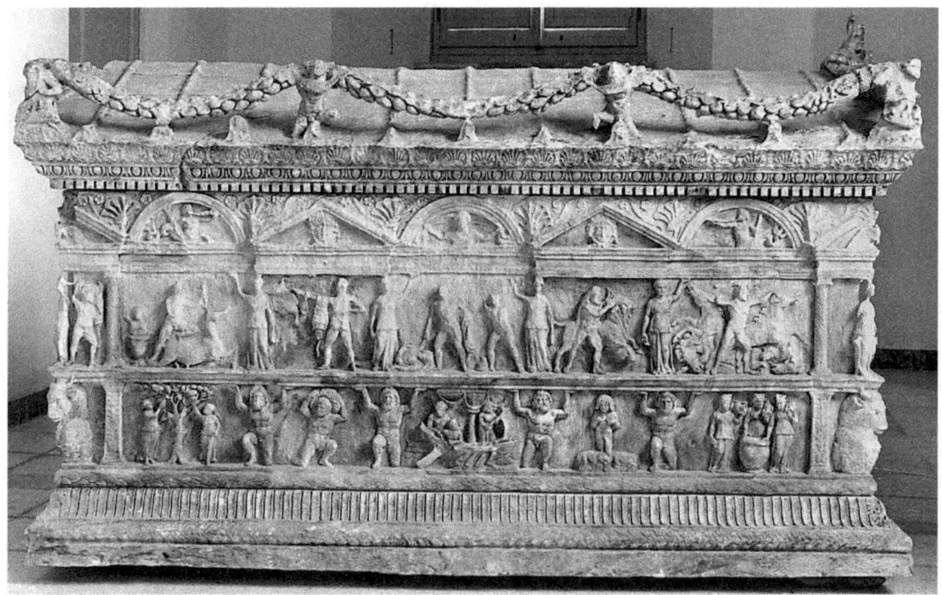

Figure 12.7: Velletri sarcophagus, rear side. Museo Civico, Velletri. Photograph: DAIR 59.52.

cave beneath, and, above them, Jupiter and Neptune. Overall, the sarcophagus looks like a work of sculptural theatre composed to illustrate how in the *mimus vitae* the metaphor of architectural support was a vivid image of the human burden in life and death.[112]

The patron of this extraordinary object is a puzzle. It was found in the Contrada Arcione on a side street off the Via Ariana which runs along the south side of the Alban Hills, about four miles from Velletri, but it had evidently been removed by grave robbers from its original location and dropped in a vineyard. Nine skeletons were inside, seven adults and two children, and an instrument in the chest showed that it was broken into in the nineteenth century. However, the dating of seven of the skeletons to between the twelfth and fourteenth centuries suggests that the sarcophagus had already been pillaged and re-used then (raising intriguing questions about the continued efficacy of its symbolic language), so even the location from which it had been removed was perhaps only secondary.[113] Nonetheless, as such a weighty object can hardly have travelled far from its original site, it is worth considering the ancient topography of the

112 For the *mimus vitae* (σκήνη ὁ βίος), see Curtius 1953, 138–144; Andreae 1963, 75–79; Ewald 1999, 130.

113 Bartoccini 1958, 129; Caldelli 2005, 109 n.2, citing Rubini 1989, 146. See also Bonanno Aravantinos 2005, 53.

neighbourhood.[114] Of the many Roman villas around Velletri, the closest to the findspot of the sarcophagus is the villa of Fontana Sant'Antonio, about four kilometres east of Velletri.[115] In 1872 three athletic statues of Pentelic marble, now in the Capitoline Museum, were found here amid substantial remains suggesting a 'sumptuous villa': ancient walls of *opus mixtum*; abundant architectural fragments, including coloured marbles; and a Hadrianic brick-stamp.[116] The cultivated, Hellenising taste implied by such finds could also have produced the Velletri sarcophagus.

The telamons in the lowest register of the sarcophagus find a parallel in an example in the Villa Borghese (Rome A, *c.* 155–160) with an arcade of five arches supported at the corners by prisoner support figures.[117] The arcade motif was applied to representations of Hercules during the same period and became more favoured than the horizontal entablature. The hero's significance as a symbol of strength for arcaded architecture is implied by the resolution of a building-workers' dispute over arcades and cross-vaults through 'supplication to Pallas Tritogeneia and strong Heracles'.[118] Of seven other contemporary arcaded Asiatic sarcophagi, at least four also depicted Hercules.[119] Typically, the arches are decorated with Lesbian cymatium, the columns spirally-fluted, and the spandrels filled with figures or heads.[120] On a reused fragment from Nicaea the figures of Hercules are also set on pedestals.[121] This alternative structural arrangement is paralleled by the arcaded courts seen from that time in eastern cities.[122] A fragment from Ephesus (*c.* 165) with a rosette in the spandrel between two arches mirrors the form of an arcade at the temple in Cyzicus drawn by Cyriac of Ancona.[123] The inner court of the temple at Aizanoi had a similar arcade.[124]

114 Caldelli 2005, 113.

115 Ibid., 110.

116 Pelzer Wagener and Ashby 1913, 405–428.

117 Wiegartz 1965, 33, 168.

118 Buckler 1923, 34–36 (Miletus); see Thomas 2007a, 90.

119 Aydın (*c.* 155–160): Wiegartz 1965, pl. 32b; Rome M (Vatican, *c.* 160): Morey 1924, fig. 82; Denizli E (*c.* 160): Ferrari 1966, pl. 2.1; Iznik (n. 121 below). The subject matter of Üskübü A and Denizli D (both *c.* 155–160) is irrecoverable: Wiegartz 1965, pl. 33e. Only Antalya E (below) clearly shows a different scene.

120 Antalya V (*c.* 165–170): Wiegartz 1965, 148, pl. 30 f; Rome I (*c.* 170): ibid., 169 pl. 42c; Rome M (prev. note).

121 Iznik Museum, inv. 1755, *c.* 150–155; Fıratlı 1974, 919–920, pl. 329a; Waelkens 1982, 71 no. 3 (Iznik T).

122 Thomas 2007a, 40, 201 f., fig. 169.

123 Ephesus D: Wiegartz 1965, 155; Waelkens 1982, 75 no. 26. Cyzicus: Ashmole 1956, 185 f. pl. 36; Lyttelton 1974, pl. 178. For a reconstruction of this arcade, see the drawing by Anthony Smith in Thomas 2007a, 39 fig. 25.

124 Lyttelton 1974, 262.

Aedicular architecture: pediments, spirals, and shells

From about 160 a variant form was produced with a significant addition, the carving of a shell-niche behind each figure's head. Its first known occurrence is on a fragment from Termessus. An armed warrior with bowed head is shown below a shell-niche out of which appears a female head. This looks like Paris, favourite of Aphrodite, bowing out of his duel with Menelaus: hovering overhead is his protecting goddess, who 'caught up Paris easily, since she was divine, and wrapped him in a thick mist and set him down again in his own perfumed bedchamber'.[125] An obvious funerary symbolism can be inferred from the scene, whereby the soul of the deceased is rescued from death by divine aid and granted immortality in the afterlife represented by the funerary chamber. A similar sense may attach to the next surviving uses of the shell form on column sarcophagi, from Rome and Beirut.[126] In each case a young rider, nude but for a chlamys, is enshrined under the central shell-niche; the juxtaposition with the myth of Daedalus and Icarus in the better-preserved Beirut fragment (Figure 12.8) suggests that this commemorates the premature death of a young man or boy. Another fragment in Antalya applies the setting to the myth of Achilles, brought from Scyros and hastened towards mortality and celebrity.[127] In these three cases the sarcophagus takes a new aedicular form, with triangular pediment over the central niche, segmental ones over the lateral niches, and shells over all niches and intermediate intercolumniations. Such forms are used in earlier Roman funerary tradition to contribute to the suggestion of an after-life. On the urn of Lucius Volusius Diodorus (Figure 12.9) a shell framed by spirally-fluted columns holds the funerary bust; shells enclose the busts on the temple-tomb of the main relief of the Haterii while plants spiral around the columns; and on a smaller relief from the same tomb two shells hang poised over garlands above the lifeless body of the deceased.[128] In the tomb of Isidora at Tuna el-Gebel, necropolis of Hermopolis Magna, the back niche suggesting the funerary bed of the deceased is framed on either side by spirally-fluted columns and above by a large conch shell.[129] Inscriptions on the inner walls of the *prothuron*, declaring that the tomb belongs to a young girl apparently drowned in the river Nile, explain the significance of conch and columns: the former, an

125 *Iliad* 3.380–1, trans. Lattimore; Antalya E, *c.* 160, Archaeological Museum, Antalya, inv. 310. Wiegartz 1965, 146 pl. 27a-b.

126 Rome E: Lawrence 1951, 143–145 fig. 31; Wiegartz 1965, 169. Beirut A: Lawrence 1951, 134 f. fig. 19; Wiegartz 1965, 152 f.; Strocka 1984, 208–211 fig. 11.

127 Antalya K: Wiegartz 1965, 146, pl. 27d, reinterpreted by Strocka 1984, 218–220.

128 Ash urns: Koch and Sichtermann 1982, pl. 39. Haterii relief: Sinn and Freyberger 1996, 51–9, no. 6, pl. II and 136 fig. 6.

129 Graindor 1932, 98, pl. II: dated by a preponderance of coinage to the late Hadrianic or Antonine period.

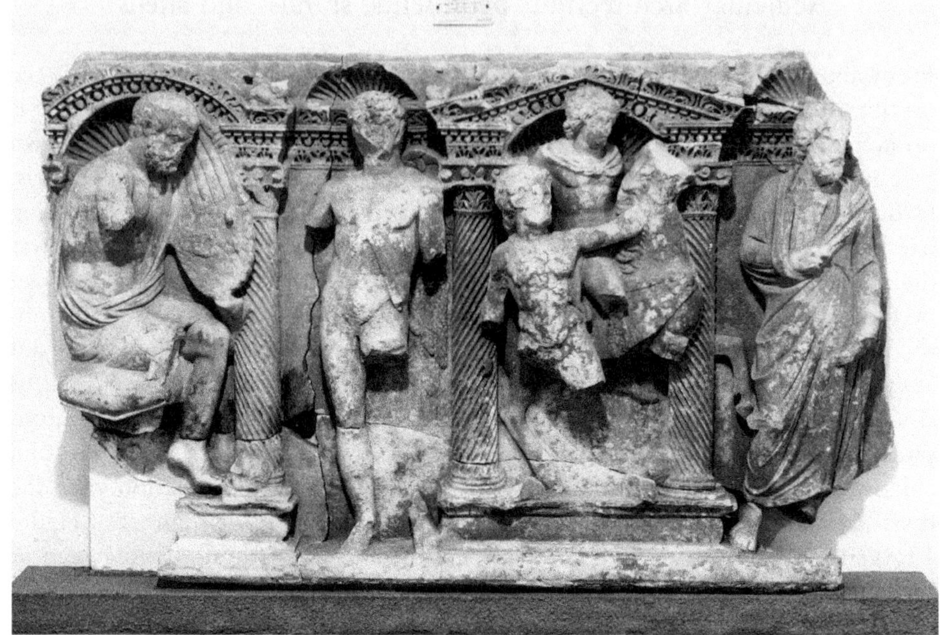

Figure 12.8: Fragment of sarcophagus from Beirut. Beirut Museum.
Photograph: Foto Oehler.

icon of the river bed, forms a 'grotto' with the columns on either side and a 'columnless' inner curved recess, symbolically painted with stars like a heaven.[130] This heavenly grotto is supported by the nymph, again highlighting the importance of this metaphor in the iconography of the Roman dead. The explicit text helps to understand the meaning of the combination of spirally-fluted columns and shell-niche around a funerary image, both for the micro-architecture of column sarcophagi and for some tomb interiors.[131] These forms were seen as securing the afterlife of the heroised deceased.

The three sarcophagus fragments above represent experimental versions of a new archetype, which became established by about 170, after which the arcade type virtually disappeared from the Docimian output until a late revival in the final years of the workshop.[132] This new scheme, Morey's 'principal type', which

130 Ibid.,101–8, text I.

131 E.g. Vatican Necropolis, Tomb I ('Tomb of the Quadriga'), early 3rd century: Toynbee and Ward-Perkins 1956, 78, pl. 5.

132 A single, later example is Hierapolis E, *c.* 180–185: Ferrari 1966, pls. 11.1, 11.3. At Aphrodisias the arcade continued longer. The two arcaded examples surviving from the variant Iznik Group (Iznik R, *c.* 170–175; Iznik K, *c.* 250) belong to the workshop's first phase or final years, mirroring Docimian practice: Wiegartz 1965, 161 f.

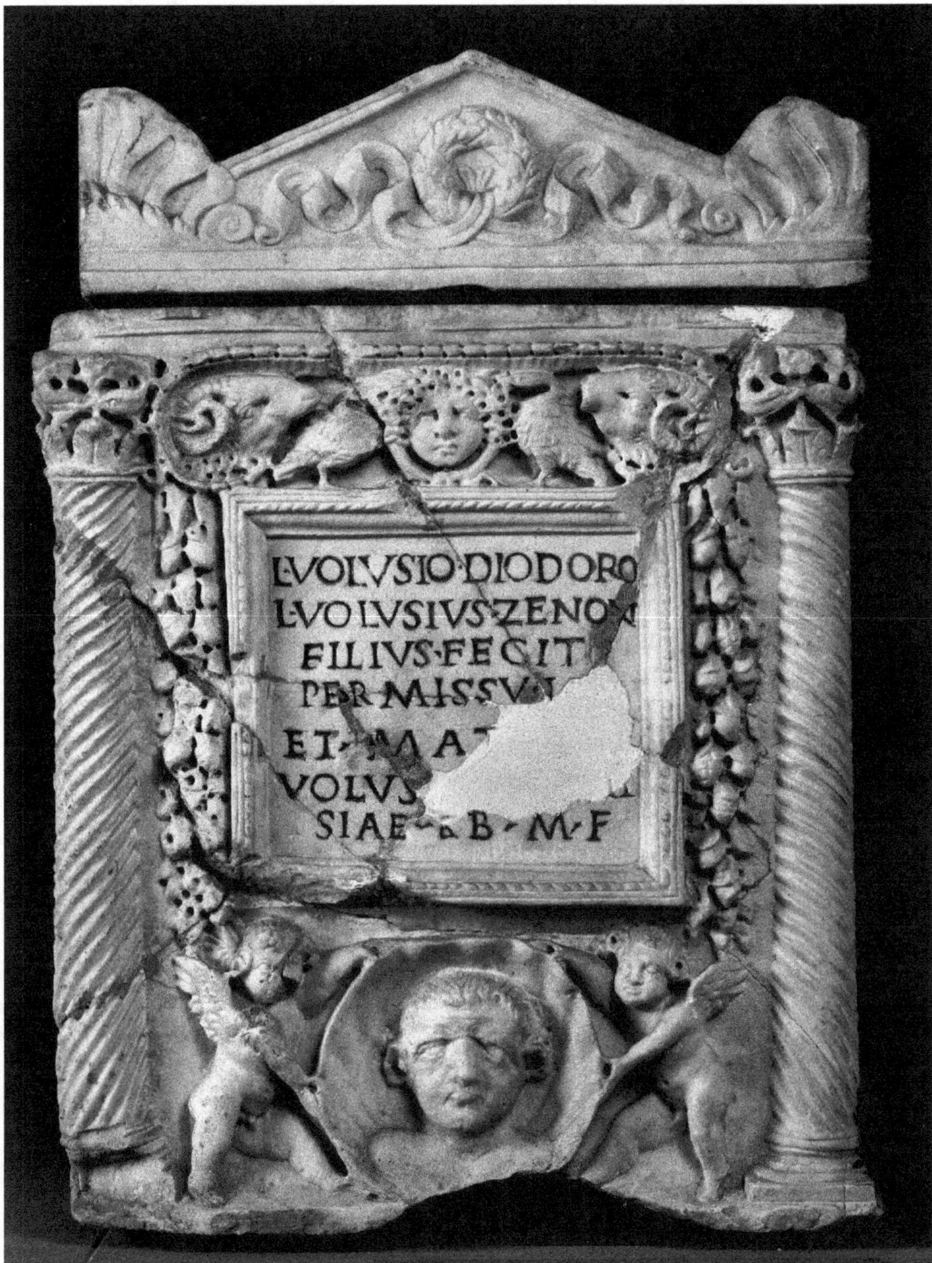

Figure 12.9: Cinerary urn for Lucius Volusius Diodorus. Vatican Museums, Rome, 9813/ 14. Photograph: Forschungsarchiv für Römische Plastik, Cologne.

had shells in the pedimented niches, but omitted them from the intermediate intercolumniations, dominated column sarcophagi produced in Docimium for ninety years.[133] In its figured decoration, it is striking for including apparently historical images of the deceased alongside mythological and divine or semi-divine figures. In its 'micro-architecture' it is also innovative. The lid no longer presents a temple roof, but reclining figures in Etruscan manner, and this style of lid was now also applied to arcaded sarcophagi.[134] There was now no longer a desire to make sarcophagi appear as miniature temples in the older Attic and Asiatic manner. The sides evoke the aedicular architecture of contemporary public buildings. The period when column sarcophagi emerged as a major event in Asiatic sculpture was also the highpoint of aedicular architecture, when the theatrical mode of presenting statues in pedimented columnar niches, projecting from a continuous wall, was applied to public buildings.[135] In column displays on fountains, baths, libraries and bouleuteria in the Roman East imperial, civic and mythological statues, framed between columns, overlooked the activities of the community.[136] Some statue niches had shell forms too, as in the propylon near the agora at Cremna (*c.* 150) and in 'Building M' at Side, where a statue of Nemesis was enshrined in a corner niche with a shell in the semi-dome between freestanding columns.[137]

In the first surviving complete Asiatic column sarcophagus of aedicular form, the spectacular instance from Rapolla (*c.* 170), the figures are elegantly fitted into the micro-architecture.[138] The long sides (Figures 12.10 and 12.11) are each formed by three pedimented shell-niches: a central one with triangular gable within an outer concave niche, suggested by the curved, receding entablature in which the figures stand on either side, and two with segmental pediments. The short sides have a single niche with triangular pediment contained within a concave niche. The whole arrangement can be understood when 'folded out' to show one short side between two long sides as a continuous façade.[139] This schema mirrors the first storey of the scene building at Aizanoi (Figures 12.12 and 12.13), where projecting columnar bays are also combined

133 Morey 1924, 29. This is what Wiegartz and Waelkens call the 'geläufiger Typ'.

134 E.g. Rome K (Torlonia, *c.* 170), also with forward and backward projections of the podium: Morey 1924, 47–48, figs. 83–84; Waelkens 1982, 76 no. 35; and the fully preserved Perge A (dated before 170 by Wiegartz 1965, 167, but neither the sarcophagus nor the photos of it in Lanckoronski's collection in Vienna can now be traced).

135 MacDonald 1986, 183–203; Burrell 2006.

136 Fountains: Dorl-Klingenschmid 2001; bath-gymnasia and libraries: Burrell 2006, 437, 455–457; bouleuteria: Balty 1991, 444–450, 511–518.

137 Cremna: Vandeput 1997, 78 pl. 93.1. Side: Mansel 1956, 59–62, fig. 21; Mansel 1978, 169–186; cf. Vandeput 1997, pl. 117.1.

138 'The Melfi Sarcophagus'. Wiegartz 1965, 164–165; Ghiandoni 1995.

139 Kranz 1978, 375–376 uses the same technique to compare funerary altars and cinerary urns with western aedicular sarcophagi.

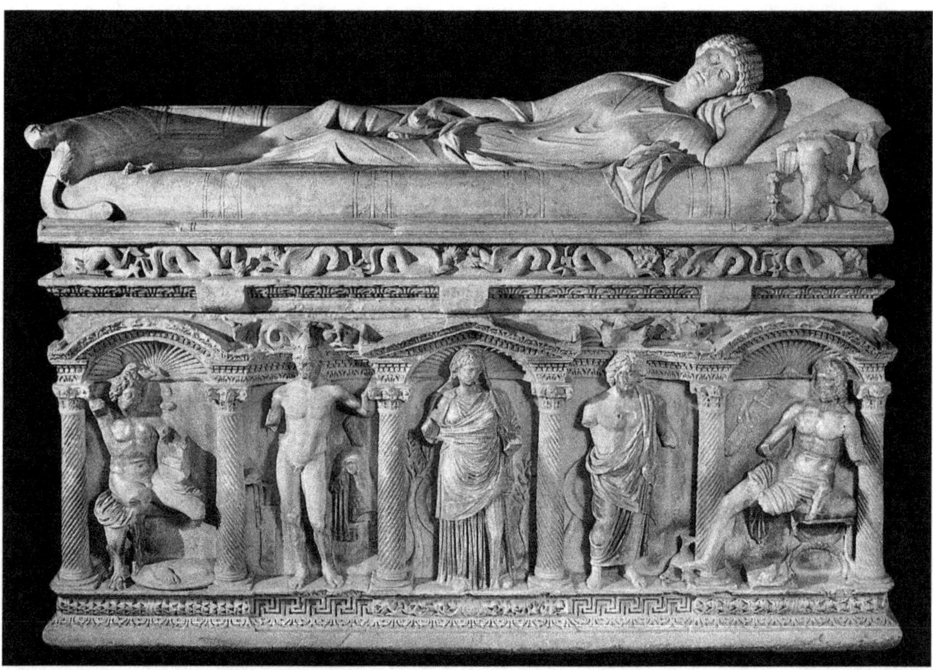

Figure 12.10: Sarcophagus from Rapolla. Castello di Melfi. Original reverse face, presented as the front face in modern display, following incorrect orientation of the lid. Photograph: Nicola Figluolo, courtesy of the Archivio Fotografico della Soprintendenza per i Beni Archeologici della Basilicata, Potenza, Italy.

with a broad curved niche of 'western' type.[140] However, the design on the sarcophagus is more dynamic than the built versions, because the niches have pediments, shell forms and spirally-fluted columns, whereas in the theatre such columns are restricted to the central pair of the second storey, and on all faces they are enclosed by concave forms.

Seen in this way, the two short sides become the focus: originally below the feet of the reclining effigy was the niche containing the door of the tomb, with the deceased, in characteristic 'Hygieia' mode of Roman aristocratic ladies, guided inside by Hermes Psychopompos; below her head, the exemplar Helen. The side facing the ancient viewer showed Aphrodite at the centre, the Roman Venus Victrix in the familiar 'Capua' type extending her shield in victory and

140 Shapley 1923, 73, regarding the Borghese-Louvre muse sarcophagus; cf. Morey 1921, pl. XV.6; Morey 1924, 92; Waelkens 1982, 123; Sear 2006, 113. The first storey of the scene building is dated by architectural ornament to the Hadrianic period, the second and third storeys to a few decades later, when the stadium-theatre complex was remodelled: Hoffmann *et al.* 1993, 455–460; Jes 2007, 163; Rohn 2008, 204. The scene building at Sagalassus is similar in form.

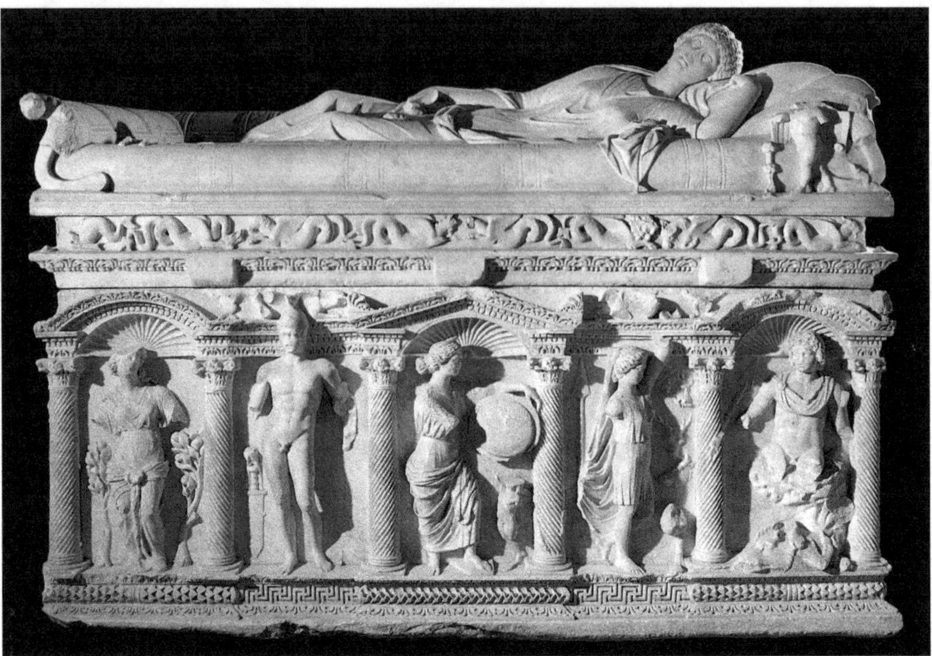

Figure 12.11: Sarcophagus from Rapolla. Castello di Melfi. Original front face, presented by photomontage. Photograph: Nicola Figluolo, courtesy of the Archivio Fotografico della Soprintendenza per i Beni Archeologici della Basilicata, Potenza, Italy.

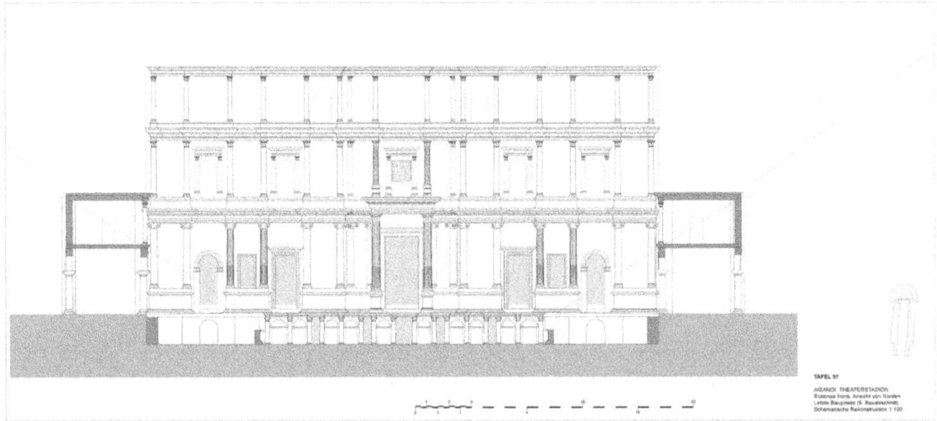

Figure 12.12: Theatre at Aizanoi, scene building. Restored elevation courtesy of Corinna Rohn.

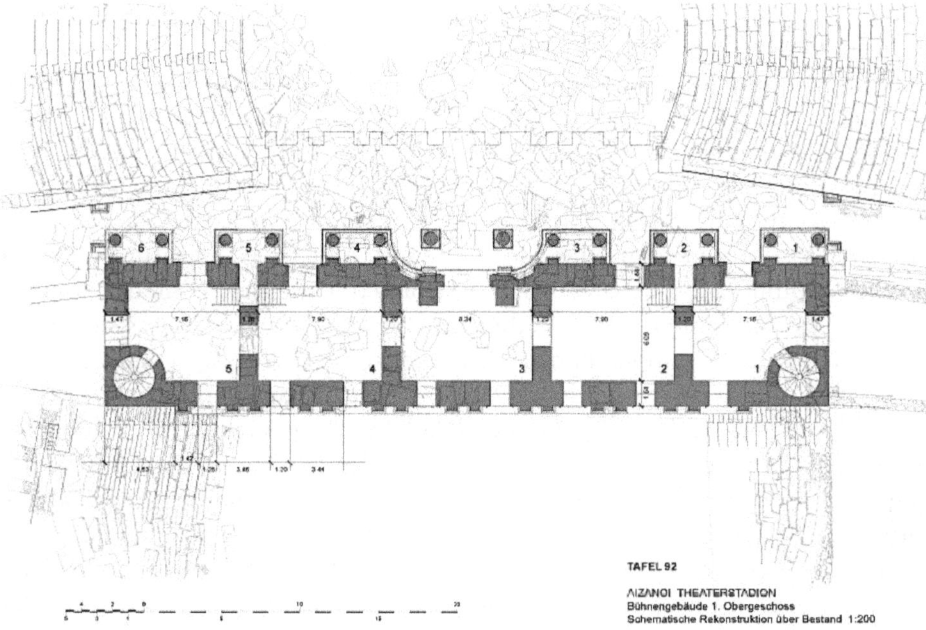

Figure 12.13: Theatre at Aizanoi, scene building. Restored plan of the first storey by Corinna Rohn.

flanked by the legendary couples Achilles and Briseis and Meleager and Atalanta, *exempla* of female power over men.[141] Conches shroud the three central females Venus, Thetis and Helen, the door, and the seated figures on the long sides: on the front, Briseis and, in a chiastic arrangement like the Velletri sarcophagus, not the huntress Atalanta, but Meleager, whom she beat to the boar; on the rear, sitting languorously, the *nemeseis* of Achilles, Apollo and Agamemnon. Unlike the earliest fragments of aedicular type, there is no shell hood for the intermediate, 'masculine' figures – Achilles (to the left of both Venus and Thetis), the 'ephebe' Hephaestus, and Atalanta – or the statuesque figures of Odysseus and Diomedes on the short right side.[142] All figures in shell-niches are comfortably enshrined by the conch; those in the intermediate intercolumniations reach the top of the entablature to maintain harmony with the central figures; only the helmet of superhuman Achilles exceeds this. The form of the figures also echoes public architecture. Although only Odysseus and

141 Ghiandoni 1995, 5 f., fig. 1; cf. Pera 1971–74. Meleager's wife Cleopatra would fit better a theme of conjugal love and is so used by Briseis herself in Ovid, *Heroides* 3.92; but iconography and dress point to Atalanta.

142 Cf. also sarcophagi at Myra and Iznik; for the common Hermes type cf. Izmir, Rome K, Afyon A.

Diomedes are presented as statues on pedestals, many other figures resemble types used for contemporary statuary. Some mirror statues found in public buildings;[143] others are known from coins and medals, or reliefs;[144] and others lacking formal parallels appear on other column sarcophagi, so may have been modelled on contemporary statue types now lost.[145] Significant hand and foot gestures integrate these figures into the surrounding aedicular architecture, reinforcing the links between human bodies and adjacent columns.[146]

Architecture and figures here show the fusion of Greek and Roman culture in the Antonine age. The sarcophagus was placed in a relatively modest tomb of the temple type common in the suburban streets of Rome.[147] It was situated in Lucania, off the Via Appia, midway between Rome and Brindisi and a strategic site on the route between Rome and Greece despite its apparent remoteness; this fertile hinterland of Venusia saw the villas of a prosperous, urban ruling class into the third century.[148] It would not be surprising if the influential Lucanian family of the Bruttii was linked with this costly and portentous work of art. As proconsul of Asia the younger Gaius Bruttius Praesens (cos. 150 and 180) might have seen products of the Docimian workshop.[149] Tantalisingly, an undated Publius Aelius Bruttius Lucianus, could, as proconsul of Lycia and Pamphylia, have known experimental forms of aedicular sarcophagi such as the one in Antalya which might have inspired that at Melfi.[150]

The principal type lasted to the end of the Docimian workshops in the mid-third century. Early examples show sensitivity to the harmony between columns and human figures. In an instance in the Vatican (*c.* 175) an arch under the pediment forms a crown for the figure's head reminiscent of the arched lintel in contemporary buildings; individual elements of the Corinthian capitals are

---

143 E.g. Venus (Capua, amphitheatre, and Ephesus, Vedius gymnasium); Thetis (Ephesus, Library of Celsus, 'Episteme'): Ghiandoni 1995, 20 f., 26.

144 Coins (Venus, Atalanta): Ghiandoni 1995, 21. Reliefs (Achilles, Apollo, Vulcan, Helen): ibid., 19 f., 24, 26, 31 f.

145 E.g. Meleager: cf. Ostia C (*c.* 165): Wiegartz 1965, pl. 40c.

146 E.g. Achilles (rear), extending left arm towards adjacent capital; Agamemnon, right foot on adjacent column base 'in an unnatural manner' (Ghiandoni 1995, 27); Diomedes, right hand on column.

147 Ghiandoni 1995, 5 fig. 6 (8 m. square).

148 Klein-Andreau 1976, 35; Gualandi *et al.* 1981, 163. E.g. the villa at the Contrada Tesoro: Klein-Andreau 1980; and that at Atella: Simpson 1982. See, in general, Small 1994, esp. 40.

149 Groag and Stein 1933, I, 370 no. 164; Rémy 2005, 119; Raepsaet-Charlier 1987, 150; Ghiandoni 1995, 47 f. For costs of such column sarcophagi, see Wiegartz 1974, 365 n. 47.

150 Paris and Radet 1885, 436 no. II. (One wonders whether the fourth name ΛΟΥΚΙΑ-ΝΟΝ was a mistake on the stone for ΛΟΥΚΑΝΙΟΝ, 'Lucanian'). Antalya K: Wiegartz 1965, pl. 27d; Waelkens 1982, 74 no. 21.

clearly articulated.[151] In the Colonna sarcophagus (*c.* 180) figures fill the niches with their heads under the conches, and a shell is added over the tomb door.[152] In a fragment from Nicaea (*c.* 180–185), a figure stands with his feet at the base of the adjacent columns and his head in the arched conch niche; his left hand rests against the upper column shaft, and his right hand touches the capital.[153]

From the last decade of the second century, however, the architectural ornament was increasingly schematic. This led Morey, incorrectly, to distinguish a later 'Sidamara' school from earlier 'Lydian' versions.[154] Yet the lack of attention to ornament only highlights the overall architectural scheme, its relation to a monumental archetype and its continuing symbolic significance. In the Severan period the aedicular model of column sarcophagi remained paramount; its most iconic features, the shell-niches and spirally-fluted columns, were indispensable. These forms were echoed in contemporary monumental buildings. At Hierapolis, not far from Docimium, the lower proscenium wall of the Severan scene building strikingly resembles contemporary column sarcophagi: an alternately projecting and receding entablature; spirally-fluted columns with composite capitals; and ornate conch forms in the semicircular niches. The alternately rectilinear and round-headed niches almost certainly contained statues in antiquity.[155] Similar designs also influenced new architecture beyond theatres. At Ephesus spirally-fluted columns flanked the stairway to the Harbour Baths from the third-century atrium.[156] The aedicular façade continued as the prime focus of architectural display. It occurs in the Marble Court at Sardis, an *aleipterion* ('anointing place') dedicated in 211 to Caracalla and Geta, and probably characterised similar structures with statues as at nearby Daldis.[157] The prestige of this archetype was a sufficient reason for the principal type to outlive other forms of Docimian column sarcophagi.

The repeated use of a set repertoire of figure types shows that aedicular architecture became a recognised frame for presenting the deceased in their social context.[158] The form became a natural medium for allegorical images of a cultivated élite linked to circles of Roman power. On the end of the sarcophagus of Claudia Antonia Sabina (Istanbul G, *c.* 190), replacing earlier mythological figures, a standing, bearded man holds a scroll; on the front, a standing man and seated, veiled woman are under the lateral segmental pediments.[159] Yet now

151 Rome L: Morey 1924, fig. 37; Waelkens 1982, 78 no. 50.
152 Rome D: Morey 1924, fig. 55; Waelkens 1982, 80 no. 61.
153 Iznik A: Morey 1924, fig. 34; Waelkens 1982, 80 no. 65.
154 Morey 1924, 82–84; Wiegartz 1965, 30.
155 *Hierapolis di Frigia* (1987), 38–48; Sear 2006, 338 f., with further literature.
156 Chapot 1907, 125 (there called the Thermae Constantinianae).
157 Yegül 1986; Burrell 2006, 460.
158 Wiegartz 1965, 81–118.
159 Morey 1924, figs. 12–14; Wiegartz 1965, 158.

there was a move away from the formerly close, proportionate relationship between figure and column. By contrast with Melfi, the heads of the figures on the front are not enclosed within the arching shell-niches, but break through the upper mouldings. On a corner fragment from Izmit-Nicomedia (*c.* 195) a half-nude figure leans out from the arched niche; his feet stretch to the foot of the column pedestals, no longer the column base.[160] On a well-preserved sarcophagus from Perge (*c.* 210), the seated figures under the side aedicules no longer show an equivalent proportion between column and figure. Whereas on the rear of the Melfi sarcophagus, despite the seated posture, the heads remain close to the capitals and the feet beside the bases, here the heads touch the upper rim of the segmental pediments and the feet stretch well into the adjacent niche.[161]

As marble sarcophagi became more widespread in the third century, the Docimian aedicular form helped to distinguish the highest ranks of society. An instance from Laodicea has the name of the asiarch Euethios Pyrrhon inscribed under the couch lid.[162] In front of, rather than within, the central aedicule is a seated, bearded man, flanked by two women, one veiled, one not; on the outside, under the segmental pediments, two young male figures, one in tunic armed with a shield, the other nude apart from a chlamys around his neck. The spirally-fluted columns rest on bulky pedestals that seem designed to create space for the figures rather than as harmonious extensions of the column. But if the micro-architecture no longer provided a proportionate setting, it still communicated an iconic language related to larger civic projects. The deceased presumably held his office after Caracalla's visit in 214/15, when the emperor restored the city's neocorate which it had previously lost. This visit was the occasion for the inauguration of a new era as a marker of local identity, celebrated perhaps by a new monumental fountain whose aedicular statue niches echoed the forms of Euethios's sarcophagus.[163] As the aedicular idiom of the nymphaeum was grounded in a cultural dialect common to cities of Asia Minor which expressed their adherence to an imperial ideology, so the asiarch's use of the same exemplar of classical style in his sarcophagus expressed both his civic authority and imperial rank.

From the later Severan period, the architectural ornament of such sarcophagi became increasingly stylised. On a fragment from Mersin-Zephyrion

160 Istanbul C (Istanbul Archaeological Museum, inv. 1886): Morey 1924, fig. 32; Waelkens 1982, 83 no. 81.

161 Antalya, Archaeological Museum, inv. 1005 (Antalya N): Wiegartz 1965, 147, pl. 29b; Waelkens 1982, 82 no. 80 (dating to *c.* 190–195, from bearded heads in manner of Marcus Aurelius); redated by Strocka 1971, 71 no. 6 because of Philisca's bun.

162 Hierapolis Museum, inv. 6527. Şimşek 1997.

163 Howgego 2005, 10; Des Gagniers 1969, 125 fig. 46 (Stage 1).

in Cilicia (*c.* 225), the dart of the egg-and-dart is replaced by simple foliage.[164] In the 230s such aedicular architecture was mere background, the column little more than a colonnette.[165] This lack of attention to the role played by columnar architecture reflected macro-architectural realities in Asia Minor. By then there were few new projects of aedicular architecture, little further work on scene buildings, and many theatres were converted for gladiatorial shows or water spectacles.[166] The symbolic language expressed in the micro-architecture of sarcophagi was almost obsolete. Such changes, however, did not result from shortages in supply of building materials, but should be linked with behavioural changes in élite self-representation. The erosion of the column sarcophagus as a medium of display in the Roman East was part of a larger shift from grand building towards ostentation in costume and shows.[167]

The lavish sarcophagi produced in the twilight of the Docimian workshops show that such a setting was still, in miniature, considered capable of conveying the educated values of late Severan society. An intellectual occupies the place of honour at the centre of the front of the sarcophagus from Selifkeh-Seleuceia; at the corners, the Dioscuri are arranged symmetrically in western style; and a mounted hunter fills the niche of one short side.[168] However, all equivalence between figures and surrounding columns was lost. In the central aedicule on the front of a sarcophagus from Konya, the conch covers the figure's shoulders, rather than his head; the latter reaches the sima of the pediment above, and the women's clothes extend to the base of the column pedestals.[169] It seems that now eastern élites no longer understood aedicular architecture as directly correlated to human representation. A late work from near Nicaea follows the standard aedicular type on three sides, but its right short side presents three shell-niches, as if of an arcade, but without the central columns, which are replaced by a hunting scene; many architectural details are lightly worked, suggesting that the figures were produced first and the architecture added later was of secondary importance.[170] In the final decade of production at Docimium the arcade experienced a brief revival.[171] It occurs again on a right side of the Sidamara

164 Adana A: Wiegartz 1965, pl. 24.

165 E.g. London C (BM, *c.* 230–235), from Rome, showing a seated, bearded poet and a Muse, Thalia, with comic theatre mask: Morey 1924, fig. 52; Waelkens 1982, 90 no. 132.

166 Sear 2006, 44, 112.

167 Borg and Witschel 2001, 90–116.

168 Istanbul A, inv. 466, *c.* 230–235; Morey 1924, 39 f. figs. 61–64; cf. also the similar, fully preserved, but damaged Afyon K from Şuhut-Synnada: Waelkens 1982, 90 no. 133.

169 Konya A (old inv. 28–29/30/32), *c.* 245; Morey 1924, 33 f. figs. 36–37.

170 Istanbul I (inv. 5123), *c.* 245; Özgan 2004, 550 f., fig. 3.

171 Wiegartz 1965, 48 (from *c.* 245).

sarcophagus (*c.* 250–260), masked by figures; this scene is the focus of the column-less front side, and the aedicular architecture is shown only on the rear, on which the reclining images of the deceased turn their backs and where the central seated figure, raised on a huge pedestal, dominates the columnar architecture. The figures dominate, the columns are understated background. In comparison with the Melfi sarcophagus, and even that from Sardis, architecture now played a drastically reduced role in the semiotics of display.

The aedicular form continued to be made in Docimian workshops until the early 260s, when an ornate example was displayed in Antioch, rediscovered in 1993 with contents of gold jewellery and coins helping to establish the date.[172] The elongated figures and heavily drilled, leaf-like architectural ornament exceed even the Sidamara example. To the same era belongs a temple-like sarcophagus found in Konya. A comparison has been observed between the two sarcophagi because of their similar 'Lycian motif' of seated corner figures, and it was concluded that the Konya example reflected evidence of economic and artistic decline corroborating Rodenwaldt's claim that 'the last decades of the third century meant the dissolution of antiquity and beginning of late antiquity.'[173] Yet, with its pitched, tiled roof and medusa's head, now not in the tympanon, but in enlarged scale on the side face below, and with the ornate calligraphy of its inscription which alone occupies the void between the seated figures, the Konya sarcophagus lacks neither expense nor artistic ambition. It shows, rather, a return to the earlier tradition of temple-like sarcophagi, now freed of the outmoded and short-lived fashion of aedicular architecture; together the human figure and written word present a new, non-columnar mode of representation.[174] In other workshops, however, and in larger architecture the spirally-fluted columns explored in the creative micro-architectural designs of column sarcophagi were by the late Empire almost 'the obligatory frame for any niche where a notable person is represented.'[175]

172 Özgan 2000, 365–376, fig. 1; Öğüş 2004.

173 Özgan 2000, 387; Rodenwaldt 1936, 83.

174 Framing by seated figures is already well-attested in western sarcophagi, e. g. the chest of Sosia Iuliana at Ravenna, but within a columnar setting (Museo Nazionale, large cloister: Gabelmann 1973, 220, pls. 50–51; *ASR* VIII, 2, A 35 pls. 14.2–4, 15.1–4, 16.1), perhaps second century.

175 Chapot 1907, 113.

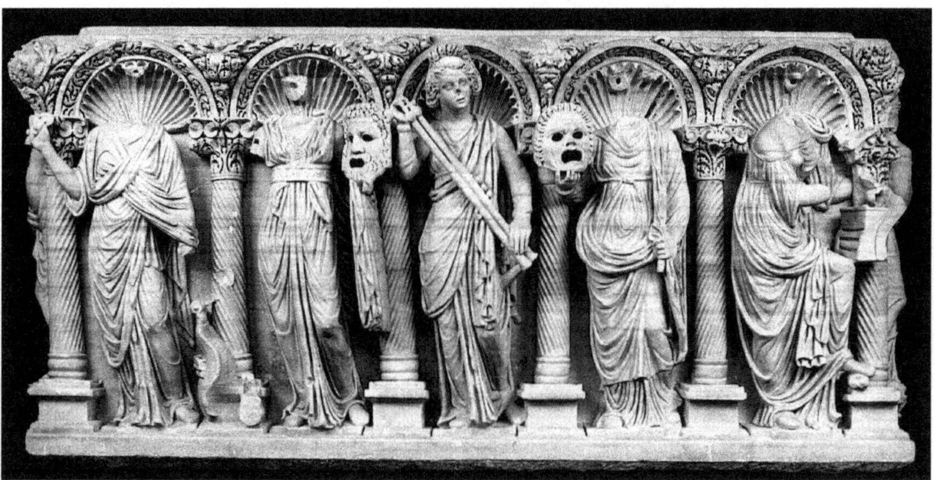

Figure 12.14: The Mattei muse sarcophagus, *c.* 280–290. Museo Nazionale Romano 80711, Rome. Photograph: DAIR 6535.

The triumph of the arcade

When the quarries of Docimium ceased to export marble sarcophagi, its artists went elsewhere to ply their trade.[176] The Berlin piece with Christ and apostles (Figure 12.2), which brought column sarcophagi so much attention, was a result of this migration, as too was the Mattei Muse sarcophagus, adorned on three sides with arcades with shell-niches.[177] Here muses hold masks paronomastically over the two central capitals (Figure 12.14).

The market in Italy for aedicular style at its height is attested not only by the many Asiatic sarcophagi found there, but also by one in Florence, a direct imitation presumably commissioned by an Italian patron.[178] But the latter's roof-like lid and garlanded intercolumniations suggest a poor understanding of the semiotics of the Asiatic model. Such works were a rarefied taste, intended perhaps, like the aedicular façades of Severan Rome, as a sign of accentuated Hellenism or regional identity.[179] More popular was the 'Lanuvium type' scheme developed in Severan Rome and imitated elsewhere, with a pediment between

176 Wiegartz et al. 1971, 98–100; Waelkens 1982, 70.

177 Morey 1924, 30 fig. 25 (Berlin A); 49 f. figs. 87–89 (Rome I); Wiegartz 1965, 21 (dating to 270s). Cf. also Vatican, Galleria Lapidaria: Morey 1924, 37, 57 (Rome C), fig. 54; and Bari below.

178 Medici-Riccardi wedding sarcophagus, *c.* 190–200, Museo dell'Opera del Duomo, Florence: Koch 1980, 99–102; Wrede 2001, 117, pl. 10.1–3.

179 E.g. the Severan scene building of Pompey's Theatre and the Septizodium; cf. Thomas 2007b.

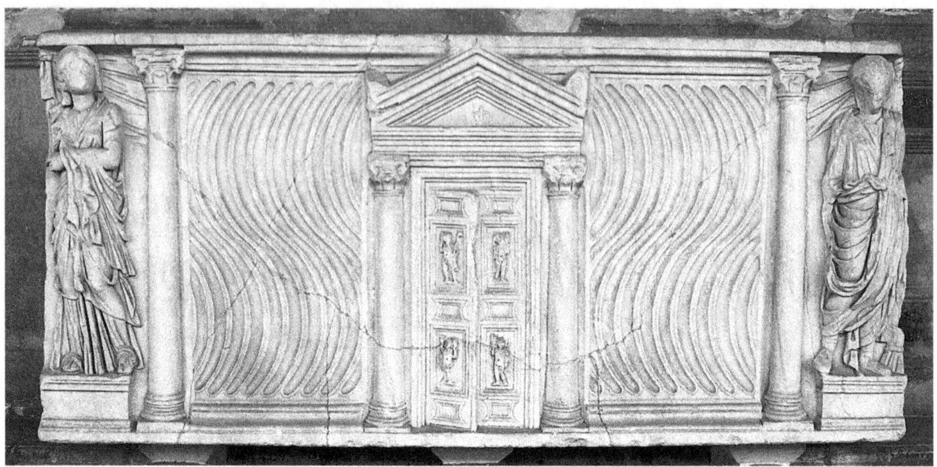

Figure 12.15: Strigillated sarcophagus in the Camposanto, Pisa. Photograph: J. Elsner.

two arches, derived from earlier cinerary traditions.[180] Senatorial patrons used its triptych format to place huge figures in civic dress under the lateral segmental arches.[181] Unlike contemporary Asiatic sarcophagi, this aedicular structure lacks the projections and recessions of a scenic, micro-architectural façade. As on earlier tombs, the statue's aedicular frame was what mattered most. Thus other senators chose strigillated forms with a single, central aedicular vignette to display their images.[182] Spirally-fluted columns and a conch hood were no longer inseparable, but dispensable additions. Sometimes only a door with columns and pediment was suggestively displayed at the centre, with further smooth columns at the side, aligned with statuary (Figure 12.15).[183]

Elsewhere in the West column sarcophagi followed a simpler arcaded scheme based on the architecture of the streetside portico.[184] Unlike first-century prototypes, the arcades of column sarcophagi in late-Antonine Italy flank a central pediment; spirally-fluted columns separate amorini representing the seasons, but show little replication of architectural ornament on the

180 Kranz 1978, 363 n. 83a.

181 Notably the Medici-Riccardi sarcophagus (Florence, Museo dell'Opera del Duomo, *c.* 220–230, with single figures under low lateral arches, either side of a pedimented doorway) and the Belvedere wedding sarcophagus (Vatican 866, *c.* 250–260, showing a couple with attendants): Wrede 2001, 119–121, pls. 11.2–3. The couple is replaced by seasons on Palazzo dei Conservatori 1185: Hanfmann 1951, ii, no. 336 fig. 33 (*c.* 240).

182 E.g. Munich, Glyptothek 533, and Pisa, Camposanto C 1 est: Wrede 2001, 122–124, pl. 13.1–3.

183 Pisa, Campo Santo: Arias 1977, 59 f. A est., figs. 13–16. Cf. also Genzano, Villa Riva: Koch and Sichtermann 1982, pl. 291; Pisa, Campo Santo: Hanfmann 1951, no. 316.

184 Weidhaas 1968.

archivolts seen on contemporary Docimian instances.[185] The arcade occurred not only on the chest, but even in acroteria on the lid.[186] The Herculean Labours are presented under an arcade of six arches on a well-preserved instance from the Via Cassia (*c.* 175–185), which depicts the myths on three sides in the same order as on Asiatic column sarcophagi and was presumably inspired by the latter.[187] Here spirally-fluted columns are replaced by narrow pilasters, foliage in the spandrels by masks and winged victories, and the flat arches lack decoration. An impressive five-bay example from Rome that reappeared at a sale in December 2009 has spirally fluted columns with western capitals, masks in the spandrels, and entablatures again lacking the florid ornament of Asiatic examples, but its central, pedimented opening shows Dionysus and a satyr within a shell-niche before a squared stone wall.[188] Elsewhere a Mauretanian senator is shown sacrificing in military robes and joining in marriage in civil dress, within a four-arch frame distinguished by composite capitals and ornamented only by masks in the spandrels.[189]

The perceived 'Romanness' of the arcade may be exploited on a sarcophagus in Palazzo Mattei di Giove (*c.* 200), where the five arches with pilasters and schematic Corinthian columns enclose figures associated with the city's origin, Mars and Venus, Mars and Rhea Silvia, and Faustulus, alongside also Cupid and Psyche, serenaded in the spandrels by trumpeting amorini.[190] At Aphrodisias, when the number of marble sarcophagi rose sharply after the mass extension of Roman citizenship through the *Constitutio Antoniniana* in 212, the costliest ones had arcades with a preference for spirally-fluted columns, conch niches, and a Lesbian cymatium around each arch.[191] The western aspect of the arcade as an element of civic architecture might explain how this form could

185 Prototypes, e.g. Campana plaques, Villa Giulia sarcophagus, and many funerary altars: Kranz 1978, 368. Late-Antonine, S. Lorenzo in Panisperma, Rome, and Rehalp-Friedhof, Zurich, *c.*160–180: ibid., 361–365, pl. 157.1–2; Koch and Sichtermann 1982, 221. A later, more florid version from Tunis substitutes the Three Graces for the central door: Tunis, Musée Bardo: Hanfmann 1951, ii, no. 504. Cf. also Ferentillo, Badia di S. Pietro in Valle: *ASR* IV,4, 276, with Dionysus and satyr in the middle intercolumniation, spirally-fluted columns, Corinthian capitals, masks in spandrels, and rather agile figures on pedestals, later second century.

186 Endymion sarcophagus, New York, Metropolitan Museum 47.100.4; cf. Rome, Palazzo Venezia, with alternating pediments and arches: Koch and Sichtermann 1982, 70, pls. 159, 251.

187 Rome, MNR 154592; Jacopi 1972, pls. 73–75.

188 *ASR* IV,4, no. 278, pl. 303.1; Sotheby's New York, sale N08603 (10/12/09).

189 Tipasa, Archaeological Park, *c.* 190: Gsell 1894, 431–437; Wrede 2001, 116 f. pl. 11.1. Cf. Pisa, Camposanto C 14 est, *c.* 203–220 (5 arches): Arias 1977, pls. 82, 172–174; Wrede 2001, 118 pl. 12.1.

190 *ASR* IV,4, no. 246, 277 pl. 261, 302; Perry 2005, 136–138, figs. 36–37.

191 Smith 2008, 386 f., Table 1; Işik 1984. E.g. Pisa, Camposanto C 22 est, *c.* 250: Arias 1977, 152–154, pls. XCIV-XCV.

demonstrate 'a new, proud sense of belonging' to the Roman Empire and civic ideology.[192] Rarer was the horizontal entablature form, though an elegant example with temple roof, Ionic capitals, two spirally-fluted columns between vertically-fluted pilasters, and three animated maenads was produced in late Antonine Tyre.[193] The arcade revived by artists from Docimium around 250 naturally included conches and spirally-fluted columns, but they also sometimes avoided columns altogether.[194] The arcades depicted on later fragments of local origin from Ephesus and Konya had flatter arch and leaf-like conch forms or empty niche-heads as on western sarcophagi.[195] Single arches upon spirally-fluted columns had an iconic power, whether they contained figures or not.[196] In northern Italy and Dalmatia arcades with spirally-fluted columns were used on pagan and Christian sarcophagi until the late fourth century.[197] A four-arch version at Arles has spirally-fluted columns but little architectural ornament; five- and seven-arch versions are common among fourth-century Christians, the former exemplified by the lavish sarcophagus of Probus, decorated on all sides with a combination of forms, the latter well-suited to accommodate Christ and the Apostles.[198] Others present fantastic images of Jerusalem, the prototype for medieval micro-architectural imaginings.[199] It was in the context of western, not Asiatic, aedicular forms, that the two-storey columnar façades of Junius Bassus and St Trophime were conceived: in the former, spirally-fluted columns frame Old and New Testament scenes, while the central columns framing Christ's enthronement and triumph are wrapped with vines; the enthroned Christ stepping over the arch of Caelus recalls the Velletri sarcophagus; the latter, showing Christ and the Apostles, with spirally-fluted columns throughout, was re-used as a font (Figure 12.16).[200] The use of trees as architectonic elements, already latent in pagan sarcophagi, came to the fore in Christian configu-

192 Smith 2008, 388–392.

193 *ASR* IV,4, no. 275 A figs. 133–136; Koch and Sichtermann 1982, 562 f. fig. 555.

194 E.g. Sagalassus B, c. 250, where the kneeling figure seems almost in place of a column: Wiegartz 1965, 170.

195 Izmir A (early fourth-century) and Konya G (*c.* 250–275): Wiegartz 1965, 159 f. and 163, pls. 36b, 39e.

196 E.g. Arles, containing only masks either side of an inscribed tabula ansata: Espérandieu 1907, 148 f. no. 183.

197 E.g. Tortona, S. Marciano: *ASR* III, 3, 432–435 no. 350; Split: Koch and Sichtermann 1982, 316–320, pls. 348, 350–351; cf. Lawrence 1932, 178 no. 6.

198 Wrede 2001, pl. 21.2; Lawrence 1932, 140–148, 167–171; cf. Koch 2000, 147.

199 St Peter's, Cappella Colonna; Milan: Wrede 2001, pls. 22.3, 23.1–2; Bucher 1976.

200 Bassus, Vatican: Lawrence 1932, 171 no. 69; Malbon 1990, 39 f., fig. 44. Figure 11.1 in this volume. St Trophime, Arles: ibid., fig. 2; Elsner 2009, 191, fig. 12.

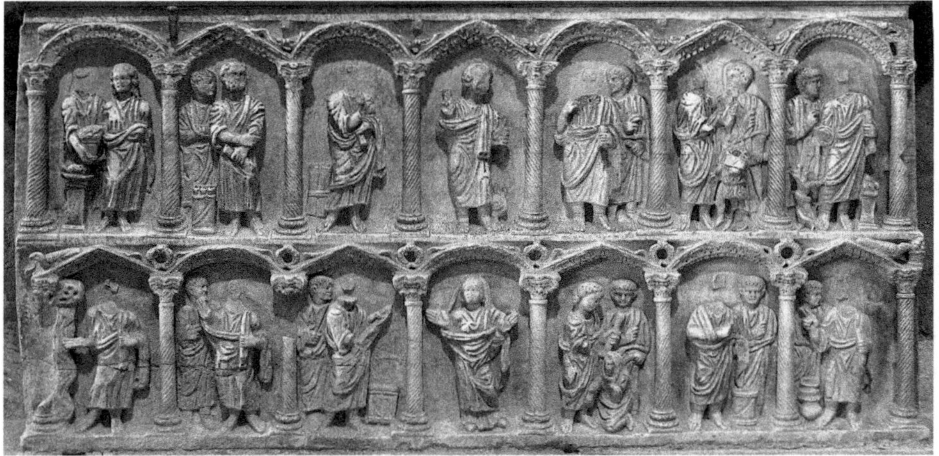

Figure 12.16: Two-tier column sarcophagus re-used as a font at St Trophîme, Arles. Photograph: Jaś Elsner.

rations.[201] The caryatid motif was revitalised in Christian images of the good shepherd, although the animal-bearing posture there seems closer to the Archaic Moschophoros.[202]

The transfer of pagan columnar symbolism to Christian art and thought ensured the continued life of the column sarcophagus. The Psamathia Relief (Figure 12.2) was first re-used as an ornamental relief in a sacred building, perhaps the church of St Stephen.[203] Then built into a wall in an underground chamber of the Sulu Monastery, it was framed by icons of the Virgin and the Archangel Michael.[204] The sarcophagus of Barbatianus (*c.* 440), re-used in Ravenna cathedral in the thirteenth century, is decorated with shell-niches and spirally-fluted columns, with a figure of Christ at the centre.[205] More than one column sarcophagus were combined to make a bishop's tomb at Myra.[206] The eleventh-century image of Christ and the Apostles on a marble lintel at St-

201 Villa Medici sarcophagus, with Dionysiac scenes, third century (Koch and Sichtermann 1982, 116, fig. 121); Attic sarcophagus, Academy, Athens (ibid., 426, fig. 460); Lawrence 1932, 171–173 fig. 64.

202 E.g. 'Three Shepherds sarcophagus' (Vatican, Lat. 191 A): caryatid-like shepherds hold sheep like baskets; their leggings, on ornate pedestals, are 'spirally-fluted'; vintage-gathering cupids play on vines behind.

203 Schemann 1999, with previous literature.

204 Effenberger 1990, 79.

205 *ASR* VIII,2, 63 f., B10, pl. 50; cf. B12 (pl. 49.2), Ariosti-Fontana family, S. Francesco, Ferrara, 5th century.

206 Morey 1924, 35 f. fig. 42; Wiegartz 1965, 165.

Genis-des-Fontaines seems modelled on early Christian column sarcophagi.[207] In S. Nicola at Bari the tomb of Archbishop Helias recycled a row of bearded 'philosopher' figures in conches with spiral columns, one of the latest works of the Docimian masters, converting the third-century image of the intellectual into one of the church fathers.[208] His marble throne rests on support figures in the classical tradition straining under its weight, illustrating, like the reuse of the Velletri sarcophagus, how the metaphor of support lying behind the creation of column sarcophagi under the Antonines remained vital in medieval micro-architecture over a millennium later.[209]

Bibliography

Ainalov, D. *Ellenisticheskiia osnovy vizantiiskago iskusstva* (St Petersburg, 1901).

Ainalov, D. *The Hellenistic origins of Byzantine art*, translated by E. and S. Sobolevitch, edited by Cyril Mango (New Brunswick, 1961).

Alföldy, G. Traianus pater und die Bauinschrift des Nymphäums von Milet. *Revue des études anciennes* 100 (1998), 367–399.

Altmann, W. *Architektur und Ornamentik der antiken Sarkophage* (Berlin, 1902).

Andreae, B. *Studien zur römischen Grabkunst.* (Heidelberg, 1963).

Andreae, B. Il grande sarcofago di Velletri a cinquant'anni dalla sua scoperta, in: M. Angle, A. Germano and F. Zevi (eds.), *Museo e territorio.* Atti del IV convegno, Velletri, 7–8 maggio 2004 (Rome, 2005), 31–36.

Arias, P. *Camposanto monumentale di Pisa, 1. Le antichità* (Pisa, 1977).

Arnheim, R. *The dynamics of architectural form* (Berkeley, 1977).

Ashmole, B. Cyriac of Ancona and the Temple of Hadrian at Cyzicus. *Journal of the Warburg and Courtauld Institutes* 19 (1956), 179–191.

Ashmole, B. and Yalouris, N. *Olympia: the sculptures of the temple of Zeus* (London, 1967).

Aurigemma, S. *I monumenti della necropoli romana di Sarsina* (Rome, 1963).

Balty, J. Ch. *Curia Ordinis. Recherches d'architecture et d'urbanisme antiques sur les curies provinciales du monde romain* (Brussels, 1991).

Banchelli, C. Sotto il tribunale, un tempio di Iside. *Corriere Fiorentino*, 28 May 2009. http://corrierefiorentino.corriere.it/notizie/arte_e_cultura/2009/28-maggio-2009/sotto-tribunale-tempio-iside-1501407274233.shtml.

Baratte, F. and Metzger, C. *Catalogue des sarcophages en pierre d'époques romaine et paléochrétienne, Musée du Louvre* (Paris, 1985).

Bartoccini, R. Il sarcofago di Velletri. *Rivista del Istituto di Archeologia e Storia dell'Arte* 7 (1958), 129–214.

Benson, J. L. Spirally fluted columns in Cyprus. *American Journal of Archaeology* 60 (1956), 385–387.

Benson, J. L. Spirally fluted columns in Greece. *Hesperia* 28 (1959), 253–272.

207 Hearn 1981, 27 f. fig. 5 (dated 1020/1).

208 Morey 1924, fig. 79; cf. Zanker 1995, Borg and Witschel 2001, 112 f.

209 Hearn 1981, 80–85, figs. 56–57 (dated 1098).

Beyen, H. *Die Pompejanische Wanddekoration vom zweiten bis zum vierten Stil* (The Hague, 1938).

Bieber, M. Roman men in Greek himation (*Romani palliati*), a contribution to the history of copying. *Proceedings of the American Philological Association* 103, no. 3 (1959), 374–417.

Bieber, M. The Velletri sarcophagus carved for the family of the Octaviani. *American Journal of Archaeology* 70 (1966), 65.

Blake, M. *Roman construction in Italy from Tiberius through the Flavians* (New York, 1968).

Boardman, J. et al. Herakles, in: *Lexicon Iconographicum Mythologiae Classicae V* (1990), 1–192.

Boldrick, S. and Fehrmann, A. Microarchitecture and the afterlife. Session 1219, of International Medieval Congress, Wednesday 12 July 2000, Institute for Medieval Studies, University of Leeds (unpublished).

Bonanno Aravantinos, M. Il sarcofago con le fatiche di Ercole e altri sarcofagi rinvenuti in area Veliterna, in: M. Angle, A. Germano and F. Zevi (eds.), *Museo e territorio.* Atti del IV convegno, Velletri, 7–8 maggio 2004 (Rome, 2005), 37–56.

Borchhardt, J. Sarkophage der Klassik und ihre Aufstellung in Lykien und Karien, in: *Bildergeschichte. Festschrift Klaus Stähler*, edited by J. Gebauer, E. Grabow, F. Jünger and D. Metzler (Möhnesee, 1984), 29–58.

Borg, B. (ed.). *Paideia: the world of the second sophistic* (Berlin, 2004).

Borg, B. and Witschel, C. Veränderungen im Repräsentationsverhalten der römischen Eliten während des 3. Jhs. n. Chr., in: *Inschriftliche Denkmäler als Medien der Selbstdarstellung in der römischen Welt*, edited by G. Alföldy and S. Panciera (Stuttgart, 2001), 47–120.

Bucher, F. Micro-architecture as the 'idea' of Gothic theory and style. *Gesta* 15/1–2 (1976), 71–89.

Buckler, W. H. Labour disputes in the Province of Asia, in: *Anatolian Studies presented to Sir William Mitchell Ramsay*, edited by W. H. Buckler and W. M. Calder (Manchester, 1923), 27–50.

Buckler, W. H., Calder, W. M. and Guthrie, W. K. C. (eds.). *Monumenta Asiae Minoris Antiqua, 4. Monuments and documents from Eastern Asia and Western Galatia* (Manchester, 1933).

Buckler, W. H., Calder, W. M. and Guthrie, W. K. C. (eds.). *Monumenta Asiae Minoris Antiqua, 6. Monuments and documents from Phrygia and Caria* (Manchester, 1939).

Cagiano de Azevedo, M. L'autenticità del sarcofago di Orvieto da Torre San Severo. *Mitteilungen des Deutschen Archäologischen Instituts, Römische Abteilung* 77 (1970), 10–18.

Caldelli, M. L. Personaggi eminenti di Velletri imperiale, in: M. Angle, A. Germano and F. Zevi (eds.), *Museo e territorio.* Atti del IV convegno, Velletri, 7–8 maggio 2004 (Rome, 2005), 107–114.

Carroll, M. *Spirits of the dead: Roman funerary commemoration in Western Europe* (Oxford, 2006).

Cascella, S. *Il teatro romano di Sessa Aurunca* (Marina di Minturno, 2002).

Castagnoli, F. Gli edifici rappresentati in un rilievo del sepolcro degli Haterii. *Bullettino Comunale* 69 (1941), 59–69.

Chapot, V. *La colonne torse et le décor en hélice dans l'art antique* (Paris, 1907).

Chausson, F. Une dédicace monumentale provenant du théâtre de Suessa Aurunca, due à Matidie la Jeune, belle-soeur de l'empereur Hadrien. *Journal des Savants* (2008), 233–259.

Cumont, F. Un sarcophage d'enfant trouvé à Beyrouth. *Syria* 10 (1929), 217–237.
Curtius, E. *European Literature and the Latin Middle Ages*, translated by W. R. Trask (London, 1953).
De Angelis, F. *La 'Periegesi' di Pausania: il viaggio in Grecia e la fruizione delle opere d'arte nel II sec. d.C.* (Unpublished Tesi di Laurea, University of Pisa, 1991–92).
De Luca, G. *I monumenti antichi di Palazzo Corsini in Roma* (Rome, 1976).
Deschamps, L. L'harmonie des sphères dans les *Satires Ménippées* de Varron. *Latomus* 38 (1979), 9–27.
Des Gagniers, J. *Laodicée du Lycos: le nymphée; campagnes 1961–1963* (Quebec, 1969).
Di Vita, A. Il mausoleo punico-ellenistico B di Sabratha. *Mitteilungen des Deutschen Archäologischen Instituts, Römische Abteilung* 83 (1976), 273–285.
Dorl-Klingenschmid, C. *Prunkbrunnen in kleinasiatischen Städten: Funktion im Kontext* (Munich, 2001).
d'Orsi, L. *Gli Scavi di Stabia* (Naples, 1954).
Effenberger, A. Studien zu den Bildwerken der Frühchristlich-byzantinischen Sammlung VI: Das Christusrelief von Psamathia. *Forschungen und Berichte. Staatliche Museen zu Berlin* 29 (1990), 79–116.
Elsner, J. The birth of late antiquity: Riegl and Strzygowski in 1901. *Art History* 25 (2002), 358–379.
Elsner, J. The Christian museum in southern France: antiquity, display, and liturgy from the Counter-Reformation to the aftermath of Vatican II. *Oxford Art Journal* 32 (2009), 181–204.
Engemann, J. *Untersuchungen zur Sepulkralsymbolik der späteren römischen Kaiserzeit* (Münster, 1973).
Espérandieu, E. *Recueil Général des Bas-reliefs de la Gaule romaine*, vol. I (Paris, 1907).
Ewald, B. *Der Philosoph als Leitbild: ikonographische Untersuchungen an römischen Sarkophagreliefs* (Mainz, 1999).
Fano Santi, M. La colonna tortile nell'architettura di età romana. *Rivista di Archeologia* 17 (1993), 71–83.
Ferrari, G. *Il commercio dei sarcophagi asiatici* (Rome, 1966).
Ficoroni, F. *Le vestigia e rarità di Roma antica, ricercate e spiegate* (Rome, 1744).
Fıratlı, N. An early Byzantine hypogeum discovered at Iznik, in: *Mansel'e Armağan = Mélanges Mansel* (Ankara, 1974), 919–932.
Fleischer, R. *Der Klagefrauensarkophag aus Sidon*, Istanbuler Forschungen 34 (Tübingen, 1983).
French, D. Isinda and Lagbe, in: *Studies in the history and topography of Lycia and Pisidia. In memoriam A. S. Hall*, edited by D. French (London, 1994), 53–92.
Gabelmann, H. *Die Werkstattgruppen der oberitalischen Sarkophage* (Bonn, 1973).
Gabelmann, H. Zur Tektonik oberitalischer Sarkophage, Altäre und Stelen. *Bonner Jahrbücher* 177 (1977), 199–244.
Galli, M. Teatro della memoria: mito e *paideia* sul sarcofago di Velletri, in: M. Angle, A. Germano and F. Zevi (eds.), *Museo e territorio.* Atti del IV convegno, Velletri, 7–8 maggio 2004 (Rome, 2005), 73–90.
Garner, G. Das Monument bei Tarragona und andere Bauten in der Nachfolge des Mausoleums von Halikarnass. *Madrider Mitteilungen* 23 (1982), 296–317.
Gasparri, C. Il sarcofago romano del Museo di Villa Giulia. *Rendiconti dell'Accademia dei Lincei* ser. 8, 27 (1972), 95–139.
Ghiandoni, O. Il sarcofago asiatico di Melfi. Ricerche mitologiche, iconografiche e stilistiche. *Bollettino d'Arte* 89–90 (1995), 1–58.

Giuliano, A. (ed.). *Museo Nazionale Romano: le sculture, I.1 Sale di esposizione* (Rome, 1979).
Graindor, P. Inscriptions de la Nécropole de Touna el-Ghebel (Hermoupolis). *Bulletin de l'Institut Français d'Archéologie Orientale du Caire* 32 (1932), 97–119.
Groag, E. and A. Stein (eds.). *Prosopographia Imperii Romani* (Berlin, 1933).
Gros, P. Le mausolée des Julii et le statut de *Glanum*. *Revue Archéologique* (1986), 65–80.
Gros, P. La fonction symbolique des édifices théâtraux dans le paysage urbain de la Rome augustéenne, in: *L'Urbs: espace urbain et histoire (Ier siècle av. J.-C.– IIIe siècle ap. J.-C.)*. Actes du colloque international organisé par le Centre national de la recherche scientifique et l'École française de Rome, Rome, 8–12 mai 1985 (Rome, 1987), 319–346.
Gros, P. La sémantique des ordres à la fin de l'époque hellénistique et au début de l'Empire. Remarques préliminaires, in: *Splendida civitas nostra. Studi archeologici in onore di Antonio Frova*, edited by G. Cavalieri Manasse and E. Roffia (Rome, 1995), 23–33.
Gros, P. *L'architecture romaine*, 2 vols. (Paris, 1996–2001).
Gros, P. Ornamentum chez Vitruve: le débat sur le décor architectural à la fin de l'époque hellénistique, in: *Vitruve et la tradition des traités d'architecture. Fabrica et ratiocinatio. Recueil d'études*, CEFR 366, edited by Pierre Gros (Rome, 2006), 389–398.
Gsell, S. Tipasa, ville de la Maurétanie Césarienne. *Mélanges d'archéologie et d'histoire* 14 (1894), 291–450.
Gualandi, M. L., Palazzi, C. and Paoletti, M. La Lucania orientale, in: *Società romana e produzione schiavistica, 1. L'Italia: insediamenti e forme economiche*, edited by A. Giardina and A. Schiavone (Rome and Bari, 1981), 155–179.
Hales, S. *The Roman house and social identity* (Cambridge, 2003).
Hanfmann, G. *The Seasons Sarcophagus in Dumbarton Oaks* (Cambridge, MA, 1951).
Hauschild, T., Mariner Bigorra, S. and Niemeyer, H. G. Torre de los Escipiones, ein römischer Grabturm bei Tarragona. *Madrider Mitteilungen* 7 (1966), 162–188.
Haynes, S. *Etruscan civilization. A cultural history* (London, 2000).
Hearn, M. F. *Romanesque sculpture: the revival of monumental stone sculpture in the eleventh and twelfth centuries* (Oxford, 1981).
Henzen, W. Sarcofago antico reperto in via Macera nel distretto di Melfi, provincia di Basilicata. *Bullettino dell'Istituto di Corrispondenza Archeologica* (1856), 158–164.
Hesberg, H. von. Bauornament als kulturelle Leitform, in: W. Trillmich and P.Zanker (eds.). *Stadtbild und Ideologie: die Monumentalisierung hispanischer Städte zwischen Republik und Kaiserzeit.* Kolloquium in Madrid vom 19. bis 23. Oktober, 1987 (Munich, 1990), 341–366.
Hierapolis di Frigia, 1957–1987 (Milan, 1987).
Hoffmann, A. Aizanoi 1988. Arbeiten im Stadion. *XI. Kazı sunuçları toplantısı*, 2 (Istanbul, 1989), 266.
Hoffmann, A., Meyer-Schlichtmann, C. and von Mosch, H.-C. Aizanoi. Zweiter Vorbericht über die Arbeiten im Stadion 1987, 1988 und 1990. *Archäologischer Anzeiger* (1993), 437–473.
Holwerda, J. Der römische Sarkophag von Simpelveld. *Archäologischer Anzeiger* (1933), 56–75.
Homes for the Soul: Micro-Architecture in Medieval and Contemporary Art. Leeds, Henry Moore Institute, 17 January – 18 March 2000.
Hope, V. *Death in ancient Rome: a source book* (London and New York, 2007).

Horn-Oncken, A. *Über das Schickliche. Studien zur Geschichte der Architekturtheorie*, Abhandlungen der Akademie der Wissenschaften in Göttingen, phil.-hist. Klasse, 3rd series, 70 (Göttingen, 1967).

Howgego, C. Coinage and identity in the Roman provinces, in: *Coinage and identity in the Roman provinces*, edited by C. Howgego, V. Heuchert and A. Burnett (Oxford, 2005), 1–17.

Işik, F. Die Sarkophage aus Aphrodisias, in: B. Andreae (ed.). *Symposium über die antiken Sarkophage.* Pisa 5.–12. September 1982 (*Marburger Winckelmann-Programm* 1984) (Marburg/Lahn, 1984), 243–281.

Jacopi, I. Sarcofago con scene di dodecatlo dalla Via Cassia. *Archeologia Classica* 24 (1972), 283–333.

Kähler, H. Die rheinischen Pfeilergrabmäler. *Bonner Jahrbücher* 139 (1934), 145–172.

Klein-Andreau, C. La romanizzazione, in: *Civiltà antiche del Medio Ofanto*, edited by G. Tocco (Naples, 1976), 35.

Klein-Andreau, C. Trouvailles d'époque romaine sur le territoire de Melfi, in: *Attività archeologica in Basilicata, 1967–1977. Scritti in onore di Dinu Adamesteanu*, edited by E. Lattanzi (Matera, 1980), 345–366.

Koch, G. Einige Überlegungen zu den Sarkophagen der kleinasiatischen Hauptgruppe. Handelt es sich um eine Produktion auf Vorrat oder auf besondere Bestellung?, in: *Munus: Festschrift für Hans Wiegartz*, edited by T. Mattern (Münster, 2000), 139–148.

Koch, G. Östliche Sarkophage in Rom. *Bonner Jahrbücher* 182 (1982), 167–208.

Koch, G. Stadtrömisch oder östlich? Probleme einiger kaiserzeitlicher Sarkophage in Rom. *Bonner Jahrbücher* 180 (1980), 51–104.

Koch, G. and Sichtermann, H. *Römische Sarkophage* (Munich, 1982).

Kockel, V. *Die Grabbauten vor dem Herculaner Tor in Pompeji* (Mainz, 1983).

Kranz, P. Zu den Anfängen der stadtrömischen Säulensarkophage. *Mitteilungen des Deutschen Archäologischen Instituts, Römische Abteilung* 85 (1978), 349–380.

La Regina, A. (ed.). *Museo Nazionale Romano* (Milan, 2005).

La Regina, A. (ed.). *Palazzo Massimo alle Terme* (Milan, 1998).

Lattimore, R. *Themes in Greek and Latin Epitaphs* (Urbana, 1962).

Lawrence, M. Columnar sarcophagi in the Latin West: ateliers, chronology, style. *Art Bulletin* 14 (1932), 103–185.

Lawrence, M. Additional Asiatic sarcophagi. *Memoirs of the American Academy at Rome* 20 (1951), 119–166.

Lawrence, M. The Velletri sarcophagus. *American Journal of Archaeology* 69 (1965), 207–222.

Lévêque, P. La date de la frise du théâtre de Delphes. *Bulletin de Correspondance Hellénique* 75 (1951), 247–263.

Levick, B. (ed.). *Monumenta Asiae Minoris Antiqua 9. Monuments from the Aezanitis recorded by C.W.M. Cox, A. Cameron, and J. Cullen* (London, 1988).

Lipiński, E. *Itineraria Phoenicia* (Leuven, 2004).

Lyttelton, M. *Baroque architecture in classical antiquity* (London, 1974).

MacDonald, W. *The architecture of the Roman Empire, 2. An urban appraisal* (New Haven and London, 1986).

Maiuri, Amedeo. Pompei. Studi e ricerche intorno alla 'Casa del Criptoportico' sulla Via dell'Abbondanza (Reg. I, ins. VI, n. 2 e 4). *Notizie degli Scavi di Antichità* (1933), 252–276.

Malbon, E. *The iconography of the sarcophagus of Junius Bassus* (Princeton, 1990).

Mansel, A. M. Bericht über Ausgrabungen und Untersuchungen in Pamphylien in den Jahren 1946–1955. *Archäologischer Anzeiger* (1956), 104–120.

Mansel, A. M. 1946–1955 yıllarında Pamphylia'da yapılan kazılar ve araştırmalar. *Belleten* 22 (1958), 211–240.

Mansel, A. M. *Side 1947–1966: yılları Kazıları ve Araştırmalarının Sonuçları* (Ankara, 1978).

Mansuelli, G. Aedicula columnis adornata. Nuove osservazioni sugli archi romani italici e provenzali. *Rivista di Studi Liguri* 36 (1970), 103–109.

Mansuelli, G. Review of Staccioli 1969. *Studi Etruschi* 38 (1970), 411–413.

Mari, Z. and Sgambaro, S. The Antinoeion of Hadrian's Villa: interpretation and architectural reconstruction. *American Journal of Archaeology* 111 (2007), 83–104.

Massari, A. and Setti, B. Architettura delle urne a capanna, in: *Preistoria e protostoria in Etruria. L'Etruria tra Italia, Europa e mondo mediterraneo. Ricerche e scavi.* Atti del Quarto incontro di studi, Manciano, Montalto di Castro, Valentano, 12–14 September 1997 (Milan, 2000), 325–337.

Mattingly, H. (ed.) *Coins of the Roman Empire in the British Museum* vol. IV (London,1940).

Menéndez Pidal, J. El Mausoleo de los Atilios. *Archivo Español de Arqueología* 43 (1970), 89–112.

Micro-architectures. L'Architecture d'Aujourd'hui, 328 (June 2000), 29–121.

Mirabella Roberti, M. (ed.). *Monumenti sepolcrali romani in Aquileia e nella Cisalpina.* Atti della 26. Settimana di studi aquileiesi, 24–28 aprile 1995, Antichità Altoadriatiche 43 (Aquileia, 1997).

Mitchell, S. *Anatolia. Land, Men and Gods in Asia Minor* (Oxford, 1993).

Moretti, G. Rovine di Lagòn. *Annuario della Scuola Archeologica di Atene* 3 (1921), 135–141.

Morey, C. R. *Roman and Christian sculpture, Part 1 The sarcophagus of Claudia Antonia Sabina and the Asiatic sarcophagi*, Sardis 5 (Leyden, 1924).

Mylius, H. Die Krufter Grabdenkmäler und ihre Rekonstruktion. *Bonner Jahrbücher* 130 (1925), 180–192.

Newby, Z. Reading programs in Greco-Roman art: reflections on the Spada Reliefs, in: *The Roman Gaze: vision, power, and the body*, edited by D. Fredrick (Baltimore, 2002), 110–149.

Nünnerich-Asmus, A. *Basilika und Portikus: die Architektur der Säulenhallen als Ausdruck gewandelter Urbanität in später Republik und früher Kaiserzeit* (Cologne, Vienna, and Weimar, 1994).

Onians, J. *Bearers of Meaning* (Princeton, 1988).

Ortalli, J. La ricostruzione del mausoleo di Rufus. Nuovi interventi sul museo archeologico sarsinate a un secolo della fondazione. *Rivista storica dell'antichità* 21 (1991), 97–136.

Öğüş, E. The Antakya sarcophagus: aspects of decoration, transportation and dating. *Bilkent University, Department of Archaeology & History of Art Newsletter* 3 (2004), 28–32.

Özgan, R. Säulensarkophage, und danach. *Istanbuler Mitteilungen* 50 (2000), 365–388.

Özgan, R. Ein Säulensarkophag aus Nikaia (Iznik), in: *Anadolu'da dogdu. 60. yasinda Fahri Işika armagan. Festschrift für Fahri Işik zum 60. Geburtstag*, edited by T. Korkut (Istanbul, 2004), 549–559.

Özoral, F. Herakles Lahdi. [A Hercules Sarcophagus] *Türk arkeoloji dergisi* 24 (1977), 145–149.

Palagia, O. Hephaestion's pyre and the royal hunt of Alexander, in: *Alexander the Great in fact and fiction*, edited by A. B. Bosworth and E. Baynham (Oxford, 2000), 167–206.

Paris, P. and Radet, G. Deux nouveaux gouverneurs de provinces. *Bulletin de Correspondance Hellénique* 9 (1885), 433–436.

Pelzer Wagener, A. and Ashby, T. Roman remains in the town and territory of Velletri. *American Journal of Archaeology* 17 (1913), 399–428.

Pensabene, P. Edilizia pubblica e committenza. Marmi e officine in Italia meridionale e Sicilia durante il II e III secolo d.C. *Revue des Archéologues et Historiens d'art de Louvain* 69 (1996–97), 3–88.

Pensabene, P. and Mesolella, G. Il sarcofago di Velletri: officine attiche e architetture teatrali in Grecia, in: M. Angle, A. Germano and F. Zevi (eds.), *Museo e territorio.* Atti del IV convegno, Velletri, 7–8 maggio 2004 (Rome, 2005), 57–72.

Pera, R. La figura di Venere e il suo significato nella monetazione degli Antonini. *Notizie dal chiostro del Monastero maggiore. Rassegna di studi del Civico museo archeologico e del Civico gabinetto numismatico di Milano* 11–14 (1971–1974), 15–21.

Perry, E. *The aesthetics of emulation in the visual arts of ancient Rome* (Cambridge, 2005).

Petersen, L. H. *The freedman in Roman art and art history* (Cambridge, 2006).

Pierro, E. A proposito di un sarcofago nella Collezione Astor a Hever Castle. Indagine preliminare sul patrimonio scultoreo di San Cesareo, in: *Scritti di antichità in memoria di Sandro Stucchi, 2. La Tripolitania. L'Italia e l'Occidente*, edited by L. Bacchielli and M. Bonanno Aravantinos (Rome, 1996), 279–289.

Poulle, B. Le théâtre de Marcellus et la sphère. *Mélanges de l'École française de Rome, Antiquité* 111 (1999), 257–272.

Prayon, F. Architecture, in: *Etruscan life and after-life: a handbook of Etruscan studies*, edited by L. Bonfante (Detroit, 1986), 174–201.

Precht, G. *Das Grabmal des Lucius Poblicius: Rekonstruktion und Aufbau* (Cologne, 1975).

Preisshofen, F. and Zanker, P. Reflex einer eklektischen Kunstanschauung bei Auctor ad Herennium. *Dialoghi di Archeologia* 4–5 (1970–71), 100–119.

Quenemoen, C. The Portico of the Danaids: a new reconstruction. *American Journal of Archaeology* 110 (2006), 229–250.

Quilici, L. and Quilici Gigli, S. Sulla Conocchia di Capua, in: *Αειμνηστος. Miscellanea di studi per Mauro Cristofani*, edited by B. Adembri (Florence, 2005), 726–737.

Raepsaet-Charlier, M.-T. *Prosopographie des femmes de l'ordre sénatorial (I-II siècles)* (Louvain, 1987).

Ramsay, W. Antiquities of Southern Phrygia and the Border Lands (II). *American Journal of Archaeology* 4 (1888), 6–21.

Rapoport, A. *House form and culture* (London, 1969).

Reinach, S. *Répertoire de la statuaire grecque et romaine, 1. Clarac de poche* (Paris, 1904).

Rémy, B. *Antonin le Pieux: le Siècle d'Or de Rome, 138–161* (Paris, 2005).

Retzleff, A. The Dresden Type Satyr-Hermaphrodite Group in Roman Theaters. *American Journal of Archaeology* 111 (2007), 459–472.

Riegl, A. *Die spätrömische Kunstindustrie nach den Funden in Österreich-Ungarn* (Vienna, 1901).

Rodenwaldt, G. Säulensarkophage. *Mitteilungen des Deutschen Archäologischen Instituts, Römische Abteilung* 38–39 (1923–24), 1–40.

Rodenwaldt, G. Sarkophage aus Aphrodisias. *Archäologischer Anzeiger* (1933), 46–56.

Rodenwaldt, G. Zur Kunstgeschichte der Jahre 220 bis 270. *Jahrbuch des Deutschen Archäologischen Instituts* 51 (1936), 82–113.

Rodenwaldt, G. Sarkophag–Miscellen. 5. Ein kleinasiatischer Kindersarkophag. *Archäologischer Anzeiger* (1938), 414–420.
Romanelli, P. (ed.). *Corpus Vasorum Antiquorum: Italia 4, Museo provinciale Castromediano di Lecce*, fasc. 1 (Milan, 1928).
Roth, R. From clay to stone. Monumentality and traditionalism in Volterran urns. *American Journal of Archaeology* 113 (2009), 39–56.
Roth-Congès, A. Le mausolée de l'île du Comte, in: *Ugernum. Beaucaire et le Beaucairois à l'époque romaine,* vol. 2, edited by J.-C. Bessac, M. Christol, and J.-L. Fiches (Caveirac, 1987), 47–128.
Rubini, M. Scheda VI.21, in: *Museo Civico di Velletri* (*Catalogo dei Musei locali e delle Collezioni del Lazio,* 6) (Rome, 1989).
Rykwert, J. *The dancing column* (Cambridge MA, 1996).
Sapelli, M. Terme di Diocleziano. Nuove acquisizioni di scultura funeraria. *Bollettino di Archeologia* 23–24 (1993), 171–174.
Schefold, K. *Orient, Hellas und Rom in der archäologischen Forschung seit 1939* (Bern, 1949).
Schefold, K. *Pompejanische Malerei: Sinn und Ideengeschichte* (Basel, 1952).
Schemann, M. Beobachtungen an den Köpfen des sogenannten Psamathia-Reliefs in Berlin. *Istanbuler Mitteilungen* 49 (1999), 443–466.
Schmidt, E. *Geschichte der Karyatide. Funktion und Bedeutung der menschlichen Träger- und Stützfigur in der Baukunst* (Würzburg, 1982).
Schreiter, C. Römische Schmuckbasen. *Kölner Jahrbuch* 28 (1995), 161–347.
Sear, F. *Roman theatres: an architectural study* (Oxford, 2006).
Sevinç, N. A new sarcophagus of Polyxena from the Salvage excavations at Gümüşçay. *Studia Troica* 6 (1996), 251–264.
Shapley, J. Another Sidamara sarcophagus. *Art Bulletin* 5 (1923), 61–75.
Silvestrini, F. *Sepulcrum Marci Artori Gemini: la tomba detta dei Platorini nel Museo Nazionale Romano* (Rome, 1987).
Simpson, C. J. The Roman villa at Atella. *Echos du Monde Classique* 26 (1982), 191–198.
Sinn, F. and Freyberger, K. *Die Ausstattung des Hateriergrabes* (Georg Daltrop and Hansgeorg Oehler (eds.), *Museo Gregoriano Profano ex-Lateranense. Katalog der Skulpturen, 1, Die Grabdenkmäler,* no. 2), Monumenta Artis Romanae 24 (Mainz, 1996).
Small, A. Villa building in Roman Lucania, in: *The excavations of San Giovanni di Ruoti,* 1, *The Villas and their environment,* edited by A. Small and R. Buck (Toronto, Buffalo and London, 1994), 37–42.
Smith, R.R.R. Sarcophagi and Roman citizenship, in: *Aphrodisias Papers, 4. New Research on the City and its Monuments, JRA* Supplement 70, edited by C. Ratté and R.R.R. Smith (Providence, RI, 2008), 347–394.
Smith, T. G. *Vitruvius on Architecture* (New York, 2003).
Spratt, T. and Forbes, E. *Travels in Lycia, Milyas and the Cibyratis,* 2 vols. (London, 1847).
Staccioli, R. A. *Modelli di edifici etrusco-italici. I modelli votivi, Archeologia Classica,* suppl. 6 (Florence, 1969).
Stewart, P. *Statues in Roman society: representation and response* (Oxford, 2003).
Stillwell, R. (ed.) *The Princeton Index of Classical Sites* (Princeton, 1976)
Strocka, V. Kleinasiatische Klinensarkophag-Deckel. *Archäologischer Anzeiger* (1971), 62–86.

Strocka, V. *Das Markttor von Milet*, Winckelmannsprogramm der Archäologischen Gesellschaft zu Berlin, 128 (Berlin, 1981).

Strzygowski, J. *Orient oder Rom? Beiträge zur Geschichte der Spätantiken und Frühchristlichen Kunst* (Leipzig, 1901).

Sturgeon, M. *Sculpture: the reliefs from the theatre, Corinth* IX.2 (Princeton, 1977).

Sturgeon, M. A new monument to Herakles at Delphi. *American Journal of Archaeology* 82 (1978), 226–235.

Sturgeon, M. Review of Schmidt 1982. *American Journal of Archaeology* 88 (1984), 415–416.

Sturgeon, M. *Sculpture: the assemblage from the theatre, Corinth* IX.3 (Princeton, 2004).

Sturgeon, M. A new feature in the civic landscape. The theater façade at Corinth, in: *Common ground. Archaeology, art, science, and humanities.* Proceedings of the XVIth International Congress of Classical Archaeology, Boston, August 23–26, 2003 (Oxford, 2006), 386–390.

Şimşek, C. Laodikya sütunlu lahti [A column sarcophagus in Laodicea]. *Türk arkeoloji dergisi* 31 (1997), 269–289.

Tchalenko, G. *Villages antiques de la Syrie du Nord: le massif du Bélus à l'époque romaine*, 3 vols. (Paris, 1953–58).

Theuer, M. Der Sarkophag des Celsus, in: *Forschungen in Ephesos* V.1, *Die Bibliothek* (Vienna, 1953).

Thomas, E. *Monumentality and the Roman Empire: architecture in the Antonine age* (Oxford, 2007a).

Thomas, E. Metaphor and identity in Severan architecture: the Septizodium between reality and fantasy, in: *Severan culture*, edited by S. Swain, J. Elsner and S. Harrison (Cambridge, 2007b), 327–367.

Türktüzün, M. Zwei Säulensarkophage aus der Südwestnekropole in Aizanoi. *Archäologischer Anzeiger* (1993), 517–526.

Vandeput, L. *The architectural decoration of Roman Asia Minor. Sagalassos: a case study* (Leuven, 1997).

Waelkens, M. *Dokimeion. Die Werkstatt der repräsentativen kleinasiatischen Sarkophage: Chronologie und Typologie ihrer Produktion* (Berlin, 1982).

Wallace-Hadrill, Andrew. *Houses and society in Pompeii and Herculaneum* (Princeton, 1994).

Wallace-Hadrill, A. Housing the dead: the tomb as house in Roman Italy, in: *Commemorating the Dead. Texts and Artifacts in Context. Studies of Roman, Jewish and Christian Burials*, edited by R. Saller, L. Brink, and D. Green (Berlin and New York, 2008), 39–78.

Webb, P. *Hellenistic architectural sculpture: figural motifs in western Anatolia and the Aegean Islands* (Madison WI, 1996).

Wegner, M. *Schmuckbasen des antiken Rom* (Münster, 1966).

Weir, R. Nero and the Herakles frieze at Delphi. *Bulletin de Correspondance Hellénique* 123 (1999), 397–404.

Weickert, C. *Das lesbische Kymation* (Leipzig, 1913).

Weidhaas, H. Porticussarkophage der Spätantike, in: J. Irmscher (ed.). *Studia byzantina.* Beiträge aus der byzantinischen Forschung der DDR zum XIII. Internationalen Byzantinistenkongress in Oxford 1966 (Halle, 1968), 133–148.

Wiegartz, H. *Kleinasiatische Säulensarkophage. Untersuchungen zum Sarkophagtypus und zu den figürlichen Darstellungen* (Berlin, 1965).

Wiegartz, H. Marmorhandel, Sarkophagherstellung und die Lokalisierung der kleinasiatischen Säulensarkophage, in: *Mansel'e Armağan = Mélanges Mansel* (Ankara, 1974), 345–383.

Wiegartz, H. et al. Symposium über die antiken Sarkophagreliefs. *Archäologischer Anzeiger* (1971), 86–122.

Wilson Jones, M. *Principles of Roman architecture* (New Haven, 2000).

Wrede, H. *Consecratio in formam deorum. Vergöttlichte Privatpersonen in der römischen Kaiserzeit* (Mainz, 1981).

Wrede, H. *Senatorische Sarkophage Roms. Der Beitrag des Senatorenstandes zur römischen Kunst der hohen und späten Kaiserzeit* (Mainz, 2001).

Yegül, F. *The bath-gymnasium complex at Sardis. Archaeological exploration of Sardis Report*, 3 (Cambridge, MA, and London, 1986).

Zampieri, G. *La tomba di San Luca Evangelista: la cassa di piombo e l'area funeraria della Basilica di Santa Giustina in Padova* (Rome, 2003).

Zanker, P. *The mask of Socrates: the image of the intellectual in antiquity* (Berkeley CA, 1995).

Zanker, P. and Ewald, B. *Mit Mythen leben. Die Bilderwelt der römischen Sarkophage* (Munich, 2004).

List of Contributors

Donato Attanasio is a chemist and spectroscopist, and works as senior scientist at the Istituto di Struttura della Materia of the National Research Council in Rome. Since the mid 1990's he has systematically explored the problem of marble provenance, using different physico-chemical techniques and developing statistical procedures of data analysis.

Stine Birk completed her PhD in Classical Archaeology ('Reading Roman Sarcophagi, Aspects of Identity, Commemoration and Chronology') at Aarhus University, Denmark. Her research has mainly focused on sarcophagi made in Rome during the third and early fourth century, particularly on forms of self-representation and role models as expressions of ideal identity constructions. She is currently working on a project related to expressions of individuality on Roman grave monuments in the eastern and western parts of the Empire. Forthcoming articles include: Adaptable Craftsmen: The Production of Sculpture and Sarcophagi in the Later Roman Empire *JRA,* supplement (edited by B. Poulsen and T. Myrup Kristensen) and The Christian Muse and the Pagan Christophoros: The Ambiguity of Late Antique Sarcophagi in *Sarkophag-Studien* (edited by G. Koch*).*

Glenys Davies is a Senior Lecturer in Classical Art in the School of History, Classics and Archaeology at the University of Edinburgh. Her PhD thesis ('Fashion in the Grave', University of London 1979) was a study of Roman ash chests, grave altars and early sarcophagi, so the present article represents a return to the subject 30 years later. She has recently published a detailed catalogue of the funerary monuments in the Ince Blundell Collection, Liverpool.

Jaś Elsner is Humfry Payne Senior Research Fellow in Classical Archaeology at Corpus Christi College Oxford and Visiting Professor of Art History at the University of Chicago. He works on Roman and early Christian art and his most recent book is *Roman Eyes: Visuality and Subjectivity in Art and Text* (2007).

Björn C. Ewald is an Assistant Professor of Art History at the University of Toronto. His areas of research are the Roman appropriation of Greek art; Roman imperial art; myth and funerary art; gender, subjectivity and the body in Roman art; ancient spatialities; the history and theory of Roman art history. The present contribution is related to a book he is currently finishing on 'Attic sarcophagi' and the Second Sophistic. His previous publications include *Der Philosoph als Leitbild* (1999); (as co-author, with Paul Zanker) *Mit Mythen leben* (2004; English translation forthcoming); (as co-editor) *The Emperor and Rome: Space, Representation, and Ritual* (2010).

L. Peter Gromet earned a B.S. from SUNY Stony Brook (1972) and a PhD from the California Institute of Technology (1979) in the fields of geology and geochemistry. He conducts research in the areas of geochemistry and global tectonics, with an emphasis in the application of radiogenic age dating to plate tectonic problems, particularly the tectonic evolution of ancient collisional mountain belts. He has worked in the North American Cordillera in California and Baja California, Mexico, the New England Appalachians, the Scandinavian and Svalbard (High Arctic) Caledonides in Norway and Sweden, and the Sierras Pampeanas in Argentina. He became acquainted with the archaeological community through interactions with Frances Van Keuren, and has greatly enjoyed contributing geological and mineralogical observations to marble and limestone provenance determinations.

John J. Herrmann, Jr., Curator of Classical Art, Emeritus of the Museum of Fine Arts, Boston, received his doctorate from the Institute of Fine Arts of New York University in 1973, working on architectural decoration in Early Christian Rome under the direction of Richard Krautheimer. His book, *The Ionic Capital in Late Antique Rome* (1988) was the fruit of this line of research. Working with conservators at the Museum of Fine Arts, Boston from 1976–2004, he developed his interests in scientific identification of ancient marble. Contact with the Association for the Study of Marble and Other Stones in Antiquity (ASMOSIA), of which he is now the Vice President, has encouraged these interests further and led to frequent collaboration with chemists and geologists, as well as other archaeologists. Past projects in this field have especially involved tracking marble from the Greek island of Thassos, and in recent years he has been working on interdisciplinary studies of quarries and marble use in ancient Algeria.

Janet Huskinson was Reader in Classical Studies at the Open University until her retirement in October 2008, since when she has held an Leverhulme Emeritus Fellowship. Her research interests are in Roman private art of the third and fourth centuries, focusing in particular on the imagery on sarcophagi used in the city of Rome, and on its social and cultural implications. She is currently completing a book on Roman strigillated sarcophagi.

Katharina Lorenz is Associate Professor in Classical Studies at the University of Nottingham. Her main research interests are the visual cultures of Greece and

Rome, and in particular the use of mythological imagery and image-text interaction. She has written a book on mythological imagery in the Roman domestic context and articles on visual story-telling on Greek pots; she is currently completing a critical discussion of three analytical methods – iconology, semiotics and image studies – used in the study of ancient art.

Zahra Newby is Reader in Classics and Ancient History at the University of Warwick. She studied at Corpus Christi College, Oxford and the Courtauld Institute of Art, University of London. She is author of *Greek Athletics in the Roman World: Victory and Virtue* (Oxford, 2005), co-editor of *Art and Inscriptions in the Ancient World* (Cambridge, 2007) and has written a number of articles on aspects of ancient art and the Second Sophistic. Her current research is on the representation of Greek mythology in Roman art.

Francisco Prado-Vilar is Ramón y Cajal Professor in the History of Art at the Complutense University in Madrid. After obtaining his PhD from Harvard University in 2002, he was named Cotsen Fellow at the Princeton Society of Fellows in the Liberal Art, and has subsequently held academic positions at Princeton University and the University of London, Birkbeck. His research and publications cover topics of wide chronological, thematic, and methodological range (arts of al-Andalus, medieval manuscript illumination, Romanesque sculpture, Hispano-Flemish and Golden Age Spanish painting). He is a member of the advisory board of the Centre for Iberian and Latin American Visual Studies (CILAVS) at Birkbeck, and the scientific committee for the Restoration Project of the Cathedral of Santiago de Compostela, as well as a fellow of the Real Colegio Complutense at Harvard University.

Ben Russell is a post-doctoral researcher affiliated to the British School at Rome. He is currently working on a project on the Roman sarcophagus trade funded by the Leverhulme Trust. Prior to this he held the doctoral studentship on the Oxford Roman Economy Project. His doctoral thesis (University of Oxford, 2009) looked at what a detailed examination of stone-use – the exploitation of stone resources and the production and distribution of stone objects – could add to understanding of the wider Roman economy. He has a BA in Classical Archaeology and Ancient History and an MSt in Classical Archaeology from the University of Oxford.

Edmund Thomas is Lecturer in Ancient Visual and Material Culture at Durham University. He has taught at the Universities of Oxford and Exeter and the National University of Ireland Galway and has published widely on Roman architecture. His *Monumentality and the Roman Empire: architecture in the Antonine age* was published by Oxford University Press, and he is now preparing a book on the relations between architecture and inscribed text in antiquity and later periods.

Dennis Trout is Associate Professor of Classics at the University of Missouri. His recent publications have been focused upon Late Latin epigraphy, especially the tradition of *carmina epigraphica* on display in the *elogia* of Damasus, and the roles of public memory and the cult of the saints in the reshaping of social identity in late ancient Rome.

Frances Van Keuren received her doctorate in Classical Archaeology, under the direction of R. Ross Holloway, from Brown University in 1973. She has been teaching Ancient Art History at the Lamar Dodd School of Art, the University of Georgia, since 1980. Thanks to the path-finding geological research into stable isotopes by her colleague Norman Herz, she became interested in collaborative research projects to determine the provenances of the marbles of Roman sarcophagi and altars. This article presents the results of the largest collaborative project that she has worked on. The project also involves the most comprehensive multi-method analysis of Roman sarcophagi to date. She is most grateful for all the outstanding contributions of her scientific and art historical collaborators.

Index

(The main focus of this index is on aspects of sarcophagi covered in the main text, and on individual examples which are the subject of specific discussion.)

www.ingramcontent.com/pod-product-compliance
Lightning Source LLC
LaVergne TN
LVHW081322110826
845149LV00007B/1566
* 9 7 8 3 1 1 0 4 8 2 3 1 7 *